T0180312

Lecture Notes in Computer Science 14107

The series Lecture Notes in Computer Science (LNCS), including its subseries Lecture Notes in Artificial Intelligence (LNAI) and Lecture Notes in Bioinformatics (LNBI), has established itself as a medium for the publication of new developments in computer science and information technology research, teaching, and education.

LNCS enjoys close cooperation with the computer science R & D community, the series counts many renowned academics among its volume editors and paper authors, and collaborates with prestigious societies. Its mission is to serve this international community by providing an invaluable service, mainly focused on the publication of conference and workshop proceedings and postproceedings. LNCS commenced publication in 1973.

Osvaldo Gervasi · Beniamino Murgante ·
Ana Maria A. C. Rocha · Chiara Garau ·
Francesco Scorza · Yeliz Karaca ·
Carmelo M. Torre
Editors

Computational Science and Its Applications – ICCSA 2023 Workshops

Athens, Greece, July 3–6, 2023
Proceedings, Part IV

Editors
Osvaldo Gervasi
University of Perugia
Perugia, Italy

Beniamino Murgante
University of Basilicata
Potenza, Italy

Ana Maria A. C. Rocha
University of Minho
Braga, Portugal

Chiara Garau
University of Cagliari
Cagliari, Italy

Francesco Scorza
University of Basilicata
Potenza, Italy

Yeliz Karaca
University of Massachusetts Medical School
Worcester, MA, USA

Carmelo M. Torre
Polytechnic University of Bari
Bari, Italy

ISSN 0302-9743 ISSN 1611-3349 (electronic)
Lecture Notes in Computer Science
ISBN 978-3-031-37113-4 ISBN 978-3-031-37114-1 (eBook)
https://doi.org/10.1007/978-3-031-37114-1

This Springer imprint is published by the registered company Springer Nature Switzerland AG
The registered company address is: Gewerbestrasse 11, 6330 Cham, Switzerland

Preface

These 9 volumes (LNCS volumes 14104–14112) consist of the peer-reviewed papers from the 2023 International Conference on Computational Science and Its Applications (ICCSA 2023) which took place during July 3–6, 2023. The peer-reviewed papers of the main conference tracks were published in a separate set consisting of two volumes (LNCS 13956–13957).

The conference was finally held in person after the difficult period of the Covid-19 pandemic in the wonderful city of Athens, in the cosy facilities of the National Technical University. Our experience during the pandemic period allowed us to enable virtual participation also this year for those who were unable to attend the event, due to logistical, political and economic problems, by adopting a technological infrastructure based on open source software (jitsi + riot), and a commercial cloud infrastructure.

ICCSA 2023 was another successful event in the International Conference on Computational Science and Its Applications (ICCSA) series, previously held as a hybrid event (with one third of registered authors attending in person) in Malaga, Spain (2022), Cagliari, Italy (hybrid with few participants in person in 2021 and completely online in 2020), whilst earlier editions took place in Saint Petersburg, Russia (2019), Melbourne, Australia (2018), Trieste, Italy (2017), Beijing, China (2016), Banff, Canada (2015), Guimaraes, Portugal (2014), Ho Chi Minh City, Vietnam (2013), Salvador, Brazil (2012), Santander, Spain (2011), Fukuoka, Japan (2010), Suwon, South Korea (2009), Perugia, Italy (2008), Kuala Lumpur, Malaysia (2007), Glasgow, UK (2006), Singapore (2005), Assisi, Italy (2004), Montreal, Canada (2003), and (as ICCS) Amsterdam, The Netherlands (2002) and San Francisco, USA (2001).

Computational Science is the main pillar of most of the present research, industrial and commercial applications, and plays a unique role in exploiting ICT innovative technologies, and the ICCSA series have been providing a venue to researchers and industry practitioners to discuss new ideas, to share complex problems and their solutions, and to shape new trends in Computational Science. As the conference mirrors society from a scientific point of view, this year's undoubtedly dominant theme was the machine learning and artificial intelligence and their applications in the most diverse economic and industrial fields.

The ICCSA 2023 conference is structured in 6 general tracks covering the fields of computational science and its applications: Computational Methods, Algorithms and Scientific Applications – High Performance Computing and Networks – Geometric Modeling, Graphics and Visualization – Advanced and Emerging Applications – Information Systems and Technologies – Urban and Regional Planning. In addition, the conference consisted of 61 workshops, focusing on very topical issues of importance to science, technology and society: from new mathematical approaches for solving complex computational systems, to information and knowledge in the Internet of Things, new statistical and optimization methods, several Artificial Intelligence approaches, sustainability issues, smart cities and related technologies.

In the workshop proceedings we accepted 350 full papers, 29 short papers and 2 PHD Showcase papers. In the main conference proceedings we accepted 67 full papers, 13 short papers and 6 PHD Showcase papers from 283 submissions to the General Tracks of the conference (acceptance rate 30%). We would like to express our appreciation to the workshops chairs and co-chairs for their hard work and dedication.

The success of the ICCSA conference series in general, and of ICCSA 2023 in particular, vitally depends on the support of many people: authors, presenters, participants, keynote speakers, workshop chairs, session chairs, organizing committee members, student volunteers, Program Committee members, Advisory Committee members, International Liaison chairs, reviewers and others in various roles. We take this opportunity to wholehartedly thank them all.

We also wish to thank our publisher, Springer, for their acceptance to publish the proceedings, for sponsoring part of the best papers awards and for their kind assistance and cooperation during the editing process.

We cordially invite you to visit the ICCSA website https://iccsa.org where you can find all the relevant information about this interesting and exciting event.

July 2023

Osvaldo Gervasi
Beniamino Murgante
Chiara Garau

Welcome Message from Organizers

After the 2021 ICCSA in Cagliari, Italy and the 2022 ICCSA in Malaga, Spain, ICCSA continued its successful scientific endeavours in 2023, hosted again in the Mediterranean neighbourhood. This time, ICCSA 2023 moved a bit more to the east of the Mediterranean Region and was held in the metropolitan city of Athens, the capital of Greece and a vibrant urban environment endowed with a prominent cultural heritage that dates back to the ancient years. As a matter of fact, Athens is one of the oldest cities in the world, and the cradle of democracy. The city has a history of over 3,000 years and, according to the myth, it took its name from Athena, the Goddess of Wisdom and daughter of Zeus.

ICCSA 2023 took place in a secure environment, relieved from the immense stress of the COVID-19 pandemic. This gave us the chance to have a safe and vivid, in-person participation which, combined with the very active engagement of the ICCSA 2023 scientific community, set the ground for highly motivating discussions and interactions as to the latest developments of computer science and its applications in the real world for improving quality of life.

The National Technical University of Athens (NTUA), one of the most prestigious Greek academic institutions, had the honour of hosting ICCSA 2023. The Local Organizing Committee really feels the burden and responsibility of such a demanding task; and puts in all the necessary energy in order to meet participants' expectations and establish a friendly, creative and inspiring, scientific and social/cultural environment that allows for new ideas and perspectives to flourish.

Since all ICCSA participants, either informatics-oriented or application-driven, realize the tremendous steps and evolution of computer science during the last few decades and the huge potential these offer to cope with the enormous challenges of humanity in a globalized, 'wired' and highly competitive world, the expectations from ICCSA 2023 were set high in order for a successful matching between computer science progress and communities' aspirations to be attained, i.e., a progress that serves real, place- and people-based needs and can pave the way towards a visionary, smart, sustainable, resilient and inclusive future for both the current and the next generation.

On behalf of the Local Organizing Committee, I would like to sincerely thank all of you who have contributed to ICCSA 2023 and I cordially welcome you to my 'home', NTUA.

On behalf of the Local Organizing Committee.

Anastasia Stratigea

Organization

ICCSA 2023 was organized by the National Technical University of Athens (Greece), the University of the Aegean (Greece), the University of Perugia (Italy), the University of Basilicata (Italy), Monash University (Australia), Kyushu Sangyo University (Japan), the University of Minho (Portugal). The conference was supported by two NTUA Schools, namely the School of Rural, Surveying and Geoinformatics Engineering and the School of Electrical and Computer Engineering.

Honorary General Chairs

Norio Shiratori	Chuo University, Japan
Kenneth C. J. Tan	Sardina Systems, UK

General Chairs

Osvaldo Gervasi	University of Perugia, Italy
Anastasia Stratigea	National Technical University of Athens, Greece
Bernady O. Apduhan	Kyushu Sangyo University, Japan

Program Committee Chairs

Beniamino Murgante	University of Basilicata, Italy
Dimitris Kavroudakis	University of the Aegean, Greece
Ana Maria A. C. Rocha	University of Minho, Portugal
David Taniar	Monash University, Australia

International Advisory Committee

Jemal Abawajy	Deakin University, Australia
Dharma P. Agarwal	University of Cincinnati, USA
Rajkumar Buyya	Melbourne University, Australia
Claudia Bauzer Medeiros	University of Campinas, Brazil
Manfred M. Fisher	Vienna University of Economics and Business, Austria
Marina L. Gavrilova	University of Calgary, Canada

Sumi Helal	University of Florida, USA and University of Lancaster, UK
Yee Leung	Chinese University of Hong Kong, China

International Liaison Chairs

Ivan Blečić	University of Cagliari, Italy
Giuseppe Borruso	University of Trieste, Italy
Elise De Donker	Western Michigan University, USA
Maria Irene Falcão	University of Minho, Portugal
Inmaculada Garcia Fernandez	University of Malaga, Spain
Eligius Hendrix	University of Malaga, Spain
Robert C. H. Hsu	Chung Hua University, Taiwan
Tai-Hoon Kim	Beijing Jaotong University, China
Vladimir Korkhov	Saint Petersburg University, Russia
Takashi Naka	Kyushu Sangyo University, Japan
Rafael D. C. Santos	National Institute for Space Research, Brazil
Maribel Yasmina Santos	University of Minho, Portugal
Elena Stankova	Saint Petersburg University, Russia

Workshop and Session Organizing Chairs

Beniamino Murgante	University of Basilicata, Italy
Chiara Garau	University of Cagliari, Italy

Award Chair

Wenny Rahayu	La Trobe University, Australia

Publicity Committee Chairs

Elmer Dadios	De La Salle University, Philippines
Nataliia Kulabukhova	Saint Petersburg University, Russia
Daisuke Takahashi	Tsukuba University, Japan
Shangwang Wang	Beijing University of Posts and Telecommunications, China

Local Organizing Committee Chairs

Anastasia Stratigea	National Technical University of Athens, Greece
Dimitris Kavroudakis	University of the Aegean, Greece
Charalambos Ioannidis	National Technical University of Athens, Greece
Nectarios Koziris	National Technical University of Athens, Greece
Efthymios Bakogiannis	National Technical University of Athens, Greece
Yiota Theodora	National Technical University of Athens, Greece
Dimitris Fotakis	National Technical University of Athens, Greece
Apostolos Lagarias	National Technical University of Athens, Greece
Akrivi Leka	National Technical University of Athens, Greece
Dionisia Koutsi	National Technical University of Athens, Greece
Alkistis Dalkavouki	National Technical University of Athens, Greece
Maria Panagiotopoulou	National Technical University of Athens, Greece
Angeliki Papazoglou	National Technical University of Athens, Greece
Natalia Tsigarda	National Technical University of Athens, Greece
Konstantinos Athanasopoulos	National Technical University of Athens, Greece
Ioannis Xatziioannou	National Technical University of Athens, Greece
Vasiliki Krommyda	National Technical University of Athens, Greece
Panayiotis Patsilinakos	National Technical University of Athens, Greece
Sofia Kassiou	National Technical University of Athens, Greece

Technology Chair

Damiano Perri	University of Florence, Italy

Program Committee

Vera Afreixo	University of Aveiro, Portugal
Filipe Alvelos	University of Minho, Portugal
Hartmut Asche	University of Potsdam, Germany
Ginevra Balletto	University of Cagliari, Italy
Michela Bertolotto	University College Dublin, Ireland
Sandro Bimonte	CEMAGREF, TSCF, France
Rod Blais	University of Calgary, Canada
Ivan Blečić	University of Sassari, Italy
Giuseppe Borruso	University of Trieste, Italy
Ana Cristina Braga	University of Minho, Portugal
Massimo Cafaro	University of Salento, Italy
Yves Caniou	Lyon University, France

Ermanno Cardelli	University of Perugia, Italy
José A. Cardoso e Cunha	Universidade Nova de Lisboa, Portugal
Rui Cardoso	University of Beira Interior, Portugal
Leocadio G. Casado	University of Almeria, Spain
Carlo Cattani	University of Salerno, Italy
Mete Celik	Erciyes University, Turkey
Maria Cerreta	University of Naples "Federico II", Italy
Hyunseung Choo	Sungkyunkwan University, Korea
Rachel Chieng-Sing Lee	Sunway University, Malaysia
Min Young Chung	Sungkyunkwan University, Korea
Florbela Maria da Cruz Domingues Correia	Polytechnic Institute of Viana do Castelo, Portugal
Gilberto Corso Pereira	Federal University of Bahia, Brazil
Alessandro Costantini	INFN, Italy
Carla Dal Sasso Freitas	Universidade Federal do Rio Grande do Sul, Brazil
Pradesh Debba	The Council for Scientific and Industrial Research (CSIR), South Africa
Hendrik Decker	Instituto Tecnológico de Informática, Spain
Robertas Damaševičius	Kausan University of Technology, Lithuania
Frank Devai	London South Bank University, UK
Rodolphe Devillers	Memorial University of Newfoundland, Canada
Joana Matos Dias	University of Coimbra, Portugal
Paolino Di Felice	University of L'Aquila, Italy
Prabu Dorairaj	NetApp, India/USA
Noelia Faginas Lago	University of Perugia, Italy
M. Irene Falcao	University of Minho, Portugal
Cherry Liu Fang	U.S. DOE Ames Laboratory, USA
Florbela P. Fernandes	Polytechnic Institute of Bragança, Portugal
Jose-Jesus Fernandez	National Centre for Biotechnology, CSIS, Spain
Paula Odete Fernandes	Polytechnic Institute of Bragança, Portugal
Adelaide de Fátima Baptista Valente Freitas	University of Aveiro, Portugal
Manuel Carlos Figueiredo	University of Minho, Portugal
Maria Celia Furtado Rocha	PRODEB–PósCultura/UFBA, Brazil
Chiara Garau	University of Cagliari, Italy
Paulino Jose Garcia Nieto	University of Oviedo, Spain
Raffaele Garrisi	Polizia di Stato, Italy
Jerome Gensel	LSR-IMAG, France
Maria Giaoutzi	National Technical University, Athens, Greece
Arminda Manuela Andrade Pereira Gonçalves	University of Minho, Portugal

Andrzej M. Goscinski	Deakin University, Australia
Sevin Gümgüm	Izmir University of Economics, Turkey
Alex Hagen-Zanker	University of Cambridge, UK
Shanmugasundaram Hariharan	B.S. Abdur Rahman University, India
Eligius M. T. Hendrix	University of Malaga, Spain and Wageningen University, The Netherlands
Hisamoto Hiyoshi	Gunma University, Japan
Mustafa Inceoglu	EGE University, Turkey
Peter Jimack	University of Leeds, UK
Qun Jin	Waseda University, Japan
Yeliz Karaca	University of Massachusetts Medical School, Worcester, USA
Farid Karimipour	Vienna University of Technology, Austria
Baris Kazar	Oracle Corp., USA
Maulana Adhinugraha Kiki	Telkom University, Indonesia
DongSeong Kim	University of Canterbury, New Zealand
Taihoon Kim	Hannam University, Korea
Ivana Kolingerova	University of West Bohemia, Czech Republic
Nataliia Kulabukhova	St. Petersburg University, Russia
Vladimir Korkhov	St. Petersburg University, Russia
Rosa Lasaponara	National Research Council, Italy
Maurizio Lazzari	National Research Council, Italy
Cheng Siong Lee	Monash University, Australia
Sangyoun Lee	Yonsei University, Korea
Jongchan Lee	Kunsan National University, Korea
Chendong Li	University of Connecticut, USA
Gang Li	Deakin University, Australia
Fang Liu	AMES Laboratories, USA
Xin Liu	University of Calgary, Canada
Andrea Lombardi	University of Perugia, Italy
Savino Longo	University of Bari, Italy
Tinghuai Ma	Nanjing University of Information Science & Technology, China
Ernesto Marcheggiani	Katholieke Universiteit Leuven, Belgium
Antonino Marvuglia	Research Centre Henri Tudor, Luxembourg
Nicola Masini	National Research Council, Italy
Ilaria Matteucci	National Research Council, Italy
Nirvana Meratnia	University of Twente, The Netherlands
Fernando Miranda	University of Minho, Portugal
Giuseppe Modica	University of Reggio Calabria, Italy
Josè Luis Montaña	University of Cantabria, Spain
Maria Filipa Mourão	Instituto Politécnico de Viana do Castelo, Portugal

Giuseppe A. Trunfio	University of Sassari, Italy
Pablo Vanegas	University of Cuenca, Equador
Marco Vizzari	University of Perugia, Italy
Varun Vohra	Merck Inc., USA
Koichi Wada	University of Tsukuba, Japan
Krzysztof Walkowiak	Wroclaw University of Technology, Poland
Zequn Wang	Intelligent Automation Inc, USA
Robert Weibel	University of Zurich, Switzerland
Frank Westad	Norwegian University of Science and Technology, Norway
Roland Wismüller	Universität Siegen, Germany
Mudasser Wyne	SOET National University, USA
Chung-Huang Yang	National Kaohsiung Normal University, Taiwan
Xin-She Yang	National Physical Laboratory, UK
Salim Zabir	France Telecom Japan Co., Japan
Haifeng Zhao	University of California, Davis, USA
Fabiana Zollo	University of Venice "Cà Foscari", Italy
Albert Y. Zomaya	University of Sydney, Australia

Workshop Organizers

Advanced Data Science Techniques with Applications in Industry and Environmental Sustainability (ATELIERS 2023)

Dario Torregrossa	Goodyear, Luxemburg
Antonino Marvuglia	Luxembourg Institute of Science and Technology, Luxemburg
Valeria Borodin	École des Mines de Saint-Étienne, Luxemburg
Mohamed Laib	Luxembourg Institute of Science and Technology, Luxemburg

Advances in Artificial Intelligence Learning Technologies: Blended Learning, STEM, Computational Thinking and Coding (AAILT 2023)

Alfredo Milani	University of Perugia, Italy
Valentina Franzoni	University of Perugia, Italy
Sergio Tasso	University of Perugia, Italy

Advanced Processes of Mathematics and Computing Models in Complex Computational Systems (ACMC 2023)

Yeliz Karaca	University of Massachusetts Chan Medical School and Massachusetts Institute of Technology, USA
Dumitru Baleanu	Cankaya University, Turkey
Osvaldo Gervasi	University of Perugia, Italy
Yudong Zhang	University of Leicester, UK
Majaz Moonis	University of Massachusetts Medical School, USA

Artificial Intelligence Supported Medical Data Examination (AIM 2023)

David Taniar	Monash University, Australia
Seifedine Kadry	Noroff University College, Norway
Venkatesan Rajinikanth	Saveetha School of Engineering, India

Advanced and Innovative Web Apps (AIWA 2023)

Damiano Perri	University of Perugia, Italy
Osvaldo Gervasi	University of Perugia, Italy

Assessing Urban Sustainability (ASUS 2023)

Elena Todella	Polytechnic of Turin, Italy
Marika Gaballo	Polytechnic of Turin, Italy
Beatrice Mecca	Polytechnic of Turin, Italy

Advances in Web Based Learning (AWBL 2023)

Birol Ciloglugil	Ege University, Turkey
Mustafa Inceoglu	Ege University, Turkey

Blockchain and Distributed Ledgers: Technologies and Applications (BDLTA 2023)

Vladimir Korkhov	Saint Petersburg State University, Russia
Elena Stankova	Saint Petersburg State University, Russia
Nataliia Kulabukhova	Saint Petersburg State University, Russia

Bio and Neuro Inspired Computing and Applications (BIONCA 2023)

Nadia Nedjah	State University of Rio De Janeiro, Brazil
Luiza De Macedo Mourelle	State University of Rio De Janeiro, Brazil

Choices and Actions for Human Scale Cities: Decision Support Systems (CAHSC–DSS 2023)

Giovanna Acampa	University of Florence and University of Enna Kore, Italy
Fabrizio Finucci	Roma Tre University, Italy
Luca S. Dacci	Polytechnic of Turin, Italy

Computational and Applied Mathematics (CAM 2023)

Maria Irene Falcao	University of Minho, Portugal
Fernando Miranda	University of Minho, Portugal

Computational and Applied Statistics (CAS 2023)

Ana Cristina Braga	University of Minho, Portugal

Cyber Intelligence and Applications (CIA 2023)

Gianni Dangelo	University of Salerno, Italy
Francesco Palmieri	University of Salerno, Italy
Massimo Ficco	University of Salerno, Italy

Conversations South-North on Climate Change Adaptation Towards Smarter and More Sustainable Cities (CLAPS 2023)

Chiara Garau	University of Cagliari, Italy
Cristina Trois	University of kwaZulu-Natal, South Africa
Claudia Loggia	University of kwaZulu-Natal, South Africa
John Östh	Faculty of Technology, Art and Design, Norway
Mauro Coni	University of Cagliari, Italy
Alessio Satta	MedSea Foundation, Italy

Computational Mathematics, Statistics and Information Management (CMSIM 2023)

Maria Filomena Teodoro	University of Lisbon and Portuguese Naval Academy, Portugal
Marina A. P. Andrade	University Institute of Lisbon, Portugal

Computational Optimization and Applications (COA 2023)

Ana Maria A. C. Rocha	University of Minho, Portugal
Humberto Rocha	University of Coimbra, Portugal

Computational Astrochemistry (CompAstro 2023)

Marzio Rosi	University of Perugia, Italy
Nadia Balucani	University of Perugia, Italy
Cecilia Ceccarelli	University of Grenoble Alpes and Institute for Planetary Sciences and Astrophysics, France
Stefano Falcinelli	University of Perugia, Italy

Computational Methods for Porous Geomaterials (CompPor 2023)

Vadim Lisitsa	Russian Academy of Science, Russia
Evgeniy Romenski	Russian Academy of Science, Russia

Workshop on Computational Science and HPC (CSHPC 2023)

Elise De Doncker	Western Michigan University, USA
Fukuko Yuasa	High Energy Accelerator Research Organization, Japan
Hideo Matsufuru	High Energy Accelerator Research Organization, Japan

Cities, Technologies and Planning (CTP 2023)

Giuseppe Borruso	University of Trieste, Italy
Beniamino Murgante	University of Basilicata, Italy
Malgorzata Hanzl	Lodz University of Technology, Poland
Anastasia Stratigea	National Technical University of Athens, Greece
Ljiljana Zivkovic	Republic Geodetic Authority, Serbia
Ginevra Balletto	University of Cagliari, Italy

Gender Equity/Equality in Transport and Mobility (DELIA 2023)

Tiziana Campisi	University of Enna Kore, Italy
Ines Charradi	Sousse University, Tunisia
Alexandros Nikitas	University of Huddersfield, UK
Kh Md Nahiduzzaman	University of British Columbia, Canada
Andreas Nikiforiadis	Aristotle University of Thessaloniki, Greece
Socrates Basbas	Aristotle University of Thessaloniki, Greece

International Workshop on Defense Technology and Security (DTS 2023)

Yeonseung Ryu	Myongji University, South Korea

Integrated Methods for the Ecosystem-Services Accounting in Urban Decision Process (Ecourbn 2023)

Maria Rosaria Guarini	Sapienza University of Rome, Italy
Francesco Sica	Sapienza University of Rome, Italy
Francesco Tajani	Sapienza University of Rome, Italy

Carmelo Maria Torre	Polytechnic University of Bari, Italy
Pierluigi Morano	Polytechnic University of Bari, Italy
Rossana Ranieri	Sapienza Università di Roma, Italy

Evaluating Inner Areas Potentials (EIAP 2023)

Diana Rolando	Politechnic of Turin, Italy
Manuela Rebaudengo	Politechnic of Turin, Italy
Alice Barreca	Politechnic of Turin, Italy
Giorgia Malavasi	Politechnic of Turin, Italy
Umberto Mecca	Politechnic of Turin, Italy

Sustainable Mobility Last Mile Logistic (ELLIOT 2023)

Tiziana Campisi	University of Enna Kore, Italy
Socrates Basbas	Aristotle University of Thessaloniki, Greece
Grigorios Fountas	Aristotle University of Thessaloniki, Greece
Paraskevas Nikolaou	University of Cyprus, Cyprus
Drazenko Glavic	University of Belgrade, Serbia
Antonio Russo	University of Enna Kore, Italy

Econometrics and Multidimensional Evaluation of Urban Environment (EMEUE 2023)

Maria Cerreta	University of Naples Federico II, Italy
Carmelo Maria Torre	Politechnic of Bari, Italy
Pierluigi Morano	Polytechnic of Bari, Italy
Debora Anelli	Polytechnic of Bari, Italy
Francesco Tajani	Sapienza University of Rome, Italy
Simona Panaro	University of Sussex, UK

Ecosystem Services in Spatial Planning for Resilient Urban and Rural Areas (ESSP 2023)

Sabrina Lai	University of Cagliari, Italy
Francesco Scorza	University of Basilicata, Italy
Corrado Zoppi	University of Cagliari, Italy

Gerardo Carpentieri	University of Naples Federico II, Italy
Floriana Zucaro	University of Naples Federico II, Italy
Ana Clara Mourão Moura	Federal University of Minas Gerais, Brazil

Ethical AI Applications for a Human-Centered Cyber Society (EthicAI 2023)

Valentina Franzoni	University of Perugia, Italy
Alfredo Milani	University of Perugia, Italy
Jordi Vallverdu	University Autonoma Barcelona, Spain
Roberto Capobianco	Sapienza University of Rome, Italy

13th International Workshop on Future Computing System Technologies and Applications (FiSTA 2023)

Bernady Apduhan	Kyushu Sangyo University, Japan
Rafael Santos	National Institute for Space Research, Brazil

Collaborative Planning and Designing for the Future with Geospatial Applications (GeoCollab 2023)

Alenka Poplin	Iowa State University, USA
Rosanna Rivero	University of Georgia, USA
Michele Campagna	University of Cagliari, Italy
Ana Clara Mourão Moura	Federal University of Minas Gerais, Brazil

Geomatics in Agriculture and Forestry: New Advances and Perspectives (GeoForAgr 2023)

Maurizio Pollino	Italian National Agency for New Technologies, Energy and Sustainable Economic Development, Italy
Giuseppe Modica	University of Reggio Calabria, Italy
Marco Vizzari	University of Perugia, Italy
Salvatore Praticò	University of Reggio Calabria, Italy

Geographical Analysis, Urban Modeling, Spatial Statistics (Geog-An-Mod 2023)

Giuseppe Borruso — University of Trieste, Italy
Beniamino Murgante — University of Basilicata, Italy
Harmut Asche — Hasso-Plattner-Institut für Digital Engineering Ggmbh, Germany

Geomatics for Resource Monitoring and Management (GRMM 2023)

Alessandra Capolupo — Polytechnic of Bari, Italy
Eufemia Tarantino — Polytechnic of Bari, Italy
Enrico Borgogno Mondino — University of Turin, Italy

International Workshop on Information and Knowledge in the Internet of Things (IKIT 2023)

Teresa Guarda — Peninsula State University of Santa Elena, Ecuador
Modestos Stavrakis — University of the Aegean, Greece

International Workshop on Collective, Massive and Evolutionary Systems (IWCES 2023)

Alfredo Milani — University of Perugia, Italy
Rajdeep Niyogi — Indian Institute of Technology, India
Valentina Franzoni — University of Perugia, Italy

Multidimensional Evolutionary Evaluations for Transformative Approaches (MEETA 2023)

Maria Cerreta — University of Naples Federico II, Italy
Giuliano Poli — University of Naples Federico II, Italy
Ludovica Larocca — University of Naples Federico II, Italy
Chiara Mazzarella — University of Naples Federico II, Italy

Stefania Regalbuto	University of Naples Federico II, Italy
Maria Somma	University of Naples Federico II, Italy

Building Multi-dimensional Models for Assessing Complex Environmental Systems (MES 2023)

Marta Dell'Ovo	Politechnic of Milan, Italy
Vanessa Assumma	University of Bologna, Italy
Caterina Caprioli	Politechnic of Turin, Italy
Giulia Datola	Politechnic of Turin, Italy
Federico Dellanna	Politechnic of Turin, Italy
Marco Rossitti	Politechnic of Milan, Italy

Metropolitan City Lab (Metro_City_Lab 2023)

Ginevra Balletto	University of Cagliari, Italy
Luigi Mundula	University for Foreigners of Perugia, Italy
Giuseppe Borruso	University of Trieste, Italy
Jacopo Torriti	University of Reading, UK
Isabella Ligia	Metropolitan City of Cagliari, Italy

Mathematical Methods for Image Processing and Understanding (MMIPU 2023)

Ivan Gerace	University of Perugia, Italy
Gianluca Vinti	University of Perugia, Italy
Arianna Travaglini	University of Florence, Italy

Models and Indicators for Assessing and Measuring the Urban Settlement Development in the View of ZERO Net Land Take by 2050 (MOVEto0 2023)

Lucia Saganeiti	University of L'Aquila, Italy
Lorena Fiorini	University of L'Aquila, Italy
Angela Pilogallo	University of L'Aquila, Italy
Alessandro Marucci	University of L'Aquila, Italy
Francesco Zullo	University of L'Aquila, Italy

Modelling Post-Covid Cities (MPCC 2023)

Giuseppe Borruso	University of Trieste, Italy
Beniamino Murgante	University of Basilicata, Italy
Ginevra Balletto	University of Cagliari, Italy
Lucia Saganeiti	University of L'Aquila, Italy
Marco Dettori	University of Sassari, Italy

3rd Workshop on Privacy in the Cloud/Edge/IoT World (PCEIoT 2023)

Michele Mastroianni	University of Salerno, Italy
Lelio Campanile	University of Campania Luigi Vanvitelli, Italy
Mauro Iacono	University of Campania Luigi Vanvitelli, Italy

Port City Interface: Land Use, Logistic and Rear Port Area Planning (PORTUNO 2023)

Tiziana Campisi	University of Enna Kore, Italy
Socrates Basbas	Aristotle University of Thessaloniki, Greece
Efstathios Bouhouras	Aristotle University of Thessaloniki, Greece
Giovanni Tesoriere	University of Enna Kore, Italy
Elena Cocuzza	University of Catania, Italy
Gianfranco Fancello	University of Cagliari, Italy

Scientific Computing Infrastructure (SCI 2023)

Elena Stankova	St. Petersburg State University, Russia
Vladimir Korkhov	St. Petersburg University, Russia

Supply Chains, IoT, and Smart Technologies (SCIS 2023)

Ha Jin Hwang	Sunway University, South Korea
Hangkon Kim	Daegu Catholic University, South Korea
Jan Seruga	Australian Catholic University, Australia

Spatial Cognition in Urban and Regional Planning Under Risk (SCOPUR23)

Domenico Camarda	Polytechnic of Bari, Italy
Giulia Mastrodonato	Polytechnic of Bari, Italy
Stefania Santoro	Polytechnic of Bari, Italy
Maria Rosaria Stufano Melone	Polytechnic of Bari, Italy
Mauro Patano	Polytechnic of Bari, Italy

Socio-Economic and Environmental Models for Land Use Management (SEMLUM 2023)

Debora Anelli	Polytechnic of Bari, Italy
Pierluigi Morano	Polytechnic of Bari, Italy
Benedetto Manganelli	University of Basilicata, Italy
Francesco Tajani	Sapienza University of Rome, Italy
Marco Locurcio	Polytechnic of Bari, Italy
Felicia Di Liddo	Polytechnic of Bari, Italy

Ports of the Future - Smartness and Sustainability (SmartPorts 2023)

Ginevra Balletto	University of Cagliari, Italy
Gianfranco Fancello	University of Cagliari, Italy
Patrizia Serra	University of Cagliari, Italy
Agostino Bruzzone	University of Genoa, Italy
Alberto Camarero	Politechnic of Madrid, Spain
Thierry Vanelslander	University of Antwerp, Belgium

Smart Transport and Logistics - Smart Supply Chains (SmarTransLog 2023)

Giuseppe Borruso	University of Trieste, Italy
Marco Mazzarino	University of Venice, Italy
Marcello Tadini	University of Eastern Piedmont, Italy
Luigi Mundula	University for Foreigners of Perugia, Italy
Mara Ladu	University of Cagliari, Italy
Maria del Mar Munoz Leonisio	University of Cadiz, Spain

Smart Tourism (SmartTourism 2023)

Giuseppe Borruso	University of Trieste, Italy
Silvia Battino	University of Sassari, Italy
Ainhoa Amaro Garcia	University of Alcala and University of Las Palmas, Spain
Francesca Krasna	University of Trieste, Italy
Ginevra Balletto	University of Cagliari, Italy
Maria del Mar Munoz Leonisio	University of Cadiz, Spain

Sustainability Performance Assessment: Models, Approaches, and Applications Toward Interdisciplinary and Integrated Solutions (SPA 2023)

Sabrina Lai	University of Cagliari, Italy
Francesco Scorza	University of Basilicata, Italy
Jolanta Dvarioniene	Kaunas University of Technology, Lithuania
Valentin Grecu	Lucian Blaga University of Sibiu, Romania
Georgia Pozoukidou	Aristotle University of Thessaloniki, Greece

Spatial Energy Planning, City and Urban Heritage (Spatial_Energy_City 2023)

Ginevra Balletto	University of Cagliari, Italy
Mara Ladu	University of Cagliari, Italy
Emilio Ghiani	University of Cagliari, Italy
Roberto De Lotto	University of Pavia, Italy
Roberto Gerundo	University of Salerno, Italy

Specifics of Smart Cities Development in Europe (SPEED 2023)

Chiara Garau	University of Cagliari, Italy
Katarína Vitálišová	Matej Bel University, Slovakia
Paolo Nesi	University of Florence, Italy
Anna Vaňová	Matej Bel University, Slovakia
Kamila Borsekova	Matej Bel University, Slovakia
Paola Zamperlin	University of Pisa, Italy

Smart, Safe and Health Cities (SSHC 2023)

Chiara Garau	University of Cagliari, Italy
Gerardo Carpentieri	University of Naples Federico II, Italy
Floriana Zucaro	University of Naples Federico II, Italy
Aynaz Lotfata	Chicago State University, USA
Alfonso Annunziata	University of Basilicata, Italy
Diego Altafini	University of Pisa, Italy

Smart and Sustainable Island Communities (SSIC_2023)

Chiara Garau	University of Cagliari, Italy
Anastasia Stratigea	National Technical University of Athens, Greece
Yiota Theodora	National Technical University of Athens, Greece
Giulia Desogus	University of Cagliari, Italy

Theoretical and Computational Chemistry and Its Applications (TCCMA 2023)

Noelia Faginas-Lago	University of Perugia, Italy
Andrea Lombardi	University of Perugia, Italy

Transport Infrastructures for Smart Cities (TISC 2023)

Francesca Maltinti	University of Cagliari, Italy
Mauro Coni	University of Cagliari, Italy
Francesco Pinna	University of Cagliari, Italy
Chiara Garau	University of Cagliari, Italy
Nicoletta Rassu	University of Cagliari, Italy
James Rombi	University of Cagliari, Italy

Urban Regeneration: Innovative Tools and Evaluation Model (URITEM 2023)

Fabrizio Battisti	University of Florence, Italy
Giovanna Acampa	University of Florence and University of Enna Kore, Italy
Orazio Campo	La Sapienza University of Rome, Italy

Urban Space Accessibility and Mobilities (USAM 2023)

Chiara Garau	University of Cagliari, Italy
Matteo Ignaccolo	University of Catania, Italy
Michela Tiboni	University of Brescia, Italy
Francesco Pinna	University of Cagliari, Italy
Silvia Rossetti	University of Parma, Italy
Vincenza Torrisi	University of Catania, Italy
Ilaria Delponte	University of Genoa, Italy

Virtual Reality and Augmented Reality and Applications (VRA 2023)

Osvaldo Gervasi	University of Perugia, Italy
Damiano Perri	University of Florence, Italy
Marco Simonetti	University of Florence, Italy
Sergio Tasso	University of Perugia, Italy

Workshop on Advanced and Computational Methods for Earth Science Applications (WACM4ES 2023)

Luca Piroddi	University of Malta, Malta
Sebastiano Damico	University of Malta, Malta
Marilena Cozzolino	Università del Molise, Italy
Adam Gauci	University of Malta, Italy
Giuseppina Vacca	University of Cagliari, Italy
Chiara Garau	University of Cagliari, Italy

Sponsoring Organizations

ICCSA 2023 would not have been possible without the tremendous support of many organizations and institutions, for which all organizers and participants of ICCSA 2023 express their sincere gratitude:

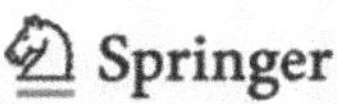

Springer Nature Switzerland AG, Switzerland
(https://www.springer.com)

Computers Open Access Journal
(https://www.mdpi.com/journal/computers)

National Technical University of Athens, Greece
(https://www.ntua.gr/)

University of the Aegean, Greece
(https://www.aegean.edu/)

University of Perugia, Italy
(https://www.unipg.it)

University of Basilicata, Italy
(http://www.unibas.it)

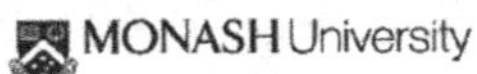

Monash University, Australia
(https://www.monash.edu/)

Kyushu Sangyo University, Japan
(https://www.kyusan-u.ac.jp/)

Universidade do Minho
Escola de Engenharia

University of Minho, Portugal
(https://www.uminho.pt/)

Referees

Francesca Abastante	Turin Polytechnic, Italy
Giovanna Acampa	University of Enna Kore, Italy
Adewole Adewumi	Algonquin College, Canada
Vera Afreixo	University of Aveiro, Portugal
Riad Aggoune	Luxembourg Institute of Science and Technology, Luxembourg
Akshat Agrawal	Amity University Haryana, India
Waseem Ahmad	National Institute of Technology Karnataka, India
Oylum Alatlı	Ege University, Turkey
Abraham Alfa	Federal University of Technology Minna, Nigeria
Diego Altafini	University of Pisa, Italy
Filipe Alvelos	University of Minho, Portugal
Marina Alexandra Pedro Andrade	University Institute of Lisbon, Portugal
Debora Anelli	Polytechnic University of Bari, Italy
Mariarosaria Angrisano	Pegaso University, Italy
Alfonso Annunziata	University of Cagliari, Italy
Magarò Antonio	Sapienza University of Rome, Italy
Bernady Apduhan	Kyushu Sangyo University, Japan
Jonathan Apeh	Covenant University, Nigeria
Daniela Ascenzi	University of Trento, Italy
Vanessa Assumma	University of Bologna, Italy
Maria Fernanda Augusto	Bitrum Research Center, Spain
Marco Baioletti	University of Perugia, Italy

Ginevra Balletto	University of Cagliari, Italy
Carlos Balsa	Polytechnic Institute of Bragança, Portugal
Benedetto Barabino	University of Brescia, Italy
Simona Barbaro	University of Palermo, Italy
Sebastiano Barbieri	Turin Polytechnic, Italy
Kousik Barik	University of Alcala, Spain
Alice Barreca	Turin Polytechnic, Italy
Socrates Basbas	Aristotle University of Thessaloniki, Greece
Rosaria Battarra	National Research Council, Italy
Silvia Battino	University of Sassari, Italy
Fabrizio Battisti	University of Florence, Italy
Yaroslav Bazaikin	Jan Evangelista Purkyne University, Czech Republic
Ranjan Kumar Behera	Indian Institute of Information Technology, India
Simone Belli	Complutense University of Madrid, Spain
Oscar Bellini	Polytechnic University of Milan, Italy
Giulio Biondi	University of Perugia, Italy
Adriano Bisello	Eurac Research, Italy
Semen Bochkov	Ulyanovsk State Technical University, Russia
Alexander Bogdanov	St. Petersburg State University, Russia
Letizia Bollini	Free University of Bozen, Italy
Giuseppe Borruso	University of Trieste, Italy
Marilisa Botte	University of Naples Federico II, Italy
Ana Cristina Braga	University of Minho, Portugal
Frederico Branco	University of Trás-os-Montes and Alto Douro, Portugal
Jorge Buele	Indoamérica Technological University, Ecuador
Datzania Lizeth Burgos	Peninsula State University of Santa Elena, Ecuador
Isabel Cacao	University of Aveiro, Portugal
Francesco Calabrò	Mediterranea University of Reggio Calabria, Italy
Rogerio Calazan	Institute of Sea Studies Almirante Paulo Moreira, Brazil
Lelio Campanile	University of Campania Luigi Vanvitelli, Italy
Tiziana Campisi	University of Enna Kore, Italy
Orazio Campo	University of Rome La Sapienza, Italy
Caterina Caprioli	Turin Polytechnic, Italy
Gerardo Carpentieri	University of Naples Federico II, Italy
Martina Carra	University of Brescia, Italy
Barbara Caselli	University of Parma, Italy
Danny Casprini	Politechnic of Milan, Italy

Piero Di Bonito	University of Campania Luigi Vanvitelli, Italy
Chiara Di Dato	University of L'Aquila, Italy
Michele Di Giovanni	University of Campania Luigi Vanvitelli, Italy
Felicia Di Liddo	Polytechnic University of Bari, Italy
Joana Dias	University of Coimbra, Portugal
Luigi Dolores	University of Salerno, Italy
Marco Donatelli	University of Insubria, Italy
Aziz Dursun	Virginia Tech University, USA
Jaroslav Dvořak	Klaipeda University, Lithuania
Wolfgang Erb	University of Padova, Italy
Maurizio Francesco Errigo	University of Enna Kore, Italy
Noelia Faginas-Lago	University of Perugia, Italy
Maria Irene Falcao	University of Minho, Portugal
Stefano Falcinelli	University of Perugia, Italy
Grazia Fattoruso	Italian National Agency for New Technologies, Energy and Sustainable Economic Development, Italy
Sara Favargiotti	University of Trento, Italy
Marcin Feltynowski	University of Lodz, Poland
António Fernandes	Polytechnic Institute of Bragança, Portugal
Florbela P. Fernandes	Polytechnic Institute of Bragança, Portugal
Paula Odete Fernandes	Polytechnic Institute of Bragança, Portugal
Luis Fernandez-Sanz	University of Alcala, Spain
Maria Eugenia Ferrao	University of Beira Interior and University of Lisbon, Portugal
Luís Ferrás	University of Minho, Portugal
Angela Ferreira	Polytechnic Institute of Bragança, Portugal
Maddalena Ferretti	Politechnic of Marche, Italy
Manuel Carlos Figueiredo	University of Minho, Portugal
Fabrizio Finucci	Roma Tre University, Italy
Ugo Fiore	University Pathenope of Naples, Italy
Lorena Fiorini	University of L'Aquila, Italy
Valentina Franzoni	Perugia University, Italy
Adelaide Freitas	University of Aveiro, Portugal
Kirill Gadylshin	Russian Academy of Sciences, Russia
Andrea Gallo	University of Trieste, Italy
Luciano Galone	University of Malta, Malta
Chiara Garau	University of Cagliari, Italy
Ernesto Garcia Para	Universidad del País Vasco, Spain
Rachele Vanessa Gatto	Università della Basilicata, Italy
Marina Gavrilova	University of Calgary, Canada
Georgios Georgiadis	Aristotle University of Thessaloniki, Greece

Ivan Gerace	University of Perugia, Italy
Osvaldo Gervasi	University of Perugia, Italy
Alfonso Giancotti	Sapienza University of Rome, Italy
Andrea Gioia	Politechnic of Bari, Italy
Giacomo Giorgi	University of Perugia, Italy
Salvatore Giuffrida	Università di Catania, Italy
A. Manuela Gonçalves	University of Minho, Portugal
Angela Gorgoglione	University of the Republic, Uruguay
Yusuke Gotoh	Okayama University, Japan
Mariolina Grasso	University of Enna Kore, Italy
Silvana Grillo	University of Cagliari, Italy
Teresa Guarda	Universidad Estatal Peninsula de Santa Elena, Ecuador
Eduardo Guerra	Free University of Bozen-Bolzano, Italy
Carmen Guida	University of Napoli Federico II, Italy
Kemal Güven Gülen	Namık Kemal University, Turkey
Malgorzata Hanzl	Technical University of Lodz, Poland
Peter Hegedus	University of Szeged, Hungary
Syeda Sumbul Hossain	Daffodil International University, Bangladesh
Mustafa Inceoglu	Ege University, Turkey
Federica Isola	University of Cagliari, Italy
Seifedine Kadry	Noroff University College, Norway
Yeliz Karaca	University of Massachusetts Chan Medical School and Massachusetts Institute of Technology, USA
Harun Karsli	Bolu Abant Izzet Baysal University, Turkey
Tayana Khachkova	Russian Academy of Sciences, Russia
Manju Khari	Jawaharlal Nehru University, India
Vladimir Korkhov	Saint Petersburg State University, Russia
Dionisia Koutsi	National Technical University of Athens, Greece
Tomonori Kouya	Shizuoka Institute of Science and Technology, Japan
Nataliia Kulabukhova	Saint Petersburg State University, Russia
Anisha Kumari	National Institute of Technology, India
Ludovica La Rocca	University of Napoli Federico II, Italy
Mara Ladu	University of Cagliari, Italy
Sabrina Lai	University of Cagliari, Italy
Mohamed Laib	Luxembourg Institute of Science and Technology, Luxembourg
Giuseppe Francesco Cesare Lama	University of Napoli Federico II, Italy
Isabella Maria Lami	Turin Polytechnic, Italy
Chien Sing Lee	Sunway University, Malaysia

Filipe Mota Pinto	Polytechnic Institute of Leiria, Portugal
Maria Mourao	Polytechnic Institute of Viana do Castelo, Portugal
Eugenio Muccio	University of Naples Federico II, Italy
Beniamino Murgante	University of Basilicata, Italy
Rocco Murro	Sapienza University of Rome, Italy
Giuseppe Musolino	Mediterranean University of Reggio Calabria, Italy
Nadia Nedjah	State University of Rio de Janeiro, Brazil
Juraj Nemec	Masaryk University, Czech Republic
Andreas Nikiforiadis	Aristotle University of Thessaloniki, Greece
Silvio Nocera	IUAV University of Venice, Italy
Roseline Ogundokun	Kaunas University of Technology, Lithuania
Emma Okewu	University of Alcala, Spain
Serena Olcuire	Sapienza University of Rome, Italy
Irene Oliveira	University Trás-os-Montes and Alto Douro, Portugal
Samson Oruma	Ostfold University College, Norway
Antonio Pala	University of Cagliari, Italy
Maria Panagiotopoulou	National Technical University of Athens, Greece
Simona Panaro	University of Sussex Business School, UK
Jay Pancham	Durban University of Technology, South Africa
Eric Pardede	La Trobe University, Australia
Hyun Kyoo Park	Ministry of National Defense, South Korea
Damiano Perri	University of Florence, Italy
Quoc Trung Pham	Ho Chi Minh City University of Technology, Vietnam
Claudio Piferi	University of Florence, Italy
Angela Pilogallo	University of L'Aquila, Italy
Francesco Pinna	University of Cagliari, Italy
Telmo Pinto	University of Coimbra, Portugal
Luca Piroddi	University of Malta, Malta
Francesco Pittau	Politechnic of Milan, Italy
Giuliano Poli	Università Federico II di Napoli, Italy
Maurizio Pollino	Italian National Agency for New Technologies, Energy and Sustainable Economic Development, Italy
Vijay Prakash	University of Malta, Malta
Salvatore Praticò	Mediterranean University of Reggio Calabria, Italy
Carlotta Quagliolo	Turin Polytechnic, Italy
Garrisi Raffaele	Operations Center for Cyber Security, Italy
Mariapia Raimondo	Università della Campania Luigi Vanvitelli, Italy

Bruna Ramos	Universidade Lusíada Norte, Portugal
Nicoletta Rassu	University of Cagliari, Italy
Roberta Ravanelli	University of Roma La Sapienza, Italy
Pier Francesco Recchi	University of Naples Federico II, Italy
Stefania Regalbuto	University of Naples Federico II, Italy
Rommel Regis	Saint Joseph's University, USA
Marco Reis	University of Coimbra, Portugal
Jerzy Respondek	Silesian University of Technology, Poland
Isabel Ribeiro	Polytechnic Institut of Bragança, Portugal
Albert Rimola	Autonomous University of Barcelona, Spain
Corrado Rindone	Mediterranean University of Reggio Calabria, Italy
Maria Rocco	Roma Tre University, Italy
Ana Maria A. C. Rocha	University of Minho, Portugal
Fabio Rocha	Universidade Federal de Sergipe, Brazil
Humberto Rocha	University of Coimbra, Portugal
Maria Clara Rocha	Politechnic Institut of Coimbra, Portual
Carlos Rodrigues	Polytechnic Institut of Bragança, Portugal
Diana Rolando	Turin Polytechnic, Italy
James Rombi	University of Cagliari, Italy
Evgeniy Romenskiy	Russian Academy of Sciences, Russia
Marzio Rosi	University of Perugia, Italy
Silvia Rossetti	University of Parma, Italy
Marco Rossitti	Politechnic of Milan, Italy
Antonio Russo	University of Enna, Italy
Insoo Ryu	MoaSoftware, South Korea
Yeonseung Ryu	Myongji University, South Korea
Lucia Saganeiti	University of L'Aquila, Italy
Valentina Santarsiero	University of Basilicata, Italy
Luigi Santopietro	University of Basilicata, Italy
Rafael Santos	National Institute for Space Research, Brazil
Valentino Santucci	University for Foreigners of Perugia, Italy
Alessandra Saponieri	University of Salento, Italy
Mattia Scalas	Turin Polytechnic, Italy
Francesco Scorza	University of Basilicata, Italy
Ester Scotto Di Perta	University of Napoli Federico II, Italy
Nicoletta Setola	University of Florence, Italy
Ricardo Severino	University of Minho, Portugal
Angela Silva	Polytechnic Institut of Viana do Castelo, Portugal
Carina Silva	Polytechnic of Lisbon, Portugal
Marco Simonetti	University of Florence, Italy
Sergey Solovyev	Russian Academy of Sciences, Russia

Maria Somma	University of Naples Federico II, Italy
Changgeun Son	Ministry of National Defense, South Korea
Alberico Sonnessa	Polytechnic of Bari, Italy
Inês Sousa	University of Minho, Portugal
Lisete Sousa	University of Lisbon, Portugal
Elena Stankova	Saint-Petersburg State University, Russia
Modestos Stavrakis	University of the Aegean, Greece
Flavio Stochino	University of Cagliari, Italy
Anastasia Stratigea	National Technical University of Athens, Greece
Yue Sun	European XFEL GmbH, Germany
Anthony Suppa	Turin Polytechnic, Italy
David Taniar	Monash University, Australia
Rodrigo Tapia McClung	Centre for Research in Geospatial Information Sciences, Mexico
Tarek Teba	University of Portsmouth, UK
Ana Paula Teixeira	University of Trás-os-Montes and Alto Douro, Portugal
Tengku Adil Tengku Izhar	Technological University MARA, Malaysia
Maria Filomena Teodoro	University of Lisbon and Portuguese Naval Academy, Portugal
Yiota Theodora	National Technical University of Athens, Greece
Elena Todella	Turin Polytechnic, Italy
Graça Tomaz	Polytechnic Institut of Guarda, Portugal
Anna Tonazzini	National Research Council, Italy
Dario Torregrossa	Goodyear, Luxembourg
Francesca Torrieri	University of Naples Federico II, Italy
Vincenza Torrisi	University of Catania, Italy
Nikola Tosic	Polytechnic University of Catalonia, Spain
Vincenzo Totaro	Polytechnic University of Bari, Italy
Arianna Travaglini	University of Florence, Italy
António Trigo	Polytechnic of Coimbra, Portugal
Giuseppe A. Trunfio	University of Sassari, Italy
Toshihiro Uchibayashi	Kyushu University, Japan
Piero Ugliengo	University of Torino, Italy
Jordi Vallverdu	University Autonoma Barcelona, Spain
Gianmarco Vanuzzo	University of Perugia, Italy
Dmitry Vasyunin	T-Systems, Russia
Laura Verde	University of Campania Luigi Vanvitelli, Italy
Giulio Vignoli	University of Cagliari, Italy
Gianluca Vinti	University of Perugia, Italy
Katarína Vitálišová	Matej Bel University, Slovak Republic
Daniel Mark Vitiello	University of Cagliari

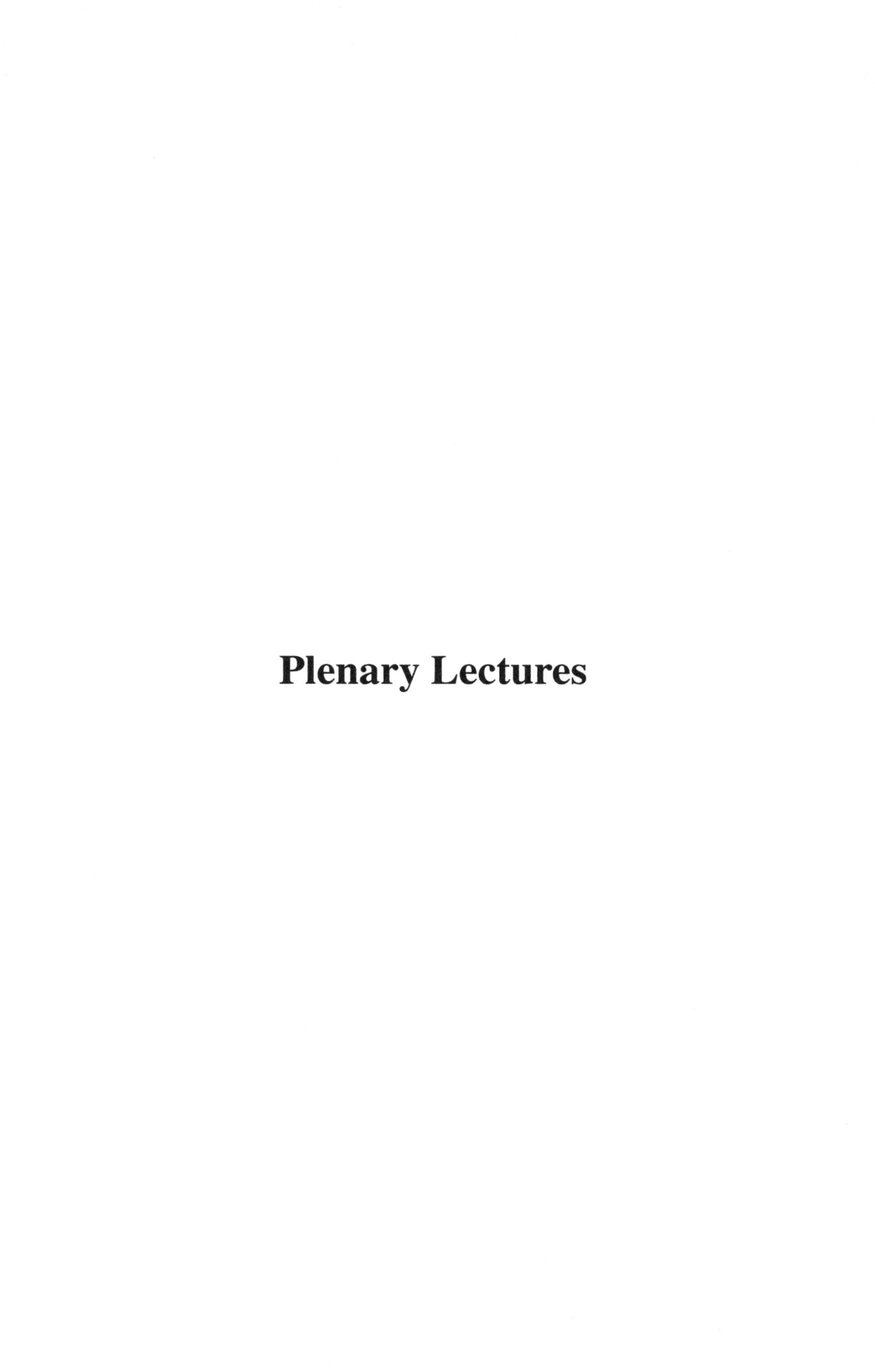

Plenary Lectures

A Multiscale Planning Concept for Sustainable Metropolitan Development

Pierre Frankhauser

Théma, Université de Franche-Comté, 32, rue Mégevand, 20030 Besançon, France
pierre.frankhauser@univ-fcomte.fr

Keywords: Sustainable metropolitan development · Multiscale approach · Urban modelling

Urban sprawl has often been pointed out as having an important negative impact on environment and climate. Residential zones have grown up in what were initially rural areas, located far from employment areas and often lacking shopping opportunities, public services and public transportation. Hence urban sprawl increased car-traffic flows, generating pollution and increasing energy consumption. New road axes consume considerable space and weaken biodiversity by reducing and cutting natural areas. A return to "compact cities" or "dense cities" has often been contemplated as the most efficient way to limit urban sprawl. However, the real impact of density on car use is less clear-cut (Daneshpour and Shakibamanesh 2011). Let us emphasize that moreover climate change will increase the risk of heat islands on an intra-urban scale. This prompts a more nuanced reflection on how urban fabrics should be structured.

Moreover, urban planning cannot ignore social demand. Lower land prices in rural areas, often put forward by economists, is not the only reason of urban sprawl. The quality of the residential environment comes into play, too, through features like noise, pollution, landscape quality, density etc. Schwanen et al. (2004) observe for the Netherlands that households preferring a quiet residential environment and individual housing with a garden will not accept densification, which might even lead them to move to lower-density rural areas even farther away from jobs and shopping amenities. Many scholars emphasize the importance of green amenities for residential environments and report the importance of easy access to leisure areas (Guo and Bhat 2002). Vegetation in the residential environment has an important impact on health and well-being (Lafortezza et al. 2009).

We present here the Fractalopolis concept which we developed in the frame of several research projects and which aims reconciling environmental and social issues (Bonin et al., 2020; Frankhauser 2021; Frankhauser et al. 2018). This concept introduces a multiscale approach based on multifractal geometry for conceiving spatial development for metropolitan areas. For taking into account social demand we refer to the fundamental work of Max-Neef et al. (1991) based on Maslow's work about basic human needs. He introduces the concept of satisfiers assigned to meet the basic needs of "Subsistence, Protection, Affection, Understanding, Participation, Idleness, Creation, Identity and Freedom". Satisfiers thus become the link between the needs of everyone and society and may depend on the cultural context. We consider their importance, their location and their accessibility and we rank the needs according to their importance for individuals or households. In order to enjoy a good quality of life and to shorten trips and to reduce automobile use, it seems important for satisfiers of daily needs to be easily accessible. Hence, we consider the purchase rate when reflecting on the implementation of shops which is reminiscent of central place theory.

The second important feature is taking care of environment and biodiversity by avoiding fragmentation of green space (Ekren and Arslan 2022) which must benefit, moreover, of a good accessibility, as pointed out. These areas must, too, ply the role of cooling areas ensuring ventilation of urbanized areas (Kuttler et al. 1998).

For integrating these different objectives, we propose a concept for developing spatial configurations of metropolitan areas designed which is based on multifractal geometry. It allows combining different issues across a large range of scales in a coherent way. These issues include:

- providing easy access to a large array of amenities to meet social demand;
- promoting the use of public transportation and soft modes instead of automobile use;
- preserving biodiversity and improving the local climate.

The concept distinguishes development zones localized in the vicinity of a nested and hierarchized system of public transport axes. The highest ranked center offers all types of amenities, whereas lower ranked centers lack the highest ranked amenities. The lowest ranked centers just offer the amenities for daily needs. A coding system allows distinguishing the centers according to their rank.

Each subset of central places is in some sense autonomous, since they are not linked by transportation axes to subcenters of the same order. This allows to preserve a linked system of green corridors penetrating the development zones across scales avoiding the fragmentation of green areas and ensuring a good accessibility to recreational areas.

The spatial model is completed by a population distribution model which globally follows the same hierarchical logic. However, we weakened the strong fractal order what allows to conceive a more or less polycentric spatial system.

We can adapt the theoretical concept easily to real world situation without changing the underlying multiscale logic. A decision support system has been developed allowing to simulate development scenarios and to evaluate them. The evaluation procedure is based on fuzzy evaluation of distance acceptance for accessing to the different types of amenities according to the ranking of needs. We used for evaluation data issued from a great set of French planning documents like Master plans. We show an example how the software package can be used concretely.

References

Bonin, O., et al.: Projet SOFT sobriété énergétique par les formes urbaines et le transport (Research Report No. 1717C0003; p. 214). ADEME (2020)

Daneshpour, A., Shakibamanesh, A.: Compact city; dose it create an obligatory context for urban sustainability? Int. J. Archit. Eng. Urban Plann. **21**(2), 110–118 (2011)

Ekren, E., Arslan, M.: Functions of greenways as an ecologically-based planning strategy. In: Çakır, M., Tuğluer, M., Fırat Örs, P.: Architectural Sciences and Ecology, pp. 134–156. Iksad Publications (2022)

Frankhauser, P.: Fractalopolis—a fractal concept for the sustainable development of metropolitan areas. In: Sajous, P., Bertelle, C. (eds.) Complex Systems, Smart Territories and Mobility, pp. 15–50. Springer, Cham (2021). https://doi.org/10.1007/978-3-030-59302-5_2

Frankhauser, P., Tannier, C., Vuidel, G., Houot, H.: An integrated multifractal modelling to urban and regional planning. Comput. Environ. Urban Syst. **67**(1), 132–146 (2018). https://doi.org/10.1016/j.compenvurbsys.2017.09.011

Guo, J., Bhat, C.: Residential location modeling: accommodating sociodemographic, school quality and accessibility effects. University of Texas, Austin (2002)

Kuttler, W., Dütemeyer, D., Barlag, A.-B.: Influence of regional and local winds on urban ventilation in Cologne, Germany. Meteorologische Zeitschrift, 77–87 (1998) https://doi.org/10.1127/metz/7/1998/77

Lafortezza, R., Carrus, G., Sanesi, G., Davies, C.: Benefits and well-being perceived by people visiting green spaces in periods of heat stress. Urban For. Urban Green. **8**(2), 97–108 (2009)

Max-Neef, M. A., Elizalde, A., Hopenhayn, M.: Human scale development: conception, application and further reflections. The Apex Press (1991)

Schwanen, T., Dijst, M., Dieleman, F. M.: Policies for urban form and their impact on travel: The Netherlands experience. Urban Stud. **41**(3), 579–603 (2004)

Graph Drawing and Network Visualization – An Overview – (Keynote Speech)

Giuseppe Liotta

Dipartimento di Ingegneria, Università degli Studi di Perugia, Italy
giuseppe.liotta@unipg.it

Abstract. Graph Drawing and Network visualization supports the exploration, analysis, and communication of relational data arising in a variety of application domains: from bioinformatics to software engineering, from social media to cyber-security, from data bases to powergrid systems. Aim of this keynote speech is to introduce this thriving research area, highlighting some of its basic approaches and pointing to some promising research directions.

1 Introduction

Graph Drawing and Network Visualization is at the intersection of different disciplines and it combines topics that traditionally belong to theoretical computer science with methods and approaches that characterize more applied disciplines. Namely, it can be related to Graph Algorithms, Geometric Graph Theory and Geometric computing, Combinatorial Optimization, Experimental Analysis, User Studies, System Design and Development, and Human Computer Interaction. This combination of theory and practice is well reflected in the flagship conference of the area, the *International Symposium on Graph Drawing and Network Visualization*, that has two tracks, one focusing on combinatorial and algorithmic aspects and the other on the design of network visualization systems and interfaces. The conference is now at its 31st edition; a full list of the symposia and their proceedings, published by Springer in the LNCS series can be found at the URL: http://www.graphdrawing.org/.

Aim of this short paper is to outline the content of my Keynote Speech at ICCSA 2023, which will be referred to as the "Talk" in the rest of the paper. The talk will introduce the field of Graph Drawing and Network Visualization to a broad audience, with the goal to not only present some key methodological and technological aspects, but also point to some unexplored or partially explored research directions. The rest of this short paper briefly outlines the content of the talk and provides some references that can be a starting point for researchers interested in working on Graph Drawing and Network Visualization.

2 Why Visualize Networks?

Back in 1973 the famous statistician Francis Anscombe, gave a convincing example of why visualization is fundamental component of data analysis. The example is known as the *Anscombe's quartet* [3] and it consists of four sets of 11 points each that are almost identical in terms of the basic statistic properties of their x– and y– coordinates. Namely the mean values and the variance of x and y are exactly the same in the four sets, while the correlation of x and y and the linear regression are the same up to the second decimal. In spite of this statistical similarity, the data look very different when displayed in the Euclidean plane which leads to the conclusion that they correspond to significantly different phenomena. Figure 1 reports the four sets of Anscombe's quartet. After fifty years, with the arrival of AI-based technologies and the need of explaining and interpreting machine-driven suggestions before making strategic decision, the lesson of Anscombe's quartet has not just kept but even increased its relevance.

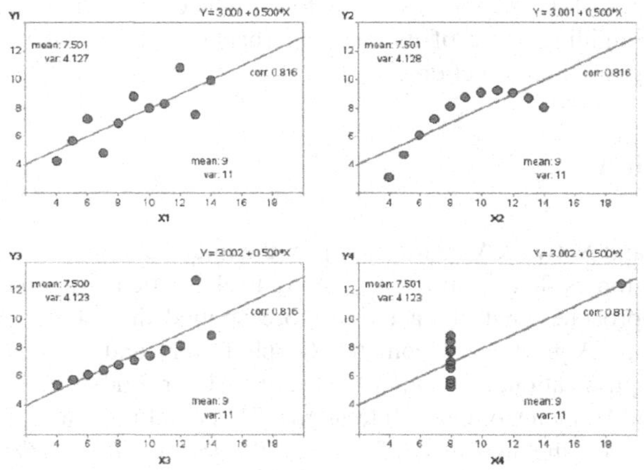

Fig. 1. The four point sets in Anscombe's quartet [3]; the figure also reports statistical values of the x and y variables.

As a matter of fact, nowadays the need of visualization systems goes beyond the verification of the accuracy of some statistical analysis on a set of scattered data. Recent technological advances have generated torrents of data that area relational in nature and typically modeled as networks: the nodes of the networks store the features of the data and the edges of the networks describe the semantic relationships between the data features. Such networked data sets (whose algebraic underlying structure is a called graph in discrete mathematics) arise in a variety of application domains including, for example, Systems Biology, Social Network Analysis, Software Engineering, Networking, Data Bases, Homeland Security, and Business Intelligence. In these (and many other) contexts, systems that support the visual analysis of networks and graphs play a central role in critical decision making processes. These are human-in-the-loop processes where the continuous interaction between humans (decision makers) and data mining or optimization algorithms (AI/ML components) supports the data exploration, the development of verifiable theories about the data, and the extraction of new knowledge that is used to make strategic choices. A seminal book by Keim et al. [33] schematically represents the human-in-the-loop approach to making sense of networked data sets as in Fig. 2. See also [46–49].

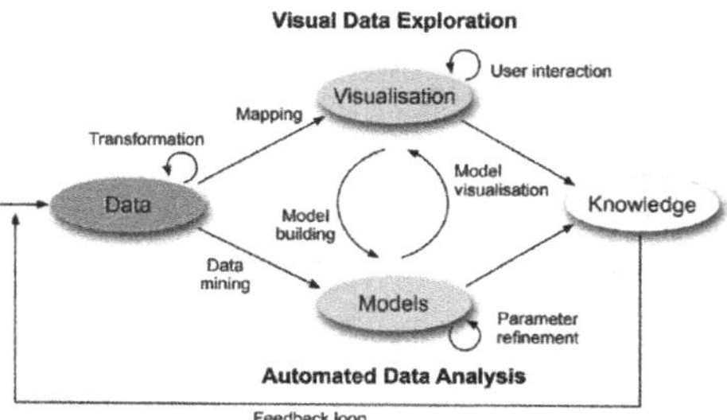

Fig. 2. Sense-making/knowledge generation loop. This conceptual interaction model between human analysts and network visualization system is at the basis of network visual analytics system design [33].

To make a concrete application example of the analysis of a network by interacting with its visualization, consider the problem of contrasting financial crimes such as money laundering or tax evasion. These crimes are based on relevant volumes of financial transactions to conceal the identity, the source, or the destination of illegally gained money. Also, the adopted patterns to pursue the illegal goals continuously change to conceal the crimes. Therefore, contrasting them requires special investigation units which must analyze very large and highly dynamic data sets and discover relationships between different subjects to untangle complex fraudulent plots. The investigative cycle begins with data collection and filtering; it is then followed by modeling the data as a social network (also called *financial activity network* in this context) to which different data mining and data analytic methods are applied, including graph pattern matching, social network analysis, machine learning, and information diffusion. By the network visualization system detectives can interactively explore the data, gain insight and make new hypotheses about possible criminal activities, verify the hypotheses by asking the system to provide more details about specific portions of the network, refine previous outputs, and eventually gain new knowledge. Figure 3 illustrates a small financial activity network where, by means of the interaction between an officer of the Italian Revenue Agency and the MALDIVE system described in [10] a fraudulent pattern has been identified. Precisely, the tax officer has encoded a risky relational scheme among taxpayers into a suspicious graph pattern; in response, the system has made a search in the taxpayer network and it has returned one such pattern. See, e.g., [9, 11, 14, 18, 38] for more papers and references about visual analytic applications to contrasting financial crimes.

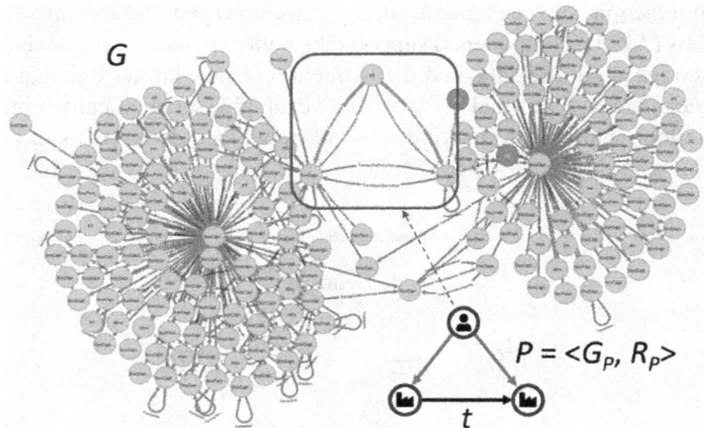

Fig. 3. A financial activity network from [10]. The pattern in the figure represents a SuppliesFromAssociated scheme, consisting of an economic transaction and two shareholding relationships.

3 Facets of Graph Drawing and Network Visualization

The Talk overviews some of the fundamental facets that characterize the research in Graph Drawing and Network Visualization. Namely:

- Graph drawing metaphors: Depending on the application context, different metaphors can be used to represent a relational data set modeled as a graph. The talk will briefly recall the matrix representation, the space filling representation, the contact representation, and the node-link representation which is, by far, the most commonly used (see, e.g., [43]).
- Interaction paradigms: Different interaction paradigms have different impacts on the sense-making process of the user about the visualized network. The Talk will go through the full-view, top-down, bottom-up, incremental, and narrative paradigms. Pros and cons will be highlighted for each approach, also by means of examples and applications. The discussion of the top-down interaction paradigm will also consider the hybrid visualization models (see, e.g., [2, 24, 26, 28, 39]) while the discussion about the incremental paradigm will focus on research about graph storyplans (see, e.g., [4, 6, 7]).
- Graph drawing algorithms: Three main algorithmic approaches will be reviewed, namely the force-directed, the layered), and the planarization-based approach; see, e.g., [5]. We shall also make some remarks about FPT algorithms for graph drawing (see, e.g., [8, 19, 20, 25, 27, 40, 53]) and about how the optimization challenges vary when it is assumed that the input has or does not have a fixed combinatorial embedding (see, e.g., [12, 13, 16, 17, 23]).
- Experimental analysis and user-studies: The Talk will mostly compare two models to define and experimentally validate those optimization goals that define a "readable"

network visualization, i.e. a visualization that in a given application context can easily convey the structure of a relational data set so to guarantee efficiency both in its visual exploration and in the elaboration of new knowledge. Special focus will be given to a set emerging optimization goals related to edge crossings that are currently investigated in the graph drawing and network visualization community unedr the name of "graph drawing beyond planarity" (see, e.g., [1, 15, 29, 35]).

The talk shall also point to some promising research directions, including: (i) Extend the body of papers devoted to user-studies that compare the impact of different graph drawing metaphors on the user perception. (ii) Extend the study of interaction paradigms to extended reality environments (see, e.g., [21, 30, 36, 37]); (iii) Engineer the FPT algorithms for graph drawing and experimentally compare their performances with exact or approximate solutions; and (iv) Develop new algorithmic fameworks in the context of graph drawing beyond planarity.

We conclude this short paper with pointers to publication venues and key references that can be browsed by researchers interested in the fascinating field of Graph Drawing and Network Visualization.

4 Pointers to Publication venues and Key References

A limited list of conferences where Graph Drawing and Network Visualization papers are regularly part of the program includes *IEEE VIS, EuroVis, SoCG, ISAAC, ACM-SIAM SODA, WADS,* and *WG.* Among the many journals where several Graph Drawing and Network Visualization papers have appeared during the last three decades we recall *IEEE Transactions on Visualization and Computer Graphs, SIAM Jounal of Computing, Computer Graphics Forum, Journal of Computer and System Sciences, Algorithmica, Journal of Graph Algorithms and Applications, Theoretical Computer Science, Information Sciences, Discrete and Computational Geometry, Computational Geometry: Theory and Applications, ACM Computing Surveys,* and *Computer Science Review.* A limited list of books, surveys, or papers that contain interesting algorithmic challenges on Graph Drawing and Network Visualization include [5, 15, 22, 29, 31–35, 41–45, 50–52].

References

1. Angelini, P., et al.: Simple k-planar graphs are simple (k+1)-quasiplanar. J. Comb. Theory, Ser. B, **142**, 1–35 (2020)
2. Angori, L., Didimo, W., Montecchiani, F., Pagliuca, D., Tappini, A.: Hybrid graph visualizations with chordlink: Algorithms, experiments, and applications. IEEE Trans. Vis. Comput. Graph. **28**(2), 1288–1300 (2022)
3. Anscombe, F.J.: Graphs in statistical analysis. Am. Stat. **27**(1), 17–21 (1973)
4. Di Battista, G., et al.: Small point-sets supporting graph stories. In: Angelini, P., von Hanxleden, R. (eds.) Graph Drawing and Network Visualization. GD 2022, LNCS, vol. 13764, pp. 289–303. Springer, Cham (2022). https://doi.org/10.1007/978-3-031-22203-0_21

5. Battista, G.D., Eades, P., Tamassia, R., Tollis, I.G.: Graph Drawing: Algorithms for the Visualization of Graphs. Prentice-Hall, Hoboken (1999)
6. Binucci, C., et al.: On the complexity of the storyplan problem. In: Angelini, P., von Hanxleden, R. (eds.) Graph Drawing and Network Visualization. GD 2022. LNCS, vol. 13764, pp. 304–318. Springer, Cham (2023). https://doi.org/10.1007/978-3-031-22203-0_22
7. Borrazzo, M., Lozzo, G.D., Battista, G.D., Frati, F., Patrignani, M.: Graph stories in small area. J. Graph Algorithms Appl. **24**(3), 269–292 (2020)
8. Chaplick, S., Giacomo, E.D., Frati, F., Ganian, R., Raftopoulou, C.N., Simonov, K.: Parameterized algorithms for upward planarity. In: Goaoc, X., Kerber, M. (eds.) 38th International Symposium on Computational Geometry, SoCG 2022, June 7–10, 2022, Berlin, Germany, LIPIcs, vol. 224, pp. 26:1–26:16. Schloss Dagstuhl - Leibniz-Zentrum für Informatik (2022)
9. Didimo, W., Giamminonni, L., Liotta, G., Montecchiani, F., Pagliuca, D.: A visual analytics system to support tax evasion discovery. Decis. Support Syst. **110**, 71–83 (2018)
10. Didimo, W., Grilli, L., Liotta, G., Menconi, L., Montecchiani, F., Pagliuca, D.: Combining network visualization and data mining for tax risk assessment. IEEE Access **8**, 16073–16086 (2020)
11. Didimo, W., Grilli, L., Liotta, G., Montecchiani, F., Pagliuca, D.: Visual querying and analysis of temporal fiscal networks. Inf. Sci. **505**, 406–421 (2019)
12. W. Didimo, M. Kaufmann, G. Liotta, and G. Ortali. Didimo, W., Kaufmann, M., Liotta, G., Ortali, G.: Rectilinear planarity testing of plane series-parallel graphs in linear time. In: Auber, D., Valtr, P. (eds.) Graph Drawing and Network Visualization. GD 2020. LNCS, vol. 12590, pp. 436–449. Springer, Cham (2020). https://doi.org/10.1007/978-3-030-68766-3_34
13. Didimo, W., Kaufmann, M., Liotta, G., Ortali, G.: Rectilinear planarity of partial 2-trees. In: Angelini, P., von Hanxleden, R. (eds.) Graph Drawing and Network Visualization. GD 2022. LNCS, vol. 13764, pp. 157–172. Springer, Cham (2023). https://doi.org/10.1007/978-3-031-22203-0_12
14. Didimo, W., Liotta, G., Montecchiani, F.: Network visualization for financial crime detection. J. Vis. Lang. Comput. **25**(4), 433–451 (2014)
15. Didimo, W., Liotta, G., Montecchiani, F.: A survey on graph drawing beyond planarity. ACM Comput. Surv. **52**(1), 4:1–4:37 (2019)
16. Didimo, W., Liotta, G., Ortali, G., Patrignani, M.: Optimal orthogonal drawings of planar 3-graphs in linear time. In: Chawla, S. (ed.) Proceedings of the 2020 ACM-SIAM Symposium on Discrete Algorithms, SODA 2020, Salt Lake City, UT, USA, January 5–8, 2020, pp. 806–825. SIAM (2020)
17. Didimo, W., Liotta, G., Patrignani, M.: HV-planarity: algorithms and complexity. J. Comput. Syst. Sci. **99**, 72–90 (2019)
18. Dilla, W.N., Raschke, R.L.: Data visualization for fraud detection: practice implications and a call for future research. Int. J. Acc. Inf. Syst. **16**, 1–22 (2015)
19. Dujmovic, V., et al.: A fixed-parameter approach to 2-layer planarization. Algorithmica **45**(2), 159–182 (2006)
20. Dujmovic, V., et al.: On the parameterized complexity of layered graph drawing. Algorithmica **52**(2), 267–292 (2008)

21. Dwyer, T., et al.: Immersive analytics: an introduction. In: Marriott, K., et al. (eds.) Immersive Analytics, LNCS, vol. 11190, pp. 1–23. Springer, Cham (2018)
22. Filipov, V., Arleo, A., Miksch, S.: Are we there yet? a roadmap of network visualization from surveys to task taxonomies. Computer Graphics Forum (2023, on print)
23. Garg, A., Tamassia, R.: On the computational complexity of upward and rectilinear planarity testing. SIAM J. Comput. **31**(2), 601–625 (2001)
24. Di Giacomo, E., Didimo, W., Montecchiani, F., Tappini, A.: A user study on hybrid graph visualizations. In: Purchase, H.C., Rutter, I. (eds.) Graph Drawing and Network Visualization. GD 2021. LNCS, vol. 12868, pp. 21–38. Springer, Cham (2021). https://doi.org/10.1007/978-3-030-92931-2_2
25. Giacomo, E.D., Giordano, F., Liotta, G.: Upward topological book embeddings of dags. SIAM J. Discret. Math. **25**(2), 479–489 (2011)
26. Giacomo, E.D., Lenhart, W.J., Liotta, G., Randolph, T.W., Tappini, A.: (k, p)-planarity: a relaxation of hybrid planarity. Theor. Comput. Sci. **896**, 19–30 (2021)
27. Giacomo, E.D., Liotta, G., Montecchiani, F.: Orthogonal planarity testing of bounded treewidth graphs. J. Comput. Syst. Sci. **125**, 129–148 (2022)
28. Giacomo, E.D., Liotta, G., Patrignani, M., Rutter, I., Tappini, A.: Nodetrix planarity testing with small clusters. Algorithmica **81**(9), 3464–3493 (2019)
29. Hong, S., Tokuyama, T. (eds.) Beyond Planar Graphs. Springer, Singapore (2020). https://doi.org/10.1007/978-981-15-6533-5
30. Joos, L., Jaeger-Honz, S., Schreiber, F., Keim, D.A., Klein, K.: Visual comparison of networks in VR. IEEE Trans. Vis. Comput. Graph. **28**(11), 3651–3661 (2022)
31. Jünger, M., Mutzel, P. (eds.) Graph Drawing Software. Springer, Berlin (2004). https://doi.org/10.1007/978-3-642-18638-7
32. Kaufmann, M., Wagner, D. (eds.): Drawing Graphs, Methods and Models (the book grow out of a Dagstuhl Seminar, April 1999), LNCS, vol. 2025. Springer, Berlin (2001). https://doi.org/10.1007/3-540-44969-8
33. Keim, D.A., Kohlhammer, J., Ellis, G.P., Mansmann, F.: Mastering the Information Age - Solving Problems with Visual Analytics. Eurographics Association, Saarbrücken (2010)
34. Keim, D.A., Mansmann, F., Stoffel, A., Ziegler, H.: Visual analytics. In: Liu, L., Özsu, M.T. (eds.) Encyclopedia of Database Systems, 2nd edn. Springer, Berlin (2018)
35. Kobourov, S.G., Liotta, G., Montecchiani, F.: An annotated bibliography on 1-planarity. Comput. Sci. Rev. **25**, 49–67 (2017)
36. Kraus, M., et al.: Immersive analytics with abstract 3D visualizations: a survey. Comput. Graph. Forum **41**(1), 201–229 (2022)
37. Kwon, O., Muelder, C., Lee, K., Ma, K.: A study of layout, rendering, and interaction methods for immersive graph visualization. IEEE Trans. Vis. Comput. Graph. **22**(7), 1802–1815 (2016)
38. Leite, R.A., Gschwandtner, T., Miksch, S., Gstrein, E., Kuntner, J.: NEVA: visual analytics to identify fraudulent networks. Comput. Graph. Forum **39**(6), 344–359 (2020)

39. Liotta, G., Rutter, I., Tappini, A.: Simultaneous FPQ-ordering and hybrid planarity testing. Theor. Comput. Sci. **874**, 59–79 (2021)
40. Liotta, G., Rutter, I., Tappini, A.: Parameterized complexity of graph planarity with restricted cyclic orders. J. Comput. Syst. Sci. **135**, 125–144 (2023)
41. Ma, K.: Pushing visualization research frontiers: essential topics not addressed by machine learning. IEEE Comput. Graphics Appl. **43**(1), 97–102 (2023)
42. McGee, F., et al.: Visual Analysis of Multilayer Networks. Synthesis Lectures on Visualization. Morgan & Claypool Publishers, San Rafael (2021)
43. Munzner, T.: Visualization Analysis and Design. A.K. Peters visualization series. A K Peters (2014)
44. Nishizeki, T., Rahman, M.S.: Planar Graph Drawing, vol. 12. World Scientific, Singapore (2004)
45. Nobre, C., Meyer, M.D., Streit, M., Lex, A.: The state of the art in visualizing multivariate networks. Comput. Graph. Forum **38**(3), 807–832 (2019)
46. Sacha, D.: Knowledge generation in visual analytics: Integrating human and machine intelligence for exploration of big data. In: Apel, S., et al. (eds.) Ausgezeichnete Informatikdissertationen 2018, LNI, vol. D-19, pp. 211–220. GI (2018)
47. Sacha, D., et al.: What you see is what you can change: human-centered machine learning by interactive visualization. Neurocomputing **268**, 164–175 (2017)
48. Sacha, D., Senaratne, H., Kwon, B.C., Ellis, G.P., Keim, D.A.: The role of uncertainty, awareness, and trust in visual analytics. IEEE Trans. Vis. Comput. Graph. **22**(1), 240–249 (2016)
49. Sacha, D., Stoffel, A., Stoffel, F., Kwon, B.C., Ellis, G.P., Keim, D.A.: Knowledge generation model for visual analytics. IEEE Trans. Vis. Comput. Graph. **20**(12), 1604–1613 (2014)
50. Tamassia, R.: Graph drawing. In: Sack, J., Urrutia, J. (eds.) Handbook of Computational Geometry, pp. 937–971. North Holland/Elsevier, Amsterdam (2000)
51. Tamassia, R. (ed.) Handbook on Graph Drawing and Visualization. Chapman and Hall/CRC, Boca Raton (2013)
52. Tamassia, R., Liotta, G.: Graph drawing. In: Goodman, J.E., O'Rourke, J. (eds.) Handbook of Discrete and Computational Geometry, 2nd edn., pp. 1163–1185. Chapman and Hall/CRC, Boca Raton (2004)
53. Zehavi, M.: Parameterized analysis and crossing minimization problems. Comput. Sci. Rev. **45**, 100490 (2022)

Understanding Non-Covalent Interactions in Biological Processes through QM/MM-EDA Dynamic Simulations

Marcos Mandado

Department of Physical Chemistry, University of Vigo, Lagoas-Marcosende s/n, 36310 Vigo, Spain
mandado@uvigo.es

Molecular dynamic simulations in biological environments such as proteins, DNA or lipids involves a large number of atoms, so classical models based on widely parametrized force fields are employed instead of more accurate quantum methods, whose high computational requirements preclude their application. The parametrization of appropriate force fields for classical molecular dynamics relies on the precise knowledge of the non-covalent inter and intramolecular interactions responsible for very important aspects, such as macromolecular arrangements, cell membrane permeation, ion solvation, etc. This implies, among other things, knowledge of the nature of the interaction, which may be governed by electrostatic, repulsion or dispersion forces. In order to know the balance between different forces, quantum calculations are frequently performed on simplified molecular models and the data obtained from these calculations are used to parametrize the force fields employed in classical simulations. These parameters are, among others, atomic charges, permanent electric dipole moments and atomic polarizabilities. However, it sometimes happens that the molecular models used for the quantum calculations are too simple and the results obtained can differ greatly from those of the extended system. As an alternative to classical and quantum methods, hybrid quantum/classical schemes (QM/MM) can be introduced, where the extended system is neither truncated nor simplified, but only the most important region is treated quantum mechanically.

In this presentation, molecular dynamic simulations and calculations with hybrid schemes are first introduced in a simple way for a broad and multidisciplinary audience. Then, a method developed in our group to investigate intermolecular interactions using hybrid quantum/classical schemes (QM/MM-EDA) is presented and some applications to the study of dynamic processes of ion solvation and membrane permeation are discussed [1–3]. Special attention is paid to the implementation details of the method in the EDA-NCI software [4].

References

1. Cárdenas, G., Pérez-Barcia, A., Mandado, M., Nogueira, J.J.: Phys. Chem. Chem. Phys. **23**, 20533 (2021)
2. Pérez-Barcia, A., Cárdenas, G., Nogueira, J.J., Mandado, M.: J. Chem. Inf. Model. **63**, 882 (2023)

3. Alvarado, R., Cárdenas, G., Nogueira, J.J., Ramos-Berdullas, N., Mandado, M.: Membranes **13**, 28 (2023)
4. Mandado, M., Van Alsenoy, C.: EDA-NCI: A program to perform energy decomposition analysis of non-covalent interactions. https://github.com/marcos-mandado/EDA-NCI

Contents – Part IV

Geographical Analysis, Urban Modeling, Spatial Statistics (Geog-An-Mod 2023)

Integrated Methods for the Ecosystem-Services Accounting in Urban Decision Process (Ecourbn 2023)

Research, Development and Innovation Projects for Territorial Cohesion in Inland Marginal Areas: Economic Analysis of Social and Cultural Benefits

Gabriella Maselli[1(✉)], Pasquale Persico[2], Antonio Nesticò[1], and Federica Russo[1]

[1] Department of Civil Engineering, University of Salerno, Fisciano, SA, Italy
{gmaselli,anestico,frusso}@unisa.it
[2] C.U.G.RI - interUniversity Centre for the Prediction and Prevention of Major Hazards, Fisciano, SA, Italy
ppersico@unisa.it

Abstract. To counteract the phenomena of demographic decline and marginalisation of inland areas, there is an urgent need for strategies and policy interventions to prevent the loss of a vast historical and cultural heritage and to trigger development and territorial cohesion processes. Various programmes and intervention strategies introduced by European and non-European governments show that investing in Research, Development, and Innovation (RDI) can be a crucial line of action for the economic valorisation of marginalised urban contexts. However, there is a lack of an operational framework that can support analysts in selecting effective intervention strategies. RDI projects are in fact complex interventions that, first, involve a multiplicity of actors and target groups. In addition, they are initiatives that generate a series of socio-cultural and environmental externalities that need to be adequately considered in the evaluations in order to make a correct judgement on the social profitability of the investments under analysis.

The aim of this study is to define a decision support model for RDI projects promoted within innovation ecosystems, which in turn must be included in a programmatic design of an ecoregion or macro-region. By means of such an economic analysis model, we intend to address the analyst in the: (a) estimation of social costs and benefits deriving from a RDI infrastructure; (b) evaluation of the social return on investment; (c) assessment of the investment risk variables and critical issues to be addressed to define strategic guidelines for the establishment and management of innovation ecosystems.

The conducted research is a starting point for application to real case studies that will allow the defined model to be tested.

(*) The paper is attributed equally to all authors.

Keywords: Internal Marginalized Areas · Ecoregions · RDI Projects · Economic Analysis

O. Gervasi et al. (Eds.): ICCSA 2023 Workshops, LNCS 14107, pp. 3–18, 2023.
https://doi.org/10.1007/978-3-031-37114-1_1

1 Introduction

In recent decades, the increasing migration from inland to urban areas is exacerbating the already marked imbalance between metropolises and small municipalities worldwide. On the one hand, cities and urban areas are growing very rapidly. According to the United Nations [1], the urban population now accounts for more than 55% of the global population and is expected to grow steadily to 68% by 2050. This translates into the presence – again according to United Nations estimates [2] – of 43 megacities by 2030, where megacity means an urban complex with at least ten million inhabitants. On the other hand, there is a relentless depopulation of small towns, mainly due to new housing and employment needs that lead citizens to prefer metropolises to rural areas. Added to this are the few or no job opportunities, the considerable distance from large service centres and the inadequacy of infrastructure and transport [3].

It is evident that these migratory dynamics are leading to a stark contrast between: (i) urban areas, which cover only 0.4–0.9 per cent of the global surface area, but are home to more than half the world's population and are responsible for about three quarters of the world's final energy use [4]; (ii) small towns, which are increasingly isolated economically, socially and culturally, and where the main risks concern productive impoverishment and the degradation of the existing building stock [5].

According to the latest data from the European Commission (2018), inland areas cover 83% of the territory of the European Union, hosting around 30% of its population. They are places with a higher percentage of citizens at risk of poverty and social exclusion than cities. This is in fact 22.4% for inland areas, while it is around 21.3% and 19.2% for large cities and medium-sized towns respectively [6]. If the marginality they suffer has caused, on the one hand, cultural, social and economic isolation; on the other, it has allowed them to preserve intact a vast material and immaterial heritage «in an autonomy that, although not devoid of contemporaneity, represents an object of great interest not only in terms of memory conservation, but also in terms of its potential to compose qualitative social and settlement models». [7] (p. 15). Awareness of the potential of these realities has been growing in recent decades and began with the crisis of the metropolis: the rapid process of urbanization has in fact led to an exponential growth in the use of resources, making it increasingly difficult to guarantee the principles of sustainability within urban systems [8]. It is exactly this crisis, therefore, that is increasingly leading to marginal realities being considered as a possible solution to mend the city-countryside relationship [9].

For all the above reasons, enhancing and protecting inland and marginal areas becomes an opportunity for the sustainable development of nations. It is therefore fundamental to proceed with a well-structured programme of interventions that is coherent and compatible with the culture of the local population and that is in step with the dynamics of the global economy and the technological revolution [10]. Starting from the analysis of problems and resources, in an integrated planning perspective it is necessary to define strategies that aim not only at building reuse, but also at environmental and landscape protection, infrastructural redevelopment and especially at social cohesion [11]. This territorial cohesion can be pursued if one invests in knowledge and applied knowledge, the latter representing a winning strategy to curb depopulation in the active and youth age [12–16].

On the basis of these premises, the aim of the paper is to demonstrate that within the framework of strategies and actions aimed at fostering the revitalisation of inland areas, a crucial role can be played by programmes and projects that contribute to defining 'innovation ecosystems'. In fact, promoting systems in which different actors - institutions, associations, universities, individual entrepreneurs and society – work together to generate, test and develop innovative solutions means investing in «knowledge of knowledge» and, as a consequence, supporting sustainable and effective development plans for the benefit of communities.

To address this issue, it becomes essential to first investigate the multiple socio-cultural, environmental, and economic repercussions that can result from the establishment of Ecosystems of Innovation (EI), and then to define operational tools useful for selecting effective intervention strategies [17]. Therefore, this research aims to characterise a decision-support model in processes aimed at the establishment of EI, with the objective of promoting social and environmental regeneration in inner and marginalised urban contexts.

The paper is divided into the following sections. Section 2 analyses the main strategies promoted by governments for the enhancement of marginal inland areas, with a focus on those based on the promotion of innovation. Section 3 first clarifies the meaning of innovation ecosystem, then defines characteristics and target groups of RDI infrastructures, then characterises the economic evaluation model. Section 4 returns conclusive remarks and research perspectives.

2 Innovation-Based Strategies for the Enhancement of Marginal Inland Areas

The growing institutional interest in inland areas, induced by the awareness of their great potential, is evident in the actions and strategies that governments are introducing to counter depopulation.

These include the Long-term Vision for the EU's rural areas (2021), which identifies actions to be taken to ensure more connected, prosperous, and resilient rural areas and communities. Specifically, 'flagship initiatives' are envisaged that aim to: (i) create new opportunities for the emergence of innovative businesses and, consequently, new jobs; (ii) strengthen territorial cohesion; (iii) improve the infrastructure and service system; (iv) promote the dissemination of diversified economic activities and sustainable agricultural practices [6].

Among the first European countries to undertake actions to counter the phenomenon of depopulation of inland areas is Spain, which already in 1984 established the *Programa Experimental de Recuperaciòn y Utilizaciòn Educativa de Pueblos Abandonados*, with the aim of revitalising small towns through cultural and educational projects [18].

France in 2015 adopted the Town-Country Reciprocity Agreements to promote inter-municipal partnerships between large, small and medium-sized towns, villages and rural areas in order to reduce economic and social gaps between the different parties and strengthen the most disadvantaged ones [19].

In Ireland, the Rural Regeneration and Development Fund (RRDF) offers an unprecedented opportunity for the revitalisation of small rural towns. It is a EUR 1 billion commitment by the government to invest in rural Ireland from 2019 to 2027, as the strengthening of rural economies and communities is one of the national strategic outcomes of the Ireland 2040 project [20].

Through the Bioenergy Villages strategy, Germany has chosen to invest in renewable energy production for the enhancement of small municipalities: currently in 120 small towns farmers and local cooperatives produce and distribute sustainable energy [21].

With the aim of countering the demographic decline and promoting the development of smaller centres, the *Strategia Nazionale per le Aree Interne* (SNAI) was launched in Italy in 2013, financed by the ordinary funds of the Stability Law. This strategy adopted a perimeter and prioritisation of inland areas according to their degree of 'peripherality' with respect to the poles, understood as centres of delivery of essential services, such as education, health, and mobility [10]. In addition to providing the perimeter of the inland areas, the SNAI has identified priority areas of intervention throughout the national territory where pilot projects of territorial enhancement are currently underway [22, 23].

Recently, more and more intervention programmes are demonstrating that investing in Research, Development and Innovation (RDI) can be a winning strategy to counter depopulation and the exodus of young people from inland areas to large urban centres. This is because, in addition to fostering a deeper awareness of the resources and problems of marginalised areas, RDI projects allow for the creation of new jobs and generate a set of social benefits for the community resulting from the production and dissemination of new knowledge.

According to Hosseini et al. [24], it is becoming increasingly important to look at intermediate and sparsely populated regions as arenas for digital innovation. In other terms, sparsely populated areas need technological innovation to address a complex set of local challenges related to specific geographical, economic, social and ecological conditions. Similarly, Provenzano et al. [25] also emphasise the fundamental importance of linking the innovation process with rural areas if the sustainable growth of peripheral areas is to be promoted.

The possibility of fostering the revitalisation of inland areas through innovation is also evidenced by the 'Smart Villages' strategy promoted by the European Network for Rural Development, which disseminates models and programmes for the regeneration of rural areas, sharing experiences and information. Specifically, this strategy aims at transforming 'marginal' cities into active and participative places, where the use of technology plays a decisive role in outlining new development paths [9]. In the literature, there are several authors who study the advantages of the Smart Village model, also analysing virtuous and successful experiences [26–28].

Again, the Organisation for Economic Cooperation and Development (OECD) in its recent report 'Unlocking Rural Innovation' [29] points out that innovation must be at the heart of the challenges facing rural regions. This is because innovation in rural regions can take very different forms than in cities. Just think that the main innovation systems are typically found in larger cities, with universities and companies large enough to have a formal R&D function. Whereas in rural areas, while it is true that science-based activities can be very successful, the uptake and implementation of these innovations requires: (i) connections to the places where the idea was developed; (ii) the resources to acquire and introduce the new technology.

Therefore, in less densely populated areas – where access to labour, capital, markets and public services is hindered by the lack of physical and digital infrastructure – only the realisation of networks and partnerships between institutions, universities, companies, associations and society can make the diffusion of innovation possible, so as to generate positive spill-over effects for the territory [30–32].

Within this framework is the Italian government's initiative «Ecosystems for Innovation in the South in Marginalised Urban Contexts» financed by the Supplementary Fund to the National Recovery and Resilience Plan (PNRR) with EUR 350 million. The aim of the investment is to promote the social and environmental regeneration of the most degraded urban areas in Southern Italy, characterised by depopulation and abandonment of inland areas. The objective is the creation of Innovation Hubs to offer highly qualified training, encourage multidisciplinary research and the birth of innovative economic activities [33].

3 Research Method

The paper intends to address the issue of the enhancement of inland areas through the creation of innovation ecosystems. While the literature and the actions implemented so far by governments demonstrate the importance of innovation as a driver of opportunities for marginalised areas, there is a lack of a systematic frame of reference that can support analysts in selecting effective intervention strategies. These are complex interventions involving a multiplicity of actors and target groups. In addition, such initiatives generate a series of socio-cultural and environmental externalities that need to be adequately considered in evaluations in order to be able to make a correct judgement on the social profitability of investments.

Therefore, the aim of this paper is to define a decision support model for processes aimed at setting up EI. To this end, we first clarify the meaning of an innovation ecosystem. Then, the characteristics of RDI projects and the effects they generate on the community are analysed. Finally, we define the logical-operational steps of the model.

3.1 What is an Innovation Ecosystem?

The concept of 'ecosystem' is rapidly gaining ground in the literature on innovation, strategy, and entrepreneurship [34]. In an increasingly specialised world, a single company generally lacks internal resources for the development of innovation. Therefore, to build a value proposition, it is increasingly necessary for individual organisations to rely on the contributions of various stakeholders, both internal and external to the institution [35, 36].

The term ecosystem was first used in a context different from its original scope, i.e. biological systems, in 1993 by Moore to describe a collection of producers and users that contribute to the performance of an organisation [37]. Subsequently, this concept has been employed in the field of innovation management, where an ecosystem is defined as a network of organisations interconnected or operating around an organisation or a technology platform with the aim of producing valuable goods and services [38–40].

Gomes et al. [34] for the first time clarify the differences between business ecosystems and innovation ecosystems, formerly used with the same meaning. In fact, it is possible to speak of an innovation ecosystem when «the value creation predominates over value capture. Also, in these cases, the relationships among actors are unstable and unclear, co-evolving in unforeseen ways, which may be changing from cooperation to competition» [34] (p.46).

In this sense, the innovation ecosystem allows us to work collectively to enable the flow of knowledge and support technological development with the aim of generating innovation [41]. According to Su et al., an innovation ecosystem must be composed of different stakeholders, including government, associations, practitioners, and others who inhabit the same scenario and appropriate new values through innovation [42].

According to Dias Sant'Ana et al., the main classifications regarding the structure of an innovation ecosystem relate to: (i) life cycle; (ii) level; (iii) layered structure [36]. With reference to lifecycle (i), innovation ecosystems are structured in four stages: emergence, expansion, leadership and self-renewal. Regarding level (ii), ecosystems can be distinguished into: macroscopic (national or international), medium (regional) or microscopic (organisational). At the macro or national level, the creation of innovation ecosystems requires the establishment of new governmental institutions, new policies, and regulations to promote interactions and the capacity for diffusion [43]. At the micro level, the ecosystem consists of: (i) social entrepreneurship organisations and technology platforms, whose purpose is to disseminate expertise; (ii) external organisations that provide access to additional resources [38]. Finally, regarding the layered structure, we identify: (a) the core-periphery structure, which consists of a 'core' company and peripheral actors; (b) the triple-layer structure, which holds a central layer, platform layer, and development and application layer; (c) the core-periphery triple-layer structure, which brings together the two models described [36].

Therefore, in the light of the above, by Ecosystem of Innovation (EI) we mean a network of universities, research organisations, territorial public bodies, and highly qualified public and private entities that promote and implement Research, Development and Innovation (RDI) infrastructures. This is to facilitate technology transfer and accelerate the digital transformation of companies' production processes with a view to economic and environmental sustainability and social impact on the territory. Such processes can be fostered by innovation ecosystems, more effectively if they are embedded in a programmatic design of an Ecoregion, i.e. a more or less large portion of ecologically homogeneous territory, or in a Macro-Region context, i.e. an area characterised by common problems and which can be conceived as an application of multi-level governance. In this case, policy implementation takes place on several levels, through (loyal) cooperation between EU institutions, states and local levels and thus as an instrument to ensure greater policy coordination between actors [44].

3.2 RDI Projects: Social Benefits and Target Groups

To understand how RDI projects can foster social cohesion in marginalised urban contexts, it is first necessary to investigate the social benefits and the relevant user-target groups.

Building RDI infrastructures in inland areas by making them areas of technological specialisation means:

- attracting resources to the area from outside (scholars, researchers and specialised professionals);
- activate in the short- and medium-term cross-fertilisation processes between businesses, between public administrations, between public administrations themselves, both local and non-local;
- facilitate the professional growth of operators;
- enable the increase and dissemination of know-how, also through the involvement of banks and venture capital;
- encourage the circulation of knowledge, also among the community [45, 46].

It follows that the model of the innovation ecosystem promoting RDI infrastructures represents a strategic network capable of fostering the circulation of knowledge and determining a series of spill-over effects on a multiplicity of user-target groups. These target groups are specifically represented by:

1. companies and laboratories that are part of the innovation ecosystem;
2. other enterprises and laboratories, already existing but outside the network, that benefit from the positive externalities generated by the research infrastructure, in terms of production and dissemination of new knowledge, and in more general terms of effects deriving from learning-by-doing processes;
3. new enterprises, i.e. start-ups and technology spin-offs, which are created as a result of the activities carried out by the RDI infrastructure. These enterprises can enjoy benefits in terms of reduced business mortality rate, cost savings and/or development of innovative products and processes;
4. researchers involved in the design, development and use of innovative machinery and technologies, as well as academics benefiting from scientific production. Specifically, the potential benefits for academic researchers are publications and citations in academic journals and the registration of patents;
5. young professional researchers working in companies. In this case, the expected benefit is expressed in terms of an increase in human capital, as well as social capital represented by the development of networks among colleagues and the establishment of new research groups;
6. students, usually post-graduates or doctoral students, but also graduates, who by attending higher education courses can certainly contribute to the increase in social and human capital;
7. population residing in the areas targeted for intervention and technological experimentation. The implementation of applied research activities enables the population to benefit from the reduction in mortality and accident rates associated with these risky events;

8. the public and the community at large. Those interested in the themes of the innovative technologies experimented in the area benefit from the possibility of access to the infrastructure, to participate directly in the training activities and local workshops promoted by the promoters of the ecosystem, to benefit from all the activities conveyed through the media and social networks or through awareness campaigns [45, 46].

3.3 Methodology

This research intends to characterise a decision-support model for innovative projects promoted in the context of EI that can guide the analyst in: (a) estimating the social costs and benefits deriving from a RDI infrastructure; (b) assessing the social return on investment; (c) analysing the investment's risky variables and the critical issues to be addressed in order to define strategic guidelines for setting up and managing EI.

The logical-operational steps on which the model is based are detailed below.

1. *Definition of project goals and evaluation parameters*
2. Having clarified the goals to be achieved with the investment in research, development, and innovation, it is necessary to define: the time horizon of the evaluation; the social discount rate; and the pricing system [47–49].
3. *Cost analysis of the RDI infrastructure.* The second step translates into the estimation of: investment costs, which are incurred during the design and construction phases; operation and maintenance costs, which concern the operational phase of the RDI infrastructure; end-of-life costs, which relate to the decommissioning phase and residual value of the works at the end of the analysis period. Being an economic analysis, the investment cost is net of VAT, while the operating, maintenance and decommissioning costs are multiplied by appropriate conversion coefficients [40].
4. *Identification of target groups and analysis of social benefits.* As highlighted in the previous section, there are eight groups of social agents whose welfare is potentially affected by the services offered by a RDI infrastructure. Once the beneficiaries have been identified, one or more benefits can be associated with each group. Although the estimation of benefits may vary considerably depending on specific project characteristics, a set of benefits resulting from the implementation of RSI infrastructures can be identified. Specifically, these are:
   A. Development of new/improved products, services and technologies;
   B. New patents;
   C. Increased birth rate and longevity of start-ups and spin-offs;
   D. Knowledge spillovers (not protected by patents);
   E. Learning-by-doing benefits;
   F. Human capital formation;
   G. Knowledge outcomes and their impact;
   H. Social benefits of RDI services for target groups;
   I. Recreational benefits for the general public [45, 46].

A. The development of new/improved products, services and technologies is a direct benefit of the project. The social value of these assets can be obtained by estimating the incremental shadow profits expected from their sale. In formula:

$$E(Z) = \sum_{i=1}^{I} \sum_{t=0}^{\tau} s_t \cdot E(\Pi_{it})$$

In which: E(Z) is the expected present value of new (or improved) products, services and technologies; *i* is the number of innovations over time *t*; $E(\Pi_{it})$ represents the incremental profit directly attributable to innovation; s_t is the discount factor.

B. The benefit generated by new patents produced and registered by the RDI infrastructure can be estimated in terms of incremental social value. Let I be the number of patents over time τ; $VSM(pv_{it},ex_{it})$ the Marginal Social Value of the i-*th* patent, which takes into account both the private value (pv_{it}) and the externality (ex_{it}) in terms of knowledge spillover; s_t the discount factor. Then the expected present value E(P) of the patent can be expressed as:

$$E(P) = \sum_{i=1}^{I} \sum_{t=0}^{\tau} s_t \cdot E(VSM_{pv_{it},,ex_{it}}) \quad (1)$$

If: 'use' is the average utilisation rate of granted patents; 'ref' is the average number of references included in granted patents in the technology sector under consideration; pv_{it} is the private value of granted patents in the specific technology sector; then in the formula (1), $E(ex_{it})$ is:

$$E(ex_{it}) = \sum_{i=1}^{I} \sum_{t=0}^{\tau} use \cdot \frac{E(pv_{it})}{ref} \quad (2)$$

C. Since the RDI infrastructure contributes to an increase in the birth and survival rate of start-ups and spin-offs, this benefit can be evaluated as the incremental profit expected and obtained by the firms, since they are able to live longer than in the counterfactual scenario. In a marginal area, it is reasonable to assume that the main contribution of the RDI project is to increase the number of start-ups in the area where the investment has fallen. Therefore, the analysis can be conducted by estimating the overall profit generated by the largest number of start-ups during their life cycle. It follows that the *ex-ante* evaluation of spin-off and start-up profits requires the determination of the following parameters:

- annual number of spin-offs/start-ups expected to be created as a result of the RDI investment;
- expected value of annual profits of spin-offs/start-ups in the country and in the reference sector;
- average duration of spin-offs/start-ups in the country and in the reference sector.

D. Research projects also generate knowledge spillovers (industry databases or software) for companies not directly benefiting from the project. The value of this benefit is estimated by assuming that the software and databases are not currently available on the market and that the cost of the individual product is estimated as a function of the time spent by the researchers on its realisation.

E. The approach in point D can also be applied to estimate the benefits of the learning-by-doing processes enjoyed by the high-tech providers involved in the design, development, or operation of the technological innovation infrastructure. Companies that can access the innovations produced by the research centre can in turn use them to produce further innovations. Again, the benefit is assessed through the shadow profit of non-user companies attributable to the RDI project or through the estimated avoided costs.

F. The benefit in terms of human capital formation is mainly enjoyed by young researchers and graduates involved in the RDI Centre's activities. These human resources, having the opportunity to work in the RDI infrastructure, acquire an advantage in terms of professional experience and career prospects, compared to a situation of non-participation in the project. This advantage is expressed in terms of incremental salary accumulated over a working life compared to the scenario without the project.

The expected present value of the benefits inherent in the accumulation of human capital E(H) equals the sum of the expected increasing earnings $E(E_{it})$ for each i-*th* student and commonly indexed from the moment φ when they leave the research centre:

$$E(H) = \sum_{i=1}^{I} \sum_{t=\varphi}^{\tau} s_t \cdot E(E_{it}) \tag{3}$$

The estimation of incremental remuneration can be conducted through: the benefit transfer approach; surveys and opinions of experts working in the relevant field; the willingness-to-pay (WTP) approach of young researchers and students for a period of study and training at the Centre, in anticipation of the salary increases they expect to realise once they enter the labour market.

G. For researchers and academics, one of the main benefits of working in the Research Centre is the opportunity to access experimental data, to contribute to the production of technological innovation, and to disseminate knowledge results through scientific publications.

The marginal value of publication is estimated through the marginal scientific cost of production approach. This marginal scientific cost is representative of the time spent by scientists to conduct research activities and produce the related output at appropriate shadow wages. Obviously, if one wants to consider that not all scientific production has the same impact on the community, one has to multiply the expected value of the scientific publication E(O) by an impact index, which summarises the level of influence of that knowledge on the academic community. In formula:

$$E(O) = \sum_{t=0}^{\tau} (s_t \cdot E(Y_t) \cdot E(m)) \tag{4}$$

where: $E(Y_t)$ is the expected social cost of scientific production at time t; s_t is the discount factor; E(m) is the impact index (or multiplier).

Specifically:

$$E(Y_t) = \text{number of academics} \times \text{average annual productivity} \times \text{unit production cost per paper} \tag{5}$$

The unit cost of production per knowledge output (paper) can be estimated using the ratio between the author's gross salary and the number of scientific outputs produced per year, considering only the amount of salary related to the time dedicated to research within the RDI Centre. Finally, the use of bibliometric techniques (e.g. by predicting the median number of citations per scientific publication) makes it possible to estimate the impact multiplier E(m), expressed by the ratio between the number of citations and the number of bibliographic references for each article.

H. RDI infrastructures use new knowledge to provide innovative services and products needed, for instance, to tackle climate change, find new ways to ensure energy security and efficiency, mitigate the risk of natural disasters, improve health.

The methods for evaluating the overall benefits resulting from the application of a research result depend on the type of innovative service or product made available by the infrastructure. However, these methods are generally based on willingness to pay or avoided costs. Given the innovative nature of the service/product provided, the challenge is to predict the probability of success and the different levels of effectiveness associated with the innovation implemented.

I. Finally, the involvement of the community in educational and scientific activities, the organisation of awareness campaigns and the promotion of the area will generate recreational benefits for all visitors to the infrastructure. In this case, the marginal social value of the benefit is expressed through the visitors' implicit willingness to pay. The most common approach to assessing WTP is the travel cost method. The catchment area is then defined and the number of visitors over the time horizon of the project is estimated. From a theoretical point of view, WTP corresponds to the sum of the following contributions: the cost of the return ticket, in the case of travel by train, coach or plane, or the cost of fuel, tolls and other operating costs in the case of travel by car; the value of the time spent travelling; the cost of hotel accommodation and food, for visitors coming from more than 150 km.

Table 1 summarises the main expected benefits of the RDI infrastructure, its users and possible methodological approaches to be implemented for evaluations.

4. *Assessment of social profitability.* Once the expected benefits of the project have been estimated, the economic viability and hence the social profitability of the investment can be assessed in terms of Net Present Value (NPV), which expresses the positive or negative difference, or equality, between the discounted sum of the benefits and the discounted sum of the costs of the project; Internal Rate of Return (IRR), which represents the return of the project within the structural, economic and financial system in which the investment is placed; Benefit-Cost Ratio (B/C), which indicates the amount of euros gained or lost for every euro spent on the intervention.
5. *Analysis of critical variables and investment risk assessment.* The complexity inherent in the implementation of RDI infrastructure requires the assessment of project-related risks. This assessment, whose objective is to manage the inherent riskiness and uncertainty in the data and assumptions underlying the ex-ante investment appraisal, requires: sensitivity analysis; qualitative risk analysis; probabilistic risk analysis; possible definition of risk mitigation and containment measures [50].

Figure 1 summarises the steps of the model.

Table 1. Expected benefits of RDI infrastructure [45, 46].

Benefit	Marginal social value	Evaluation approach	Target group
A. Development of new/improved products, services and technologies	Incremental shadow profits	Enterprise surveys; Statistical inference from enterprise data	(1), (2), (3)
B. New patents	Marginal social value of the patent	Inventor surveys; Statistical inference from data on the decision to renew patents or the economic terms of patent transactions	(1), (2), (3), (4)
C. Increased birth rate and longevity of start-ups and spin-offs	Incremental shadow profits	Start-up and spin-off surveys; Statistical inference from start-up and spin-off data; Transfer of benefits	(1), (2), (3)
D. Knowledge spillovers (not protected by patents)	Increased shadow profits; Avoided costs; Willingness to pay for time savings	Enterprise surveys; Avoided cost of producing or purchasing a technology; Cost avoided through the exploitation of a new technology; Benefit transfer	(1), (2), (3), (8)
E. Learning-by-doing benefits	Increased shadow profits; Avoided costs	Enterprise surveys; Statistical inference from enterprise data; Benefit transfer	(1), (2), (3)
F. Human capital formation	Incremental salary over working life	Survey of alumni; Benefit transfer	(5), (6)
G. Knowledge outcomes and their impact	Marginal cost of production	Gross salary of scientists; Value of time; Value of scientific publications	(4), (5)
H. Social benefits of RDI services for target groups	Willingness to pay avoided costs	Costs-damages avoided due to risk reduction	(7), (8)
I. Recreational benefits for the general public	Willingness to pay for time savings	Travel cost method; Contingent valuation; Benefit transfer	(8)

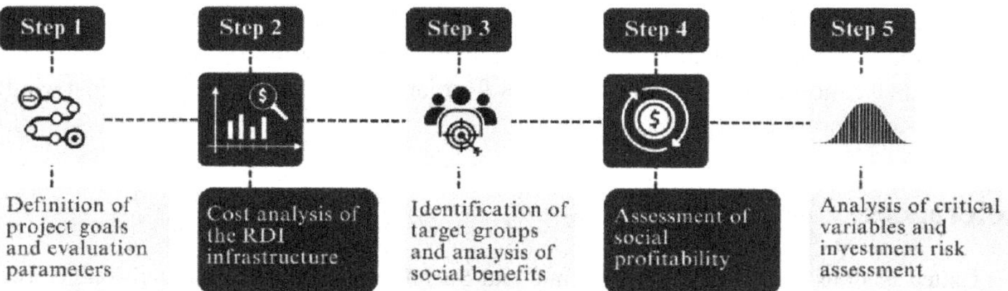

Fig. 1. Steps of the model.

4 Concluding Remarks and Research Perspectives

The crisis of the metropolitan city model and the accentuation of environmental degradation phenomena lead to the need to enhance and protect inland and marginal areas. There is therefore an urgent need for well-structured intervention programmes aimed not only at building reuse, but also at environmental and landscape protection, infrastructure redevelopment and social cohesion. The actions and programmes implemented so far by governments show that investing in research, development and innovation can be a crucial course of action to foster territorial cohesion in marginalised areas. However, there is a lack of a systematic frame of reference that can support analysts in selecting effective intervention strategies.

In line with the above, this paper aims to define a Cost-Benefit Analysis model for RDI projects promoted within innovation ecosystems, which, it has been said, in order to function must themselves be included in a programmatic design of an ecoregion or macro-region. The RSI projects generate social and cultural impacts involving a multiplicity of actors and target groups and represent one of the main items of cost-benefit testing. However, these externalities are often difficult to estimate and are therefore not always adequately taken into account in economic evaluations.

The proposed economic model consists of the following four steps: (i) definition of project objectives and evaluation benchmarks; (ii) analysis of RDI infrastructure costs; (iii) identification of target groups and analysis of social benefits; (iv) analysis of critical variables and investment risk assessment.

From the characterisation of the model, it emerges that crucial steps to be able to make a correct judgement on the social profitability of the investments under analysis concern first of all the identification of the categories of potential beneficiaries of the project. Then, by means of specific estimation approaches, the evaluation of social externalities, which for RDI projects concern: the development of new/improved products, services and technologies; the filing of new patents; the increase in the birth rate and longevity of start-ups and spin-offs; the spillover of knowledge (not protected by patents); learning-by-doing benefits; the training of human capital; the results of knowledge and its impact; social benefits of RDI services deriving from the dissemination of new knowledge; recreational benefits for the community related to scientific promotion activities. Finally, the assessment of project-related risks is a further crucial step to be able to consider the complexity inherent in the implementation of the RDI infrastructure.

In a research perspective, the application to case studies will allow both to validate the defined model and to demonstrate how investment in 'knowledge and applied knowledge' can become a concrete driver of opportunities for marginalised urban contexts, fostering their long-term productivity and growth.

References

1. United Nations Department of Economic and Social Affairs, Population Division: World Urbanization Prospects: The 2018 Revision (ST/ESA/SER.A/420). United Nations, New York, NY (2019)
2. United Nations Department of Economic and Social Affairs, Population Division: World Population Prospects 2019: Highlights (ST/ESA/SER.A/423). United Nations, New York, NY (2019)
3. Sau, A.: La Rivitalizzazione Dei Borghi e Dei Centri Storici Minori Come Strumento per il Rilancio Delle Aree Interne. Federalismi.it. Rivista di Diritto Pubblico Italiano, Comparator, Europeo, 3 (2018). Available online: www.federalismi.it. Accessed on 1 March 2023
4. Marvuglia, A., Havinga, L., Heidrich, O., Fonseca, J., Gaitani, N., Reckien, D.: Advances and challenges in assessing urban sustainability: an advanced bibliometric review. Renew. Sustain. Energy Rev. **124**, 109788 (2020)
5. Nesticò, A., Fiore P., D'Andria, E.: Enhancement of small towns in inland areas. A novel indicators dataset to evaluate sustainable plans. Sustainability **12**(16), 6359 (2020). https://doi.org/10.3390/su12166359
6. ENRD: Long Term Vision for Rural Areas. 1st ed., Publications Office of the European Union: Luxembourg (2021)
7. Paolella, A.: Il Riuso Dei Borghi Abbandonati. Esperienze Di Comunità, 1st ed. Pellegrini Editore, Cosenza, Italy (2019)
8. Zucaro, A., Maselli, G., Ulgiati, S.: Insights in urban resource management: a comprehensive understanding of unexplored patterns. Frontiers in Sustainable Cities **3**, 807735 (2022). https://doi.org/10.3389/frsc.2021.807735
9. D'Andria, E, Fiore, P.: The RI.P.R.O.VA.RE. Project for the Regeneration of Inland Areas: A Focus on the Ufita Area in the Campania Region (Italy). Buildings **13**(2), 336 (2023). https://doi.org/10.3390/buildings13020336
10. Russo, F., Marra, A., Gerundo, R., Nesticò, A.: On the phenomenon of depopulation of inland areas. In: Gervasi, O., Murgante, B., Misra, S., Rocha, A.M.A.C., Garau, C. (eds.) Computational Science and Its Applications – ICCSA 2022 Workshops. ICCSA 2022. Lecture Notes in Computer Science, vol. 13382. Springer, Cham (2022). https://doi.org/10.1007/978-3-031-10592-0_28
11. Coletta, T.: I Centri Storici Minori Abbandonati della Campania. Conservazione, Recupero e Valorizzazione, 1st ed. Edizioni Scientifiche Italiane, Naples, Italy (2010)
12. Calabrò, F., Cassalia, G., Lorè, I.: A Project of enhancement and integrated management: the cultural heritage agency of locride. In: Calabrò F., Della Spina L., Piñeira Mantiñán M.J. (eds.), New Metropolitan Perspectives, NMP 2022. Lecture Notes in Networks and Systems, LNNS, 482, pp. 278–288. Springer Science and Business Media Deutschland GmbH (2022). https://doi.org/10.1007/978-3-031-06825-6_27
13. Manganelli, B., Morano, P., Tajani, F.: The impact of studentification on the residential real estate market. Analysis of external factors and dynamics of the phenomenon generated by the university campus of Potenza (Italy) [L'impatto della studentizzazione sul mercato immobiliare residenziale. Analisi dei fattori esterni e della dinamica del fenomeno generato dal campus universitario di Potenza (Italia)], Valori e Valutazioni (30), 59–69 (2022)

14. Spatari, G., Lorè, I., Viglianisi, A., Calabrò, F.: Economic feasibility of an integrated program for the enhancement of the byzantine heritage in the aspromonte national park. The case of staiti. In: Calabrò, F., Della Spina, L., Piñeira Mantiñán, M.J. (eds.) New Metropolitan Perspectives, NMP 2022. Lecture Notes in Networks and Systems, LNNS, Vol. 482, pp. 313–323. Springer Science and Business Media Deutschland GmbH (2022). https://doi.org/10.1007/978-3-031-06825-6_30
15. Troisi, R., Alfano, G.: Proximity and inter-firm corruption: a transaction cost approach. Small Business Economics 1–16 (2022)
16. Tajani, F., Anelli, D., Di Liddo, F., Morano, P.: An innovative methodology for the assessment of the social discount rate: an application to the European states for ensuring the goals of equitable growth. Smart and Sustainable Built Environment (2023)
17. Del Giudice, V., De Paola, P., Morano, P., Tajani, F., Del Giudice, F.P.: A multidimensional evaluation approach for the natural parks design (2021). Applied Sciences **11**(4), 1767, 1–15 (2021). https://doi.org/10.3390/app11041767
18. Del Molino, S.: La Spagna Vuota, 1st ed., Sellerio Editore: Palermo, Italy (2019)
19. D'Andria, E., Fiore, P., Nesticò, A.: Small towns recovery and valorisation. An innovative protocol to evaluate the efficacy of project initiatives. Sustainability **13**(18), 10311 (2021). https://doi.org/10.3390/su131810311
20. Government of Ireland: Rural Regeneration and Development Fund Fourth Call for Category 1 Applications: Information Booklet. Department of Rural and Community Development (2021). Available online: http://www.assets.gov.ie, last accessed 21 February 2023
21. Wüste, A., Schmuck, P.: Bioenergy villages and regions in germany: an interview study with initiators of communal bioenergy projects on the success factors for restructuring the energy supply of the community. Sustainability **4**(2), 244–256 (2012). https://doi.org/10.3390/su4020244
22. Strategia Nazionale Aree Interne. Available online: https://www.agenziacoesione.gov.it/strategia-nazionale-aree-interne/, last accessed 24 March 2023
23. Lucatelli, S.: La strategia nazionale, il riconoscimento delle aree interne. Territorio **74**, 80–86 (2015)
24. Hosseini, S., Frank, L., Fridgen, G., Heger, S.: Do not forget about smart towns. Bus. Inf. Syst. Eng. **60**(3), 243–257 (2018). https://doi.org/10.1007/s12599-018-0536-2
25. Provenzano, V., Arnone, M., Seminara, M.R.: Innovation in the rural areas and the linkage with the quintuple helix model. Procedia. Soc. Behav. Sci. **223**, 442–447 (2016). https://doi.org/10.1016/j.sbspro.2016.05.269
26. Doloi, H., Green, R., Donovan, S.: Planning, Housing and Infrastructure for Smart Villages, 1st edn. Routledge, London, UK (2018)
27. Simonato, A.: Villaggi intelligenti: Il Piano d'azione europeo. Aggiornamenti Sociali **11**, 779–780 (2019)
28. Visvizi, A., Lytras, M., Mudri, G.: Smart Villages in the EU and Beyond, 1st edn. Emerald Publishing, Bingley, UK (2019)
29. OECD: Unlocking Rural Innovation, OECD Rural Studies. OECD Publishing, Paris (2022). https://doi.org/10.1787/9044a961-en
30. Ahrend, R., Farchy, E., Kaplanis, I., Lembcke, A.C.: What makes cities more productive? evidence from five OECD countries on the role of urban governance. J. Reg. Sci. **57**(3), 385–410 (2017). https://doi.org/10.1111/jors.12334
31. Lengyel, B., Bokányi, E., Di Clemente, R., Kertész, J., González, M.C.: The role of geography in the complex diffusion of innovations. Scientific Reports **10**(1) (2020) https://doi.org/10.1038/s41598-020-72137-w
32. Maloney, W.F. Valencia Caicedo, F.: Engineering Growth. J. European Econ. Asso. **20**(4), 1554–1594 (2022). https://doi.org/10.1093/jeea/jvac014

33. Agenzia della Coesione Territoriale Hompage, https://www.agenziacoesione.gov.it/opportunita-e-bandi/manifestazione-ecosistemi/, last accessed 24 February 2023
34. Gomes, L.A.de V., Facin, A.L.F., Salerno, M.S., Ikenami, R.K.: Unpacking the innovation ecosystem construct: evolution, gaps and trends. Technological Forecasting and Social Change **136**, 30–48 (2018)
35. Talmar, M., Walrave, B., Podoynitsyna, K.S., Holmström, J., Georges, L.A., Romme, A.G.L.: Mapping, analyzing and designing innovation ecosystems: the ecosystem pie model. Long Range Plan. **53**(4), 101850 (2020). https://doi.org/10.1016/j.lrp.2018.09.002
36. Dias Sant'Ana, T., de Souza Bermejo, P.H., Moreira, M.F., de Souza, W.V.B.: The structure of an innovation ecosystem: foundations for future research. Management Decision **58**(12), 2725–2742 (2020). https://doi.org/10.1108/MD-03-2019-0383
37. Moore, J.F.: Predators and prey: a new ecology of competition. Harv. Bus. Rev. **71**, 75–86 (1993)
38. Adner, R.: Match your innovation strategy to your innovation ecosystem. Harv. Bus. Rev. **148**, 98–107 (2006)
39. Autio, E., Thomas, L.D.W.: Innovation ecosystems: implications for innovation management?, The Oxford Handbook of Innovation Management. Oxford University Press, Oxford, UK, pp. 204–224 (2014)
40. Senyo, P.K., Liu, K., Effah, J.: Digital business ecosystem: literature review and a framework for future research. Int. J. Inf. Manage. **47**, 52–64 (2019)
41. Wessner, C.W., Affairs, G.: Innovation Policies for the 21st Century. National Academies Press, Washington, DC (2007)
42. Su, Y.S., Zheng, Z.X., Chen, J.: A multi-platform collaboration innovation ecosystem: the case of China. Manag. Decis. **56**, 125–142 (2018)
43. Surie, G.: Creating the innovation ecosystem for renewable energy via social entrepreneurship: insights from India. Technol. Forecast. Soc. Chang. **121**, 184–195 (2017)
44. Berionni, L.: La strategia macroregionale come nuova modalità di cooperazione territoriale. Note e commenti. Available online: http://www.fondieuropei.regione.emilia-romagna/, last accessed 2 February 2023
45. European Commission. Guide to Cost-Benefit Analysis of Investment Projects. Economic Appraisal Tool for Cohesion Policy 2014–2020. Directorate-General for Regional and Urban Policy: Brussells, Belgium (2014)
46. Florio, M., Forte, S., Pancotti, C., Sirtori, E., Vignetti, S.: Exploring Cost-Benefit Analysis of Research, Development and Innovation Infrastructures: An Evaluation Framewor (2016). Available at SSRN: https://ssrn.com/abstract=3202170
47. Maselli, G., Nesticò, A.: A probabilistic model for the estimation of declining discount rate [Un modello probabilistico per la stima del saggio di sconto declinante]. Valori e Valutazioni **24**, 181–194 (2020). https://siev.org/14-24-2020/
48. Nesticò, A., Maselli, G.: A protocol for the estimate of the social rate of time preference: the case studies of Italy and the USA. Journal of Economic Studies **47**(3), 527–545 (2020). https://doi.org/10.1108/JES-02-2019-0081
49. Nesticò, A., Maselli, G., Ghisellini, P., Ulgiati, S.: A dual probabilistic discounting approach to assess economic and environmental impacts. Environ. Resource Econ. **85**, 239–265 (2023). https://doi.org/10.1007/s10640-023-00766-6
50. Maselli, G., Macchiaroli, M., Nesticò, A.: ALARP criteria to estimate acceptability and tolerability thresholds of the investment risk. Appl. Sci. **11**(19), 9086 (2021). https://doi.org/10.3390/app11199086

The Role of Renewable Energy Communities in the Sustainable Urban Development

Maria Rosaria Sessa[1(✉)] and Francesco Sica[2]

[1] Department of Business Sciences – Management and Innovation Systems, Via Giovanni Paolo II, 132, 84084 Fisciano, SA, Italy
masessa@unisa.it
[2] Department of Architecture and Design, Sapienza University of Rome, 00196 Rome, Italy

Abstract. Economic, social, and environmental sustainability is becoming increasingly important in territorial development policies in Europe and internationally. Among the sustainable development goals, the theme of the energy transition is particularly important, which translates not only into a move away from energy from fossil fuels in favor of renewable ones but also into an improvement in energy efficiency linked to energy production and greater awareness of energy consumption by citizens. To achieve a paradigm of sustainable development, combating the problem of resource scarcity and biodiversity loss, as well as the unsustainability of today's consumption and production systems, the Renewable Energy Communities (CER) can be a suitable model to support urban space redevelopment projects. Actions that aim to recover the pre-existing building heritage to give new life to abandoned areas are increasingly necessary for the protection of the environment. This encourages the propensity to act responsibly, promoting virtuous circles for the territories and communities of reference. This work aims to analyse and understand the actual benefits of the Renewable Energy Communities model for sustainable urban development. An additional aim is to consider Renewable Energy Communities as criteria for identifying industrial areas to convert or redevelop into sustainable industrial areas (SIAs) through a logical-mathematical approach.

Keywords: Energy community · renewable energy · transition · sustainable development · logical-mathematical approach

1 Introduction

The sustainability paradigm, already central at the international level with the Agenda 2030 and at the community level with new policies of the European Union (i.e. European Green Deal) has acquired increasing importance in the business choices of enterprises, also considering the social and environmental dimension when defining their corporate objectives. In this regard, it is necessary to overcome or integrate the conventional business model based on maximizing economic well-being, with objectives aimed at other issues such as environmental protection, enhancement of natural resources, equity, inclusion, solidarity, and social cohesion, in order to create value for themselves and their

O. Gervasi et al. (Eds.): ICCSA 2023 Workshops, LNCS 14107, pp. 19–30, 2023.
https://doi.org/10.1007/978-3-031-37114-1_2

stakeholders in the long term. Thus, the adoption of a holistic approach, also pursuable through the latest ESG criteria (Environmental, Social, and Governance) implies that companies will be required to an evolution in the management of production processes or the provision of services, starting with the supply of raw materials. For example, reducing the use of certain fossil fuels through an energy-efficiency operation is one of the ways to integrate the ESG approach into business strategies [1]. Fundamental is the use of renewable energy sources in the pursuit of ESG criteria and sustainability policies.

Therefore, in today's economic and geopolitics scenario, energy efficiency is an absolute priority that assumes a "triple value", economic, social, and environmental.

This new interpretation of the management of business activities finds full consistency in the phenomenon of the Renewable Energy Communities, which can contribute to the energy transition. The Energy Community can be considered as an integrated model in which the entire territory is involved producing local energy, through interventions calibrated on the local availability of resources and respectful of the patrimonial values of the territory, overcoming upstream the environmental criticalities that arise from an approach oriented to the intensive exploitation of resources. Its creation is an opportunity to experiment with a model of energy capitalization of the territory.

In particular, sustainable development of urban areas has become the prime challenge in the energy sector, promoting objectives such as energy consumption and carbon footprint reduction; low-cost and low-carbon electricity supply; a smart European electricity grid; alternative fuels and mobile energy sources; innovative knowledge and technologies; market uptake of energy and ICT innovation; robust decision making and public engagement.

In this regard, the European Commission (2016) presented the "Clean Energy for All Europeans" package, also known as the "Clean energy package", which includes several measures in the fields of energy efficiency, renewable energy, and internal energy market power [2], making a clear reference to Energy Communities. These can be understood as a way to "organise" collective energy actions around open, democratic participation and governance and the provision of benefits for the members of the local community [3]. There are two formal definitions of Energy Communities: "citizen Energy Communities" [4], and "renewable Energy Communities" [5]. These Directives represent the first time an enabling EU legal framework for collective citizen participation in the energy system. They describe Energy Communities as new types of non-commercial entities that, although they engage in economic activity, their primary purpose is to provide environmental, economic, or social community benefits rather than prioritise profit-making [6].

To give substance to international and community policies regarding the diffusion of the sustainability paradigm, the use of renewable sources must, first of all, take shape in the local dimension, acting on territorial contexts with appropriate and locally defined solutions based on the specificities of the places.

Therefore, the objectives of this research are 1) to analyse and understand the actual benefits of the Renewable Energy Communities model for sustainable urban development; 2) to consider Renewable Energy Communities as criteria for identifying industrial areas to convert or redevelop into Sustainable Industrial Areas through a logical-mathematical approach.

2 Methods and Materials

Energy Communities can support the redevelopment of industrial areas into Sustainable Industrial Areas through the transition to decentralised energy. Producing, storing, and consuming electricity in the same area produced by a local generation plant allows the prosumer to actively contribute to the energy transition, encourages energy efficiency, and promotes the development of renewable energy sources and the sustainable development of the territory. Today, self-consumption can be implemented not only in an individual form but also in a collective form within apartment blocks, local Energy Communities, or precisely in the context of Sustainable Industrial Areas where there is already a unitary manager who could also take care of the management of the operational schemes underlying the Renewable Energy Communities.

2.1 The Energy Communities Model

The change in today's production and consumption systems towards more sustainable and eco-efficient forms is more stringent than ever. The energy transition towards more suitable forms that allow a reduction in consumption and a lower impact on the environment, is one of the processes implemented by society in response to the reduction of environmental impacts.

In this regard, there is growing attention to the Energy Community model, in order to consider new forms of energy sharing in the energy transition. Being a concept of recent development, this cannot be identified as unitary, being accessible to multiple interpretations, connoting it with a widely acceptable flexible meaning. This would facilitate the spread of the concept of an Energy Community, functioning as a bridge concept that facilitates the treatment and dialogue concerning the theme between subjects and their different interests [7].

Already in the early 2000s, the concept of the Energy Community referred to the idea of energy sharing to address issues related to climate change, the use of renewable resources, and sustainability [8].

Over the years, the field of investigation of Energy Communities changes considerably and brings with it the succession of different terminologies adopted to identify the phenomenon. Alongside Energy Community, expressions such as Renewable Energy Community [9] collective and politically motivated renewable energy projects [10], Energy Democracy [11], Sustainable Energy Communities [12]. Despite the different terminology used, the intrinsic meaning is shared: Energy Community identifies initiatives in which the community itself benefits from the collaboration that is established between the participants in terms of energy, obtaining advantages regarding the generation, management, acquisition, and consumption of the same. These initiatives have a positive impact on the community through the development of renewables promoted and the significant reduction of energy consumption, in a context of social cohesion and innovation. The activity carried out by Energy Communities can be different and multiple [13]: a local activity; an interest-based activity; a collaborative, citizens-managed process with locally distributed benefits in an equitable manner; an activity at the intermediate level between the individual and that of enterprises; an energy management agency; an experiment by a few.

Whatever definition is given of the Energy Community concept, there is no doubt that the benefits of this new model of energy sharing are multiple and disparate. The sense of identity, the sharing of places, values, visions, and interests, solidarity, the ability to participate and mobilize collectively, and resilience, give Energy Community the appointment of an ideal model to identify sustainable ways to produce, use and share energy from a technological, organizational and economic point of view. Hence, Energy Communities represent a new model that promotes the link between energy choices and economic, environmental, and social perspectives [14]. The Community becomes a place where the willpower of different actors (citizens, enterprises, public administrations), located in a specific area, to share the will to self-produce and self-consume energy from renewable energy sources is expressed.

In this paper, the concept of Renewable Energy Communities will be considered.

2.2 Sustainable Industrial Areas: A Conceptual Overview

The growing attention to the environmental sustainability of products and production processes led to the transformation of the current global production system. Therefore, in recent years, interest in industrial areas and their redevelopment in Sustainable Industrial Areas.

In the Declaration of Toledo (2010), the European Ministers for regional development, in light of the principles of sustainability, defined the territory as a complex system, comprising not only urbanized, rural, and other spaces, e.g., industrial land, but nature as a whole and the environment surrounding mankind; therefore, a holistic multidisciplinary approach should be adopted, capable of harmonizing the various of variables, economic, environmental, and social sustainability locally. In contrast, production systems can be understood as a set of many interdependent and different elements. These have the objective to transform input resources into output finished products. This definition of the production system fits into a larger context, which is the industrial area defined as the territory in which they are located to achieve economies of scale due to common services and infrastructure [15].

Internationally, the sustainability of a territory is defined using the concept of Eco-Industrial Parks (EIPs), within which mutually beneficial relationships are established between organizations and their environment, through the management of raw materials, by-products, and waste shared as indicated by the principles of industrial ecology [16]. Actually, different terminologies and definitions are used by various organizations around the world to refer to Sustainable Industrial Areas or relatively similar concepts, the most accredited one is Eco-Industrial Park.

One of the most accredited definitions of EIP is given by Lowe and Moran (1995), for which the eco-industrial parks can be understood as a community of manufacturing and service businesses located together on common property. Member businesses seek enhanced environmental, economic, and social performance through collaboration in managing environmental and resource issues [17]. By working together, the community of businesses seeks a collective benefit that is greater than the sum of benefits each company would realize by only optimising its performance [17].

One of the most significant drivers of EIPs is the opportunity to increase business, industrial competitiveness, and sustainable growth. Support for the development of EIPs can be offered through the provision of economically, environmentally, and socially aligned services and a plan to meet the sustainability agenda for an industrial area. In particular, it is possible to identify key environmental, economic, and social drivers of EIPs (Table 1).

Table 1. Main key drivers of Eco-Industrial Parks.

Economic	Environmental	Social
Direct and indirect employment creation	Climate change commitments at global and national levels	Better working and labour conditions
Skills upgrading of the labour force	Increased demand to improve efficiency and growth	Transition to more sustainable land use
Technology and knowledge transfer through foreign direct investment	Responding to environmental and social concerns from consumers	Improved occupational health and safety
	Ensuring infrastructure is resilient to higher resource costs and adapts to climate change risks	Provision of vocational training
Linkages between the industrial park firms and small and medium-sized enterprises (SMEs) and communities outside the industrial park	Greening the supply chain and alleviating resource constraints, which can lead to improved resource management and resource conservation	Support to local community well-being and community outreach
		Provision of social infrastructure to workers and community
Demonstration effects arising from the application of good international industry practices and regional development approaches	The presence of relevant policy mechanisms (for example, taxes and market mechanisms, such as carbon pricing)	Improvement of gender equality
		Creation of local jobs
		Better security and crime prevention

Reaching these targets will require deep and long-lasting changes by organizations in different industrial sectors. Therefore, in this context, EIPs have the potential to play an important role.

However, it is interesting to note that nationally, an industrially developed area could be configured differently on the territory. In Italy, it can also refer to two specific patterns when analysing an industrialized area: industrial districts and sustainable productive areas. Most of the time, both are defined similarly or as aggregates of production realities, not specifying that the aggregation concerning sustainability requires the development of policies and practices different than the traditional way of managing an industrial district. It is possible to have a district every time several undertakings belonging to the same industry or producers of the same product are located on a relatively small territory, to determine a series of processes of exchange of raw materials, ideas, and knowledge between them [18]. The district so defined is more of a territorial productive model. That territory, due to its historical, geographical, cultural, and administrative role, becomes the connective tissue of relationships between businesses and enterprises and the local community. In contrast, the concept of a Sustainable Productive Area refers to a set of enterprises that do not necessarily need to be in the same production sector. The objective of the area is to obtain high environmental and social performance through a unified management system. Sustainable productive areas can be considered as an evolution of industrial districts and could support the process of revitalization of the numerous Italian industrial districts, today characterized by a great crisis that could lead to increased risk of disappearance of the same.

Then, implementing the principles of sustainability in a production area means not only improving the environmental performance of each production sector but, rather, implementing harmonious sustainable development in the municipality of productive activities and the territory, whereby the strategic objectives of single-unit production must be coincident with those of other units belonging to the same area. In fact, for sustainable economic development, a production area needs to focus not only on technological and managerial innovations aimed at maximizing profits and optimization of production efficiency but also, on improving environmental performance and enhancement of human resources. This implies a greater willingness of the business community to cooperate with the other actors, both public and private, in the area to improve the governance of the territory.

This means that creating synergy between enterprises through joint management processes and/or exchange of raw materials and sharing energy can lead to economies of scale, an increase in the innovation potential, a reduction in environmental impacts, an increase in their competitive advantage, to promote the conservation of ecosystem functions in the long term, environmental protection, and the development of the urban spaces, through a land system.

Sustainable Industrial Areas represent the management structures and governance of the urban space which are the closest to the concept of a land system.

3 Data Analysis: Benefits of CER in Italy

In Italy the Renewable Energy Communities result is divided as follows: 35 operational, 41 planned and 24 being established [19]. The Energy Communities that are being born are extremely heterogeneous in the social, environmental, and geographical contexts in which they develop, for the actors involved and their motivations. What unites their constitution is undoubtedly the desire to seek sustainable and responsible ways of producing, consuming, and using energy, in addition to the incentives that come from it in economic terms. Concerning the impacts of the implementation of Renewable Energy Communities, four macro-categories of benefits can be identified [20]:

- Technical-energetic: The electricity system benefits from considerable positive effects deriving from the collective action of producers and consumers who, by aggregating collectively in local energy projects, contribute to the reduction of network losses, to the improvement of voltage profiles as well as the lower stress of the distribution network, with a consequent increase in self-consumption and self-sufficiency indicators.

- Environmental: With the CER model, there is a proportional increase in the production and share of renewable energy consumption at a local level. For Italy, it is quantified in 17.2 GW the new renewable capacity expected by 2030 through the establishment of Renewable Energy Communities and self-consumption models that would allow a reduction in CO_2eq emissions by 2030 estimated at 47.1 million tons, considering the average consumption of 2700 kWh of Italian families [19]. To these direct benefits can be added the indirect effect of increasing awareness of the use of energy resources by members.
- Social: social impacts can be seen both in the process of construction and operation of the CER (increase in participation in the decision-making process), and in the allocation of the value generated.
- Direct and indirect economic impact on sustainable urban development: The direct benefits were given by the cost reduction, deriving from a conscious use of energy. The indirect benefits are associated with the possibility that the coordination between the organisations of the territory (i.e. industrial areas) experienced within the CERs and the collaboration with other relevant local actors, can trigger virtuous processes of shared construction of strategies and actions for sustainable local and urban development.

Other researchers of the sector have investigated the benefits deriving from Energy Communities in a report on Smart grids, providing four classes of recipients [21]: energy users, the electricity system, the territory, and the consumer. In order to obtain these benefits will be necessary to consider the key factors for the success of Renewable Energy Communities, that are [22]:

- Group: a group of members that synergistically and in an organized and cohesive way, acts for a common purpose, and overcomes adversity.
- Project: an idea supported by relevant knowledge and skills, financial and material resources.
- Community: benefits from the implementation of projects.
- Support network: adequate information on Renewable Energy Communities for the realisation of sustainable projects.
- Policy: Without a policy framework to support CERs, their development is not desirable. The diffusion of Energy Communities shows that renewable technologies are now ripe to give life to communities, but also that the obstacles concern the political-regulatory support for these projects.

This highlights that it is necessary to create new tools, models, and approaches, which allow for identifying, realisation, and evaluating urban industrial areas redevelopment projects in SIAs through also Renewable Energy Communities. Therefore, the implementation of the SIA model through the Renewable Energy Community's contribution can promote the highest environmental, economic, and social repercussions in the territorial context of reference.

4 The Diffusion of SIA Through a Logical-Mathematical Approach

The use of Operations Research techniques and tools allows for the structuring of optimisation models aimed at solving specific evaluation questions by defining an objective function and identifying one or more constraint conditions of various kinds [23].

The expressions of the mathematical model referred to the decisional problem posed is constructed based on the linearity principle of Linear Programming, useful, for example, to support the selection process between design alternatives aimed at the redevelopment of the urban industrial area in Sustainable Industrial Areas [24–26], by assessing the suitability of exploiting the Renewable Energy Communities schemes as the dominant criteria. Since in the first instance each design alternative must be evaluated in its entirety to establish whether to carry it out or whether to exclude it, the algorithms of Discrete Linear Programming (DLP) are used. In analogy to how specifically it proceeds in the resolution of choice cases between investment projects within urbanized fabrics to be redeveloped through integrated intervention programs, also for the optimal selection of areas to be allocated to projects that respect the eco-functional logic at the base of SIAs, the mathematical models to be used are to be considered characterized by the integer constraint placed on the decision variables and resolved through the algorithms of the Discrete Linear Programming (DLP). The use of multi-criteria assessment techniques – capable of taking into account, both in the programming and management phases of the individual initiatives to be implemented, multi-dimensional aspects relating to the same type of work – appears useful when it comes to redeveloping an urban industrial area in Sustainable Industrial Area [27, 28]. Depending on the productive sector of interest and available data, it is possible to use different assessment tools that can express the multi-dimensional nature of initiatives related to the redevelopment of territory according to the SIA model. In particular, by resorting to the Operations Research optimization algorithms [29], it is possible to resolve decision-making problems regarding the selection of the site on which to carry out interventions that include actions to transform industrial areas into SIAs through the use of multiple evaluation criteria, able to consider both the morphological characteristics that socio-economic of the area and in this study energy choices also, through the construction of functional relationships between variables.

Intending to pursue the objectives deriving from interventions carried out according to principles of eco-efficiency, the problem arises of selecting, among some areas to be redeveloped, those most suitable to be transformed through actions of this type. Each area is assessed by identifying certain criteria defined according to the objective attributable to the target to be reached (e.g. possibility of integrating the functional schemes of Renewable Energy Communities to achieve the target of a Sustainable Industrial Area).

DLP makes it possible to solve both cases of selection between urban areas that are better suited to be redeveloped with forestation [26], as well as cases related, for example, the composition of the best portfolio of investment projects evaluated through urban sustainability criteria (for example, the atmospheric CO2 emissions and acoustic pollution, the use of renewable energy sources, the land and water use, the circular economy models) [25].

In general, models of linear programming can be implemented through specific mathematical programming tools, such as, for example, MatLab, A Mathematical Programming Language (AMPL), Excel, Lingo, and Lindo. The selection of the type of software to be used is a function of the number of parameters and the number of win-win conditions that characterise the evaluation problem to be solved.

Among the most used are those of dynamic programming, implicit enumeration (such as the Branch & Bound), the algorithms of the cutting planes, and the Brunch & Cut algorithm [30]. The model proposed for the selection and evaluation to implement transformation actions of industrial areas in SIAs can be implemented through the software A Mathematical Programming Language (AMPL).

AMPL software corresponds to a mathematical language used to describe and solve optimisation problems [31], in particular those of scheduling problems [32]. This language is well suited to modeling decision-making cases related to urban industrial redevelopment projects according to eco-system logic [33].

Theoretically, in the present study, to pursue the m objectives deriving from interventions carried out based on the eco-functional principles of the SIA, the problem arises of selecting, among the n industrial areas to be redeveloped, those most suitable to be transformed through sustainability actions, in particular, through the role that Renewable Energy Communities can play in supporting the redevelopment project. Each area – assumed as variable Xi of the problem – is evaluated based on k evaluation criteria defined according to the objective attributable to the m-th target to be reached. In consideration of the investment cost, Ci of the project carried out on the i-th area and of the budget available, which define the financial constraint characterizing the system. A logical-mathematical approach proposed by Discrete Linear Programming can be written as:

$$Xij = f(Ci, K, kj).$$

where:

Xi = Area (i = 1,..., n)

Ci = Costs

K = Budget

kj = Evaluation criteria (j = 1,..., m)

Therefore, the mathematical logic approach considered, using the AMPL software, will be able to support the implementation of the SIA model through some fundamental steps, such as: identifying the elements of the problem (specific objectives with the targets, number of areas, evaluation criteria) as a set; specifying the parameters of the problem (Budget, Costs, Multi-criteria Evaluation Matrix) to be inserted in the system; defining the value of the variables (var X binary); structuring the objective function as a linear algebraic expression that maximises the capacity to pursue the multiple aims of the sustainable development initiatives of the urban industrial areas; specifying the constraints of the problem to be solved.

In addition, the use of a logical-mathematical approach developed in terms of Linear Programming allows rationalising the decision-making problem considered with the sustainability objectives underlying the interventions aimed at realising Sustainable Industrial Areas. This is made possible through the writing of simple algebraic expressions in which the variables, the parameters relating to the characteristics (economic, social, and environmental type) of the reference territorial context of the industrial areas are transformed into SIAs, as well as the effects produced by redevelopment initiatives, developed according to the eco-functional principles of the SIAs in the area expressed through appropriate performance indicators, they are placed in correspondence with each other. The choice of which indicators to use during the construction of the model depends on the evaluation questions to be solved, which in turn depends on the type of target considered [34].

The use of multi-criteria analysis models of such structural and formal characteristics, such as the one proposed in the present work, can support the implementation of territorial and local development sustainable policies. This approach can be useful for decision-makers (public and private) in implementing a program of investment in Renewable Energy Communities able to contribute to the pursuit of targets at the base of the SIA respecting the available financial resources. Thus, it is possible to encourage a form of territorial governance shared in which the design, implementation, or conversion of industrial areas in SIAs can involve enterprises, consumers, and citizens and benefit the entire community; contributing to the achievement of objectives for improving environmental and social performance and territorial development according to principles of sustainable development paradigm.

5 Conclusions

The diffusion of CERs represents a great opportunity to experiment with new energy models based on the self-organization of members and on the enhancement of the resources available to the territories. The CERs have above all great social value as well as economic and environmental, as they can represent models of synergy and cooperation spread throughout the national territory, helping to experiment with innovative solutions in the management of the common good, and in the implementation of new urban and local development policies.

The theoretical model must adapt to the nascent concrete cases, starting from the ability to penetrate urban systems, facilitated by self-consumption schemes, which remains a great challenge for any ecological transition policy. All this must be combined with the rational exploitation of resources, compatible with environmental constraints, which respects the territories, encouraging the development of 'ethical' initiatives.

Therefore, in this study, it was suggested that a mathematical logic approach be adopted to select criteria of a different nature to favour redevelopment projects. Among the different selection options, it is suggested to also include Renewable Energy Communities that could support SIA participants from the point of view of energy efficiency. Renewable Energy Communities can be acting beyond the energy sector and play a more transformative role at the local level. They are characterised by the participation of a wide range of actors, and local administrations often play a key role in facilitating implementation and future development. These are actions that, besides energy savings, promote other initiatives including sustainable mobility, local employment, educational and dissemination programs, building renovation, and/or urban redevelopment projects.

Future findings of this research will be through the application of learning in a specific local context, quantifying the economic, environmental, and social benefits of a Renewable Energy Community implementation that promotes green services and infrastructures for sustainable urban redevelopment.

References

1. Elliott, R.N., Langer, T., Nadel, S.: Reducing oil consumption through energy efficiency: opportunities in the industry. Environ. Qual. Manage. **15**(4), 81–91 (2006)
2. Lowitzsch, J.: Consumer Stock Ownership Plans (CSOPs). The prototype business model for renewable energy communities. Energies **13**, 1–24 (2019)
3. Roberts, J., Frieden, D., Gubina, A.: Energy Community Definitions. Compile Project: Integrating Community Power in Energy Islands (2019). https://main.compile-project.eu/wp-content/uploads/Explanatory-note-on-energy-community-definitions.pdf. Last accessed 11 April 2023
4. European Commission: Directive (EU) 2019/944 on Common Rules for the Internal Market for Electricity and Amending Directive 2012/27/EU. No. July 2009 (2019)
5. European Parliament & Council of the European Union: Directive (EU) 2018/2001 on the Promotion of the Use of Energy from Renewable Sources. Official Journal of the European Union. vol. 2018, No. November (2018)
6. REScoop.EU: Q & A: What Are "Citizen" and "Renewable" Energy Communities?. Policy Paper (2019). https://www.rescoop.eu/uploads/rescoop/downloads/QA-What-are-citizens-energy-communities-renewable-energy-communities-in-the-CEP.pdf, last accessed: 11 April 2023
7. Star, S.L., Griesemer, J.R.: Institutional ecology, translations, and boundary objects: amateurs and professionals in Berkeley's Museum of Vertebrate Zoology, 1907–39. Soc. Stud. Sci. **19**(3), 387–420 (1989)
8. Pellizzoni, L.: Energy Community. A critical survey of the literature (2018). https://www.openstarts.units.it/bitstream/10077/22309/1/2_BSA5Energia_innovazione.pdf, last accessed: 11 April 2023
9. Walker, G., Devine-Wright, P.: Community renewable energy: what should it mean? Energy Policy **36**, 497–500 (2008)
10. Becker, S., Kunze, C.: Transcending community energy: collective and politically motivated projects in renewable energy (CPE) across Europe. People, Place & Policy **8**(3), 180–191 (2014)
11. Szulecki, K.: Conceptualizing energy democracy. Environmental Policy **27**(1), 21–41 (2018)
12. Romero-Rubio, C., de Andrés Díaz, J.R.: Sustainable energy communities: a study contrasting Spain and Germany. Energy Policy **85**, 397–409 (2015)
13. Burchell, K., Rettie, R., Roberts, T.C.: Community, the very idea!: perspectives of participants in a demand-side community energy project. People, Place and Policy **8**(3), 168–179 (2014)
14. Torabi Moghadam, S., Di Nicoli, M.V., Manzo, S., Lombardi, P. Integrating energy communities in the transition to a low-carbon future: a methodological approach. Energies 1597 (2020)
15. Cariani, R.: Eco-Aree Produttive. In: Guida all'eco-Innovazione, Alle Politiche per la Sostenibilità e ai Progetti Operativi nelle Aree Produttive Ecologicamente Attrezzate (APEA). Ambiente Editore, Milano, Italy (2013)
16. Beltramo, R., Vesce, E., Pairotti, M.B.: L'area industriale di Pescarito: Introduzione allo studio. In: Beltramo, R., Vesce, E. (eds.) Prove di APEA. Strumenti per l'Evoluzione verso le Aree Produttive Ecologicamente Attrezzate. Il caso Pescarito. Ambiente Editore, Milano, Italy (2014)

17. Lowe, E., Moran, D.H.: A fieldbook for the development of eco-industrial parks. In: Report for the U.S. Environmental Protection Agency. Indigo Development International, Oakland, CA, USA (1995)
18. Cutaia, L., Morabito, R.: Sostenibilità dei Sistemi Produttivi. In: Strumenti e Tecnologie verso Lagreen Economy. ENEA: Roma, Italy (2012)
19. Legambiente: Report on Renewable Energy Communities (2022). https://legambiente.it/wp-content/uploads/2021/11/Comunita-Rinnovabili-2022_Report.pdf, last accessed: 11 April 2023
20. Giusti, A.: Energy Communities: The protagonists of the ecological transition (2022). https://www.quotidianolegale.it/wp-content/uploads/2022/10/Comunita-energetiche_le-protagoniste-della-transizione-ecologica._Giusti.pdf, last accessed: 11 April 2023
21. Chiaroni, D., Frattini, F., Franzo, S.: Smart Grid Report. Prospects for the development of Energy Communities in Italy. Energy & Strategy Group. Politecnico di Milano, Italy (2014)
22. Seyfang, G., Park, J.J., Smith, A.: Community Energy in the UK. In: Working Paper, p. 11. University of East Anglia, Norwich (2012)
23. Korte, B., Fonlupt, J., Vygen, J.: Optimisation combinatoire: Theorie et algorithms. Springer, Germany, Berlin (2010)
24. Chakhar, S., Mousseau, V., Pusceddu, C., Roy, B.: Decision map for spatial decision making in urban planning. In: Batty, M. (ed.) The 9th International Computers in Urban Planning and Urban Management Conference, London, UK, 29 June - 1 July. University College London: the Centre for Advanced Spatial Analysis (CASA), UK, pp. 1–18 (2005)
25. Nesticò, A., Sica, F.: The sustainability of urban renewal projects: a model for economic multi-criteria analysis. J. Prop. Invest. Finan. **35**(4), 397–409 (2017)
26. Nesticò, A., Guarini, M.R., Morano, P.: An economic analysis algorithm for urban forestry projects. Sustainability **11**(2), 314 (2019)
27. Guarini, M.R., Nesticò, A., Morano, P., Sica, F.: A Multicriteria Economic Analysis Model for Urban Forestry Projects, pp. 564–571. Springer, International Symposium on New Metropolitan Perspectives. Cham. Switzerland (2018)
28. Guarini, M.R., Morano, P., Sica, F.: Historical School Buildings. A Multi-Criteria Approach for Urban Sustainable Projects. Sustainability **12**(3), 1076 (2020)
29. Gilardino, A., Rojasa, J., Mattosa, H., Larrea-Gallegos, G., Vàzquez-Rowe, I.: Combining operational research and life cycle assessment to optimize municipal solid waste collection in a district in Lima (Peru). J. Clean. Prod. **156**, 589–603 (2017)
30. Ventura, P.: Alcuni Contributi alla separazione primale e duale per problemi di programmazione lineare intera. vol. 6(8). Bollettino dell'Unione Matematica Italiana (2003)
31. Schoen, F.: Modelli di ottimizzazione per le decisioni. Società Editrice Esculapio, Italy, Bologna (2006)
32. Dolan, E., Moré, J.J.: Benchmarking optimization software with performance profiles. Math. Program. **91**, 201–213 (2002)
33. Bagstad, K.J., Semmens, D.J., Waage, S., Winthrop, R.: A comparative assessment of decision–support tools for ecosystem services quantification and valuation. Ecosyst. Serv. **5**, 27–39 (2013)
34. Sessa, M.R., Esposito, B., Sica, D., Malandrino, O.: A logical-mathematical approach for the implementation of ecologically equipped productive urban areas. Sustainability **13**(1365) (2021)

The Infrastructure Sector Sustainability: Using of the Deterministic Frontier Analysis for Performance-Accounting Measurement

Raffaele Maria Sica[1], Francesco Sica[2](✉), Maria Rosaria Sessa[3], and Nicola Sica[4]

[1] Spike Reply S.R.L, Robert Koch St. 1/4, 20152 Milan, Italy
[2] Department of Architecture and Design, "Sapienza" University of Rome, 00196 Rome, Italy
francesco.sica@uniroma1.it
[3] Department of Management and Innovation Systems, University of Salerno, 84084 Salerno, Italy
[4] Department of Economics and Statistics, University of Salerno, 84084 Salerno, Italy

Abstract. The capacity of the infrastructure sector to generate value for the territory in terms of social inclusion, economic growth, and employment may be determined as of today (2023) on the basis of empirical evidence. With the technological advancements and the development of other modes of transportation over time, the system of roads and highways in particular has come to play a crucial role in the growth of a territory. It is also necessary for the infrastructure system, particularly the transportation sector, to adapt to international norms for sustainable growth. Operationally, this means that projects must be planned and carried out that have the potential to influence the territory's strategic progress from three different angles: economic, social, and environmental.

The goal of the current study is to provide a quantitative methodology to aid in the analysis of infrastructure sector performance, particularly that of the transportation one. The framework suggested directs evaluation of the infrastructure sector in terms of sustainability and takes into consideration potential performance indicators in order to develop accounting procedures for the sustainability performance. The formalization of the analytical tool based on the proposed framework adheres to the logical rules of Deterministic Frontier Analysis (DFA). The transport infrastructure sector is evaluated by the DFA in relation to the achievement of the sustainability goals set at the European Union level. In the conclusions, it is discussed how the use of the proposed framework may affect the allocation of initiatives related to the sector being tested on the territory's sustainable development.

Keywords: infrastructure sector · sustainable development · multicriteria analysis · DFA

O. Gervasi et al. (Eds.): ICCSA 2023 Workshops, LNCS 14107, pp. 31–41, 2023.
https://doi.org/10.1007/978-3-031-37114-1_3

1 Introduction

The 17 Sustainable Development Goals in the UN Agenda 2030 (2015), which are generally aimed at economic prosperity, social inclusion, and environmental sustainability, are the perspective that individual territorial contexts adopt when planning investments in various production sectors in order to address the new challenges of the 21st century [1]. Infrastructure investments are essential to attaining sustainable development and enhancing the capacity of communities in many nations. Infrastructure includes investments in transportation, irrigation, electricity, and information and communication technology. Infrastructure investment is necessary for productivity and income development as well as for improved health and educational results [2–6].

The Connecting Europe Facility (CEF) 2.0 (2021–2027) program in Europe aims to build, develop, modernize, and complete trans-European networks in the energy, digital, and transportation sectors with the goal of creating a unique global market while taking into account the goals of environmental, social, and economic cohesion [7]. Il CEF 2.0 emphasizes the value of collaboration across the transportation, energy, and digital sectors. A green, digital, and resilient Europe is another goal of the Next Generation EU (2020) for post-pandemic socio-economic recovery from COVID-19. The Recovery and Resilience initiative, which aims to encourage investment to promote post-pandemic recovery in Europe, is a crucial component of the Next Generation EU package. An average of 191.5 billion euros have been placed at Italy's disposal for projects and reforms associated with the National Recovery and Resilience Plan (NRRP) [8]. Separately, the Italian government commits an additional 30.6 billion euros to initiatives considered strategically important for the development and improvement of the country's infrastructure sector (e.g., the initiatives "Safe Roads - Implementation of a dynamic monitoring system for the remote control of bridges, viaducts and tunnels of the main road network" and "Interventions of the Complementary Plan in the territories affected by the 2009–2016 earthquake, Infrastructure and Mobility, Investments on the State Road Network"). The EU proposes the Green Deal plan (2019) as the foundation for CEF 2.0 (2021) and Next Generation (2020), aiming to focus sustainable investments to boost environmental-ecological trans-action in Europe. The Green Deal aims to reduce atmospheric pollutant emissions by 55% from 1990 levels by 2030 in order to have a "climate-neutral" economy by 2050 [9]. Based on a balanced participation of the public and private sectors in the processes of financing the initiatives, an investment plan (2020–2030) of about one trillion euros is put into place to support initiatives for the sustainable development of the sectors deemed to be the most energy-intensive (e.g., the infrastructure sector) [10, 11].

The basic objectives of the Green Deal (2019), which were also re-proposed in the more recent CEF 2.0 (2021), include: ecological transition; energy consumption; sustainable forms of transportation; circular economy; digital transactions.

The previously specified goals for the transportation infrastructure sector deviate as follows: *i*) resilience, with emphasis on energy efficiency and renewable energy generation; *ii*) sustainable mobility; *iii*) forms of circular economy; and *iv*) transport safety measures for the system's primary users.

i) Due to the ongoing conflict in Ukraine (2023), there is currently a great deal of uncertainty surrounding the energy supply, making energy efficiency and the generation of energy from renewable sources increasingly important. Infrastructure system operators are being forced to come up with customized ways to reduce energy consumption without compromising the safety of road users because to the high running expenses of electric power plants and the strict am-environmental requirements that must be satisfied. The installation of more energy-efficient lighting fixtures, whose usage is maximized by the use of IoT-based sensors, has shown potential solutions. It is necessary to implement a transition from a carbon emission-heavy energy system based on fossil fuels to one with lower carbon emissions in order to reduce energy consumption [4, 12, 13].
ii) Due to the restrictions imposed by the single member states of the Parigi Agreement, a gradual conversion of the circular park to other feeding mechanisms is taking place. It is predicted that there won't be any more internal combustion engines in the EU after 2035, only electric vehicles. Hence, as a result of this scenario, a single manager must act in order to prevent the use of electric vehicles [14–16].
iii) The existing road pavement production process is designed to use enormous amounts of virgin raw materials and natural resources in order to get ready for a circular economy. Discussions and disputes revolve on the effects of this element, which force a shift in perspective that the NRRP itself imposes. Thus, the usage of novel materials is being investigated in order to extend a pavement's lifespan and minimize maintenance. Because of their intimate ties to energy saving, these pavements may be used to advance both the circular economy and ecological transition [17–19].
iv) Also, the requirement to maintain infrastructure assets by actions that extend the infrastructure's useful life with an eye to road safety should be taken into account. There is a need to implement systems of monitoring and inspection vigilance on roads, capable of dealing in a predictive and timely manner with catastrophic events that can generate irreversible consequences on human life, due to the heterogeneity of materials and construction techniques that characterize the existing infrastructure sector. In the European environment, there is a propensity to support measures to assess the level of vulnerability of the current infrastructure network as well as monitoring activities of infrastructure located in seismic and hydrogeological risk zones. To that end, the Ministry of Infrastructure and Sustainable Mobility has allocated 450 million euros to the NRRP in Italy for the monitoring and remote management of bridges, viaducts, and tunnels on state and private roads [20–24].

So, setting up a system to track the performance of the infrastructure system in terms of sustainability plays a key role in achieving each of the objectives listed in *i*) through *iv*) in the best possible way. Through the use of appropriate performance indicators and evaluation tools, an auditing system may conceptualize valuation frameworks while accounting for the performance of infrastructure in relation to European sustainability targets. The challenge facing infrastructure managers, especially those in charge of constructing roads, is to plan and implement initiatives that take into account the effects that their actions would have on the local community and environment, particularly in light of territorial cohesion principles.

2 Aims

In light of the foregoing, the proposed work seeks to address the following research questions:

- What indicators may be used to assess a territory's infrastructure system's sustainability in terms of performance? Which letter-writing sustainability indicators are directly related to system infrastructure analysis, and which others are less so?
- Which evaluation methodology enables measuring the infrastructure system's performance in relation to the sustainable targets to achieve?

In order to respond to earlier concerns, the present contribution aims to provide a description of a methodological-operational apparatus based on processes for evaluating the sustainability of infrastructure systems, particularly transportation systems. The performance measurement framework proposed takes into account the use of efficiency potential indicators, as well as a system of analysis developed using Deterministic Frontier Analysis (DFA). This last one (DFA), as we shall see, allows for the execution of static comparative analyses between components of a homogeneous research field as well as the provision of preliminary predictions regarding the development of the same (components) in comparison to reference targets.

The work is structured as follows: Sect. 3 provides an overview of sustainability indicators and potential methods and tools for evaluating the sustainability performance of an infrastructure system; Sect. 4 is devoted to the discussion of the valuative framework proposed to support the sustainability analysis of the transportation infrastructure system. The conclusions are presented in Sect. 5, where you also analyse the methodology's limitations and outline the research directions that follow the presented work.

3 Materials and Method

To respond in a way that is in line with the new challenges of the twenty-first century, it is becoming more and more imperative for European states to align themselves with the sustainable development goals imposed at the community level. After the presentation and analysis of the various European-level objectives, it is intended to provide a methodology for evaluating the effectiveness of the road infrastructure system in terms of the degree to which sustainability objectives are pursued. The proposed methodological apparatus was developed with the intention of comparing the performance of the road network in relation to community sustainability goals. To do this, a preliminary overview of sustainability indicators used in scientific and grey literature to assess the sustainability of infrastructure systems is provided (3.1), along with a description of valuation models and tools used to assess sustainability performance (3.2). What is described in the two following subparagraphs is helpful in clarifying the framework of Sect. 4.

3.1 Accounting the Sustainability of Infrastructure Sector: Suite of Proper Performance Indicators

The measurement of sustainability, which is generally intended to be in terms of its three aspects of economic, social, and environmental, is done by using appropriate indicators for each one. With the first international instances of "sustainability" being defined, the term's meaning has gradually declined both linguistically and conceptually, especially when taking into account the various applicative and reference contexts [25]. In contrast to the scientific community's increased desire to define sustainability as a unique aggettivation of a country's social and economic system throughout the twentieth century, the interest in discussing sustainability in relation to a country's environmental and ecological aspects has increased significantly in the twenty-first one. In particular, especially due to phenomena related to climate change, renewable energy production, and the protection of terrestrial and marine ecosystems, sustainability has assumed an increasingly practical value. As such, it is used as a theoretical reference point to guide the planning and implementation of initiatives at various scales that may be able to respond to United States-level sustainability objectives. In this hypothetical, each individual initiative is initially assessed for its impact on environmental assets first, followed by its impact on increasing economic wealth and improving people's quality of life [26, 27].

A number of indicators have been proposed at the community level in completing the operations of impact assessment, and not. The assessment of the effects is feasible at several levels of analysis, including sub-urban, city, metropolitan, extra-metropolitan, national, and continental. There are suggested reference indicators for each that are more suited to measuring sustainability at that particular scale. It follows that we can make reference to a larger number of independently collected indicators that broaden the analysis's geographic scope. a basis for which it is possible to find a significant number of sustainability indicators at the national level, including economic, social, and environmental factors.

The indicators used in documentation to assess the current state of infrastructure in Europe with regard to the transportation system include the description of the system's physical structure, the level of usage, the management style, and even the most recent accessibility measures [11].

3.2 Approaches for Evaluating Efficiency in Assessment Procedures

The majority of writing on efficiency analysis focuses on comparing components of a standard studio set or different types of sets using key performance indicators, often of the financial variety, without taking into account relationships with exogenous factors of the environmental, social, and economic kinds. The studies that focus on evaluating products according to their life cycles while taking into account each stage of production are those that have received the most current in-depth attention [28–32].

It is feasible to determine that by studying existing literature the two main approaches to measuring effectiveness are *i*) traditional and *ii*) of frontier. Regardless of the method employed, the effectiveness measurements obtained at the end of an empirical analysis represent relative measurements: each decisional unit is evaluated in relation to the best performance obtained from the collection of the decisional units put to the test.

i) Using data on the amounts of input used and the levels of output obtained from a group of productive units, the construction of the production function is carried out while referring to the standard regression model. The level of effectiveness was determined by comparing the observed performance of the decision-making unit with the average observational field performance [33, 34].
ii) With information on the amount of input used and the output levels achieved by a group of production units, one proceeds to building a production possibility frontier that "circles" the points that correspond to the observed units. The measurement of effectiveness is based on a comparison of observed performance with literary references made to models (*best practice*) [35–37]. These last establish the analytical element's optimal efficiency boundary, which may be distinguished in:
    - Effective: The units are placed along the border;
    - Ineffective: The units are located just within the border.

As a result, the efficiency measurement is calculated in terms of distance from the border. The residuals from the regression are used to get the efficiency measurement.

I methods for measuring borderlines generally can be classified as *a*) parametric or *b*) not.

a) The frontier is expressed just by returning to a mathematical function notation that depends on a certain number of unknown parameters. Deterministic Frontier Analysis (DFA) and Stochastic Frontier Analysis are examples of parametric methods [38].
b) A collection of gathered information is used to reconstruct the production combination, with the border being constructed by taking into account certain characteristics and constituting the envelope. Among the non-parametric methods are the following: Data Envelopment Analysis and Free Disposal Hull.

The framework for performance analysis efficiency in the context of sustainable development is described in the section that follows with regard to the transportation infrastructure support system.

4 Proposal of a Framework DFA-Based for Transport System

As shown in Fig. 1, this aims to provide a framework for evaluating the sustainability of the transportation infrastructure system's performance. The proposed framework is organized into three sequential steps:

1. Identification of sustainable goals,
2. measurement of performance using appropriate indicators,
3. and selection of an efficient technique are the first three steps.

Everyone is described in the subsequent subparagraphs.

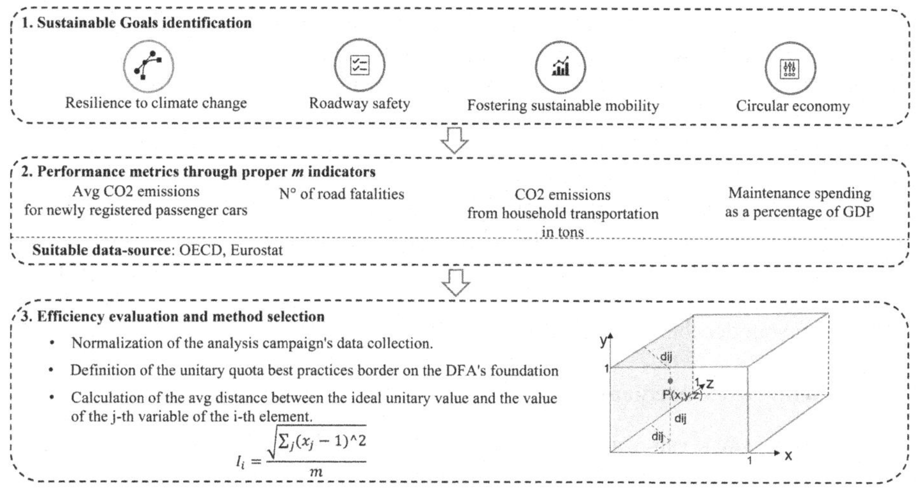

Fig. 1. Assessment framework DFA-based.

4.1 Sustainable Goals Identification and Performance Metrics

The European objectives that were sought to be examined were:

1. climate change resilience;
2. road safety;
3. promotion of sustainable mobility, and
4. circular economy and sustainable materials.

Each of the following objectives has been assigned a set of varying proxy variables that might depict the system's infrastructure's level of tracking relative to potential reference points. To be more explicit, the following conditions have been met:

1. for the goal of "road safety," the number of traffic accidents per 1,000 inhabitants is taken into consideration; this indicator is one of the SDG in the EU's collection of indicators. It is used to track progress on SDG 11 about making cities and human settlements inclusive, secure, resilient, and sustainable and SDG 3 about good health and wellbeing, which are included in the European Commission's top priorities for the European Green Deal. The indicator is comparable to SDG Global Indicator 3.6.1, "Rate of Mortality Due to Road Incidents." In 2010, the Commission adopted the communication "Toward a European Road Safety Space: Political Directions for Road Safety 2011–2020," with the goal of reducing the total number of traffic fatalities in the EU by 2020 in comparison to 2010. A reduction of 50% in fatalities and serious injuries by 2030 compared to 2019 is the goal set out in the EU's Strategic Road Safety Action Plan and its Road Safety Policy Framework for the 2021–2030 period. Ambitious goals have also been set for road safety to reach zero road fatalities by 2050;
2. in order to achieve the goal of "resilience to climate change," it was decided to use CO2 emissions from transportation for residents;

3. for the objective of "a circular economy and sustainable materials," data on investments in road infrastructure as a percentage of GDP are used; this type of data is used to be able to represent maintenance investments to ensure a longer lifespan for the infrastructure;
4. the "median CO2 emission of new automobiles" can be used as a variable proxy for the objective of "promot[ing] sustainable mobility." The indicator is a part of the set of indicators for the EU's sustainable development goals. It is used to track progress towards SDG 12 on ensuring sustainable consumption and production models and SDG 13 on adopting urgent measures to counteract climate change and its effects. These sustainable development goals are included in the European Commission's list of priorities under the "Green Deal Europe."

4.2 Efficiency Measurement

The effectiveness analysis was conducted by referring to the DFA's underlying principles. This was initially developed in the economic sector for decision-makers who used several production factors to obtain more goods without explicitly stating the functional relationship. A frontier approach is used, where the distinctive feature is that the data are not surrounded or ignored rather than being interspaced by a function.

In this instance, a methodological approach to performance evaluation has been tested. It is based on the definition of the probability-optimal frontier for each analytical parameter and the measurement of the distance between the performance level at present and the ideal reference level. The series of values for each parameter has been appropriately normalized to an interval of $[0 \div 1]$ in order to combat the data set's inhomogeneity, which is distinctive to the study field. This operation allows for the ability to deal with various sets of data of various types while also allowing for the consideration of an ideal boundary that is discretized in an original post-quota unitarian piano. Each piano's front edge determines the calculation of the distance relating to the country's performance level, which, in nautical terms, is defined as the vector to the number of evaluation factors, in our case four. Because of each veterinarian's multidimensional characteristics, it was decided to calculate the relative distance using the Euclidean mathematical expression for distance.

5 Conclusions

It is crucial for the individual European States to respond to the new challenges of the twenty-first century [39–43]; as a result, it is necessary to analyze the modes of intervention in order for the individual European States to adhere to the new European directions in addition to understanding where to focus their investment.

In order to address the four community-level objectives of promoting sustainable mobility, addressing traffic safety, addressing climate change, and addressing circular economy, underling the Green New Deal, it has been decided to provide a quantitative methodology for assessing the efficiency of infrastructure system in sustainable perspective. Every single one of them was represented by a variable proxy. By doing an efficiency analysis based on the Deterministic Frontier Analysis, it is possible to obtain results in terms of relative average efficiency while also getting a global indication of how far a territory infrastructure system is from the boundaries of best practices.

It is clear the value of the evaluation method proposed for economic policy goals, particularly in the effort to implement an investment plan within a production-focused sector in sustainable development perspective. With an emphasis on that in Italy, the suggested evaluation approach will be used to analyse the sustainable performance of the European highway transportation system. Future findings from the effort will be based on a comparison of the European nations' respective transportation systems using the previously described methodology. It will be feasible to illustrate the limitations and potentials of the suggested assessment framework in connection to geographical elements of analysis by going over the data we will get.

References

1. Campbell, D.A.: An update on the United Nations millennium development goals. J. Obstet. Gynecol. Neonatal. Nurs. **46**(3), e48–e55 (2017)
2. Alampi, D., Messina, G.: Time-is-money: i tempi di trasporto come strumento per misurare la dotazione di infrastrutture in Italia. Le infrastrutture in Italia: dotazione, programmazione, realizzazione, 137–174 (2011)
3. Benfratello, L., Iozzi, A., Valbonesi, P.: Technology and incentive regulation in the italian industry. The journal of regulatory economics **35**, 201–222 (2009)
4. Blackmon, G., Zeckhauser, R.: Fragile commitments and the regulatory process. Yale Journal of Regulation **9**, 73–100 (1992)
5. Bonanni, A.: Van Miert: Italia fuorilegge sull'Iri. Archivio storico Corriere della Sera, 23 (1997)
6. Bruinsma, F.R., Rietveld, P.: The accessibility of European cities: theoretical framework and comparison approaches. Environ Plan A **30**, 449–521 (1998)
7. Vetorazzi, S.: Establishing the Connecting Europe Facility 2021–2027 (2018)
8. Tajani, F., Di Liddo, F., Guarini, M.R., Ranieri, R., Anelli D.: An assessment methodology for the evaluation of the impacts of the COVID-19 pandemic on the Italian housing market demand. Buildings **11**(592), 1–28 (2021). ISSN: 2075-5309
9. Sessa, M.R., Russo, A., Sica, F.: Opinion paper on green deal for the urban regeneration of industrial brownfield land in Europe. Land Use Policy **119**, 106198 (2022). https://doi.org/10.1016/j.landusepol.2022.106198
10. Martínez-Zarzoso, I., Suárez-Burguet, C.: Transport costs and trade: empirical evidence for Latin American imports from the European Union. J. Int. Trade & Economic Develop. **14**(3), 353–371 (2005)
11. Hart, O., Shleifer, A., Vishny, R.W.: The proper scope of government: theory and an application to prisons. Q. J. Econ. **112**(4), 1127–1161 (1997)
12. Bronzini, R., Casadio, P., Marinelli, G.: Quello che gli indicatori territoriali sulle infrastrutture di trasporto possono, e non possono dire. Le infrastrutture in Italia: dotazione, programmazione, realizzazione 101 (2011)
13. Spatari G., Lorè I., Viglianisi A., Calabrò F.: Economic feasibility of an integrated program for the enhancement of the byzantine heritage in the aspromonte national park. The case of staiti. In: Calabrò, F., Della Spina, L., Piñeira Mantiñán, M.J. (eds.) New Metropolitan Perspectives, NMP 2022. Lecture Notes in Networks and Systems, LNNS, vol. 482, pp. 313–323. Springer Science and Business Media Deutschland GmbH (2022). https://doi.org/10.1007/978-3-031-06825-6_30

14. European Commission: Territorial Agenda 2030. A future for all places (2020)
15. Venter, Z.S., Barton, D.N., Gundersen, V., Figari, H., Nowell, M.: Urban nature in a time of crisis: recreational use of green space increases during the COVID-19 outbreak in Oslo. Norway. Environ. Res. Lett. **15**(10), (2020)
16. European Commission: EU Biodiversity Strategy for 2030 Bringing nature back into our lives. https://eur-lex.europa.eu/legal-content/EN/TXT/?qid=1590574123338&uri=CELEX:52020DC0380, last accessed: 26 November 2021
17. Giorgiantonio, C., Giovanniello, V.: Infrastrutture e project financing in Italia: il ruolo (possibile) della regolamentazione. Banca d'Italia (2009)
18. Dixon, P.B., Jorgenson, D. (eds.): Handbook of computable general equilibrium modeling, 1st edn (2012)
19. IMD: World competitiveness report (2008)
20. KPMG: Benchmarking highways england: a report to the office of rail and road (2016)
21. Link, H., Nash, R., Shires, A.: Jd in "International journal of sustainable transport" (2014)
22. Massiani, J., Ragazzi, G.: Costi ed efficienza delle concessionarie autostradali: un'indagine sugli operatori italiani. Trasporti europei **38**, 85–106 (2008)
23. Iozzi, A.: La riforma della regolamentazione del settore autostradale. La riforma della regolamentazione del settore autostradale, pp. 1000–1030 (2002)
24. Ministero delle infrastrutture e dei trasporti: Conto nazionale delle infrastrutture e dei trasporti (1995)
25. Sheppard, S.R., Meitner, M.: Using multi-criteria analysis and visualisation for sustainable forest management planning with stakeholder groups. For. Ecol. Manage. **207**(1–2), 171–187 (2005)
26. United Nations: System of Environmental Economic Accounting 2012—Central Framework (2012)
27. Diaz-Balteiro, L., Romero, C.: Making forestry decisions with multiple criteria: a review and an assessment. For. Ecol. Manage. **255**(8–9), 3222–3241 (2008)
28. Sica, F., Nesticò, A.: The Benefit Transfer Method for the Economic Evaluation of Urban Forests. In: Gervasi, O., et al. (eds.) ICCSA 2021. LNCS, vol. 12954, pp. 39–49. Springer, Cham (2021). https://doi.org/10.1007/978-3-030-86979-3_3
29. Guarini, M.R., Morano, P., Sica, F.: Eco-system Services and Integrated Urban Planning. A Multi-criteria Assessment Framework for Ecosystem Urban Forestry Projects. In: Mondini, G., Oppio, A., Stanghellini, S., Bottero, M., Abastante, F. (eds.) Values and Functions for Future Cities. GET, pp. 201–216. Springer, Cham (2020). https://doi.org/10.1007/978-3-030-23786-8_11
30. Mondini, G.: Valutazioni di sostenibilità: dal rapporto brundtland ai sustainable development goal. Valori e Valutazioni 23 (2019)
31. Guarini, M.R., Morano, P., Sica, F.: Integrated ecosystem design: an evaluation model to support the choice of eco-compatible technological solutions for residential building. Energies **12**(14), 2659 (2019). https://doi.org/10.3390/en12142659
32. Morano, P., Tajani, F., Guarini, M.R., Sica, F.: A systematic review of the existing literature for the evaluation of sustainable urban projects. Sustainability **13**(9), 4782 (2021). https://doi.org/10.3390/su13094782
33. Páez, A., Scott, D.M., Morency, C.: Measuring accessibility: positive and normative implementations of various accessibility indicators. J. Transp. Geogr. **25**, 141–153 (2012)
34. Spencer-Bickle, A.: Initial benchmarking of highways england's regional maintenance spending. European transport conference (2017)
35. Manganelli, B., Tajani, F.: Optimised management for the development of extraordinary public properties. J. Property Invest. Fina. **32**(2), 187–201 (2014). ISSN: 1463-578x

36. Tajani, F., Morano, P.: Evaluation of vacant and redundant public properties and risk control. A model for the definition of the optimal mix of eligible functions. J. Property Invest. Fina. **35**(1), 75–100 (2017). ISSN: 1463-578x
37. Tajani, F., Morano, P., Ntalianis, K.: Automated valuation models for real estate portflios: a method for the value updates of the property assets. J. Property Invest. Fina. **36**(4), 324–347 (2018). ISSN: 1463–578x
38. O'Donnell, C. J., O'Donnell, C. J.: Deterministic frontier analysis. Productivity and Efficiency Analysis: An Economic Approach to Measuring and Explaining Managerial Performance, pp. 281-324 (2018)
39. Dolores, L., Macchiaroli, M., De Mare, G.: Financial impacts of the energy transition in housing. Sustainability **14**, 4876 (2022). https://doi.org/10.3390/su14094876
40. Macchiaroli, M., Dolores, L., De Mare, G., Nicodemo, L.: Tax policies for housing energy efficiency in italy: a risk analysis model for energy service companies. Buildings **13**, 582 (2023). https://doi.org/10.3390/buildings13030582
41. Cambini, C., Nash, C.: Benchmarking in roads and tolled highways. Benchmarking and Regulation in Transport 53–71 (2021)
42. Anelli, D., Tajani, F., Ranieri, R.: Urban resilience against natural disasters: mapping the risk with an innovative indicators-based assessment approach. J. Clean. Prod. **371**, 133496 (2022)
43. Wheat, P., Stead, A.D., Greene, W.H.: Robust stochastic frontier analysis: a Student'st-half normal model with application to highway maintenance costs in England. J. Prod. Anal. **51**(1), 21–38 (2019)

Unveiling the Potential Use of Euler Equations in the Utility Additive Analysis for Mass Appraisal

Francesco Tajani[1], Francesco Sica[1], Maria Rosaria Guarini[1](✉), Pierluigi Morano[2], and Rossana Ranieri[1]

[1] Department of Architecture and Design, "Sapienza" University of Rome, 00196 Rome, Italy
mariarosaria.guarini@uniroma1.it

[2] Department of Civil, Environmental, Land, Building Engineering and Chemistry, Polytechnic University of Bari, 70125 Bari, Italy

Abstract. Using mass appraisal techniques has become strategically important in case of plans property assets, investments in technical and economic renewals, alienation of structures no longer suitable for public needs. Multiple operators implement mass appraisal procedures for residential properties. The UTility Additive (UTA) approach for mass residential property evaluation is tested in this research. The UTA considers the process of deciding a property's price as a multi-criteria typology, with the market-determining attributes of the property acting as the selection criteria to which be capable of assigning marginal utility functions. The Euler equations technique makes use of a variety of margin utility functions, including logistic, exponential, and linear ones. The purpose of this research is to provide a novel operational paradigm for figuring out a property's value in relation to UTA and optimization roles. We wished to investigate the applicability of the Euler Equation (linear, exponential, logistic) as marginal utility functions in particular. We look at the results of independently applying several marginal utility functions, illustrating the various performance stances toward the price formation process. The conclusions discuss the potential for using Euler equations as utility marginal functions throughout the UTA, with following extensions of the work in view to evaluate the performance of the operative model UTA on real case studies.

Keywords: Property Valuation · Mass Appraisal · Utility functions · Euler Equations

1 Introduction

In 2021, the global real estate market size was valued 3.69 trillion of US dollars and is expected to expand of 5.2% from 2022 to 2030 at a compound annual growth rate. The market is supposed to grow both in the residential segment and in the commercial sector, and, as happened for the 2021, commercial spaces have been the most important element driving industry expansion [1]. In Europe, real estate investments in the first half of 2022 increased by approximately 70% compared to the same period in 2021. However, high

O. Gervasi et al. (Eds.): ICCSA 2023 Workshops, LNCS 14107, pp. 42–53, 2023.
https://doi.org/10.1007/978-3-031-37114-1_4

inflation levels, increasing financing rates and escalating levels of economic uncertainty - also due to rising energy costs because of the continuing Russian-Ukrainian conflict - led to a slowdown in growth. Despite this, significant economic transactions took place in the second half of 2022, causing total volumes to exceed 2021 levels, with an overall increase of around 20% [2, 3].

The World Economic Outlook Update (January 2023) estimates that global growth will fall to 2.9 percent in 2023 but increase to 3.1 percent in 2024. The 2023 forecast is 0.2 percentage point higher than predicted in the October 2022 World Economic Outlook. Furthermore, global inflation is expected to drop to 6.6 percent in 2023 and 4.3 percent in 2024, still above pre-pandemic levels [4, 5].

In addition to this complex economic and financial situation, effects of the Covid-19 pandemic are still present. In fact, the Covid-19 pandemic has globally and deeply changed the real estate market and, also, many and different aspects of everybody's daily life, causing effects on both the social dynamics and the mental well-being of the population [6]. Since the end of 2019, collective preventive measures have been taken all over the world, with numerous limitations. Social distancing, obligatory confinement, access's reduction to public places, interruption of theatre, cinema or concert programs, and reduction of national and international trade have forced almost all the world's population to carry out different functions in their homes (i.e., remote working and distance learning activities, or sports and recreational activities) by leading to considerable variation in the ways of using domestic spaces [7–9]. Furthermore, the pandemic has changed the way of living the cities, exacerbating the resilience of urban spaces and making it more difficult to plan and manage the cities in general [10].

On the real estate market, the impact of the pandemic was visible directly in the first semester of 2020, especially from a retail point of view, due to strict lockdown measures and movement restrictions. The lockdowns imposed across the world, also, caused an interruption in new construction projects and led to slow-moving industry growth. Despite the pandemic's huge reduction in home sales, in 2022 real estate activity began to recover, returning to pre-pandemic levels. According to the National Association of Realtors [11], awaiting sales in U.S. metro areas, were down more than 30% in April 2020. After that period, potential buyers began to search again for and purchase of homes, enhancing the growth of the real estate market. Additionally, the influence of the e-commerce has increased awareness among consumers regarding online real estate services, live-streaming rooms, that are used still nowadays.

As well, the Covid-19 pandemic and the energy issue resulting from the geopolitical crisis that flare up in January 2022 have exacerbated some latent critical issues inherent in the residential building segment.

In fact, the effects of the pandemic – which, as already mentioned, have substantially altered the way of living in domestic spaces - and the effects of energy price restrictions have overlaid their effects. When analyzing the evolution of the real estate sector, it is possible to see how abnormal events of a varied nature have significantly modified market dynamics and make it complex and difficult to make appropriate market forecasts, because this type of events could increase situations of uncertainty and market instability. The real estate sector has been directly and indirectly impacted by the state of uncertainty and evolutionary dynamics, which have at various points during the last year affected and shaped all of the real estate segments, particularly in Italy.

However, uncertainty regarding the real estate sector's direction in the near future is significant and projected to rise. Real estate markets are structurally unstable in Italy and have undergone significant changes and ongoing transformations because of social, economic, and fiscal factors. On the other hand, the real estate sector will be also affected by the development of projects using funds from National Recovery and Resilience Plan (NRRP) and National Plan of Complementary Investments (PNC) works and interventions.

In Italy the NRRP has been definitively endorsed on 13 July 2021 for a total of 222.1 billion euros and provides a general framework of reforms and measures to be implemented from 2021 to 2026 within the six pillars identified in the European Green Deal: i) green transition, ii) digital transformation, iii) social and territorial cohesion, iv) health, v) policies for the next generation and sustainable and vi) smart and inclusive growth.

It is important to highlight that the construction sector first, and the real estate sector after, are central to the effective development of the missions envisaged in the NRRP. In particular using instruments for the evaluation of property values has become crucial for the definition of effective projects that meet the needs of the community, and beyond that, for the proper allocation of public resources. This context of changing dynamics and of persisting uncertainty requires the employment of models that, in addition to having a solid theoretical and methodological foundation, can automatically capture the causal relationships between explanatory factors and prices and estimate property values to plan and develop effective projects.

2 Objectives and Sections of the Work

The strategic use of mass appraisal methodologies includes the development of management and upgrading plans for both public and private property assets [12] regarding: expenditures in technological and economic refun tionalization [13]; alienation of structures that are no longer appropriate [14] for societal demands (military barracks, hospitals, areas in disuse, etc.); risk associated with the credit institutions' supply of mortgage loans [15]. For example, Harrison et al. (2001), Lewis (2003), Hefferan and Boyd (2010), all discuss the taxation system, programming territorial transitions, and reviewing current or ex post planning choices made by the public administration [16–18].

An experimental property assessment approach has been used in the current paper. It is based on the Utility Additive (UTA) technique, which views the process of a property's price formation by means of the property's attributes serving as assessment criterion of reference market. The multi-attribute utility theory is an extension of the UTA technique, which is based on the idea that preferences may be broken down using additive utility functions. There aren't many examples of this approach being used in literature to analyze the real estate market. Gomes and Rangel (2009) explained the utility functions of variables often taken into account in the appraisal of residential properties in Volta Redonda using the UTA technique (Brazil) [19]. When there is little information on recent sales of comparable properties and their supply only partially reflects the values of the properties, Aouni and Martel (2004) advised using the UTA approach to support property assessments [20]. The UTA technique has been employed by Greco et al. (2008) and Figueira et al. (2009) by taking into account all potential marginal value functions that are consistent with the decision-indicated maker's preferences [21, 22]. The research's novelty lies in the adaption of several additive utility function types under the UTA umbrella. The typologies were discovered using the Euler Equation technique, which is often used in consumer theory and appreciation of relative properties. The technique takes into account the most important characteristics that characterize utility functions, such as the coefficients of relative and absolute risk aversion, the intertemporal elasticity of substitution, and the coefficients of relative and absolute prudence.

With reference to the Italian real estate market, the application of UTA as it is impacted by the Euler method to creating the utility functions is investigated. In particular, four scenarios were developed based on the kind of utility function that was taken into account. It is of particular relevance to compare the results of UTA implementation to the case study as the utility function under examination differs. This was accomplished using AMPL software to develop an optimization model in accordance with the UTA method's principles.

The paper is set up as follows. Outlines for the UTA and Euler approach for utility function definition are presented in Sect. 3. Section 4 describes the appropriate non-linear optimization algorithms for constructing model UTA-performance. In the same section, an optimization model is presented in which the user can develop alternatives utility functions. The work is concluded in Sect. 5 with a brief summary of the conclusions.

3 Overlooking the UTA Approach

The UTA approach posits that throughout the ordering phase of the eligible alternatives, each decision-maker tries to maximize - consciously or subconsciously - all the variables that form the global utility function (U) associated with each option.

The $v_{i,j}$ shows how the i-*th* option follows the j-*th* criterion whereas a_i ($i = 1,\ldots,$ n) denotes the potential alternatives and c_j ($j = 1,\ldots,$ m) the criteria that characterize the alternatives. $V_{i,j}$ specifies a marginal utility ($u^{'}_{i,j}$), which is the contribution of the alternative i-*th* in reference to the j-*th* criterion to the accomplishment of the global utility U regarding the alternative under consideration.

The UTA technique verifies the following relation by designating C and A, respectively, as the set of criteria of c_j unit (with $j = 1, \ldots, m$) and the set of alternatives of a_i unit (with $i = 1, \ldots, n$):

$$\forall a_i \in A \cup \forall c_j \in C : U(a_i^j) = f(v_{i,j}) \cong f(u'_{i,j}) \tag{1}$$

The global utility of an alternative (a_i) may be calculated using the additive technique Eq. (2), which needs the assumption of independence among the criteria studied and allows for the consideration of a constant term $\sigma(a_i)$:

$$U(a_i) = \sum_{j=1}^{m} u'_{i,j} + \sigma(a_i) \tag{2}$$

The UTA method enables one to quantify the contribution of each criteria to the price formation, otherwise global utility, of each alternative in the population of the detected sample.

In the optimization optic, the global utility functions are approximated as closely as possible to the price reported for each apartment, using a goal programming approach that aims to minimize the error $\varepsilon(a_i)$ corresponding to the difference between the value of the global utility $U(a_i)$ estimated for the apartment and its global utility detected, i.e. the respective selling price $P(a_i)$. So, the objective function takes the following form:

$$\min_{i=1,\ldots,n} \sum_{i=1}^{n} \varepsilon(a_i) = \overline{\varepsilon} = \sum_{i=1}^{n} |P(a_i) - U(a_i)| \tag{3}$$

The UTA method's restrictions are connected to the construction of the marginal utility functions for each criteria used. The marginal utility function should reflect the phenomena under investigation, followed by the connection seen between input value $(v_{i,j})$ and the appropriate marginal utility function $(u_{i,j})$. The piecewise linear function is typically thought of as the functional form that represents the marginal utility. Yet, when using an Eulerian mathematical method, it is also feasible to discover the existence of other functions that describe the marginal utility.

3.1 The Utility Functions Under an Eulerian Mathematical Approach

The most common utility functions used in the literature on the Euler problem are quadratic, exponential, and isoelastic preferences. In this part, we present an overview of these functions and discuss their key advantages and disadvantages.

The marginal utility, for each functional form, is shown in the Table 1. After the suggested summary table, specifics of each type of utility function and its marginal formulation are described separately.

Table 1. Overview of utility functions typologies.

Utility functions types U (A)	Marginal utility function $u'_{i,j}$
a) *Quadratic*	
$\mathrm{U}_{(\mathrm{A})} = \mathrm{qc} \pm \frac{\mathrm{m}}{2}\mathrm{c}^2$	$\mathrm{q} \pm \mathrm{mc}$
b) *Exponential*	
$\mathrm{U}_{(\mathrm{A})} = -\frac{\mathrm{e}^{-\mathrm{ac}}}{\mathrm{a}}$	e^{-ac}
c) *Isoelastic*	
$\mathrm{U}_{(\mathrm{A})} = \frac{\mathrm{c}^{1-\gamma}}{1-\gamma}$	$\frac{\gamma}{c}$

a) **Quadratic function**

In earlier studies, the particular situation of quadratic preferences was used to evaluate the conventional model of consumption. The Permanent Income model with confidence equivalence is the name given to this situation in the literature [23].

In light of this supposition, the Euler equation is as follow:

$$E_{j-1}[u'(C_j)] = u'(C_{j-1}) \tag{4}$$

updates to:

$$\mathrm{C_j = C_{j-1}} + \varepsilon_\mathrm{j} \tag{5}$$

where the ε_j term is representative that every new knowledge concerning the consumer's sources of uncertainty has an influence on consumption. As a result, in the exceptional situation of quadratic preferences, consumption acts like a martingale: ex ante, present consumption is the greatest predictor of next period's consumption; ex post, consumption changes only if expectations are not met.

When expectations are replaced by realizations, the consumption function is the same as under certainty, which is what quadratic utility implies. The person spends as much as they would if their future wages were guaranteed to match their means. Because there is no precautionary saving in the confidence equivalence situation, the model can be quite deceptive when there is uncertainty.

The quantity of consumption that people are prepared to forgo in order to eliminate a specific degree of consumption uncertainty climbs as people get wealthier since quadratic utility implies growing absolute risk aversion. As riskier portfolios are often owned by richer households, this trait is undesirable theoretically and strongly counterfactually.

b) **Exponential function**

In the literature on consumption, exponential utility has been frequently employed, notably in the well-known model put out by Caballero (1990), where a closed form solution for consumption is found [24].

This functional type stands out because it Consistently exhibits Absolute Risk Aversion (CARA). On the other hand, consumption of relative risk aversion is rising, which is a completely erroneous premise. Intertemporal elasticity of substitution is also declining, just as it was in the case of quadratic preferences.

Because of these characteristics, exponential utility is an unrealistic description of individual preferences.

c) **Isoelastic function**

Since Hansen and Singleton's works from 1982 and 1983, a highly common preference definition known as isoelastic utility has been utilized in the consumption literature. It has also been used extensively in numerous theoretical asset pricing studies [25, 26]. In reality, the isoelastic utility assumption and the lognormality of the joint distribution of consumption and stock returns lead to a closed-form, empirically tractable specification of the model's constraints.

Such a specification, however, also places severe constraints on preferences: in this case, the elasticity of consumption's ability to be substituted over time is constant and equal to the reciprocal of the degree of risk aversion. As a result, there are two functions for the curvature parameter. It summarizes consumers' attitudes toward risk since it is equivalent to the coefficient of relative risk aversion on the one hand. Conversely, its reciprocal measures changes in consumption growth when the relative prices of current and future consumption vary since it is equal to the elasticity of intertemporal substitution.

4 Non-linear Optimization Algorithms for Operative Models UTA-Performance

Using approaches from operational research, it is possible to address the many aspects of the smart city using mathematical formalizations that are responsive to changes in the analysis system. When it comes to manage dynamic flow in optimization optic, it is helpful to apply programming approaches. Due to the true functional relationships between the variables that govern the system, it is feasible to handle the multi-dimensionality of the analysis relatively simply.

The approach that should be used is expressed as an optimization process in the construction of an analytical mathematical model, which including:

$$\begin{cases} \max(\text{or } \min) C(x_1, \ldots, x_n) \\ \varphi_m(x_1, \ldots, x_n) \leq b_m \\ x \in X \end{cases} \tag{6}$$

with the set of variables x, the objective function C(x), the system of constraints φ_m.

There are two types of programming problems that can be distinguished:

1. linear programming problems, where the objective function and the functions that define the constraints are both linear, and
2. non-linear programming problems, where at least one of the functions that define the problem is not linear.

The algorithm for addressing the problem must be chosen in every case. The more popular resolution strategies in the context of all linear programming include dynamic programming, implicit enumeration techniques like Branch&Bound (B&B), cutting plane algorithms, and the Brunch & Cut approach [27–31].

The purpose of the section that follows is to give an operational tool UTA-performance based that can be customized according to the kind of utility function the user wants to provide in the analysis. This is accomplished by developing a simple rational model using the syntax of AMPL software, which is capable of resolving various optimization issues while taking into account and respecting the relationships between inputs and outputs. About this, AMPL contains a number of solvers (KNITRO, CPLEX, MINOS, etc.) that are intended to resolve linear, as opposed to optimization problems, while taking into account a variety of different types of predetermined constraints. The real estate market's features, which might affect how prices are built, are taken into consideration while calibrating the suggested analytical model.

4.1 Describing UTA-Performance Model for Mass Appraisal

The AMPL syntactic rules were employed for developing the proposed optimization model [32]. The system has the same structure as in (6), and the AMPL tool was used to implement the Simplex optimization approach, which allows for the resolution of both linear and non-linear programming problems.

The use of AMPL enables the following:

- construction of a parametric model through the file.mod;
- writing of the data of the problem with a file.dat separated from the corresponding file.mod;
- characterization of the system's components such as a series of objects (set);
- establishment of the unknown values,
- to articulate the objective function using an equation based on linear algebra that maximizes/minimize the utility function.

The *m* criteria are used to evaluate the *n* alternatives (set CASES). The division PARAMETERS contains the numerical values for each factor used to characterize the mass appraisal instance. These are the price of each option (param PRZ) and the j-*th* Criterion (C) for evaluating each option (param CRITERION).

The problem's unknown values are determined by the type of margin utility function used (linear, exponential, isoelastic) in the respect to the Euler Equation approach. In accordance with Eq. (3), the objective function is expressed as follows:

$$\min imize\,\overline{\varepsilon} : \ \mathrm{sum\{i\,in\,CASES\}(PRZ[i]{-}{-}(U[i] = f(u_i^j))} \tag{7}$$

It makes sense to associate the i-th marginal utility function with numerical intervals of defined extremes of the j-*th* characteristics because each marginal utility function is denoted by a different mathematical formula and therefore has a different numerical significance depending on the type of analysis variable under consideration. To put it another way, it makes logical to discretize the j-*th* variable's numerical series into discrete k-*th* intervals and connect the marginal utility function of study with each. This implies that the mass appraisal optimization problem should include algebraic formulations of continuity of characteristics at the end ($^-$) and beginning ($^+$) extremes of each interval, as follow:

$$u_{ijk}^{-} = u_{ijk+1}^{+} \tag{8}$$

Depending on the marginal utility function to be used, the (8) might be described by foreseeing various mathematical structures. The three different types of Euler Equations (Linear, Exponential, and Isoelastic) are then used to arrange the potential algebraic configurations of the number (8), as in Table 2.

Table 2. Overview of constraints per margin utility functions typologies.

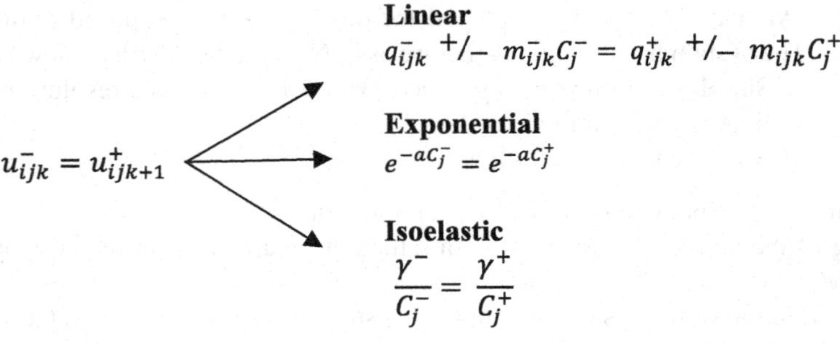

Linear
$q_{ijk}^{-}\ {}^{+}/{-}\ m_{ijk}^{-}C_j^{-} = q_{ijk}^{+}\ {}^{+}/{-}\ m_{ijk}^{+}C_j^{+}$
Exponential
$e^{-aC_j^{-}} = e^{-aC_j^{+}}$
$u_{ijk}^{-} = u_{ijk+1}^{+}$
Isoelastic
$\frac{\gamma^{-}}{C_j^{-}} = \frac{\gamma^{+}}{C_j^{+}}$

Table 3 then shows the entire layout of the AMPL programming standards-compliant UTA-performance based optimization system. The characteristics of the model in Table 2 are then provided while taking into account the linear, exponential and isoelastic marginal utility functions. A system example with four instances and one criterion (SURF) is suggested in the Fig. 1 below.

Table 3. Structuring UTA-performance model according to AMPL editing-rules.

#Sets-system#
set CASES: = 1..n;
#Parameters#
param PRZ {*i* in CASES};
param CRITERION {*i* in CASES};
#Objective function clarification#
minimize $\overline{\varepsilon\varepsilon}$: : sum{i in CASES}(PRZ[i] – (U[i] = f(u_i^j));
#Constraints#
subject to (s.t.) constraints: $u_{ijk}^{-} = u_{ijk+}^{+}$

Linear

```
set CASI := 1..4;

param PRZ{CASI};
param SURF{CASI};

var q1;
var m1;
var q2;
var m2;
var q3;
var m3;
var q4;
var m4;

minimize somma: sum{i in CASI}(PRZ[i] - (q1 + m1*SURF[1]) - (q2 + m2*SURF[2]) - (q3 + m3*SURF[2])- (q4 + m4*SURF[4]))^2;

s.t. vincolo_0 {i in CASI}: q1 + m1*SURF[1] - q2 - m2*SURF[1] = 0;
s.t. vincolo_1 {i in CASI}: q2 + m2*SURF[2] - q3 - m3*SURF[2] = 0;
s.t. vincolo_2 {i in CASI}: q3 + m3*SURF[3] - q4 - m4*SURF[3] = 0;
```

Exponential

```
set CASI := 1..4;

param PRZ{CASI};
param SURF{CASI};

var a1;
var a2;
var a3;
var a4;

minimize somma: sum{i in CASI}(PRZ[i] - (exp(-a1*SURF[1])) - (exp(-a2*SURF[2])) - (exp(-a3*SURF[3]))- (exp(-a4*SURF[4])))^2;

s.t. vincolo_0 {i in CASI}: exp(-a1*SURF[1]) - exp(-a2*SURF[2]) = 0;
s.t. vincolo_1 {i in CASI}: exp(-a2*SURF[2]) - exp(-a3*SURF[2]) = 0;
s.t. vincolo_2 {i in CASI}: exp(-a3*SURF[3]) - exp(-a4*SURF[3]) = 0;
```

Isoelastic

```
set CASI := 1..4;

param PRZ{CASI};
param SURF{CASI};

var γ1;
var γ2;
var γ3;
var γ4;

minimize somma: sum{i in CASI}(PRZ[i] - (γ1/SURF[1]) - (γ2/SURF[2]) - (γ3/SURF[3]) - (γ4/SURF[4])^2;

s.t. vincolo_0 {i in CASI}: (γ1/SURF[1]) - (γ2/SURF[2]) = 0;
s.t. vincolo_1 {i in CASI}: (γ2/SURF[2]) - (γ3*SURF[2]) = 0;
s.t. vincolo_2 {i in CASI}: (γ3*SURF[3]) - (γ4*SURF[3]) = 0;
```

Fig. 1. AMPL files. Mod for linear, exponential and isoelastic functions

5 Conclusions

The application potential of the proposed UTA approach for mass appraisal, which is capable of producing an efficient management of both public and private property, is connected to the consequences of this research for valuation practice. To improve the properties with the most convenience and to reduce management costs in order to streamline the management of public assets, public administrations may use the suggested operative models. They may also determine the effects of property tax policies and investments in urban redevelopment, as expressed in variations in property prices, and update the property values of their assets over time.

Private operators, on the other hand, could use the proposed methodologies with relative assessment tools for a variety of purposes, including: updating and periodically verifying the market values of properties as securities for credit exposures; allowing the adoption of possible balancing measures aimed at reducing credit risks; real estate funds, periodically assessing the market values of their assets; and private companies, monitoring the congruency of their assets.

The models, whose structures resemble those in Fig. 1, will be adopted to various marginal utility functions obtained using the Euler Equation method. The Euler approach's benefit of referencing mass appraisal experiences is tractable on evaluating how well the three models—linear, exponential, and isoelastic—perform in terms of the utility goal following the application of the specific marginal function. To this, the model will be applied to several case studies in order to evaluate its efficacy, highlight its benefits, and draw attention to its drawbacks.

Additional results from this research could be related to the potential for combining together the marginal utility function of each section of the UTA model taking in practice more than one assessment criterion, in order to obtain functional forms rather than necessarily linear functions that are more closely related to the empirical phenomenon under study. A further area that needs to be investigated is whether it is possible to define a universal valuation function for all markets. This research was unable to do so because the examined markets were opaque, the influencing factors for selling prices were too specific, and the sample size was too small.

References

1. CBRE: https://www.cbre.it/insights/reports/italy-real-estate-market-outlook-2023, last 01 March 2023
2. Gupta, A., Mittal, V., Peeters, J., Van Nieuwerburgh, S.: Flattening the curve: pandemic-induced revaluation of urban real estate. J. Financ. Econ. **146**(2), 594–636 (2022)
3. PWC: https://www.pwc.com/gx/en/industries/financial-services/real-estate/emerging-trends-real-estate/europe-2023.html#report, last 01 March 2023
4. IMF: https://www.imf.org/en/Publications/WEO, 21 February 2023
5. MSCI: https://www.msci.com/documents/10199/8f62c2a3-8374-cbf9-a7d2-a8c2c5e63e62, last accessed 28 February 2023
6. Inoue, H., Todo, Y.: The propagation of economic impacts through supply chains: the case of a mega-city lockdown to prevent the spread of Covid-19. In: PLoS ONE **15**(9 September), 1–10 (2020)
7. Li, H.Y., Cao, H., Leung, D.Y.P., Mak, Y.W.: The psychological impacts of a Covid-19 outbreak on college students in China: a longitudinal study. In: International Journal of Environmental Research and Public Health **17**(11) (2020)
8. Tajani, F., Liddo, F.D., Guarini, M.R., Ranieri, R., Anelli, D.: An assessment methodology for the evaluation of the impacts of the COVID-19 pandemic on the Italian housing market demand. Buildings **11**(12), 592 (2021)
9. Tajani, F., Morano, P., Di Liddo, F., Guarini, M.R., Ranieri, R.: The Effects of Covid-19 Pandemic on the Housing Market: A Case Study in Rome (Italy). In: Gervasi, O., et al. (eds.) ICCSA 2021. LNCS, vol. 12954, pp. 50–62. Springer, Cham (2021). https://doi.org/10.1007/978-3-030-86979-3_4
10. Anelli, D., Ranieri, R.: Resilience of complex urban systems: a multicriteria methodology for the construction of an assessment index. In: New Metropolitan Perspectives: Post COVID Dynamics: Green and Digital Transition, between Metropolitan and Return to Villages Perspectives, pp. 690–701. Springer International Publishing, Cham (2022)
11. NAR REALTOR: https://www.nar.realtor/blogs/economists-outlook/where-people-moved-in-2022, last accessed 28 February 2023
12. Bourassa, S.C., Cantoni, E., Hoesli, M.: Spatial dependence, housing submarkets, and house price prediction. The Journal of Real Estate Finance and Economics **35**(2), 143–160 (2007)

13. McCluskey, W., Deddis, W., McBurney, R.D., Mannis, A., Borst, R.: Interactive application of computer assisted mass appraisal and geographic information systems. J. Prop. Valuat. Invest. **15**(5), 448–465 (1997)
14. Lee, S., Park, I., Choi, J.K.: Spatial prediction of ground subsidence susceptibility using an artificial neural network. Environ. Manage. **49**(2), 347–358 (2012)
15. Lentz, G., Wang, K.: Residential appraisal and the lending process: a survey of issues. Journal of Real Estate Research **15**(1), 11–39 (1998)
16. Harrison, D.T., Smersh, G., Schwartz, A.: Environmental determinants of housing prices: the impact of flood zone status. Journal of Real Estate Research **21**(1/2), 3–20 (2001)
17. Lewis, B.D.: Property tax in Indonesia: measuring and explaining administrative (under-) performance. Public Administration and Development **23**(3), 227 (2003)
18. Hefferan, M.J., Boyd, T.: Property taxation and mass appraisal valuations in Australia adapting to a new environment. Prop. Manag. **28**(3), 149 (2010)
19. Gomes, L.F.A.M., Rangel, L.A.D.: Determining the utility functions of criteria used in the evaluation of real estate. Int. J. Prod. Econ. **117**(2), 420–426 (2009)
20. Aouni, B., Martel, J.M.: Property assessment through an imprecise goal programming model. Info. Sys. Operat. Res. **42**(3), 189–200 (2004)
21. Greco, S., Mousseau, V., Słowinski, R.: Ordinal regression revisited: multiple criteria ranking using a set of additive value functions. Eur. J. Oper. Res. **191**(2), 416–436 (2008)
22. Figueira, J.R., Greco, S., Słowinski, R.: Building a set of additive value functions representing a reference preorder and intensities of preference: GRIP method. Eur. J. Oper. Res. **195**(2), 460–486 (2009)
23. Jappelli, T., Pistaferri, L.: The consumption response to income changes. Annual Review of Economics **2**, 479–506 (2010)
24. Caballero, R.J.: Consumption puzzles and precautionary savings. J. Monet. Econ. **25**(1), 113–136 (1990)
25. Merton, R.B.: Rational theory of option pricing. Bell J. Econ. Manag. Sci. **4**, 141–183 (1973)
26. Rubinstein, M.: The strong case for the generalized logarithmic utility model as the premier model of financial markets. Journal of Finance (1976)
27. Vercellis, C.: Ottimizzazione: teoria, metodi, applicazioni. McGraw-Hill, Milano (2008)
28. Guarini, M.R., Morano, P., Sica, F.: Eco-system Services and Integrated Urban Plan-ning. A Multi-Criteria Assessment Framework for Ecosystem Urban Forestry Projects. In: Values and Functions for Future Cities, pp. 201–216. Springer, Cham (2020)
29. Guarini, M.R., Morano, P., Sica, F.: Integrated ecosystem design: an evaluation model to support the choice of eco-compatible technological solutions for residential building. Energies **12**(14), 2659 (2019). https://doi.org/10.3390/en12142659
30. Morano, P., Tajani, F., Di Liddo, F., Amoruso, P.: The public role for the effectiveness of the territorial enhancement initiatives: a case study on the redevelopment of a building in disuse in an Italian small town. Buildings **11**(3), 87 (2021)
31. Calabrò, F.: Integrated programming for the enhancement of minor historical centres. The SOSTEC model for the verification of the economic feasibility for the enhancement of unused public buildings. [La programmazione integrata per la valorizzazione dei centri storici minori. Il Modello SOSTEC per la verifica della fattibilità economica per la valorizzazione degli immobili pubblici inutilizzati]. ArcHistoR **13**(7), 1509–1523 (2020). https://doi.org/10.14633/AHR280
32. Bruglieri, M., Cordone, R., Liberti, L., Iuliano, C.: Manuale essenziale di AMPL. Dipartimento di Elettronica e Informazione. Politecnico di Milano (2010)

Evaluation Aspects in the Strategic Planning of a Reticular DMO for the Promotion of Inner Areas of Calabria

Francesco Calabrò(✉) and Immacolata Lorè

Mediterranea University, 89124 Reggio Calabria, Italy
francesco.calabro@unirc.it

Abstract. The study, first phase of an applied research on the Metropolitan City of Reggio Calabria, aims to identify the best organizational solutions for the cultural-tourist offer of specific territorial contexts, such as inner areas. The paper intends to deepen the contribution of economic-estimative evaluations to the construction of an experimental reticular DMO (Destination Management Organization) to support the local development processes of areas with an unexpressed cultural potential. The study deals with the implications connected with an organizational-managerial model of the Destination, as a support tool for the decision-making process of the network construction in order to guarantee an added value in the tourist chain.

Keywords: Economic-Estimative Evaluations · Strategic Planning · DMO · Widespread Heritage · Cultural Tourism · Inner Areas · Local Development

1 Introduction

The paper explains the methodological approach and the first results of the research activities carried out by the UNESCO Med Lab of the Mediterranean University (RC) on the territory of the Metropolitan City of Reggio Calabria.

The research activities are aimed at promoting the development of the investigated areas, through the valorization of their Cultural Heritage, mainly from a tourist point of view. The research is structured in two connected fields: one oriented towards the best organization of the tourist offer, the other focused on issues more closely related to Cultural Heritage, in particular on the management aspects associated with its fruition.

The paper focuses on the first research line, starting from the state of the art of the scientific debate on DMO (Destination Management Organization), to then develop an innovative hypothesis of Reticular Destination Management Organization (R-DMO), based on the common themes of the territories and not on their geographical contiguity.

Particular attention is then dedicated to the different contributions that the culture of economic and estimative evaluation can bring to the topic.

After the presentation of the methodological approach, the paper introduces the innovative hypothesis of R-DMO, to finally present the first results of the research activities on the case study.

O. Gervasi et al. (Eds.): ICCSA 2023 Workshops, LNCS 14107, pp. 54–72, 2023.
https://doi.org/10.1007/978-3-031-37114-1_5

2 State of the Art

In a country like Italy where it continues to discuss a wide and different cultural-tourist offer, the era of importing a foreign model is over, strategic planning through the construction of a Destination seems feasible above all for those places that, minor by nature (less known and at risk of depopulation or abandonment), are crushed by the globalized tourism market which tends to cut them off from the international circuits [1].

The Tourist Destination represents the fundamental unit of analysis in the management and organization of the tourist systems: in addition to its role as a tourist attraction, it represents the *value chain* of the tourist product and experience [2]. In this sense, a DMO plays a leading role in the management of the destination network (integration of services, definition of a territorial product) and in establishing and maintaining cooperation between the local interested parties (tour operators, businesses and administrations) [3].

In the complex and global scenario, the DMO has become the core of all destination development activities, as a catalyst and facilitator for the tourism improvement.

Although its notion has been extensively addressed in the literature over the past twenty years, much fewer models have been empirically developed to optimize its activity [4]. While some authors amplify the marketing component, others in recent years have underlined its global character from a management point of view [5], with attention to a smart approach [6].

From the DMO point of view, each territories of the network can be interpreted as hubs of a complex system, as "systems of systems" on varying of socio-economic and cultural contexts. In this sense, the enhancement of the Widespread Heritage of specific territories can be a potential asset for a conscious strategic plan based on the enhancement of endogenous resources [7], as local drivers of sustainable development [8]. This perspective is able to recover the dimension of the Widespread Museum [9], that due to its flexible nature is able to face many of the current challenges that cultural institutions are facing. It represents the most complete, complex and innovative form in which the protection and enhancement of heritage [10, 11] on a wide scale is combined with the aim of promoting tourism that gives again centrality to inner areas and their territories and communities [12, 13].

These reflections are even more felt in the most fragile areas such as Calabria, where the need for integrated management of the widespread heritage overcome the fragmentation of policies and interventions, raising questions on the issue of protection and quality of tourist offer.

3 Methodology

In application to the principles of the Economics of Welfare [14–16], the contribution deals with the issue of enhancing the Cultural Heritage of a Wide Area through the tool of the DMO (Destination Management Organization) for the construction of a Tourist Destination.

A DMO can be considered as the basis of the tourism system, whose production criteria are organizational efficiency and effectiveness; it plays a leading role in the management of the Destination's network, in establishing and maintaining cooperation between the interested parties (local institutions and organizations, economic entities, service providers, residents, groups and entities such as second houses) and in supporting tourists [17, 18].

The methodology started from a synthetic analysis of the characteristics of the Calabrian heritage: a territory in which, for different reasons, there are no characteristic sites of a given era, which individually have the attractive potential, for example, of a place like Pompei (Campania, IT). In particular, the earthquakes that have followed over the centuries, have destroyed significant parts of the Heritage, whose distinctive character today is given precisely by its heterogeneity and widespread availability.

This distinctive character suggested a strategy for the construction of the Destination that would enhance its features (tangible and intangible heritage): for this reason, rather than using a geographical logic, a thematic one was opted for in relation to multi-stratification, considering at the same time the weaknesses of Calabrian infrastructure.

With reference to the DMO concept as a formal organization that serves a tourist destination with a geographical area of responsibility, generally of a supra-municipal level between contiguous territories [19], it has been identified the possibility that this organization could favor the promotion of territories also not contiguous, but characterized by a common heritage.

Based on this reasoning, two types of DMO have been distinguished:

– one on a geographical basis (characterized by a network of contiguous territories);
– one on a thematic basis (characterized by a network of territories that may not be contiguous, but with common assets).

It is with regard to the second one that, starting from the concept of Widespread Heritage and borrowing the components of a DMO (Attractors, Public Orgs, Attraction Managers, Accessibility and Transport, Services: Accommodation Providers, Restaurants and Retail Outlets, Complementary Services), the hypothesis of a reticular DMO (R-DMO) is developed as a Destination made up of interoperable systems (see Table 1) [20]. In this sense, the R-DMO can be considered a response to the fragmentation and heterogeneity of a widespread heritage such as the Calabrian one, through the search not for geographical continuity, but for the interactions connected to the heritage and the landscape. Consequently, the choice of the case study fell on three non-contiguous areas of the same province and characterized by the presence of a Widespread Heritage (different in nature, eras and characteristics), but with a common element that influences the landscapes, the wine tradition.

In this context, the culture of evaluation can make it possible to identify the organizational-management models most suited to the specific characteristics of the territories, resources and stakeholders and to verify their feasibility and economic sustainability (see Table 2).

The methodological approach consists of four different phases as specified below. The first, of a theoretical nature, is dedicated to bibliographic and documentary recognition, the subsequent ones, of an applicative-experimental nature, concern the elaboration of the strategy and the evaluation tools.

- Phase 1: bibliographic and documentary recognition
- Phase 2: identification and cataloging of resources (Attractors) – analysis of the DMO components (system of services) → objective: definition of a cognitive framework functional to the construction of a Tourist Destination

  Phase 2.0: Construction of the Attractors Selection Criteria

- Phase 3: development of support tools for decisions and impact estimation (in progress)

  Phase 3.0: Construction of the Actions Selection Criteria

Specifically, the theorized evaluation plan (see Table 2) concerns:

2.0 – the structuring of the Attractors Selection Criteria (subject of the paper);
3.0 – the identification of the Actions Selection Criteria (in progress).

Table 1. Methodological Approach. Elaboration by the authors, 2023.

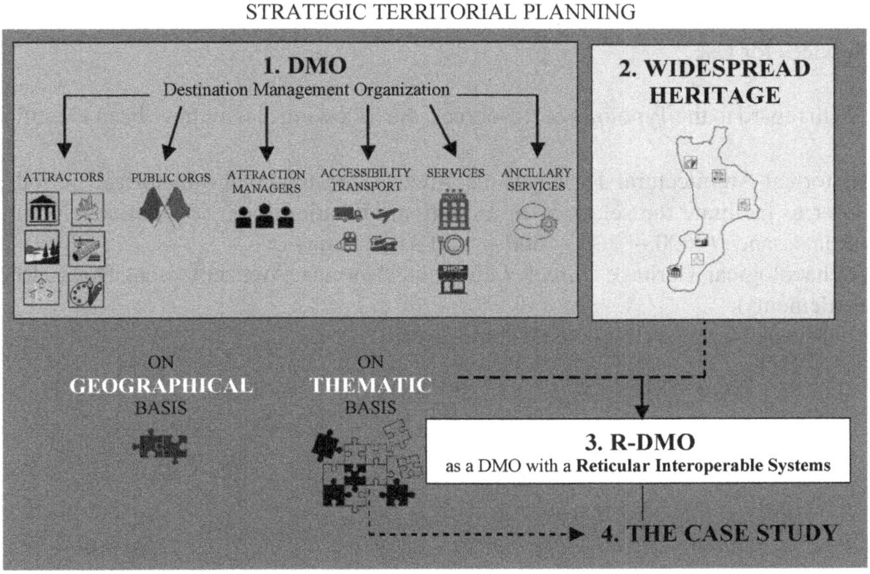

STRATEGIC TERRITORIAL PLANNING

1. DMO
Destination Management Organization

ATTRACTORS
PUBLIC ORGS
ATTRACTION MANAGERS
ACCESSIBILITY TRANSPORT
SERVICES
ANCILLARY SERVICES

2. WIDESPREAD HERITAGE

ON **GEOGRAPHICAL** BASIS

ON **THEMATIC** BASIS

3. R-DMO
as a DMO with a **Reticular Interoperable Systems**

4. THE CASE STUDY

Table 2. Evaluation plan. Elaboration by the authors, 2023.

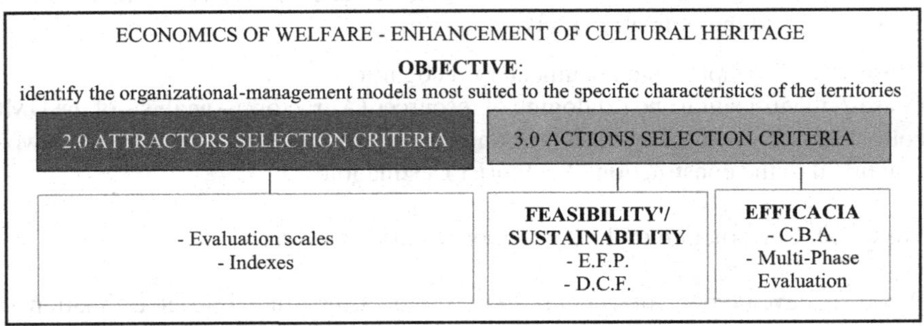

The Attractors Selection Criteria. With reference to the selection of tangible resources (see point 4), the evaluation plan saw the structuring of the Attractors Selection Criteria in order to understand the levels of their attractiveness. Therefore, the method and criteria were explained, on the basis of the following informations:

- Type of Resources;
- Period of Construction;
- Ownership Structure;
- Relevance;
- State of Conservation;
- Services for Use.

With regard to the Typology of Resources, the following classes have been identified:

- Historical-Architectural Heritage, classified according to the historical period in order to facilitate the selection in a multi-stratification logic (Byzantine / Norman / Renaissance / '600 – '700 – '800 – '900 Architectures);
- Archaeological Heritage (Greek / Roman / Norman Archaeological Parks; Rock Settlements);
- Landscape Heritage (Protected Natural Areas).

For each of theme, the Ownership Structure (public/private) were surveyed and the State of Conservation assessed, identifying three possible situations:

- *sufficient* (required interventions)
- *good* (small maintenance interventions required)
- *excellent* (no interventions required)

The Relevance was assessed on a four-point evaluation scale, based on its reporting in different publications, crossed with the judgment of experts. The Services for Use were assessed on a four-point evaluation scale, based on:

- presence of a management model;
- maintenance levels;
- provision of: website, electronic ticketing and online reservations; parking spaces; public toilets; informative materials; reporting of routes; tourist guides or audio guides;
- opening time;
- entrance ticket.

The Actions Selection Criteria. The identification of the Actions Selection Criteria (Point 3 – in progress) will take place on the basis of:

- evaluation of economic and financial feasibility/sustainability;
- evaluation of effectiveness.

Specifically, the verification of the economic-financial feasibility/sustainability of the organizational and managerial models of the R-DMO will take place on the basis of the construction of the Economic and Financial Plan (E.F.P.) and the Discounted Cash Flow Analysis – D.C.F.).

With regard to the evaluation of effectiveness, the first reasoning connected to the multidimensional evaluation of the overall effects generated by the R-DMO is reported, through a Multi-Phase (see point 5) and integrated approach (use of monetary and non-monetary techniques), focusing in particular on:

- the multidimensional evaluation of the overall effects generated by the R-DMO, in terms of economic development and revitalization of social and territorial contexts such as Inner Areas, of changes in social welfare and promotion of local identity on the basis of participatory processes;
- the identification of the public and private conveniences' system and of the economic aspects for their balancing for the feasibility and sustainability, in a long-term time.

The construction of a wide area DMO – with poorly connected territories and devoid of a large ranging planning – constitutes the obstacle to its innovative charge and its range of action, despite the presence of a widespread cultural heritage.

In relation to the areas under examination, characterized by dynamics of physical and socio-economic marginalization but by the heterogeneity and quality of cultural resources (tangible and intangible), the construction of a reticular DMO (R-DMO – Reticular Destination Management Organization) has been identified as a functional tool for the development strategy. Therefore, the proposed R-DMO suggests a new way of planning a Tourist Destination for non-contiguous, heterogeneous and functionally connected territories, such as a network of hubs selected through appropriate indicators and considerations.

This methodology can contribute to the optimal construction of Tourist Destinations in inner areas, presenting a current framework of the processes and interdependencies connected to a single management organization. This can be the basis for the development of a decision support tools in order to optimize activities and operations in R-DMO.

3.1 Good Practices

These considerations include different examples of creative planning and tools. In the national territory (IT), the experiences of the *Sistema Puglia* are particularly interesting. In this case the Wide Area Planning, in line with the provisions of *Documento Strategico Regionale 2007/2013* and of the FESR European Programme, has had a strong development into the *Strategic Plans of Wide Area* (Piani Strategici di Area Vasta) of ten territorial aggregations (Lead institution: Bari, Brindisi, Foggia, Lecce, Taranto, Casarano, Gravina, Barletta, Comunità Montana Monti Dauni Meridionali, Monopoli); these plans outline specific and shared objectives by addressing human and economic resources in the same direction (*Linee Guida per la pianificazione strategica territoriale di Area Vasta – NVVIP Regione Puglia*). These aggregations include the cases of:

- TARANTINA WIDE AREA (twenty-eight municipalities). Strategic objectives of the Plan: construction of a new identity and a unitary image of the territory; promotion of a renewed economic and productive mission; development of an integrated infrastructure system.
- WIDE AREA OF MURGIANA CITY (six municipalities). Strategic objectives of the Plan: to strengthen municipal cooperation; ensure the protection and enhancement of the heritage; open up to the world by improving internal and external accessibility.
- VISION 2020 WIDE AREA (ten non-contiguous municipalities of the new polycentric BAT Province). The vision is based on seven creative cities and visions that represent as many theme-places, proposed as "territorial intuitions", which interpret the themes and opportunities for the development of the territory and its evolution: the City of Rurality; the City of Typical Production; the City of Art; the City of the Sea; the City of Design; the City of Entertainment; the City of Government.

Among other experiences, *Le Vie Dei Tesori* in Sicily, a project dedicated to the story and discovery of the island's heritage (places, people, landscapes, experiences, traditions, productions) as a widespread museum. Born in 2006 in Palermo on the occasion of the

Bicentenary of the city's University, the project has gradually expanded involving twenty of the capital municipalities, large cities and over fifty villages. In 2017 one of its spin-offs was born in the Lombardy Region with the aim of growing communities starting from their heritage. The project, carried out by the *Le Vie dei Tesori Onlus Foundation*, produces an induced income of over 5 million euros every year (data source: Otie – Observatory on Tourism for Islands Economy). It collaborates with local authorities and over two-hundred public and private partners on participatory enhancement projects, such as the *Borghi dei Tesori Fest* in 2021, that digitized, narrated and opened the heritage of small municipalities to the public.

4 The Study Context

The Areas. In connection with the reasoning, the choice of the case study fell on three non-contiguous Areas (see Fig. 1) of the Metropolitan City of Reggio Calabria (IT) not particularly developed from a tourist point of view but characterized by the presence of cultural resources of value, and contiguous to territories with well-known heritage (Reggio Calabria: Bronzi di Riace; Palmi: Varia – UNESCO IH; Gerace: Borgo di Eccellenza; Scilla: Borgo Marinaro of Chianalea; Locri: Archaeological Park of Locri Epizefiri; Casignana: Roman Villa).

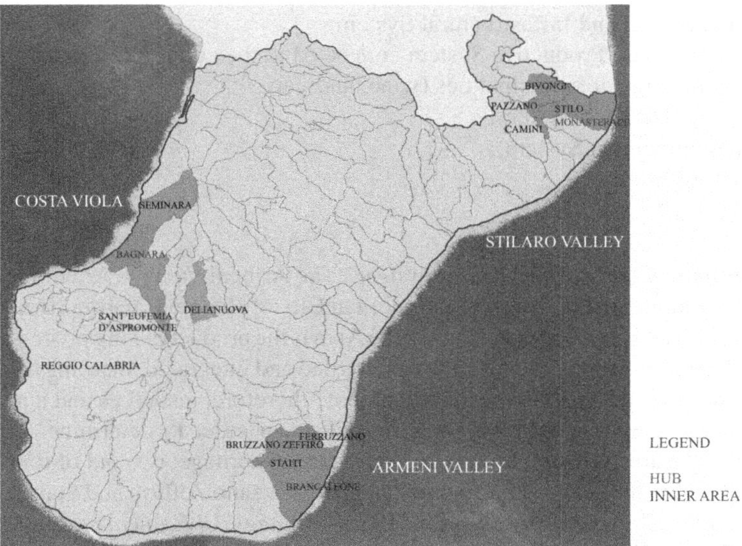

Fig. 1. The study context, Metropolitan City of Reggio Calabria (IT), Armeni Walley – Stilaro Walley – Costa Viola. Elaboration by the authors, 2023.

In identifying the case study and in a geographical and territorial reasoning to support the inner areas, a Coast Hub with a connection function was identified for each Area under examination (see Table 3).

Table 3. Case study – Areas.

AREA	MUNICIPALITY	
	COAST HUB	INNER AREA
1. Valle degli Armeni	Brancaleone	Bruzzano Zeffirio, Ferruzzano, Staiti
2. Vallata della Stilaro	Monasterace	Bivongi, Camini, Pazzano, Stilo
3. Costa Viola	Bagnara	Delianuova, Sant'Eufemia d'Aspromonte, Seminara

The Common Theme. In relation to the concept of R-DMO referred to the point 3, the examined areas are characterized by the presence of a widespread heritage, but with a common element that influences their landscapes, the wine tradition [21]; they constitute, in fact, the main areas of quality wine in different production in the province (Armeni Valley: Greco di Bianco D.O.C., Mantonico D.O.C., I.G.T. Rosso di Palizzi; Stilaro Valley: Rosso di Bivongi D.O.C.; Costa Viola: Zibibbo – Bianco I.G.T.).

The Area Under Examination. Specifically, the contribution reports the analyses conducted on the Armeni Valley (Area 1), while the investigations on the remaining areas are in progress. In particular, the analyses concerned:

- the Geographical and Infrastructural System;
- the Economic and Productive System connected to the cultural resources and to the common heritage of municipalities (wine landscapes);
- the Cultural Heritage System;
- the Accommodation System;
- the Tourist Flows;
- the SWOT.

The Geographical and Infrastructural System. The Armeni Valley – Area 1 (see Fig. 2) includes four municipalities of the Metropolitan City of Reggio Calabria (Brancaleone, Bruzzano Zeffirio, Ferruzzano and Staiti); the Area is the product of long processes of historical and identity stratification, which have settled and integrated, marking and designing the landscapes that are still perceptible today; therefore, resources and anthropic or natural emergencies and vocations were examined in order to determine a cognitive framework. The area is characterized by a rich natural heritage: two out of four municipalities fall within the Aspromonte National Park (Bruzzano Zeffirio and Staiti) or have a *Sito di Interesse Comunitario – SIC* (IT9350160- *Spiaggia di Brancaleone*; IT9350159- *Bosco di Rudina*, Ferruzzano); three out of four municipalities fall within the *Costa dei Gelsomini* Regional Marine Park (Brancaleone, Bruzzano Zeffirio, Ferruzzano).

The Economic and Productive System connected to the cultural resources and to the common heritage. From an economic and productive point of view, the Armeni Valley is known for the richness of its biodiversity and its wine heritage with over one hundred vines with a unique genome currently kept in the *Kepòs Conservation Field* (Ferruzzano). From Roman times to the Middle Ages, the production of wine was an important resource for the area, connoting it as one of the main production centers of Calabria; historical and cultural evidence of this heritage is the MiC (Ministry of Culture) census of over one hundred and sixty millstone – *palmenti* (ancient tanks dug into the rock where the grapes were pressed to produce the must). During the 20th century, wine production underwent a period of decline due to national economic redirection policies with the consequent emigration of farmers to the cities and the abandonment of vineyards. However, in recent years, there has been a return to the production of quality wine (eleven wineries surveyed by the authors as of 2023 and three quality designations – D.O.C., I.G.T., D.O.P.), with the adoption of modern techniques and the enhancement of local varieties (Zibibbo, Greco di Bianco and Mantonico), appreciated on the national and international market (see Fig. 3).

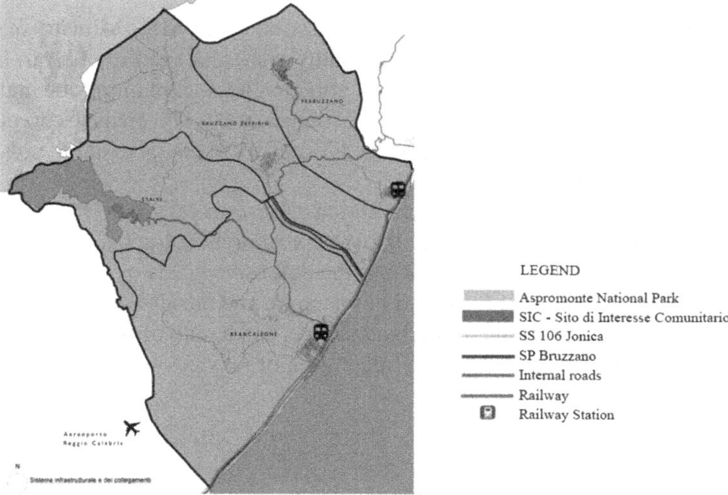

Fig. 2. Area 1 – The Territorial Context. Elaboration by the authors, 2023.

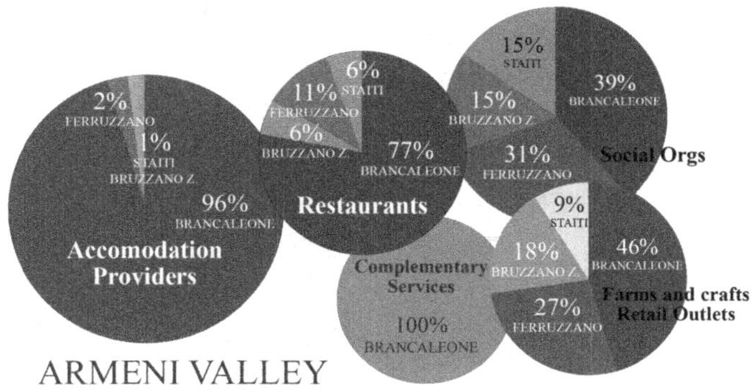

Fig. 3. Area 1 – Summary of winery data collection, Armeni Valley (RC). Elaboration by the authors, 2023.

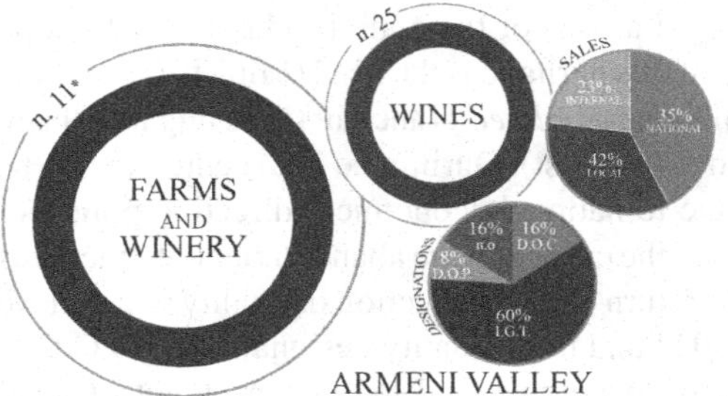

Fig. 4. Area 1 – Summary of data collection on economic-productive services connected to cultural heritage, Armeni Valley (RC). Elaboration by the authors, 2023.

The Cultural Heritage System. After outlining the context, the MiC (Ministry of Culture) data on the cultural resources of each municipality were analyzed in order to highlight their distribution and understand the levels of attractiveness, explaining the method and evaluation criteria that allowed it the selection (see point 3). The analyses do not derive exclusively from studies based on documents and statistical data, but are the result of an applied research by the authors.

The analyses revealed a strong concentration of resources which confirm the landscape and naturalistic value of the area, the variety of archaeological and architectural assets [22, 23], among which the evidence of the defensive needs of the Norman period (towers, walls, castles and other fortification systems), and the signs of rurality linked to the economies of the Aspromonte hinterland. Therefore, a map of the Cultural Heritage concentration was drawn up through the integration of services (see Figs. 4 and 5).

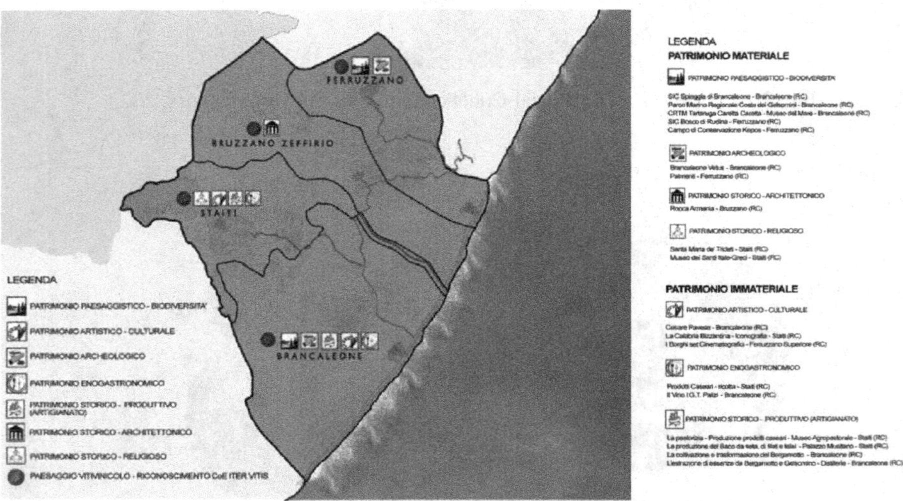

Fig. 5. Area 1 – Summary of cultural heritage data collection, Armeni Valley (RC). Elaborations by the authors, 2023

The Accommodation System. The analysis of the relevance and consistency of the cultural heritage was a necessary but not sufficient operation for the study of the attractiveness under a tourist profile, if not correlated to a study of the visitor flows and the accommodation offer [24, 25], key factors for understanding whether the territories are prepared to welcome an innovative, inclusive and sustainable tourism planning. Therefore, the Istat (Istituto Nazionale di Statistica) data up to 2021 on accommodation facilities divided by municipality and type was examined, cross-referenced with the data of the main OTA (Online Travel Agencies) up to 2023 (see Table 4). The capacity of the Area 1 consists of 91.4% of beds in hotel structures (Brancaleone), 6.6% of B&Bs and 1.9% of Holiday Homes (see Table 4); even if it is not possible to make a subdivision of the flows based on the reason for the stay, this share of the offer concerns a demand related to tourist-bathing and return reasons. By comparing the distribution of the accommodation offer with the cultural one (see Table 4, Fig. 5), substantial coincidences emerge between the areas with the greatest concentration of cultural resources and those in which the accommodation offer is more structured (Brancaleone); on the other hand, the less dense areas in terms of censed cultural heritage are also those in which the availability of beds is more limited (Staiti).

The Tourist Flow. The tourist flow of the metropolitan city of Reggio Calabria reveals a strong dichotomy on a provincial and regional scale, which has its roots in the attractiveness of some seaside and coastal destinations which only increases the divergence with inner areas. If the proposed strategy is able to integrate cultural heritage and inner centers that otherwise would not have the strength to generate a tourist demand, the discontinuity of the accommodation offer could be an obstacle. The Istat data collected up to 2021 attest that 89.3% of arrivals and 91.7% of presences in the province were absorbed by the city of Reggio Calabria and by the large centers along the coast (e.g. Locri, Siderno, Roccella Jonica). In fact, it is no coincidence, that the data on the tourist flows of the four municipalities cannot be deduced from the Istat surveys since, to protect the privacy of the economic subjects involved, the data on arrivals and presences in the minor municipalities are merged (unlike the data on the consistency and quality of

Table 4. Area 1 – Analysis of tourist flows and accommodation system (Sources: Istat 2021 data cross-referenced with the main OTAs up to 2023). Elaboration by the authors, 2023.

TOURIST FLOWS		ACCOMMODATION CAPACITY		
Armeni Valley		Municipality	Structure Typology	Number of Beds
Arrivals	6.200	BRANCALEONE	B&B	40
			Hotel	858
Presences	44.600	BRUZZANO ZEFFIRIO	Holiday Home	10
		FERRUZZANO	B&B	22
Average Stay	7,2 days	STAITI	Holiday Home	8
		Tot. Beds		938

the structures which are detailed); the tourist movement was, therefore, analyzed in a comparative perspective for disaggregated data.

The SWOT Analysis. From the SWOT analysis (see Table 5) a great endogenous potential emerged for tourism development that, however, requires on the one hand a project for the sustainable use of individual resources, and on the other the elaboration of an integrated project and system capable of promoting sustainable economic, social and environmental development.

Table 5. The SWOT Analysis. Elaborations by the authors.

STRENGTHS	WEAKNESSES
• **Tangible Heritage** of high cultural value (*Brancaleone Vetus, Rocca Armenia, Santa Maria De Tridetti*, ancient distilleries, *Costa dei Gelsomini-* Caretta Caretta Turtle, Aspromonte National Park – Geopark UNESCO) • **Wine landscape** (*Palmenti, Kepòs Conservation Field, Quality wine production cellars, International Quality Denominations, CoE Cultural Route – Iter Vitis*) • **Intangible Heritage** (art of cooking: bergamot, dairy products; craftsmanship: production of silkworms, yarns and looms, essences of bergamot and jasmine) • **A well-established sense of hospitality** as a • behavioral culture of the communities	• **Insufficient infrastructural equipment** • **Low level of the Standards of tourist services** • **Seasonality of tourist flows and employment in the sector** • **Dismiss of rural areas** in the absence of interventions to support geographical isolation • **Progressive abandonment of centers** – youth emigration • **Few presence of tour operators** • **State of conservation of heritage** • **Access to financial resources** – Insufficient capacity of entrepreneurship to use the resources financed by rural development and tourism policies • **Difficulty of entering national and international commercial circuits** • **Poor functionality of the PA** • **Low level of coordination between stakeholders** • **Scarce presence of associations** • **Inadequate media coverage of positive actions**
OPPORTUNITIES	**THREATS**
• **Market trend of cultural tourism** • **Improvement of the attractiveness of the territory through the integrated management of resources** • **Diversification of the economy** – creation of employment opportunities • **Intersectoral integration of food production and valorization of local crafts** • **empowerment of decision makers** • **Rationalization and renewal of the offer**	• **Competition and globalization of the tourism market** • **Prevalence of return and transit tourism and of nearby seaside area on the coast** • **Perception of the local economy as a specialized issue and a sectoral policy** • The plurality of subjects and services as a strong point, in the absence of **adequate coordination,** can produce fragmentation and a difficulty in monitoring the evolutionary scenarios

5 The Enhancement and Networking Strategy

The proposed strategy takes into account the existing resources and, at the same time, the new resources that the project can generate, taking into account the model of *multi-polar* networks [26], in which a complementarity between centers of dimension and of different hierarchical level [27].

The poly-centrality and poly-functionality of urban contexts, the cultural diversity that characterizes them, the being inhabited by heterogeneous flows, paves the way for new tourism opportunities beyond the best-known resources [28].

On the basis of these considerations, the network was built starting from connections in which the role of a center does not depend on its size but on the ability to fit into the exchange circuits, not only economic, but also environmental and cultural, synthesizing the complexity of the connections present at the local level [29]; each hub of the network assumes, therefore, a specific role according to the relationship it develops with the theme of the R-DMO (in this specific case, the wine landscape) and the role of signifier it assumes in the local context.

5.1 Objectives and Actions

General Objective (GO) of the strategy, the structuring of an experimental reticular DMO (R-DMO). In line with the Specific Objectives (SO), seven Actions (A) are envisaged as shown in Table 6.

Table 6. Specific Objectives (SO) and Actions (A). Elaborations by the authors.

Specific Objectives (SO)	Actions (A)
SO1 – foster collaboration forms between public and private stakeholders	A1 – identification and implementation of partnership forms
SO2 – promote the protection, enhancement and promotion of tangible and intangible cultural heritage	A2 – research activity (filing and heritage mapping), design and implementation of knowledge tools (information and dissemination material, storytelling)
	A3 – identification of public buildings with historical-cultural value to be recovered for the promotion and localization of productive activities of excellence (in the specific case it should be emphasized how much this operation refers to a back-ground lacking in experience)
SO3 – promote and enhance typical local products through quality tourism	A4 – construction of a cooperation technology platform (e-commerce)
SO4 – involve the owners of the services around the cultural system	A5 – design of integrated circuits and tourist packages (attractors and services)
SO5 – make the territory a competitive product	A6 – development of territorial marketing forms through the elaboration of a communication and rebranding plan
SO6 – seasonal variations of the offer	A7 – membership in national and international circuits

6 The Economic and Estimative Implications

In a historical moment in which community awareness is completely different from the past and in a regulatory framework made up of a particularly intense planning season, it appears evident that neither the Municipalities nor the Regions may be able to manage these opportunities directly, but it also appears useful to identify territorial aggregates ready to welcome and finalize the needs of one and the other and to summarize them. In this situation the Municipalities prove to be completely unsuitable as they are not able to respond to the managerial breadth that this form of enhancement of the territory requires; therefore, the need arises to build a management framework which, in addition to the linearity of the DMO, is able to support aware and coherently constructed territorial aggregates.

In this context, the proposed R-DMO can be defined as a complex network with a series of hubs that are extremely interesting for the search for optimal functional programs and related management models on a wide area [30, 31].

On the numerous expectations placed on development opportunities connected to the enhancement of cultural tourism, it is also important to evaluate the expected impact of such operations [32–34].

In this context, the culture of evaluation can make it possible to identify the organizational-management models most suited to the specific characteristics of the territories. Specifically, the study reports the first reasoning on the identification of the Actions Selection Criteria on the basis of economic feasibility and sustainability and effectiveness [35–37].

With regard to the effectiveness, an interesting impact assessment was the one launched by the Toscana Region starting in 2009 for the Cultural Itinerary of the Council of Europe under its responsibility, the *Via Francigena*, through the use of three methodologies [38]:

a) a counterfactual approach focused on areas that are currently less developed in terms of tourist attraction, which saw the comparison of the evolution of tourist presences in rural areas crossed or excluded from the *Francigena*, demonstrating a differential of 34% of presences (290,000 unit);
b) the application of a multi-regional input-output model, for which the presences directly attributable to the *Via Francigena* were isolated with the application of a geographical method for estimating GDP (Gross Domestic Product) and work units (ULA – Unità di Lavoro) activated by public investment and local tourism spending. In the evaluation phase (investment phase), an activation of 10.8 million euros of GDP and 200 full-time work units (ULA) was estimated, for the total expenditure when fully operational, an estimated activation of 49.1 million euros of GDP (0.04% of regional GDP) and 881 work units (0.05% of Tuscan employment).
c) the elaboration of long-term evolutionary scenarios (until 2022), based on the application of the dynamics of tourist presences experienced in comparable territories, assuming that the *Francigena* evolves in four different ways, according to the different sizes:
   1) the regional average (WTO – World Trade Organization Organization);
   2) the dynamics of the English Cotswold, a rural area comparable to the Tuscan hill;

3) the dynamics of the similar Camino de Santiago;
4) the dynamics of another prestigious rural area of the region, the Chianti.

In relation to the case study, the impact assessment will refer to two phases, *pre* and *post*. Specifically, the reasoning reported relates to the *pre-phase* and concerns the applicability of the *counter-factual* and *input-output method* to the examined territories.

With regard to the *counter-factual method*, the isolation of a control group was identified as a condition, which has characteristics similar to those of the examined territories, but which will not benefit from the R-DMO. In fact, the area concerned a very heterogeneous territory, made up of large rural and seaside parts and contiguous to well-known destinations (see point 4). Therefore, the first step should consist in isolating the rural municipalities from the mature ones from a tourist point of view. The former can then be compared with rural territories not affected by the Destination.

The *input-output model* can instead be applied to estimate the economic and employment impact in two different ways:

a) in the pre-phase, it will be able to measure the income and employment attributable to the investments of the last few years in the cultural and tourist heritage sector (see Table 7);

Table 7. Area 1 – Implemented Strategies in the cultural heritage and tourist sector. Sources: Open Cohesion, Amministrazione Trasparente of Brancaleone, Bruzzano Zeffirio, Ferruzzano and Staiti. Elaboration by the authors, 2023.

IMPLEMENTED STRATEGIES CULTURAL HERITAGE AND TOURIST SECTOR		
SECTOR	MUNICIPALITY	EXPENSE
INFRASTRUCTURE	BRANCALEONE	€ 430.387,21
	BRUZZANO ZEFFIRIO	€ 652.115,10
	FERRUZZANO	€ 322.335,00
	STAITI	€ 350.000,00
TOT. ARMENI VALLEY INFRASTRUCTURE		**€ 1.754.857,31**
CULTURE AND TOURISM	BRANCALEONE	€ 569.294,20
	BRUZZANO ZEFFIRIO	€ 820.688,22
	FERRUZZANO	€ 661.552,58
	STAITI	€ 1.401.860,10
TOT. ARMENI VALLEY CULTURE AND TOURISM		**€ 3.453.395,10**
COMPANY INCENTIVES	BRANCALEONE	€ 65.000,00
	BRUZZANO ZEFFIRIO	€ 21.981,00
	FERRUZZANO	-
	STAITI	-
TOT. ARMENI VALLEY COMPANY INCENTIVES		**€ 86.981,00**
TOT. ARMENI VALLEY		**€ 5.295.233,41**

b) in the post-phase, it will be able to estimate the income and employment deriving from the total tourist expenditure connected to the R-DMO.

For the estimation of economic results and employment according to a more integrated approach, the hypothesized approach is based on the development of microdata bases on local economic activities to determine the range of variation in labor productivity; this approach also opens up new possibilities for analyzing the estimate of employment and the economic results of companies starting from local level productivity maps (on the basis of parameters identified in the cost and revenue relationships of the selected companies) consistent with the basic data and with the estimation inputs of the national aggregates.

7 First Conclusions and Research Perspectives

The research carried out has allowed, on the one hand, to recognize the value necessary for heritage and the landscape for it to contribute to the construction of a Tourist Destination, but more striking is the recognition of the absence of tools that manage the cultural system in an integrated way. Recognizing this dependence is the preliminary step for its strengthening, necessary to recognize the importance of the identity function exercised by the territories. In this context, the work offers possible guidelines and a framework of strategic choices outlining various opportunities for the territories concerned. Among the possibilities that emerged it finds the continuity of reading of the territories and their landscapes regardless of the territorial borders.

The contribution aims to demonstrate the innovative character of a new way of planning a Tourist Destination, not necessarily for geographically contiguous territories, but characterized by a common heritage, with the aim of providing with the next studies, a quantitative evaluation of the potential competitiveness of a R-DMO, understood as the ability to enhance the attractiveness on the market of disadvantaged territories [39].

For this reason, the transversal nature of a R-DMO, which includes several territories, even non-contiguous ones, and the collaboration between heterogeneous associations and foundations that manage the development of the destination in a participatory manner, can produce widespread and non-selective effects, combining economic-employment development with the protection and enhancement of the heritage and guaranteeing visibility to minor territories that is perceptible by potential visitors and investors [40].

References

1. Campolo, D., Calabrò, F., Cassalia, G.: A cultural route on the trail of Greek monasticism in Calabria. In: Bevilacqua, C., Calabrò, F., Della Spina, L. (eds.) New Metropolitan Perspectives. Local Knowledge and Innovation dynamics towards territory attractiveness through the implementation of Horizon/Europe2020/Agenda2030. Smart Innovation, Systems and Technologies, SIST, vol. 101, pp. 475–483. Springer Science and Business Media Deutschland GmbH (2019). https://doi.org/10.1007/978-3-319-92102-0_50
2. CNR-IRISS: XXV Rapporto sul Turismo Italiano, 2020–2022 (2023)

3. Korzh, N., Onyshchuk, N.: Integrated business strategy of the organization for the Destination Management Organisations (DMO). Sci. Notes of Ostroh Acad. National Univ., "Econ." Ser. **1**(26(54)), 30–36 (2022)
4. Triandafil A., Dinu A., Puie F., Şerbănescu A.: Destination Management organizations: a systematization of recent literature with a focus on new research trends. Cactus Tourism J. **3**, 56–63 (2022)
5. Bogacz-Wojtanawska, E., Gòral, A.: Network or structures? Organizing cultural routes around heritage values. Humanistic Manag. J. **3**, 253–277 (2018)
6. Del Chiappa G., Buonincontri P., Errichiello L., Micera R.: Tourism, Hospitality and Culture 4.0: Shifting Towards the Metaverse (2022)
7. Calabrò, F., Cassalia, G., Lorè, I.: A project of enhancement and integrated management: the cultural heritage agency of Locride. In: Calabrò, F., Spina, L.D., Mantiñán, M.J.P. (eds.) New Metropolitan Perspectives: Post COVID Dynamics: Green and Digital Transition, between Metropolitan and Return to Villages Perspectives, pp. 278–288. Springer International Publishing, Cham (2022). https://doi.org/10.1007/978-3-031-06825-6_27
8. Barca, F., Carrosio, G.: Un modello di policy place-based: la Strategia nazionale per le aree interne. In: AttivAree. Un disegno di rinascita delle aree interne. Il Mulino (2020)
9. Van Aalderen, M.: Il bello dell'Italia. Il Belpaese visto di corrispondenti di stampa estera. Albeggi Editore, Fiumicino (2015)
10. CoE: Convenzione Europea del Paesaggio, art. 30. Florence (2000)
11. ICOMOS: Impact Heritage Assessment for Cultural World Heritage Properties. Paris (2011)
12. Graf, M., Popesku, J.: Cultural routes as innovative tourism products and possibilities of their development. Int. J. Cult. Dig. Tourism **3**(1), 24–44 (2016)
13. Sabir, B.: Developing a multidisciplinary tourism. Planning approaches on cultural routes. J. Multidiscip. Acad. Tourism **4**(1), 37–47 (2019)
14. Pigou, A.: The Economics of Welfare. Macmillan and Co., London (1932)
15. Tenaglia S.: Gli indicatori di benessere nella programmazione economica in Italia. Un esempio virtuoso di sinergia tra ricerca e policy making. Sinappsi, XII, n. 1, pp.14–25 (2022)
16. Magrini M.: L'economia circolare. Un paradigma della sostenibilità applicabile anche al turismo. Università Ca' Foscari Venezia (2022)
17. Erbas A.: Tourism planning through the system of national Destination Management Organization. In: Destinasyon Canavarına Karşı Ulusal Turizm Planlamasıve Maliyet Kontrolü Detay Publishing, Ankara (2023)
18. Manganelli, B., Tajani, F.: Optimised management for the development of extraordinary public properties. J. Property Investment Finance **32**(2), 187–201 (2014)
19. Reinhold, S., Beritelli, P.: Destination Management Organization (DMO). In: Encyclopedia of Tourism Management and Marketing. Edward Elgar Publishing (2022). https://doi.org/10.4337/9781800377486.destination.management.organization
20. Lanucara, S., Praticò, S., Modica, G.: Harmonization and interoperable sharing of multi-temporal geospatial data of rural landscapes. In: Calabrò, F., Della Spina, L., Bevilacqua, C. (eds.) ISHT 2018. SIST, vol. 100, pp. 51–59. Springer, Cham (2019). https://doi.org/10.1007/978-3-319-92099-3_7
21. Praticò, S., Solano, F., Di Fazio, S., Modica, G.: A multitemporal fragmentation-based approach for a dynamics analysis of agricultural terraced systems: the case study of costa viola landscape (Southern Italy). Land **11**(4), 482 (2022). https://doi.org/10.3390/land11040482
22. Fragomeni, P., Lorè, I.: VR as (In)Tangible representation of cultural heritage. scientific visualization and virtual reality of the doric temple of punta stilo: interference ancient-modern. In: Bevilacqua, C., Calabrò, F., Della Spina, L. (eds.) NMP 2020. SIST, vol. 178, pp. 1851–1861. Springer, Cham (2021). https://doi.org/10.1007/978-3-030-48279-4_175

23. Fotia, A., Caccamo, F., Buda, R.: Cultural heritage recovery interventions through steel endoskeletons: a case study. In: Calabrò, F., Spina, L.D., Mantiñán, M.J.P. (eds.) New Metropolitan Perspectives: Post COVID Dynamics: Green and Digital Transition, between Metropolitan and Return to Villages Perspectives, pp. 2024–2034. Springer International Publishing, Cham (2022). https://doi.org/10.1007/978-3-031-06825-6_194
24. Spatari, A., Calabrò, F., Lorè, I., Viglianisi, A.: Economic feasibility of an integrated program for the enhancement of the byzantine heritage in the Aspromonte national park. the case of Staiti. In: New Metropolitan Perspectives, Conference proceedings NMP2022. Springer (2022).https://doi.org/10.1007/978-3-031-06825-6_30
25. Coscia, C., Fregonara, E., Rubino, I.: To what extent is the Airbnb market segment resilient? Evidence from the tourism and short-term rental trends of Turin (Italy) during the 2020 COVID-19 pandemic crisis (2023)
26. Dematteis, G., Bonavero, P.: Il sistema urbano italiano nello spazio unificato europeo. Milano, F. Angeli (1997)
27. Gumuchian, H., Pecqueur, B.: La ressource territoriale. Paris, Anthropos (2007)
28. Maitland, R., Newman, P.: Developing world tourism cities. In: Maitland, R., Newman, P. (eds.) World Tourism Cities: Developing Tourism off the Beaten Track, pp. 3–21. Routledge, London-New York (2009)
29. Moroni, S., Rauws, W., Cozzolino, S.: Forms of self-organization: urban complexity and planning implications. Env. Plann. B: Urban Anal. City Sci. **47**(2), 220–234 (2020)
30. Anelli, D., Tajani, F.: Valorization of cultural heritage and land take reduction: an urban compensation model for the replacement of unsuitable buildings in an Italian UNESCO site. J. Cult. Herit. **57**, 165–172 (2022)
31. Del Giudice, V., Massimo, D.E., Salvo, F., De Paola, P., De Ruggiero, M., Musolino, M.: Market price premium for green buildings: a review of empirical evidence. Case study. In: Bevilacqua, C., Calabrò, F., Della Spina, L. (eds.) NMP 2020. SIST, vol. 178, pp. 1237–1247. Springer, Cham (2021). https://doi.org/10.1007/978-3-030-48279-4_115
32. Fregonara, E., Ferrando, D.G.: The discount rate in the evaluation of project economic-environmental sustainability. Sustainability **15**(3), 2467 (2023)
33. Martini, A., Sisti, M.: Valutare il successo delle politiche pubbliche. Il Mulino, Bologna (2009)
34. Nesticò, A., Galante, M.: An estimate model for the equalisation of real estate tax: a case study. Int. J. Bus. Intell. Data Min. **10**(1), 19 (2015). https://doi.org/10.1504/IJBIDM.2015.069038
35. Gravagnuolo, A., Angrisano, M., Fusco, G.L.: Circular economy strategies in eight historic port cities: criteria and indicators towards a circular city assessment framework. Sustainability **11**(13), 3512 (2019)
36. Calabrò, F.: Promoting peace through identity. Evaluation and participation in an enhancement experience of Calabria's endogenous resources | Promuovere la pace attraverso le identità. Valutazione e partecipazione in un'esperienza di valorizzazione delle risorse endogene della Calabria. ArcHistoR **12**(6), 84–93 (2019). https://doi.org/10.14633/AHR146
37. Troisi, R., Alfano, G.: Proximity and inter-firm corruption: a transaction cost approach. Small Bus. Econ. **60**(3), 1105–1120 (2023)
38. Conti, E., Iommi, S., Piccini, L., Rosignoli, S.: Itinerari culturali europei e sviluppo sostenibile: il caso della via Francigena. AISRe (2015)
39. Santagata, W.: Cultural districts and their role in economic development. In: Ginsbourg, V., Throsby, D. (eds.) Handbook on the Economics of Art and Culture, pp. 1101–1119. Elsevier, Amsterdam (2006)
40. Murgante, B., Berardi, L., Di Donato, P.: Plan4all: Rete europea delle Buone Pratiche per l'interoperabilità degli strumenti di Pianificazione territoriale. In: 13a Conference Proceedings ASITA, Bari (2009)

Integrating Ecosystem Services Value in the Economic Assessment of Urban Projects. Proposal of an Analytical-Operative Approach

Maria Rosaria Guarini[1](✉), Francesco Sica[1], Pierluigi Morano[2], and Francesco Tajani[1]

[1] Department of Architecture and Design, "Sapienza" University of Rome, 00196 Rome, Italy
mariarosaria.guarini@uniroma1.it

[2] Department of Civil, Environmental, Land, Building Engineering and Chemistry, Polytechnic University of Bari, 70125 Bari, Italy

Abstract. Urban project evaluation methods frequently rely on the assessment of costs and benefits that are directly tied to monetary measurement. They do not account for the additional advantages to society and economy that ecosystems, depending on their conditions and in response to rising community need, might provide. What might therefore be developed to support the inclusion of the ecosystem services assessment within the framework of economic evaluation procedures in urban system?

The work attempts to offer a viable and adaptable framework capable of guiding private and/or public entities' actions while also taking into consideration the ecosystem's advantages, more specifically the ecosystem services. The proposed workflow is constituted by series of steps that support the development of decision-making processes that can assess a single intervention from several perspectives, from environmental to economic in nature. It can support the implementation of economic evaluation strategies that take into account the importance of ecosystem services provided by urban habitats. The research highlights how different land use patterns, socioeconomic systems, and environmental conditions can change the project's potential to deliver ecosystem services.

The conclusions outline the practical implications and the limits of the developed assessment framework.

Keywords: Economic evaluation · Ecosystem services · Urban · Analytical framework

1 Introduction

Cities and towns have the biggest and most significant influence on ecological processes and biological variety (biodiversity) of all land uses because to their structures, transportation infrastructure, parks, and demands for goods and services. This effect is expected to persist given the ongoing trend of urbanization and the production needed to feed it [1, 2].

O. Gervasi et al. (Eds.): ICCSA 2023 Workshops, LNCS 14107, pp. 73–84, 2023.
https://doi.org/10.1007/978-3-031-37114-1_6

The definition of biodiversity given by the 2005 Millennium Ecosystem Assessment [3], which was based on the 1992 Convention on Biological Diversity [4], consists in the variety of life on Earth, which is made up of many components, including genes, species, populations, and ecosystems, on a variety of geographical scales, from local to global [5–7].

Although though cities and their surrounding areas might pose a danger to biodiversity, they also offer a variety of chances for various species to coexist in various ecosystems and with various land uses. Cities are frequently situated near areas with high biodiversity, such estuaries, coasts, ecotones, and fertile plains [8, 9]. The following ways that they can sustain biodiversity if they are well-managed:

- cities serve as refuges for animals whose habitats have been devastated by intense agriculture and forestry;
- cities are socio-ecological systems where new species communities and habitats can emerge;
- urban green spaces give cities advantages (ecosystem services) that cannot be imported, such noise reduction and pollution absorption [10].

Ecosystem services refer to the products and services that nature offers. Together with the life necessities like food and water, they also offer other services like water filtration and cultural and therapeutic advantages. The yearly value of ecosystem services worldwide was tentatively estimated in 1997 to be USD 32 trillion, or nearly twice the world's GDP [11–14].

The following categories of ecosystem services were established by the Millennium Ecosystem Assessment in 2005:

- Provisioning service, provide food, water, raw materials, biofuels, and medicinal resources;
- Regulating services regulate the quality of air, soil and water, provide flood and disease control, provide pollination services and regulate pests and prevent disease;
- Habitat or supporting services provide living spaces for plants or animals; they also maintain a diversity of different breeds of plants and animals;
- Cultural services include the non-material benefits people obtain from contact with ecosystems, including aesthetic, spiritual, educational and psychological benefits; public health and recreational opportunities [3].

The Economic of Ecosystems and Biodiversity (TEEB) program seeks to highlight the benefits of biodiversity to the global economy. During their conference in Germany in 2007, the G8 + 5 environment ministers decided to "start the process of examining the global economic value of biological variety, the costs of the loss of biodiversity, and the failure to adopt protective measures versus the costs of successful conservation." To help decision-makers manage the planet's limited ecological resources wisely, the TEEB method approaches environmental challenges from an economic viewpoint [15, 16].

This emphasizes the significance of cities for biodiversity on a global scale, as well as the significance of urban green spaces and biodiversity for the sustainability of cities and the welfare of its inhabitants in sustainable economy perspective. As cities expand and the line separating urban and rural regions becomes less distinct, plants and animals adapt to the shifting urban environment, reflecting the ongoing evolution of the connection between humans and nature. With rising city growth come more habitats, and both purposefully and accidentally introduced species may be found in cities [17].

Because the society and the economy depend on the ecosystem products and services that the environment provides, protecting biodiversity is essential to ensuring a healthy local economy. Ecosystem services, which comprise both natural resources (products) and activities that offer a service, such as clean air, fuel, and water purification, are supported by biodiversity. Conserving the ecosystem and taking advantage of the clean water it produces is less expensive than replacing an ecosystem function, for as by constructing and operating a water treatment facility [18, 19].

When a species that may offer medical services or other benefits becomes extinct and cannot be replaced, the loss of biodiversity has an even bigger negative impact.

The current governmental-territorial scenario, both international and domestic, calls for a shift in the transformation processes of human settlements on the territory toward the reduction of biodiversity loss, the enhancement of value-adding practices related to it (biodiversity), and the definition of trajectories of social, economic, and environmental integration. In order to define and identify those settlement transformation interventions that, from the perspective of a sustainable economy, are able to produce the least impacts on human and natural ecosystems, environmental, economic, and social, and preserve and/or increase natural capital, it is necessary to encourage the adoption of an integrated, multidimensional, multiscale approach. What tools and techniques, though?

2 Aims

It is critical to highlight how various strategies and tools are employed in practice to aid in the incorporation of environmental value into decision-making processes for land use and/or urban planning. Some of them are based on multi-criteria logic, in which several indicators are considered and meant to express distinct impacts both numerically and qualitatively.

To progress toward an integrated strategy that protects and advances the environmental component, decision-makers, educators, and land development professionals must change their perspectives. It is crucial to encourage information-sharing throughout collaborative decision-making procedures.

Based on these fundamental assumptions, the work makes an attempt to provide a framework for assessing in eco-systemic terms the consequences that settlement transformation processes may have in the urban environments of cities. This methodology enables the evaluation of projects in urban environments using the socioeconomic and ecological conditions of the reference environment.

The work is articulated as follows. Section 3 describes the techniques, and assessment tools that support interventions that protect the biotic component. Section 4 describes the economic evaluation approach proposed for urban initiatives, together with its supporting documentation. Section 5 shows the work's results, and the application potential of the suggested analytical scheme is analysed, as a complement to the acknowledged evaluation processes that are increasingly used in contemporary practice.

3 Mainstreaming Economic-Environmental Assessment: Main Approaches and Methods

With a preference for a integration logic among many elements, it is aimed to suggest a multi-criteria evaluation technique in which several considerations are concurrently incorporated, among them the ecological and environmental features of the relevant urban system with that concern social and economic nature. It is conceivable to enable co-participatory processes of identifying the kinds of interventions to be carried out on the existing, favoring an integrated ecosystem approach, by supporting an assessment workflow through the suggested methodological framework [20]. Figure 1 depicts the articulation of one of the key worldwide standards for environmental-economic accounting of reference, the System of Environmental Economic Accounting-Central Framework (SEEA-CF) by the United Nations, in conjunction with various methodologies and instruments for assistance [20].

To concern the SEEA-CF, it is based on quantifying the stocks of assets and flows of ecosystem services that habitats offer to the economy, particularly to the regional production system. Operationally, it consists of successive steps starting with the accounting of the extension and condition regarding the kind of ecosystem, followed by the assessment of the ecosystem service that it generates. It immediately moves to the economic accounting of ecosystem services from the biophysical measurement [20]. You can read the structure of SEEA-CF flowchart in Fig. 1.a.

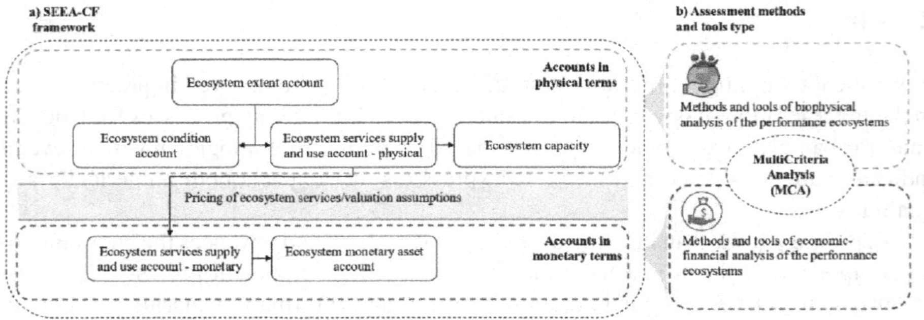

Fig. 1. SEEA-CF framework with methods/tools clusters.

Depending on the type of evaluation problem to be solved, the evaluation methodology and tool to be used, and the potential application of participatory processes for gathering stakeholder expressions of interest, different methodologies for evaluating urban-territorial projects from an ecosystem perspective may be used. It is possible to categorize three distinct types of approaches and tools of assistance in line with the phase relating to the biophysical accounting and the economic-based one (Fig. 1.b). They are: *i*) multi-criteria, *ii*) biophysical, and *iii*) economic-financial in nature. In particular, biophysical techniques are used to characterize ecosystems' contributions to the provision of ecosystem services for the community through the enhancement of natural processes. The measurement of several biotic and abiotic configurational aspects of existing ecosystems serves as their theoretical underpinning. Some examples of biophysical approaches include direct measurements, such as field observations and surveys, indirect measurements, such as remote sensing techniques, the use of analysis-tools (such as i-Tree software), and analytical-mathematical modeling tools, such as ecological and statistical analysis tools [21–23]. Economic-financial strategies explore how a habitat's generation of ecosystem services influences land development economically, as assessed just in monetary terms. These strategies include creating an assessment framework that integrates the costs and benefits of the proposed activity. The direct and indirect costs and benefits of eco-system conservation, restoration, and service supply for biodiversity protection may be assessed. Costs for ecosystem restoration, particularly those that promote the provision of habitat for biodiversity, are included. Because the installation of ecosystem restoration can also reduce the effects of urban heat islands, the phenomena being examined may have a direct economic impact. There are references for estimating the equivalent economic value for the natural assets, water resource, and atmospheric carbon dioxide concentration to be put into the valuation frameworks supporting the economic-financial approaches. Otherwise, the multi-criteria assessment approaches allow economic, environmental, and socio-cultural factors to be considered independently or together within the same domain of research. This is accomplished using suitable evaluation methods and associated instruments that enable comprehensive analyses and investigations of several elements of various kinds, represented in monetary and/or nonmonetary terms [21, 24–26]. There are several noteworthy ones among them, including the Benefit-Transfer (BT) method [22], or even the tools implementing the Analytic Hierarchy Process (AHP) [27], Techniques for Order of Preference Based on Similarity to the Ideal Solution (TOPSIS) [21], Natural-Capital Accounting (NCPT), and optimization algorithms specific to operations research [27]. By designing multi-objective mathematical optimization models according to the multidimensional nature of SEEA-CF, they may be used to answer a large number of multi-criteria matrix assessment issues. It is feasible to define and select the kind of settlement transformation intervention to be implemented using a sustainable economy strategy by cultivating an integrated, multidimensional, multiscale evaluative logic that takes into account the usage of various evaluation instruments and methodologies [28, 29].

4 Proposal of an Economic-Environmental Accounting System for Urban Projects

4.1 Methodological Framework Approach for Integrated Economic-Environmental Assessments

The structuring of the proposed evaluation approach can be succinctly described methodologically (Fig. 2) as an interactive and integrated process consisting of the following stages, based on the logical-functional links of SEEA-CF in Fig. 1:

- Stage 1 (Identification of Objectives): definition of the objectives, general and specific to be achieved and identification of potential tactics for achieving the ecological targets related to the bioclimatic, environmental, human settlement, infrastructural and socio-economic conditions of the urban reference context;

- Stage 2 (Evaluation criteria and performance indicators): identification of the main direct and indirect drivers of ecosystem service provision in terms of suitable indicators to be used in the evaluation procedure, both biophysical and economic;
- Stage 3 (Assessment methods and tools): identification of the appropriate evaluation models to support the decision-making systems of public and private entities when evaluating the cost-effectiveness of the process.

In particular, the proposed economic-environmental evaluation scheme can be taken as the framework that substantiates the operational framework outlined next. The identification of sustainability goals to be pursued (Stage 1) is necessary to ensure the production of services aimed at: regulating the natural and climatic conditions of the place; socially and culturally educating the population; and sustaining the local economy through supply enhancement and/or new commercial-recreational activities (cultural and recreational services). Each goal, or type of ecosystem service, can be articulated using appropriate evaluation criteria and particular performance indicators (Stage 2). The indicators that can be used concern both the conditions that represent the urban ecosystem in its naturalistic and biodiversity characteristics and the performance in terms of the impact that the intervention solution is able to express with respect to the economic, social, and environmental characteristics of the urban environment and the area in which it is located. The identification (and implementation in the operational framework) of appropriate multi-criteria matrix techniques for the study and evaluation of interventions (Stage 3), is aimed at identifying the evaluation tools that allow the proposed intervention solution(s) to be screened from a variety of angles, and the various options to be considered in relation to one or more sustainability objectives.

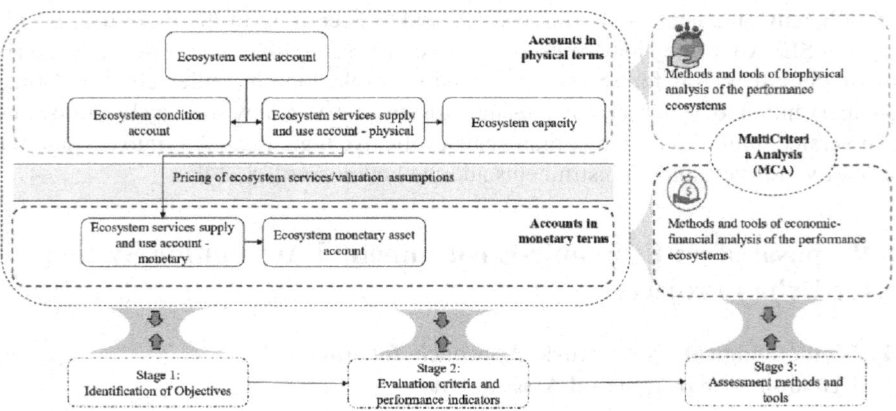

Fig. 2. Methodological framework approach for integrated economic-environmental assessments.

4.2 Operative Framework

Figure 2 shows the outlines of the logical-functional relationships that enable integrated economic-environmental assessments; it serves as the backbone structure for the Operational Framework described in Fig. 3 for the economic assessment of urban transformation initiatives. It is intended to direct intervention planners to adopt solutions chosen from an integrated and sustainable economic-environmental perspective and then, to direct public and private decision-makers in identifying, for example, the best intervention alternative taking into account the effects generated in terms of ecosystem services on the territory, according to the sustainability objective to be achieved-re and the interests of the stakeholders involved in the specific urban area transformation initiative.

The creative process of defining the solutions to be adopted in a settlement transformation intervention can be structured in three stages that lead to the evaluation of the economic and environmental effects generated by the adopted design solutions and then in the case of several alternative solutions to the possibility of choosing the one that meets the best level of sustainability. They are:

- Step 1 (Context analysis and definition of the objectives of the intervention): study of the current state of the urban context, including bioclimatic, infrastructural, urban planning, economic and social aspects, among others. This is done to gather information on the situation of the area prior to the intervention (ex-ante), including in terms of ecosystem services, and identify advantages, disadvantages, opportunities and potential hazards associated with the type of intervention to be designed/implemented, and finally to define the specific objectives to be achieved as well as identify potential strategies to be adopted to achieve the ecological objectives related to the bioclimatic, environmental, human settlement, infrastructural and socioeconomic characteristics present in the urban context of reference;
- Step 2 (meta-planning): in this phase, taking into account what emerged in the previous phase, the actions and solutions to be adopted (masterplan) in the intervention in order to reduce and/or contain impacts on the environment, ecosystems, and at the social-economic level and ensure the production of eco-system services must be defined and systematized with respect to the general and specific objectives.
- Step 3 (impact assessment): quantification, measurement, and evaluation of the financial costs and revenues of the intervention, as well as the economic benefits; evaluation of the effects produced by the intervention in terms of the provision of ecosystem services; use of economic models to support the decision-making systems of public and private entities when assessing the cost-effectiveness of the process.

In Step 1, information is gathered on the set of economic, social, and environmental factors of the intervention context. In particular, those key factors that in terms of their effects can be "improved" or worsened" with the urban transformation project should be identified, assessed, and emphasized, and thus those on which action can be taken for the provision of ecosystem services to the community and for the maintenance or improvement of the existing natural capital. Among the key factors, land-use and land-cover patterns, socio-demographic characteristics of the population, physical-natural implications of ecosystems, and the situation of the surrounding environment can have a strong impact on the supply of regulating, supporting, providing, and cultural services. In order to assess project success after project implementation (ex-post), the ecosystem services survey and quantification of the natural capital present prior to the implementation of the intervention is an indispensable reference. The use of tools often employed in biophysical and environmental studies of ecosystems, such as the i-Tree program (in particular, in Fig. 3 describing the proposed Operational Framework, the i-Tree Canopy Tool is indicated) can allow to quantify ex ante the ecosystem services and natural capital in the intervention area and then (Step 3) to foreshadow the change in their consistence and quality in relation to the design choices adopted (ex-post) by simulating in the application of the tool the configuration adopted. According to the logic of SWOT analysis, the results of the context analysis and those derived from the use of tools designed to quantify in the pre-intervention state of affairs the ecosystem services (e.g., i-Tree Canopy) can be used as components in the development and creation of an intervention context assessment matrix. In fact, the application of the SWOT matrix is aimed, in the proposed Operational framework, at expressing and synthesizing information about the current situation of the area in terms of the advantages, disadvantages, opportunities, and potential hazards associated with the type of intervention to be carried out, and at identifying the type of ecosystem services that predominantly characterize or may characterize the intervention area.

Through the identification of the type of ecosystem services to be considered in order to enhance the context and the intervention area and to maintain or improve of the existing natural capital, it is possible to define the specific programmatic objectives to be pursued in the drafting of the intervention master plan (Step 2). Already, the aims and methods of implementation of the first phase alone provide evidence of the usefulness of the proposed 'integrated evaluation approach (Fig. 2) from the earliest stages of intervention definition and elaboration.

In Step 3, in addition to the usual assessments of financial and economic feasibility and sustainability based on estimates of costs, revenues, and benefits, the ecosystem services of interest are recalculated, as already highlighted, to determinate the possible influence and effects that the intervention, as foreshadowed in the master plan, may have on the supply of ecosystem services, either directly or indirectly through the preservation, modification, or addition of new components to the existing natural capital. The value of ecosystem services that change as a result of project implementation is also quantified in monetary terms at this stage using an appropriate multicriteria valuation technique. Figure 3, which illustrates the proposed Operational Framework, shows the use of a particular tool, such as the Natura-Capital Planning tool. Developed by the Consultancy for Environmental Economics & Policy in March 2018, this tool is based on the calculation of the environmental net benefit relative to the inhibitory transformation intervention. The environmental net-gain illustrates the potential of the impact a single project may have on the existing natural resources and vegetation, as well as the ability to provide ecosystem services. It allows the scoring of the effect of the intervention for each ecosystem service to be represented, starting precisely from the implementation of the data of the initial set-up and then those following the intervention. Changes in the value of ecosystem services are particularly significant because they describe the impact produced by the way the spatial economic asset was changed. The implementation of this procedure on alternative intervention solutions (master plans) makes it possible to

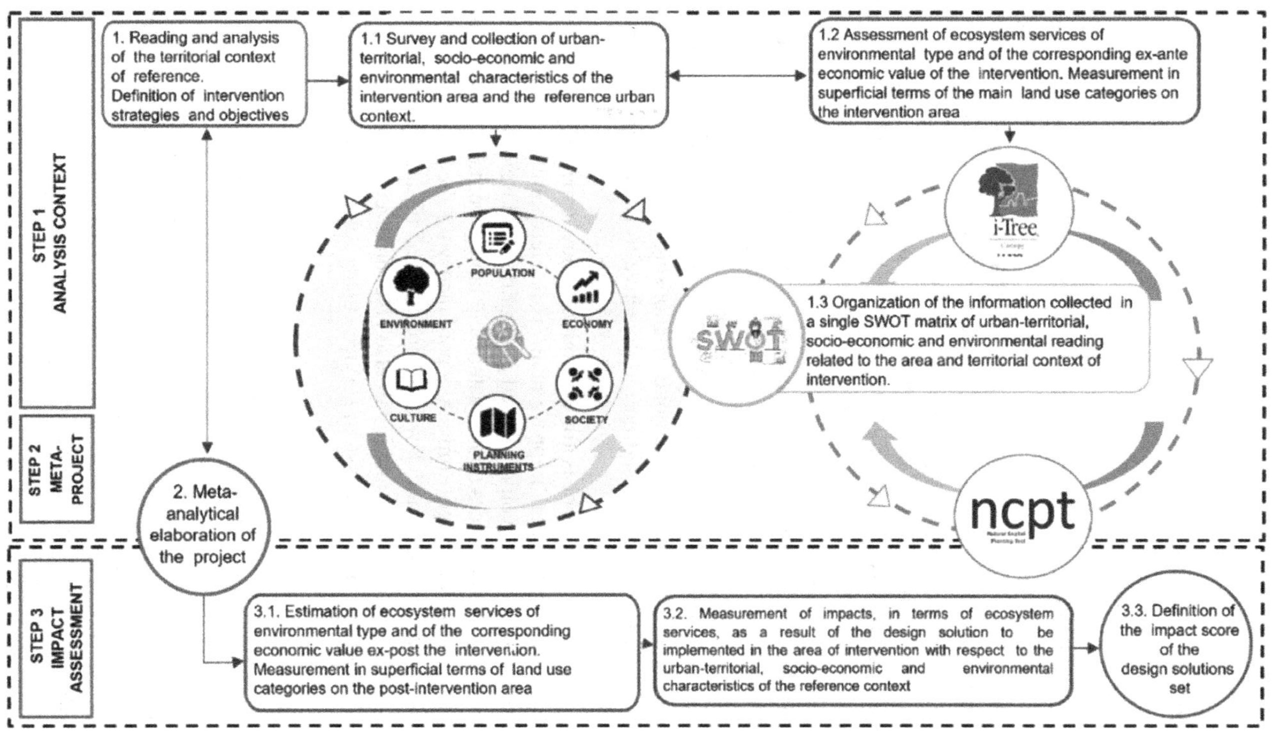

Fig. 3. Operative framework for economic-environmental assessment of urban projects.

choose, among the different prefigured intervention solutions, the one that in the complex produces the least impacts on human and natural environmental, economic and social ecosystems.

5 Conclusions

Multicriteria supporting tools are necessary in order to include the biophysical and financial advantages of ecosystem services into the decision-making processes. They want to instill a range of values—including social, environmental, and economic ones—in nature so that both public and private subjects can orient their choices upon a variety of considerations. The benefits of using tools with many criteria may first be observed in the transformational city development processes where the built and natural environments interact in order to meet the sustainable goals set at an international level.

To activate sustainable policies and decision-making processes, it is crucial to use appropriate assessment models to take into account the variety of effects produced by this type of intervention, including with respect to the morphological characteristics of the reference context. This is because the SEEA-CF shows how the environmental asset interacts with the value system of the urban context. In order to create settlement transformation processes from the standpoint of sustainable urban development, the study suggests an assessment procedure that is inspired by SEEA-CF. The option to create several assessment models is provided by the use of evaluation procedures based on multi-criteria analysis. This may also be done by choosing the proper condition and performance indicators, which vary based on the objective to be met and the kind of ecosystem service to be quantified.

It is clear how important this tool is for economic policy, especially with a view to urban renewal and environmental improvement. This viewpoint assumes that the suggested assessment framework would be used as a guide for developing operational models to assist public-private choices about sustainable land governance. Such models will be built using optimization algorithms in accordance with the syntactic patterns of the operational research. Each model will be constructed in accordance with the assessment issue under consideration, and it will also take into account the biophysical-economic measurement of certain ecosystem services using relevant software suitable to the problem at hand.

References

1. Mader, A.: Biodiversity, climate change and sustainable human settlements. In: Laros, M.T., Jones, F.E. (eds.) ICLEI – Local Governments for Sustainability. Local Action for Biodiversity Guidebook: Biodiversity Management for Local Governments (2010)
2. Von Haaren, C., Galler, C., Ott, S.: Landscape planning. The basis of sustainable landscape development. Bundesamt für naturschutz/Federal Agency for Nature Conservation, Gebr. Klingenberg Buchkunst Leipzig GmbH, vol. 51 (2008)
3. Assessment, M.E.: Ecosystems and Human Well-Being: Wetlands and Water. World Resources Institute (2005)
4. Un, I.R.B.: Convention on Biological Diversity. Treaty Collection (1992)

5. Werner, P., Zahner, R.: Biodiversity and cities. A review and bibliography. BfN-Skripten, Bonn, 245 (2009)
6. TEEB – The Economics of Ecosystems and Biodiversity. Mainstreaming the Economics of Nature: a Synthesis of the Approach, Conclusions and Recommendations of TEEB (2010)
7. Forman, R.T.T.: Urban Regions: Ecology and Planning Beyond the City. Cambridge University Press (2008)
8. Heynen, N., Kaika, M., Swyngedouw (eds.) In the Nature of Cities: Urban Political Ecology and the Politics of Urban Metabolism. London. Routledge, New York (2006)
9. Agger, A.: Towards tailor-made participation: how to involve different types of citizens in participatory governance. The Town Plann. Rev. **83**(1), 29–45 (2012)
10. Grima, N., Corcoran, W., Hill-James, C., Langton, B., Sommer, H., Fisher, B.: The importance of urban natural areas and urban ecosystem services during the COVID-19 pandemic. PLOS ONE **15**(12), e0243344 (2020)
11. European Commission: Territorial Agenda 2030. A future for all places (2020)
12. Venter, Z.S., Barton, D.N., Gundersen, V., Figari, H., Nowell, M.: Urban nature in a time of crisis: recreational use of green space increases during the COVID-19 outbreak in Oslo. Norway. Environ. Res. Lett. **15**(10), 104075 (2020)
13. European Commission: EU Biodiversity Strategy for 2030 Bringing nature back into our lives. https://eur-lex.europa.eu/legal-content/EN/TXT/?qid=1590574123338&uri=CELEX:52020DC0380. Last accessed: 26 Nov 2021
14. Klapper, L., El-Zoghbi, M., Hess, J.: Achieving the sustainable development goals. The role of financial inclusion (2016)
15. Pettifor, A.: The Case for the Green New Deal. Verso Books, London (2020)
16. Faludi, A.: Cohesion, coherence, cooperation: European spatial planning coming of age? Routledge (2010)
17. Spampinato, G., Malerba, A., Calabrò, F., Bernardo, C., Musarella, C.: Cork oak forest spatial valuation toward post carbon city by co2 Sequestration. In: Bevilacqua, C., Calabrò, F., Della Spina, L. (eds.) NMP 2020. SIST, vol. 178, pp. 1321–1331. Springer, Cham (2021). https://doi.org/10.1007/978-3-030-48279-4_123
18. Santos-Martin, F., et al.: Creating an operational database for ecosystems services mapping and assessment methods. One Ecosyst. **3**, e26719 (2018)
19. Sheppard, S.R., Meitner, M.: Using multi-criteria analysis and visualisation for sustainable forest management planning with stakeholder groups. For. Ecol. Manage. **207**(1–2), 171–187 (2005)
20. United Nations: System of Environmental Economic Accounting 2012—Central Framework (2012)
21. Diaz-Balteiro, L., Romero, C.: Making forestry decisions with multiple criteria: a review and an assessment. For. Ecol. Manage. **255**(8–9), 3222–3241 (2008)
22. Sica, F., Nesticò, A.: The benefit transfer method for the economic evaluation of urban forests. In: Gervasi, O., et al. (eds.) ICCSA 2021. LNCS, vol. 12954, pp. 39–49. Springer, Cham (2021). https://doi.org/10.1007/978-3-030-86979-3_3
23. Guarini, M.R., Morano, P., Sica, F.: Eco-system services and integrated urban planning. A multi-criteria assessment framework for ecosystem urban forestry projects. In: Mondini, G., Oppio, A., Stanghellini, S., Bottero, M., Abastante, F. (eds.) Values and Functions for Future Cities. GET, pp. 201–216. Springer, Cham (2020). https://doi.org/10.1007/978-3-030-23786-8_11
24. Mondini, G.: Valutazioni di sostenibilità: dal rapporto Brundtland ai Sustainable Development Goal, vol. 23. Valori e Valutazioni (2019)
25. Guarini, M.R., Morano, P., Sica, F.: Integrated ecosystem design: an evaluation model to support the choice of eco-compatible technological solutions for residential building. Energies **12**(14), 2659 (2019). https://doi.org/10.3390/en12142659

26. Morano, P., Tajani, F., Guarini, M.R., Sica, F.: A systematic review of the existing literature for the evaluation of sustainable urban projects. Sustainability **13**(9), 4782 (2021)
27. Vercellis, C.: Ottimizzazione. Teoria, metodi, applicazioni, pp. i-470. McGraw-Hill (2008)
28. Guarini, M.R., Chiovitti, A., Battisti, F., Morano, P.: An integrated approach for the assessment of urban transformation proposals in historic and consolidated tissues. In: Gervasi, O., et al. (eds.) ICCSA 2017. LNCS, vol. 10406, pp. 562–574. Springer, Cham (2017). https://doi.org/10.1007/978-3-319-62398-6_40
29. Tajani, F., Di Liddo, F., Guarini, M.R., Ranieri, R., Anelli, D.: An assessment methodology for the evaluation of the impacts of the COVID-19 pandemic on the Italian housing market demand. Buildings **11**(592), 1–28 (2021)

Ethical AI Applications for a Human-Centered Cyber Society (EthicAI 2023)

Ethical Artificial Intelligence in Telerehabilitation of Neurodevelopmental Disorders: A Position Paper

Aurora Castellani[1](✉), Mariagrazia Benassi[2], and Giulia Balboni[1]

[1] University of Perugia, 06123 Perugia, PG, Italy
Aurora.castellani@studenti.unipg.it, Giulia.balboni@unipg.it
[2] University of Bologna, 40127 Bologna, BO, Italy
Mariagrazia.benassi@unibo.it

Abstract. Neurodevelopmental disorders are a cluster of mental disorders with neurobiological origins that occur during the development of children and lead to cognitive deficits with possible behavioral and emotional consequences. Intensive and individualized interventions are required to take action on these deficits timely. Recently, telerehabilitation techniques for neurodevelopmental disorders have been implemented by automating the rules to set up the intervention protocol. The use of artificial intelligence algorithms primarily applies to this automation. Although these methods have several advantages, such as automatizing personalization and self-adaptation, ethical implications emerged. In detail, it remains unclear how ethical principles can be applied to these new interventions. The present paper outlines a framework of ethical recommendations for using artificial intelligence in telerehabilitation for children with neurodevelopmental disorders. For this aim, a review of the use of artificial intelligence in adults as users is presented and the European Union requirements for trustworthy artificial intelligence for children are explored. The paper proposes some practical applications of ethical principles for artificial intelligence systems in the telerehabilitation of neurodevelopmental disorders and research strategies in line with the European Union guidance. This review of the ethical implication of artificial intelligence is intended to be an opportunity to improve artificial intelligence telerehabilitation of children with neurodevelopmental disorders.

Keywords: Artificial Intelligence · Artificial Intelligence Algorithms · Telerehabilitation · Rehabilitation Care · Neurodevelopmental Disorders · Ethics · European Union guidelines · Ethical Recommendations

1 Introduction

1.1 Telerehabilitation of Neurodevelopmental Disorders

Telerehabilitation is a branch of telemedicine concerning the delivery of remote rehabilitative treatment with the individual working independently in a familiar environment and with clinician monitoring through the Internet and telecommunication technology [1].

O. Gervasi et al. (Eds.): ICCSA 2023 Workshops, LNCS 14107, pp. 87–103, 2023.
https://doi.org/10.1007/978-3-031-37114-1_7

Telerehabilitation has been applied for years to treat children with neurodevelopmental disorders (NDDSs) [2]. According to the International Classification of Diseases 11th (ICD-11) Revision, the most recent version of a system used by healthcare providers to classify and code diseases [3], neurodevelopmental disorders are classified into:

1. Disorders of intellectual development (6A00-6A0Z)
2. Developmental speech or language disorders (6A01)
3. Developmental learning disorder (6A03)
4. Developmental motor coordination disorder (6A04)
5. Autism spectrum disorder (6A02)
6. Attention deficit hyperactivity disorder (6A05)
7. Stereotyped movement disorder (6A06)

These disorders imply cognitive deficits and can also affect the behavioral, emotional, and relational development of children [4]; these characteristics require the intervention of several professionals working together to enhance impaired abilities and avoid long-term cascade effects on other abilities [5]. Rehabilitation is a complex process that may require telerehabilitation to strengthen impaired functional or instrumental skills; this often occurs within integrated intervention programs. An intervention that integrates classical treatment in the clinician's presence with remote treatment, thus rehabilitative treatment in mixed delivery, can ensure effective treatment. These interventions offer the possibility of making the rehabilitation course intensive but customizable, to achieve less repetitiveness of activities, and respect for the zone of proximal development [1]. The activities are challenging but possible for the user who performs them; the activities are at a slightly higher level of difficulty than the child's current performance. This contributes to a positive effect on both child and family motivation [6].

Various platforms for the telerehabilitation of neurodevelopmental disorders have been developed recently. These platforms allow both "skills" work (training of deficit abilities) and "processes" work (training of substrate abilities for the development of more complex skills) [7–9]. The effectiveness of telerehabilitation treatments has been demonstrated in various studies involving, for example, specific learning disorders such as dyscalculia [10], dyslexia [11], or other neurodevelopmental disorders such as attention deficit hyperactivity disorder [12] or autism spectrum disorder and intellectual disability [13]. Tele-rehabilitation can partly answer the challenges posed by the COVID-19 pandemic but also the limitations of national healthcare systems. Examples are difficulties in moving frequently from one's home to perform treatment at the clinic or such in Italy the clashing with long waiting lists and the organization of public health services [2] The child connects remotely from a computer and performs many rehabilitative activities from home with adult monitoring and the clinician visiting the child in the outpatient setting only periodically. This type of intervention reduces costs for families and increases the number of children who simultaneously receive treatment from the clinician [14].

1.2 Artificial Intelligence in Telerehabilitation of Neurodevelopmental Disorders

Technology development has added the study of new applications of computing power to the opportunities of telerehabilitation. Indeed, in the last fifty years, we have witnessed the development of Artificial Intelligence (AI) [15]. AI represents the new design of digital environments and has also begun to be integrated into the telerehabilitation of neurodevelopmental disorders in different forms. Robotics [16–19], virtual reality [20–23], and online platforms [24–26] are just some of the most popular applications of AI models in rehabilitation and learning contexts [27]. Several studies have demonstrated the effectiveness of implementing these models for the skill enhancement of children with neurodevelopmental disorders [28–30]. For example, Melis et al., (2001) [31] presented ActiveMath, a web-based intelligent tutoring system for mathematics. ActiveMath dynamically generates interactive courses based on a student's goals, preferences, skills, and knowledge. It uses various AI techniques to create self-adaptive courses, feedback, and dynamic exercises. Riedl et al. (2009) [32] designed a computer game to help adolescents with autism spectrum disorders with social skills. Teens can practice in different social scenarios with minimal monitoring by caregivers, teachers, and health professionals. Baschera & Gross (2008) [33] developed an intelligent and adaptive tutoring system that children and adolescents can use with spelling difficulties. Drigas & Ioannidou (2013) [27], in a systematic review, showed that most of the AI tools used for learning had positive results. Although these interventions have several advantages and application opportunities, fundamental ethical implications must be considered, such as those related to privacy or explainability [34]. Moreover, it is still unclear how ethical principles can be applied to these new interventions.

1.3 Ethics of Artificial Intelligence

Many definitions of AI have been proposed over the years. In 2019, the European Union defined AI as a set of software and/or hardware systems designed by humans capable of acting in both the physical and digital environment through data acquisition. They are systems with complex goals that can interpret data, make decisions, and act according to the set goal [35]. AI systems have wide applications and significant impacts in various areas of society [36].

A worldwide debate has been generated about what principles should guide AI design, use, and deployment. Organizations worldwide have worked to answer these questions [37–39] through national and international workshops attended by hundreds of AI experts. This work has led to the drafting of different policy, business, and research papers that aim to guide ethical AI [37]. A scoping review [40] of existing global ethical guidelines for AI through 2019 revealed that most documents agree on some essential principles to guide AI design and use: transparency, justice, non-maleficence, accountability, and privacy (see Table 1).

However, we believe there is a lack of a unified view of the many contributions concerning the ethics of AI and that there remain some open questions related to how ethical principles should be interpreted and implemented.

In 2020, the European Union partially answered these questions by publishing a tool for evaluating the trustworthiness of AI: The Assessment List for Trustworthy Artificial Intelligence (ALTAI) [41]. This is the first tool for the AI assessment according to the European Union's Ethical Guidelines for Trustworthy AI [42]. The ALTAI is a flexible tool that is primarily intended for organizations that want to evaluate the trustworthiness of their AI systems. It seeks to help them understand the meaning of trustworthy AI and

Table 1. Ethical principles for AI shared by worldwide guidelines.

PRINCIPLES	DEFINITION
Transparency	Concerns the concepts of explainability, interpretability, communication processes, and information diffusion. This principle covers the use of data and its objectives, human-system interaction, and automated decisions
Justice	It includes the concepts of fairness and avoidance, monitoring and minimization of bias and discrimination (such as respect for diversity, inclusion, and equality), the ability to challenge decisions, the right to redress and remedy, equitable access to data, and the benefits of AI
Non-Maleficence	Includes the concepts of safety and avoidance of foreseeable or unintended harm such as discrimination, invasion of privacy, or physical harm
Accountability	Includes the concepts of acting with "integrity," defining the allocation of responsibility in advance, paying attention to processes that could lead to harm, promoting diversity, and introducing ethics into scientific research
Privacy	Includes the concepts of protection, data security, trust, and freedom

know the risks and strategies to reduce them while simultaneously trying to enhance AI's benefits. The basic idea is to make people understand that AI affects society but also different actors, including citizens (with special attention to children and minority people). The tool envisions a systems assessment through a multidisciplinary team that also includes experts in the different application areas of AI, e.g., researchers, designers, staff who will use or work with the AI system, ethicists, and legal officers. The tool includes self-assessment questions in agreement with the seven requirements of the European Union for trustworthy AI:

1. Human Agency and Oversight
2. Technical Robustness and Safety
3. Privacy and Data Governance
4. Transparency
5. Diversity, Non-discrimination, and Fairness
6. Societal and Environmental Well-being
7. Accountability

1.4 Ethical Artificial Intelligence for Children

There is an increase in the breadth of ethical discourse related to AI applications with adults as users. However, the increased presence of intelligent systems in children's everyday lives poses fundamental ethical questions for researchers, healthcare professionals, and stakeholders [43].

In recent years, some organizations (e.g., UNICEF, UNESCO) have published documents that have addressed the issue of trustworthy AI for children as primary users [44–46]. These papers have sought to understand whether the ethical principles guiding

AI are also valid when children are involved with the aim to help develop reliable AI for children and youth and to help them and their caregivers use it safely.

AI can also impact children, so there is a need to address the ethical issues affecting them in this area. Often in technology development, children do not have the opportunity to communicate their ideas, needs, or worries, and there is a lack of figures to encourage them in this communication. Very often, children do not have all information to understand how their data are used or if they are discriminated against by a system [47]. In 2022, the European Union tried to address these needs by publishing "Artificial Intelligence and the Right of Children" [48]. This document identified some key requirements, application strategies, and research gaps that still need to be addressed to protect children when interacting with AI systems. Some key points of the paper are summarized in Table 2.

Table 2. Requirements and strategies of the European Union for trustworthy AI for children.

Artificial Intelligence and the Right of Children	
REQUIREMENTS	*AI minimization methods.* It is important to consider AI technology as a limited resource
	Transparency, explainability, communication, and accountability. Minor users must be informed and made accountable for using AI systems
	Inclusion and non-discrimination. AI must be suitable for children. Prejudice and discrimination must be avoided
	Privacy, data protection, and security. Children and their caregivers must have decision-making power over what data AI systems use, and how it is used and shared
	Respect for children's agency. Children must be aware of their interaction with AI systems. Research must respect and foster the construct of children's agency
METHODOLOGY	*Prediction, evaluation, and monitoring.* Evaluation tools and guidelines must be designed for AI stems that have children as users
	Multi-stakeholder collaboration. Multidisciplinary professional teams and users can be a resource in the design and use of AI
	Children's participation. At all stages of the process leading to the production of an AI system for children, the users' cognitive, social, and emotional developmental stages must be taken into account, not just their age
	Balancing conflicting rights. In the case of conflicting rights, there must be regulations that establish the trade-off between them

Certainly, the ethical issues raised for child users, including concerns about privacy, transparency, agency, and inclusion, also apply in the case of neurodevelopmental disorders. However, using these systems by children with neurodevelopmental disorders, most of whom use them remotely, raises the need for in-depth reflections [43].

This paper aims to conduct a comprehensive and updated review of the application of AI in telerehabilitation for children with neurodevelopmental disorders. In detail, we aim to reflect on the current literature to understand whether the guidelines for trustworthy AI for children can be applied to the characteristics of telerehabilitation for children with neurodevelopmental disorders. Further proposed is developing a possible research framework to fill some of the gaps in the ethics of AI in these telerehabilitation interventions. The first part of this paper is a general introduction to applications of AI models to the telerehabilitation of neurodevelopmental disorders. Next, a literature review is presented on the ethical principles that should guide the design and use of AI with both adults and children as users. The second part discusses EU requirements for trustworthy AI to make these requirements applicable to the telerehabilitation of children with neurodevelopmental disorders. Finally, the last part presents a proposal for a research framework.

2 EU Requirements in the Telerehabilitation of Neurodevelopmental Disorders: Some Proposals

This section of the paper will discuss the EU requirements for trustworthy AI with children as users in depth. The goal is to develop some solutions to apply these principles when AI systems are applied to the telerehabilitation of neurodevelopmental disorders.

To develop trustworthy telerehabilitation AI tools for children with neurodevelopmental disorders, the paper aims to emphasize two central elements. The first element refers to the importance of considering the needs and characteristics of these children in the processes of AI design and use. To this end, the paper proposes: solutions that can promote awareness and information about the use of AI for these children; strategies to support children's self-actualization and give them a role in design; and inclusion of caregivers. The second element refers to the importance of considering AI as an opportunity to implement the effectiveness of treatments and personalization; however, it is important to use AI with the understanding that it is a resource that may be subject to errors and limitations and cannot completely replace the therapeutic relationship with the clinician, whose presence remains central to the treatment process.

The aim will not be to discuss aspects concerning general and sectoral policies but to propose application possibilities to which research can contribute. For this reason, this paper also does not address all EU requirements for trustworthy AI for children. The requirements that have been addressed are those most related to the role of researchers, designers, and experts in the rehabilitation of neurodevelopmental disorders. This choice is also motivated by the professional background of the authors.

2.1 AI Minimization

AI minimization refers to understanding that intelligent systems are not unlimited resources and may have a potential impact on sustainable development. AI should be used only for tasks that can have a real positive impact [49].

In the telerehabilitation of neurodevelopmental disorders, AI minimization can be translated into the possibility of an integrated type of treatment with AI used in conjunction with the clinician's presence meetings. Why, however, is AI necessary in this rehabilitation context? Because it can lead to benefits in different situations. As described previously, it could be a system to be used when treatment in the clinician's presence is limited due to accessibility problems for the user (transportation, family's work problems, covid-19 pandemic, and residence in rural areas) or in case of financial difficulties [50]. The 2012 National Guidelines for Telemedicine of the Italian Ministry of Health specify that telemedicine can be compared to other types of therapeutic intervention but that it does not replace the therapeutic clinician-patient relationship. Telemedicine can be a way to complement classical treatments, and it can improve the effectiveness of rehabilitation [51]. In this sense, AI is no exception. Families, users, and clinicians could be oriented to the application of these systems in a combined way. A substantial part of the treatment is carried out in the child's living places through a computer, supervised by a caregiver. The clinician then establishes periodic meetings to monitor and evaluate the progress of the rehabilitation training. Also, the caregiver may initiate the rehabilitation session with the patient having audio and video contact with the clinician remotely, who tracks what is happening through the data received from the system. In this way, the clinician can respond to concerns, monitor the progress of the rehabilitation training, evaluate the situation overall, and make decisions about it.

Minimization of AI can also mean, for example, that the systems aimed to promote skill generalization, autonomy, or self-regulation are used in the early stages of treatment. When the child has reached a good level of competence, gradually, the use of the system can be reduced until treatment is stopped [48].

2.2 Transparency, Explainability, and Communication

The principles of transparency, explainability, and communication refer to the need to make children knowledgeable and informed users when they use an AI system [45, 48, 52]. Critical thinking is a central element for children to have the right confidence in AI regarding risks and benefits. However, what are the most appropriate ways to explain an AI system to children with neurodevelopmental disorders? An analysis is needed that focuses on the developmental stages and types of difficulties of these children.

A pre-treatment phase could be developed to allow children to familiarize themselves with the system, with the activities proposed by the system, and ask questions about the technology as they experience it. The clinician can then provide the information appropriately to the child's level of understanding and/or intellectual functioning but needs specific training about the technology. For example, children with autism spectrum disorder can have deficits in language pragmatics. Social pragmatics is the ability to effectively use and regulate communication for several purposes, with different interlocutors, and in various circumstances [53]. For children, this involves difficulties, such as paying attention to an auditory message when they are stressed, a tendency to ask repetitive questions, or difficulties listening while doing something else simultaneously [54]. In this case, to effectively explain AI the telerehabilitation system could include some features such as a pre-treatment phase with an introduction with social stories (short stories with pictures) or comic conversations. These are widely used tools for behavioral interventions [55, 56]. In addition, the use of visual aids can provide cues or sequential steps for potential situations that may be difficult to understand.

Lemaignan et al. (2021) [57] adopted such an approach for a social robot used to support children with autism spectrum disorders in schools. The data obtained from children's questions could provide a unique perspective to guide the application of the principles of transparency, explicability, and communication in the case of AI systems for children with autism spectrum disorders.

The principles of transparency, explainability, and communication may also concern the reliability of the information provided by the AI system. For example, the system could provide intelligent warnings about the child's lack of attention during treatment or a system malfunction [46, 48]. These warnings can appear on the child's computer screen and be seen by the caregiver monitoring the treatment but also be sent to the clinician as well. The system thus provides smart warnings if the treatment does not occur as expected. However, the system must also provide information regarding the reliability of the warning. It is possible, for example, that an interruption in activity has occurred due to an external event that the system cannot detect. Therefore the possibility of an error in detection must be recognized. In this case, both the clinician and the caregiver have the choice of whether or not to accept the alert. Information on warnings' reliability is essential to allow individuals to be truly involved in the human-IA interaction [46].

Also, the involvement of caregivers is important in applying the principles of transparency, explainability, and communication. Caregivers could be trained on the AI system their child will use to avoid any negative effects on the treatment [58]. It would be useful, for example, a demo version for caregivers that could address potential questions, doubts, or curiosities raised by users during the beta test. Alternatively, a pre-treatment phase could also be provided for caregivers to allow the clinicians to answer doubts or questions or for data collection that could help to design the informative demo version.

2.3 Inclusion and Non-Discrimination

Two additional requirements for trustworthy AI for children are inclusion and non-discrimination. Various papers addressed bias and prejudices in AI systems from different points of view: gender, ethnicity, disability, and age [59–61]. Some of these documents also referred to children as victims of possible discrimination [62–64].

A possible approach in the field of neurodevelopmental disorders may be knowledge sharing. Designing systems for rehabilitating users of different ages, evolutionary needs, and stages of development also requires including the children themself. A design that includes children, caregivers, healthcare professionals, researchers, and stakeholders can help reduce the risk of discrimination and prejudice while respecting children's preferences, demands, and rehabilitation needs.

Very often, children are given little space in the design of technology [65]. For example, children with neurodevelopmental disorders may be characterized by disorders in the expressive, receptive, or pragmatic language modality or involving multiple processes [66] that can significantly restrict their access to technology. It is possible to foresee modes of activity administration and response by children that they may understand, such as the use of Alternative Augmented Communication, the use of buttons, or visual agendas integrated into the system [57, 67].

Child-centered methodologies should include children. However, critical reflections are needed to understand how children with neurodevelopmental disorders can be included and heard in designing and implementing these AI systems [68, 69]. A possible solution could be to propose research designs that try to include and evaluate different co-design modes to find the ideal solution.

2.4 Agency

The concept of agency concerns the right of children to self-realize. Children must be free to have control, make decisions, influence their environment and events, have their own goals, and conduct themselves to achieve them [70]. As argued by Bandura, the agency is about beliefs of self-efficacy [71]. Children and young people must be helped to understand the importance of having freedom in making decisions and achieving their goals. Perceiving themself unable to engage in behaviors to achieve their goals or that their behaviors have no effects may impact the children's self-efficacy and self-esteem [43].

Spiel et al. (2019) [72] showed that children with autism spectrum disorders rarely have freedom of choice when interacting with computers. In most cases, technologies address the needs of people who care for children with autism spectrum disorders but not directly the needs of children affecting the children's sense of self-determination.

A possible solution could be to allow children to establish their treatment objectives in agreement with the clinician. The child can thus experience being the master of his own decisions and personal goals, also affecting their treatment motivation. However, the proposed solution is less related to AI and more to the approach taken by the physician.

2.5 Privacy and Data Protection

Personal data and other sensitive data can be used to train AI models. Thanks to these data, the system can make decisions, predictions or propose activities. Data protection becomes a central issue, especially for children with disabilities performing remote treatment with online access [73].

The General Data Protection Regulation (GDPR) makes it clear that in the European Union, children must have special protection for children because they may be less aware of the risks and consequences of sharing data. Parental consent is thus needed, and agencies have to make a reasonable effort to check that such consent is truly given in line with the law [74]. The need for technology to minimize the sharing of sensitive data and to protect the privacy of families and users will not be discussed here. The aim is instead to make privacy statements understandable to children with neurodevelopmental disorders. It is important to ensure the protection of children and freedom in the choice of what they want to share and to guarantee the possibility of withdrawing consent to provide and share their data at any time.

For this purpose, informed consent may be provided that is suitable for them and that they can understand although it would not be required by law. Informed consent can be a tool to make children aware and leave them free to choose concerning information about them. For example, Strickler & Havercamp (2023) [75] designed an informed consent process to help adults with intellectual disabilities understand critical aspects of research. In this process, the different dimensions of informed consent were explained to participants through multiple and dynamic approaches. The process was repeated until participants understood all the content, gradually reducing the information provided. Similar approaches can help children with neurodevelopmental disorders understand the necessary information about using their data.

3 Proposed Search Framework

AI systems applied to the telerehabilitation of neurodevelopmental disorders could have numerous advantages: reducing treatment costs for families, the possibility of intensive and personalized rehabilitation, and a more significant number of children who benefit from rehabilitation treatments. Nevertheless, it is necessary to consider the ethical implications.

Current literature provides numerous ethical guidelines for AI. Still, these have only recently begun focusing on children's rights and so far they do not concern the ethics of AI applied to telerehabilitation for children with neurodevelopmental disorders. It is, therefore, necessary to expand the research in this field to develop trustworthy AI for children with neurodevelopmental disorders as well. For this aim, we have planned a proposal for a search framework shown in Fig. 1.

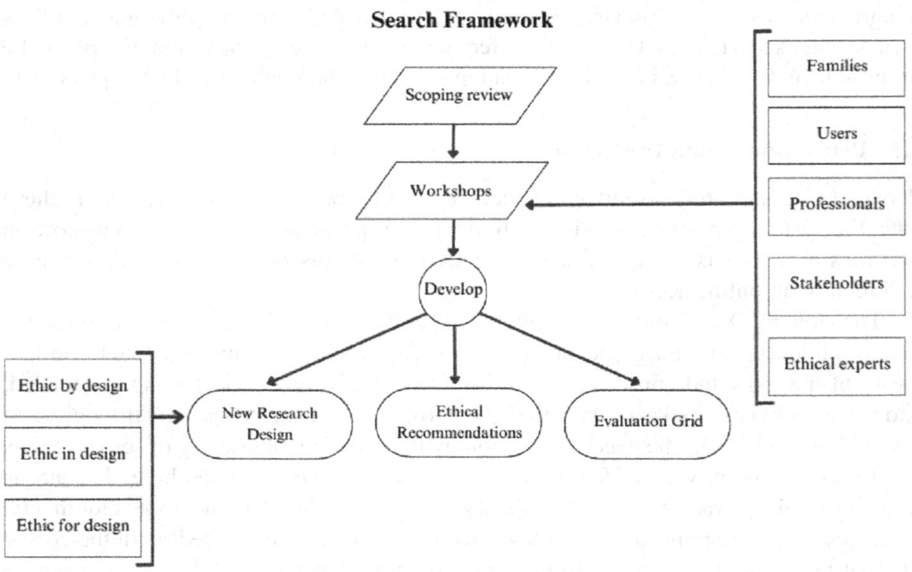

Fig. 1. Flowchart of the search framework proposed for trustworthy AI in telerehabilitation of neurodevelopmental disorders.

First, we propose a scoping review of the literature on ethical guidelines for AI with children as the primary users. It will outline a comprehensive framework for understanding what ethical principles should be applied when children come into contact with AI systems. In agreement with the protocol used by Jobin et al. (2019) [40] inspired by the PRISMA protocol [76], multiple screening strategies will be applied, including searching with both classic databases search engines and some lists of ethics guidelines [77, 78].

Different published guidelines on trustworthy AI for children have shown that the developers of AI as well as the children must be included in the development of the AI systems to provide a complete picture of different points of view [46–48]. Therefore workshops will be conducted with experts in rehabilitation and telerehabilitation for neurodevelopmental disorders who are familiar with or use intelligent systems. These experts might be: health professionals, i.e., educators, neuropsychiatrists, psychiatrists, psychologists, speech and language therapists, occupational and neuro-psych motility therapists; stakeholders, i.e., professionals in the field of intelligent systems applied to the rehabilitation of children with disabilities as designers, professionals working as Data Privacy Officers or research and ethics officers in companies developing intelligent systems for rehabilitation; experts in AI ethics, i.e., are those who have published articles or books on the ethics of AI in rehabilitation and telerehabilitation (scientific, legal, deontological, and ethical aspects); parents, and minor users with neurodevelopmental disorders who already benefit from AI telerehabilitation (see Fig. 1). In agreement with the literature [79], the workshops will cover the participants' knowledge, personal opinions, and ideas concerning:

1. The link between professional/personal background and telerehabilitation with intelligent systems
2. Perception about telerehabilitation with AI, both from a personal perspective and the perspective of the specific profession/category of membership
3. Structural issues of AI telerehabilitation that have ethical implications and how can be overcome
4. Ethical principles that are involved in the development and implementation of an AI telerehabilitation program, both for the patient and the clinician
5. Strategies that need to be implemented to achieve improved ethics in AI telerehabilitation

The data derived from these workshops can be processed and analyzed by qualitative content analysis [80]. The workshop results and the scoping review will have three goals:

1. Producing ethical recommendations to guide the research, design, and use of intelligent systems for the telerehabilitation of neurodevelopmental disorders.
2. Creating an ethical criteria evaluation grid to be used as a guide to assess whether a telerehabilitation intervention aligns with the guidance provided by all participants involved in the process.
3. Developing a research design for AI applied to the telerehabilitation of neurodevelopmental disorders.

The research design will integrate the review and the results of the workshops with the three ethical levels that should structure AI design (see Fig. 1) [81]:

1. Ethics by design. AI is capable of ethical reasoning
2. Ethics in design. Design methods include an assessment of the ethical implications of AI systems

3. Ethics for design. There are standards of conduct that ensure the integrity of developers and users in all stages of system development

The research design has to be adapted to the characteristics of children with neurodevelopmental disorders and the telerehabilitation context.

Having recommendations that are based on the literature investigation but also on giving voice to key actors (families, caregivers, stakeholders, and children) could also have an impact on the effectiveness of treatments. Adherence to the proposed criteria could act on dimensions such as children's agency, family information, and motivation. This would mean revaluing ethics in terms of protecting professionals and children and as a central aspect of the care and effectiveness dimension of rehabilitation.

4 Conclusion

This article described current literature about telerehabilitation with intelligent systems and the ethics to propose how to implement ethical principles for a trustworthy AI for the telerehabilitation of children with neurodevelopment disorders. We have developed a proposal for a future research framework that, through a systematic review of the literature and workshops with stakeholders, could lead to ethical recommendations for AI applied to the telerehabilitation of neurodevelopment disorders; an evaluation grid of ethical criteria to be used as a guide to assess the adherence of these types of treatments with the recommendations provided; and the development of a research design for AI applied to the telerehabilitation of neurodevelopment disorders.

This ambitious proposal must clash with the feasibility and timelines of research and the realities of companies, clinicians, and families. Multi-parties collaboration presents significant challenges. For example, the parties involved may have different goals, ideas, and strategies; these can sometimes conflict. The EU paper highlighted how even in various situations, principles that want to protect children's rights might conflict with each other such as protecting privacy with the need for data to train algorithms. Complex and joint work between multiple parties will be needed to develop concrete solutions respectful of children with special needs.

References

1. Casalini, C., Mazzotti, S.: Problems and prospects of telemedicine in neurodevelopmental disorders. Psicologia Clinica Dello Sviluppo **25**(3), 389–416 (2021). https://doi.org/10.1449/100597
2. Bachmann, C., Gagliardi, C., Marotta, M.: Teleriabilitazione nei disturbi di apprendimento. Principi e evidenze di efficacia per presa in carico a distanza. Edizioni Centro Studi Erickson spa, Trento (2020)
3. Stein, D.J., et al.: Mental, behavioral and neurodevelopmental disorders in the ICD-11: an international perspective on key changes and controversies. BMC Med. **18**, 21 (2020). https://doi.org/10.1186/s12916-020-1495-2
4. American Psychiatric Association: Neurodevelopmental disorders: DSM-5® selections. American Psychiatric Publishing, USA (2015)

5. Chacko, A., Uderman, J., Feirsen, N., Bedard, A.-C., Marks, D.: Learning and cognitive disorders: multidiscipline treatment approaches. Child Adolesc. Psychiatr. Clin. **22**, 457–477 (2013). https://doi.org/10.1016/j.chc.2013.03.006
6. Báez-Suárez, A., Padrón-Rodriguez, I., Santana-Cardeñosa, D., Santana-Perez, L., Lopez-Herrera, V.M., Pestana-Miranda, R.: Implementation of a telerehabilitation program for children with neurodevelopmental disorders during the lockdown caused by COVID-19. Br. J. Occup. Ther. **86**(4), 284–292 (2022). https://doi.org/10.1177/03080226221141322
7. Lorusso, M.L., Borasio, F., Molteni, M.: Remote neuropsychological intervention for developmental dyslexia with the Tachidino platform: no reduction in effectiveness for older nor for more severely impaired children. Children **9**(1), 71 (2022). https://doi.org/10.3390/children9010071
8. Tucci, R., Savoia, V., Bertolo, L., Vio, C., Tressoldi, P.: Efficacy and efficiency outcomes of a training to ameliorate developmental dyslexia using the online software Reading Trainer. Bollettino Di Psicologia Applicata **64**(273), 53–60 (2015)
9. Simons, D.J., et al.: Do "brain-training" programs work? Psychol. Sci. Public Interest **17**(3), 103–186 (2016). https://doi.org/10.1177/1529100616661983
10. Drigas, A., Pappas, M., Lytras, M.: Emerging technologies for ICT-based education for dyscalculia: Implications for computer engineering education. Int. J. Eng. Educ. **32**, 1604–1610 (2016)
11. Pecini, C., et al.: Training RAN or reading? A telerehabilitation study on developmental dyslexia. Dyslexia **10769242**(25), 318–331 (2019). https://doi.org/10.1002/dys.1619
12. Aksayli, N.D., Sala, G., Gobet, F.: The cognitive and academic benefits of Cogmed: a meta-analysis. Educ. Res. Rev. **29**, 229–243 (2019). https://doi.org/10.1016/j.edurev.2019.04.003
13. Benyakorn, S., et al.: Computerized cognitive training in children with autism and intellectual disabilities: feasibility and satisfaction study. JMIR Ment Health **5**(2), e40 (2018). https://doi.org/10.2196/mental.9564
14. Falcone, R., Capirci, O., Lucidi, F., Zoccolotti, P.: Prospettive di intelligenza artificiale: mente, lavoro e società nel mondo del machine learning. G. Ital. Psicol. **45**(1), 43–68 (2018). https://doi.org/10.1421/90306
15. Wilks, Y.A.: Artificial Intelligence: Modern Magic or Dangerous Future? The Illustrated Edition. MIT Press (2023)
16. Nasri, N., et al.: Assistive robot with an AI-based application for the reinforcement of activities of daily living: technical validation with users affected by neurodevelopmental disorders. Appl. Sci. **12**(19), 9566 (2022). https://doi.org/10.3390/app12199566
17. Wood, L.J., Zaraki, A., Robins, B., Dautenhahn, K.: Developing Kaspar: a humanoid robot for children with autism. Int. J. Soc. Robot. **13**(3), 491–508 (2019). https://doi.org/10.1007/s12369-019-00563-6
18. Berrezueta-Guzman, J., Pau, I., Martin-Ruiz, M.-L., Maximo-Bocanegra, N.: Assessment of a robotic assistant for supporting homework activities of children with ADHD. IEEE Access **9**, 93450–93465 (2021). https://doi.org/10.1109/ACCESS.2021.3093233
19. Mcvey, S.M., Chew, E., Caroll, F.: The review of dyslexic humanoid robotics for reinforcement learning. In: European Conference on e-Learning, vol. XVII, pp. 654–657 (2021). https://doi.org/10.34190/EEL.251.132
20. Senno, B., Barcha, P.: Customizing user experience with adaptive virtual reality. In: Proceedings of the 23rd International Conference on Intelligent User Interfaces Companion, pp. 1–2. ACM, Tokyo (2018)
21. Barba, M.C., et al.: BRAVO: a gaming environment for the treatment of ADHD. In: De Paolis, L.T., Bourdot, P. (eds.) AVR 2019. LNCS, vol. 11613, pp. 394–407. Springer, Cham (2019). https://doi.org/10.1007/978-3-030-25965-5_30

22. Moon, J., Ke, F., Sokolikj, Z.: Automatic assessment of cognitive and emotional states in virtual reality-based flexibility training for four adolescents with autism. Br. J. Educ. Technol. **51**, 1766–1784 (2020). https://doi.org/10.1111/bjet.13005
23. McMahan, T., Duffield, T., Parsons, T.D.: Feasibility study to identify machine learning predictors for a virtual school environment: virtual reality stroop task. Front. Virtual Real. **2**, 673191 (2021). https://doi.org/10.3389/frvir.2021.673191
24. Poornappriya, T., Gopinath, R.: Application of machine learning techniques for improving learning disabilities. Int. J. Electr. Eng. Technol. **11**(10), 392–402 (2020). https://doi.org/10.34218/IJEET.11.10.2020.051
25. Gilbert, B., et al.: Dyslexia and AI: the use of artificial intelligence to identify and create font to improve reading ability of individuals with Dyslexia. In: Langran, E., Christensen, P., Sanson J. (eds.) Proceedings of Society for Information Technology & Teacher Education International Conference. pp. 856–865. Association for the Advancement of Computing in Education (AACE), New Orleans, LA, United States (2023). https://www.learntechlib.org/primary/p/221937/
26. Devi, A., Kavya, G.: Dysgraphia disorder forecasting and classification technique using intelligent deep learning approaches. Prog. Neuropsychopharmacol. Biol. Psychiatry **120**, 110647 (2023). https://doi.org/10.1016/j.pnpbp.2022.110647
27. Drigas, A.S., Ioannidou, R.-E.: A Review on artificial intelligence in special education. In: Lytras, M.D., Ruan, D., Tennyson, R.D., Ordonez De Pablos, P., García Peñalvo, F.J., Rusu, L. (eds.) WSKS 2011. CCIS, vol. 278, pp. 385–391. Springer, Heidelberg (2013). https://doi.org/10.1007/978-3-642-35879-1_46
28. Dhingra, K., Aggarwal, R., Garg, A., Pujari, J., Yadav, D.: Mathlete: an adaptive assistive technology tool for children with dyscalculia. Disabil. Rehabil.: Assistive Technol **ahead-of-print**, 1–7 (2022). https://doi.org/10.1080/17483107.2022.2134473
29. Barua, P.D., et al.: Artificial intelligence enabled personalised assistive tools to enhance education of children with neurodevelopmental disorders—a review. IJERPH **19**, 1192 (2022). https://doi.org/10.3390/ijerph190311921
30. Wang, M., Muthu, B., Sivaparthipan, C.B.: Smart assistance to dyslexia students using artificial intelligence based augmentative alternative communication. Int. J. Speech Technol. **25**, 343–353 (2021)
31. Melis, E., et al.: ActiveMath: a generic and adaptive web-based learning environment. Int. J Artif. Intell. Educ. (IJAIED) **12**, 385–407 (2001)
32. Riedl, M., Arriaga, R., Boujarwah, F., Hong, H., Isbell, J., Heflin, J.: Graphical social scenarios: toward intervention and authoring for adolescents with high functioning autism. In: AAAI Fall Symposium: Virtual Healthcare Interaction, Arlington, VA (2009)
33. Baschera, G.M., Gross, M.: Poisson-based inference for perturbation models in adaptive spelling training. Int. J. Artif. Intell. Educ. **20**(4), 333–360 (2010). https://doi.org/10.3233/JAI-2010-011
34. Dignum, V., Penagos, M., Pigmans, K., Vosloo, S.: Policy guidance on AI for children. UNICEF Office of Global Insight and Policy, New York. https://www.unicef.cn/en/reports/policy-guidance-ai-children (2020)
35. High Level Expert Group on Artificial Intelligence: A definition of AI: Main capabilities and disciplines. Brussels (2019). https://ec.europa.eu/digital-single-market/en/news/definition-artificial-intelligence-maincapabilities-and-scientific-disciplines
36. Schwartz, R., Vassilev, A., Greene, K., Perine, L., Burt, A., Hall, P.: Towards a Standard for Identifying and Managing Bias in Artificial Intelligence. National Institute of Standards and Technology, Gaithersburg, MD (2022). https://doi.org/10.6028/NIST.SP.1270
37. United Nations Educational, Scientific and Cultural Organization: Recommendations on the Ethics of Artificial Intelligence. UNESCO Digital Library, Paris (2022). https://unesdoc.unesco.org/ark:/48223/pf0000381137

38. Yeung, K.: Recommendation of the council on artificial intelligence (OECD). Int. leg. mater. **59**, 27–34 (2020). https://doi.org/10.1017/ilm.2020.5
39. Jelinek, T., Wallach, W., Kerimi, D.: Policy brief: the creation of a G20 coordinating committee for the governance of artificial intelligence. AI Ethics **1**(2), 141–150 (2020). https://doi.org/10.1007/s43681-020-00019-y
40. Jobin, A., Ienca, M., Vayena, E.: The global landscape of AI ethics guidelines. Nat. Mach. Intell. **1**(9), 389–399 (2019). https://doi.org/10.1038/s42256-019-0088-2
41. Ala-Pietilä, P., et al.: The Assessment List for Trustworthy Artificial Intelligence (ALTAI). European Commission, Brussels (2020)
42. Smuha, N.A.: The EU approach to ethics guidelines for trustworthy artificial intelligence. Comput. Law Rev. Int. **20**(4), 97–106 (2019). https://doi.org/10.9785/cri-2019-200402
43. Antle, A.N., Kitson, A.: 1, 2, 3, 4 tell me how to grow more: a position paper on children, design ethics and wearables. Int. J. Child-Comput. Interact. **30**, 100328 (2021). https://doi.org/10.1016/j.ijcci.2021.100328
44. Unicef: Policy guidance on AI for children 2.0. UNICEF Office of Global Insight and Policy, New York (2021)
45. WEF: Artificial Intelligence for Children. World Economic Forum (2022). https://www.weforum.org/reports/artificial-intelligence-for-children?_gl=1*c7aij2*_up*MQ..&gclid=CjwKCAjw6IiiBhAOEiwALNqncfkpoSPkbQJ-m4BT4J3EqIVkBFLMhYonXqTtUWOM_oqm6jMK4KUsBRoCqW8QAvD_BwE (2022). Last accessed 30 Mar 2023
46. Fengchun, M., Wayne, H., Huang, R., Zhang, H., UNESCO: AI and Education: A Guidance for Policymakers. UNESCO Publishing, Paris (2021)
47. Dignum, V., Penagos, M., Pigmans, K., Vosloo, S.: Policy Guidance on AI for Children. UNICEF Office of Global Insight and Policy, New York (2020)
48. European Commission: Artificial intelligence and the rights of the child: towards an integrated agenda for research and policy. Joint Research Centre: Publications Office, LU (2022). https://doi.org/10.2760/012329
49. Lee, B.X., et al.: Transforming our world: implementing the 2030 agenda through sustainable development goal indicators. J. Public Health Pol. **37**, 13–31 (2016). https://doi.org/10.1057/s41271-016-0002-7
50. Ogourtsova, T., Boychuck, Z., O'Donnell, M., Ahmed, S., Osman, G., Majnemer, A.: Telerehabilitation for children and youth with developmental disabilities and their families: a systematic review. Phys. Occup. Ther. Pediatr. **43**(2), 129–175 (2023). https://doi.org/10.1080/01942638.2022.2106468
51. Ministero della Salute: Linee d'indirizzo nazionali sulla telemedicina. Salute.gov. https://www.salute.gov.it/portale/documentazione/p6_2_2_1.jsp?lingua=italiano&id=2129 (2012). Last accessed 24 Mar 2023
52. Mahmud, M., et al.: Towards explainable and privacy-preserving artificial intelligence for personalisation in autism spectrum disorder. In: Antona, M., Stephanidis, C. (eds.) Universal Access in Human-Computer Interaction. User and Context Diversity, pp. 356–370. Springer International Publishing, Cham (2022). https://doi.org/10.1007/978-3-031-05039-8_26
53. Baron-Cohen, S.: Social and pragmatic deficits in autism: cognitive or affective? J. Autism. Dev. Disord. **18**, 379–402 (1988). https://doi.org/10.1007/BF02212194
54. Botting, N., Conti-Ramsden, G.: Autism, primary pragmatic difficulties, and specific language impairment: can we distinguish them using psycholinguistic markers? Dev. Med. Child Neurol. **45**(08), 515–524 (2003). https://doi.org/10.1017/S0012162203000963
55. Güler, T.D., Erdem, M.: Use of mobile social story maps in the development of cognitive and social skills of children with autism spectrum disorder. J. Spec. Educ. Technol. **37**, 482–497 (2022). https://doi.org/10.1177/01626434211037547

56. Terlouw, G., Van't Veer, J.T.B., Prins, J.T., Kuipers, D.A., Pierie, J.-P.E.N.: Design of a digital comic creator (it's me) to facilitate social skills training for children with autism spectrum disorder: design research approach. JMIR Ment. Health **7**(7), e17260 (2020). https://doi.org/10.2196/17260
57. Lemaignan, S., Newbutt, N., Rice, L., Daly, J., Charisi, V.: UNICEF guidance on AI for children: Application to the design of a social robot for and with autistic children. arXiv preprint arXiv:2108.12166 (2021). https://doi.org/10.48550/arXiv.2108.12166
58. WEF: Generation AI: Establishing Global Standards for Children and AI. World Economic Forum. https://www.weforum.org/reports/generation-ai-establishing-global-standards-for-children-and-ai/ (2019)
59. Franzoni, V.: Gender differences and bias in artificial intelligence. In: Vallverdú, J. (ed.) Gender in AI and Robotics: The Gender Challenges from an Interdisciplinary Perspective, pp. 27–43. Springer International Publishing, Cham (2023). https://doi.org/10.1007/978-3-031-21606-0_2
60. Whittaker, M., et al.: Disability, bias, and AI. In: Noseworthy, P.A., Attia, Z. (eds.) AI Now Institute 8. Springer International Publishing, Cham (2019)
61. Noseworthy, P.A., et al.: Assessing and mitigating bias in medical artificial intelligence: the effects of race and ethnicity on a deep learning model for ECG analysis. Circ.: Arrhythmia Electrophysiol. **13**(3), e007988 (2020). https://doi.org/10.1161/CIRCEP.119.007988
62. Trewin, S.: AI fairness for people with disabilities: Point of view. arXiv preprint arXiv:1811.10670 (2018). https://doi.org/10.48550/arXiv.1811.10670
63. Miller, K.: A matter of perspective: discrimination, bias, and inequality in AI. In: Jackson, M., Shelly, M. (eds.) Advances in Information Security, Privacy, and Ethics, pp. 182–202. IGI Global (2020)
64. Baker, R.S., Hawn, A.: Algorithmic bias in education. Int. J. Artif. Intell. Educ. **32**, 1–41 (2021). https://doi.org/10.1007/s40593-021-00285-9
65. Potapov, K., Marshall, P.: LifeMosaic: co-design of a personal informatics tool for youth. In: Proceedings of the Interaction Design and Children Conference, pp. 519–531. Association for Computing Machinery, New York (2020)
66. Georgiou, N., Spanoudis, G.: Developmental language disorder and autism: commonalities and differences in language. Brain Sci. **11**(5), 589 (2021). https://doi.org/10.3390/brainsci11050589
67. Neamtu, R., Camara, A., Pereira, C., Ferreira, R.: Using artificial intelligence for augmentative alternative communication for children with disabilities. In: Lamas, D., Loizides, F., Nacke, L., Petrie, H., Winckler, M., Zaphiris, P. (eds.) INTERACT 2019. LNCS, vol. 11746, pp. 234–243. Springer, Cham (2019). https://doi.org/10.1007/978-3-030-29381-9_15
68. Zaman, B.: Designing technologies with and for youth: Traps of privacy by design. Media Commun. **8**(4), 229–238 (2020). https://doi.org/10.17645/mac.v8i4.326
69. Charisi, V., Malinverni, L., Schaper, M.-M., Rubegni, E.: Creating opportunities for children's critical reflections on AI, robotics and other intelligent technologies. In: Proceedings of the 2020 ACM Interaction Design and Children Conference: Extended Abstracts, pp. 89–95. ACM, London (2020)
70. Siegler, R.S., DeLoache, J.S., Eisenberg, N., Gershoff, E.T., Saffran, J., Leaper, C.: How Children Develop, 5th edn. Worth Publishers Macmillan Learning, New York (2017)
71. Bandura, A.: Adolescent development from an agentic perspective. In: Pajares, F., Urdan, T. (Eds.), Self-Efficacy Beliefs of Adolescents 2006, pp. 1–43. Greenwich, CT: Information Age (2006)
72. Spiel, K., Frauenberger, C., Keyes, O., Fitzpatrick, G.: Agency of autistic children in technology research—A critical literature review. ACM Trans. Comput.-Human Interaction (TOCHI) **26**(6), 1–40 (2019). https://doi.org/10.1145/3344919

73. Chatterjee, S., Sreenivasulu, N.S.: Personal data sharing and legal issues of human rights in the era of artificial intelligence: moderating effect of government regulation. Int. J. Electr. Government Res. (IJEGR) **15**(3), 21–36 (2019). https://doi.org/10.4018/IJEGR.2019070102
74. Zaeem, R.N., Barber, K.S.: The effect of the GDPR on privacy policies: Recent progress and future promise. ACM Trans. Manag. Inform. Syst. (TMIS) **12**(1), 1–20 (2020). https://doi.org/10.1145/3389685
75. Strickler, J.G., Havercamp, S.M.: Evaluating an informed consent process designed to improve inclusion of adults with intellectual disability in research. Res. Dev. Disabil. **134**, 104413 (2023). https://doi.org/10.1016/j.ridd.2022.104413
76. Liberati, A., et al.: The PRISMA statement for reporting systematic reviews and meta-analyses of studies that evaluate health care interventions: explanation and elaboration. PLoS Med. **6**(7), e1000100 (2009). https://doi.org/10.1371/journal.pmed.1000100
77. AlgorithmWatch.: AI Ethics Guidelines Global Inventory. https://algorithmwatch.org/en/ai-ethics-guidelines-global-inventory/. Last accessed 30 Mar 2023
78. Linking Artificial Intelligence Principles (LAIP) Homepage. https://www.linking-ai-principles.org. Last accessed 30 Mar 2023
79. Guy, M., Blary, A., Ladner, J., Gilliaux, M.: Ethical issues linked to the development of telerehabilitation: a qualitative study. Int. J. Telerehabi. **13**(1), e6367 (2021). https://doi.org/10.5195/ijt.2021.6367
80. Mayring, P.: Qualitative Content Analysis: A Step-by-Step Guide. Sage Publications Ltd., London (2021)
81. Dignum, V.: Ethics in artificial intelligence: introduction to the special issue. Ethics Inf. Technol. **20**(1), 1–3 (2018). https://doi.org/10.1007/s10676-018-9450-z

Natural Language Processing Techniques for Hate Speech Evaluation for Brazilian Portuguese

Cássia C. S. Rosa(✉), Fábio V. Martinez, and Renato Ishii

Faculdade de Computação, Universidade Federal de Mato Grosso do Sul, Campo Grande, Brazil
{cassia.c,fabio.martinez,renato.ishii}@ufms.br

Abstract. The numerous harmful publications generated from large amounts of data expelled daily on social media make it necessary to adopt automated technologies for online content moderation. Sentence classification and sentiment analysis are Natural Language Processing (NLP) techniques used to detect hate speech on social media platforms such as Facebook and Instagram. However, some difficulties reduce the effectiveness of these tools in the Portuguese language. Previous research has shown how NLP models have high accuracy when trained with datasets centered on mastering the Brazilian Portuguese language. In this work, we propose the creation of a large-scale linguistic corpus for Brazilian Portuguese composed of publications collected from the social network Twitter. The experiments were performed by tuning a pretrained transformer model.

Keywords: Hate Speech · Brazilian Portuguese · NLP

1 Introduction

From the creation of social networks, assumptions about the formation of these spaces began to be studied. Among them, the idealization that a social network would be an environment free of social problems such as racism, misogyny, and LGBTQIA+Phobia stands out. However, it is possible to see that this is a flawed estimate, most likely because the Internet is not fully inclusive, as according to the UN, 37% of the world's population does not have access to the World Wide Web. Thus, it is notable that there is a predominance of only a fraction of society on the Internet since its construction and, as this is a hegemonic space, it is noticeable the engendering of discrimination not only through social networks, but also through blogs, websites, and forums. See for instance the case of the forum called "StormFront" [7], created in 1995 and removed from the Internet in 2017 for propagating Nazi and white supremacist ideas.

Removing content from the Internet is not an easy task, as there are a large number of devices connected daily and countless posts made by them. For this and other reasons, social networks began to use mechanisms capable of automatically detecting violations of their terms of use, causing failures where these

O. Gervasi et al. (Eds.): ICCSA 2023 Workshops, LNCS 14107, pp. 104–117, 2023.
https://doi.org/10.1007/978-3-031-37114-1_8

systems ignored complaints, classified them incorrectly, or even took a long time to remove some discriminatory content. In this way, as the use of social networks and other online socialization platforms increases, the need for more efficient and fair systems for detecting and removing offensive content is growing.

A strategy often applied for this purpose is the use of Natural Language Processing (NLP), a branch of the Artificial Intelligence (AI) area that aims to understand human languages automatically. Several techniques such as Bag of Words, Naïve Bayes, and Support Vector Machines (SVM) have been created and are now used for sentiment analysis, construction of search tools, and automatic correction of words and texts. Among the extensive purposes of the NLP, the detection of hate speech is still being consolidated due to the difficulty in detecting the presence of hate in a sentence. This is due both to the lack of consensus on the concept of hate speech and also to the lack of balanced databases that contain different types of hate speech correctly cataloged.

This paper is organized as follows. Section 2 displays important background for the foundation of the research with highlights of some work carried out previously and some problems faced through the analysis of hate speech. Section 3 shows the methodology applied for data collection and annotation. Finally, in Sect. 4 the results are presented, and Sect. 5 the conclusions and future work are discussed.

2 Preliminaries

In this section, important concepts for developing this work will be presented, as well as the techniques and technologies used and their characteristics.

2.1 Natural Language Processing

Natural Language Processing (NLP) is a branch of Artificial Intelligence that aims to understand human languages in an automated way. The Bag of Words [18] is a technique that counts the frequency of words in a text and rearranges them into a list in which information about the word order is discarded. Thus, it is possible to use this result as an input to machine learning models like Naïve Bayes [29], which has a probability table containing the ratio between the occurrence of words and their total number in each corpus. Support Vector Machines (SVM) [10] is another machine learning model that divides the data space into dimensions according to the number of classes of the problem to be treated. The objective of this model is to maximize the margin between the generated spaces to correctly categorize as much data as possible. Other NLP techniques such as lemmatization and stemming are adopted during the data preprocessing stage and are used to reduce and normalize the large volume of words that will be analyzed in the future. While lemmatization transforms a word into its base, stemming transforms a word into its trunk or root.

Despite being widely used in other applications, the techniques mentioned above may be ineffective for detecting hate speech. Because of figures of speech such as ambiguity, sarcasm, and irony, the context of a sentence is essential in determining toxicity. Therefore, there is an urgent need to use more sophisticated techniques for evaluating hate speech, such as those mentioned below.

A *transformer* [28] is an artificial neural network architecture that has an encoding and decoding framework. The Bidirectional Encoder Representations of Transformers (BERT) [14] is a model based on transformer architecture that has achieved state-of-the-art and was developed by Google's Artificial Intelligence team to be applied in NLP tasks. It uses masked language modeling (MLM), where some vocabulary words are encoded and the model tries to predict them from their context. Normally, MLM uses unidirectional models, in which the context is understood from left to right or from right to left. BERT, however, uses a bidirectional approach, which combines unidirectional contexts.

Tokenizing a string is an important process for linguistic models (LM). In particular, BERT performs the subtokenization of word pieces, a process in which a word is divided into its prefixes, if they exist, and, with the result of this segmentation, the identified terms are called *tokens*. Hence, the generated tokens are provided as input to the model that performs the *embedding activity*, or *embedding*, to represent them as a vector of weights in which each position represents information about them. The tokenization step is assigned as input to the LM which has 12 layers in its basic form and 24 layers in its extensive form.

BERTimbau [26] is a BERT model trained for Brazilian Portuguese that initially implements text similarity, text element recognition, and named entity recognition tasks. In this work, this model was adapted to classify sentences that contain some type of hate speech.

2.2 Hate Speech

The Brazilian Law Number 7716, of January 5, 1989, defines that acts of discrimination or prejudice based on race, color, ethnicity, religion, or national origin resulting from hate speech must be criminalized. However, the crimes of racism and racial/discriminatory injury are seen as different because, in the first, it is understood that the aggressor's intention would be to offend the entire group to which the victim belongs, while in the second, it is understood that his intention would be to offend only the victim. As in the legal sphere, these definitions contribute to the emergence of problems that can make it difficult to classify hate speech.

Thus, to accomplish the detection of hate speech, it is necessary to have a well-defined parameter about what are the main characteristics of a manifestation of hate and how it can manifest itself in different situations. Hate speech can be identified through two basic characteristics, which are the insult or offense to a person who is included in a socially vulnerable group and speeches, gestures, or expressions that incite violence explicit or implicit [22].

Another ingredient that also contributes to wrong classifications of hate speech is the way in which the aggressor manages to disguise the hatred through sentences that can be considered opinions, political ideologies, or freedom of speech. Rosenfied [23] defines two ways of expressing hate. For him, *hate speech in form* are explicitly hateful manifestations, such as racist insults aimed at racial groups. While *hate speech in substance* are veiled manifestations of hatred, such as denial of the Holocaust or other type of message that does not contain injuries.

Because there are still many discussions on the subject, in this work only explicitly hateful manifestations will be classified as hate speech, since this is a generally well-defined category in research that surround this subject.

2.3 Related Works

The debate on hate speech is covered by several areas of knowledge such as Computer Science, Law, and Literature. In the former, several researchers seek to improve their techniques for evaluating words, phrases, and speeches to contribute to less toxic virtual environments. However, the majority of research is developed by English-based texts [6,12,13,30], making it difficult for these systems to operate in other languages [1,3,8,9]. In this way, to increase the performance of hate speech detection in Portuguese, some previous works were done.

Pelle and Moreira [21] collected 10,000 comments from the Brazilian news page called G1 and created two databases: OFFCOMBR-2, in which at least two annotators agreed with the chosen class, and OFFCOMBR -3, where all three annotators agreed with the chosen class, namely "offensive" and "non-offensive". The "offensive" class is categorized into the subclasses "racism", "sexism", "xenophobia", "homophobia", "religious intolerance", and "swearing". The Naïve Bayes and SVM algorithms were used to classify these comments. The best classifier, SVM, achieved a score of 80% on the F measure.

Fortuna and colleagues [16] collected 5,668 tweets to compose their database, which was divided into "hate speech" and "non-hate speech" classes. The class "hate speech" was subdivided into subtypes called "sexism", "corporal", "origin", "homophobia", "racism", "ideology", "religion", "health", and "other lifestyle". For classification, the LSTMs deep learning model was used, which obtained a score of 78% on the F measure.

Leite et al. [20] presented TOLD-Br, a database with around 21,000 tweets in Brazilian Portuguese. The "toxic" and "non-toxic" classes were used for binary classification, while the "LGBTQ+Phobia", "xenophobia", "racism", "misogyny", "obscene", and "insulting" were used for multi-classification. Pretrained natural language processing models together with a model created from Bag-of-Words techniques and automated machine learning were used for both classifications. Their best models, which used the BR-BERT and M-BERT-BR architecture, scored on the F measure of 76% and 75%, respectively.

Silva [25] used the dataset provided by Fortuna et al. In addition, the SVM, MLP Neural Network, Logistic Regression, and Naïve Bayes algorithms had some configurations tested to obtain better performance. The SVM algorithm outperformed the others and obtained an F measure of 71%.

This work arises with the premise of collecting Twitter publications to compose an extensive database, which will be cataloged in three different classes and will later be applied to detect sentences constituted by some type of explicitly hateful manifestation. A deep learning model will be used to classify the previously collected items.

2.4 Scope

For identifying possible hate speech, it is first necessary to verify whether this is content that discriminates against a person or a minority social group to which he belongs. Even more so if this is content that instigates violence against that person or against socially vulnerable groups. In addition, the dynamics between users, the social, cultural, and regional contexts, as well as the context of the phrase and issues related to the resignification of words among groups marginalized by society, among other issues, need to be considered to guarantee the legitimacy of possible classifications made by linguistic models.

Other issues related to the automation of publication analysis also need to be considered. For Duarte et al. [15], the tools used for moderating content online have certain limitations related to the NLP, such as the need for a specific domain, relatively low reliability and inferior classification ability to humans. Those issues that can disproportionately marginalize and censor discriminated groups, such as with the Perspective API, which ranked Twitter profiles of drag queens as more toxic than profiles of white supremacists and far-right leaders [2].

Algorithmic biases are also present in natural language processing tools and large models [5] used for content moderation on social media platforms. Therefore, to prevent these technologies from being inefficient and biased, it is essential to create a robust, balanced, and correctly annotated database, as well as to train more accurate models and investigate the presence of bias in existing datasets [11,19]. Together, the results obtained by these models must be evaluated by humans to guarantee their correctness. Furthermore, it is important to emphasize that discrimination also happens outside of social networks and the application of hate detectors is just a small step towards mitigating discrimination, which needs to be fought in a significant way outside of the Internet.

Because of the amount of data used in the training process, BERT is classified as a Large Language Model (LLM). The high consumption of resources like energy to train these models can cause big environmental impacts [27]. Furthermore, ethical and social issues can be effect by biased dissemination [31] arising from a lack of representativeness on data [5]. Additionally, the identity terms used in this work can increase the discrimination and marginalization of minority groups [11]. This occurs because offensive words and expressions could have different meanings, depending on the context in which they are applied [17]. Thus, it is important to invest in mitigation and evaluation of bias techniques in language models and datasets [32].

3 Databases

In this section, we described how the construction of the database was accomplished, its annotations, and other characteristics.

3.1 Data Collection and Preprocessing

The *snscrape*[1] is tool for data mining that support social media services like Facebook, Instagram, Reddit, and Telegram. Differently from the Twitter API, available only to developers, this is an open-source tool that can be used by anyone and does not require registration, as well as there is no need to perform any type of authentication beforehand and there is also no limit for requests, nor a maximum capacity for extracting publications. For these reasons, *snscrape* was the tool chosen to achieve the data collection process.

As the intention is to collect only *hate in form* publications, queries were carried out to capture publications that contain any of the terms mentioned below, which are arguments for a search.

The hashtag "eleições2022" was consulted after the second round of the 2022 Brazilian presidential elections. It was chosen because of its overlap with other hashtags such as "vaidatpt" and "brasilvota22", which were frequently used in that same period. Publications that contained the terms "favelado", "nordestino", "indigenous" or "african" were consulted in the months of October and November, with the intention of capturing possibly xenophobic terms. In this same time interval, posts consisting of the terms "vagabunda" (slut), "piranha" (whore), "feminazi" or "macumbeira" (witch) were also consulted. The words "humor negro" (black humor), "negro" and "escravo" (slave) were searched between August and November to evaluate publications with racist content. Adjectives commonly used in ableist sentences, such as "retardado" (retarded), "débil" (moron) and "demente" (demented), were analyzed from September to November of the same year. As well as "obeso" (obese) and "gordo" (fat), which were also surveyed in the same period. Finally, more broadly, the terms "traveco" (tranny), "afeminado" (effeminate), and "opção sexual" (sexual option) were used to capture tweets from January 2019 to November 2022. The step-by-step of this process can be seen in Fig. 1. Also, the word cloud of the entire corpus is show in Fig. 2.

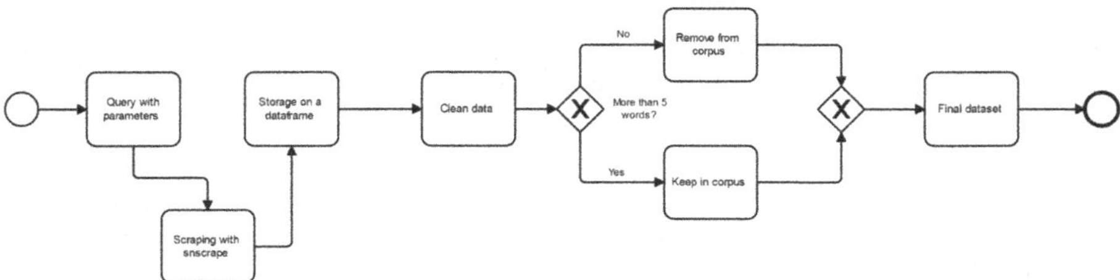

Fig. 1. Process of data collection and data cleaning.

[1] https://github.com/JustAnotherArchivist/snscrape.

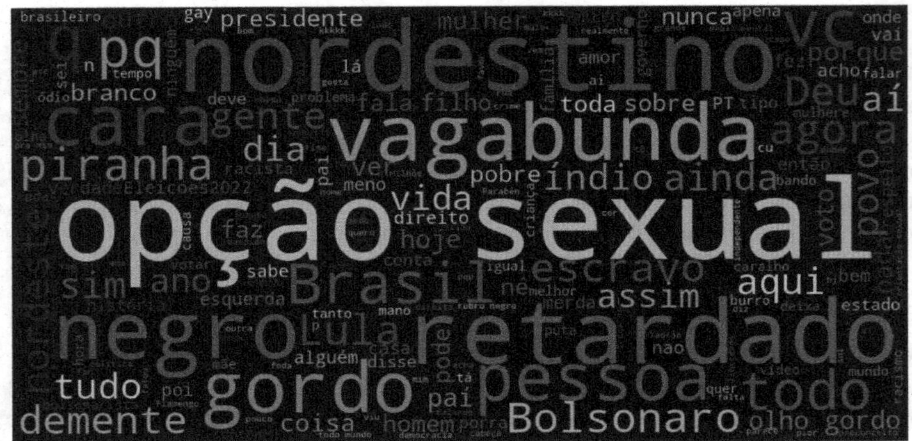

Fig. 2. Our corpus shown as a word cloud.

In this process, usernames were replaced by "@user" and hypertexts were removed, to avoid possible identifications. If a publication has less than five words or is identical to another one in the set, it is excluded from the database. Furthermore, we observed that hashtags were not removed because they can add information necessary for the context of a sentence. Finally, we emphasize that the tokenizer used is capable of identifying the "#" symbol and ignoring it.

3.2 Data Annotation

A total of 848 sentences were randomly chosen for manual labeling, which was performed using the annotation platform Label Studio. Of these, 108 were classified as hate speech, 370 as offensive, and 370 as neutral. The sentences were annotated by the author, a 21 years black woman, naturally from the north of Brazil. Therefore, it is possible the existence of bias, due to the lack of representativeness during the annotation. Furthermore, cultural and social factors can influence the process, even if adopting a hate speech definition addressed by specialists.

Examples classified as hateful follow the evaluation premise explained in Sect. 2. It is worth noting that offenses directed at other groups, which do not suffer from the social stigma directed at marginalized groups, were not considered hateful. In addition to this reason, the offense class was added due to the large number of examples that were not neutral statements, as well as not explicitly hateful manifestations. Based on this assumption, it is possible to see that some labeling of the offense class can be interpreted as *hate speech in substance* and that, notoriously, can compose the corpus of hateful tweets. However, as the annotation was not achieved by any specialist or person with previous experience in hate speech categorization, this was a measure adopted to mitigate the number of words mistakenly annotated as neutral, which may trigger a possibility that implicitly hateful speeches be treated as non-toxic. Furthermore, tweets classified as neutral were not necessarily identified as po sitive, as they may contain offensive words, but which are not intended for a person or are not harmful in the context used.

To clarify the classification performed in this work, Table 1 shows some annotated examples.

Table 1. Examples of annotated sentences in Portuguese. Three types of annotations are presented: Hate speech, Offense, and Neutral.

Text in Portuguese (English translation)	Annotation
Que negros de merda (What fucking niggers)	Hate speech
Sua loira vagabunda do caralho morte p vc é pouco... (You fucking blonde slut death to you is little...)	Hate speech
Essa enquete prova que o brasileiro é um povo MT retardado... (This poll proves that Brazilians are a VERY retarded people...)	Offense
tenho muito nojo de gordo suado cheio de banha kkk (I'm really disgusted with sweaty fat people full of lard lol)	Offense
Amiga mas nem todo mundo tem o sonho de ser piranha (Friend, but not everyone has the dream of being a slut)	Neutral
Homens negros falem sobre amor, isso motiva outros negros (Black men talk about love, it motivates other black people)	Neutral

Furthermore, Fig. 3 shows the process of data annotation adopted in this work.

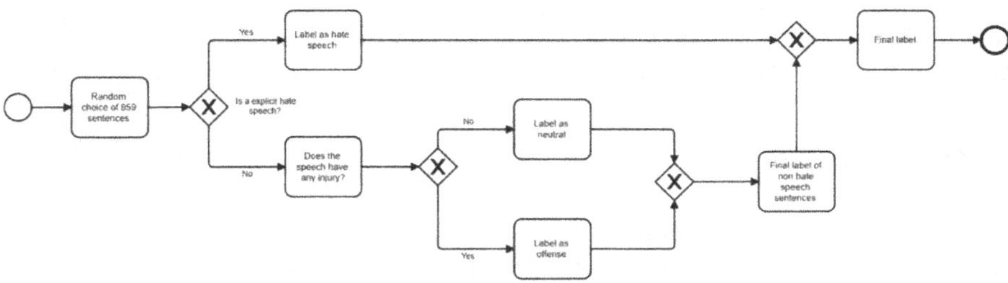

Fig. 3. Process of data annotation.

An exploratory text data analysis was conducted in the annotated dataset to acquire more knowledge about it. Figure 4 shows the most frequent words present on the dataset. By this, it is possible to recognize that the dispersion of data is compatible with the chosen words and hashtags used during the collection

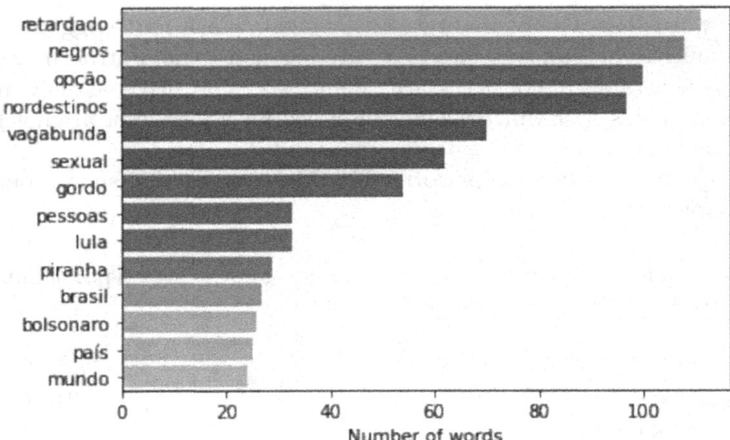

Fig. 4. The most frequent words in the annotated dataset.

process. Thus, the sentences selected to compose the annotated dataset represent the original corpus.

To exemplify the composition of data in each category, i.e. neutral, offensive, and hateful, four bigrams were created. In Fig. 5, except for "sexual option", which predominates in all sets, the other bigrams demonstrate, mainly, the differences between the definitions of hate speech and offense. Notice that, in the hate speech class, there is a high correlation between the bigrams and misogyny speech.

As seen in Fig. 6, the variation between the number of words present in a sentence in the annotated data set is also representative of the evaluation. This is because the tweets produced, containing hate or not, do not follow a pattern and can vary in different ways, one of which is the number of words. However, it is also possible to notice that as the number of words increases, the number of tweets decreases, since social media users usually post with less than 30 words.

4 Results

Due to the small number of labeled publications, the *hatecheck-portuguese* dataset, by Röttger and colleagues [24], which contains 2581 sentences annotated as *hateful* and 1110 annotated as *not-hateful*, was chosen for fine-tuning the pretrained model BERTimbau. This is the process in which a deep learning model has its parameters adjusted to perform tasks from a different dataset than the one it was previously trained on. Data were originally used for functional tests obtained in the language model for sentiment analysis XLM-T [4] and Google's Perspective API. Functional testing is an evaluation performed to measure the

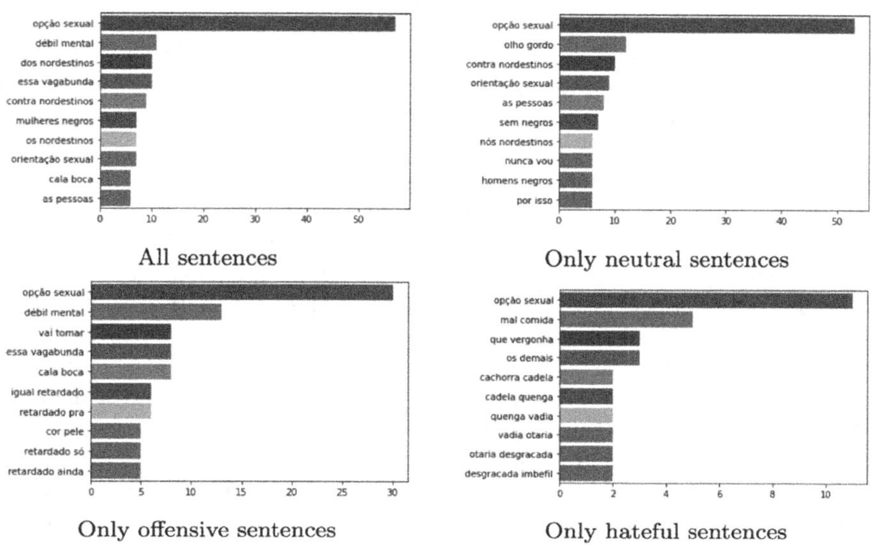

Fig. 5. The composition of data as a bigram in each category of annotated dataset: Neutral, Offensive, and Hateful.

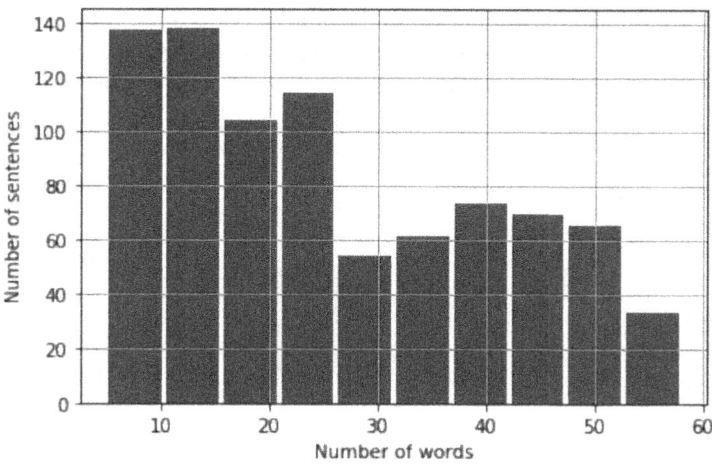

Fig. 6. Number of words per sentence in the annotated dataset.

quality of software through the analysis of the outputs generated by a program from a certain set of data provided as input.

Determining factors for choosing this database were (1) the examples contained in the corpus "hateful" being explicitly hateful manifestations, and (2) the process of generating test cases, done manually by specialists in the Portuguese language who have experienced previous research or annotation of hate speech. Additionally, the OffComBR-2 [21] database, which contains a corpus of 831 examples annotated as '*no*', and a corpus of 419 examples annotated as '*yes*', was also used to compose the evaluation step. Although the functional test set has more examples, the texts extracted from news comments by Pelle and Moreira [21] have a structure similar to that of the collected tweets and, for this reason, can positively influence the learning of the model.

In this way, the BERTimbau adjustment was performed from these data, and each set was applied separately to generate a model. In both sets, a random division of the data of 80% for training and 20% for validation was performed. Fine-tuning was defined in 4 steps with batch sizes equal to 16 and a learning rate starting at 0.00001. The resulting models were tested with collected data that were labeled "neutral" and "hate speech". As seen in Fig. 7, the first model using the functional test set, obtained an F measure of 68% and a accuracy of 66%. The second model, using the set of offensive comments, obtained an F measure of 74% and a accuracy of 73%. Another test was also performed with the second model to evaluate the "offense" corpus of the collected database. The F measure remained at 74% while the accuracy increased to 74%. The F measure, or simply F1, is a metric for evaluating the performance of machine learning models. More specifically, it is responsible for observing other metrics that it evaluates: precision and recall, which are used to measure how well the model performed in avoiding false positives and false negatives, respectively. The Table 2 helps to elucidate the performance of all models and points out how even with few examples, the collected database has a huge potential for hate speech detection task. All results obtained can be found at TwitterHateBR.

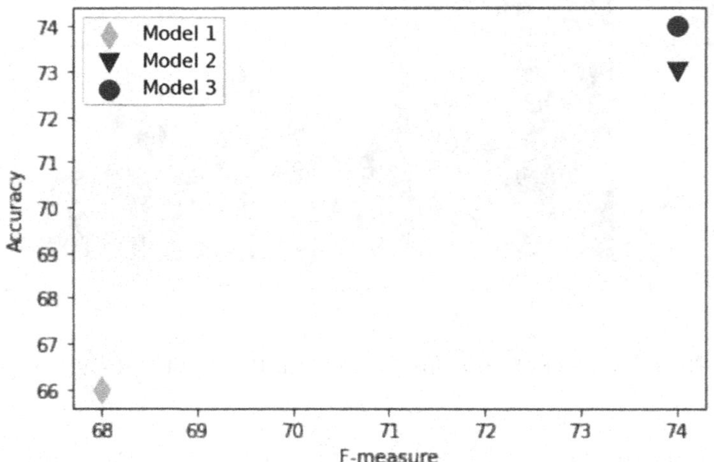

Fig. 7. F-measure and Accuracy of each model.

Table 2. Each model and his respective metrics and database. Two types of metrics are presented: F-measure and accuracy. Three databases are used: Functional test set, offensive comments and the collected database.

Model	F-measure	Accuracy	Database
Model 1	68%	66%	Functional test set
Model 2	74%	73%	Offensive comments
Model 3	74%	74%	Collected database

5 Conclusion

As with other AI problems, to perform hate speech detection, determining a database is an essential step in training good models. Therefore, it is important to collect large amounts of examples belonging to the analyzed domain, as well as to correctly catalog them based on the fundamentals and discussions about expressions of hate.

Like the previous, this work has been faced with obstacles to find examples for the hateful class, since the vast majority of the sentences contained in databases are neutral or offensive. This imbalance, in addition to generating false classifications, can also bring bias, since the low amount of data makes the model not able to learn correctly the hate speech concept.

This work presented the process achieved to collect Twitter publications used to create a large database in Brazilian Portuguese, as well as its criteria for evaluating instances and labeling of sentences called hate speech. The result of applying the database created to two models trained from previous works is also presented, in which the F measure obtained in the second model is within the range found in previous works.

Future work consists of including the annotation of more tweets by volunteers with previous experience in hate speech annotation and the fine-tuning of other pretrained models from this data. Additionally, it is feasible to apply techniques of evaluation and mitigation of bias in the dataset and models and also to accomplish adjustments in the dataset to reach the balance of classes.

Acknowledgments. We thank the support of the UFMS (Universidade Federal de Mato Grosso do Sul). We also thank the support of the INCT of the Future Internet for Smart Cities funded by CNPq, proc. 465446/2014-0, Coordenação de Aperfeiçoamento de Pessoal de Nível Superior - Brasil (CAPES) - Finance Code 001, and FAPESP, proc. 2014/50937-1 and 2015/24485-9.

Any opinions, findings, and conclusions or recommendations expressed in this material are those of the authors and do not necessarily reflect the views of, FAPESP, CAPES, and CNPq.

References

1. Aluru, S.S., Mathew, B., Saha, P., Mukherjee, A.: Deep learning models for multilingual hate speech detection. arXiv preprint arXiv:2004.06465 (2020)
2. Antonialli, D.: Drag queen vs. David Duke: Whose tweets are more 'toxic'. Wired. Retrieved (July/August 2019)
3. Plaza-del Arco, F.M., Molina-González, M.D., Urena-López, L.A., Martín-Valdivia, M.T.: Comparing pre-trained language models for Spanish hate speech detection. Expert Syst. Appl. **166**, 114120 (2021)
4. Barbieri, F., Anke, L.E., Camacho-Collados, J.: XLM-T: multilingual language models in twitter for sentiment analysis and beyond. In: Proceedings of the Thirteenth Language Resources and Evaluation Conference, pp. 258–266 (2022)
5. Bender, E.M., Gebru, T., McMillan-Major, A., Shmitchell, S.: On the dangers of stochastic parrots: can language models be too big? In: Proceedings of the 2021 ACM Conference on Fairness, Accountability, and Transparency, pp. 610–623 (2021)
6. Biere, S., Bhulai, S., Analytics, M.B.: Hate speech detection using natural language processing techniques. Master Business AnalyticsDepartment of Mathematics Faculty of Science (2018)
7. Bowman-Grieve, L.: Exploring "stormfront": a virtual community of the radical right. Stud. Conflict Terror. **32**(11), 989–1007 (2009)
8. Corazza, M., Menini, S., Cabrio, E., Tonelli, S., Villata, S.: Cross-platform evaluation for italian hate speech detection. In: CLiC-it 2019–6th Annual Conference of the Italian Association for Computational Linguistics (2019)
9. Corazza, M., Menini, S., Cabrio, E., Tonelli, S., Villata, S.: A multilingual evaluation for online hate speech detection. ACM Trans. Internet Technol. **20**(2), 1–22 (2020)
10. Cortes, C., Vapnik, V.: Support-vector networks. Mach. Learn. **20**, 273–297 (1995)
11. Davidson, T., Bhattacharya, D., Weber, I.: Racial bias in hate speech and abusive language detection datasets. arXiv preprint arXiv:1905.12516 (2019)
12. Davidson, T., Warmsley, D., Macy, M., Weber, I.: Automated hate speech detection and the problem of offensive language. In: Proceedings of the International AAAI Conference on Web and Social Media, vol. 11, pp. 512–515 (2017)
13. De Gibert, O., Perez, N., García-Pablos, A., Cuadros, M.: Hate speech dataset from a white supremacy forum. arXiv preprint arXiv:1809.04444 (2018)
14. Devlin, J., Chang, M.W., Lee, K., Toutanova, K.: BERT: pre-training of deep bidirectional transformers for language understanding. arXiv preprint arXiv:1810.04805 (2018)
15. Duarte, N., Llanso, E., Loup, A.: Mixed messages? The limits of automated social media content analysis. In: Friedler, S.A., Wilson, C. (eds.) Proceedings of the 1st Conference on Fairness, Accountability and Transparency. Proceedings of Machine Learning Research, vol. 81, pp. 106–106. PMLR (23–24 February 2018)
16. Fortuna, P., Rocha da Silva, J., Soler-Company, J., Wanner, L., Nunes, S.: A hierarchically-labeled Portuguese hate speech dataset. In: Proceedings of the Third Workshop on Abusive Language Online, pp. 94–104. Association for Computational Linguistics, Florence, Italy (August 2019)
17. Garg, T., Masud, S., Suresh, T., Chakraborty, T.: Handling bias in toxic speech detection: a survey. ACM Comput. Surv. (2023, just accepted). https://doi.org/10.1145/3580494
18. Harris, Z.S.: Distributional structure. Word **10**(2–3), 146–162 (1954)

19. Huang, X., Xing, L., Dernoncourt, F., Paul, M.J.: Multilingual twitter corpus and baselines for evaluating demographic bias in hate speech recognition. arXiv preprint arXiv:2002.10361 (2020)
20. Leite, J.A., Silva, D.F., Bontcheva, K., Scarton, C.: Toxic language detection in social media for Brazilian Portuguese: New dataset and multilingual analysis. arXiv preprint arXiv:2010.04543 (2020)
21. de Pelle, R., Moreira, V.: Offensive comments in the Brazilian web: a dataset and baseline results. In: Anais do VI Brazilian Workshop on Social Network Analysis and Mining. SBC, Porto Alegre, RS, Brasil (2017)
22. Rocha, J.L.A., Mendes, A.P.T.: Guidance Booklet for Victims of Hate speech (in Protuguese) (2020)
23. Rosenfeld, M.: Hate speech in constitutional jurisprudence: a comparative analysis. Soc. Sci. Res. Netw. **41**, 1–63 (2001)
24. Röttger, P., Seelawi, H., Nozza, D., Talat, Z., Vidgen, B.: Multilingual hateCheck: functional tests for multilingual hate speech detection models. arXiv preprint arXiv:2206.09917 (2022)
25. Silva, A.S.R.: Study of distributional models for detecting hate speech in Portuguese.. Ph.D. thesis, Universidade de São Paulo (2021). (in Portuguese)
26. Souza, F., Nogueira, R., Lotufo, R.: BERTimbau: pretrained BERT Models for Brazilian Portuguese. In: Cerri, R., Prati, R.C. (eds.) Intelligent Systems: 9th Brazilian Conference, BRACIS 2020, Rio Grande, Brazil, October 20–23, 2020, Proceedings, Part I, pp. 403–417. Springer International Publishing, Cham (2020). https://doi.org/10.1007/978-3-030-61377-8_28
27. Strubell, E., Ganesh, A., McCallum, A.: Energy and policy considerations for deep learning in nlp. arXiv preprint arXiv:1906.02243 (2019)
28. Vaswani, A., et al.: Attention is all you need. In: Guyon, I., et al. (eds.) Advances in Neural Information Processing Systems. vol. 30. Curran Associates, Inc. (2017)
29. Vikramkumar, B,V., Trilochan: Bayes and naive bayes classifier. CoRR abs/1404.0933 (2014)
30. Waseem, Z., Hovy, D.: Hateful symbols or hateful people? Predictive features for hate speech detection on twitter. In: Proceedings of the NAACL Student Research Workshop, pp. 88–93 (2016)
31. Weidinger, L., et al.: Ethical and social risks of harm from language models. arXiv preprint arXiv:2112.04359 (2021)
32. Xia, M., Field, A., Tsvetkov, Y.: Demoting racial bias in hate speech detection. arXiv preprint arXiv:2005.12246 (2020)

From Black Box to Glass Box: Advancing Transparency in Artificial Intelligence Systems for Ethical and Trustworthy AI

Valentina Franzoni[1,2(✉)]

[1] Department of Mathematics and Computer Science, University of Perugia, PG 06123 Perugia, Italy
[2] Department of Computer Science, Hong Kong Baptist University, Kowloon, Hong Kong, China
valentina.franzoni@unipg.it

Abstract. The rapid development of Artificial Intelligence (AI) systems has raised significant ethical concerns, particularly with the problem of transparency in their decision-making processes. As AI systems become increasingly integrated into various aspects of society, there is an urgent need to transform these 'black box' models into more transparent and understandable 'glass-box' systems. This paper explores the methods, challenges, and implications associated with supplementing transparency in AI systems in the promotion of ethical and trustworthy AI. We will examine the significance of transparency for stakeholders (i.e., users, developers, and policymakers), and the trade-offs between transparency and other objectives, e.g. accuracy and privacy. Recent US legislation prohibiting copyright claims on neural network-generated documents is used to illustrate the issues presented by the opaque nature of black-box AI models.

A thorough literature review is carried out to investigate current approaches and tools for AI transparency and identify gaps and areas for future research.

By moving from black box to glass box AI systems, we can ensure that AI technologies are not only powerful but also ethically sound and aligned with human values. This study adds to the ongoing debate about AI ethics and prepares the way for future research into the complex landscape of transparency, trust, and decision-making in AI systems.

Keywords: transparency · artificial intelligence · black box · neural networks · deep learning ethics · explainable AI · trust · decision-making · algorithmic auditing

1 Introduction

Transparency is increasingly important in AI systems as these technologies permeate various areas, e.g., natural language processing, computer vision, and even AI-generated material (e.g., text documents, images, animations, and music).

O. Gervasi et al. (Eds.): ICCSA 2023 Workshops, LNCS 14107, pp. 118–130, 2023.
https://doi.org/10.1007/978-3-031-37114-1_9

Transparency is critical in AI systems for fostering trust, promoting fairness, and ensuring accountability, which is critical given their far-reaching effect on society.

Trust is a fundamental aspect of human-AI interactions. As AI systems become more sophisticated and integrated into everyday life, users need to trust these technologies to make informed decisions and engage with them effectively. Transparency in AI systems allows users to understand the underlying decision-making processes, engenders trust and promotes acceptance. E.g., AI-generated content can be used in various applications, from content creation to customer support: ensuring transparency in how these models generate content helps users trust and use their outputs responsibly. Another critical aspect of AI systems is fairness, as biased or discriminatory outcomes can have critical repercussions for people and society [7,8]. Transparent AI systems allow users, developers, and regulators to spot and address potential bias in data or algorithms. Transparency in the context of AI-generated content can help expose any unintended biases in the generated documents, ensuring the fairness of the content given to users. Accountability is another relevant value for AI systems because it allows for the assignment of responsibility for their actions and results. Transparent AI systems enable stakeholders to track decisions back to specific system components, which is critical for holding developers and organizations accountable for any negative outcomes. Transparency in the realm of AI-generated documents can help users, developers, and lawmakers identify the source of any problematic content, allowing for appropriate corrective actions and informed policy decisions.

Unfortunately, transparency in AI systems is not always possible by design because of the black-box nature of the techniques used for training, and the consequent difficulty in providing sources for the final output.

The emergence of many content-generating AI models, e.g. *ChatGPT* [1], *Midjourney* [2], and *Artbreeder* [3], has sparked a revolution in various industries and applications. Initial issues related to accountability are generating scepticism and resistance towards the adoption of AI technologies: if people reject AI systems based on these early challenges, it could result in significant missed opportunities for innovation, efficiency, and societal progress, stifling innovation and impeding the potential benefits that AI can offer. AI-generated content has the potential to transform industries such as journalism, entertainment, education, and marketing, automating tasks and enabling new creative possibilities. AI can indubitably save time and resources, leading to increased productivity and economic growth. AI-generated content can help address global challenges, such as providing access to information and educational resources in underserved areas or creating sample synthetic data sets for domains of research where there is a lack of data (e.g., see Fig. 1 for a transformation of the facial emotion expression of a given image), and where collecting or accessing data may arise ethical issues

Fig. 1. Example of synthetic data transformation of emotional faces made with Artbreeder, [3] starting from a given image (on the left) to a happier one (in the center) and an angry one (on the right), which in this case inherited a cartoonish style from the training data and discrimination model.

Fig. 2. Example of synthetic data of emotional faces created with Midjourney [2].

(e.g., collecting data about unpleasant emotions, [4] which cannot be aroused on purpose, and would be difficult to track, see Fig. 2).

It is critical to understand that the early adoption of AI technologies will unavoidably be fraught with difficulties. These problems, however, ought to be viewed as chances for development rather than as objections. Governments and stakeholders should put their attention on finding solutions for these problems through research, development, and collaboration rather than ignoring or limiting AI. AI can be used responsibly by developing *glass-box* systems (i.e., supporting additional information to black-box systems, especially for algorithm training), establishing ethical standards, and putting transparency measures in place. This will pave the way for a time when AI-generated content is both accountable and useful. Such a direction could be more beneficial than just avoiding any copyrighted use of AI-generated content.

While the United States government decided that in the USA it is not legit to claim copyright on any document (e.g., text, image, music) generated by AI, [5] ten companies, including *OpenAI*, *TikTok*, *Adobe*, the *BBC*, and *Bumble*, have signed up for a new set of guidelines on building, creating, and sharing AI-generated content responsibly, in the *Partnership on AI* (PAI), an AI research nonprofit [6]. PAI suggestions urge both technology developers and creators and distributors of digitally-created synthetic media to be more open about what the technology can and cannot do, as well as to disclose when people may be interacting with this type of content. The same direction is taken by many researchers, associations, and editors, highlighting such clarity as a relevant outcome of any AI-related research. One of the most essential aspects of the PAI guidelines is the companies' agreement to include research methods to notify users when they are interacting with something generated by AI. A crucial aspect of the guidelines is the commitment of the participating companies to explore and implement methods to inform users when they are engaging with AI-generated content. Potential approaches include the use of watermarks, disclaimers, or traceable elements in the AI model's training data or metadata, highlighting the importance of both transparency and user awareness in the responsible deployment of AI-generated content.

In this paper, the recent development of AI Ethics will be studied providing novel laws and guidelines, and then the state of the art is provided for scientific research on the topic. Some considerations are added to each proposal, and examples are provided of critical issues that remain unsolved. Final conclusions are then drawn.

2 Recent Development of AI Ethics

In recent years, there have been several key developments and milestones in the field of AI ethics. In November 2021, UNESCO's General Conference adopted the Recommendation on the Ethics of Artificial Intelligence, which is the first-ever global standard-setting instrument on the subject [9]. This recommendation aims to protect and promote human rights and human dignity and serves as an ethical guiding compass for building respect for the rule of law in the digital world.

The European Commission suggested a regulation establishing harmonized rules on artificial intelligence (Artificial Intelligence Act) [10] and amending certain Union legislative acts on April 21, 2021. The proposal seeks to guarantee that AI systems placed on and used in the Union market are safe and adhere to existing legislation on fundamental rights and Union values. It also aims to improve governance and effective enforcement of previously existing laws on fundamental rights and safety requirements applicable to AI systems and to facilitate the development of a single market for lawful, safe, and trustworthy AI applications while preventing market fragmentation. The final rules to be given are still unknown.

Such a plan establishes harmonized rules for the development, market placement, and use of AI systems in the European Union, based on a risk-based strategy. It suggests a single, future-proof definition of artificial intelligence (still not agreed upon), where certain particularly harmful AI practices are prohibited as violating Union values, while specific restrictions and safeguards are proposed in connection to certain law enforcement uses of remote biometric identification systems. The plan establishes a solid risk methodology for defining high-risk AI systems that endanger people's health and safety or fundamental rights. Before these AI systems can be introduced on the Union's market, they must comply with a set of mandatory requirements for trustworthy AI, and conformity assessment processes. No rules are given for researchers, yet.

The ongoing efforts by various organizations and initiatives to establish ethical guidelines and best practices for AI development and deployment, engaging in dialogue with various stakeholders [6], will ideally develop practical solutions for ensuring that AI technologies benefit people and society.

The U.S. Copyright Office has launched an initiative to examine the copyright law and policy issues raised by artificial intelligence (AI) technology [5]. This includes the scope of copyright in works generated using AI tools and the use of copyrighted materials in AI training. The Office convened public listening sessions in the first half of 2023 to gather information about current technologies and their impact and published a notice of inquiry in the Federal Register. The current response is that no copyright can be claimed on AI-generated content.

On February 28, 2020, also the Vatican issued the *Rome Call for AI Ethics*, [15] a document agreed upon by Catholics and leaders of other religions, together with experts from *IBM*, *Microsoft*, and other scientists, outlining six main principles that they all agree should be followed to ensure that AI does not damage humanity, i.e.: Transparency, Inclusion, Accountability, Impartiality, Reliability, Security (and Privacy). The idea is to foster a feeling of shared responsibility among international organizations, governments, institutions, and the private sector to establish a future in which digital innovation and technological progress give humanity primacy.

3 Literature Review of Ethics in AI

The scientific literature on AI ethics has identified several key principles and challenges related to the development and deployment of AI systems. Transparency, privacy, accountability, and fairness are among the most commonly cited principles, while lack of ethical knowledge and vague principles are significant challenges for considering ethics in AI.

A systematic literature review of AI ethics principles and challenges conducted by Khan et al. [11] revealed that the global convergence set consists of 22 ethical principles and 15 challenges. A lack of ethical knowledge and vague principles were reported as significant challenges for considering ethics in AI.

The study also found that there is still debate about the implications of these principles and that various research organizations, lawyers, think-tankers, and regulatory bodies are involved in developing AI ethics guidelines and principles. The findings of this study are preliminary inputs for proposing a maturity model that assesses the ethical capabilities of AI systems and provides best practices for further improvements.

However, recent studies have found that the current guidelines created for AI ethics are ineffective and are not being implemented in practice, with no impact on ethical decisions [12,13]. There are no tools, methods, or frameworks that bridge the gap between AI concepts and their practical application. More research in this area is needed to discuss AI ethics principles, and challenges, providing evaluation standards and models that guide the AI industry in considering ethics in practice.

Thilo Hagendorff's *The Ethics of AI Ethics: An Evaluation of Guidelines* [14] evaluates 22 key AI ethics guidelines and makes recommendations on how to overcome their relative ineffectiveness. While AI ethics guidelines have been created in recent years to gather principles that technology developers should adhere to, the author contends that these guidelines frequently lack methods to reinforce their own normative claims. The article contends that researchers, politicians, consultants, managers, and activists must address this fundamental flaw in ethics and offers suggestions for improving the efficacy of AI ethics guidelines. Researchers in the field of AI are not considered in the list of relevant subjects for this sensitization idea.

Madhulika Srikumar et al.'s article *Advancing ethics review practices in AI research*, published in Nature Machine Intelligence in 2022, [16] discusses the adoption of ethics review procedures as an important first step in anticipating and mitigating the potential harms of AI research. The authors contend that long-term success will necessitate a coordinated community effort to support experimentation with various ethics review procedures, study their impact, and provide opportunities for diverse voices from the community to share insights and foster norms.

4 Discussion and Considerations on Unsolved Issues

4.1 General Discussion

In the scientific works and the recent contributions from various governments, considered in the previous sections, governments are almost always considered the main guarantors for ethics in AI, but the shortcoming of this point of view is trivially clear: governments can only legislate after they are aware of existing problems on AI, whereas only researchers in public or private universities and private or supranational research organisations have a real grasp of the problems before they already have the first side effects on society.

Among the others, the Vatican Rome call actually hopes for the emergence of a completely new discipline, i.e. *algorethics*, which is defined as the ethics of algorithms shared by all actors and contains both scientific knowledge and ethical principles as prerequisites for the new knowledge required to ensure AI ethics. This goal seems a long way off: good for raising awareness, but with no immediate practical application.

Scientific research in this matter, instead, provides several works on specific issues, e.g., gender bias, [17] dataset bias [8], overconfidence in AI systems, [7]. Researchers are thus called now, more than ever, at speaking, explaining, and publishing their contribution to the better ethical management of Artificial Intelligence. A critical effort is nowadays invested by researchers in the field of AI to support neural networks and other black-box systems to provide additional information [18] to support the output with sources to guarantee accountability [19] or make the process of data elaboration and classification transparent [20] and explainable, with the recent creation of a new branch of AI called *explanable AI* [21].

4.2 Unsolved Issues and Considerations

The issues that remain unsolved and untreated in the public debate for practical solutions are numerous. The current high hype of ChatGPT, which is arising in acknowledgement of how generative neural networks work and are used to generate content for the final user, highlighted the most evident issues. E.g., there is an objective gap in the law about how to treat the copyright (used in the USA to protect creative products) or author's rights (as it is called in Europe) for content generated by Artificial Intelligence. The US government decided that the personal contribution of the author to write the prompt instructions for the content generation is not enough to state the copyright, because this law is meant to protect personal creations and not ones made by machines. Other countries don't agree and are discussing finding a good compromise, which looks difficult because of the borderline situation, where deciding how much personal creative contribution is generally needed to use a command prompt to generate consistent creations using AI.

A similar problem for copyright can be found by looking at the problem of content generation from a bottom-up point of view: if the content is generated using an algorithm which is trained on material covered by copyright, does the generated document infringe such copyright? The answer could not be trivial: in fact, the main gap is the lack of knowledge about the training data (see the example in Fig. 3 and actual seed image fed as a starting point, used for the generation of a particular document, which is not possible to retrieve for standard black-box neural networks.

Fig. 3. Example of image generated with Midjourney [2] in the style of Van Gogh. Can the application by AI of the style of an existing author infringe the author's copyright? What if a manually painted image is fed to the algorithm as a starting point, will it be as if the image is modified with an editing software?

Furthermore, the hype of generative neural networks is rising interest in almost each and every discipline and field of application: when everybody speaks about generative AI, most of them will speak without the necessary background knowledge, providing the public with countless imprecisions and mistakes that spread virally in the interpretation of the problem, of the right way to use the AI tools, of the goals and skills of generative AI, and, last but not least, of the dangers of AI, which is often seen as the production of a singularity that will self-train, rule the worlds and destroy humanity. Such surreal concerns stemming from an imperfect and insufficient knowledge of the issue are generating

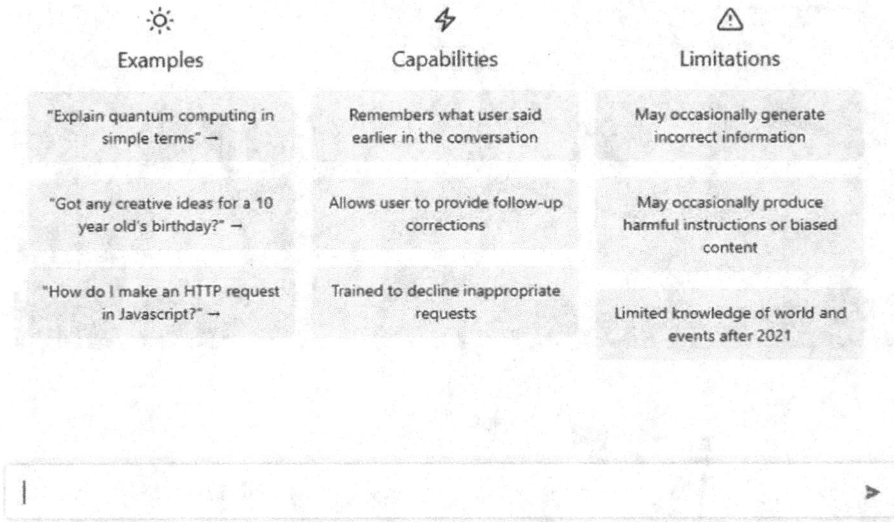

Fig. 4. Homepage of ChatGPT [1]. On the right side the warning about the AI limitations is visible, listing incorrect information, harmful instructions, biased content, and limited knowledge among the potential output results.

serious misunderstandings in the general public and in everyday discussions in the media, which tend to exaggerate in stirring up clickbait controversy. This resonance effect could lead to disdain and rejection by many of the artificial intelligence tools that are being studied to improve the lives of mankind, e.g. in the fields of medicine and wellness. Already today, there is much resistance in the public to believing that what appears to be made to replace human intelligence rather than, as is more correct, to support decision-making or improve the productivity of jobs that are humanly difficult to sustain over a long period of time because they are mentally or physically exhausting. This misunderstanding is producing a rejection similar to that of the AI dark ages of the 1980s, but at a time when the development of AI cannot be slowed down without extreme side effects in research and development.

The need to regulate, rather than AI, the communication and dissemination of information on AI is therefore increasingly evident, to convey correct information in a way that is useful to avoid misuse or inconsistent fears with uncontrolled consequences. A clear example of the need of a different approach to communication is the fact that people do not read the rules and articles of agreement to which they are asked to consent, nut just automatically click the consent button with no clue of its consequences, and then complain about alleged rights they

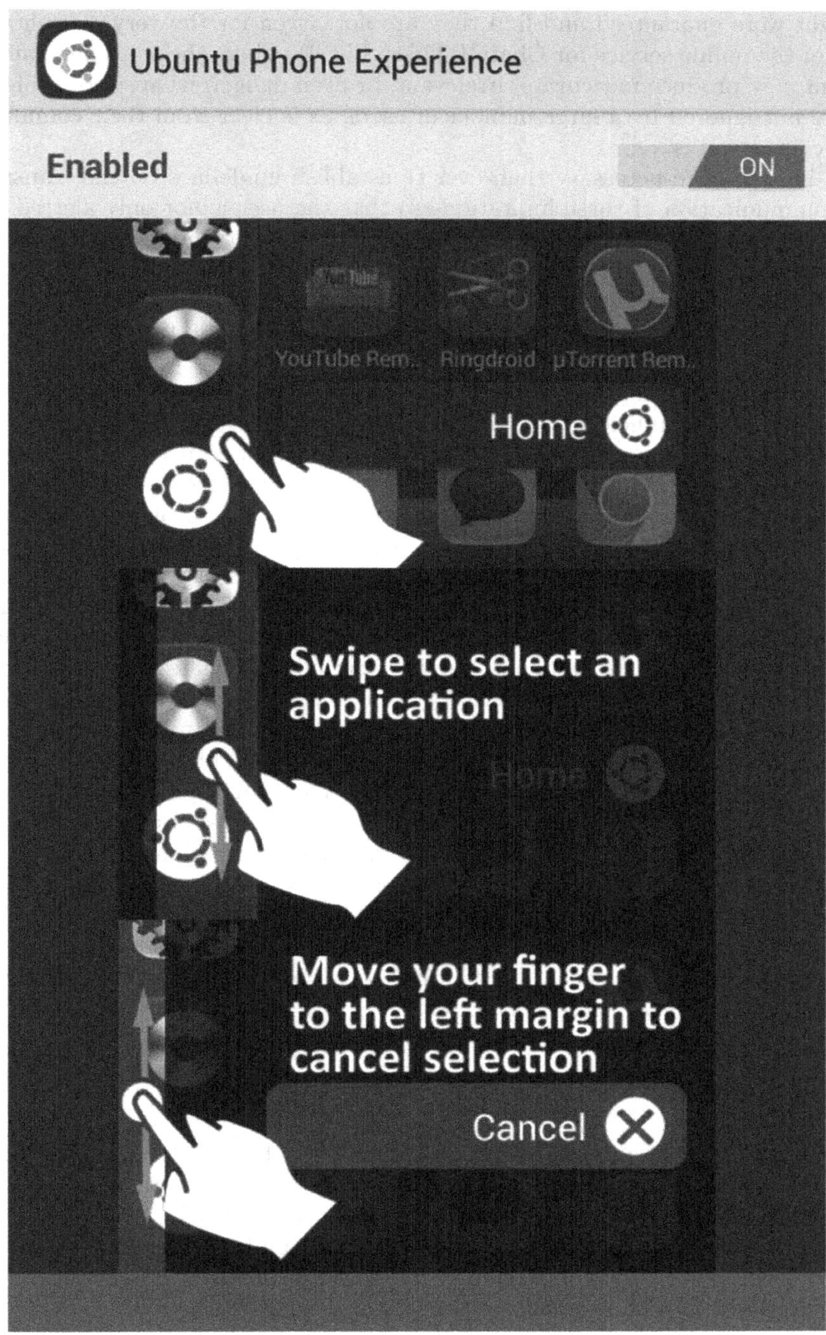

Fig. 5. UI design of a tutorial (in this case, for the Ubuntu phone experience) for the first-time use of an app.

thought were guaranteed and find they are not. Even for the very clear homepage of the online service for ChatGPT (see Fig. 4), where the warning that the system may produce inaccurate, irrelevant, or even dangerous answers is highly visible but ignored by a large number of users, as is clear from their comments on social networks.

It is now more necessary than ever to establish guidelines on the transparent communication of these limitations so that the user is not only alerted but aware of them. One modality could be taken from the tutorials often used for user-interface design when first opening an interface (see the example in Fig. 5), constraining the user to interact with the information provided to him by checking its comprehension (e.g., with clicks, answering basic questions, or gamification).

Concerning misuse, then, a distinction must be made. On the one hand, there is misuse due to insufficient training, for which developers and companies operating AI tools have declared themselves frightened and for which they are already fighting back with guidelines, training, debates and scientific dissemination. On the other hand, there is deliberate misuse, which is already forbidden by law and is not the responsibility of the developers, except perhaps in a tiny part. We can compare this problem to that of developing a bottle: the bottle is designed to contain a liquid and not to be (or not to be) used as a blunt weapon. If there are contexts and situations where it is necessary to regulate to prevent misuse, e.g. by preventing people from entering the stadium with glass bottles or corked water bottles, it is certainly not the duty of bottle designers to put a disclaimer on the label announcing not to throw the bottle at people. In fact, this use is so clearly conscious of illegality that no responsibility can be placed on the designer of the object. The same can be said about AI ethics. On the one hand, it is certainly necessary to train users to correct and conscious use, but surely it must be considered apart from any deliberately criminal use that should be made of generative AI tools, e.g. to generate the animation of a face and make him speak words that he did not say pretending that it is an original video. Such criminal uses are the responsibility of the user and not of the researcher or designer and it is unlikely to expect that a tool will not be made available to the public if it does not prevent any misuse of this kind.

5 Conclusions

The current hype of generative AI raised concerns about Artificial Intelligence that could lead to rejecting AI. There are evident gaps in laws and rules for several issues, e.g., providing sources for content created using generative AIs, copyright, fair use, and education or dissemination of information, among others. Research is the only stage of development where it is possible to intervene before the side effects of AI on society spread.

It is paramount that a debate about ethics in AI is raised among researchers, to avoid misuse and misinformation that could lead to the rejection of AI by the general public opinion. It is important to distinguish misuse due to a lack of education and information from the voluntary and conscious criminal use of AI tools and provide different solutions to different cases.

Among the issues raised by the recent hype of generative AI, there is the need for a glass-box approach, considering explainable AI to support data for checking the sources, to avoid breach of copyright, and to guarantee the security and privacy of information protected by law.

6 Ethical Statements

AI has been used to support this paper in image generation (i.e., Midjourney), information retrieval (i.e., Bing), language correctness, clarity (i.e., Grammarly), and text translation (i.e., DeepL). No textual content has been included which is generated by AI and not creatively and professionally elaborated by the author's human mind. Figure 5 is under IPRight policy and its use is free, provided that it is clear that this paper is in no way speaking for or on behalf of Canonical and that there is no endorsement by Canonical for this paper. The author acknowledges support by PRIN "PHRAME" Grant n. 20178XXKFY.

References

1. https://openai.com/blog/chatgpt
2. https://www.midjourney.com/
3. https://www.artbreeder.com/
4. Franzoni, V., Biondi, G., Milani, A.: A web-based system for emotion vector extraction. In: Gervasi, O., et al. (eds.) ICCSA 2017. LNCS, vol. 10406, pp. 653–668. Springer, Cham (2017). https://doi.org/10.1007/978-3-319-62398-6_46
5. https://copyright.gov/ai/
6. https://syntheticmedia.partnershiponai.org/
7. Franzoni, V., Vallverdù, J., Milani, A.: Errors, biases and overconfidence in artificial emotional modeling. In IEEE/WIC/ACM International Conference on Web Intelligence-Companion Volume, pp. 86–90. (2019, October)
8. Franzoni, V., Biondi, G., Milani, A.: Defining classification ambiguity to discover a potential bias applied to emotion recognition data sets. In 2022 IEEE/WIC/ACM International Joint Conferences on Web Intelligence (WI) and Intelligent Agent Technologies (IAT). IEEE (2022 December)
9. https://www.unesco.org/en/artificial-intelligence/recommendation-ethics
10. https://eur-lex.europa.eu/legal-content
11. Khan, A. A, et al,: Ethics of AI: A systematic literature review of principles and challenges. arXiv preprint arXiv:2109.07906 (2021)
12. Vakkuri, V., Kemell, K.-K.: Implementing AI ethics in practice: an empirical evaluation of the RESOLVEDD strategy. In: Hyrynsalmi, S., Suoranta, M., Nguyen-Duc, A., Tyrväinen, P., Abrahamsson, P. (eds.) ICSOB 2019. LNBIP, vol. 370, pp. 260–275. Springer, Cham (2019). https://doi.org/10.1007/978-3-030-33742-1_21
13. Ray Eitel-Porte. Beyond the promise: implementing ethical AI. AI Ethics **1**(1) 73–80 (2021)
14. Hagendorff, T.: The ethics of AI ethics: an evaluation of guidelines. Minds Mach. **30**, 99–120 (2020)

15. https://www.romecall.org/the-call/
16. Srikumar, M., et al.: Advancing ethics review practices in AI research. Nat. Mach. Intell. **4**, 1061–1064 (2022)
17. Franzoni, V.: Gender differences and bias in artificial intelligence. In: Vallverdú, J. (ed.) Gender in AI and Robotics. Intelligent Systems Reference Library, vol. 235. Springer, Cham (2023). https://doi.org/10.1007/978-3-031-21606-0_2
18. Räukur, T., Ho, A., Casper, S., Hadfield-Menell, D.: Toward transparent ai: A survey on interpreting the inner structures of deep neural networks. arXiv preprint arXiv:2207.13243 (2022)
19. Kim, B., Park, J., Suh, J.: Transparency and accountability in AI decision support: explaining and visualizing convolutional neural networks for text information. Decis. Supp. Syst. **134**, 113302 (2020)
20. Wang, J., Liu, H., Wang, X., Jing, L.: Interpretable image recognition by constructing transparent embedding space. In: Proceedings of the IEEE/CVF International Conference on Computer Vision, pp. 895–904 (2021)
21. Xu, F., Uszkoreit, H., Du, Y., Fan, W., Zhao, D., Zhu, J.: Explainable AI: a brief survey on history, research areas, approaches and challenges. In: Tang, J., Kan, M.-Y., Zhao, D., Li, S., Zan, H. (eds.) NLPCC 2019. LNCS (LNAI), vol. 11839, pp. 563–574. Springer, Cham (2019). https://doi.org/10.1007/978-3-030-32236-6_51

13th International Workshop on Future Computing System Technologies and Applications (FiSTA 2023)

Towards a Dynamic Computation Offloading Mechanism with Twin Delayed DDPG in Edge Computing

Aiichiro Oga and Bernady O. Apduhan(✉)

Department of Information Science, Kyushu Sangyo University, Fukuoka, Japan
k20rs023@st.kyusan-u.ac.jp, bob@is.kyusan-u.ac.jp

Abstract. A potential pitfall of edge computing is that processing delays occur when the load is concentrated on a single edge server. To alleviate this issue, computation offloading technology has been proposed to solve this problem. In this research, we aim to realize an efficient computation offloading for edge server load balancing and real-time processing by an offloading mechanism using Twin Delayed DDPG (TD3) algorithm. In the preliminary experiment, the offload destination was determined by considering the location information, load ratio, and CPU utilization of the offload destination edge server, and using DDPG reinforcement learning algorithm. In the main experiments, we used the TD3 reinforcement learning algorithm. The experiments results show that higher episodic reward and learning stability can be achieved by using TD3 with the optimal noise parameters applied compared to DDPG.

Keywords: Computation Offloading · Edge Computing · Twin Delayed DDPG (TD3)

1 Introduction

1.1 Background of Research

In recent years, the Internet of Things (IoT), a technology that connects objects in various industries to the Internet, such as home appliances, industrial robots, and factory line maintenance, in addition to Internet terminals such as PCs and smartphones, is being utilized. Due to this influence, the number of such Internet-connected objects (IoT devices) is expected to further increase in the future. Cloud computing is currently being used as the technology to process the large amount of data generated by IoT devices. Cloud computing is a service that allows users to use software and applications over a network on an on-demand basis. However, as the number of IoT devices being used increases, data transmission capacity grows, and there are problems such as communication delays caused by the squeeze on communication bandwidth and the difficulty in responding to real-time requests due to the distance to the cloud data center.

Edge computing is a technology that has been attracting attention to addressing such issues. Edge computing is a technology in which an edge server is installed near

O. Gervasi et al. (Eds.): ICCSA 2023 Workshops, LNCS 14107, pp. 133–149, 2023.
https://doi.org/10.1007/978-3-031-37114-1_10

a device, and the edge server processes data and tasks emitted by the device on behalf of the device. Since edge computing allows processing to be performed near the device, it allows for more real-time processing than cloud computing via the Internet and can reduce communication delays between the device and the cloud server. In addition, since processing can be performed solely on the edge server, it is possible to reduce the amount of communication by sending only the processing results to the cloud server without overloading the network. However, the problem of processing delays caused by the concentration of load on a single edge server has been cited. To solve this problem, a technique called computation offloading was considered.

Computation offloading is a technology that reduces the load on the main system by transferring part of the processing to an external system [6–10]. Research is being conducted to solve the edge computing problem by transferring the processing of one edge server to another edge server to reduce the load.

1.2 Research Objective

The objective of this study is to achieve efficient computation offloading, which is a real-time processing of tasks and load balancing of edge servers by an offloading mechanism using deep reinforcement learning to solve the processing delays on edge servers. We will verify whether the offload mechanism using deep reinforcement learning learns optimal offloading decisions and behaves in a way that increases rewards.

The paper is organized as follows. In Sect. 2, we provide a brief review of related technologies. Section 3 cites related research, while Sect. 4 describes the system model and experiment environment. Sections 5 and 6 describe experiments with DDPG and TD3, respectively. Lastly, Sect. 7 discusses our concluding remarks and cites future work.

2 Review of Related Technologies

2.1 Deep Deterministic Policy Gradient(DDPG)

Deep Deterministic Policy Gradient (DDPG) is a deep reinforcement learning algorithm for handling continuous action spaces. DDPG is based on the deterministic policy gradient method because it is a method that applies deep reinforcement learning to the deterministic policy gradient method [1, 2]. While general policy learning methods maximize the expected reward, DDPG is characterized by maximizing the total estimated reward. The learning model of DDPG is shown in Fig. 1. First, the Actor outputs actions from the state, and Critic evaluates Actor's actions with the state and Actor's actions as input and outputs the value of the actions. Then, based on the evaluation from Critic, Actor updates the strategy and selects an action. By repeating these flows, the optimal behavior that can obtain more reward is learned.

In DDPG, the behavioral value function (Q function) is updated using the following target values. This equation represents the sum of the reward at time step t and the discounted future Q value. The future Q value is obtained from the target Critic network using as input the next states_(t + 1) and the action by the target policy in that state.

The DDPG Eq. 1:

$$Q_{target}(t) = r_t + \gamma Q_{target}(s_{t+1}, \pi'(s_{t+1})) \tag{1}$$

where,

- $\mathbf{r}_t$ is the reward at time step t
- γ is the discount rate
- $\mathbf{Q_{target}}$ $(\mathbf{s_{(t+1)}}, \boldsymbol{\pi}'(\mathbf{s_{(t+1)}}))$ is the **Q** value of the action of the target policy $\boldsymbol{\pi}'(\mathbf{s_{(t+1)}})$ in the next state's$_{\mathbf{(t+1)}}$ by the target Critic network.

Critic's loss function $\mathbf{L_{critic}}$ is then defined as the mean squared error between the **Q** value $\mathbf{Q(s_t,a_t)}$ predicted by the network and its target value $(\mathbf{r_t} + \boldsymbol{\gamma}\mathbf{Q_{target}}(\mathbf{s_{(t+1)}}, \boldsymbol{\mu}_{\mathbf{target}}(\mathbf{s_{(t+1)}})))$.

The DDPG Eq. 2:

$$L_{critic} = \frac{1}{N}\sum (r_t + \gamma Q_{target}(s_{t+1}, \mu_{target}(s_{t+1})) - Q(s_t, a_t))^2 \tag{2}$$

where,

- $\mathbf{r_t}$ is the reward at time step t.
- γ is the discount rate
- $\mathbf{Q_{target}}$ is the target Critic network.
- $\mathbf{s_{(t+1)}}$ is the next state.
- $\boldsymbol{\mu}_{\mathbf{target}}$ is the target Actor network (target policy)
- $\mathbf{a_t}$ is the action at time step t
- $\mathbf{Q(s_t,a_t)}$ is the Q value generated by the current Critic network.
- $\boldsymbol{\Sigma}$ represents the sum over all samples in the batch, and **N** is the batch size.

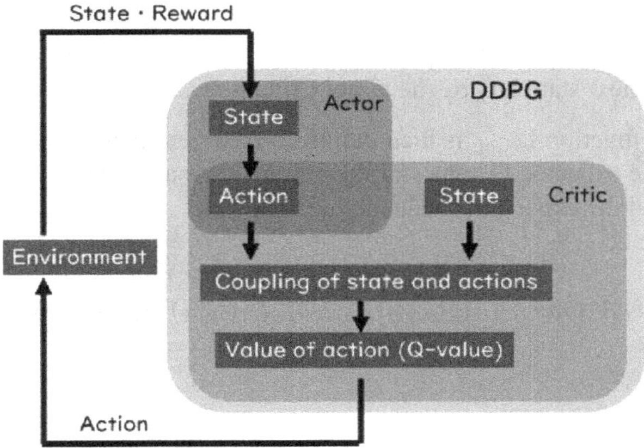

Fig. 1. The DDPG learning model.

2.2 The Twin Delayed Deep Deterministic Policy Gradient(TD3)

Twin Delayed Deep Deterministic Policy Gradient (hereinafter referred to as TD3) is one of the deep reinforcement learning algorithms in continuous action space. TD3 is an extension of Deep Deterministic Policy Gradient (hereinafter referred to as DDPG) and is designed to deal with the problem of overestimation of action value functions with noise [1]. The algorithm estimates the minimum value of the action value function using two independent networks of Critic and suppresses overestimation. In addition, to achieve smooth policy updates in the action space, noise is added to the actions from the target policy network, and the noise is clipped to stabilize the actions.

The learning model of TD3 is shown in Fig. 2. In the learning process of TD3, Actor generates actions from the state, and two Critics evaluate the value of the actions using the state and Actor's actions as inputs. In addition, the minimum value estimates obtained from the two Critic networks are used to update the policy. By delaying the timing of policy update, TD3 ensures that the learning of the value function is stable before updating the policy, thereby improving the learning stability. Through these original innovations, TD3 can achieve higher performance and stability in the continuous action space.

In TD3, the behavioral value function (Q function) is updated using the following target values. This equation represents the sum of the reward at time step t and the discounted future Q-value (the minimum of the outputs of the two target Critic networks). The future Q-value is obtained from each target Critic network using as input the next state and the action taken by the target policy in that state.

The TD3 Eq. 1:

$$Q_{target}(t) = r_t + \gamma min_{i=1,2}(Q_{i,target}(s_{t+1}, \pi'(s_{t+1}))) \tag{3}$$

where,

- $\mathbf{r_t}$ is the reward at time step t
- γ is the discount rate
- $\mathbf{min}_{i=1,2}$ $(\mathbf{Q}_{i,\, target}$ $(\mathbf{s_{t+1}}, \pi'(\mathbf{s_{t+1}})))$ are the $\mathbf{Q}$ values of the target policy π' $(\mathbf{s_{t+1}})$ actions in the next state $\mathbf{s_{t+1}}$ by the target Critic network respectively.

Critic's loss function L_{critic} is then defined as the goal that minimizes the squared error between the expected Q value for the current state and action and the sum of the actual reward and the expected Q value in the next state.

The TD3 Eq. 2:

$$L_{critic} = \sum (r_t + \gamma min_{i=1,2}(Q_{target}(s_{t+1}, \mu_{target}(s_{t+1}) + \mathrm{N}(0, \sigma))) - Q(s_t, a_t))^2 \tag{4}$$

where,

- $\mathbf{r_t}$ is the reward at time step t
- γ is the discount rate
- $\mathbf{min_{i=1,2}}$ $(\mathbf{Q_{target}}$ $(\mathbf{s_{t+1}}, \mathbf{\mu_{target}}$ $(\mathbf{s_{t+1}})$ + $\mathbf{N(0,\sigma)}))$ is the Q value of two target Critic networks for the action of target policy μ_{target} (s_{t+1}) plus noise N (samples from a

normal distribution with mean 0 and clipping value σ) in the following state. The smaller Q values of the two target Critic networks for the action of the target policy μ_{target}.

- $\mathbf{Q(s_t,a_t)}$ is the Q-value that the current Critic network predicts for state s_t and action a_t.

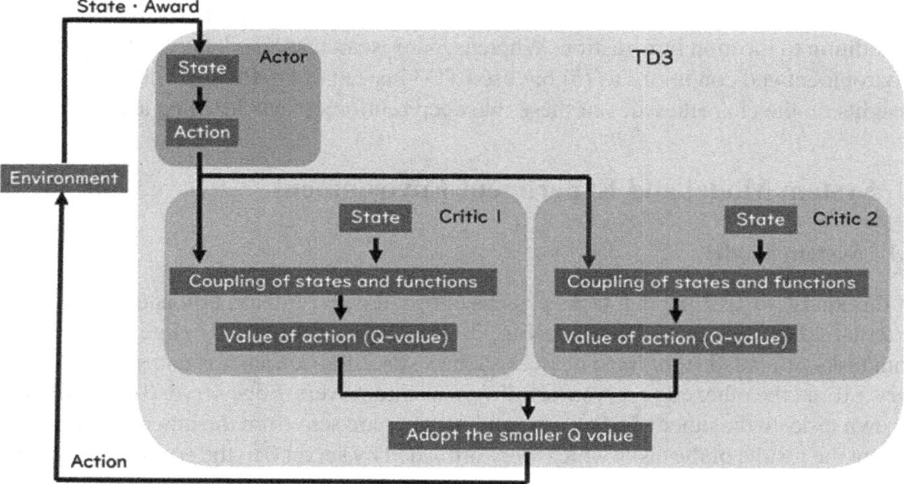

Fig. 2. The TD3 learning model.

3 Related Research

Yunzhao Li, et.al. [3] developed a system using the deep reinforcement learning algorithm DDPG for the problem of computational offloading with unbalanced edge server load, aiming to optimize computational offloading decisions. The system using the DDPG algorithm was compared with the Deep Q Network (DQN) algorithm and the Asynchronous Advantage Actor-Critic (A3C) algorithm to demonstrate the superiority of the system using the DDPG algorithm. This study was able to show the superiority of the system using the DDPG algorithm over the Deep Q Network (DQN) algorithm and the Asynchronous Advantage Actor-Critic (A3C) algorithm on a mobile edge computing environment.

Our research considers data consolidated into tasks from non-mobile devices, such as surveillance cameras and sensors, which can be offloaded to another edge server as the need arises.

Ide, S. [3] conducted research aimed at developing a high-performance edge computing system using the deep reinforcement learning algorithm DDPG to achieve both load balancing and real-time processing in edge computing. In developing the high-performance edge computing system, they investigated the problems that edge computing faces, studied methods to overcome the problems of conventional and related methods, verified the operation of the proposed method and evaluated its effectiveness. Likewise, they conducted a comprehensive review of both domestic and overseas related research papers. His research assumes that the optimal offload destination from a mobile to each edge server is determined based on the location information of the mobile (e.g., smartphone) and each edge server.

While Tsurumaru, R, et al.[5] share the same main research objectives and used DDPG algorithm with [4], his research attempts to determine the optimal offload destination from one edge server to another based on CPU, memory, and hard disk utilization in addition to location information. Whereas, our research adopted the same experiment environment and conditions as [5] but used TD3 instead of DDPG to evaluate and learn insights on the characteristics of these two deep reinforcements learning algorithms.

4 System Model and Experiment Environment

4.1 System Model

In this study, we assume that tasks possessed by edge server 0 are offloaded to multiple external edge servers, as shown in Fig. 3. The tasks possessed by edge server 0 are data/tasks offloaded from fixed devices such as surveillance cameras and sensors. Edge server 0 and the other edge servers are different edge servers. Edge server 0 only offloads its own tasks to the other edge servers, and no tasks are sent from the other edge servers, except the results of the tasks which were offloaded by server 0 to the concerned servers.

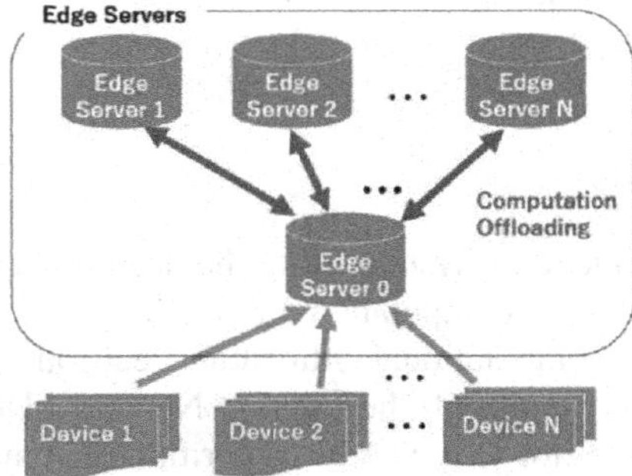

Fig. 3. Data consolidation and tasks offloading between edge servers.

4.2 Proposed Methodology

To perform efficient computation offloading from Edge Server 0, which possesses the task, to multiple external edge servers, we proposed a task offloading mechanism that makes continuous action decisions assuming a single-agent scenario with Broker Server as the agent. The interaction between the Broker Server and the environment is shown in Fig. 4.

To achieve complex decision making of the agent, a deep reinforcement learning algorithm Deep Deterministic Policy Gradient (DDPG) based on the Actor-Critic model is employed. The DDPG algorithm is capable of learning dynamic load-balancing policies because it is characterized by its ability to deal with continuous action spaces.

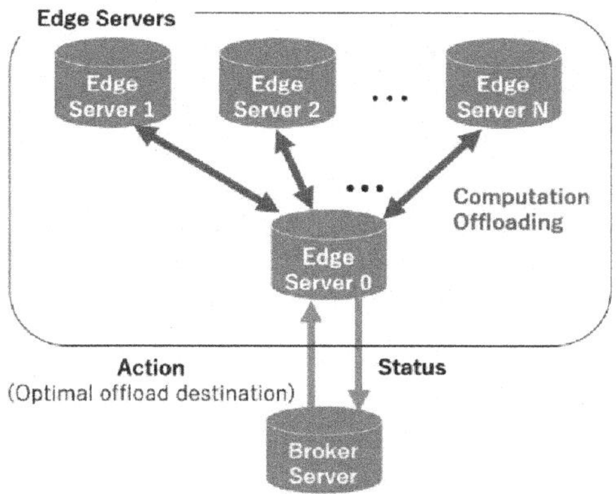

Fig. 4. Interaction between the broker server and concerned edge server.

4.3 Experiment Environment

See (Tables 1, 2 and 3)

Table 1. Machine Specifications

OS	Windows10 Home
CPU	Intel(R) Core(TM) i7-9700K CPU@3.60GHz
GPU	NVIDIA GeForce RTX2070 SUPER
Memory	16.00 GB
Storage	464 GB

5 Experiments with DDPG

5.1 Experiment Objective

In this experiment, we will assume an environment that is close to a real-world situation. That is, the edge server that owns the tasks makes the offloading decisions on which destination servers to offload and confirm whether the offloading mechanism can make the optimal offload decision.

Table 2. Software used in the experiments.

Package	Anaconda
Programming language	Python (ver3.7.1)
Integrated Development Environment (IDE)	PyCharm Community
Library	TensorFlow(ver2.3)

Table 3. Simulation Parameters

Parameter	Value
Learning Steps	3000steps
Data Size	50MB
Migration Bandwidth	1GB/s
No. of Tasks	90
No. of Edge Servers	10
Maximum number of simultaneous edge servers	10

5.2 Experiment Methods

In addition to the task size used in the preliminary experiments and numerical data on the location of each randomly generated edge server, numerical data on the CPU utilization, memory utilization, and hard disk utilization of randomly generated offload destination edge servers were input to the agent. The optimal offload destination is determined based on the utilization rate, memory utilization rate, hard disk utilization rate, load factor, and location information of each edge server. The experiments were conducted on a virtual edge computing environment. Here, the system administrator will set the parameters such as edge servers to be deployed in the environment and task size to be generated in advance (Table 4).

5.3 Results and Discussion

In addition to the location information and load ratio of each edge server, the system was tested to see if it could make optimal offload destination decisions considering the CPU utilization, memory utilization, and hard disk utilization of the offload destination edge servers. Tasks are assumed to be those generated by fixed devices such as surveillance cameras and sensors. We defined the reward value to increase or decrease depending on the number of tasks processed, as well as to provide an additional reward if the offloading decision is made to an edge server with the lowest CPU utilization, memory utilization, and hard disk utilization (less than 50%).

Figure 5 shows the average of the results of 10 experiments for the value of the reward per episode obtained from the training in this experiment. The rewards increased with each successive episode. The learning was terminated when the reward was about

Table 4. DDPG Model Parameters

Parameter	Value
No. of Layers	5
Activation Function	ReLu Function
Actor Learning Rate	1.0×10^{-4}
Critic Learning Rate	2.0×10^{-4}
Discount Rate	0.9
Soft Update Renewal Rate	1.0×10^{-2}
Experience Replay Buffer Size	1.0×10^{4}
Batch Size	32

202,000, because the learning was set to terminate when the maximum reward value was not updated in the last 30 episodes, and the learning was completed (Table 5 and Fig. 6).

Table 5. Summary of results of 10 studies using DDPG

Average number of overall episodes	308.30
Mean value of rewards for the last 30 episodes	199393.80
Median reward of last 30 episodes	199330
Mode of reward of last 30 episodes	198203
Standard deviation of the reward of the last 30 episodes	2534.86
Range of the reward of the last 30 episodes (difference between the maximum and minimum values)	10005
Number of times the mean value of the reward of the last 30 episodes exceeded 198000	7 times

The average amount of reward in the last 30 episodes was 199393.80, with an average number of episodes of 308. Sometimes the study ended with a small number of episodes near 100 and other times with many episodes near 500, and the nature of the graph of averages shows a variation in rewards in the latter part of the study where the population of data is small.

It can be observed that the value of rewards obtained from the environment increases as the episodes progress. This suggests that an appropriate offloading policy is being learned. The increase in the reward value indicates that the system can process many tasks, and that it is successfully learning an appropriate offload policy considering the CPU utilization, memory utilization, and hard disk utilization of the edge server where the offload is to be performed. It is thought that the system can successfully perform

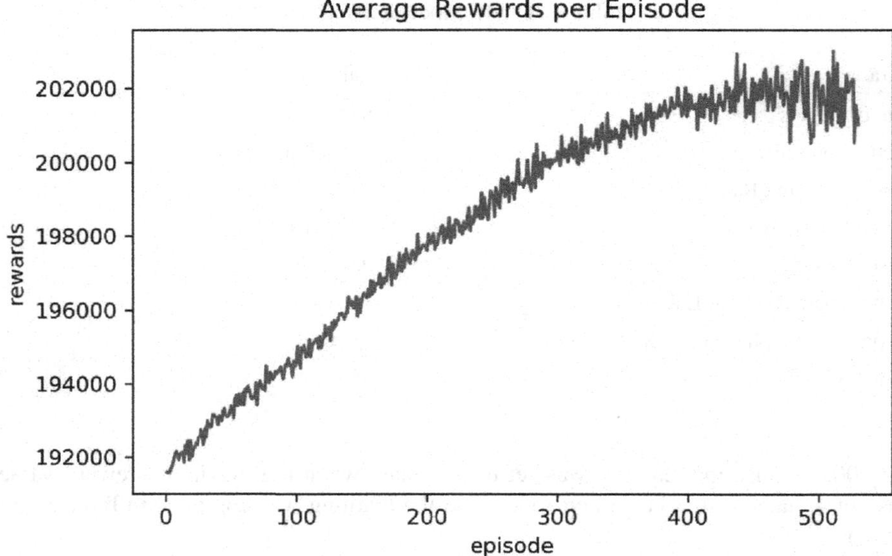

Fig. 5. Average reward of 10 times per episode for the reward of learning results using DDPG (Vertical axis: average amount of reward/horizontal axis: number of episodes)

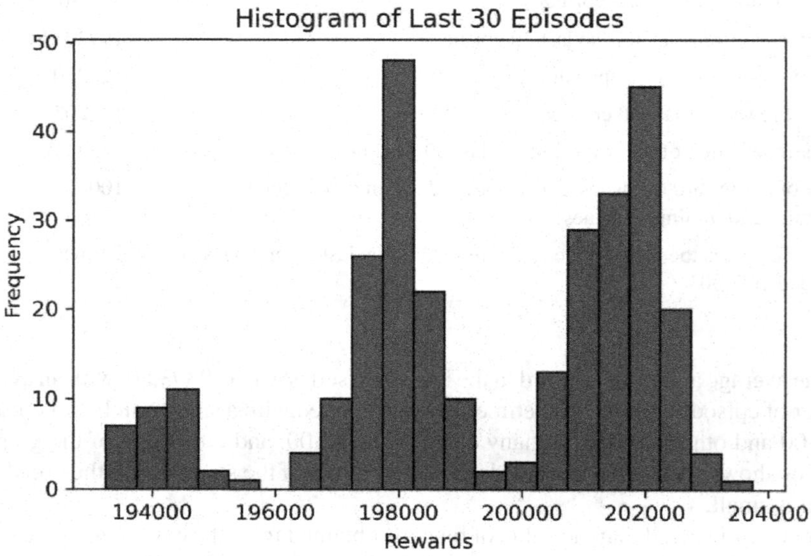

Fig. 6. Histogram summarizing the amount of reward for the last 30 episodes of the 10 learning results using DDPG

learning considering the CPU utilization, memory utilization, and hard disk utilization of the offload destination edge server.

As can be seen from the histogram, the most frequent reward for the last 30 episodes was around 198000, followed by 202000, with a slight outlier appearing around 194000. It is clear that the learning process is relatively stable. Thereafter, we will use 198000, which was the most frequent final reward for DDPG, as a baseline to see if the TD3 reward exceeds this value.

6 Experiments with TD3

We conducted experiments on the same simulation environment using the Twin Delayed DDPG reinforcement learning algorithm.

6.1 The TD3 model parameters

See Table 6.

Table 6. TD3 model parameters

Parameter	Value
No. of layers	5
Activation function	ReLu function
Actor Learning rate	1.0×10^{-4}
Critic Learning rate	2.0×10^{-4}
Discount rate	0.9
Soft Update Renewal rate	1.0×10^{-2}
Experience Replay Buffer size	1.0×10^{4}
Batch size	32
Policy Network Delay Update Interval	2
Clipping value of action noise	0.5–0.6
Standard deviation of action noise	0.2–0.3

6.2 Experiments and Results

To search for the optimal noise parameters, we set the clipping value of the action noise to 0.5 or 0.6 and the standard deviation of the action noise to 0.2 or 0.3. Rewards increase as the episodes progress. The learning was completed when the amount of reward was between 202,000 and approximately 204,000 without updating the previous maximum reward in the last 30 episodes, and when the reward was judged to be stable and high. The following are the learning results for each noise parameter.

6.2.1 TD3 (Noise Clipping Value 0.5, Standard Deviation of Noise 0.2)

See (Table 7, Figs. 7 and 8).

Table 7. Summary of the results of 10 training sessions with TD3 (noise = 0.5/0.2)

Average number of overall episodes	266.50
Mean value of rewards for the last 30 episodes	198383.69
Median reward of last 30 episodes	199278.5
Mode of reward of last 30 episodes	199267
Standard deviation of the reward of the last 30 episodes	3232.94
Range of the reward of the last 30 episodes (difference between the maximum and minimum values)	11131
Number of times the mean value of the reward of the last 30 episodes exceeded 198000	6 times

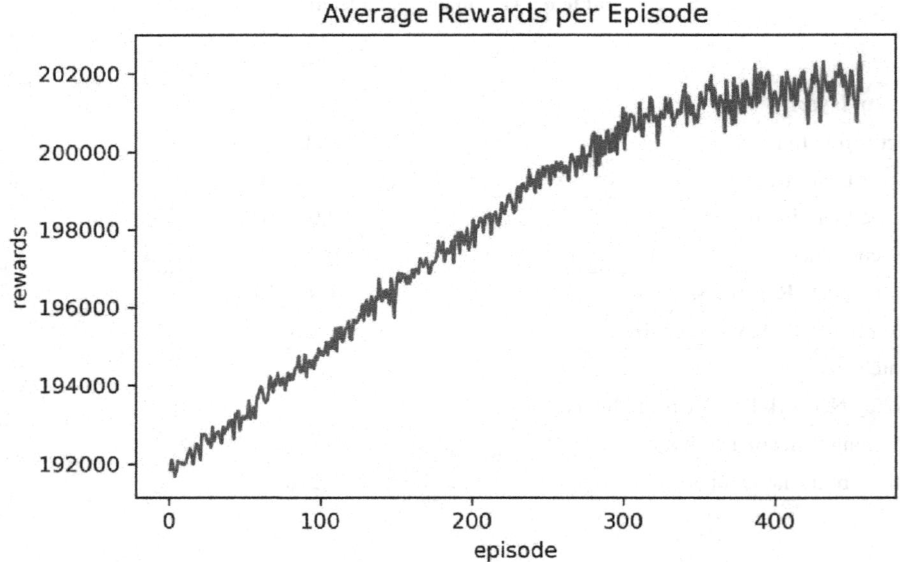

Fig. 7. Reward for learning results using TD3 (noise = 0.5/0.2), Average reward for 10 times per episode (vertical axis: average amount of reward/horizontal axis: number of episodes)

The learning was performed with a clipping value of 0.5 for noise and a standard deviation of 0.2 for noise, with an average reward value of 198383.69 for the last 30 episodes and an average of 266.50 for the number of episodes. The histogram shows a noticeable mountain of learning that was terminated early. It is inferred that the noise was too small, and the search was not sufficient, resulting in a locally optimal solution.

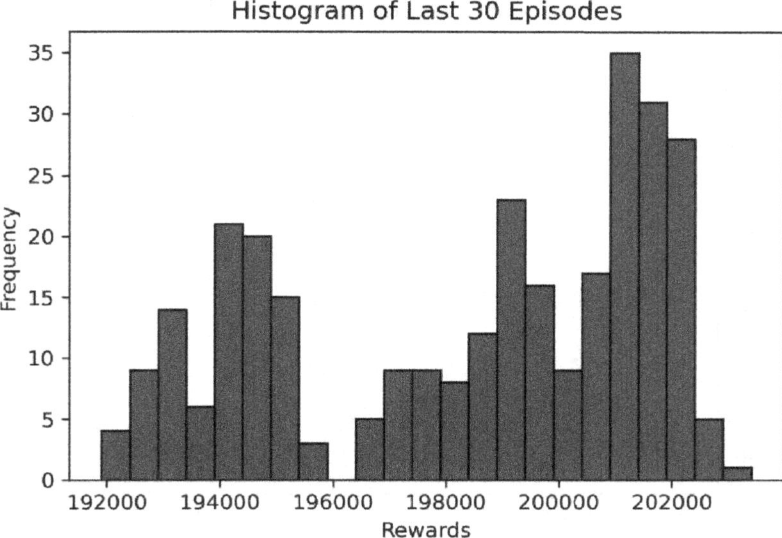

Fig. 8. Histogram summarizing the amount of reward for the last 30 episodes of the 10 learning results using TD3 (noise = 0.5/0.2)

The most frequent reward amount was around 201000, which is an improvement compared to DDPG, but the number of times it was below 198000, the DDPG's most frequent value, increased, raising questions about its stability.

6.2.2 TD3 (Clipping Value of Noise 0.5, Standard Deviation of Noise 0.3)

See Table 8 and Figs. 9 and 10.

Table 8. Summary of 10 training results using TD3 (noise = 0.5/0.3)

Average number of overall episodes	351.00
Mean value of rewards for the last 30 episodes	199606.51
Median reward of last 30 episodes	201058.5
Mode of reward of last 30 episodes	201104
Standard deviation of the reward of the last 30 episodes	3239.91
Range of the reward of the last 30 episodes (difference between the maximum and minimum values)	11842
Number of times the mean value of the reward of the last 30 episodes exceeded 198000	9 times

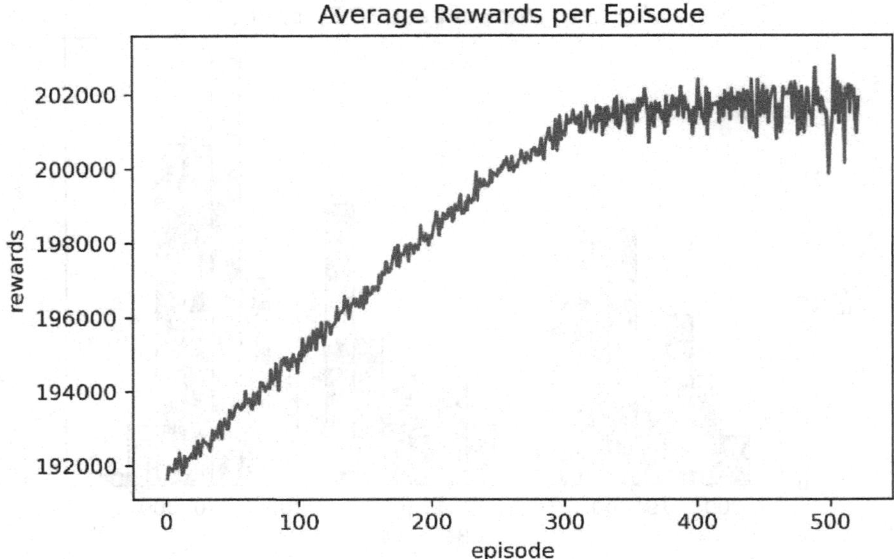

Fig. 9. Reward for learning results using TD3 (noise = 0.5/0.3), Average reward for 10 times per episode (vertical axis: average amount of reward/horizontal axis: number of episodes)

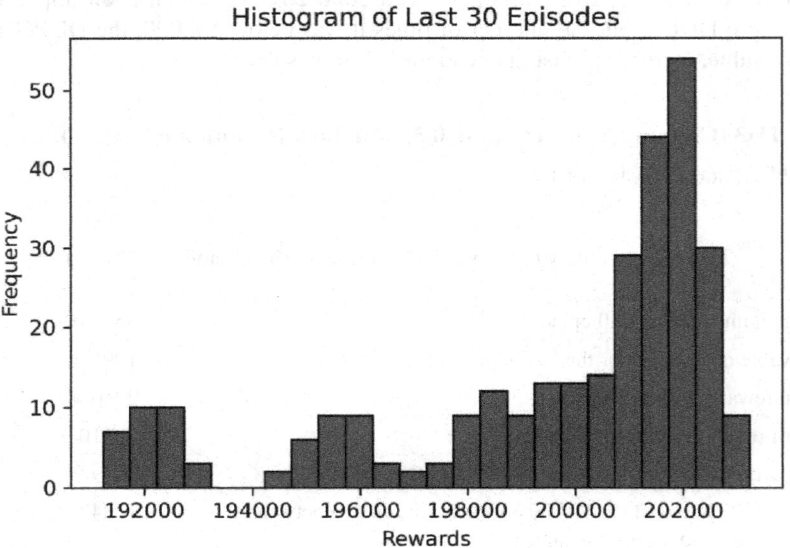

Fig. 10. The rewards of the learning results using TD3 (noise = 0.5/0.3), Histogram summarizing the amount of reward for the last 30 episodes of the 10

(Noise clipping value 0.5, standard deviation of noise 0.3), resulting in an average reward of 199606.51 for the last 30 episodes and 351 for the total number of episodes. As can be seen from the histogram, high episodic rewards were obtained consistently.

The average episode reward exceeded 198,000 9 out of 10 times, making it difficult to find outliers. In addition, the average reward was higher than that of DDPG in all comparisons of the number of episodes (200, 300, 400, and 500 episodes).

6.2.3 TD3 (Clipping Value of Noise 0.6, Standard Deviation of Noise 0.2)

See Table 9 and Figs. 11 and 12.

Table 9. Summary of 10 training results using TD3 (noise = 0.6/0.2)

Average number of overall episodes	314.20
Mean value of rewards for the last 30 episodes	199052.55
Median reward of last 30 episodes	200003
Mode of reward of last 30 episodes	200151
Standard deviation of the reward of the last 30 episodes	3457.62
Range of the reward of the last 30 episodes (difference between the maximum and minimum values)	12907
Number of times the mean value of the reward of the last 30 episodes exceeded 198000	7 times

(Noise clipping value of 0.6, standard deviation of noise of 0.2) was used for training, and the average amount of reward for the last 30 episodes was 19,952, and the overall episode count average was 314.20. As can be seen from the histogram.

The most frequent reward volume is around 203,000. Increasing the noise (clipping value of noise 0.5, standard deviation of noise 0.3) resulted in the mountains shifting to the right and higher rewards compared to (clipping value of noise 0.5, standard deviation of noise 0.3). However, it can also be observed that learning is more often terminated prematurely at 192000–194000. The number of times the average episodic reward exceeded 198000 was slightly less than 7 times. It is considered that when the noise is too large, although the rewards are high because of sufficient exploration, the stability of learning is reduced, and outliers are more likely to be obtained.

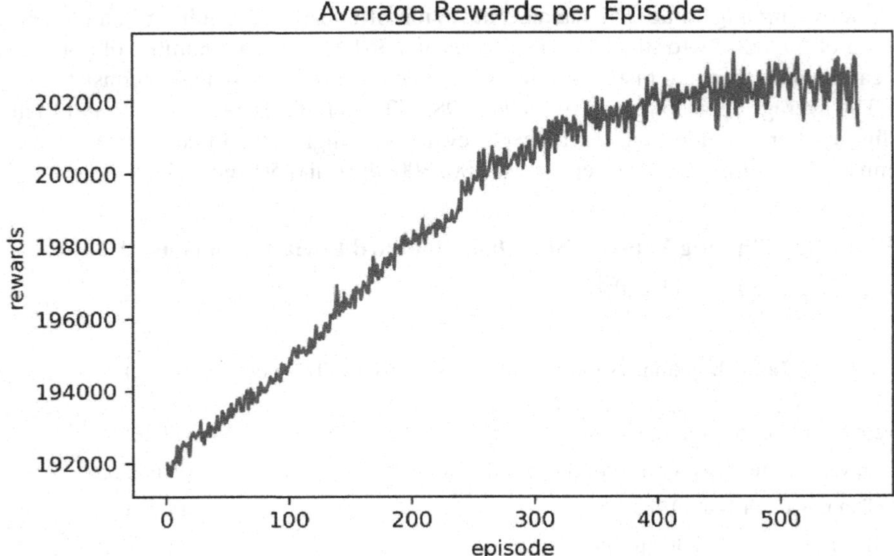

Fig. 11. Reward for learning results using TD3 (noise = 0.6/0.2),Average reward for 10 times per episode (vertical axis: average amount of reward/horizontal axis: number of episodes)

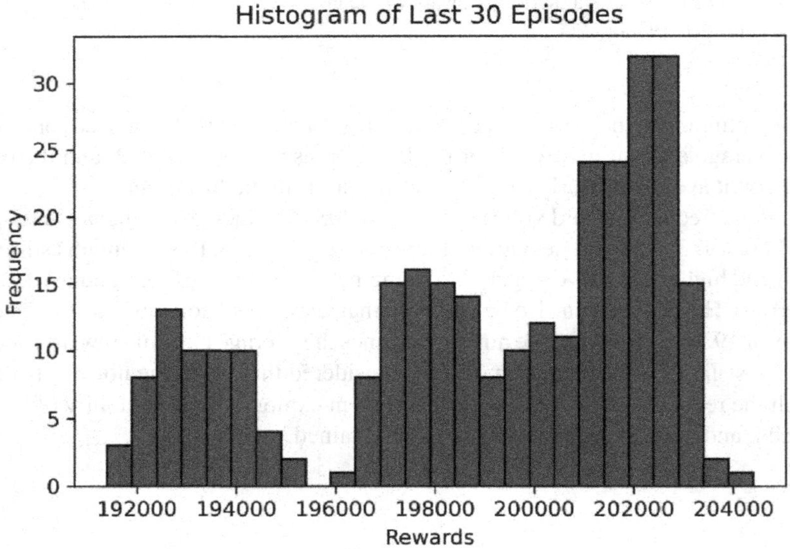

Fig. 12. The rewards of the learning results using TD3 (noise = 0.6/0.2), Histogram summarizing the amount of reward for the last 30 episodes of the 10

7 Concluding Remarks and Future Work

Increasing the parameters of clipping value and standard deviation of the behavioral noise increased the episodic reward but decreased the success rate of learning. From this, we infer that excessive noise impairs learning stability. The noise parameter that minimizes the standard deviation of the episode reward in the final 30 episodes is the combination of a clipping value of 0.5 for action noise and a standard deviation of 0.3 for action noise, which is estimated to be the optimal noise parameter in this experiment. Higher episodic reward and learning stability can be achieved by using TD3 with the optimal noise parameters applied, compared to DDPG.

In the conducted experiments, the task sizes were all set to the same value. However, it is assumed that in a real environment, there will be a variety of tasks and task sizes which differ from each other. To realize a more practical system, we believe it is necessary to conduct experiments with random task sizes. In addition, the experiments were conducted on a virtual edge computing environment, and actual edge servers were not used. Therefore, we consider it necessary to conduct experiments to verify the effectiveness of the offloading mechanism in a real environment.

References

1. Studying Reinforcement Learning from the Basics after All These Years, DDPG/TD3 Edition (Continuous Action Space.) https://qiita.com/pocokhc/items/6746df2eb9e7840e6814 (2022). (in Japanese)
2. Fujimoto, S., Hoof, H., Meger, D.: Addressing function approximation error in actor-critic methods. In: Proceedings of the 35th International Conference on Machine Learning (ICML) (2018). https://arxiv.org/abs/1802.09477
3. Li, Y., Qi, F., Wang, Z., Xiuming, Y., Shao, S.: Distributed edge computing offloading algorithm based on deep reinforcement learning. IEEE Access **8**, 85204–85215 (2020)
4. Ide, S.: Development of a Dynamic Offloading Mechanism for Edge Computing Using Deep Reinforcement Learning: Master Thesis, Graduate School of Information Science, Kyushu Sangyo University (2021). (in Japanese)
5. Tsurumaru, R., Apduhan, B.: Improving a dynamic offloading mechanism in edge computing using deep reinforcement learning. In: Proceedings 2023 Hinokuni Symposium (2023). (in Japanese)
6. Sadiki, A., Bentahar, J., Dssouli, R., En-Nouaary, A.: Deep Reinforcement Learning for the Computation Offloading in MIMO-based Edge Computing: TechRxiv (2021). https://doi.org/10.36227/techrxiv.16869119.v1
7. Li, S., Hu, X., Du, Y.: Deep Reinforcement Learning for Computation Offloading and Resource Allocation in Unmanned-Aerial-Vehicle Assisted Edge Computing. Sensors **21**, 6499 (2021). https://doi.org/10.3390/s21196499
8. J. Li, Z. Chen, X. Liu: Deep reinforcement learning for partial offloading with reliability guarantees. In: Proceedings of the 2021 IEEE ISPA/BDCloud/SocialCom/SustainCom, pp. 1027–1034 (2021)
9. Hazarika, B., Singh, K., Biswas, S., Li, C.-P.: DRL-based resource allocation for computation offloading in IoV networks. IEEE Trans. Indus. Inform. **18**(11), 8027–8038 (2022)
10. Xi, H., Huang, Y.: Deep reinforcement learning based offloading decision algorithm for vehicular edge computing. Peer J. Comput. Sci. **8**, e1126 (2022). https://doi.org/10.7717/peerj-cs.1126

Data-Flow Visual Programming Environment for Small IoT Devices

Sota Ogura[1], Kazuaki Tanaka[1(✉)], Ko-ichiro Sugiyama[2], and Miu Kawahara[2]

[1] Kyushu Institute of Technology, Kitakyushu, Japan
kazuaki@ics.kyutech.ac.jp
[2] National Institute of Technology, Matsue College, Matsue, Japan

Abstract. Embedded systems, such as smartphones, home appliances, and automotive cars, are widely used in various settings. Furthermore, demand for embedded systems continues to rise, driven by factors such as the aging population, declining birthrate, and the need to reduce labor costs in factories and companies.

To address the shortage of C and C++ programmers and enhance the accessibility of embedded systems development, we propose a method that utilizes Node-RED, a visual programming tool. And then mruby/c, a language that combines the benefits of Ruby and C/C++, and enable even programming novices to develop embedded systems. We also incorporate Docker Compose to simplify the process of building a development environment, and release as a open source software.

Our approach offers a promising solution for engineers seeking to improve their embedded systems development skills or those who want to enhance the productivity and readability of their code. By leveraging Node-RED and mruby/c, this study provides an innovative solution that can enable a wider range of developers to participate in embedded systems development, ultimately contributing to the growth of this field.

Keywords: mruby/c · IoT · Node-RED · Programming Environment

1 Introduction

1.1 Background

These days, embedded systems are used in various places and situations, and their demand is increasing year after year. Factors such as a declining birth rate, an aging population, and cost reduction in companies and factories are contributing to this rise in demand. For embedded systems, development in C is preferred because of its immediacy. As a result, there is a need for an embedded development environment that is easily used for beginners who have never used C before.

In recent years, the importance of utilizing data such as IoT and AI as critical technological elements are highlighted. To satisfy this demand, we focused on data-flow visual programming tools, which are good for understanding data flow

O. Gervasi et al. (Eds.): ICCSA 2023 Workshops, LNCS 14107, pp. 150–161, 2023.
https://doi.org/10.1007/978-3-031-37114-1_11

when developing IoT applications. In this study, we propose a method for building an embedded development environment that enables a wider range of users to develop embedded systems using Node-RED, a data-flow visual programming tool, and mruby/c, which shares the productivity and readability characteristics of Ruby compared to C.

1.2 Objective

The objective of this research is to develop a programming environment for small devices that allows users to intuitively comprehend the flow of data between devices for IoT development. To provide an environment that enables a wider range of users to develop IoT applications, we use a data-flow type visual programming language, which is easy to comprehend. Developers can implement application programs by visually placing nodes and wiring among them. The programs for microcontrollers are automatically generated from these visual programs. This approach allows users to develop IoT applications with ease and enhances development efficiency.

2 Application Configurations

Table 1 shows the development environment used in this work. We choose the programming language Ruby, which offers better readability and productivity than C. The data-flow visual programming tool we choose is the Node-RED environment. All these environments are coded as a docker-compose copen-source software.

Table 1. Development Environment

OS	Windows 11
Chrome browser	>89
Node.js	> ver.16.17.1
Node-RED	> ver.3.0.2
mruby/c IDE	> ver.1.03
Docker Compose	> ver.3.7

2.1 mruby/c

murby/c is a language for embedded development that inherits the high productivity and readability characteristics of Ruby, making it easy to use for beginning programmers [4]. Furthermore, its compiler can convert Ruby code to byte-code that can be executed on a VM (Virtual Machine), reducing memory consumption during program execution. This feature allows for development on microcontrollers with limited computing resources. If a low-power microcontroller chip is used, it can be implemented in a power-saving manner. In this study, we aim to construct a programming environment using the Ruby language by introducing mruby/c.

2.2 Node-RED

This study leverages Node-RED [5], a data-flow visual programming tool developed by IBM to interconnect hardware devices, APIs, online services, etc. Node-RED is built on Node.js to leverage an event-driven, non-blocking model. It can also run on low-cost hardware, such as a Raspberry Pi at the edge of the network, as well as in the cloud.

The programming method is to create a flow by arranging blocks, called nodes, each of which is given a function, and connecting them with wires. Nodes send and receive data to and from each other, and perform various processes (Fig. 1). This programming method is more visually represented in the editor, making it an easy-to-use tool for a wide range of users.

Node-RED also allows users to create their own nodes. Node design and layout of configuration items are done in HTML, and the processing within nodes is done in JavaScript.

Nodes process external events such as messages and GPIO hardware changes from the forward node to which they are basically connected and send them out to the backward node. Each node has one input port and multiple output ports as needed. There are also three types of nodes implemented.

Input Nodes: Has only output ports.
Flow can be started manually or at regular intervals.
Output Nodes: Has only an input port.
Displays messages in the sidebar in the editor.
Functional Nodes: Has both input and output ports.
Performs conditional branching and various other processes.

In this study, we developed a node for microcontrollers using this functionality. The details are described in Sect. 3.2.

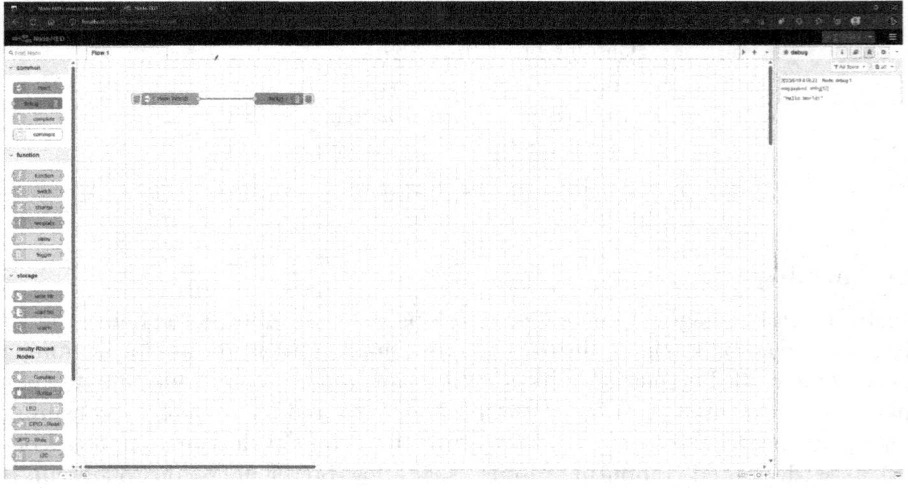

Fig. 1. Node-RED Development Environment

2.3 Docker Compose

Docker is a containerized virtualization technology provided by Docker Inc. Container-based virtualization technology is a technology that creates an execution environment in which a middleware environment called a container is built from the Docker Engine, a resident program for using Docker running on the host OS, without booting a guest OS. One advantage is that applications can run more lightly because the load on the computer is reduced by using only the minimum amount of memory and CPU required. Another advantage is resource efficiency, since an OS is not required for each application. Even complex architectures can be easily shared with a Dockerfile and the necessary files. An image of container-based virtualization is shown in Fig. 2.

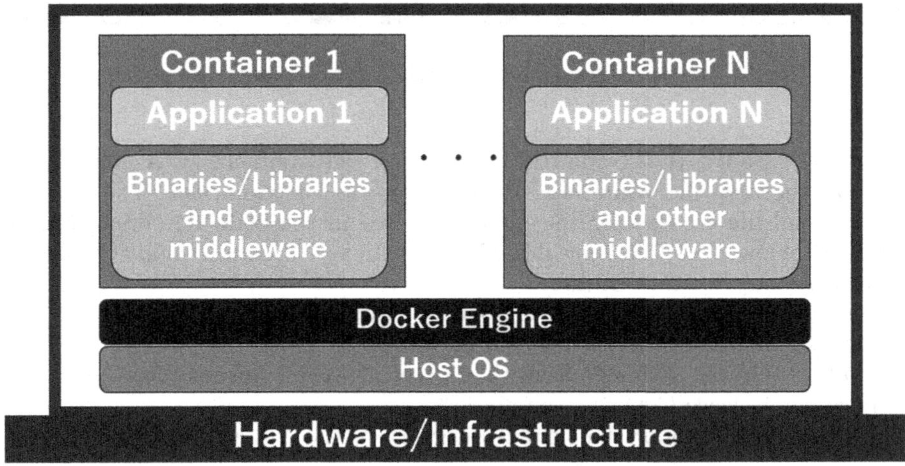

Fig. 2. Image Figure of Container-Based Virtualization Technology

However, to start a container, it is necessary to code complex commands with options, which can easily lead to mistakes and prevent smooth environment sharing. Docker Compose can automate this process by allowing you to define web servers, DB servers, etc. in the 'docker-compose.yml' file, and then start and configure all the containers needed to run them at once (Fig. 3).

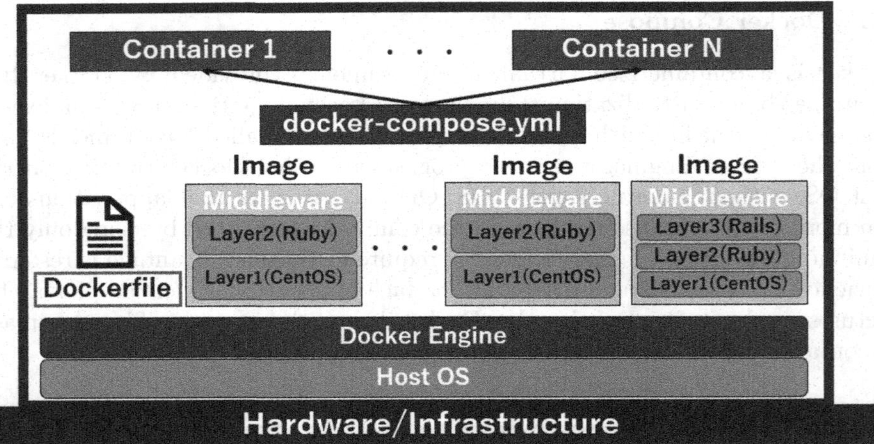

Fig. 3. Image Figure of Docker Compose

In this study, the Node-RED execution environment was automated with Docker and the container started with Docker Compose. The docker-compose.yml file created for the build is shown in the code 1.1. Each item is described below. The following describes the "Image Creation" and "Container Start" necessary to start Docker.

version: Specify the version of Docker Compose
services: Describe the service container to be started
build: Create an image from the dockerfile in the current directory
ports: Release Container number 1880
volumes: Bind-mount the current directory to the /data directory

Code 1.1. docker-compose.yml

```
version: "3.7"

services:
  node-red:
    build: ./node-red
    ports:
      - "1880:1880"
    volumes:
      - node-red-data:/data

  sinatra:
    build: ./sinatra
    ports:
# - 4567:4567
      - 80:4567
volumes:
  node-red-data:
```

Creationg an Image. An image is a collection of configuration files necessary to start a container, the application's execution environment. The same execution environment can be run on various machines by sharing this image. The image is created by making a file named "Dockerfile" and describing the settings involved in building the image in the file. The creation should describe the following. In addition, the dockerfile created in this study is shown in Code1.2.

FROM: Describe the image name and tag name based on which image you want to create.
COPY: Describes the names of files and directories to be copied into the container.
RUN: Execute commands to install middleware.

Code 1.2. Dockerfile

```
FROM nodered/node-red:latest


COPY node-red-contrib-mrubyc-rboard ./node-red-contrib-mrubyc-rboard

RUN npm install ./node-red-contrib-mrubyc-rboard

#common
RUN rm ./node_modules/@node-red/nodes/core/common/05-junction.html
RUN rm ./node_modules/@node-red/nodes/core/common/05-junction.js
RUN rm ./node_modules/@node-red/nodes/core/common/25-catch.html
RUN rm ./node_modules/@node-red/nodes/core/common/25-catch.js
RUN rm ./node_modules/@node-red/nodes/core/common/25-status.html
RUN rm ./node_modules/@node-red/nodes/core/common/25-status.js

RUN rm ./node_modules/@node-red/nodes/core/common/60-link.html
RUN rm ./node_modules/@node-red/nodes/core/common/60-link.js

RUN rm ./node_modules/@node-red/nodes/core/common/98-unknown.html
RUN rm ./node_modules/@node-red/nodes/core/common/98-unknown.js
```

Container Start. A container is a process isolated from other processes running on the OS. When it is launched, the Docker daemon first creates a process name space dedicated to the container and then executes the processes contained in the container as members of that name space.

Type "docker-compose up -d" when starting containers at the command prompt. This will start a series of containers in detached mode. By sharing the docker-compose.yml file and the dockerfile, the same development environment can be built on other machines.

3 Method

3.1 System Configurations

The system configuration to be developed in this study is shown in Fig. 4. The user creates a flow by connecting nodes on Node-RED. The JSON code stored in the created flow is extracted. Then, based on the JSON code, the Ruby code to run on the microcontroller board and convert it from the converted Ruby code to byte code. RBoard executes the program with the received byte-code.

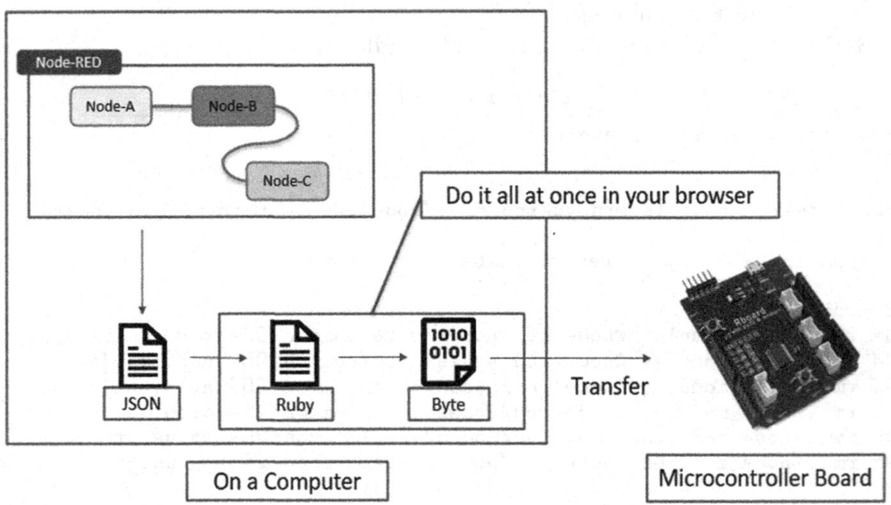

Fig. 4. System Configurations

3.2 Node Development

Node-RED allows you to create original nodes. The created node and the edit dialog for the LED node are shown in Fig. 5. Creating a node, the appearance of the node, the design of the edit dialog, and the configuration items of the node, which require JavaScript and HTML, are reflected on Node-RED by copying the file containing the node program with the COPY command and installing it with the RUN command. The reflected node is displayed as shown in the left figure of Fig. 5, and can be placed in the editor on Node-RED by drag and drop to create a flow. Nodes placed in the editor can be configured by simply selecting functions and entering numerical values in the edit dialog as shown in the center figure. The function-ruby node shown on the right can be freely written in Ruby, so it is used when you want to perform processing that is difficult to do by arranging nodes.

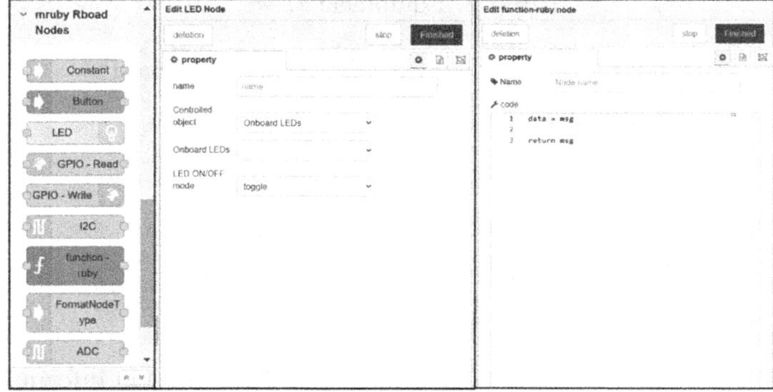

Fig. 5. List of Original Nodes (Left), Edit Node Dialog (Middle, Right)

3.3 Steps from Floe Creation to Execution

The JSON code extracted from Node-RED is converted to byte-code, the byte-code is transferred to the microcontroller using Web Serial API [6], and the program is executed. The following shows the details of the procedure from flow creation to execution in Node-RED. In addition, the screen of Web Serial API is shown in Fig. 6.

Fig. 6. Transferring Byte-code using Web Serial API

4 Operational Acceptance Testing

Using an ultra-compact analog temperature sensor (MCP9701E), create a program to control LEDs with the temperature sensor and display temperature values on a terminal. A list of the equipment used is shown in Table 2.

Table 2. Equipment Used

Equipment	quantity used
Temperature Sensor(MCP9701E)	1
RBoard	1
MicroUSB	1
LED (Red, Green)	2
Resistance 300[ohm]	2

RBoard is a microcontroller board developed by Shimane Information Processing Center Co. In addition, since it is equipped with a GROVE port, sensors and actuators can be used without soldering [7]. The RBoard was adopted for the operation verification because, as mentioned above, it is easy to handle for first-time users and inexpensive compared to other microcontroller boards.

Fig. 7. RBoard

The program created in Node-RED is shown in Code.1.3. The inject node sends data to the right node every second. The GPIO-Read node receives a signal from temperature sensor. Since received signal value from the temperature sensor is an analog voltage, the function-ruby node writes a program to convert it to a temperature in degrees Celsius.

In addition, to confirm that the device behaviour, message is logged by program (Ruby method puts).

Of course, We can convert analog voltage to temperature in degrees Celsius using Node-RED nodes instead of using Ruby code, however, the Ruby code is more brief and clear.

Code 1.3. function-ruby-node Code

```
data = msg
temp = data
V2mV = 1000
Vout = 400
temp_coef = 19.5

celsius = (temp * V2mV - Vout)/temp_coef

puts "----------------------------"
puts celsius
return celsius
```

The temperature data converted by the function-ruby node is sent to the switch node for judgment. In this operation verification, the red LED is turned on when the temperature is 22 °C or higher, and the green LED is turned on when the temperature is less than 22 °C.

Below are the steps for deploying from data-flow description in Node-RED to target device.

1. Place and program nodes on Node-RED to create a flow.
2. Extract JSON code from the created flow.
3. The extracted JSON code is converted to byte-code using the mruby/c compiler. The converted bytecode is downloaded as an mrb file.
4. Click the "onConnect" button on the Web Serial API screen to perform serial communication between the microcontroller board and the PC.
5. Click the "Attach File" button and select the mrb file saved in step 3.
6. Click the "write" button to transfer the binary code to the microcontroller.

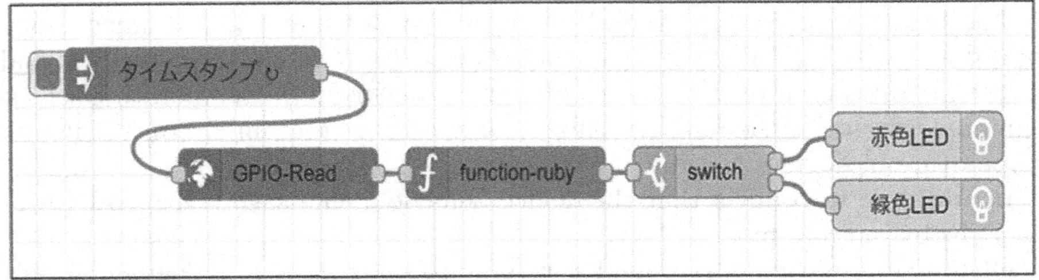

Fig. 8. Program Created in Node-RED

The results obtained from the operational verification conducted are shown below. The temperature values displayed on the terminal and the results of the red and green LEDs lighting up are shown in Fig. 9.

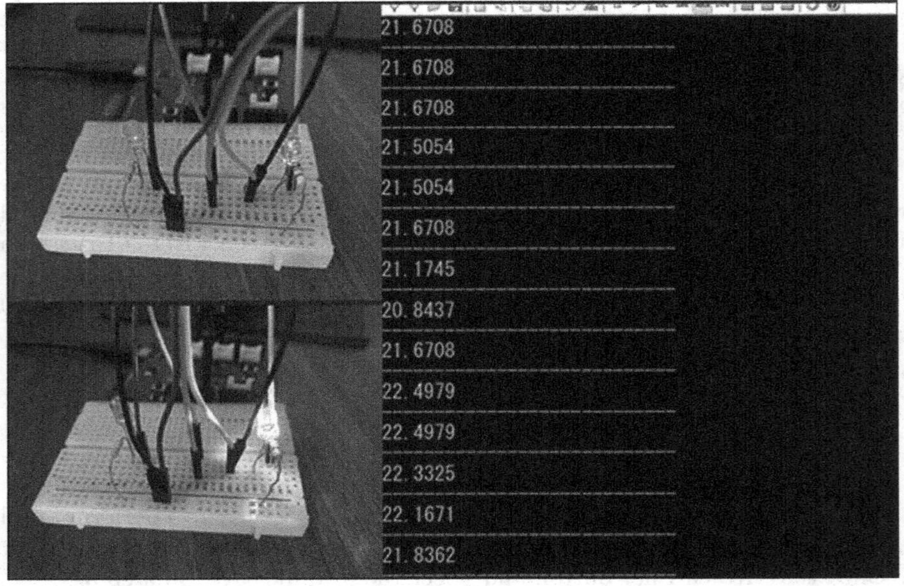

Fig. 9. Temperature below 22 °C (Upper Left), Temperature above 22 °C (Lower Left)

5 Conclusions

Our proposal for embedded software development involves using a data-flow programming environment. The developer creates a flow, which is then converted from JSON code to byte-code using the Ruby code generator mruby/c compiler, with the JSON code serving as data-flow storage information. The converted bytecode is transferred to the microcontroller, and the program is executed, resulting in an IoT development environment.

We discovered that data-flow programming allows for development irrespective of the programming language, and the created programs are easy to comprehend. As a result, even individuals with no programming experience can explain the processing of embedded systems.

In the future, we aim to implement the node under development and broaden the application's scope to other microcontroller boards beyond RBoard. Furthermore, we intend to test the system's functionality with a robotic arm for industrial purposes using this development environment.

References

1. Tanaka, K., Tsujino, C., Maeda, H.: IoT software by dataflow programming in Mruby programming environment. In: Proceedings of Computational Science and Its Applications ICCSA 2020, Cagliari, Italy, July 1–4, 2020,, Part IV, pp. 212–220 (2020) https://doi.org/10.1007/978-3-030-58811-3_15
2. Tsujino, T., Tanaka, K.: IoT application development for small devices using data flow. In: The 81st National Convention of Information Processing Society of Japan (2019)
3. Murakami, A., Tanaka, K.: Creation of a data-flow programming environment for small devices. In: The 81st National Convention of Information Processing Society of Japan (2022)
4. mruby/c, Shimane Software R&D Center. https://www.s-itoc.jp/activity/research/mrubyc/
5. Node-RED. https://nodered.jp/
6. Web Serial API, W3C Community Group Draft Report. https://wicg.github.io/serial/
7. RBoard, himane Information Processing Center Co. https://www.sjcinc.co.jp/service/rboard 2022

Tweets Sentiment Analysis of Putin's Participation at the G20 Summit in Indonesia

Syifa Auliyah Hasanah[1], Isal Firmansyah[1], Farid Azhar Lutfi Nugraha[1], Anindya Apriliyanti Pravitasari[1], Eka Novita Sari[2], and Tutut Herawan[3,4](✉)

[1] Department of Statistics, Universitas Padjadjaran, Jl. Ir. Soekarno KM. 21, Jatinangor, Sumedang, West Java 45363, Indonesia
{syifa19010,farid1900}@mail.unpad.ac.id, anindya.apriliyanti@unpad.ac.id

[2] AMCS Research Center, Jalan Griya Taman Asri, Sleman, Yogyakarta, Indonesia
eka@amcs.co

[3] Sekolah Tinggi Pariwisata Ambarrukmo Yogyakarta, Jl. Ringroad Timur No. 52, Bantul, Daerah Istimewa Yogyakarta 55198, Indonesia
tutut@stipram.ac.id

[4] Institute for Big Data Analytics and Artificial Intelligence, UiTM Shah Alam, 40450 Shah Alam, Selangor Darul Ehsan, Malaysia

Abstract. The Group of Twenty (G20) is an international economic cooperation forum established to address global and regional issues. The members are countries with large economies and the ability to have a significant impact on the global, since their GDP (Gross Domestic Product) shares about 80% of the global GDP. The dispute between Russia and Ukraine drew international attention regarding Russia's involvement in the G20. The Russian President, Vladimir Putin, played a major role and became a major source of concern in this dispute. The Western Bloc countries, such as the United States, wanted Russia to be expelled from the forum, but the Eastern Bloc believed the G20 was not a platform for discussing security matters, therefore Russia could still be included. As a result, sentiment analysis has to be conducted to determine the global community's reaction to Putin's presence at the G20 summit in Indonesia. Aside from that, the goal of this study is to automate the forecast of future public sentiments on the same subject. The Bidirectional Gated Recurrent Unit (BiGRU) architecture was employed in this work, using three sentiment labels: positive, negative, and neutral. The model created in this investigation has an accuracy value of 86.76% after being run for 20 epochs. This demonstrates that the model may get a reasonably accurate classification result when categorizing sentiments about Putin's attendance at the G20 Indonesia summit.

Keywords: Tweets · Sentiment analysis · G20 · Conflict · Russia · Vladimir Putin · BiGRU

O. Gervasi et al. (Eds.): ICCSA 2023 Workshops, LNCS 14107, pp. 162–178, 2023.
https://doi.org/10.1007/978-3-031-37114-1_12

1 Introduction

The G20 or Group 20 is a multilateral cooperation forum consisting of 19 countries and the European Union (EU), which was formed to help solve global and regional problems with two focuses, i.e., the Finance Track and the Sherpa Track. The G20 is an important world forum because it represent 2/3 of the world's population or around 5.267 billion people, covering 80% of the world's GDP and also representing about 75% of the world economy [1]. The G20 Forum does not have a permanent leader, but it does have a presidency function when one of the country's members will host the event for a full year. In 2022, Indonesia has the opportunity to hold the G20 presidency. This is a great opportunity for Indonesia to host such a big event with countries that have great economic and political influence. The G20 presidency in Indonesia will have a positive impact on Indonesia. According to Finance Minister Sri Mulyani Indrawati, the G20 forum in Indonesia can contribute to Indonesia's GDP of US $533 million, or around Rp7.4 trillion. The G20 Forum is also predicted to increase domestic consumption by up to IDR 1.7 trillion. Meanwhile, in other sectors, such as tourism, the G20 forum will contribute to the increase in foreign tourists by 1.8 million–3.6 million and will also create 600 thousand–700 thousand new jobs [1]. Besides the positive effects, Indonesia still needs to face some problems that will affect the G20 forum. The Russia-Ukraine conflict is one of them. The conflict has given rise to the political stance of the United States and several western bloc countries towards the G20 forum. They asked Indonesia not to invite Russia to the G20. The United States threatened not to attend the G20 summit if Russian President Vladmir Putin was present.

The Russia-Ukraine conflict brings a dilemma to the invitation decision of the President of Russia to the G20 summit in Indonesia. As the host, Indonesia has to invite all G20 members, including Russia, but some countries asked Indonesia not to invite Russia to the G20 forum. Indonesia needs to make the best decision for all parties. Good diplomacy skills are needed in this situation. Various responses have appeared regarding the issue of Putin's participation in the G20 Summit in Indonesia. Some narratives from some media are made to support one side of the two disputing camps. Therefore, sentiment analysis is needed to see the actual public's response based on data. Sentiment analysis will analyze a person's opinions, attitudes, and emotions towards a thing [2]. The benefit of this sentiment analysis is to know how the majority of the public responds to Putin's participation in the G20 summit in Indonesia, which can be used as a public sentiment reference and consideration by the Indonesian government on the decision to invite Putin to the G20 summit. This research is one of the first studies that discusses public sentiment on the issue of Putin's participation in the G20 summit in Indonesia. The methods that will be used in this research are deep learning methods that are expected to provide greater performance than the traditional methods.

This study tries some deep learning algorithms such as BiLSTM, CNN, and BiGRU to know which algorithm has the best performance in classifying public sentiment towards Putin's participation in the G20 issue. Three classification categories are used in this study, i.e., positive, neutral, and negative. In the end, the BiGRU algorithm shows the highest accuracy and the lowest loss, so this study decided to use BiGRU to predict public sentiment towards Putin's participation in the G20 forum.

Sentiment analysis in this study is limited to Twitter data in English with the issue of "Putin's participation at the G20 2022 Summit in Indonesia," taken from April 22 to April 30, 2022. This study focuses on public opinion on Twitter, which is used because this platform allows people to express their feelings and perceptions about things that are happening "right now" [3]. Usually, some information and issues spread faster on Twitter than on any other social media or news platforms. Aside from that, Twitter's character restriction feature influences the use of "to-the-point" sentences.

The remainder of the paper is organized as follows. In Sect. 2, we introduce some traditional machine learning and deep learning architectures. Section 3 describes the deep learning architecture we use in this research. In Sect. 4, we show the results of the sentiment analysis process and performance evaluation of the proposed BiGRU method compared to other deep learning architectures such as BiLSTM and CNN. Finally, we describe our conclusion and future work in Sect. 5.

2 Related Works

The use of Twitter data in sentiment analysis to see the public's response to an issue is a common thing for researchers [3]. Sentiment analysis on Twitter and several social media applications has become one of the trending topics for researchers. The business sector has used a lot of sentiment analysis to find out user responses and reviews related to products from a manufacturer, but now sentiment analysis is not only used to see consumer responses to an item; sentiment analysis is also used to see responses to an issue such as politics, economics, and others. In recent years, researchers have created a number of automated approaches for detecting and classifying abusive, sarcastic, and toxic language [4]. Sentiment analysis helps us to find various opinions on social media [5]. In politics, sentiment analysis is also often used as a means of effective and efficient promotion, campaigning and dissemination related to political policies so that it can generate opinions and comments from the public, in the form of positive comments, negative comments and neutral.

Caprolu et al. [6] gather and analyze data from Twitter. In particular, investigating data volumes and public perception of the Russia-Ukraine conflict by utilizing statistical analysis techniques and Aspect-Based Sentiment Analysis (ABSA). The results obtained state that the claims of some media contradict the actual situation. Therefore sentiment analysis is very important to validate results based on data found in the field.

Previously, there was no research that examined the sentiment analysis of Putin's participation in the G20. The topic that was covered in this study is a new topic that was brought up because of the Russia-Ukraine conflict that coincides with the G20 summit in Indonesia. So the data used here is a new data that will be subjected to a sentiment analysis using the appropriate machine learning model.

The machine learning models' effectiveness is based on two key factors: the availability of a huge amount of labeled data and the intelligent manual construction of a set of features that can be used to distinguish samples [7]. Many different algorithms can be used to perform sentiment analysis. Generally, two types of algorithms are used, namely traditional machine learning algorithms i.e., Naïve Bayes, SVM, KNN, decision tree, and others, as well as deep learning algorithms such as BiLSTM, BiGRU, CNN, and others.

Traditional machine learning algorithms tend to have simpler concepts. In a previous study that conducted sentiment analysis on Twitter by comparing three algorithms, i.e., SVM, Naïve Bayes, and also KNN [8], the traditional machine learning model was still sufficient to handle sentiment on Twitter data by providing an accuracy of 63% for the Naive Bayes model, 60% for the SVM model, and 61% for the KNN model. In another similar study [9], which conducted sentiment analysis by comparing the Naïve Bayes, KNN, and Decision Tree algorithms, the accuracy was around 50% for all models. Although the accuracy of the traditional machine learning algorithms in the two studies above is not high enough, several studies using traditional machine learning algorithms can achieve a higher accuracy, such as the sentiment review research of the Pedulilindungi application, which compares the Naïve Bayes model and SVM [10], which obtained an accuracy of 84.33% for SVM and 81.16% for Naïve Bayes.

To improve the performance of traditional models, deep learning models can be tried, which are conceptually more complex than traditional models but provide higher performance values based on large-scale datasets. One of the studies that uses deep learning algorithms is research with the title CNN for sentence classification [11], this study enables the easy extraction of textual information, and relational research has made significant progress in sentiment analysis. Zhang employed character-level CNN to classify text in 2015 [12]. On the other hand, CNN isn't a perfect algorithm because it can't catch long-range features [4]. Another study that uses a deep learning model is Sentiment Analysis of Comment Texts based on BiLSTM [13]. This study states that the context information is considered by the BiLSTM model, which allows for a better text representation of the comments. This study compares the BiLSTM model with other deep learning models and one traditional algorithm Naive Bayes. The accuracy value obtained in sentiment analysis using the BiLSTM algorithm in this study is 91.54%, while the traditional Naïve Bayes model provides an accuracy of 86.02%, which is smaller than other deep learning models. Not different from BiLSTM, BiGRU deep learning model in the study with a title "Sentiment analysis based on BiGRU information enhancement" [14] with binary sentiment, i.e., positive and negative, shows good accuracy, and the use of two-layer BiGRU based on BERT preprocessing gives a good accuracy value of 82.63%. The researcher says the length of the running model process is the drawback of using this algorithm. Other related studies have also demonstrated that BIGRU achieves higher accuracy. For example, a binary sentiment analysis research paper titled 'Sentiment Analysis Using an Ensemble Approach of BiGRU Model: A Case Study of AMIS Tweets' analyzed various topics on Twitter, including games, football, LGBT, Trump, and Syria, and reported an accuracy of the sentiment analysis is about 84.8% [15].

This study will use deep learning algorithm to predict public sentiment towards Putin's participation on G20 event, the more complex sentiment analysis algorithm (deep learning algorithm) is used in this study with the hope of providing good performance value.

3 Data and Proposed Method

3.1 Data

We use Twitter crawled data using the keywords "Russia G20" and "Putin G20". By using these keywords, 15213 tweets were collected. However, the data is still dirty data that must go through various processes before it can be used for analysis. The first thing to do with the data is to pre-process the data through the case folding process and data cleaning, tokenization, and stopword removal. So, we get 12462 lines of data that are ready to use which are then labeled with the help of the package in python, namely Vader. The dataset is divided into three categories of labels, namely positive, negative, and neutral with the proportions of each category obtained as follows: positive (1675 tweets), negative (4921 tweets), and neutral (5866 tweets).

3.2 Method

As in Fig. 1, this research begins with the data pre-processing step. At this step, the data will be prepared for further analysis using a predetermined algorithm. The next step is to divide the dataset into training and testing data, which will then be analyzed using several algorithms, namely LSTM, BiLSTM, GRU, BiGRU, and Convolution. The algorithm with the highest evaluation value will be used in this analysis.

3.2.1 Data Preprocessing

Pre-processing is at an early stage. It's a very important step to handling raw data. Without this process, the next process will not produce a good output. Pre-processing helps deal with various problems and produces data that is ready for analysis. The following are the steps in pre-processing data.

Case Folding and Data Cleaning

Case folding is the process of converting all existing letters to lowercase. So, words that still have capital letters will automatically turn into lowercase letters, for example, the letter "B" will become "b". This is done because with case folding, data redundancy can be reduced. Data cleaning is the process of preparing data such as detecting and correcting the arrangement of the dataset so that it can be used for analysis. In this process, words that are not needed will be removed, such as "http" and cleaning of duplicated data is also carried out. Data that has the same content even though it comes from different users will be discarded. At this stage, the author also removes several elements such as removing punctuation marks, eliminating numbers, and so on.

Stop-Word Removal

Stopword Removal is a process to remove certain words that often appear but have no meaning that has a major influence on the analysis process. Examples of words that will be deleted are conjunctions, prepositions, and slang words that are usually used but give the impression of being informal in a sentence. This stopword removal process is done by first making a list of what words are included in the stopword itself. The list will be

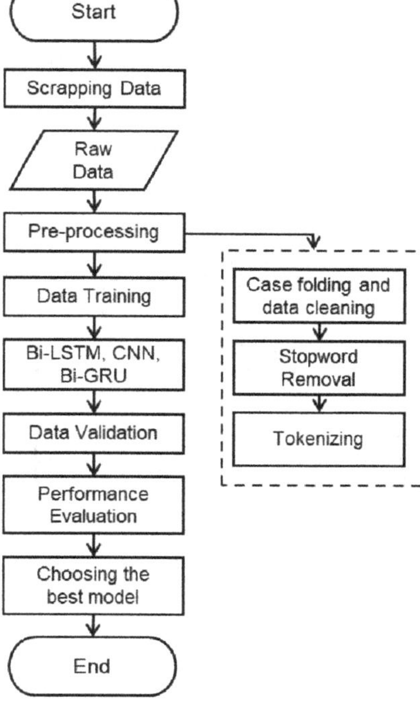

Fig. 1. Flowchart of this research

a benchmark if in the dataset we have these words will be discarded. In this process, emoticons, symbols and pictographs, transport and map symbols, flags, and Chinese characters are usually used in tweeting.

Tokenizing
Tokenizing is the process of separating words in sentences and then collecting them in an array of data which will then be weighted in each of these words. The list of words that make up the sentence will be separated by commas and spaces.

Split Data
In this study, the data will be divided into two groups, namely training data, and testing data. Training data is used to create and train the model to be used. While data testing is used to test the model that has been made.

3.2.2 Sentiment Analysis with BiLSTM

Bidirectional Long Short-Term Memory (BiLSTM) is an extension of the regular LSTM which can improve performance on classification problems. The results of the LSTM output produce global information; it is still difficult to capture the important information contained in it [16]. BiLSTM conducts data training twice, unlike LSTM which only does training once. The raw dataset from the first process is fed back into the second process. This can provide additional networking and obtain faster and more complete results. From Fig. 2, the layer below it moves forward (forward) to understand the first word to the last, while the other layers move backward (backward) to understand the word from the end to the first word.

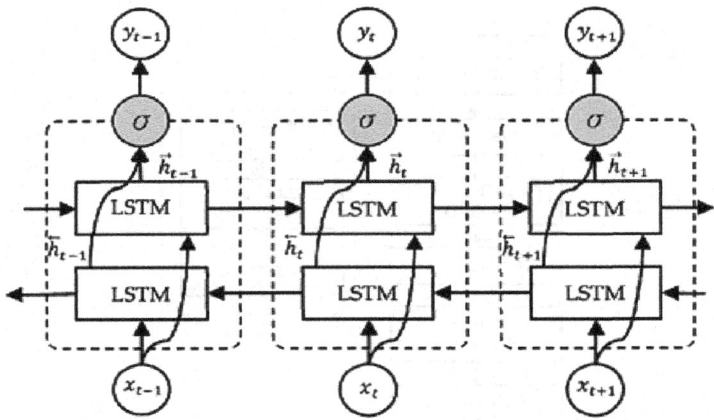

Fig. 2. BiLSTM Architecture [17]

3.2.3 Sentiment Analysis with BiGRU

The Gated Recurrent Unit (GRU) is a development of the RNN architecture because the RNN cannot record a lot of information at the time step, in addition to solving problems considering long dependencies and large text, the GRU architecture is suitable for use. GRU has two gates called Reset Gates and Updates Gates. Update gate is used to determine how much data will be discarded [18]. The two gates are used to control the flow of hidden information.

The GRU architecture has problems in the context that was used previously without considering the future context resulting in the loss of information obtained where the GRU architecture can only arrange the order from front to back [19]. Therefore, this is the basis for developing the Bidirectional Gated Recurrent Unit (BiGRU) architecture, where this architecture consists of two GRUs to take input in a forward direction and another GRU to take input in a backward direction. One of the advantages of this architecture is that the structure is not too complicated so BiGRU can train faster. The BiGRU model is obtained from replacing hidden layer neurons in the Bidirectional Recurrent Neural Network with GRU memory units, with the following structure (see Fig. 3).

The picture above shows the process that occurs in the BiGRU architecture which consists of two GRUs going back and forth. The first one functions as an input reader in the forward direction $(x_1, \ldots, x_n)$ resulting in a forward hidden state sequence $(\vec{h}_1, \ldots, \vec{h}_n)$, while the other functions as an input reader in the reverse order $(x_n, \ldots, x_1)$ and returns a sequence of backward hidden states $(\overleftarrow{h}_n, \ldots, \overleftarrow{h}_1)$. At time t, the hidden layer

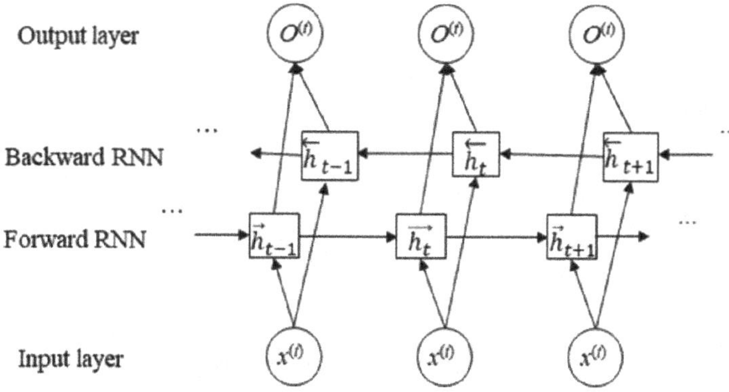

Fig. 3. BiGRU Architecture [20]

BiGRU returns h_t. The calculation process is as follows:

$$\vec{h}_t = \sigma\left(W_{x\vec{h}}x_t + W_{\vec{h}\vec{h}}\vec{h}_{t-1} + b_{\vec{h}}\right),$$

$$\vec{h}_t = \sigma(W_{x\vec{h}}x_t + W_{\vec{h}\vec{h}}\overleftarrow{h}_{t-1} + b_{\vec{h}}),$$

$$h_t = \vec{h}_t \oplus \overleftarrow{h}_t, \tag{1}$$

where W is the weight matrix connecting the two layers, b is the bias vector, σ is the activation function, $\vec{h}_t$ and $\overleftarrow{h}_t$ are the outputs of the forward and backward GRUs, and is the sum of elements.

3.2.4 Sentiment Analysis with CNN

The Deep Learning method is a method that is commonly used to solve a problem that is more complex than other methods because this method has many hidden layers that can help to solve various complex problems. One of the deep learning methods is the Convolutional Neural Network (CNN) (see Fig. 4). This method is generally used for image-based data analysis. However, now many researchers are using CNN to analyze public sentiment towards an object. Among the advantages when using CNN because it is easy to train and has connections are also fewer parameters compared to other algorithms [21].

3.2.5 Evaluation Matrix

To find out which algorithm is suitable for the problems we have, we need a tool that can calculate how well the performance of our classification model is. In this case, the confusion matrix (see Table 1) is a suitable tool to use. This table can display and compare the actual value with the predicted value of the model. The evaluation matrices commonly used include accuracy, precision, recall, and $F1$-score.

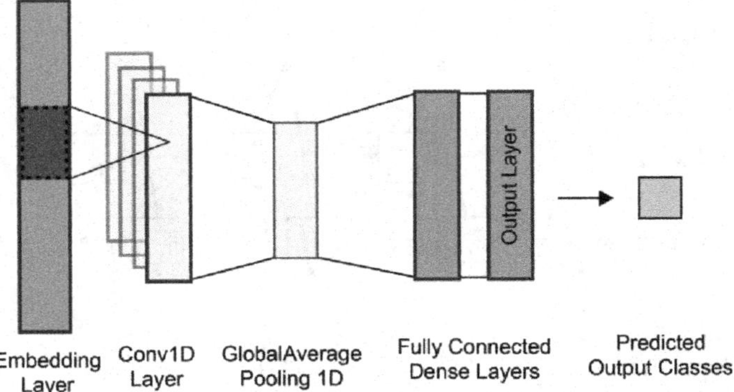

Fig. 4. CNN Architecture

Table 1. Confusion Matrix

	Positive	Negative
Positive	True Positive (*TP*)	False Positive (*FP*)
Negative	False Negative (*FN*)	True Negative (*TN*)

Accuracy

Accuracy is the value obtained from the sum positive data that is predicted to have positive value as well as negative data that is predicted to have a negative value with all the data in the dataset. The calculation of the accuracy value can be seen in the following equation:

$$\text{Accuracy} = \frac{TP + TN}{TP + FP + FN + TN} \tag{2}$$

The accuracy value is only suitable when the comparison of the actual number of data tables is relatively the same.

Precision

Precision is the value obtained from the probability that the data is predicted to have a positive value and, in fact, the data is included in the positive category. Precision may be defined as the degree of dependability of a model when the model provides a positive prediction. In computing accuracy, just the first or second line of the confusion matrix is necessary. Precision is the fraction of positively correct forecasts versus the overall positive prediction. Mathematically precision may be stated as follows:

$$\text{Precision} = \frac{TP}{TP + FP} \tag{3}$$

Recall

Recall or sensitivity is a strategy for determining how effectively a test can detect a genuine positive; recall represents a model's success in rediscovering knowledge. Recall is calculated by comparing positive accurate predictions to total positive correct data. Mathematically the recall value may be expressed as follows:

$$\text{Recall} = \frac{TP}{TP + FN} \tag{4}$$

F1-Score

Calculations that summarize accuracy and sensitivity/recall by calculating harmonic averages of each. The following formula may be used to calculate the value of the F1-Score:

$$\text{F1 - Score} = \frac{2\,x\,Precision\,x\,Recall}{Precision\,x\,Recall} \tag{5}$$

4 Results and Discussion

This section describes the data set used for experimentation and analysis of several models. The experiments are performed using the Keras Tensorflow library and the python language. Model comparison is done by comparing the accuracy validation obtained by each model. The network architecture is set homogeneously in each model used with the first layer being a vector embedding layer with dimensions of 1000 words to represent each word. Model tested is used in the second layer, for the CNN model an additional layer is needed for the pooling layer. The third layer uses a dense layer with ReLU activation and the last layer is an output layer with 3 neurons with Softmax activation. The number of epochs is set to 100 and Adam optimizer is used for optimization with learning rate set to 1e-4. Model checkpoint is applied by monitoring validation accuracy with mode max to save the best model.

4.1 Experimental

The data used in this study is the tweets with the keywords putin G20 and Russia G20 from April 22nd–30th, 2022. Dataset is obtained by crawling data from twitter using the tweepy library. This study mined the documents of about 12,462 tweets. Table 2 below shows the comparison of one example of a comment that has done through the text pre-processing stage.

The tweets have undergone changes in the text preprocessing. At this phase, the process of case folding and stopwords, non-alphanumeric and emojis removal is carried out. The results of the text reprocessing phase produce text data that are ready to enter the tokezining stage. The following is a data visualization of the results of text pre-processing.

Table 2. Sample of data preprocessing result based on problem

Raw Data	Data after Preprocessing
RT @AaronParnas: Vladimir Putin should not be allowed at this year's G20 summit	Vladimir putin not allowed g20
Brazil, China, South Africa and others still support Putin in G20 membership in spite of 'Ol Joe Biden. ✅	Brazil china south africa others still support putin g20 membership spite ol joe biden
RT @maythamdk: Indonesia invites Russian President Vladimir Putin to attend the G20 summit	Indonesia invites russian president vladimir putin attend g20

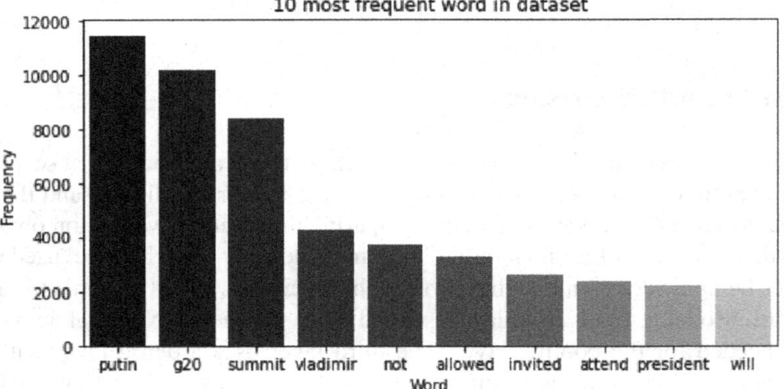

Fig. 5. Bar chart of the number of words that appear in dataset

The Fig. 5 above visualizes the number of words that appear in tweets related to Putin and the G20, the word 'putin' is the word with the highest number of occurrences, namely 11,374 words, followed by the word 'g20' with 9,679 words, "Vladimir" with 4,231 words, 'not' with 3,685 words, 'allowed' with 3,258, 'peak' with 2,863 words, the word 'invites' with 2,614 words, 'will' with 2,114 words, 'president' with 2,069 words, and the word 'invites' with 1,556 words. In this case, we can see that the words 'putin' and 'vladimir' have a different number of words, but in reality, we do not distinguish between the two words as having two different meanings. Because sometimes people write it using the full name "Vladimir Putin" or just "Putin".

The first step we do after collecting the data is labeling. We conducted our labeling using packages in Python, namely Vader. The package helps us designate 15213 tweets, forming three classifications for this case, namely positive, negative, and neutral. However, after that, we also did class validation of the labeling results manually for several sample tweets so that we were able to make clear that each tweet had entered the correct class. After carrying out several lengthy processes, such as the labeling stage on the data, followed by the data pre-processing stage such as data cleaning and case folding, stopword removal, and tokenizing, the next step is the sentiment analysis process carried out using the BiLSTM, CNN, and BiGRU algorithms on tweets regarding Putin and the G20. All data that is ready to be analyzed is then separated by 70% for training data from all data (8,723 data) and 30% for validation data from all data (3,739 data). The distribution of training data and validation data for each sentiment can be seen in the following Table 3.

Table 3. Result of the dataset labels distribution

Sentiment	Training	Validation	Total
Neutral	4106	1760	5866
Negative	3445	1476	4921
Positive	1172	503	1675

Table 3 above shows the distribution sentiment label for the data. It appears that mostly the tweets' sentiments towards this topic are negative. This information can represent sentiments from the public of twitter regarding the topic of President Putin's participation in the G20 Summit, an international event which is being discussed around the world.

4.2 Performance Analysis

The best model is determined by making comparisons between several models.The Bidirectional Gated Recurrent Unit (BiGRU) is chosen to be the best model to be used in classifying tweets.

4.2.1 BiLSTM Model Performance

The BiLSTM model is used for testing using 100 epochs. The graph of validation loss and validation accuracy in Fig. 6 below shows the graph of validation loss showing a decrease and the graph of validation accuracy showing an increase in each epoch which indicates better results and does not experience overfitting.

The highest validation accuracy was obtained for the BiLSTM model at 0.98583 with a validation loss of 0.0589 which was achieved in the 65th epoch.

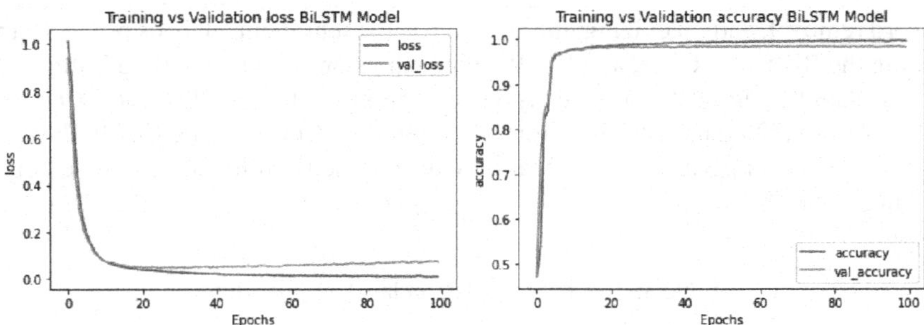

Fig. 6. Training and Validation Loss and Accuracy for BiLSTM

4.2.2 CNN Model Performance

The CNN model was also tested the same as other models with a maximum epoch of 100 epochs. The validation loss graph and the CNN model validation accuracy graph are the same as the previous model which shows good results and does not experience overfitting (see Fig. 7).

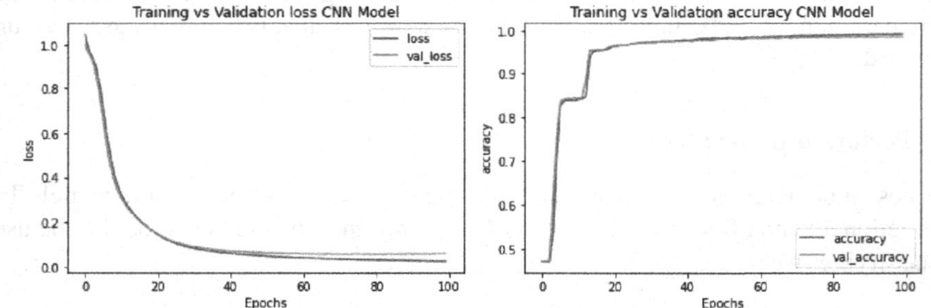

Fig. 7. Training and Validation Loss and Accuracy for CNN

In the 94th epoch, the CNN model got the highest validation accuracy at 0.98583 with a validation loss of 0.0583.

4.2.3 BiGRU Model Performance

Similar to other model tests, the BiGRU model was tested with a maximum epoch of 100 epochs. The graph in Fig. 8 below also shows the validation loss graph and the validation accuracy graph which are quite good and do not experience overfitting.

The BiGRU model gets the highest validation accuracy at 0.98636 with a validation loss of 0.0534 which can be achieved in the 29th epoch.

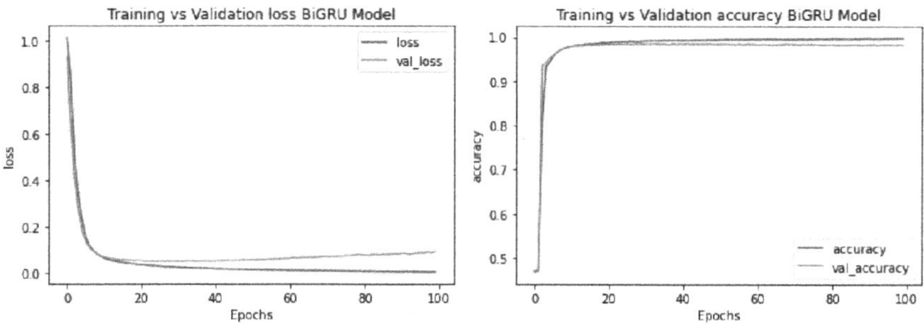

Fig. 8. Training and Validation Loss and Accuracy for BiGRU

4.3 Classification Results

The Confusion Matrix in Table 4 shows that the data that was predicted to be correct with a neutral class amounted to 1743 data, correctly predicted with a negative class totaling 1461 data, and correctly predicted with a positive class totaling 484 data. The labels that are predicted according to the actual label are represented by the main diagonal of the confusion matrix, while the elements outside the diagonal of the confusion matrix are the elements that are mislabeled by the machine learning model. A high diagonal value in the confusion matrix indicates the selected model shows good performance in classifying sentiments.

The comparison of our model with CNN and BiLSTM models to evaluate the model and conclude the results. Results of other models along with our models are tabulated in Table 4.

Table 4. Comparison of different evaluation measures of BiLSTM, CNN, and BiGRU

Model	Evaluation Metric			
	Accuracy	Precision	Recall	F1 – score
BiLSTM	0.98449	0.98	0.976	0.98
CNN	0.98583	0.98	0.98	0.98
BiGRU (our proposed model)	0.98636	0.983	0.98	0.983

The results of the classification of our proposed model as reported in Table 4 are the best among other models, this shows that our proposed model is very promising in this dataset with an accuracy of 0.98636.

The Performance Metrics in Table 5. Shows the evaluation of sentiment classification carried out using the BiGRU architecture. Sentiment classification is performed on the data used with an accuracy score of 98%. The neutral class and the negative class got an f1 score of 99%, higher than the positive class which got an f1 score of 97%. These results mean that the model used can predict the category of tweets with neutral and negative

Table 5. Performance matrix of each classes for BiGRU architecture

	Neutral	Negative	Positive
Precision	0.99	0.99	0.97
Recall	0.99	0.99	0.96
F1 – score	0.99	0.99	0.97
Accuracy		0.98636	

sentiments more accurately than the categories of tweets with positive sentiments. Table 6 is a Confusion matrix which shows data that is correctly predicted with a neutral class of 1743 data, correctly predicted with a negative class of 1461 data, and correctly predicted with a positive class of 484 data.

Table 6. Confusion matrix for BiGRU architecture

Confusion Matrix		Predicted		
		Neutral	Negative	Positive
Actual	Neutral	1743	11	6
	Negative	8	1461	7
	Positive	8	11	484

The labels that are predicted according to the actual label are represented by the main diagonal of the confusion matrix, while the elements outside the diagonal of the confusion matrix are the elements that are mislabeled by the machine learning model. A high diagonal value in the confusion matrix indicates the selected model shows good performance in classifying sentiments.

5 Conclusion and Recommendation

In this study, we have successfully compared three deep learning algorithms, i.e., BiLSTM, CNN, and BiGRU. We got BiGRU as the best algorithm with an accuracy of 98.63% and a loss of 0.053, so in this case, the BiGRU algorithm is considered the most suitable for use in predicting public sentiment on the issue of Putin's participation in the G20 in Indonesia. This study used 12,462 data tweets from April 22, 2022 to April 30, 2022. To improve performance results, additional datasets and data collection ranges can be added. This research can find out the actual public response to Putin's participation in the G20. The results of this study can be a source of reference for the government in considering the decision to invite Putin to the G20 forum.

The recommendation that can be given in future research is to compare other deep learning algorithms with traditional algorithms. We can find out whether traditional algorithms can handle sentiment analysis on the issue of Putin's participation in the G20 forum. Utilizing better labeling methods and collecting datasets over a longer period of time is also more likely to improve this research.

Acknowledgement. The authors thanks to the Department of Statistics and Research Center for Artificial Intelligence and Big Data, Universitas Padjadjaran which supports this research. The work of Tutut Herawan and Eka Novita Sari is supported by AMCS Research Center.

References

1. Ministry of Communication and Information Technology: G20pedia (2022)
2. Ananda, F.D., Pristyanto, Y.: Analisis Sentimen Pengguna Twitter Terhadap Layanan Internet Provider Menggunakan Algoritma Support Vector Machine. MATRIK: Jurnal Manajemen, Teknik Informatika dan Rekayasa Komputer **20**(2), 407–416, (2021)
3. Qiu, L., Lin, H., Ramsay, J., Yang, F.: You are what you tweet: personality expression and perception on Twitter. J. Res. Pers. **46**(6), 710–718 (2012)
4. Islam, M.S., Ghani, N.A.: A novel BiGRUBiLSTM model for multilevel sentiment analysis using deep neural network with BiGRU-BiLSTM. In: Recent Trends in Mechatronics Towards Industry 4.0: Selected Articles from iM3F 2020, Malaysia, pp. 403–414. Springer Singapore, Singapore (2021)
5. Behrendt, S., Schmidt, A.: The Twitter myth revisited: intraday investor sentiment, Twitter activity and individual-level stock return volatility. J. Bank. Finance **96**, 355–367 (2018)
6. Caprolu, M., Sadighian, A., Di Pietro, R.: Characterizing the 2022 Russo-Ukrainian Conflict Through the Lenses of Aspect-Based Sentiment Analysis: Dataset, Methodology, and Preliminary Findings. arXiv preprint arXiv:2208.04903 (2022)
7. Jabreel, M., Hassan, F., Moreno, A.: Target-dependent sentiment analysis of tweets using bidirectional gated recurrent neural networks. In: Advances in Hybridization of Intelligent Methods: Models, Systems and Applications, pp. 39–55 (2018)
8. Pratama, B.Y., Sarno, R.: Personality classification based on Twitter text using Naive Bayes, KNN and SVM. In: 2015 International Conference on Data and Software Engineering (ICoDSE), pp. 170–174. IEEE (2015)
9. Zerrouki, K., Hamou, R.M., Rahmoun, A.: Sentiment analysis of tweets using Naïve Bayes, KNN, and decision tree. In: Research Anthology on Implementing Sentiment Analysis Across Multiple Disciplines, pp. 538–554. IGI Global (2022)
10. Firmansyah, I., Asnawi, M.H., Hasanah, S.A., Novian, R., Pravitasari, A.A. A comparison of support vector machine and naïve Bayes classifier in binary sentiment reviews for PeduliLindungi application. In: 2021 International Conference on Artificial Intelligence and Big Data Analytics, pp. 140–145. IEEE (2021)
11. Chen, Y.: Convolutional neural network for sentence classification. Master's thesis, University of Waterloo (2015)
12. Zhang, X., Zhao, J., LeCun, Y.: Character-level convolutional networks for text classification. In: Advances in Neural Information Processing Systems, vol. 28 (2015)
13. Xu, G., Meng, Y., Qiu, X., Yu, Z., Wu, X.: Sentiment analysis of comment texts based on BiLSTM. IEEE Access **7**, 51522–51532 (2019)
14. Yin, X., Liu, C., Fang, X.: Sentiment analysis based on BiGRU information enhancement. J. Phys. Conf. Ser. **1748**(3), 032054. IOP Publishing (2021)

15. Hameed, Z., Shapoval, S., Garcia-Zapirain, B., Zorilla, A.M. Sentiment analysis using an ensemble approach of BiGRU model: a case study of AMIS tweets. In: 2020 IEEE International Symposium on Signal Processing and Information Technology (ISSPIT) (2021)
16. Jia, L., Jiang, T., Meng, J.H., Zhang, T.: Tibetan text classification method based on BiLSTM model. In; 2020 International Conference on Artificial Intelligence and Electromechanical Automation (AIEA), pp. 27–31. IEEE (2020)
17. Li, Y.H., Harfiya, L.N., Chang, C.C.: Featureless blood pressure estimation based on photoplethysmography signal using CNN and BiLSTM for IoT devices. Wirel. Commun. Mob. Comput. **2021**, 1–10 (2021)
18. Yu, Q., Zhao, H., Wang, Z.: Attention-based bidirectional gated recurrent unit neural networks for sentiment analysis. In: Proceedings of the 2nd International Conference on Artificial Intelligence and Pattern Recognition, pp. 116–119. ACM Press (2019)
19. Abdelgwad, M.M., Soliman, T.H.A., Taloba, A.I., Farghaly, M.F.: Arabic aspect based sentiment analysis using bidirectional GRU based models. J. King Saud Univ.-Comp. Inf. Sci. **34**(9), 6652–6662 (2022)
20. Ouyang, X., Zhou, P., Li, C.H., Liu, L.: Sentiment analysis using convolutional neural network. In: 2015 IEEE International Conference on Computer and Information Technology; Ubiquitous Computing and Communications; Dependable, Autonomic and Secure Computing; Pervasive Intelligence and Computing, pp. 2359–2364. IEEE (2015)
21. Shi, L., Du, K., Zhang, C., Ma, H., Yan, W.: Lung sound recognition algorithm based on Vggish-Bigru. IEEE Access. **7**, 139438–139449 (2019)

Droneways: Definition of Unmanned Aircraft Vehicles Airways and Traffic Management for Urban and Interurban Environments – A Survey

Rafael Marinho de Andrade[1,2], Elcio Hideiti Shiguemori[1,2], and Rafael Duarte Coelho dos Santos[1(✉)]

[1] National Institute for Space Research, São José dos Campos, SP, Brazil
rafael.santos@inpe.br

[2] Advanced Studies Institute, São José dos Campos SP, Brazil

Abstract. In the 20th century aviation has proven itself as one of the most important techno-social revolutions of modern human history. Now, Unmanned Aerial Vehicles (UAVs) are on the verge of leading the next techno-social revolution, remodeling several areas such as logistics, passengers and cargo transport, surveillance, etc., moving a global market that does not stop growing. The establishment of UAV traffic management systems (UTM) is necessary to make this revolution happen. Ten years after the establishment of the UTM concept, it has been expanded around the world and moves more and more interested parties to develop research to define, optimize and implement technologies and legal apparatuses to make UTMs something practical, real, and effective. Despite all the advances so far, the development of UTM still depends to be maturated for it to be finally implemented: it is an area rich in discoveries and definitions to be made, with problems that await solutions from all sides. In this article, a historical recapitulation and composition of the current state of development were carried out.

Keywords: UAS Traffic Management · Unmanned Aerial Vehicles · Dynamic Environmental Modeling · Artificial Intelligence

1 Introduction

In the 20th century, aviation has proven itself as one of the most important techno-social revolutions of modern human history, allowing better mobility of people and goods and being a key component in defense [5]. By the middle of that century, the remotely piloted aircraft systems (RPAS) appeared [27], also known as "unmanned aerial vehicles" (UAV), but it was only in the 21st century that remotely piloted aircraft technologies advanced and became miniaturized to the point of becoming an affordable technological trend, especially during the 2010s [13]. Then, UAVs began to draw attention to the most diverse areas as a promising and often relatively simple tool to be applied in scenarios ranging

O. Gervasi et al. (Eds.): ICCSA 2023 Workshops, LNCS 14107, pp. 179–197, 2023.
https://doi.org/10.1007/978-3-031-37114-1_13

from logistics and remote sensing to surveillance and search and rescue missions [20]; the possibilities are so wide that they can be considered in the solution of practically any conceivable problem [13].

There is research for the development of UAVs to meet the most diverse needs, establishing and moving a market that doesn't stop growing, impacting all the markets involved – it is estimated that by the end of 2022 the global UAV market was worth around USD 43 billion, and this value is expected to rise to somewhere around USD 600 billions by the year of 2030 [11]. In 2017, there were more than one million UAVs registered in the USA, of which more than 80% were registered for recreational purposes [9].

Today, just like conventional aircraft in the past, UAVs are leading a techno-social revolution by being increasingly applied as a solution to an increasingly diverse range of problems. The existence of UAVs in contemporary society is a striking reality, but the legislation and rules for the control and management of these aircraft are still incipient [2]. In fact, to date, no system for controlling and managing UAV traffic has been established in most parts of the world.

A factor that determined the success of conventional aircraft since the 20th century is its serious and efficient set of international rules since the operation of aircraft is considered a critical operation given its destructive potential [20]. It lead to the establishment of Air Traffic Management systems (ATM), and their operation with the highest rigor consolidated civil aviation as one of the safest and most efficient systems ever made. UAV systems, however, cannot follow the same rules since they have different flight capabilities due to their usually smaller sizes that allow them to fly and reach the most difficult and critical places, such as between buildings or even indoor environments. Even being used all around the world, there are currently no operational traffic monitoring systems available for UAVs.

Even though no UAV management system hasn't been implemented, there are initiatives under development so that airlines for managing activities with UAVs become something real and practical. In the USA, there is the pioneer UTM (UAS Traffic Management) from the FAA and NASA, the UAM (Urban Air Mobility), also from the FAA, and the UTFC (UAS Traffic Flow Control) from NASA, in addition to MITRE initiatives. In Europe, there is the U-Space from the European Commission, the DLR U-SPACE from the German Aerospace Center, METROPOLIS, and the LLRTM (Low-Level RPAS Traffic Management) from ONERA. In Asia, there is the UTM concept from Nanyang Technological University (Singapore), UOMS (UAS Aviation Operation Management System) from China, JAXA's UTM (Japanese Aerospace Exploration Agency) [2].

The establishment of traffic management systems for such aircraft is a latent contemporary society need, which is currently experiencing a techno-social revolution around aerial vehicles popularly known as "drones", which can assume different proportions and aerodynamic capacities, as well as operating in different regimes and for different purposes. With the establishment of such systems, mainly known as "UTM", society will be able to safely and efficiently enjoy the inherent advantages and resources of these aircraft, making society more efficient in several areas and positively moving the economy.

In this article, a historical recapitulation and composition of the current state of development are carried out by the bibliographies involving the lines of research involved in the development of traffic management systems for UAS, which can be important for the development of upcoming projects.

2 UAV Laws Around the World

All sovereign nations with an international airport follow an international statute defined by the International Civil Aviation Organization (ICAO), which means that international civil aviation follows, in general, always the same rules. For now, however, this only applies to conventional civil aviation and ICAO doesn't have a statute with centralized rules for all sovereign nations to follow when is about UAVs – however much the general recommendation is that these aircraft do not interfere with the operations of conventional aircraft, or otherwise operate just like them. As a consequence, at least for now, each nation is free to define the rules for the operation of UAVs and the like within their territories.

Although there are some standards in the establishment of legislation for UAVs – which consequently impact on the rules defined for the operation of eventual UTMs –, the influence of two agents in defining these laws and rules is somewhat clear: 1) the civil aviation local laws that already existed and was in force before the popularization of UAVs, and 2) the ideals defined by already conceptually established UTMs (such as the FAA-NASA UTM and the U-Space).

International laws and regulations – whose access links are centralized in [12] – tend to vary considerably, even though they show some standards. These standards have some consistency among sovereign nations in Europe, in addition to a certain influence from the FAA-NASA UTM (which simply limits UAV airspace to up to 120 m high and establishes concerns for meteorological and social conditions) and the U-Space. Table 1 presents general restrictions for several nations in Europe, and Table 2 for nations elsewhere [1,6,19,26].

3 The Evolution of UAV Traffic Management

Since UAVs are allowed to operate in several distance ranges (depending on their capabilities), they depend on legislation and technological resources to control their traffic, ensuring that their operations are safe and efficient.

3.1 Dawn of UTM: Early-2010

Until the mid-2010s, while UAVs were becoming popular, the laws were still incipient and also unclean [14]: an aircraft could be legally considered a toy, a model airplane, or an aircraft of conventional use. The growing popularization of UAVs made the need for definitions of laws and rules more evident, to avoid accidents and assign legal responsibilities. In general, the first organizations assigned to deal with this type of responsibility and control were the regulatory bodies linked to aeronautics.

Table 1. General restrictions for UAV in European sovereign nations [19].

Sovereign nation	Minimum distance	Constraint element
Belgium	2778 m	Airports
	926 m	Heliports
	50 m	Building, people, animals
Croatia	3 km	Airport and approach/departure zone
	150 m	Group of people
	30 m	People and structures
Czech Republic	150 m	Congested areas
	100 m	Person not directly associated with the operation
Germany	1,5 km	Airports
	No fly zone	Above people, accident and disaster areas, prisons, military installations, industrial areas and power stations
Ireland	8 km	Airports
	2 km	Aircraft in flight
	150 m	People, vessel, vehicle and structures
Italy	5 km	Airports
	150 m	Congested areas
	50 m	People and properties
Poland	5 km	Airports
Slovenia	300 m	Crowds
	50 m	Power lines, roads, railways, etc.
Spain	8 km	Airports
Sweden	50 m	People, animals and properties
Switzerland	5 km	Airfields
	100 m	Crowds
United Kingdom	150 m	Congested areas
	50 m	People, objects and vehicles

Since 1981, remotely controlled model airplanes could occupy the American airspace as long as they were at safe distances from the civilian population, airports, or areas insensitive to noise, at a height of up to 120 m [10]. This same legislation was faced with the need for updates, and by 2013 this became even more latent with research on drones for transport and logistics operations already conducted by notable companies such as Amazon, DHL, Google, etc.

By 2014, UAVs were classified into three types: high-capacity (somewhat similar to conventional aircraft), small-sized (which weighs less than 1 kg) and medium-sized (the most common classification nowadays) [14].

3.2 First Steps: Mid-2010s

As shown in Fig. 1, American legislation (defined by the FAA) divides airspace into seven classes, where A, B, C, D, and E are ATM-dependent controlled spaces, F is unused and the G is uncontrolled [8]. Class G is the low-flying height airspace that matters to whatever is immediately below (such as properties).

Table 2. General restrictions for UAV in Asian, Oceanian and Latin-American sovereign nations [19].

Sovereign nation	Minimum distance	Constraint element
Australia	30 m	People not involved in operation, buildings, properties, structures and animals.
Brazil	5,6 km	Registered aerodromes, operating on approach/takeoff zones
	2 km	Registered helipads and agricultural aviation areas
	1,9 km	Registered aerodromes, operating outside of approach/takeoff zones
	30 m	People not involved in operation, buildings, properties, structures and animals
	No fly zone	Above crowds and populated areas.
China	5 km	National boundary lines, radio observations
	2 km	Landing points for manned aircraft, borderlines, satellite earth stations
	1 km	Military reservation, thunderhead, buildings, tall towers, power grids, wind power
	500 m	High-speed railway
	200 m	Warehouses with inflammable and explosive objects, petrol stations, electric power facilities, mountains.
Japan	30 m	People and properties
	No fly zone	Over event sites with group of people
United Arab Emirates	5 km	Airports, heliports, airfields and controlled airspace
	150 m	Crowds, public and private properties

The "thin" UTM, by Foina *et al.*: [10] presented a solution based on the ideas described by NASA and operation of systems applied in autonomous cars, relying more on sensors than third-parties information. This solution considered three components: 1) electronic identification, 2) route planning system, and 3) ground identification devices. The electronic identification consists of sequences of colored light signals. The route planning system (main component) consists of a communication protocol between the aircraft and the UTM, where the starting and ending points of the routes are communicated. The UTM manages the airspace based on airspace concurrency restrictions and other particularities, thus determining the definitive route that is sent to the aircraft.

The system relies on simplicity, not requiring continuous communication between the aircraft and the UTM, where the UTM would be "thin". The identification system would be a system based on computer vision to read the aforementioned electronic identification (working similarly to a traffic radar) and thus perform the necessary validations regarding the aircraft, its route, etc.

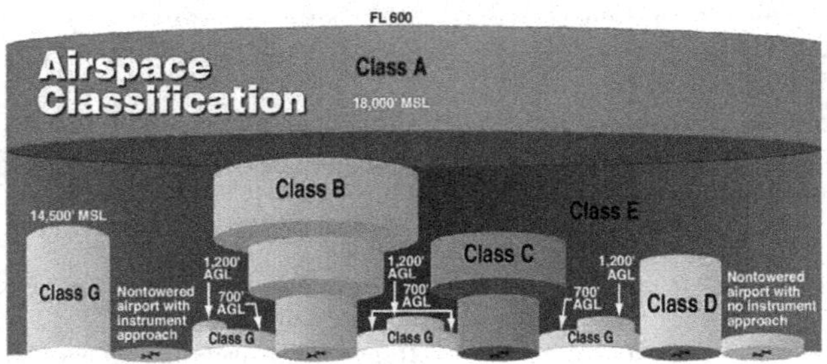

Fig. 1. Classification of the American airspace, from [8].

The Zhu and Wei Geofences: In the literature, among the approaches that are mainly concerned with safety, those that consider the geofence approach stand out, a concept that was proposed by the European Organization for Civil Aviation Equipment (EURO-CAE) together with NASA [2]. Consist of virtually delimited geographic zones following specific rules within their volume; geofences are defined as areas restricted to the flight of controlled amounts of aircraft, or even no aircraft at all, reserving them only for specific aircraft.

[28] defined that geofences are a way to ensure the use of airspace with the lowest collision probabilities and that dynamic geofences, in turn, should guarantee greater flexibility and security to the UTM, where its 3D spaces are lean and follow aircraft throughout their operations, like bubbles; the main advantage of this is to prevent geofences from becoming too complex, without becoming rudimentary like a huge bubble that envelops all presumed operational space.

This kind of solution depends on planning and high stability of the aircraft and/or continuous communication between them and the UTM, but the geofences themselves are modelled taking into account the most agile displacements. In any case, [28] consider that the only communication between the aircraft and the UTM is in the planning and deliberation for operations, with less communications as possible.

For environment modeling, everything is modeled as a graph, where the geofences are dynamically generated from the graph's vertices.

3.3 Expansion: Late-2010s

By the end of the 2010s, the UTM concept and its needs were already clear after the efforts to establish them, mainly by NASA, and so a period of research mainly to improve and optimize technologies and approaches for the implementation of UTMs begun. The concept has also expanded around the world.

A Framework for Singapore: Applying evolutionary algorithms, [23] proposed a framework with three main components: 1) traffic network construction, 2) route planning, and 3) takeoff scheduling.

The traffic network consists of the urban topography defined as a graph, where the nodes must be in safe places in relation to physical structures such as buildings, for example, and must present the greatest possible connectivity.

The routing algorithm defines both routes with intersections and without intersections, where the latter aims to minimize the chances of conflicts and, therefore, collisions. Basically, it consists of applying Dijkstra's algorithm or similar algorithms like A*; also uses tabu searches to avoid restricted areas, depth and breadth searches to define flexibility. [23] also consider the application of other linear programming resources in the algorithm.

The scheduling based on an evolutionary algorithm consists of defining the ideal takeoff and landing points and time, in order to avoid conflicts. For proof of concept purposes, they assumed that all aircraft would move at constant speed.

The validation took into account the city of Singapore and the tests were conducted with delivery activities, with previously defined take-off and landing points. On average, there were no waits of more than a few seconds for takeoff.

Not long after, [17] claimed that, although many approaches applied to define routes in UTMs have been presented, few show concern about the risks involved in the urban air environment inherent to UTM operations. They also noted that probabilistic roadmaps (PRM) and random rapid exploration trees (RRT) have improved route planning for UAVs.

Resuming the work presented by [23], [17] proposed and investigated an interesting model of risk-based UAV route planning, aiming to be safe and efficient in urban environments and low flight, considering attributes such as signal strength and population density as risk blocks.

With regard to risks, four types are considered: 1) physical obstacles (such as buildings), 2) meteorological adversities (such as wind, fog, rain, among others), 3) operational restrictions (such as GPS signal) and 4) regulatory and social constraints (socially defined, such as militarized areas and the like). These risks were also scaled in five levels, based on probability and severity.

To actually define the routes, the Dijkstra, A* and ant colony algorithms were tested, where the displacements between the nodes would have 7 directional degrees of freedom.

As well as in [17,23] simulated tests with the urban environment of Singapore. The results indicate that Dijkstra's algorithm is slightly more secure than A*, but much more expensive; the ant colony algorithm didn't perform well.

The Taiwanese UTM: [15] based their work on the legislation defined by the CAA, with rules for flights up to or above 120 m in height [3] and taking into account, in particular, suburban regions. They idealized an architecture very similar to a smart city, but having as main inspiration the ATM systems.

[15] proposed their own communication protocol and well-defined workflows for all UAV flight stages (pre-takeoff, flight and post-landing), prioritizing UTM operation with prior mission planning (ideally at least 30 min before takeoff). It also proposes circular surveillance for each aircraft for an area of about 600 m that surrounds it.

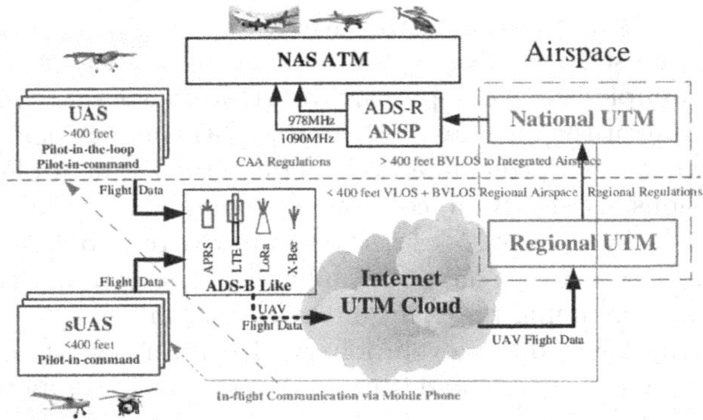

Fig. 2. UTM for Taiwan airspace control, from [16].

[15] have developed a prototype and considered that plans changes in flight time can be very chaotic for the UTM. Because of this, they suggest that such changes are not allowed.

Anticipating that as soon as UAVs would ordinarily operate below 120 m high in urban and interurban environments to fulfill their tasks, and that, depending on the capabilities and assignments of the aircraft in question, they may still be subject to occupying the conventional aircraft space, [16] noticed in communication and infrastructure the foundations for the development of UTMs, including the appropriate frequency spectrum for this type of communication.

[16] proposed a hierarchical UTM, composed of regional UTMs that sums in a larger UTM where communication is the key point, as shown in the diagram in Fig. 2 as "Regional UTM" and "National UTM", respectively, or "RUTM" and "NUTM".

A proof-of-concept test was conducted in Tainan (which comprises its own RUTM). The results indicate that the hierarchical division helps to relieve the computational cost in the realization of deconflictions, making them more agile, and without any problems in the operational safety of the system.

3.4 Maturation: Early-2020s

Entering the 2020s, UTM research was already present in several world powers and the concept was already established *de facto*. There were still no operational UTMs in operation, but studies on specific optimization applications with the aim of being employed in UTM systems became more frequent.

The Pötter Neto, Bertolli and Saotome Simulations: The A* algorithm was also addressed by [18] for route planning, in order to find optimal routes between two points. In particular, they extracted 2D and 3D maps from simulated environments, and compared the A* algorithm between 2D and 3D environments for UTMs.

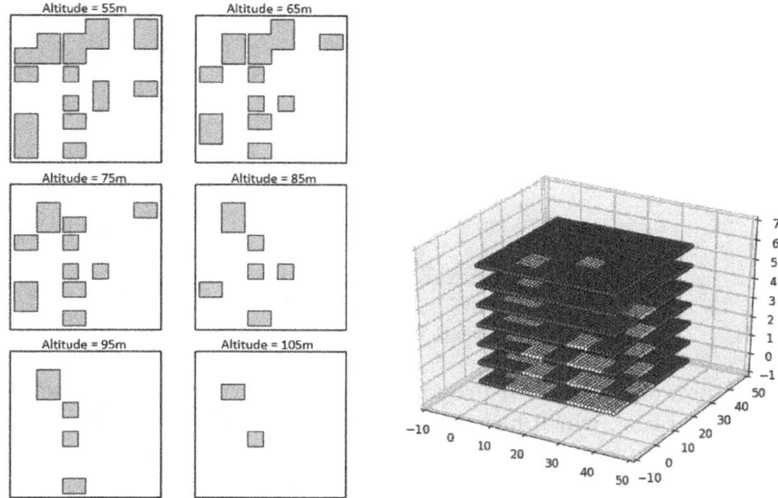

Fig. 3. Simulation environment modeling as a tensor of order 3, from [18].

First, [18] modeled the environment with buildings that occupy homogeneous areas and with varying heights. The maps are defined as a tensor of order 3, where each voxel represents $1\,\text{m}^3$, as graphically abstracted as in Fig. 3. The maps are then vectors with matrices of dimension 200×200, where the altitudes have been more discreetly separated.

To reduce the computational cost, the matrices were then simplified and grouped into sets of 5×5.

The experimentation process included the definition of a pair of voxels as a takeoff and landing points. As a practical verdict, the A* algorithm covered more space for the displacements when executed restricted to 2D displacements, while the 3D algorithms are more spatially efficient (however requiring a considerably higher computational cost); therefore, displacements in mostly horizontal traffic lines would be slower, while traffic lines with more vertical freedom would be more agile (but more complex).

In the following year, [19] returned with a update, presenting the same details but in a more elaborate form and accompanied by additional details, such as the application both Euclidean and Manhattan distance in the simulations.

An UTM Optimised by Artificial Intelligence: [25] identified both the FAA-NASA UTM and U-Space as Air Traffic Flow Management (ATFM) extensions, and declared that none of them can currently meet the needs and tactics that will be needed in the coming years in intense low-height flight operations. They proposed then an approach that combines tabu search and A* algorithm to support the UTM decision process, providing dynamic route re-planning in complex environments, achieving better results for NP-complex problems. The solution is based on four-dimensional trajectory functionalities, being resilient to uncertainties, and seeks to be safe and efficient, while reducing uncertainties. A diagram of this UTM is shown in Fig. 4.

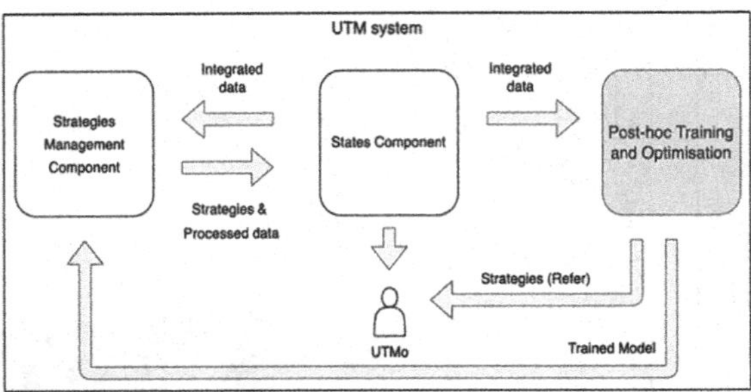

Fig. 4. IA-optimized UTM structure, from [25].

In previous works [24], they proposed a GRU recurrent network architecture for Deep Q Learning, which has components to deal with the multidimensional states of the environment and components for strategies management, as well as components for post-training optimization; in [25], the focus was on post-training optimization, with a component for generating training sets based on genetic algorithms and tabu search; the training data is stored in the strategy management component and the training data is the actual states.

The components may not always immediately achieve optimal solutions, but the data may be reintroduced into machine learning training algorithms.

Throughout the system operation, there is a continuous data exchange between the database and the route re-planning system, always integrating the data: the A* algorithm enters as a tabu search *pipeline* process, aiming always avoiding route conflicts or otherwise minimizing their effects. It also has its complexity increased as the system deal with more routes under these objectives.

[25] also conducted a case study simulating high-density operations. Finally, the tabu search presented, in comparison with the genetic algorithm, larger amounts of collision cases and a slightly smaller number of steps in the paths, also requiring time around 15% to 20% greater (roughly speaking), using modest *hardware* and *software* configurations.

The Bauranov and Rakas Review: Within this expanding universe, while several works (such as those already summarized here) make contributions to its development, [2] stand out for bringing together the most complete UTM research to date, listing, summarizing and synthesizing relevant studies grouped by factors that impact aerospace modeling.

Among the various points addressed, [2] research led them to gather knowledge to define the least problematic airspace possible, taking into account in a synthetic way problems that go beyond collision with structures and objects (including other aircraft).

The research also exposes important information, such as 1) the fact that the restriction that aircraft cannot be less than 5 nautical miles from another while in flight (or 90 s of range in cruising speed) does not aligns with the idea of small aircraft and in urban areas with low flight height; 2) the considerably high noise produced by UAVs tends to be a particularly difficult problem to deal with, and it is observed that this is becoming one of the most annoying sounds in

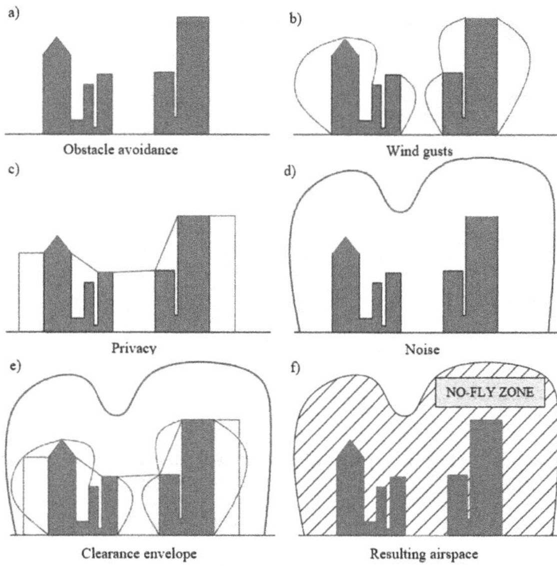

Fig. 5. Flight zones delimitation according to different constraints, from [2].

the modern world according to recent research [4]; and 3) visual pollution is also a popular concern, indicating that traffic over less populated regions (including over water) is a sensible idea for this problem.

The problems also come up against the issue of privacy and its moral, ethical and legal issues, as also observed by [19], given the fact that UAVs are usually equipped with imaging sensors (whether for recording images or for its avionics).

Other issues were also noted with regards to communication and sensors, including unreliability and errors that may be inappropriate for a system like UTM (like the ones associated with GPS).

But the most worrying problem exposed by [2] is the issue of wind gusts and weather conditions, presented as the main risk agents for UAV operations as well to any other aircraft.

More than just exposing relevant details about UTMs, [2] also suggest and support some assumptions such as the idea of avoiding regions and building critical infrastructure such as hospitals, militarized zones, schools and the like.

In summary, one of the contributions of [2] is the conservative airspace delimitation approach demonstrated in Fig. 5. This approach, however, practically eliminates the presence of UAVs in an environment where many of them must be used to fulfill their operational objectives: in the nearby urban environment, in direct or close contact with customers of their respective business models.

Additionally, [2] also summarized relationships between the amount of structure needed to establish the observed concepts, as well as plotted curves that describe the relationship between the amount of structure and various performance metrics; these relationships are shown in Fig. 6.

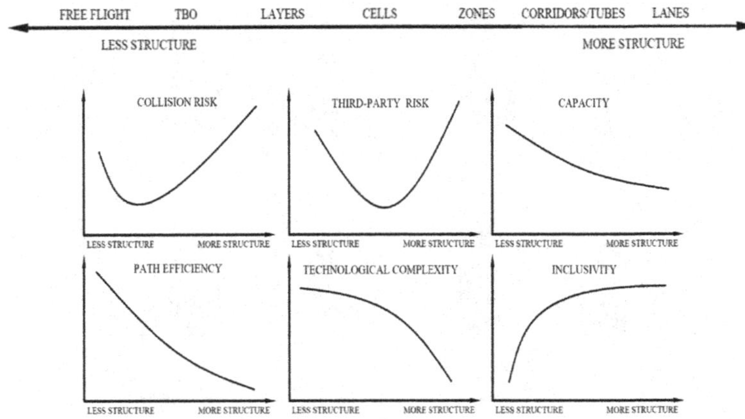

Fig. 6. Relations between the amount of structure needed for different concepts and their performances, from [2].

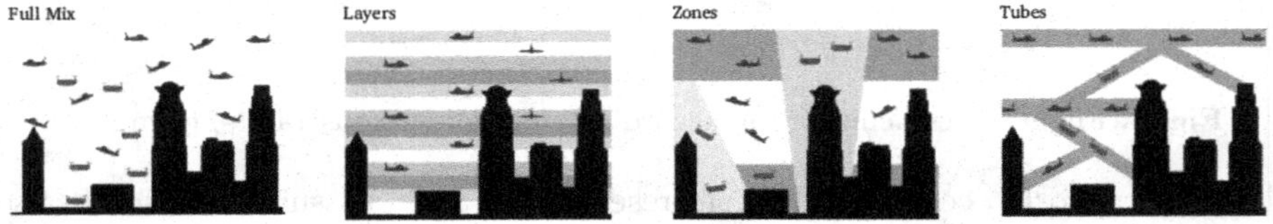

Fig. 7. Different airspace structures considered for METROPOLIS UTM, from [22].

Table 3. Comparison between considered structures for the METROPOLIS UTM [2].

Comparison attribute	Full mix	Layers	Zones	Tubes
Safety	2	1	3	4
Third party risk	2	1	3	4
Capacity	1	2	3	4
Efficiency	1	2	3	4
Noise	2	1	4	3

Finally, also in a comparative way, [2] addressed the concept of a UTM for the European Union called METROPOLIS [22] and its four different airspace structures: 1) free flight, 2) layers, 3) zones and 4) tubes, which are best graphically represented in Fig. 7 and whose comparison is summarized in Table 3.

In summary, taking into account the work of [22] when comparing these four structures, the layers approach takes 1st place in the search for the best structure, followed by the free flight approach, while the 3rd place goes to zones structure and 4th (and last) place goes to tube structure.

Dynamic Four-Dimensional Geofences: [21] considers that, with the pace of growth in the number of UAVs in circulation, it should not take long before the airspace where they travel becomes congested, either spatially or logically. To deal with such conditions, they proposed a UTM based on geofences that can be added, adjusted and removed from static and temporal definitions, with means for merging, partitioning and performing deconflictions of geofences.

In this UTM, the approved geofences would therefore be temporally organized and spatially processed to have non-conflicting boundaries. Hence, every conceivable airspace position is reserved for none or a single one geofence. They explored the theory and implementation of a geofences management system in UTMs and related algorithms, standing out for being apparently the first to offer deconfliction capabilities in three-dimensional geofences.

In practice, the geofence is an aerospace volume with spatial, temporal and permissive constraints. If a geofence conflicts with some airspace of higher priority (an airport, for example), the geofence must be defined in a way that excludes this region of higher operational priority. There may also be time restrictions on when users could define and make use of their own geofences, and the priority

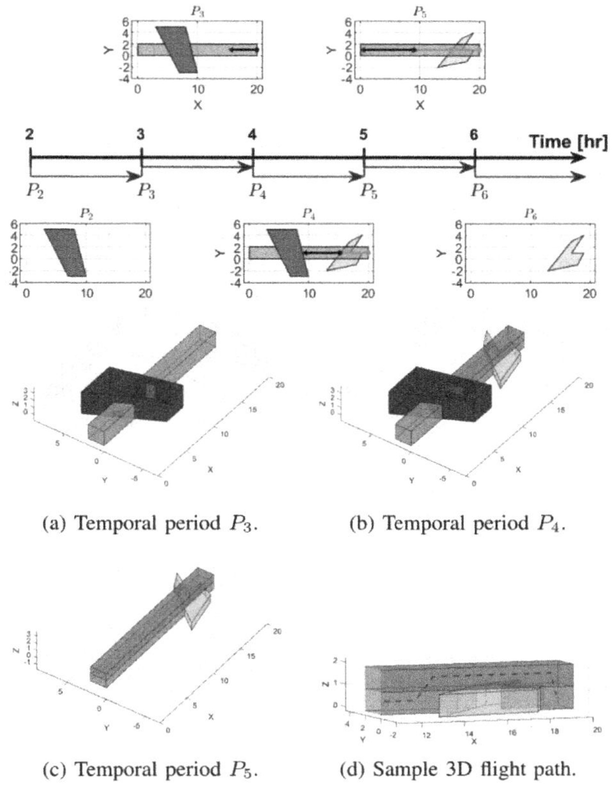

(a) Temporal period P_3.
(b) Temporal period P_4.
(c) Temporal period P_5.
(d) Sample 3D flight path.

Fig. 8. Example of spatiotemporal evolution of geofences, from [21].

tiebreaker between two geofences may be in favor of the one defined first, so that the geofences created afterwards must adapt to the existing airspace.

For operational safety reasons, minimum vertical heights and widths must be established for the definition of geofences, and they can be also vertically partitioned to create deconflictions trends in the definition of new geofences. These partitions generated from the original geofence would be assigned for the same purpose, as two or more "subgeofences" of it, and which in practice compose a whole geofences, as can be seen in Fig. 8.

Fluid-Inspired Aerial Traffic Lines: At the same time that Ella Atkins was researching dynamic four-dimensional geofences, featured in [21], she was also busy collaborating with other innovative approaches. In one these approaches, [7] adopted continuous Eulerian mechanics as a way of coordinating spatiotemporal planning, such as an ideal fluid flow governed by Laplace partial differential equations (PDE). The solution seeks to be temporally invariant, and it's inspired by physical concepts rather than just mathematics.

Assuming that 1) the design and allocation of air corridors are centralized and 2) each UTM is connected to a single local UTM cloud that manages such airspace (mainly at low flight heights), the solution seeks to define smooth aerial traffic lines between obstacles (like buildings), as shown in Fig. 9, where the direction of these streamlines rotating clockwise every 5 m.

The approach ensures that traffic lines maintain safety margins away from obstacles. The operation of the traffic lines is in order of requests, and are optimized using Markov decision processes (MDP) which, according to hierarchically organized terminal and non-terminal states, optimizes the traffic lines; these MDP have a reasonable computational cost but take into account the optimization for a single aircraft at a time – check the diagram in Fig. 10.

For experimentation, simulations were conducted based on Downtown Tucson, extracting the coordinates of the region and converting them to Euclidean space, and model the 3D buildings in the simulation environment. In this environment, building areas were defined as obstacles, as shown in Fig. 11, and very close buildings were grouped into convex envelopes.

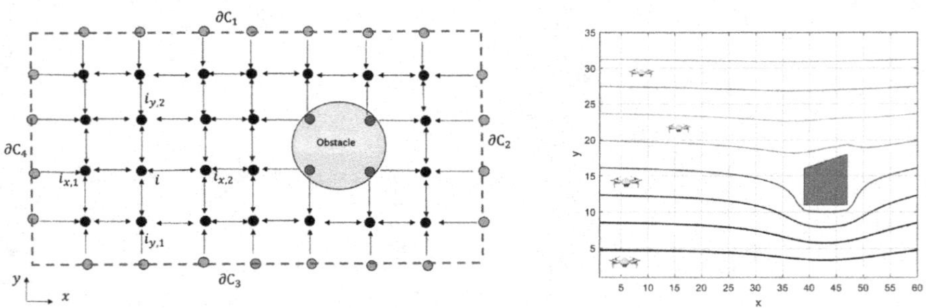

Fig. 9. Air corridors' streamline definition, from [7].

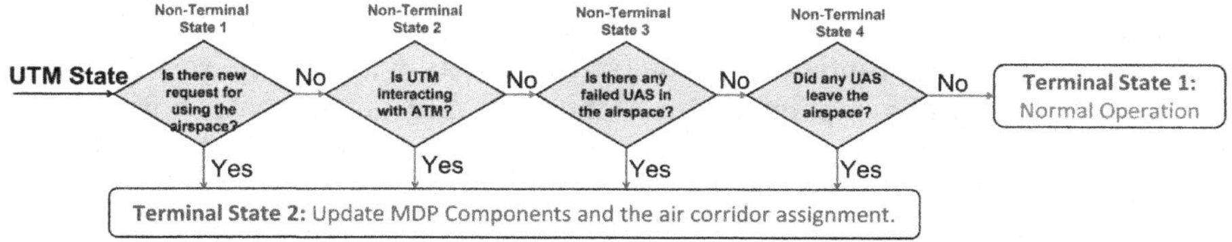

Fig. 10. MDP state machine for UAV allocation into the air corridors, from [7].

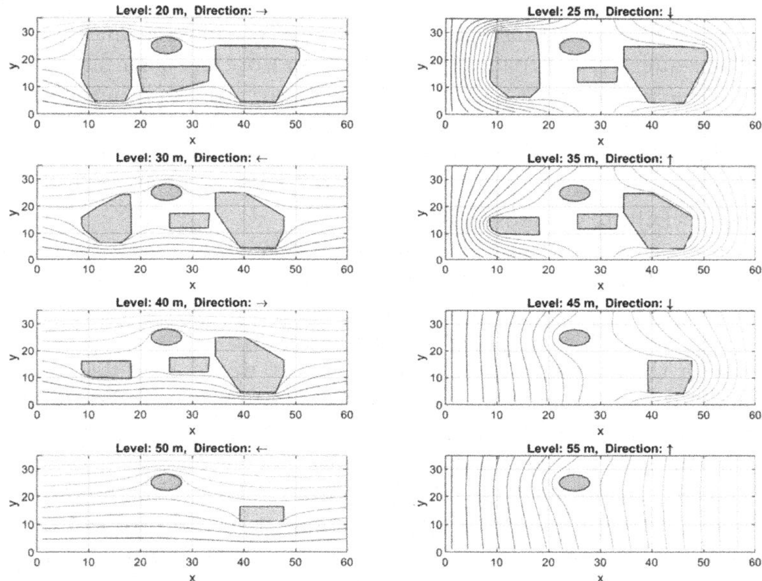

Fig. 11. Streamlines definition on layers, from [7].

Finally, from the streamlines with directions defined by height (with a 90 ° clockwise change every 5 m), the Euclidean space can be summarized as a set of graphs organized as a three-dimensional mesh that can generate routes from any linear programming algorithm.

4 Discussion

In view of the analyzed references, some patterns and preferences in technological approaches are notable, thus forming some specific lines of research that contribute directly or indirectly to the development of the UTM concept.

It is observed that several geometric abstractions were approached for modeling the environment, as well as different abstractions for defining the airspace. Figure 6 and Fig. 7 (with Table 3) summarized these abstractions in a synthetic and comparative way, showing that no approach meet all the needs of an UTM:

although the structures most recommended by [2] are free flight zones and layers. These structures stands out amongst the others with regard to safety, risk to third parties, traffic capacity, route efficiency and noise levels, but demand greater technological complexity both from the UTM and from the aircraft to work out, consequently being less inclusive.

Despite this diversity and the varied advantages and disadvantages associated with each structural abstraction, practically all approaches fall back onto the abstraction of the environment as a graph, either immediately (where the environment is in fact already modeled as a graph) or discrete (where the graph is defined after excluding obstacles and defining waypoints, among other processes). Consequently, approaches to routing and optimization are, in general, based on operation research algorithms and linear programming such as Dijkstra's algorithm, A* and ant colony algorithm.

The A* algorithm, for example, was the most common approach in both 2D and 3D abstractions, explicitly addressed in [17,18,23] and [25]. These first two also addressed Dijkstra's algorithm.

More than just generating optimal routes, however, there were concerns about the complexity of the system, with the computational cost distribution between the UTM and the aircraft, as well as the communication between them. The solutions presented by [10] stand out for considering a "thin" UTM system, where most of the computational processing cost would be outside the actual management system, distributing duties between other involved devices. [28], in turn, present a solution that relies on ideally minimal amounts of communication between the aircraft and the UTM. In contrast, [15] relied almost completely on connectivity for the efficiency of their approach, reinforced in [16]; even so, both have in common the proposal of their own communication protocol.

The need for changes in flight itineraries during flight was also a common concern in virtually every work that addressed the dynamism of air environments, considering both meteorological and systematic particularities. During prototyping exercises, [15] even assumed that this dynamism is so chaotic that they thought it best to prevent changes in itineraries from being made once the aircraft takes off, in addition to requiring the itineraries scheduling with at least half hour in advance; this more radical perception is somewhat in line with the contemporary work of [15], who argues that deconflictions do should be carried out in flight time, while making it clear that proactive deconflictions are much more desirable than reactive deconflictions. To better distribute the communication, making the problem more computationally manageable, [16] presented proposals that divide a larger UTM (linked to the ATM) into several subsystems that manage the zones in which they are responsible and establish contact with a superior centralizing unit.

For optimisation, the use of metaheuristics such as tabu search [23,25] and genetic algorithms [25] were addressed, presenting promising results. The use of more advanced artificial intelligence techniques in [24] has also applied recurrent neural networks and reinforcement learning for the definition and continuous optimization of routes, as well as Markov Decision Process [7].

Finally, since current aircraft do not necessarily follow the standards and technical approvals to be able to operate in the airspace governed by UTMs with considerable technological needs, and the very technological complexities of UTMs efficient enough to be implemented would be high, it is fair to believe that this type of service will not be implemented in the near future. Even after a decade of conceptual and theoretical development by several government institutions, research institutes and private initiative corporations, this is an area of research and development that still needs to mature.

5 Conclusion

The research and development of UAV traffic management systems comprises a relatively young area that mainly gathers around the term *UAV Traffic Management*, generally reduced to the acronym UTM. The first initiatives to establish concepts and theories about this area emerged in the early 2010s in efforts conducted mainly by the FAA in conjunction with NASA, with room for collaboration with other government agencies, academic and independent research groups, and private initiatives.

About 10 years later, the FAA-NASA UTM concept has expanded around the world and moves more and more interested parties to develop research to define, optimize and implement technologies and legal apparatuses to make UTMs something practical, real and effective, in order to insert UAVs and similar vehicles into modern society, with all their benefits that promise leading the world into the next techno-social revolution.

Despite all the advances established so far by the various research centers involved in the area (which also have the remarkable collaboration between key researchers), the development of UTM still depends to be maturated for it to be finally implemented: it is an area rich in discoveries and definitions to be made, with problems that await solutions from all sides.

We can speculate that the technologies that will allow the implementation of UTMs are already established, and that a set of them will be legally required for UAVs to operate in urban and interurban environments, as happened with conventional aircraft in the 20th century. The requirement for these technologies, which ensure the safe and efficient operation of UTMs, will also push the development of the area, while make it more expensive and therefore less accessible.

It is then concluded that the research area explored in the bibliographic review is a fertile ground for the development of several research with the proposition of new approaches on, for example: 1) definitions of routes, 2) optimization of routes, 3) techniques of airspace modeling, 4) UTM system architecture modeling, 5) establishment of communication technologies and protocols.

References

1. Agência Nacional de Aviação Civil, A. Regulamento Brasileiro da Aviação Civil Especial (RBAC-E n°94). (2021)

2. Bauranov, A., Rakas, J.: Designing airspace for urban air mobility: A review of concepts and approaches. Prog. Aerosp. Sci. **125**, 100726 (2021)
3. Civil Aeronautical Administration Civil Aviation Act. (https://www.caa.gov.tw/en/content/index.asp?sno=325 2018,4)
4. Carry, L., Coyne, J.: ICAO unmanned aircraft systems (UAS), circular 328. UVS International, Blyenburgh & Co. **2012**, 112–115 (2011)
5. Colomina, I. & Molina, P. Unmanned aerial systems for photogrammetry and remote sensing: a review. ISPRS J. Photogramm. Remote Sens **92**(2014)
6. Departamento de Controle do Espaço Aéreo Sistemas de Aeronaves Remotamente Pilotadas e o Acesso ao Espaço Aéreo Brasileiro (ICA 100–40) (2015)
7. Emadi, H., Atkins, E., Rastgoftar, H. A Finite-State Fixed-Corridor Model for UAS Traffic Management (2022)
8. FAA Pilot's Handbook of Aeronautical Knowledge. FAA-H-8083-25B. (US Department of Transportation-Federal Aviation Administration-Flight ... (2016)
9. Federal Aviation Administration FAA Aerospace Forecast: Fiscal Years 2017–2037 (FAA 2017)
10. Foina, A., Krainer, C., Sengupta, R.: An Unmanned Aerial Traffic Management solution for cities using an air parcel model. In: 2015 International Conference On Unmanned Aircraft Systems (ICUAS), pp. 1295–1300 (2015)
11. Grand View Research Commercial Drone Market Size: Share and Trends Analysis Report By Product (Fixed-wing, pp. 2023–2030. Rotary Blade, Hybrid), By Application, By End-use, By Region, And Segment Forecasts (2023)
12. International Civil Aviation Organization Current UAV State Regulations (2023). https://www.icao.int/safety/UA/UASToolkit/Pages/State-Regulations.aspx
13. Jeziorska, J.: UAS for wetland mapping and hydrological modeling. Remote Sens. **11** 1997 (2019)
14. Kopardekar, P. Unmanned Aerial System (UAS) Traffic Management (UTM): Enabling Low-Altitude Airspace and UAS Operations. (NASA 2014)
15. Lin, C., Chen, T., Shao, P., Lai, Y., Chen, T., Yeh, Y.: Prototype Hierarchical UAS Traffic Management System in Taiwan. In: 2019 Integrated Communications, Navigation And Surveillance Conference (ICNS), pp. 1–13 (2019)
16. Lin, C., Shao, P.: Development of hierarchical UAS traffic management (UTM) in Taiwan. J. Phys. Conf. Ser. **1509**(1) 2012 (2020)
17. Pang, B., Tan, Q., Ra, T., Low, K.: A risk-based UAS traffic network model for adaptive urban airspace management. In: AIAA AVIATION 2020 FORUM (June 2020)
18. Pötter Neto, C., Carvalho Bertoli, G., Saotome, O.: 2D and 3D A* algorithm comparison for UAS traffic management systems. In: 2020 International Conference on Unmanned Aircraft Systems (ICUAS), pp. 72–76 (2020)
19. Pötter Neto, C., Carvalho Bertoli, G,. Saotome, O.: A-star path planning simulation for UAS Traffic Management (UTM) application. abs/2107.13103
20. Prevot, T., Rios, J., Kopardekar, P., Robinson III, J., Johnson, M., Jung, J.: UAS Traffic Management (UTM) Concept of Operations to Safely Enable Low Altitude Flight Operations. 16th AIAA Aviation Technology, Integration, And Operations Conference. (June 2016), https://doi.org/10.2514/6.2016-3292
21. Stevens, M., Atkins, E.: Geofence definition and deconfliction for UAS traffic management. IEEE Trans. Intell. Transp. Syst. **22**, 5880–5889 (2021)
22. Sunil, E., Hoekstra, J., Ellerbroek, J., Bussink, F., Nieuwenhuisen, D., Vidosavljevic, A., Kern, S.: Metropolis: Relating airspace structure and capacity for extreme traffic densities. ATM Seminar 2015, 11th USA/EUROPE Air Traffic Management R&D Seminar (2015)

23. Tan, Q., Wang, Z., Ong, Y., Low, K.: Evolutionary optimization-based mission planning for UAS traffic management (UTM). In: 2019 International Conference On Unmanned Aircraft Systems (ICUAS), pp. 952–958 (2019)
24. Xie, Y., Gardi, A., Sabatini, R.: Reinforcement learning-based flow management techniques for urban air mobility and dense low-altitude air traffic operations. In; 2021 IEEE/AIAA 40th Digital Avionics Systems Conference (DASC), pp. 1–10 (2021)
25. Xie, Y., Gardi, A., Sabatini, R.: Hybrid AI-based demand-capacity balancing for UAS traffic management and urban air mobility. In: AIAA AVIATION 2021 FORUM (July 2021)
26. Xu, C., Liao, X., Tan, J., Ye, H., Lu, H.: Recent research progress of unmanned aerial vehicle regulation policies and technologies in urban low altitude. IEEE Access **8**, 74175–74194 (2020)
27. Zaloga, S.: Unmanned Aerial Vehicles: Robotic air Warfare 1917–2007. Osprey Publishing (2008)
28. Zhu, G., Wei, P.: Low-altitude UAS traffic coordination with dynamic geofencing. In; 16th AIAA Aviation Technology, Integration, and Operations Conference (June 2016)

Geomatics for Resource Monitoring and Management (GRMM 2023)

Integration of Copernicus Data and Services to Assess Local Aridity Conditions in the Apulian Context: The Case of Marina di Ginosa

Carlo Barletta, Alessandra Capolupo(✉), and Eufemia Tarantino

Department of Civil, Environmental, Land, Building Engineering and Chemistry (DICATECh), Politecnico Di Bari, Via Orabona 4, 70125 Bari, Italy
{carlo.barletta,alessandra.capolupo,eufemia.tarantino}@poliba.it

Abstract. Water is a fundamental element for life on the Earth. Its availability, at a local scale, depends on the climate as well as on how it is managed and distributed for human use. Nowadays, water scarcity is a major concern in many parts of the world, also in relation to the possible effects of climate change and urbanization. The aim of this study is to integrate various Copernicus and other free and open data in order to calculate the main components of the water balance as defined by ISPRA's BIGBANG procedure. The territory of a basin including the locality of Marina di Ginosa, in southern Italy, was chosen as study site. All the analyses were carried out in the Google Earth Engine cloud environment, where a proper JavaScript code was developed. The estimation made it possible to retrieve monthly maps of the hydrological variables from October 2015 to September 2018 at a geometric resolution of 10 m, and to assess local drought conditions by applying the FAO-UNEP aridity index. Even if this approach is affected by uncertainties owing to the schematic representation of the natural processes, it is a valuable tool for analyzing the spatial and temporal fluctuations of the water resource availability, especially in critical areas of southern Italy.

Keywords: GEE · Climate change · BIGBANG · desertification · drought

1 Introduction

In the next future, climate change is expected to affect the water availability for human consumption and ecosystems, leading to possible changes in the hydrological cycle and, therefore, resulting in drier conditions than in the past, especially in the semi-arid regions of southern Europe. Soil-water dynamics depend on various complex hydro-meteorological and biophysical processes, that control the hydrological balance. Indeed, not all the water that flows into a catchment area infiltrates the soil; following a conceptual scheme, there is also a part of the precipitation that runs off the soil surface and another one that returns to the atmosphere through the process of evapotranspiration. Additionally, the soil-water interaction is affected by multiple factors (climatic conditions, soil physical properties, topography, land cover, soil management practices etc.).

O. Gervasi et al. (Eds.): ICCSA 2023 Workshops, LNCS 14107, pp. 201–216, 2023.
https://doi.org/10.1007/978-3-031-37114-1_14

Climate change may endanger the amount of water in the soil for social and economic activities because of natural and anthropogenic causes, as well as variations in land use/land cover (LU/LC) [1–12].

A quantitative examination of the water balance components using models is a good technique to evaluate the impacts of climate change and urbanization on aridity conditions of soils and, thus, on water resource availability. For this purpose, the Italian National Institute for Environmental Protection and Research (ISPRA) developed the "Nationwide GIS-based regular gridded hydrological water budget" procedure, called BIGBANG, which allows the monthly evaluation of the water balance components for the Italian territory through a spatially distributed approach, with a resolution of 1 km. This model employs basic and well-established approaches from the literature, requiring only a few parameters [1, 7–9, 11, 13–15]. However, in order to enhance the analysis at the local scale, it would be essential to develop a tool that allows for a better understanding of the spatial and temporal variability of these processes at a higher geometric resolution. This would aid in water management and planning for resource protection purposes.

Today, a significant source of data and information for environmental analysis and monitoring is provided by the Copernicus initiative of the European Union (EU). The Copernicus collection consists of multispectral and radar imagery acquired by the Sentinel satellites (namely the "space component"), in-situ observations from contributing missions which are provided by international and national agencies or by private entities (the so called "in-situ component"), and value-added information from the "services component", which is made up of six thematic services (marine, land, atmosphere, emergency, climate change and security) [16, 17]. The Copernicus Climate Change Service (C3S) provides data and information in a free and open format to support the analysis of climate change impacts and the EU's adaptation and mitigation policies. The C3S is based on existing research infrastructures and knowledge available worldwide, and allows its users to freely access to a variety of climate datasets in the Climate Data Store (https://cds.climate.copernicus.eu) [18, 19]. On the other hand, the Copernicus Land Monitoring Service (CLMS) provides data and information on LU/LC and biophysical parameters at the European scale with a resolution of 10 m (https://land.copernicus.eu/pan-european/high-resolution-layers), as well as other data such as the 25 m resolution pan-European digital surface model (the "EU-DEM", available at https://land.copernicus.eu/imagery-in-situ/eu-dem/eu-dem-v1-0-and-derived-products).

The aim of this work is to integrate different free and open data provided by Copernicus program with other open informative layers, provided by national or international institutions, in order to retrieve the main water balance components, as defined by the ISPRA BIGBANG procedure, on a local scale and with a geometric resolution of 10 m. This approach, which allows for the spatial and temporal analysis of the variability of the water balance components, could be a useful tool for the detailed assessment of local aridity conditions, particularly in areas of southern Italy at risk of desertification and drought, as well as to support a sustainable water resource management.

The basin's region, including the area of Marina di Ginosa in southern Italy, was chosen as the research site since it was feasible to download Copernicus data of monthly temperature and precipitation readings from 2015 to 2018. Unlike the ISPRA's BIG-BANG model, which was developed in ArcGIS software, this study was carried out by creating and implementing a JavaScript code in the Google Earth Engine (GEE) cloud platform, a free-to-use environment developed by Google for analyzing and handling a large volume of geospatial and Earth Observation (EO) data using Google's high performance computing capabilities [20–24]. The proposed methodology, which takes advantage of the cloud technology, can speed-up the operations and computations required to obtain the results.

2 Materials and Methods

2.1 Study Area and Data

The basin including the location of Marina di Ginosa, mainly belonging to the Apulia Region and, in a very small part, to the Basilicata Region, was selected as pilot site because monthly observations of air temperature and precipitation were available from a Copernicus dataset for the period 2015–2018. The study area, located between the Bradano and Lato river basins, is part of the "Ionian Arc of Taranto", in the southern sector of a foreland basin called "Bradanic Trough" (Fig. 1).

From a geomorphological point of view, this territory is characterized by a succession of marine terraces consisting of discontinuous strips of terraced marine deposits, marly grey-blue clays, calcarenites, alluvial deposits and coastal dunes resting on calcareous rocks [25, 26].

The investigated territory covers an area of 116.2 km^2, with a maximum elevation of 92.4 m above sea level (a.s.l.) and is crossed by the Galaso stream.

The climate is typically Mediterranean, characterized by fairly hot (maximum temperatures >30–35 °C) and dry summers, and mild winters. Precipitation is mostly concentrated in the autumn-winter period; its average annual amount, in the Taranto area, is often less than 500 mm/year. In general, only the autumn-winter precipitation contributes to the aquifer recharge since the scarce summer rainfall is significantly lost for evapotranspiration. In addition, in this area of the Apulia Region, rainfall characterized by high intensity prevail, minimally contributing to the groundwater recharge and causing sudden and occasional surface runoff [27].

The LU/LC of the study area was preliminarily analyzed using the Copernicus "CORINE land cover 2018" dataset (where CORINE stands for COoRdination of INFormation for the Environment), available on the CLMS website with a geometric resolution of 100 m [28]. The distribution of the LU/LC categories is detailed in Table 1: the 84.6% of the territory is dedicated to agricultural use while only 7.1% of the total area is destinated for the artificial surfaces.

To calculate the main components of the hydrological balance, monthly observations of four variables (maximum, minimum and mean temperature, and precipitation), measured by the hydro-meteorological station of Marina di Ginosa, and available in the Climatic Research Unit (CRU) v.4.06 dataset [29] (https://cds.climate.copernicus.eu/cdsapp#!/dataset/insitu-gridded-observations-global-and-regional?tab=overview) were

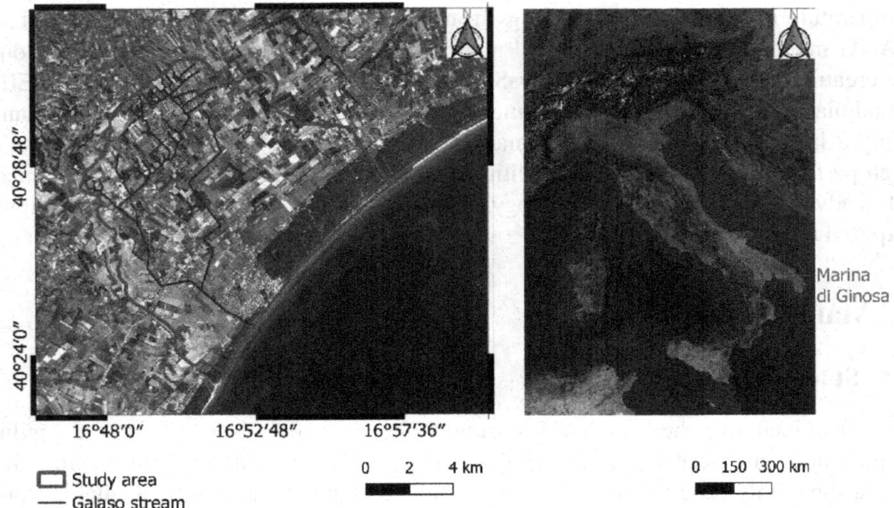

Fig. 1. Study area.

Table 1. Distribution of LU/LC classes according to CORINE land cover 2018 dataset.

	CORINE land cover class	Area [km^2]	Percentage [%]
Artificial surfaces	Continuous urban fabric	1.2	1.0
	Discontinuous urban fabric	6.2	5.3
	Dump sites	0.6	0.5
	Sport and leisure facilities	0.3	0.3
Agricultural areas	Non-irrigated arable land	34.5	29.7
	Vineyards	30.8	26.5
	Fruit trees and berry plantations	8.9	7.7
	Pastures	0.4	0.3
	Complex cultivation patterns	23.7	20.4
Forest and semi natural areas	Coniferous forest	5.6	4.8
	Sclerophyllous vegetation	3.6	3.1
	Beaches, dunes, sands	0.4	0.3

selected. Because there were no missing data in the dataset for these years, the evaluation was limited to the years 2015–2018. Moreover, the monthly temperature and precipitation values were considered constant over the entire study area.

The soil sealing maps, produced by ISPRA from the CLMS Imperviousness layers (https://land.copernicus.eu/pan-european/high-resolution-layers/imperviousness) at 10 m resolution, are essential for the implementation of the BIGBANG model [13,

30]. Because this project spanned the years 2015 to 2018, four layers, corresponding to soil sealing maps for 2015, 2016, 2017, and 2018, were acquired from the ISPRA web page (https://groupware.sinanet.isprambiente.it/uso-copertura-e-consumo-di-suolo/library/consumo-di-suolo). These classified maps were then aggregated in the GEE platform into two main macro-classes: "Impervious surface" and "Non impervious surface". Figure 2 illustrates one of the four soil sealing maps obtained in GEE after aggregating the various LU/LC classes.

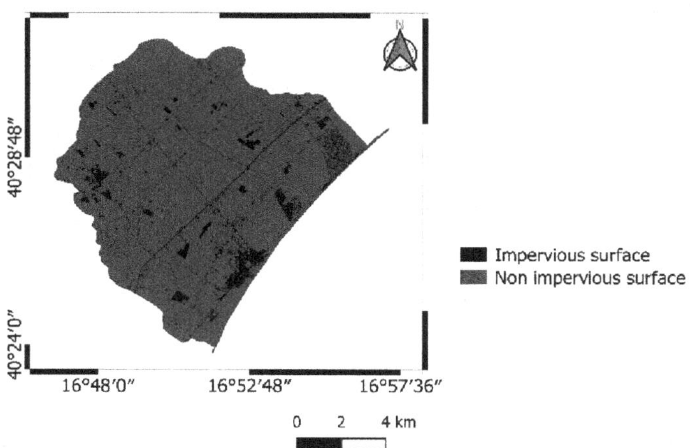

Fig. 2. The soil sealing map 2015, obtained in GEE for the study area, after aggregating the various LU/LC classes into two main categories.

Other necessary data for this work are the map of the Available Water Capacity (AWC) of the soil and the map of the Potential Infiltration Coefficient (CIP) [13]. The former, produced by the European Soil Data Center (ESDAC) [31–34] is an open data with 500 m resolution (https://esdac.jrc.ec.europa.eu/content/topsoil-physical-properties-europe-based-lucas-topsoil-data). The latter, was derived from the Mouton hydrogeological complexes map produced by ISPRA (http://www.sinanet.Isprambiente.it/it/sia-ispra/download-mais/complessi-idrogeologici/view) assigning a CIP value to each complex as reported by Celico (1998) [13, 35].

2.2 GEE and Operative Workflow

GEE is a free cloud platform that exploits Google's computational infrastructure to allow to analyze large geospatial data sets for environmental monitoring and analysis while minimizing operational and computational time. To achieve the objectives of this study, a proper code was created and implemented in the GEE Code Editor, the Integrated Development Environment (IDE) designed for the development of algorithms using the JavaScript programming language [22, 36, 37].

Figure 3 describes the operative workflow used in this investigation.

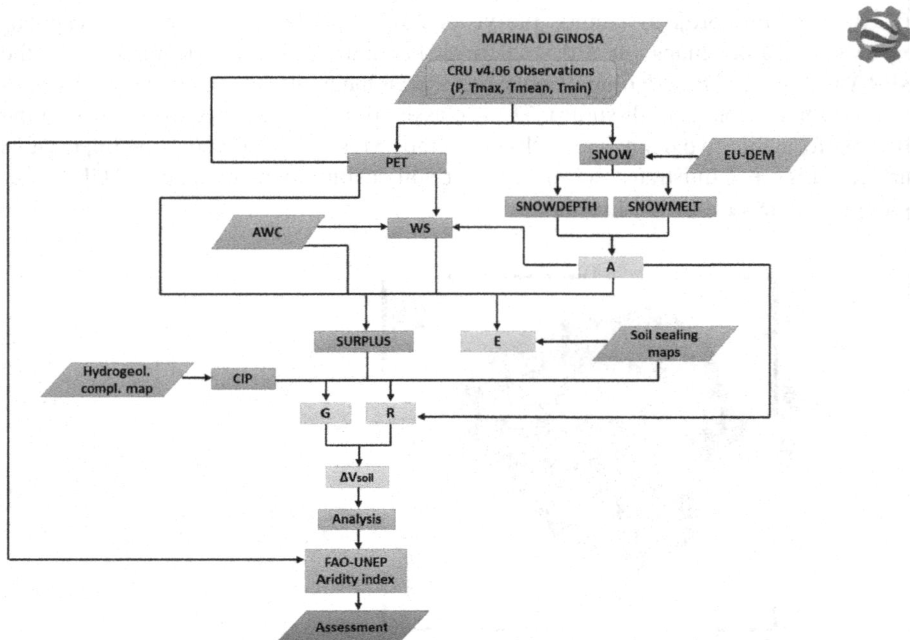

Fig. 3. Operative workflow. CRU: Climatic Research Unit; P: Precipitation; T_{max}: Maximum Temperature; T_{mean}: Mean Temperature; T_{min}: Minimum Temperature; PET: Potential Evapotranspiration; EU-DEM: European Union-Digital Elevation Model; AWC: Available Water Capacity; WS: Soil Water Content; A: Liquid Inflow; E: Actual Evapotranspiration; CIP: Potential Infiltration Coefficient; G: Groundwater Recharge; R: Surface Runoff; ΔV_{soil}: Variation in Soil Water Content; FAO: Food and Agriculture Organization; UNEP: United Nations Environmental Programme.

After selecting the monthly values of total precipitation (P), and the monthly means of daily maximum, mean and minimum air temperature (T_{max}, T_{mean} and T_{min}) from the CRU v4.06 dataset [29], related to the "Marina di Ginosa" meteorological station, four thematic maps of P, T_{max}, T_{mean} and T_{min} were obtained in the GEE environment for each month from October 2015 to September 2018. This was done to perform the analysis considering three hydrological years (2015–2016, from October 2015 to September 2016; 2016–2017, from October 2016 to September 2017; and 2017–2018, from October 2017 to September 2018). Furthermore, for each month i, it was decided to keep the monthly values of P_i, $T_{max,i}$, $T_{mean,i}$ and $T_{min,i}$ constant over the whole study area, due to the similar morphological and climatic characteristics of the whole territory, which is also relatively small.

Then, from P, T_{max}, T_{mean} and T_{min}, the maps of potential evapotranspiration (PET) and liquid inflow A were calculated for each month. The EU-DEM was used to obtain the possible monthly snow precipitation from which it is possible to derive the values of monthly snow accumulation and snowmelt, as reported in [13]. The PET and A maps were then used together with the AWC data to retrieve the soil water content (WS), the actual evapotranspiration E and the surplus, for each month. The 10 m resolution soil sealing maps were used to perform the calculation separately for "impervious" and "non impervious" classes. Moreover, the maps of groundwater recharge G and surface runoff R were calculated for each month from the CIP data, together with the surplus, A and the soil sealing maps. Then, it was possible to retrieve the variation of the soil water content for each of the investigated month. Lastly the assessment of the soil aridity conditions, for each hydrological year (2015–2016, 2016–2017, and 2017–2018) was performed by calculating the FAO-UNEP aridity index [13].

2.3 Water Balance Components Computation

According to the BIGBANG procedure, considering a generic month i, the water balance for the root zone (the layer of soil that is affected by the root system of the vegetation), is expressed as follows [13]:

$$A - E = R + G + \Delta V_{soil} \tag{1}$$

where

- A is the volume of the liquid inflow that reaches the soil, consisting of the rainfall plus the snowmelt;
- E is the volume of the actual evapotranspiration;
- R is the volume of the surface runoff;
- G is the volume of the groundwater recharge;
- ΔV_{soil} is the variation of the volume of stored water in the soil;

Once obtained, for each month i, the thematic maps of precipitation and temperature (considered constant over the entire study area) from October 2015 to September 2018, the following variables were retrieved:

- Liquid inflow A;
- Potential evapotranspiration PET;
- Soil water content WS;
- Actual evapotranspiration E;
- Groundwater recharge G;
- Surface runoff R;
- Soil water content variation ΔV_{soil}.

Liquid Inflow Because the average temperature for each month studied is always higher than the threshold for snow formation, there is no melting, and the liquid inflow A_i always corresponds with the total monthly precipitation (P_i).

Potential Evapotranspiration. This variable, expressed in mm/month, was calculated, for each month i, with the equation of Hargreaves and Samani [13]:

$$PET_i = M_i * 0.0135 * [T_{mean,i} + 17.8] * [0.17 * \sqrt{T_{\max,i} - T_{\min,i}} * R_{a,i}] \tag{2}$$

where

- M_i is the number of days of the month i;

- $T_{mean,i}$, $T_{max,i}$, $T_{min,i}$ are the monthly mean of daily mean, maximum and minimum temperature [°C], for the month i;
- $R_{a,i}$ is the monthly mean of the daily extraterrestrial radiation [mm/day of evaporated water equivalent], for the month i, calculated as in [13].

Soil Water Content. The water content in the soil depth of 1 m was computed using the scheme reported in [13]:

$$WS_i = f(A_i, PET_i, AWC, WS_{i-1}) \tag{3}$$

where

- AWC is the available water capacity [mm of water/m of soil depth];
- WS_{i-1} [mm/m] is the soil water content in the month i–1.

Since, in this model, an initial condition is required, it was assumed that in January 2015 the soil water content was equal to AWC over the entire case study territory.

Actual Evapotranspiration. The soil sealing maps at 10 m resolution were used to compute the actual evapotranspiration, for each month i, differently for "Impervious surface" and "non impervious surface" LU/LC classes.

For "impervious surface" class, according to [13]:

$$E_i = 0 \tag{4}$$

as it was assumed that these areas are without vegetation (no transpiration) and that all the liquid inflow turns into surface runoff.

For "non impervious surface" LU/LC class, instead, the expressions reported in [13] were adopted:

$$E_i = f(A_i, PET_i, AWC, WS_{i-1}) \tag{5}$$

Groundwater Recharge. In Order to Determine the Groundwater Recharge G, for Each month i, the Surplus (from Which G is Generated) Was First Calculated Using the Following Expression [13]:

$$Surplus_i = \max\{[(A_i - PET_i) - (AWC - WS_{i-1})], 0\} \tag{6}$$

Then, the G was computed in this way: for "Impervious surface" LU/LC class

$$G_i = 0 \tag{7}$$

while, for "Non impervious surface" class, the following equation was considered

$$G_i = \frac{CIP}{100} * Surplus_i \tag{8}$$

where CIP is the potential infiltration coefficient.

Surface Runoff. The Runoff, for the month i, Was Calculated [13]:

For "Impervious surface class"

$$R_i = A_i \tag{9}$$

and, for "Non impervious surface" class, as complementary

$$R_i = \left(1 - \frac{CIP}{100}\right) * Surplus_i \tag{10}$$

Variation in Soil Water Content. The Soil Water Content Variation, for Each month i, Was Retrieved by Using the Following Expression [13]:

$$\Delta V_{soil,i} = A_i - E_i - R_i - G_i \tag{11}$$

2.4 Soil Aridity Assessment

The assessment of the soil aridity condition was performed by calculating, for each hydrological year (2015–2016, 2016–2017 and 2017–2018) and for the entire period of analysis (from October 2015 to September 2018), the aridity index (AI) proposed by Food and Agriculture Organization (FAO) and United Nations Environmental Programme (UNEP) [13, 38], expressed by:

$$AI_{FAO-UNEP} = \frac{\overline{P}}{\overline{PET}} \tag{12}$$

where

- $\overline{P}$ is the mean annual precipitation [mm];
- $\overline{PET}$ is the mean annual potential evapotranspiration [mm].

The AI is a numerical indicator of aridity widely adopted for measuring the dryness of the climate at a given location. According to this index, the climate can be classified into the following types [13, 38–40]:

Table 2. Climate classification and dryland subtypes based on the FAO-UNEP aridity index.

Climate type	Subtype	Aridity index
Dry	Hyper-arid	AI < 0.05
	Arid	0.05 ≤ AI < 0.2
	Semi-arid	0.2 ≤ AI < 0.5
	Dry-subhumid	0.5 ≤ AI < 0.65
Non dry	Humid	AI ≥ 0.65

3 Results and Discussion

This research aimed at integrating various open Copernicus data in order to estimate, on a monthly scale, the components of the water balance, as defined by ISPRA's BIGBANG model [13], over the territory of Marina di Ginosa, in southern Italy, in order to assess the local aridity conditions.

As explained above, monthly maps of each variable were obtained by developing and implementing a JavaScript code in the GEE cloud environment, considering the period between October 2015 and September 2018. Therefore, it was possible to perform the analysis for three hydrological years: 2015–2016, 2016–2017 and 2017–2018.

Table 3 and Fig. 4 summarize the results of this study. Table 3 reports the annual values of A, E, R, G and ΔV_{soil} at the level of the whole study area. Figure 4A shows the annual water balance while, in Fig. 4B is represented the trend of the monthly mean values of A, E, R and G over the case study area. According to Table 3 and Fig. 4A, the wettest year was the 2015–2016 ($A = 534$ mm), while the driest year was the 2017–2018 (only 392 mm). Furthermore, based on the model, a considerable portion of the precipitation was owing to evapotranspiration in all three hydrological years and groundwater recharge was nil in 2015–2016 and 2017–2018. On the other hand, the runoff is approximately 10% of the inflow in all cases, while a value of ΔV_{soil} of + 0.1 mm was found for each hydrological year from Eq. 11. As a result, for all three years, the input (A) was approximately equal to outputs (E, R and G).

However, if we calculate the difference between A and E (i.e. the "internal flow" [13, 41], which is a measure of the availability of the water resource generated, under natural conditions, exclusively by precipitation into a territory) it is possible to notice that the natural availability of the water resource for the area in question is very low, excluding external contributions (Table 4). The lowest availability of the resource was estimated in 2017–2018 (only 32.3 mm) and corresponds to the minimum of the annual inflow (see also Fig. 4).

Figure 4B shows the large monthly variability of precipitation, although groundwater recharge is different from zero only in January 2017, coinciding to the greatest precipitation reported at the Marina di Ginosa meteorological station. As an example, due to the impossibility of showing all the maps of the water balance components retrieved in the GEE platform, the Fig. 5 reports the annual average maps of E, R and G for the hydrological year 2016–2017. All the maps have been obtained with a geometric resolution of 10 m and allow for a local investigation of each component's variability within the case study region. The predicted values are dependent on the AWC parameter, which has a 500 m resolution, thus the maps appear to be at a lower resolution.

Table 3. Annual water balance, related to the whole study area, for the hydrological years 2015–2016, 2016–2017 and 2017–2018.

Year	A [mm]	E [mm]	R [mm]	G [mm]	ΔVsoil [mm]
2015–2016	534.0	490.1	43.8	0.0	+ 0.1
2016–2017	421.0	365.0	38.9	17.1	+ 0.1
2017–2018	392.0	359.7	32.2	0.0	+ 0.1

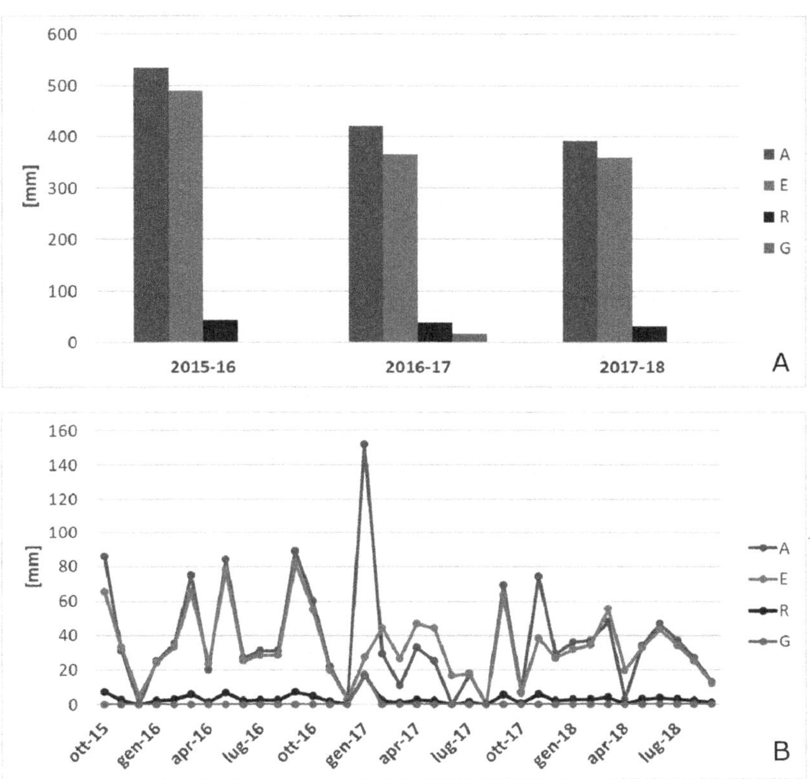

Fig. 4. Annual water balance, related to the whole study area, for the hydrological years 2015–2016, 2016–2017 and 2017–2018 (A), and monthly water balance for the whole study area (B).

Table 4. Internal flow, calculated by the difference between A and E, and annual mean temperature, related to the whole study area for the hydrological years 2015–2016, 2016–2017 and 2017–2018.

Year	Internal flow A [mm]	Annual mean temperature [°C]
2015–2016	43.9	18.0
2016–2017	56.0	18.0
2017–2018	32.3	17.9

It should be emphasized that the estimations are derived from a schematic representation of natural occurrences and so may therefore be susceptible to uncertainties. Further uncertainties could result from the extension of the monthly precipitation and temperature values, measured at the Marina di Ginosa station, to the entire study area. Furthermore, this assessment has not taken into account any anthropic contribution and any surface or underground contribution from external areas.

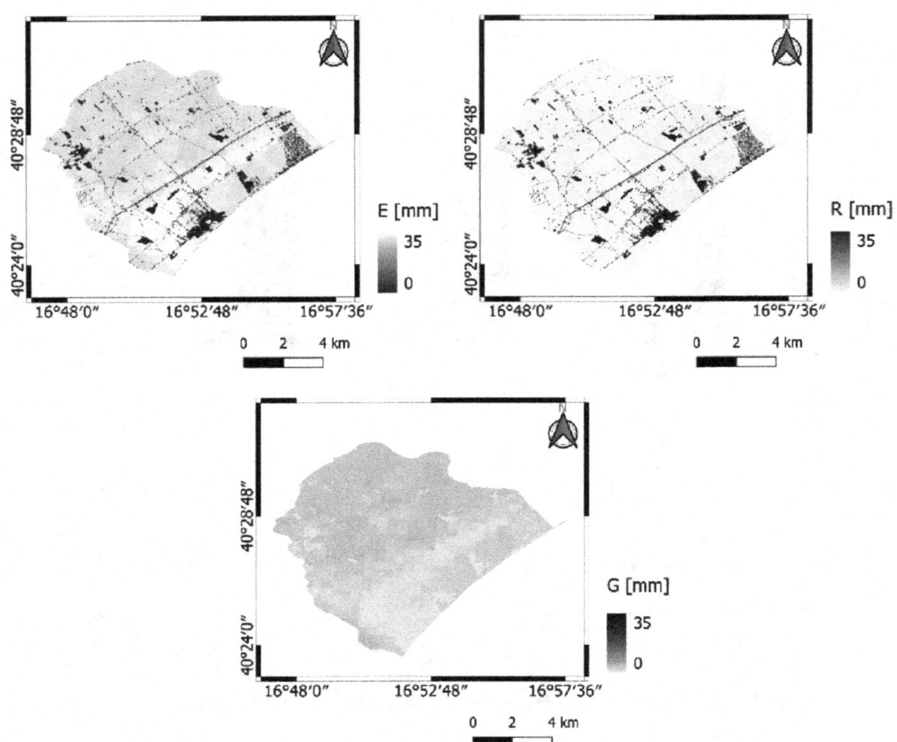

Fig. 5. Annual average maps of E, R and G for the hydrological year 2016–2017.

Table 5 reports the results of the application of the FAO-UNEP aridity index [13, 40]. In accordance with the thresholds reported in Table 2, the territory of Marina di Ginosa resulted "dry semi-arid" for all three hydrological years considered and for the whole period of analysis. Therefore, this area suffered from water scarcity in the period 2015–2018. This conclusion is consistent with the World Atlas of Desertification (WAD) [42], which states that "aridity" and "water scarcity" are biophysical issues challenges affecting this region. Furthermore, because this assessment only took three years of observations into account, and because a much longer period (at least 30 years) would be required for a more accurate evaluation of the climatic type of the area, the term "drought" could be reasonably used to define the condition of water scarcity affecting this territory from 2015 to 2018 [43–45].

Table 5. FAO-UNEP aridity index calculated for the period of analysis, and climate classification.

Year	AI	Climate type
2015–2016	0.44	Dry semi-arid
2016–2017	0.36	Dry semi-arid
2017–2018	0.32	Dry semi-arid
2015–2018	0.37	Dry semi-arid

4 Conclusion

The objective of this paper is to integrate different Copernicus and other open data for the monthly evaluation of the hydrological balance throughout the region of Marina di Ginosa, in southern Italy. To that end, a JavaScript code was written in the GEE cloud platform to calculate the primary component of the hydrological balance at a resolution of 10 m for the period 2015–2018, using the ISPRA's BIGBANG approach. Monitoring and quantitative evaluation of water resources is undoubtedly fundamental to supporting sustainable water resource management and hence decision-making in this sector, especially in light of the potential consequences of climate change and urbanization [11, 13, 14, 46–48].

Because the FAO-UNEP aridity index [13, 38–40] identifies the climate as "dry semi-arid", this research determines that this area was affected by water scarcity from 2015–2018. However, in order to correctly interpret the results, the model's simplifications and schematizations must be taken into consideration. Furthermore, to improve estimations accuracy, a greater number of precipitation and temperature measurements from nearby hydro-meteorological stations should be evaluated and interpolated using geostatistical methods.

References

1. Caretta, M.A., et al.: Water. In: Pörtner, H.-O., et al. (eds.) Climate Change 2022: Impacts, Adaptation and Vulnerability. Contribution of Working Group II to the Sixth Assessment Report of the Intergovernmental Panel on Climate Change, pp. 551–712. Cambridge University Press, Cambridge, UK and New York, NY, USA (2022)
2. Konapala, G., Mishra, A.K., Wada, Y., Mann, M.E.: Climate change will affect global water availability through compounding changes in seasonal precipitation and evaporation. Nat. Commun. **11**, 3044 (2020)
3. Haddeland, I., et al.: Global water resources affected by human interventions and climate change. PNAS **111**, 3251–3256 (2013)
4. Grillakis, M.G.: Increase in severe and extreme soil moisture droughts for Europe under climate change. Sci. Total Environ. **660**, 1245–1255 (2019)
5. Manfreda, S., Iacobellis, V., Fiorentino, M.: Appunti di idrologia superficiale, 1st edn. Aracne editrice, Roma (2010)
6. ASCE: Hydrology handbook. ASCE Manuals and Reports on Engineering Practice No. 28, 2nd edn. American Society of Civil Engineering, New York (1996)

7. Balha, A., Vishwakarma, B.D., Pandey, S., Singh, C.K.: Predicting impact of urbanization on water resources in megacity Delhi. Remote Sens. Appl.: Soc. Environ. **20**, 100361 (2020)
8. Ge Sun, C.L., et al.: Impacts of urbanization on watershed water balances across the conterminous United States. Water Resour. Res. **56** (2020)
9. Daba, M.H., Bazi, Z., Belay, A.: Effects of climate change on soil and water resources: a review. J. Environ. Earth Sci. **8**, 71–80 (2018)
10. Grusson, Y., Wesström, I., Svedberg, E., Joel, A.: Influence of climate change on water partitioning in agricultural watersheds: examples from Sweden. Agric. Water Manag. **249**, 106766 (2021)
11. Braca, G., Bussettini, M., Ducci, D., Lastoria, B., Mariani, S.: Evaluation of national and regional groundwater resources under climate change scenarios using a GIS-based water budget procedure. Rendiconti Lincei. Scienze Fisiche e Naturali **30**(1), 109–123 (2019). https://doi.org/10.1007/s12210-018-00757-6
12. Copernicus Climate Change Service: Water management. https://climate.copernicus.eu/water-management. Last accessed 31 Mar 2023
13. Braca, G., Bussettini, M., Lastoria, B., Mariani, S., Piva, F.: Il Bilancio Idrologico Gis Based a scala Nazionale su Griglia regolare – BIGBANG: metodologia e stime. Rapporto sulla disponibilità naturale della risorsa idrica. Istituto Superiore per la Protezione e la Ricerca Ambientale, Rapporti 339/21, Roma (2021)
14. Braca, G., Ducci, D.: Development of a GIS Based Procedure (BIGBANG 1.0) for Evaluating Groundwater Balances at National Scale and Comparison with Groundwater Resources Evaluation at Local Scale. In: Calvache, M.L., Duque, C., Pulido-Velazquez, D. (eds.) Groundwater and Global Change in the Western Mediterranean Area. EES, pp. 53–61. Springer, Cham (2018). https://doi.org/10.1007/978-3-319-69356-9_7
15. Moghim, S.: Assessment of water storage changes using GRACE and GLDAS. Water Resour. Manage. **34**(2), 685–697 (2020). https://doi.org/10.1007/s11269-019-02468-5
16. Jutz, S., Milagro-Pérez, M.P.: Copernicus: the European Earth Observation programme. Revista de Teledetección **56**, V–XI (2020)
17. Copernicus: Infrastructure overview. https://www.copernicus.eu/en/about-copernicus/infrastructure-overview. Last accessed 1 Apr 2023
18. Copernicus Climate Change Service. https://climate.copernicus.eu/about-us. Last accessed 31 Apr 2023
19. Thépaut, J-N., Dee, D., Engelen, R., Pinty, B.: The Copernicus programme and its climate change service. In: IGARSS 2018 – 2018 IEEE International Geoscience and Remote Sensing Symposium, pp. 1591–1593. IEEE, Valencia, Spain (2018)
20. Gorelick, N., Hancher, M., Dixon, M., Ilyushchenko, S., Thau, D., Moore, R.: Google Earth Engine: planetary-scale geospatial analysis for everyone. Remote Sens. Environ. **202**, 18–27 (2017)
21. Kumar, L., Mutanga, O.: Google Earth Engine applications since inception: usage, trends and potential. Remote Sens. **10**, 1509 (2018)
22. Barletta, C., Capolupo, A., Tarantino, E.: Exploring the potentialities of Landsat 8 and Sentinel-2 satellite data for estimating the land surface albedo in urban areas using GEE platform. In: Gervasi, O., et al. (eds.) International Conference on Computational Science and Its Applications, LNCS, vol. 13379, pp. 435–449. Springer, Cham. (2022)
23. Capolupo, A., Monterisi, C., Barletta, C., Tarantino, E.: Google Earth Engine for land surface albedo estimation: comparison among different algorithms. In: Proceedings of SPIE, vol. 11856, Remote Sensing for Agriculture, Ecosystems, and Hydrology XXIII, p. 118560F. International Society for Optics and Photonics (2021)
24. Capolupo, A., Monterisi, C., Saponaro, M., Tarantino, E.: Multi-temporal analysis of land-cover changes using Landsat data through Google Earth Engine platform. In: Proceedings of

SPIE, vol. 11524, Eighth International Conference on Remote Sensing and Geoinformation of the Environment (RSCy2020), p. 1152419. International Society for Optics and Photonics (2020)
25. Cotecchia, V.: Area idrogeologica dell'arco ionico tarantino. In: Acque sotterranee e l'intrusione marina in Puglia: dalla ricerca all'emergenza nella salvaguardia della risorsa. Memorie descrittive della carta geologica d'Italia 92, pp. 248–312. ISPRA Serv. Geologico d'Italia (2014)
26. Tropeano, M., Sabato, L., Pieri, P.: Filling and cannibalization of a foredeep: the Bradanic Trough, Southern Italy. Geol. Soc. London, Special Pub. **191**, 55–79 (2002)
27. Cotecchia, V., Simeone, V., Gabriele, S.: Caratteri climatici. In: Acque sotterranee e l'intrusione marina in Puglia: dalla ricerca all'emergenza nella salvaguardia della risorsa. Memorie descrittive della carta geologica d'Italia 92, pp. 338–369. ISPRA Serv. Geologico d'Italia (2014)
28. Copernicus Land Monitoring Service: https://land.copernicus.eu/. Last accessed 4 Apr 2023
29. Harris, I., Osborn, T.J., Jones, P., Lister, D.: Version 4 of the CRU TS monthly high-resolution gridded multivariate climate dataset. Sci. Data **7**, 109 (2020)
30. Munafò, M., Salvati, L., Zitti, M.: Estimating soil sealing rate at national level – Italy as a case study. Ecol. Ind. **26**, 137–140 (2013)
31. Ballabio, C., Panagos, P., Montanarella, L.: Mapping topsoil physical properties at European scale using the LUCAS database. Geoderma **261**, 110–123 (2016)
32. Panagos, P., et al.: European Soil Data Centre 2.0: soil data and knowledge in support of the EU policies. Eur. J. Soil Sci. **73**, e13315 (2022)
33. Panagos, P., Van Liedekerke, M., Jones, A., Montanarella, L.: European Soil Data Centre: response to European policy support and public data requirements. Land Use Policy **29**, 329–338 (2012)
34. European Commission, Joint Research Centre: European Soil Data Centre (ESDAC). http://esdac.jrc.ec.europa.eu. Last accessed 4 Apr 2023
35. Celico, P.: Prospezioni idrogeologiche. Liguori Editore, Napoli (1988)
36. Tamiminia, H., Salehi, B., Mahdianpari, M., Quackenbush, L., Adeli, S., Brisco, B.: Google Earth Engine for geo-big data applications: a meta-analysis and systematic review. ISPRS J. Photogramm. Remote. Sens. **164**, 152–170 (2020)
37. Mutanga, O., Kumar, L.: Google Earth Engine Applications. Remote Sens. **11**, 591 (2019)
38. European Commission – Joint Research Centre: World Atlas of Desertification: patterns of aridity. https://wad.jrc.ec.europa.eu/patternsaridity. Last accessed 8 Apr 2023
39. Stefanidis, K., Kostara, A., Papastergiadou, E.: Implications of human activities, land use changes and climate variability in Mediterranean lakes of Greece. Water **8**, 483 (2016)
40. United Nations Environmental Programme. World atlas of desertification. Edward Arnold, London, UK (1992)
41. Eurostat and OCSE: Data collection manual for the OECD/Eurostat joint questionnaire on inland waters and Eurostat regional water questionnaire. Concepts, definitions, current practices, evaluations and recommendations, Version 4 (2018)
42. European Commission – Joint Research Centre: World Atlas of Desertification: convergence of global change issues. https://wad.jrc.ec.europa.eu/countryreport. Last accessed 8 Apr 2023
43. NOAA: Drought vs. aridity. https://www.ncei.noaa.gov/access/monitoring/dyk/drought-aridity. Last accessed 8 Apr 2023
44. European Environment Agency: Wet and dry – aridity. https://www.eea.europa.eu/publications/europes-changing-climate-hazards-1/wet-and-dry-1/wet-and-dry-aridity. Last accessed 8 Apr 2023
45. European Environment Agency: Wet and dry – drought. https://www.eea.europa.eu/publications/europes-changing-climate-hazards-1/wet-and-dry-1/wet-and-dry-drought. Last accessed 8 Apr 2023

46. Figorito, B., Tarantino, E., Balacco, G., Fratino, U.: An object-based method for mapping ephemeral river areas from WorldView-2 satellite data. In: Proceedings of SPIE, Remote Sensing for Agriculture, Ecosystems, and Hydrology XIV, vol. 8531, p. 85310B (2012)
47. Apollonio, C., Balacco, G., Novelli, A., Tarantino, E., Piccinni, A.F.: Land use change impact on flooding areas: the case study of Cervaro Basin (Italy). Sustainability **8**, 996 (2016)
48. IDMP: Drought and water scarcity. WMO No.1284. Global Water Partnership, Stockholm, Sweden and World Meteorological Organization, Geneva, Switzerland (2022)

Integrated Use of Geomatic Methodologies for Monitoring an Instability Phenomenon

Noemi Pagano, Alberico Sonnessa, Federica Cotecchia, and Eufemia Tarantino(✉)

Department of Civil, Environmental, Land, Construction and Chemistry (DICATECh), Politecnico di Bari, Via Orabona 4, 70125 Bari, Italy
n.pagano@studenti.poliba.it, {alberico.sonnessa, federica.cotecchia,eufemia.tarantino}@poliba.it

Abstract. The growing exposure of the Italian territory to hydrogeological risk, also worsened by the influence of climate change, has made the occurrence of catastrophic phenomena, such as landslides and floods, always more impactful. In this frame, geomatic methodologies can provide a crucial support in properly characterizing a potentially critical instability phenomenon, both from the spatial and kinematic view. In this work, the integrate use of geomatic methodologies, i.e., Multi-temporal Interferometric Synthetic Aperture Radar (MTInSAR) technology and structural sensors, namely biaxial tiltmeters, were employed to kinematically investigate the behavior of an urban area affected by a landslide, located in the Apulian territory. The MTInSAR analysis carried out on Sentinel-1 SAR acquisitions showed a strong non-linear behavior in the displacement-time trends, also highlighting the presence of differential motions constituting a threat for buildings. As regards the main retaining structure, currently damaged by the landslide, automatic measurements provided by the tiltmeters confirmed the presence of more active areas, as detected by the SAR observations.

The outcomes of this work provided key information to the structures responsible for the management of the risk connected with the instability and allowed to address the proper design of the mitigation works.

Keywords: landslide geomatic monitoring · MTInSAR · tiltmeters · non-linear displacements · Sentinel-1

1 Introduction

Hydrogeological instability, triggered by natural and/or anthropogenic factors, is one of the most debated issues at global scale, which currently involves the scientific community [1]. The Italian peninsula, because of its geological structure and the growing anthropic pressure, is particularly subject to instability phenomena [2].

The study [3] developed by ISPRA (Istituto Superiore per la Protezione e la Ricerca Ambientale - Italian Institute for Environmental Protection and Research) estimates that 93.9% of Italian towns are subject to instability phenomena, such as landslides, floods

O. Gervasi et al. (Eds.): ICCSA 2023 Workshops, LNCS 14107, pp. 217–233, 2023.
https://doi.org/10.1007/978-3-031-37114-1_15

[4] and/ or coastal erosion [4]. The impact of landslides in Italy is incredibly significant, thus representing a real social and economic problem [5, 6].

In recent years, several catastrophic events affected the Italian territory, the last of which was recorded on the Ischia Island in November 2022, causing the death of 12 people and damage to the economy and tourism [7].

The availability of reliable techniques aimed at monitoring instabilities becomes then increasingly crucial to counter these events and helps to adopt effective solutions for mitigating their effects [8–10].

The risk mitigation strategies, that can help to avoid a disastrous development of an instability or support the emergency management phase of the event, encompass a deep knowledge of the phenomenon, to better understand its evolution and accurately monitor its effects [11, 12].

In this frame, the geomatic monitoring based on ground and aerial/satellite techniques and sensors, provides the ability to properly characterize the field of displacements and help the safeguard of the infrastructures and people involved [13]. The methodologies to be employed must be appropriately identified according to the magnitude of the phenomenon, the extent and accessibility of the study area.

The implementation of population warning methodologies to safeguard human lives must be carried out through Early Warning Systems, unless a routinary monitoring activity cannot be conducted or when cost-benefit analysis is unfavorable [14, 15].

In the last decades, the technological evolution has facilitated the use of more advanced sensors and has made available large databases consisting of multiple territorial information, as in the case of the European Copernicus program [16].

The Copernicus program, with its completely 'free & open' data policy, provides a huge repository of historical SAR data and allows a tight monitoring of large areas, also allowing to perform back-analyses preparatory to the design and the installation of ground-based monitoring systems. The Copernicus program allows to benefit from an additional service, known as the European Ground Motion Service (EGMS), which provides a consistent and high-quality information on natural and anthropogenic ground motion, with millimeter accuracy [17].

This work focuses on the analysis of SAR data acquired by the Sentinel-1 mission within the Copernicus program, relating to a town, situated on the Dauno Sub-Apennine in the Apulia region, damaged by a gravitational landslide phenomenon. The satellite data allowed a detailed kinematic characterization of the displacement field affecting the urban area, which is partially located on the rear scarp of the instability.

The deformation pattern was examined referring to a seven years-spanning data set, using the Multi- Temporal InSAR (MTInSAR) methodology. The study of displacement trends shown by individual scatterers was coupled with an areal analysis, aimed at highlighting differential behaviors and the possible presence of different temporal phases in the activation of the instability phenomenon.

The analysis played a key role in drawing up the design of the geomatic monitoring system currently running on the site, which included the implementation of a tiltmetric network, which measurement are also examined.

2 The Study Area

The investigated area is located in the Apulian territory, on the border with Molise region. The presence of a gravitative landslide required the intervention of the competent authorities to understand the phenomenon and plan the proper interventions. However, the instability has been observed since the late 1800 and its development could be attributed to several causes which include seismic events. In order to remediate the instability effects, a series of retaining works have been undertaken since 1950. The most recent retaining wall has been built in 2006. Moreover, the presence of differential collapses in some buildings has determined their demolition.

A comparison between the aerial images acquired in 2002 (Fig. 1A) and in 2022 (Fig. 1B) evidences the evolution of the built area.

The landslide phenomenon threatens the settlement area and also involves a zone called the Crojo spring, located north-west of the historical center.

Fig. 1. Study area plan for 2002 (A) and 2022 (B). The areas highlighted in the white square belong to the Crojo spring. The red line delineates the rear scarp of the landslide area. Source: Google Earth Pro. (Color figure online)

3 Methodologies Employed

In the present work, multi-temporal satellite interferometry MTInSAR technique and structural monitoring sensors, operated through the installation of tiltmeters along the retaining wall, are being employed. The tiltmeters implement an alert system based on the exceeding of a predetermined inclination threshold, which can provide an early warning in case of sudden variations of the tilt angle of the wall [18].

3.1 MTInSAR

Among geomatic technologies, satellite interferometer techniques play a leading role, due to its accuracy and its cost-benefit ratio. MTInSAR allows to survey ground displacements on the earth surface, providing information on a certain portion of territory with a fixed revisit time. The SAR technique, Synthetic Aperture Radar, has the potential to observe and measure deformations of the earth's surface over large areas with a high degree of detail.

The Sentinel-1 (S1) constellation, framed in the Copernicus mission, featured two satellites (S1A-B) operating in C-band and following a near-polar orbit, characterized by a revisit time of approximately 6 days until 2021. Nowadays, after the decommissioning of the S1B satellite, the revisit time has been significantly reduced to 12 days. However, the free availability of archive images, acquired from 2015 to present, and a relatively high spatial resolution (20x5m) over extensive areas, allow to obtain an accuracy of up to 1 mm in terms of displacement trend [19].

SAR interferometry (InSAR) relies on the basic principle of evaluating the potential dissimilarities between two images captured with a radar sensor under identical geometric conditions, but during two different instants of time [20].

The analysis performed by the Persistent Scatterers Interferometry (PSI) technique needs the identification of radar marks, called Permanent Scatterers (PS), both natural and anthropic (e.g., rocks or man-made structures), distinguishable in the entire image stack processed, so that they can be compared over time. The PS must not change their 'electro-magnetic signature' and phase information, to be clearly identifiable even if atmospheric or climatic conditions change. The quality of the interferometric fringes depends on the correlation between the two SAR images.

Correlation can be estimated in terms of interferometric coherence γ [21], ranging between 0 and 1, where $\gamma \approx 0$ indicates a strong measurement noise. This is generally noticeable in heavily vegetated areas or large bodies of water. By several observations during time and in the identical area, continuous monitoring of ground displacements is attained.

Therefore, MT-InSAR technique can detect ground displacements associated with pixels on the corresponding image. The main outcome of the technique is the identification of measurement points spatially georeferenced (by longitude, latitude and ellipsoidal height) and characterized by i) a coherence value defining the stability of the target and its reliability ii) the annual average value of the velocity computed along the Line of Sight (LoS), which is the direction joining the sensor and the target,perpendicular to the orbit and inclined by an angle θ - called off-nadir, iii) and the displacement time series during the monitoring period [22].

3.2 Tiltmeters

Remote biaxial tiltmeters allow the monitoring of inclination fluctuations of a structure over time along two axes [23].

Generally, the measurements acquired by this category of sensors are strongly influenced by the temperature parameter and its variation. Direct or indirect solar radiation transfer, by warming the structure where the sensor is installed, and the sensor itself, triggers a disturbing impact on the tiltmeter. To consider the impact of this parameter, the device is generally equipped with thermistors recording the temperature value.

The instrument provides punctual values, i.e., indicative of the inclination variations of a limited portion of the monitored object, Hence, to accurately describe the behavior of a complex construction, the use of several sensors is required. However, the opportunity to record long-term time series (in the order of years) at regular intervals can greatly improve the knowledge of the geometry and deformational speed of structures affected by the instability, thus providing information on the evolution of the study area [24].

4 Data Analysis

4.1 MT-InSAR Data

Considering the favorable orientation of the built area and the retaining wall (north-south) nearly perpendicular to the LoS, and the steepest path direction (west-northwest) of the slope underneath the instability zone, the study area was analyzed through the data obtained along the descending orbit from March 2015 to April 2021, with an average frequency of 6 days.

The interferometric dataset has been acquired within the European Copernicus Program from the S1 satellite constellation and processed using the approach shown in [25], and provided in the frame of a collaboration between the Polytechnic University of Bari and the Government Commissioner for the environmental risk of the Apulia region, which oversees the implementation of proper risk mitigation strategies. A simple filtering process has been applied to the historical time series; given the raw data, a moving average has been computed on five acquisitions and a 1 σ test has been assessed on the central value of the considered measures to remove possible outliers. If not accepted by the test, the measured value has been classified as an outlier and consequently replaced with the value from the moving average.

The displacement average velocity map computed along the LoS in Fig. 2, evidence the PS belonging to the settlement area most affected by the instability, which is the active retrogressive scarp at the head of the landslide. The scatterers pertaining to the Crojo spring are also displayed.

The recorded speeds are shown in the Fig. 3A. Nonetheless, in pursuit of more trustworthy information about the displacement and velocity fields, the PS characterized by a coherence ≤ 0.6, (Fig. 3B) were discarded.

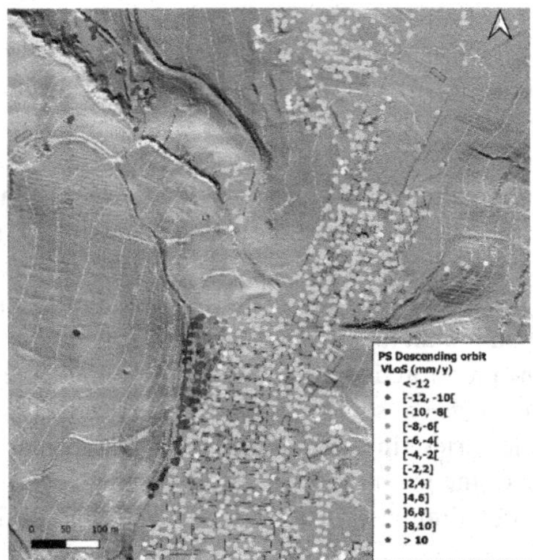

Fig. 2. Average velocity map along the Los between March 2015 and April 2021, computed on the data acquired on the descending track.

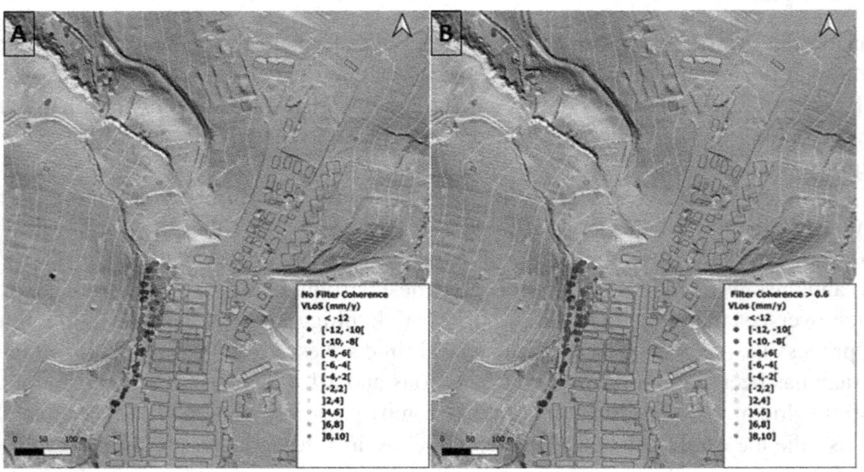

Fig. 3. Velocity map without coherence filter (A) and filtered by coherence > 0.6 (B)

As the Table 1 clearly indicates, the distribution of PSs with a velocity value of less than −4 mm/year remains almost unchanged in percentage terms [26].

Table 1. Number of PS distributed in the different ranges.

Velocity ranges (mm/ years)	Number of PSs		Per cent of PSs	
	No Filter C	C >0,6	No Filter C	C >0,6
≤-12	22	12	11,06	9,92
]-12;-10]	42	30	21,11	24,79
]-10;-8]	78	50	39,2	41,32
]-8;-6]	45	27	23,12	22,31
]-6;-4]	1	1	0,5	0,83
]-4;-2]	0	0	0	0
]-2;2]	10	1	5,03	0,83
]2;4]	0	0	0	0
]4;6]	0	0	0	0
]6;8]	0	0	0	0
]8;10]	0	0	0	0

Following these results, the analyses have been conducted on the sub-dataset characterized by a coherence value > 0.6.

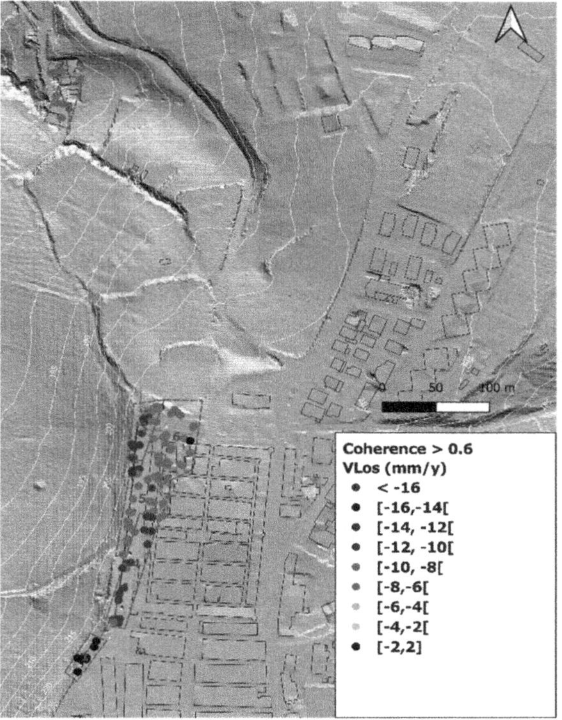

Fig. 4. Cluster characterized by a comparable average velocity along the LoS.

The evaluation of the ground motion map brought out several clusters characterized by a comparable behavior, in terms of average velocity (Fig. 4).

Table 2. Average velocity of the identified clusters

N.cluster	Average Vel (mm/y)	Std. Dev. Vel
1	-14,29	0,35
2	-13,04	0,42
3	-10,25	0,79
4	-10,22	0,37
5	-9,08	0,60
6	-7,42	0,74
7	-8,38	0,14

As described in [27] the PS trend throughout the entire observation time, validated using COSMO-SkyMed acquisitions and levelling measurements, is marked by a strongly non-linear behavior, (Fig. 5), where periods showing almost constant and relatively low velocities are interspersed with short acceleration stages of the landslide, characterized by a higher velocity. The graphs refer to nine PS belonging to the retaining structure (A-I) and one target located in the Crojo area (L).

In addition, the time series related to two points approximately adjacent to the points A and F examined in Fig. 5, available from EGMS portal, have been analysed into the present study, and the relative trend have been compared, as evidenced in Figs. 6 and 7. The points viewed through the EGMS portal considered were selected considering their coherence value, i.e., greater than 0.6, and undergone the simple filtering process as described above. The peculiar behaviour remains substantially confirmed when comparing the two datasets for both examined points.

A more refined investigation has been conducted by deepening the fourth dimension of the phenomenon, namely its spatial evolution over time, also with the purpose of evidencing possible remobilizations of the same portions of the unstable area in different periods. Starting from the peculiar displacement pattern, detected in the upper part of the instability including the north-west sector of the urban area and the Crojo spring, the whole dataset has been split in into three-month temporal intervals.

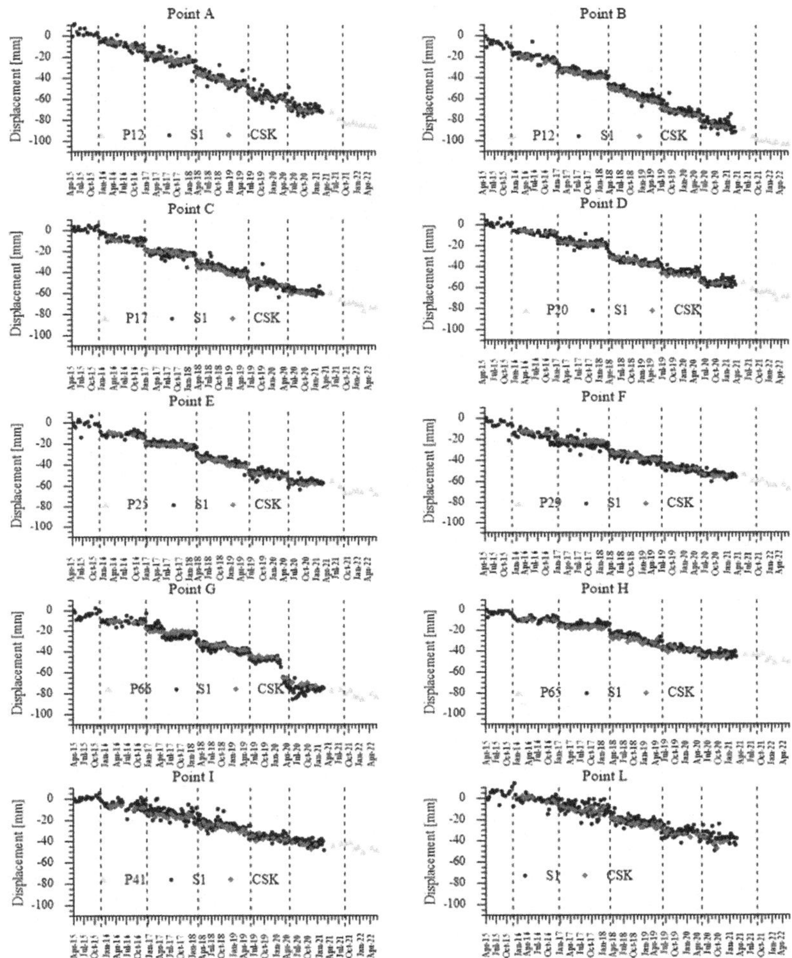

Fig. 5. PS trend evidenced by Sentinel-1 data (S1 series) and validated through COSMO-SkyMed (CSK series) data and levelling measurements (Pi series) (image source: [27]).

26 sub-datasets were then derived, processed and classified to highlight the presence of PS with a comparable behavior.

The back analysis highlighted that the whole unstable area is simultaneously involved in the acceleration phase, during which the average velocity has a sudden increase (Fig. 8a, d). The southernmost corner of the retaining structure, within the cluster 1, shows relevant velocities during the periods after the acceleration phase (Fig. 8b, c, e, f). In Fig. 8(b and c), also the northern part of the retaining structure shows significant displacement rates during the periods (Fig. 8c and e), while the section south of the latter highlight motions (Fig. 8b and f). During the stages characterized by the maximum displacement rate, approximately 50% of the sample belongs to the cluster typified by

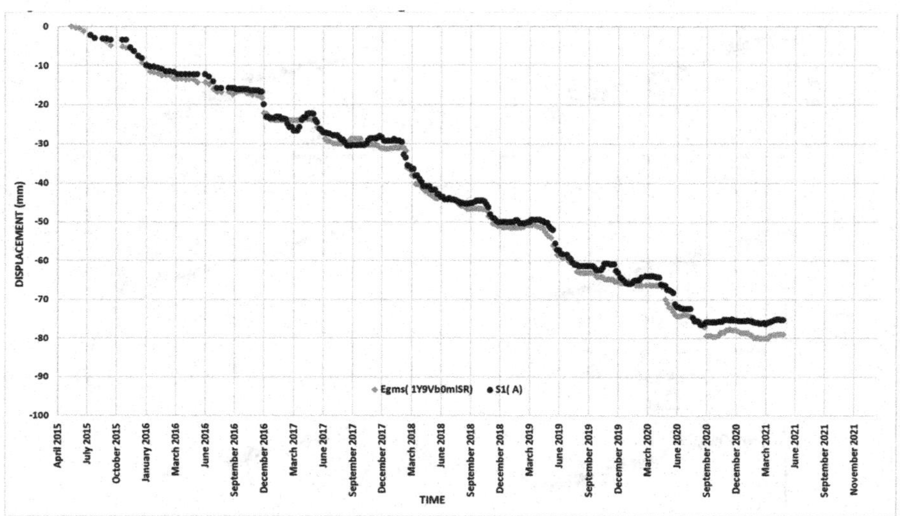

Fig. 6. PS trend evidenced by Sentinel-1 data (S1 A) compared with Egms point.

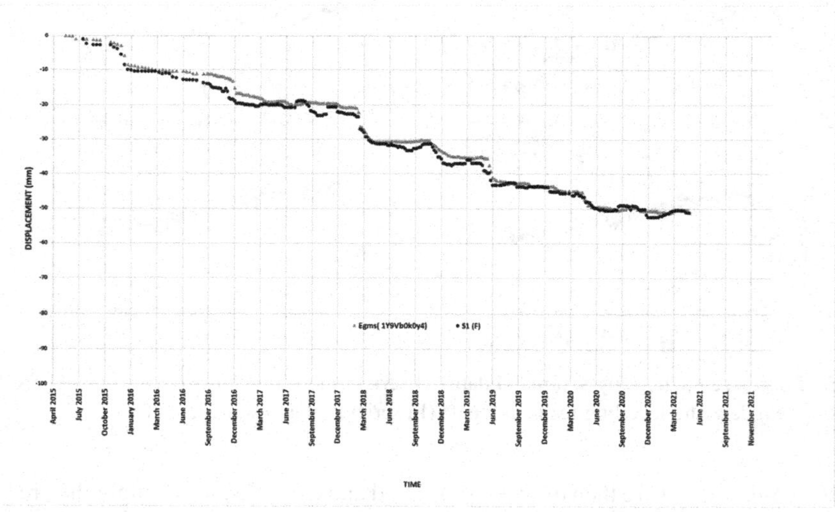

Fig. 7. PS trend evidenced by Sentinel-1 data (S1 F) compared with Egms point.

a velocity ranging from −20 to −40 mm/year, while the remainder is distributed in the two immediately contiguous classes.

The impact of the ground motion on a building is generally limited when the displacement affects the entire structure at the same time, leading to a rigid and homogeneous translation. On the contrary, a differential displacement at the foundations level, in relation to the soil-structure interaction, could trigger a gradient in the stress-strain condition

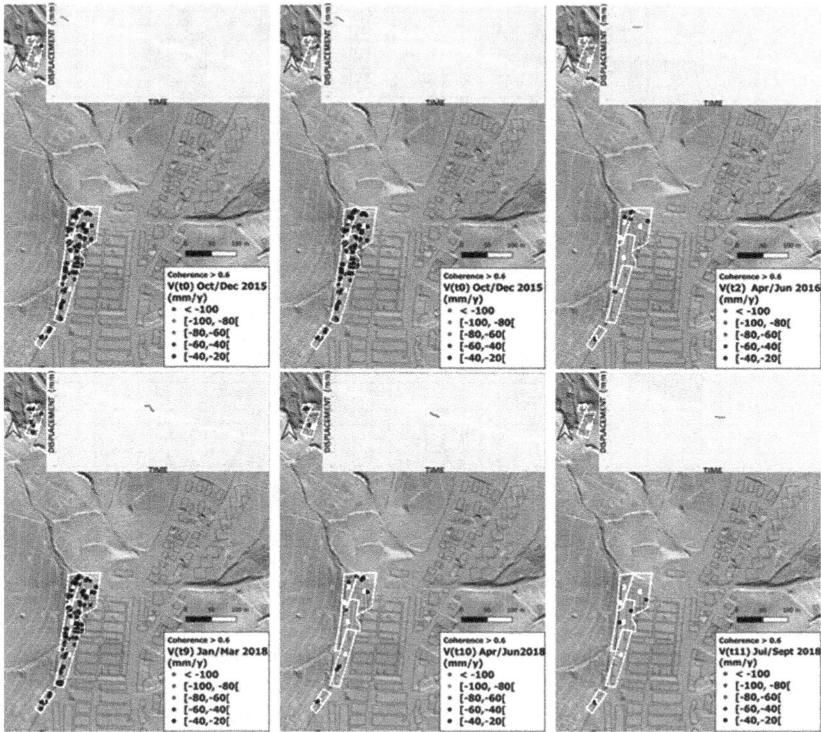

Fig. 8. 6 of 26 Sequences for planimetric velocity map

of the edifice, resulting in severe damages and, in worst cases, in the failure of the building. The effects of the differential movements can be spotted on the townhouses located across the border between the stable and unstable area, which are subject to a significant displacement component on the side of the landslide edge. The impacts of this dynamic are shown in Fig. 9. Based on these results and the damages detected on the field, the competent authorities have ordered the evacuation of the buildings within the subsiding area.

4.2 Tiltmeter Data

Following the outcomes of the MTInSAR back analysis, in September 2021, eight bi-axial tiltmeters (CE01 to CE08, Fig. 10) have been installed on the containing structure to provide high-frequency monitoring of the wall and a prompt alert in case of a sudden change in its inclination, indicative of an acceleration of the instability process. The tiltmeters are remotely controlled and record the temperature on the first channel, namely Ch1, and the tilt values along two additional channels, Ch2 and Ch3, in transverse and longitudinal direction to the structure respectively, at hourly intervals. The observed data were processed using a moving average over a range of 24 h to minimize the effects of the daily temperature fluctuations. Except for the CE08 sensor, located in the southernmost

Fig. 9. Evidence of instability

part of the structure, on the long-term period the small inclination variations recorded by the system show essentially a direct or inverse correlation on the temperature (Fig. 11), indicating the absence of planimetric displacements until January 2023. This dependence is probably related with the microclimatic conditions and mechanical features of each tiltmeter.

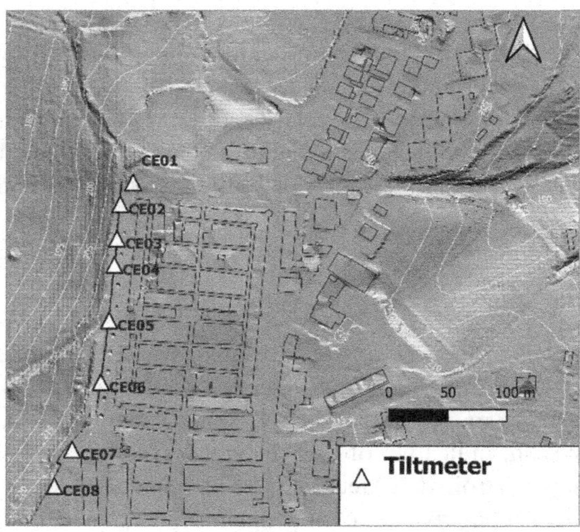

Fig. 10. Tiltmeters location.

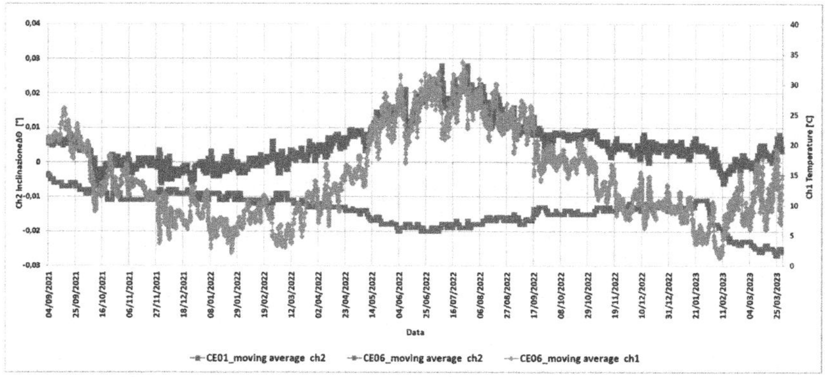

Fig. 11. Direct or inverse variation of the inclination Ch2 with temperature (Ch1)

As regards the time interval between the installation of the system and January 2023, the CE08 sensor recorded a rotation that caused an estimated shift at the head of the wall of approximately 2cm, considering the pivot coinciding with the base of the structure. However, between the end of January 2023 and the end of February 2023, fast changes in inclination with respect to the Ch2 channel (i.e., perpendicularly to the wall) were recorded also by CE03, CE04, CE07 tiltmeters. Whereas at the time of writing this paper, the small changes seem to be temperature-related again. Figures 12 and 13 show the trends of the entire series.

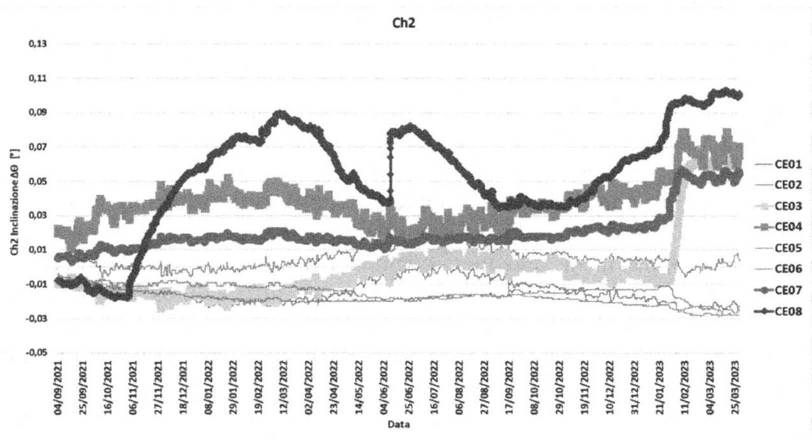

Fig. 12. Variation in tilt in direction perpendicular (Ch2) to retaining structure measured by all tiltmeters.

The tilt variation first involved CE07 and CE08, located on the south side of the retaining structure, followed by a sudden variation of inclination recorded by CE03 and CE04. This increased activity could be related the mobilization of two areas more active

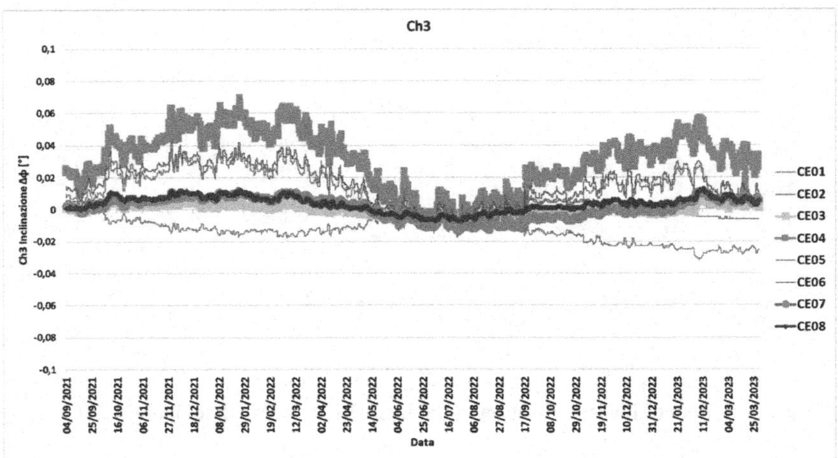

Fig. 13. Variation in tilt along the direction (Ch3) to retaining structure measured by all tiltmeters.

than the surrounding zones, as evidenced by the MTInSAR analysis. The duration of this intensity variation seems to confirm the evidence of MTInSAR analysis, where the succession of phases is typified by periods with small displacements and phases in which the magnitudes are considerably larger.

5 Conclusions

The aim of the presented work was to investigate and kinematically describe the phenomenon that affects the study area. To this purpose, several geomatic methodologies which led estimate the displacement field, were jointly applied. The results provided by the MTInSAR analysis, through processed data from the Sentinel-1 database, gave evidence of the extension of the urban area affected by the landslide, showing increasing velocities moving from the edge of the stable area towards the retaining wall.

The SAR data analysis also brought out the presence of clusters characterized by different mean displacement velocities, computed along the LoS, which can trigger differential displacements resulting in severe damages to structures. The investigation of the phenomenon from a time perspective, reveals a peculiar behaviour of the instability area, evidencing displacements along the LoS evolving by following a non-linear trend.

High-precision geometric leveling validated and reinforced the results obtained from satellite observations, confirming the detected trend. Moreover, the focus on the temporal development of the instability also highlighted zones particularly active during the considered periods. The activation of the same zones has been evidenced also by the sudden increase or the tilt angle measured by tiltmeters CE03, CE04, CE07, CE08 (Fig. 14).

Nevertheless, it must be pointed out that the definition of an interval (three months in the presented case) necessarily influences the results of the analysis, as the acceleration periods not do not repeat regularly. The a priori definition of the used interval

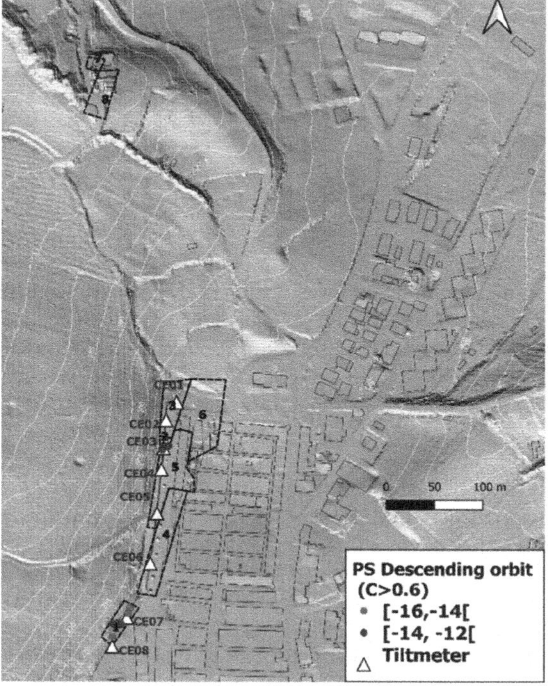

Fig. 14. Areas characterized by maximum negative displacement velocities along the LoS, with superimposition of the tiltmeters location.

may therefore have led to underestimate displacement velocity whit respect to shorter acceleration periods or overestimate it during the low velocity phases.

Until January 2023, the measurements of the tiltmetric network installed along the retaining structure indicated the absence of planimetric shift of the retaining wall. The last measurements evidence instead the non-simultaneous activation of the landslide body, which mechanisms are currently under investigation.

The outcomes of this work provided key information to the structures responsible for the management of the risk connected with the instability, and allowed the addressing of the proper design of the mitigation works. The measurements acquired by the tiltmeters constituting the early warning system, implemented after the MTInSAR analysis evidence, confirmed the peculiar trend of the phenomenon.

Future developments of this study foresee the analysis of ground topographic observations regarding the slope area underneath the town and the integration with geotechnical and geological models to gain a comprehensive understanding of the landslide evolution.

Acknowledgements. This study has been partly funded through the National Recovery and Resilience Plan (NRRP), Mission 4 Component 2 Investment 1.4 - Call for tender No. 3138 of 16 December 2021 of Italian Ministry of University and Research funded by the European Union – NextGenerationEU.

Award Number: Project code: CN00000013, Concession Decree No. 1031 of 17 February 2022 adopted by the Italian Ministry of University and Research, CUP: D93C22000430001, Project title: "National Centre for HPC, Big Data and Quantum Computing".

References

1. Notti, D., et al.: A multidisciplinary investigation of deep-seated landslide reactivation triggered by an extreme rainfall event: a case study of the Monesi di Mendatica landslide, Ligurian Alps. Landslides **18**(7), 2341–2365 (2021). https://doi.org/10.1007/s10346-021-01651-3
2. Brandolini, P., et al.: Hillslope degradation in representative Italian areas: Just soil erosion risk or opportunity for development? Land Degrad Dev. **29** (2018). https://doi.org/10.1002/ldr.2999
3. Trigila, A., Iadanza, C., Bussettini, M., Lastoria, B.: Dissesto idrogeologico in Italia: pericolosità e indicatori di rischio - Edizione 2018 (2018)
4. Viccione, G., Izzo, C.: Three-dimensional CFD modelling of urban flood forces on buildings: a case study. J. Phys.: Conf. Ser. (2022). https://doi.org/10.1088/1742-6596/2162/1/012020
5. Wilde, M., Günther, A., Reichenbach, P., Malet, J.P., Hervás, J.: Pan-European landslide susceptibility mapping: ELSUS version 2. J Maps. **14**, 97–104 (2018). https://doi.org/10.1080/17445647.2018.1432511
6. Canuti, P., Casagli, N., Ermini, L., Fanti, R., Farina, P.: Landslide activity as a geoindicator in Italy: Significance and new perspectives from remote sensing (2004). https://doi.org/10.1007/s00254-003-0952-5
7. Tomasone, M., et al.: Risk management planning on a volcanic island: fear and loathing in Ischia (Italy). Geol. Soc. Lond. Spec. Pub. **519** (2023). https://doi.org/10.1144/sp519-2021-183
8. Sonnessa, A., Tarantino, E.: Using GNSS observation for mitigating the impact of SODs and RODs on the built environment – introducing the new SNIK continuously operating reference station and its applications. In: Gervasi, O., et al. (eds.) ICCSA 2021. LNCS, vol. 12955, pp. 102–111. Springer, Cham (2021). https://doi.org/10.1007/978-3-030-87007-2_8
9. Margottini, C., et al.: Landslide hazard assessment, monitoring and conservation of Vardzia monastery complex. In: Lollino, G., Giordan, D., Marunteanu, C., Christaras, B., Yoshinori, I., Margottini, C. (eds.) Engineering Geology for Society and Territory - Volume 8, pp. 293–297. Springer, Cham (2015). https://doi.org/10.1007/978-3-319-09408-3_51
10. Marsella, M., D'Aranno, P.J.V., Scifoni, S., Sonnessa, A., Corsetti, M.: Terrestrial laser scanning survey in support of unstable slopes analysis: the case of Vulcano Island (Italy). Nat. Hazards **78**(1), 443–459 (2015). https://doi.org/10.1007/s11069-015-1729-3
11. Alcántara-Ayala, I.: Integrated landslide disaster risk management (ILDRiM): the challenge to avoid the construction of new disaster risk. Environ. Haz. 20 (2021). https://doi.org/10.1080/17477891.2020.1810609
12. Tong, X., Schmidt, D.: Active movement of the Cascade landslide complex in Washington from a coherence-based InSAR time series method. Remote Sens. Environ. **186**, 405–415 (2016). https://doi.org/10.1016/j.rse.2016.09.008
13. Fastellini, G., Radicioni, F., Stoppini, A.: The Assisi landslide monitoring: report on a multi-year activity based on geomatic techniques. In: GI4DM 2010 Conference - Geomatics for Crisis Management (2010)

14. Sapena, M., Gamperl, M., Kühnl, M., Garcia-Londoño, C., Singer, J., Taubenböck, H.: Cost estimation for the monitoring instrumentalization of Landslide Early Warning Systems. https://doi.org/10.5194/nhess-2023-41
15. Ramesh, M.V., Thirugnanam, H., Singh, B., Nitin Kumar, M., Pullarkatt, D.: Landslide early warning systems: requirements and solutions for disaster risk reduction—India. In: Alcántara-Ayala, I., et al. (eds.) Progress in Landslide Research and Technology, vol. 1, no. 2, pp. 259–286 (2022). Springer, Cham (2023). https://doi.org/10.1007/978-3-031-18471-0_21
16. Rucci, A., Ferretti, A., Fumagalli, A., Passera, E., Altamira, T.: Large-scale InSAR monitoring: status and challenges. https://doi.org/10.5194/egusphere-egu23-14963
17. Crosetto, M., et al.: The evolution of wide-area DInSAR: from regional and national services to the European ground motion service (2020). https://doi.org/10.3390/RS12122043
18. Harilal, G.T., Madhu, D., Ramesh, M.V., Pullarkatt, D.: Towards establishing rainfall thresholds for a real-time landslide early warning system in Sikkim, India. Landslides **16** (2019). https://doi.org/10.1007/s10346-019-01244-1
19. Cigna, F., Ramírez, R.E., Tapete, D.: Accuracy of sentinel-1 PSI and SBAS InSAR displacement velocities against GNSS and geodetic leveling monitoring data. Remote Sens. (Basel) **13** (2021). https://doi.org/10.3390/rs13234800
20. Hu, J., Li, Z.W., Ding, X.L., Zhu, J.J., Zhang, L., Sun, Q.: Resolving three-dimensional surface displacements from InSARmeasurements: a review (2014). https://doi.org/10.1016/j.earscirev.2014.02.005
21. Canisius, F., Brisco, B., Murnaghan, K., Van Der Kooij, M., Keizer, E.: SAR backscatter and InSAR coherence for monitoring wetland extent, flood pulse and vegetation: a study of the Amazon lowland. Remote Sens. (Basel) 11 (2019). https://doi.org/10.3390/RS11060720
22. Franceschetti, G., Lanari, R.: Synthetic Aperture Radar Processing (2018). https://doi.org/10.1201/9780203737484
23. Petrosino, S., Ricco, C., De Lauro, E., Aquino, I., Falanga, M.: Time evolution of medium and long-period ground tilting at Campi Flegrei caldera. Adv. Geosci. **52** (2020). https://doi.org/10.5194/adgeo-52-9-2020
24. Ricco, C., Aquino, I., Borgstrom, S.E., Del Gaudio, C.: A study of tilt change recorded from July to October 2006 at the Phlegraean Fields (Naples, Italy). Ann. Geophys. **50** (2007)
25. Samarelli, S., Agrimano, L., Epicoco, I., Cafaro, M., Nutricato, R., Nitti, D.O., Bovenga, F.: RheticuS®: a cloud-based geo-information service for ground instabilities detection and monitoring. In: International Geoscience and Remote Sensing Symposium (IGARSS) (2018). https://doi.org/10.1109/IGARSS.2018.8518226
26. Bonaldo, G., Caprino, A., Lorenzoni, F., da Porto, F.: Monitoring displacements and damage detection through satellite MT-InSAR techniques: a new methodology and application to a case study in Rome (Italy). Remote Sens. (Basel) 15 (2023). https://doi.org/10.3390/rs15051177
27. Sonnessa, A., di Lernia, A., Oscar Nitti, D., Nutricato, R., Tarantino, E., Cotecchia, F.: Integration of multi-sensor MTInSAR and ground-based geomatic data for the analysis of non-linear displacements affecting the urban area of Chieuti, Italy. Int. J. Appl. Earth Obs. Geoinf. **117** (2023). https://doi.org/10.1016/j.jag.2023.103194

Crowdsensing Close-Range Photogrammetry for Accurately Reconstructing a Digital Twin of a Cultural Heritage Building Using a Smartphone and a Compact Camera

Cristina Monterisi, Alessandra Capolupo(✉), and Eufemia Tarantino

Department of Civil, Environmental, Land, Construction and Chemistry (DICATECh), Politecnico di Bari, Via Orabona 4, 70125 Bari, Italy
alessandra.capolupo@poliba.it

Abstract. The development of user-friendly and cost-effective survey technologies is critical in the protection and preservation of cultural heritage structures. Although they are commonly reconstructed using digital photogrammetry techniques, and with the integration of Terrestrial Laser scanners and Remotely Piloted Aircraft Systems, they are now increasingly being modeled by crowdsensed systems, which are easily accessible even to non-expert users.

As such, the goal of this research is to evaluate the performance of a smartphone and a commercial compact camera in reconstructing a detailed and accurate digital twin of a cultural heritage object. In both cases, the close-range photogrammetric technique, based on the combination of Structure for Motion and Computer Vision approaches, was used. Those methods were tested on the Ognissanti Church, located in Valenzano, Italy. MicMac Graphic User Interface and CloudCompare, two open-source software and user-friendly interfaces, were used throughout the process. Thus, once camera calibration, preprocessing, and processing phases were completed, both collected databases were compared on the base of tie points image matching, average residuals in block-bundle adjustment resolution, and processing times. Despite variations in acquisition resolution and instrumental stability, and the fact that the point cloud from smartphone camera is 3 times less dense than that from compact camera, picture matching is equivalent after 15 to 20 orientation repetitions. The resulting two clouds were almost overlapping, with an average distance of 0.01 m. These findings also matched previous outcomes in the literature for small-volume reconstruction, substantiating the notion of performance independence from the size of the modified item.

Keywords: Digital twin · Smartphone-based photogrammetry · Cultural Heritage · 3D metric reconstruction · Computer Vision · Structure for Motion

O. Gervasi et al. (Eds.): ICCSA 2023 Workshops, LNCS 14107, pp. 234–250, 2023.
https://doi.org/10.1007/978-3-031-37114-1_16

1 Introduction

Digitization assumes a key role among the strategic axes of the National Recovery and Resilience Plan (PNRR) under the "Next Generation EU" program. The European Union has recently moved toward producing digital twins integrating data collection, aggregation, artificial intelligence, and analytic and virtual representations to preserve and make accessible cultural and historical heritage. In achieving this, it is essential to plan for continuous monitoring that ensures accurate estimates of surveyed areas and volumes [1].

Digital photogrammetry, both aerial and terrestrial, enables the reconstruction of metrically accurate and efficient digital models. It involves Computer Vision (CV) algorithms, for isolated objects and monuments with regular geometries or complex shapes modeling [2], Structure for Motion (SfM) [3–5], and Dense Multi-View 3D Reconstruction (DMVR) [6] techniques used in photographic campaigns with images overlay.

For years digital photogrammetry has been used for 3D reconstruction in Cultural Heritage (CH) applications [7, 8], often coupled with surveys using Terrestrial Laser Scanner (TLS) [9–16] and Remotely Piloted Aircraft Systems (RPAS) platforms [10, 14, 16–19]. Classical surveys (e.g. total station and Global Navigation Satellite System (GNSS)) combine effectively with TLS, which provides dense geometry information and very fine textured dense point clouds despite being a time-consuming process, and with RPAS platforms, which are characterized by high efficiency in covering large areas in a limited time. [10]. However, photogrammetry has usually been performed with commercial cameras and technologies, which are high-cost and not available to all users.

Therefore, with the increasingly widespread use of smartphones in recent years, Close-Range Photogrammetry (CRP) and crowdsensing have shown to be cheaper and user-friendly technologies, available even for all non-expert photogrammetry users, but still reliable for reconstructing 3D models [17, 20].

Nowadays, smartphones are equipped with cameras, even multiple ones, with increasing resolution, often higher than compact cameras. In addition, images can be shared on the web via Wi-Fi, providing near real-time measurements [21]. Moreover, apps such as Polycam, available on both IOS and Android devices, have recently been developed for in-app cloud-based 3D model reconstruction, with results comparable to SfM approaches [22].

During the last few years, several studies investigate the photogrammetric accuracy of 3D reconstructions obtained from smartphones, particularly for modeling geomorphological, geotechnical, and geological structures [23–25], historic buildings [26], including by stereovision [27], for industrial [28, 29] and medical [30, 31] applications. Although crowdsensing applications from smartphones are increasingly widespread, one of the limitations associated with this technology is the accuracy of model reconstruction. To achieve this, some studies include and analyze the calibration [32], pre-processing [33], and processing phase using proprietary software such as Pix4D [34] (https://www.pix4d.com/), Agisoft Metashape [35] (https://www.agisoft.com/) or open software such as Apero and MicMac (https://micmac.ensg.eu/index.php/) [36].

Only a few studies have compared the performance of smartphones and Digital Single-Lens Reflex (DSLR) cameras, both of which affordable and widely available ways of surveying. However, all studies refer to small-object modeling. In particular, Saif et al. [21] verified the reliability of the self-calibration and modeling approach with both cameras in the metric survey of areas and small geometric volumes, even though SmartPhone cameras (SPCs) had more lens distortion than DSLRs..

To respond to the lack of application of studies on large object modeling and comparison in the calibration phase, this paper aims to evaluate the potential of smartphones as on-site collection close-range photogrammetry tools for geometric modeling of CH buildings, comparing their reconstruction performance in terms of accuracy and point clouds, with digital compact cameras. In accordance with the European INfrastructure for SPatial InfoRmation in Europe (INSPIRE) directive [37] and Free-and-Open-Source Softwares (FOSS), in this study the open source MicMac software for the calibration and 3D reconstruction phase was tested, specifically using of the newly introduced user-friendly MicMac Graphic User Interface (GUI) interface [38].

The paper is organized in three main sections: i) "Material and methods" (Sect. 2), ii) "Results and discussion" (Sect. 3), and, lastly, iii) "Conclusion" (Sect. 4). In Sect. 2 background, methodology, dataset definition, pre-processing, processing, and post-processing phases needed for an accurate 3D modeling of a CH site, are described. Section 3 goes over the study findings and discussion on crowdsensing potentialities and reconstruction performances using smartphone and DSLR cameras. The final part highlights the process's merits and limitations as well as potential research advances.

2 Material and Methods

2.1 Study Site and Workflow Definition

The Romanic Church of Ognissanti, Valenzano, Italy (Fig. 1), is a historic rock building from the 12th century. Built of limestone tuff ashlars, it is located in the Apulian countryside, among olive groves. Abandoned for almost a century, it has remained almost intact in its Romanic style. Twentieth-century restorations were focused on repairing the cracks found on the roof slab, closing the entrance vestibule, maintaining the interior area, and removing the bell gable [39].

Restored in the 20th century, particularly regarding structural and roofing securing and internal maintenance efforts, it is now inaccessible and at risk of collapse. Therefore, this heritage needs careful and continuous monitoring of its static condition to plan suitable ordinary and extraordinary maintenance.

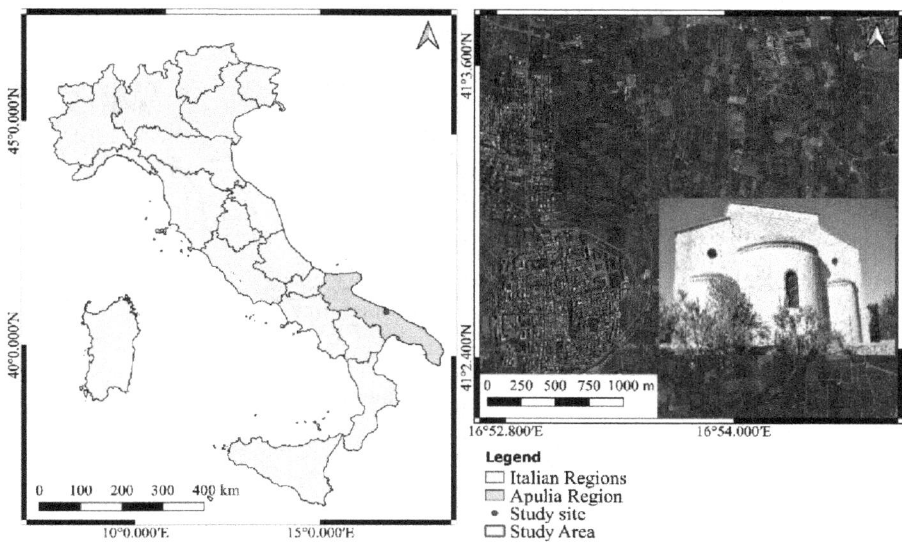

Fig. 1. Study site position in the Italian context on the left and overview of the study area on the right. A detailed of Ognissanti's Church is reported on the bottom-right.

After careful planning, the surveys carried out undershooting conditions to ensure the comparability of the surveyed data. The pre-processing and processing steps were conducted using open source MicMac (through the new user-friendly MicMac GUI interface) and CloudCompare software, focusing on the influence of the matching and calibration phases on the reconstruction accuracy, size, and noise of the generated dense point clouds. In this regard, statistical investigation methods were employed to compare reconstruction performances and estimate the accuracy of the 3D models acquired from both smartphone and DSLR cameras. Finally, the reliability of such results was investigated and discussed before statistically evaluating the correlation among the results of the previous processing phases. The operational workflow adopted is summarized in Fig. 2.

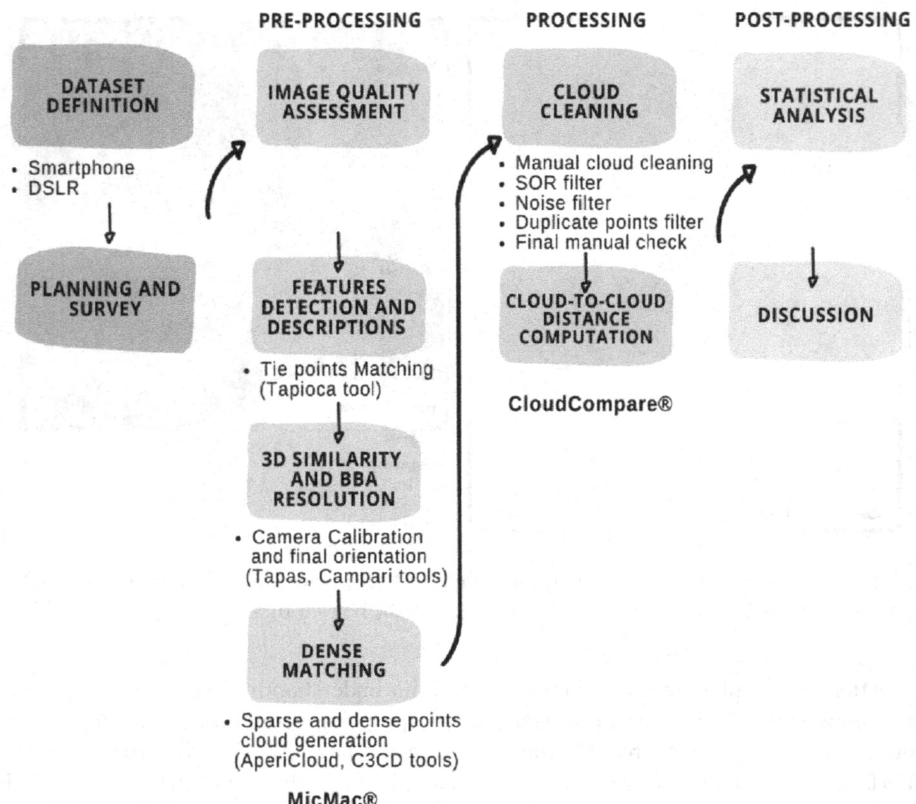

Fig. 2. Workflow of the survey from smartphone and Digital Single-Lens Reflex (DSLR) cameras. BBA: Bundle Block Adjustment; C3CD: Culture 3D Cloud; SOR filter: Statistical Outlier Removal filter.

2.2 Field Data Campaign and Dataset Description

In this research, photogrammetric data about Ognissanti's Church was captured using an ordinary DSLR camera (Nikon D-3300) and a smartphone (Xiaomi Redmi 10 C)..

The camera's specifications are listed in Table 1.

The survey was designed to be completed in a single day with uniform weather conditions (negligible cloud cover and wind) and monitoring the sun's position on the horizon to minimize direct reflections. By setting the ground pixel size as constant, depending on the focal length and the camera pixel size, the capture distance was calculated for both sensors, as shown in Table 2.

To overcome the difficulties caused by the survey's relevant noise conditions, the horizontal capture distance between the two sensors was kept constant. The presence of trees and dry-stone walls around the structure to be examined affected image matching.

Table 1. Utilized cameras Specifics.

Specifications	DSLR camera (Nikon D-3300)	Smartphone camera (Xiaomi Redmi 10C)
Camera model	D-3300	Samsung SSKKN1 Isocell
Sensor type	CMOS	CMOS
Sensor size	APS-C (23.5 mm x 15.6 mm)	~ 1/5"
Pixel size	3.84 μm	~ 0.72 μm
Camera Resolution	24 MP	Dual 50 MP + 2 MP
Focal Length (35 mm equivalent)	18- 55 mm	26.4 mm
Native ISO	10–12,800	100 – 6,400
Aperture	f/3.5-f/5.6	f/1.8-f/2.4
Image Format	RAW (NEF), JPEG	JPG

Table 2. Conditions and parameters of the acquisition survey.

Acquisition conditions and parameters	DSLR camera (Nikon D-3300)	Smartphone camera (Xiaomi Redmi 10C)
Acquisition data Acquisition hours	2022/11/17 h. 9.30 a.m. – 11.30 a.m	2022/11/17 h. 9.30 a.m. – 11.30 a.m
Acquisition distance	10.8 m	15.0 m
Captured photos number	148	152
Horizontal Photos distance	0.96 m	0.96 m
Photos Overlap	≥ 80%	≥ 80%

2.3 Data Processing

The collected images were transferred to a PC which specifications are given in Table 3.

Table 3. Configuration of the PC used for images processing.

PC model	HP Omen 45L
Operating System	Windows 64 bit
RAM	64 GB
CPU	Intel(R) Core(TM) i9–12900 K 3.20 GHz; 12th gen
GPUs	NVIDIA GeForce RTX 3090

Following a preliminary quality assessment phase that measures images contrast, blurred images are eliminated (with estimated quality less than 0.6 in a range from 0 to 1).

The program setting allowed editing the *exif* metadata (Focal Length, Focal Length equivalent to 35mm, Camera Model Name) for both acquisition sensors. The Tapioca tool, an operational interface of the bigger Pastis, was then used to perform feature detection and description, as well as the identification of matching tie points across pictures. At this step, four chunks (image blocks), one for each side of the building, were created and, for each of them, the same parameters were set to ensure comparability of results. It was possible to automatically compute the tie points by first considering pairs of images at a lower resolution and then detail matching at full resolution by using the Scale Invariant Feature Transform++ (SIFT++) algorithm [40, 41], whose advantage is to integrate the tie point generation in a way compatible with the global pipeline, with Multiple Scale (MulScale) mode.

Moreover, the ResiduesTapas tool was used to compute the camera orientation with a free-network approach. At the Internal Orientation (IO) step, the Radial Extended radial distortion model with 10 degrees of freedom (focal, principal point coordinates, distortion point coordinates, and 5 radial distortion coefficients) [42] was used. Micmac used Campari tool capabilities to address Block Bundle Adjustment (BBA) incorporating IO parameters using the Levenberg-Marquard optimization method [43, 44], which is suitable for handling nonlinear least squares problems. In the final orientation step, the four previously created chunks were merged. Lastly, using the Apericloud and Culture 3D Cloud (C3CD) tools, it was possible to automatically reconstruct the new sparse and dense points by setting the maximum resolution using the BigMag algorithm [45, 46].

After manually cleaning the point clouds to remove outliers from the object to be modeled (e.g., dry stone walls and trees), the Statistical Outlier Removal (SOR) filter and noise filter were applied [47] and duplicate points were removed.

Filtering parameters were selected through an iterative process including manual interpretation in order to offer the best cleaning of the dense point cloud while preserving relevant relief characteristics such as scattered points portraying the building's top. A last inspection allowed for the removal of any remaining isolated points or identified things that were discordant with the study site. After manual alignment and a subsample of the two clouds, the Cloud-to-Cloud (C2C) tool, in conjunction with the Multiscale Model to Model Cloud Comparison (M3C2) plugin [48], made it possible to calculate the distance between points acquired by DSLR and smartphone along the normal surface to the reference direction, while keeping track of 3D variations in the orientation of the surface, after manual alignment and a subsample of the two clouds.

It was then possible to estimate a confidence interval dependent on points cloud roughness and registration error for each measured distance.

2.4 Performance Reconstruction and Accuracy Assessment

The performance reconstruction and accuracy assessment step was aimed at testing: a) datasets quality; b) performance reconstruction in terms of processing time, quality, and cleanness of the generated point clouds; and c) accuracy of the photogrammetric measurements made with smartphones and DSLRs.

As highlighted by Triggs et al. [49], the photogrammetric products reconstruction accuracy depends on processed images quality, acquisition distance, and camera type. Therefore, the study considered these factors all. While conducting BBA using SfM (see Subsection "Data Processing"), the first factor was assessed (with the goal of minimizing its impacts) by utilizing the picture quality tool and selecting a SIFT++ technique.

Attaching an error matrix to the percentage of tie points retained in the BBA stage in matching the images and analyzing the residuals and their variation by the number of iterations in the calibration stage allows to compare calibration and modeling performance between the two cameras.

Pearson's correlation [50] was used to evaluate the alignment matrix between point clouds. Lastly, the errors that affected the final measurements of the oriented image blocks were evaluated using the Root Mean Square Error (RMSE).

3 Results and Discussion

In this study, a close-range photogrammetric crowdsensing approach was used to reconstruct a digital twin of a heritage building by comparing smartphones and compact cameras performances.

Survey planning allowed the acquisition of 152 and 146 images from smartphone and DSLR, respectively. Following the image quality assessment, 3 and 1 images were discarded from the two datasets, respectively. Inside MicMac software, all images with unsuitable lighting and environmental conditions were discarded, tie point matching and local calibration, and final alignment of the models were performed. Since MicMac is an open and programmable software, it allows to manage all preprocessing parameters. In this regard, it permits to choose the calibration model, as not all software, even commercial ones like Agisoft Metashape, does.

After the pre-processing step, the percentages of tie points kept in the image matching during the BBA resolution phase were calculated for the 112 images collected during both surveys (Table 4).

Table 4. Tie points maintained in images matching during the BBA phase (in percentage).

		DSLR (ref)				
		>99 (%)	95 - 99	80–95	50–80	<50
Smartphone	>99 (%)	89	1	1	0	0
	95–99 (%)	1	1	0	0	1
	80–95 (%)	6	3	2	1	0
	50–80 (%)	3	1	0	0	0
	<50 (%)	0	0	0	1	1

The results reveal precise image matching. Despite the significant number of trees present, only two shots from each camera had a proportion of tie points retained in the final orientation of less than 50%. A value more than 80% is represented by 84% and 94% of images shot by smartphones and DSLRs, respectively. In both smartphone and DSLR polls, 89 images had a value more than 99%. Table 5 depicts elaboration timing of whole pre-processing step.

Table 5. Elaboration time during pre-processing phases in MicMac

Pre-processing phase	Smartphone camera Elaboration time (min)	DSLR camera Elaboration time (min)
Image Quality Assessment	0.5	1.0
Tie point matching	240.0	150.0
Camera calibration and final orientation	180.0	90.0
Dense matching	8.0	12.0

Even though crowdsensing systems such as smartphones and DSLRs reduce survey time and allow for user-friendly surveying and retrieval, the preprocessing phase requires substantial processing time. When Micmac is used as a preprocessing tool in conjunction with the PC configuration outlined in Table 3, the processing times are much longer than those measured in trials using commercial software. [21]. Pre-processing times for data from mobile devices are roughly twice as lengthy as those for tiny cameras.

However, it greatly increases processing times when compared to standard photogrammetry from TLS and RPAS [11, 16–18, 51, 53], especially when utilizing MicMac, rather than black-box software like Agisoft Metashape [21, 54].

An analysis of average residual variation in relation to the number of iterations of the final orientation step (BBA resolution/ image matching) was conducted on a sample of 15 images acquired from both cameras (for a total of 30 paired images). Samples were selected by identifying 3 major clusters: 4 images with higherthan 80% BBA coverage, 4 images with about 50% BBA coverage, and 4 images with less than 20% BBA coverage. Moreover, the first and last survey images, as well as a random acquisition, were taken into account. Indicative results of the 3 identified groups are displayed in Fig. 3.

The further synthetic analysis highlights that, as environmental conditions become worse, more iterations are required before the residual achieves acceptable values (smaller than 1 px). The gap between the residual from the smartphone and the residual from the DSLR drops substantially after a series of 15 and 25 repetitions in pictures with increased noise produced by tree cover. It should be noted that the residuals from DSLR acquisitions are more stable, yielding satisfactory results even with a small number of repeats (less than 5). However, although the value of the resulting residual is always lower in images acquired from DSLR (with an average of 0.39 px), the residual from smartphone data also reaches sub-pixel values (with an average of 0,67 px).

The topographic conformation of the site and the survey distance precluded a total reconstruction of the building. The noise caused by the significant presence of trees and the dry-stone walls surrounding the building affected the modeling result.

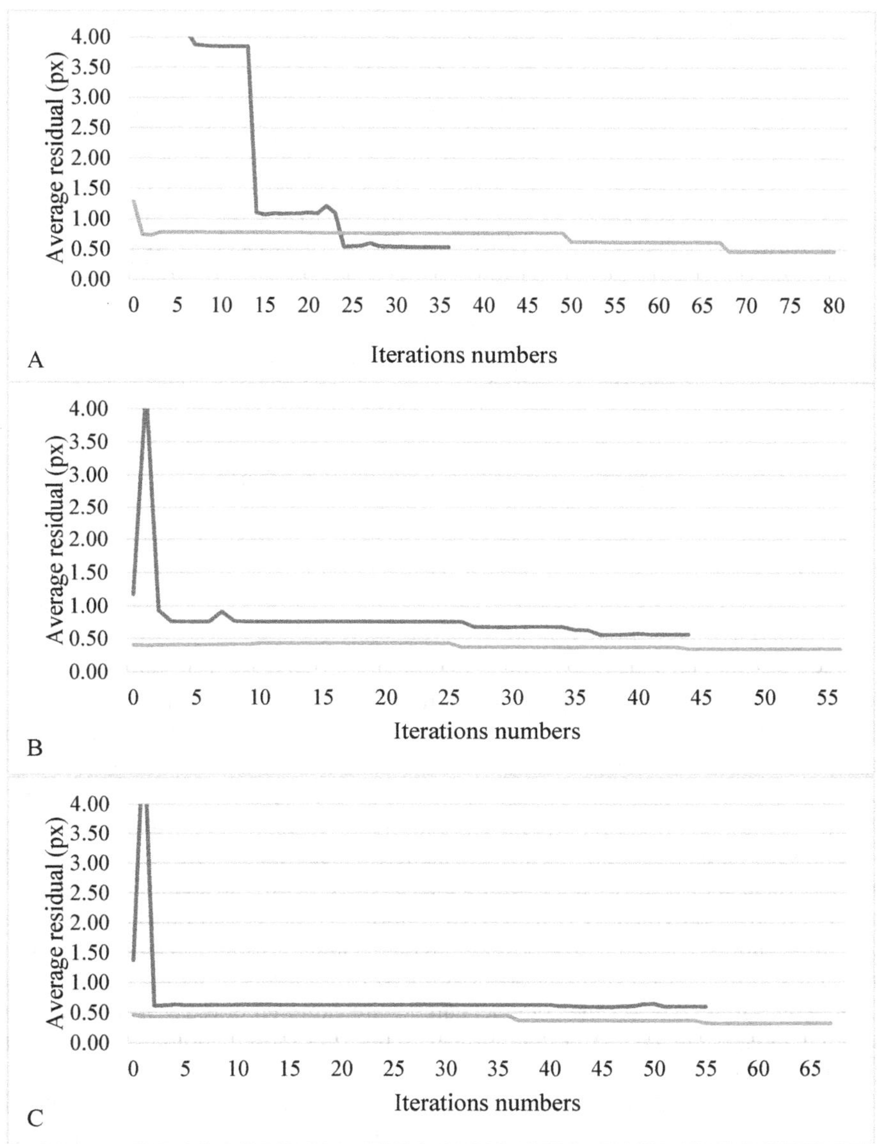

Fig. 3. Average Residual in function on iterations number in images matching during the Block Bundle Adjustment (BBA) phase. A) Reference image with more than 80% tree cover; B) Reference image with about 50% tree cover; c) Reference image with less than 20% tree cover.

The analysis of the reconstructed dense clouds is summarized in Table 6. The *DSLR camera* and *Smartphone camera* columns represent the size of each dense point cloud. The $\Delta\,(DPC_i\,points - DPC_{i\text{-}1})\,(\%)$ and $\Delta\,(DPC_i\,points - DPC_{i\text{-}1})\,(\%)$ columns represent the percentage of point decrease after applying the pre-processing filters. The point

Table 6. DPC points number on processing phases. DPC: Dense Point Cloud; SPC: Sparse Points Cloud

Points Cloud specifications	DSLR camera	Δ (DPC_i points – DPC_{i-1}) (%)	Smartphone camera	Δ (DPC_i points – DPC_{i-1}) (%)
SPC	5,750,814		957,338	
DPC	16,195,314		6,693,286	
DPC after SOR filter	9,967,825	-38.45	3,155,806	-52.85
DPC after noise filter	6,298,317	-36.81	2,329,822	-26.17
DPC after duplicate points filter	6,298,317	0.00	2,329,822	0.00
DPC after manual check	6,296,217	-0.03	2,328,969	-0.04
Δ (DPC_i points – DPC_0) (%)		-61.12		-65.20

cloud obtained by DSLR, after manually removing the elements from the survey target (dry-stone walls and trees), is approximately three times denser than that generated by a smartphone. It presents better geometric quality and a significant outlier values reduction. The data also reveal that both point clouds contain no duplicate points after applying SOR and noise filtering. The research provides evidence on cloud point number independence from the smartphone or digital camera utilized, which confirms the results reported by Saif et al. [21] on the modeling of tiny geometric objects. It also implies that the same characteristic is unaffected by the size of the discovered item. The gap indicates that the dense cloud cover provided by DSLR gives a more accurate depiction of the identified object information. Consequently, despite having a camera resolution twice that of the tested DSLR, the smartphone camera performs worse in terms of reconstructed model quality. After all, images for the compact camera are captured in RAW format, with no auto-adjustment or image compression. Instead, the JPG format compresses images to reduce their size.

In order to metrically compare the two generated models accuracy, alignment was required. The models were then uploaded to CloudCompare for the processing stage and aligned with point pairs-picking for registration. The DSLT model was scaled on a 1.68 factor. The RMSE was used to analyze the error impacting the final alignment from oriented image blocks. It yielded a reasonably low value (0.42 m), indicating that the two developed models fit well. DSLR dense point cloud, as seen in Fig. 4, provides a higher level of details and definition but does not include the reconstruction of the building roof. This is especially due to the lower acquisition distance between the camera and the object, which was selected to maintain the same detected pixel size between both cameras.

Fig. 4. Dense Points cloud alignment. A. Smartphone reconstruction; B. Reflex reconstruction; 3. Reconstruction alignment overlay.

Lastly, the distance between the modeled dense point clouds was computed using C2C tool (Fig. 5). This suggests that most of the points are less than 0.3 m away from the corresponding ones in the direction normal to the plane of the modeled surface. Building facades differ less across the two models, while roof parts, which have a lesser concentration of points, differ the most. This is explained in part by the lack of top modeling points in the DSLR data.

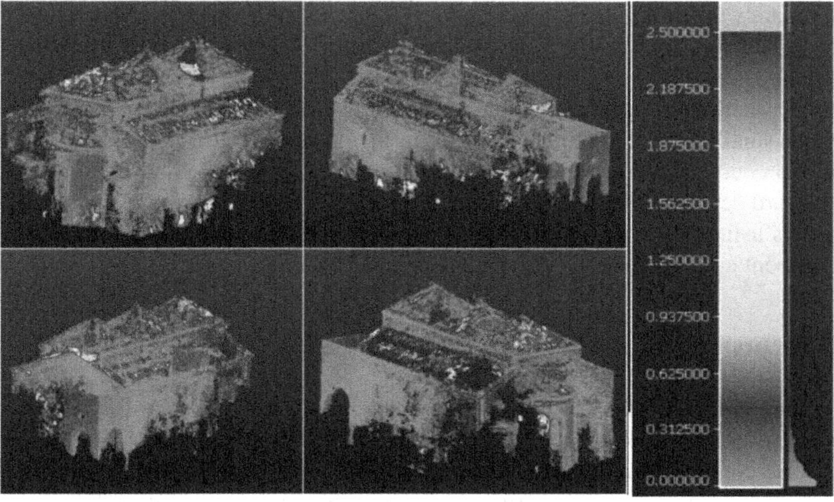

Fig. 5. Cloud-to-cloud distance computation (DSLR reference data)

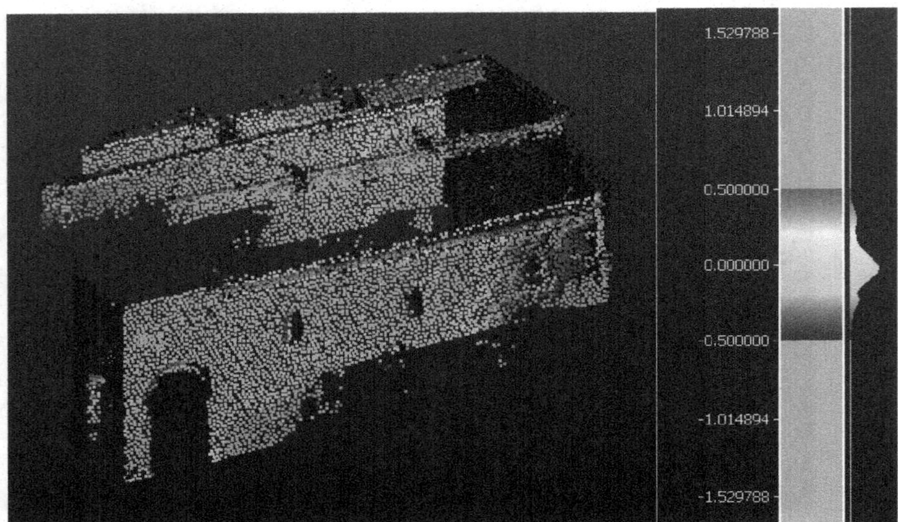

Fig. 6. M3C2 tool Dense points cloud distance

M3C2 tool results in determining the distances between the two point clouds are shown in Fig. 6. Distances distribution can be assimilated to a normal curve with values between -0.5m and 0.5m, a mean of -0.01 m, and a standard deviation of 0.29.

Although model's accuracy may be affected by factors, including image quality, image acquisition strategy, camera calibration, and SfM algorithm [55], the error obtained from a combination of TLS and drone-mounted cameras, was compared. While the average reconstruction error generated by crowdsensing is equivalent to that produced by camera reconstruction on the drone and TLS [10–12, 16], the standard deviation is approximately ten times larger than that produced by the combination of TLS and RPAS camera modeling [13]. However, the acquisition tactics employed a more approachable, user-friendly, cost-effective, and direct approach.

Moreover, this paper presents comparable results in large object monitoring to the literature on small object modeling [21], in terms of dense point clouds size ratio, gaussian distribution curve of point cloud distances between cameras, mean absolute distances, and standard deviation of 3D reconstruction. The ability to reconstruct accurate 3D metric models using user-friendly survey procedures is critical for major cultural heritage improvement and monitoring.

4 Conclusion

In literature, a few researchers have investigated the metric accuracy of reconstruction of 3-dimensional models by crowdsensing close-range photogrammetry. In particular, some works compared the metric reconstruction performance of user-friendly and readily available technologies such as smartphones and compact cameras. Among them, all have focused on the survey of small objects.

The performance of reconstruction combining smartphone and DSLR data capture to the modeling of large objects, namely a Cultural Heritage building located in Valenzano (Italy), was investigated in this work.

In both the calibration and alignment phases, the study shows encouraging results for 3D model reconstruction. Although the average preprocessing residues, processing time, and dense point cloud size are lower than that of a DSLR camera, the alignment phase reveals a consistent overlap between the two point clouds, with cloud-to-cloud differences ranging from 0.5 m to 0.5 m and, on average, settling around 0.01 m. Those findings suggests that, like compact cameras, smartphones may be used to collect on-site photogrammetric data immediately. Despite increased processing time and early residual instability in the first iterations of the BBA resolution phase, it produces an accurate reconstruction of the 3D object. Furthermore, by providing data comparable to tiny object analysis, this study solidifies the results' independence from the size of the identified items and the noise around the survey zone. Despite their speed in surveying, the processing periods of these cameras are frequently longer than those of consolidated photogrammetric acquisition methods.

This study's conclusions are confined to the testing of only two cameras and one calibration technique. Future studies might quantitatively examine the association between camera characteristics (sensor size, resolution, focal length) and model quality. Furthermore, in order to make accurate 3D heritage modeling accessible to non-expert users, further research might look at reconstruction quality in connection to calibration methodologies and pre-processing technologies, such as in-app processing.

References

1. Remondino, F.: Heritage recording and 3D modeling with photogrammetry and 3D scanning. Remote Sens. **3**, 1104–1138 (2011)
2. Remondino, F., El-Hakim, S.: Image-based 3D modeling: a review. Photogramm. Rec. **21**, 269–291 (2006)
3. Robertson, D., Cipolla, R. Structure from motion. Practical Image Processing and Computer Vision. John Wiley: Hoboken, NJ, USA (2009)
4. Capolupo, A., Saponaro, M., Borgogno Mondino, E., Tarantino, E.: Combining interior orientation variables to predict the accuracy of Rpas-Sfm 3D models. Remote Sens. **12**(17), 2674 (2020)
5. Caradonna, G., Tarantino, E., Scaioni, M., Figorito, B.: Multi-image 3D reconstruction: a photogrammetric and structure from motion comparative analysis. In: Gervasi, O., et al. ()eds. Computational Science and Its Applications–ICCSA 2018: 18th International Conference, Melbourne, VIC, Australia, July 2–5, 2018, Proceedings, Part V, vol. 18, pp. 305–316. Springer, Heidelberg (2018). https://doi.org/10.1007/978-3-319-95174-4_25
6. Furukawa, Y., Ponce, J.: Accurate, dense, and robust multiview stereopsis. IEEE Trans. Pattern Anal. Mach. Intell. **32**, 1362–1376 (2010)
7. Guarnieri, A., Pirotti, F., Vettore, A.: Cultural heritage interactive 3D models on the web: an approach using open source and free software. J. Cult. Herit. **11**(3), 350–353 (2010)
8. Balletti, C., Bertellini, B., Gottardi, C., Guerra, F.: Geomatics techniques for the enhancement and preservation of cultural heritage. Int. Arch. Photogramm. Remote Sens. Spatial Inf. Sci., **XLII-2/W11**, 133–140 (2019)

9. Cianci, M.G., Colaceci, S.: Laser scanner and UAV for the 2D and 3D reconstructions of cultural heritage. Sci. Res. Inf. Technol. Ricerca Scientifica e Tecnologie dell'Informazione **12**(2), 43–54 (2022)
10. Xu, Z., Wu, L., Shen, Y., Li, F., Wang, Q., Wang, R.: Tridimensional reconstruction applied to cultural heritage with the use of camera-equipped UAV and terrestrial laser scanner. Remote Sens. **6**, 10413–10434 (2014)
11. Tiwari, P.S., Pande, H., Gupta, S., Chandan, G., Samwal, E., Agarwal, S. Damage detection and virtual reconstruction of built heritage: an approach using high-recolution range and intensity data. J. Ind. Soc. Remote Sens. (2023)
12. Fassi, F., Fregonese, L., Ackermann, S., De Troia, V. Comparison between laser scanning and automated 3D modelling techniquesd to reconstruct complex and extensive cultural heritage areas. Int. Arch. Photogram. Remote Sens. Spat. Inf. Sci. **XL-5/W1** (2013)
13. Tysiac, P., Sieńska, A., Tarnowska, M., Kedziorski, P., Jagoda M. Combination of terrestrial laser scanning and UAV photogrammetry for 3D modelling and degradation assessment of heritage building based on a lighting analysis: case study—St. Adalbert Church in Gdansk, Poland. Herit. Sci. **11**, 53 (2023)
14. Saponaro, M., Capolupo, A., Turso, A., Tarantino, E.: Cloud-to-cloud assessment of UAV and TLS 3D reconstructions of cultural heritage monuments: the case of Torre Zozzoli. In: Eighth International Conference on Remote Sensing and Geoinformation of the Environment (RSCy2020), vol. 11524, pp. 60–71. SPIE (2020)
15. Saponaro, M., Tarantino, E., Fratino, U.: Geometric accuracy evaluation of geospatial data using low-cost sensors on small UAVs. In: Gervasi, O., et al. (eds.) ICCSA 2018. LNCS, vol. 10964, pp. 364–374. Springer, Cham (2018). https://doi.org/10.1007/978-3-319-95174-4_29
16. Capolupo, A.: Accuracy assessment of cultural heritage models extracting 3D point cloud geometric features with RPAS SfM-MVS and TLS techniques. Drones **5**(4), 145 (2021)
17. Capolupo. A.; Maltese, A.; Saponaro M.; Costantino, D. Integration of terrestrial laser scanning and UAV-SFM technique to generate a detailed 3D textured model of a heritage building. Earth Resources and Environmental Remote Sensing/GIS Applications (SPIE) XI Conference (2020)
18. Pepe, M.; Alfio, V.S.; Costantino, D. UAV platforms and the SfM-MVS approach in the 3D surveys and modelling: a review in the cultural heritage field. Appl. Sci. **12** (2022)
19. Cutugno, M., Robustelli, U., Pugliano, G.: Structure-from-motion 3D reconstruction of the historical overpass Ponte Della Cerra: a comparison between MicMac® open source software and Metashape®. Drones **6**, 242 (2022)
20. Boccia, L., Capolupo, A., Esposito, G., Mansueto, G., Tarantino, E.: A crowd-sensing system for geomatics applications. In: Misra, S., et al. (eds.) ICCSA 2019. LNCS, vol. 11622, pp. 297–312. Springer, Cham (2019). https://doi.org/10.1007/978-3-030-24305-0_23
21. Saif, W., Alshibani, A.: Smartphone-based photogrammetry assessment in comparison with a compact camera for construction management applications. Appl. Sci. **12**, 1053 (2022)
22. Eker, R., Elvanoglu, N., Ucar, Z., Bilici, 3, Aydın, A.: 3D Modelling of a historic windmill: PPK-aided terrestrial photogrammetry vs smartphone app. ISPRS—Int. Arch. Photogramm. Remote Sens. Spat. Inf. Sci. **XLIII-B2-2022 XXIV** (2022)
23. Dabove, P., Grasso, N., Piras, M.: Smartphone-based photogrammetry for the 3D modeling of a geomorphological structure. Appl. Sci. **9**, 3884 (2019)
24. Tavani, S., Granado, P., Riccardi, U., Seers, T., Corradetti, A.: Terrestrial SfM-MVS photogrammetry from smartphone sensors. Geomorphology **367**, 107318 (2020)
25. Alessandri, L., et al.: The fusion of external and internal 3d photogrammetric models as a tool to investigate the ancient human/cave interaction: the La Sassa case study. ISPRS—ISPRS—Int. Arch. Photogramm. Remote Sens. Spat. Inf. Sci. **XLIII-B2–2020**, 1443–1450 (2020)

26. Bolognesi, C. M., Fiorillo, F. Virtual representations of cultural heritage: sharable and implementable case study to be enjoyed and maintained by the community. Buildings **13**, 410 (2023)
27. Masiero, A., Fissore, F., Piragnolo, M., Guarnieri, A., Pirotti, F., Vettore, A.: Initial evaluation of 3D reconstruction of close objects with Smartphone Stereo Vision. ISPRS—Int. Arch. Photogramm. Remote Sens. Spat. Inf. Sci. **XLII-1**, 289–293 (2018)
28. Yu, L., Lubineau, G. A smartphone camera and built-in gyroscope based application for non-contact yet accurate off-axis structural displacement measurements. Measurement **167**, 108449 (2021)
29. Najathulla, B.C., Deshpande, A.S., Khandelwal, M.: Smartphone camera-based micron-scale displacement measurement: development and application in soft actuators. Instrum. Sci. Technol. **50**, 616–625 (2022)
30. Stark, E., Haffner, O., Kuˇcera, E.: Low-cost method for 3D body measurement based on photogrammetry using smartphone. Electronics **11**, 1048 (2022)
31. Matuzeviˇcius, D., Serackis, A.: Three-dimensional human head reconstruction using smartphone-based close-range video photogrammetry. Appl. Sci. **12**, 229 (2021)
32. Remondino, F., Fraser, C.S.: Digital camera calibration methods: considerations and comparisons. Int. Arch. Photogramm. Remote Sens. Spat. Inf. Sci. **36**, 266–272 (2006)
33. Jasinska, A., Pyka, K., Pastucha, E., Midtiby, H.S. A simple way to reduce 3D model deformation in smartphone photogrammetry. Sensors **23**, 728 (2023)
34. PIX4D Homepage. https://www.pix4d.com/. Accessed 27 Feb 2023
35. Agisoft Metashape Homepage. https://www.agisoft.com/. Accessed 27 Feb 2023
36. MicMac Homepage. https://micmac.ensg.eu/index.php/. 27 Feb 2023
37. Wheeler, D.A. Why Open Source Software/Free Software (OSS/FS). http://www.dwheeler.com/oss_fs_why.html. 27 Feb 2023
38. MicMac Graphic User Interface (GUI), http://clintons3d.com/plugins/other/micmacgui/index.html. Accessed 02 Mar 2023
39. De Cadilhac, R.L.:'arte della costruzione in pietra: chiese di Puglia con cupole in asse dal secolo XI al XVI. Gangemi Editore, Roma, Italy (2011)
40. Lowe, D.G.: Object recognition from local scale-invariant features. In: Proceedings of the Seventh IEEE International Conference on Computer Vision, Kerkyra, Greece, vol. 2, pp. 1150–1157 (1999)
41. GitHub SIFT++ Homepage. https://github.com/davidstutz/vedaldi2006-siftpp. Accessed 27 Feb 2023
42. Zhang, Z.: A flexible new technique for camera calibration. IEEE Trans. Pattern Anal. Mach. Intell. **22**(11), 1330–1334 (2000)
43. Levenberg, K.: A method for the solution of certain nonlinear problems in least squares. Quart. Appl. Math. **2**, 164–166 (1944)
44. Marquardt, D.W.: An algorithm for least-squares estimation of nonlinear inequalities. SIAM J. Appl. Math. **11**, 431–441 (1963)
45. MicMac documentation, MicMac, Apero, Pastis, and Other Beverages in a Nutshell! (2022)
46. Rupnik, E., Daakir, M., Pierrot Deseilligny, M.: MicMac – a free, open-source solution for photogrammetry. Open Geospat. Data Softw. Stand. **2**(1), 1–9 (2017). https://doi.org/10.1186/s40965-017-0027-2
47. Rusu, R.B., Cousins, S.: Point cloud library (pcl). In: IEEE International Conference on Robotics and Automation, pp. 1–4 (2011)
48. Lague, D., Brodu, N., Leroux, J.: Accurate 3D comparison of complex topography with terrestrial laser scanner: Application to the Rangitikei canyon (N-Z). ISPRS J. Photogramm. Remote Sens. **82**, 10–26 (2013)

49. Triggs, B., Mclauchlan, P.F., Hartley, R., FitzGibbon, A.W.: Bundle Adjustment -A Modern Synthesis. Lecture Notes in Computer Science. Springer Science and Business Media LLC, vol. 1883, pp. 298–372 (2000)
50. Pearson, K.: On the criterion that a given system of deviations from the probable in the case of a correlated system of variables is such that it can be reasonably supposed to have arisen from random sampling, the London, Edinburgh, and Dublin. Philos. Mag. J. Sci. **50**(302), 157–175 (1990)
51. Saponaro, M., Capolupo, A., Caporusso, G., Tarantino, E.: Influence of co-alignment procedures on the co-registration accuracy of multi-epoch SFM points clouds. Int. Arch. Photogramm. Remote Sens. Spat. Inf. Sci. **43**, 231–238 (2021)
52. Saponaro, M., Capolupo, A., Caporusso, G., Borgogno Mondino, E., Tarantino, E.. Predicting the accuracy of photogrammetric 3D reconstruction from camera calibration parameters through a multivariate statistical approach. Int. Arch. Photogramm. Remote Sens. Spat. Inf. Sci. XLIII-B2–2020 **43**, 479–486 (2020)
53. Saponaro, M., et al.: Data fusion of terrestrial laser scanner and remotely piloted aircraft systems points clouds for monitoring the coastal protection systems. Aquat. Ecosyst. Health Manag. **23**(4), 389–397 (2020)
54. Saponaro, M., Turso, A., Tarantino, E.: Parallel Development of Comparable Photogrammetric Workflows Based on UAV Data Inside SW Platforms. In: Gervasi, O., et al. (eds.) ICCSA 2020. LNCS, vol. 12252, pp. 693–708. Springer, Cham (2020). https://doi.org/10.1007/978-3-030-58811-3_50
55. Eker, R., Alkan, E., Aydın, A.: A comparative analysis of UAV-RTK and UAV-PPK methods in mapping different surface types. Eur. J. Forest Eng. **7**(1), 12–25 (2021)

Landsat 9 Satellite Images Potentiality in Extracting Land Cover Classes in GEE Environment Using an Index-Based Approach: The Case Study of Savona City

Alessandra Capolupo(✉) and Eufemia Tarantino

Department of Civil, Environmental, Land, Building Engineering and Chemistry (DICATECh), Politecnico di Bari, Via Orabona 4, 70125 Bari, Italy
alessandra.capolupo@poliba.it

Abstract. Land use and land cover modeling is an essential tool because it enables scientists and policymakers to foresee prospective changes in landscape heritage and examine trends to minimize potential dangers. To attain this purpose, a continuous stream of data needs be collected and examined. Landsat missions present a viable alternative since they have been collecting continuous data for five decades, and a new platform was launched at the end of September 2021 to avoid disrupting such a series. Consequently, the purpose of this research is to assess the quality of Landsat 9 data in extracting land use information using the index-based approach. Following the conclusion of the collection and pre-processing operations, two of the most often used vegetation indices, NDVI and MSAVI2, were derived from a Landsat 9 data covering Savona city, which was chosen as the pilot site due to its unique geomorphological characteristics. Lastly, maps accuracy was assessed by computing the confusion matrices, k estimator and overall, producer and users accuracy. The entire method was implemented in the free cloud computing platform Google Earth Engine by writing custom Java code. The generated land use/cover maps were both satisfactory, albeit the MSAVI2 had a greater overall accuracy (90.24% vs 79.60%) and K parameter (84.45% vs 71.70%) due to its ability to minimize soil spectral effect. Those findings are consistent with those derived from Landsat 8 images. This means that Landsat 9 is an excellent successor to Landsat 8.

Keywords: satellite open images · geospatial big data · land use classification algorithms · cloud computing · NDVI · MSAVI2

1 Introduction

Among Earth observation systems, the Landsat initiative stands out because it has gathered continuous data for five decades, allowing researchers to explore Earth's physical process laws and dynamic evolution despite its poor, or at least medium, resolution [1]. As a result, it appears to be ideal for conducting ecological analyses and detecting changes in Land Use/Cover (LU/LC) from the early 1970s [2–4] which is the primary

O. Gervasi et al. (Eds.): ICCSA 2023 Workshops, LNCS 14107, pp. 251–265, 2023.
https://doi.org/10.1007/978-3-031-37114-1_17

cause of significant environmental crises such as climate change or erosion [5–7]. Therefore, having incessant and accurate LU/LC maps looks to be critical in addressing the primary environmental challenges.

To ensure that data gathering does not cease, a new Landsat satellite mission, Landsat 9, was launched at the end of September 2021 by the National Aeronautics and Space Adminstration (NASA) and the US Geological Survey (USGS). To enhance observational timing, it was sent into orbit eight days following Landsat 8, guaranteeing the acquisition of around 1,500 new scenes every day [6]. Indeed, the geometric, temporal, and spectral resolutions of the Landsat 8 OLI sensor and the Landsat 9 OLI-2 sensor are nearly identical. The key distinction between them is the greater radiometric resolution (14 bits) of the Landsat 9 sensor against the OLI sensor's 12-bit resolution [9].

Landsat missions therefore provide an essential baseline data set, however only few images are truly helpful because the majority of them are impacted by climatic circumstances and, as a result, cannot be used to give relevant information [10]. Furthermore, two additional issues must be addressed: i) the vast number of data to be processed to meet a specific purpose, and ii) the detection of the best technique to extract LU/LC information in a short period of time. The former issue might be addressed by utilizing a web-based platform designed to manage geographical large data, such as Google Earth Engine (GEE - https://earthengine.google.org) [11]. The latter, on the other hand, might be addressed by assessing the many algorithms produced over time and picking the best one in accordance with the study goal.

GEE, in fact, allows users to review the integrated data catalogue, which is updated daily, and choose one of the actual accessible open-source geospatial data or import a proprietary layer to process in the Application Programming Interface (API) [12]. API enables to manage hundreds of geographical data at the same time by writing appropriate codes in Java or Python languages and making use of the collection of complex algorithms already integrated in such a platform [11]. As a consequence, any user has the ability to write their own code or customize existing ones. Also, each algorithm is sped up due to the number of processors engaged throughout the running phase. This even eliminates any challenges related with the storage, management, and analysis of massive volumes of geographical big data, going beyond the constraints of the frequently applied desktop software. Although they feature a smart, interactive, and user-friendly interface that can be utilized by both IT-skilled and non-IT-skilled people [13–15], in most cases, such software are black boxes, as they do not disclose any understanding about the adopted procedures. Because they are not flexible, only pre-existing algorithms may be used to process the data and, then, the optimal processing approach may not be available [16].

In fact, numerous ways to dealing with geographic big data and creating LU/LC maps have been created throughout the years. The most recurrent ones are index-based [17, 18], machine learning (ML) [19–21], and Object-Based Image Analysis (OBIA) [22, 23]. So far, none of them are without restrictions. In fact, the index-based technique can only extract information from one LU/LC category, whereas ML requires a large number of parameters that are difficult to implement, and OBIA does not deliver promising results on low/medium resolution images [24–27]. As a result, it is critical to select the optimal strategy based on the input data and study objectives.

In this research, the index-based approach was used to generate LU/LC maps from satellite images quickly. This decision was made to assess the potential of the new satellite platform Landsat 9. Furthermore, while it delivers data in continuity with Landsat 8, its potential has yet to be tapped since it is so new. Furthermore, the free cloud computing GEE platform was used to speed up the operation and customize the categorization algorithms based on study needs. The approach was tried at a pilot site in Savona, a town in the Liguria area of northern Italy, selected because of its morphological complexity.

The paper is structured as follows: Part 2 "Materials and Methods" explains the city of Savona, the chosen pilot site where the technique was evaluated (Sect. 2.1), as well as the methodology used to generate the geodatabase in the GEE environment (Sect. 2.2) and to handle Landsat 9 satellite pictures (Sects. 2.2 and 2.3). Finally, the process for determining the accuracy of the resultant maps is evaluated (Sect. 2.4). Part 3 "Results and discussion" presents and discusses the final results relating to the generating LU/LC maps, map accuracy, Landsat 9 image quality, and script performance. The Conclusion section highlights more improvements and criticality.

2 Material and Methods

This section displays the techniques used to attain the study objectives. Indeed, after consulting GEE catalogue and collecting the input Landsat 9 images, they were preprocessed to rectify the atmospheric conditions and remove cloud cover (Sect. 2.2). The pansharpenig technique was also applied to increase their spatial resolution. Following that, the index-based classification method was used to extract land use information by implementing two indices, NDVI and MSAVI2 (Sect. 2.3). The accuracy metrics, such as Overall Accuracy (OA), Producer Accuracy (PA), User Accuracy (UA), and Kappa coefficient (K) were used to estimate the reliability of the resulting classification maps (Sect. 2.4). Finally, the performance of the two indices derived from Landsat 9 images is discussed. All steps were finalized by writing appropriate code in the open-source GEE environment.

2.1 Study Area

Savona city, in Liguria region, is situated on a tiny alluvial plain produced by the Letimbro River on the Riviera di Ponente (Fig. 1). It includes a large patch of the upper basin of the Bormida from the shore to the Alpine-Appennine lake. It is mostly hilly, and it contains the Colle di Cadibona, which connects the Alps to the Appennino. The main watercourse is the Centa, which runs through Albenga.

Throughout the twentieth century, the population grew along the coast, both north and south, until it reached Vado Ligure and Albisola Marina, and it absorbed other minor towns, resulting in a conurbation of around 115,000 people. The old town, which is located between the port and the ancient fortress, is a maze of tiny and twisting alleys studded with piazzas and elegant homes (Priamar). Newer communities, on the other hand, feature a tiered plant with broad, straight roadways.

The port is the economic core of the metropolitan area, allowing the city to fulfill key economic duties since its establishment, and it is served by 18-km funicular railways

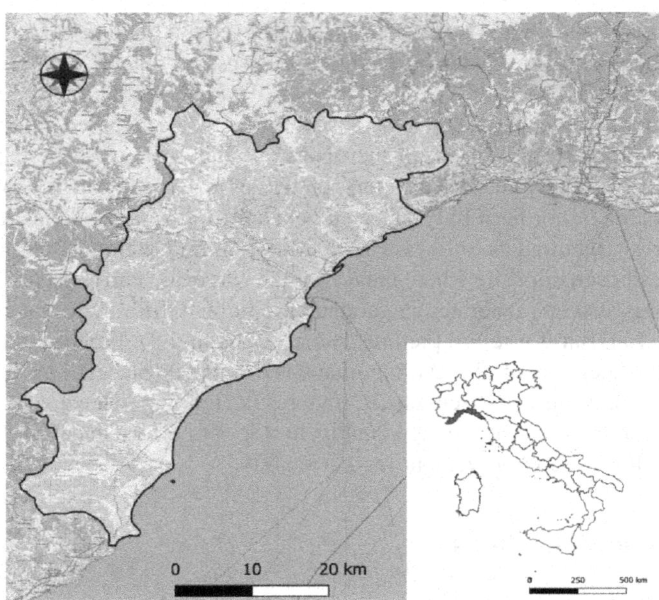

Fig. 1. The study area's location. On the bottom is an overview of the Italian context, with the Liguria Region highlighted in green, and on the top, the administrative boundaries of Savona are represented on the freely available Open Street Map (OSM) service.

designed to transfer carbon from the mountains to the city. In the 1960s, the convergence of vital freight rivers at Genoa's nearby massive port drove Savona to focus on the export of specialized products, namely petroleum. Following that, Savona's port underwent a series of transformations, resulting in a gradual shift of industrial port activities to the area of Vado Ligure, while the city seaport, which has been completely redesigned in terms of infrastructure, has emphasized its touristic vocation, focusing particularly on passenger traffic. In fact, tourism, along with the agricultural and industrial sectors, is vital to the local economy.

2.2 Database Construction and Preprocessing Step

Google created and launched GEE, a new cloud platform for storing and processing geospatial big data in 2017 [11]. It is made up of three major components: a high-performance computing (HPC) infrastructure, a large number of processors dedicated to speeding up the procedure and running custom-designed algorithms, and, lastly, a data catalogue that is updated daily with approximately 6000 freely available scenes collected by active missions and Digital Elevation Models (DEMs) with various resolution as well as vector, topographic and climate data [12]. Such data can be downloaded in both raw and pre-processed formats for use with desktop software, or they may be directly uploaded into the GEE API [28, 29]. In this case, the second option was picked. After reviewing the catalogue, indeed, the most suited Landsat 9 satellite images covering the research location were imported into GEE API. Apart from the satellite mission and pilot site location, cloud cover information was also taken into account: only scenes with a cloud cover value of less than 30% were examined. In contrast, any acquisition time constraint was not imposed due to the scarcity of Landsat data; the satellite mission was launched by the end of September 2021. Finally, only Level-2 data were examined.

Thus, after importing into the API an image collection acquired from Landsat 9 mission from November 2021 up to November 2022 and filtering the images based on the aforementioned cloud cover and level information, just one image, dated January 2022 and having a cloud cover percentage of 10%, was satisfactory and selected to be processed in the further steps. That image was given in the Universal Transverse Mercator projection and the World Geodetic System (WGS84) datum. At this stage, a cloud masking procedure was performed, which required employing suitable filters to make the clouds invisible and omitting the corresponding pixels throughout the processing phase [30, 31]. Mateo Garcia's approach [32] based on information provided by the quality assessment band was used to attain this purpose. In contrast, no further orthorectification phase was necessary since the accuracy of the process was deemed enough, and a pansharpening approach was applied to increase picture resolution using the algorithm established by Stuhler et al., (2016) [33] for handling Landsat 8 images. "Pansharpening" is the final stage of the pre-processing technique. This means that the generated image served as the categorization procedure's input data. Figure 2 depicts the entire pre-processing operation.

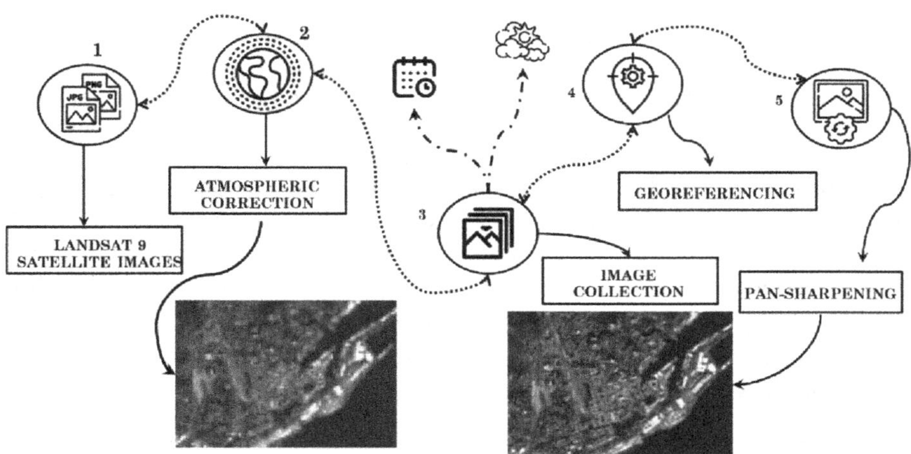

Fig. 2. Preprocessing workflow

2.3 Index-Based Classification Approach

The corrected image was then used as input data in the index-based classification method. An approach like this is useful for quickly separating LU/LC classes from satellite data [34]. This attribute makes this approach more appealing than any other classification strategies when a large number of data or a large region must be investigated. As a consequence, an enormous number of indexes that can extract Earth's characteristics based on their spectral signature have been devised. Because each object's spectral signature indicates its ability to absorb, reflect, and transmit energy, items in the same LU/LC class do not have the same trend, but rather a comparable one. Because each object's spectral signature indicates elements' ability to absorb, reflect, and transmit energy, items in the same LU/LC class do not have the same signature trend, but rather a comparable one. As a result, each index entails the incorporation of distinct bands capable of evaluating a certain LU/LC category. Red and Red Edge bands, for example, are often used to detect green regions and water [35], whereas TIR and SWIR bands are commonly utilized to identify bare soil [36] and built-up areas [37], as well as to extract information about sparse and thick vegetation [38]. Thus, only few indicators are appropriate for classifying an entire area [39]. In most circumstances, additional indexes must be merged to achieve this goal [40].

In this study, the performance of two vegetation indices, Normalized Difference Vegetation Index (NDVI) (Eq. 1) [41] and Modified Soil Adjusted Vegetation Index 2 (MSAVI2) (Eq. 2) [42], derived from Landsat 9, was test to classify the whole pilot site.

$$NDVI = \frac{\mathrm{NIR} - \mathrm{RED}}{NIR + RED} \tag{1}$$

$$\mathrm{MSAVI2} = \frac{(2 * \mathrm{NIR} + 1 - \sqrt{(2 * NIR + 1)^2 - 8 * (NIR - RED)}}{2} \tag{2}$$

As shown in Eqs. 1–2, NDVI and MSAVI2 integrate the same bands albeit in a different way. This indicates that they are both committed to identifying vegetated regions, but from distinct perspectives. Indeed, the former, which is primarily related to biomass development and plant health, is frequently used to assess vegetation phenology [43], whereas the latter is more suited when green zone are discontinuous due to its capacity to minimize soil spectral influence [42]. This means they give complimentary information and are frequently used to assess green space density and health condition [44]. Moreover, both indices are between -1 and + 1, with greater values increasing as the biomass concentration of the pixel rises. The accuracy of both maps, which is described in further detail in the next Section, was statistically determined.

2.4 Accuracy Assessment

The reliability of the resulting LULC classification maps was estimated, as indicated in [45, 46], by constructing a reference dataset with a number of testing samples proportionate to the class size. The stratified random sample point approach was utilized to produce such a data collection, and each generated sample was then manually examined and labeled according to its placement. The baseline land use information used to establish point position were produced by interpreting the satellite images overlaid on testing samples. This technique was iteratively repeated for all of the testing samples on each classified map. Based on these findings, Eqs. 3–6 were used to calculate accuracy metrics such as OA, PA, UA, and K [47, 48].

$$OA = \frac{\sum n_i}{N_{TOT}} \tag{3}$$

$$UA = \frac{n_{ii}}{n_{i+}} \quad (4)$$

$$PA = \frac{n_{ii}}{n_{+i}} \quad (5)$$

$$K = \frac{N_{TOT} \sum n_{ii} - \sum n_{iR} * n_{Pi}}{{N_{TOT}}^2 - \sum n_{iR} * n_{Pi}} \quad (6)$$

where N_{TOT} and n_i are the amount of correctly classified testing samples and the total number of testing samples, respectively. On the other hand, n_{ii} and n_{i+} represent the number of correctly identified testing samples belonging to a certain class and the number of reference samples comprising in such a category. Lastly, n_{iR} and n_{Pi} are the number of samples utilized in the test and classification classes, respectively. All parameters of the confusion matrix have a value between 0 and 1. The greater their worth, the greater the accuracy.

3 Results and Discussion

This research examined the ability of the newly developed Landsat 9 platform to extract LU/LC classes using an index-based method in GEE platform. As previously stated, while no classification technique is flawless in every situation, the index-based approach provides an efficient and resilient solution for automatically classifying the whole study area in a short period of time [49]. As a result, it was chosen as the standard for measuring the performance of the new satellite images. Thus, two distinct indices, NDVI [41] (Eq. 1) and MSAVI 2 [42] (Eq. 2), were calculated on a satellite image collected by Lansat 9 platform which was selected by consulting the GEE catalogue and imported in the API. To choose the most suitable data for the research, three primary criteria were established: i) Landsat mission, ii) a cloud cover percentage of less than 30%, and iii) a 2-level satellite data. In contrast, no assumptions were made regarding the acquisition date because the platform was newly started, and so just a few data are available. Also, most of them are ineffective due to climatic circumstances, therefore just one image, dated January 2022, was picked. Before to processing, its resolution was increased using the pan-sharpening technique (Fig. 2). The outcome was the input data for the index-based technique, the results of which are shown in Fig. 3.

Both indices distinguished four LU/LC categories: water, built-up areas, sparse and dense vegetation. Nevertheless, no significant difference was identified in water and built-up regions, represented by blue and red pixels, respectively. In contrast, the same quantity of green areas was found, even though the distribution of sparse and dense vegetation is radically different. In fact, the amount of sparse vegetation is greater than the amount of dense vegetation in MSAVI2, whereas the situation is exactly opposite in the NDVI map. This conclusion, which is obvious in Fig. 3, is accentuated in Fig. 4, where the distribution of LU/LC pixels is displayed in histogram charts. In both representations, the pixels devoted to water and built-up regions are same, as opposed to sparse and thick vegetation. This is due mostly to the disparity in information offered by the two indexes. These are vegetation indices established to differentiate green regions from others, however as mentioned by [44], they are often employed in different scenarios. The former, NDVI, is more suited to characterize plant phenology since it is linked to biomass and plant health status, whereas MSAVI2 is better suited for neutralizing the influence of soil spectral signature. When the green patches are discontinuous, MSVAI2 accuracy outperforms NDVI.

This statement is also supported by the NDVI and MSAVI2 confusion matrices reported in Tables 1 and 4, respectively. Indeed, the detection of water and built-up areas is fairly accurate in both generated maps, whereas the distinction between sparse and dense vegetation is more accurate in the MSAVI2 chart. This means that NDVI is excellent at predicting vegetation but not at differentiating the density of green areas. Such an issue affects their OA and K value, despite the fact that both indicators show a promising result. Indeed, the NDVI and MSAVI2 OA values are 79.60% and 90.24%, respectively, while the K values are 71.70% and 84.45%. K is a measure of inter-rater reliability that takes a value between -1 and 1: the higher the value, the more reliable the results are. Thus, NDVI is consistent, whereas MSAVI2 is extremely trustworthy.

In general, the classes have high accuracy values from both the PA and the CA perspectives (Tables 2, 3, 5 and 6), but there are some important differences to consider. MSAVI2 provides minor accuracy values for the UA (68,46% vs 75.24%) in the urbanization class. This means that, even though 78.76% (PA) of urban areas are correctly classified, only 68.46% are truly urban. In contrast, NDVI shows a lot of misclassifications in sparse vegetation category. The UA is approximately equivalent to 47%, while the PA is about 50%. This is because most sparse green pixels are mislabeled as built-up or dense vegetation, and dense vegetation is misidentified as sparse green areas, as is evident from Table 1.

These observations are consistent with previous research findings in terms of accuracy and LU/LC classes isolated. According to Capolupo et al., (2020) [39], who evaluated classification indices on the pilot site of Margherita di Savoia (Puglia region) with similar morphological features, both indices are capable of extracting the four categories identified in this study plus bare soil. Their OA, however, were 73.24% and 83.30%, respectively.

Moreover, to speed up the procedure, GEE cloud computing platform was used through the development of an own code in Java language. Indeed, thanks to its parallel processors, such a script ran quickly, overcoming common desktop software constraints. Furthermore, the developed code can be easily applied to other case studies by simply adjusting the indices thresholds to the site surface features. As a result, GEE appears to be the best solution for processing geospatial big data quickly and customizing the algorithms to research specific needs.

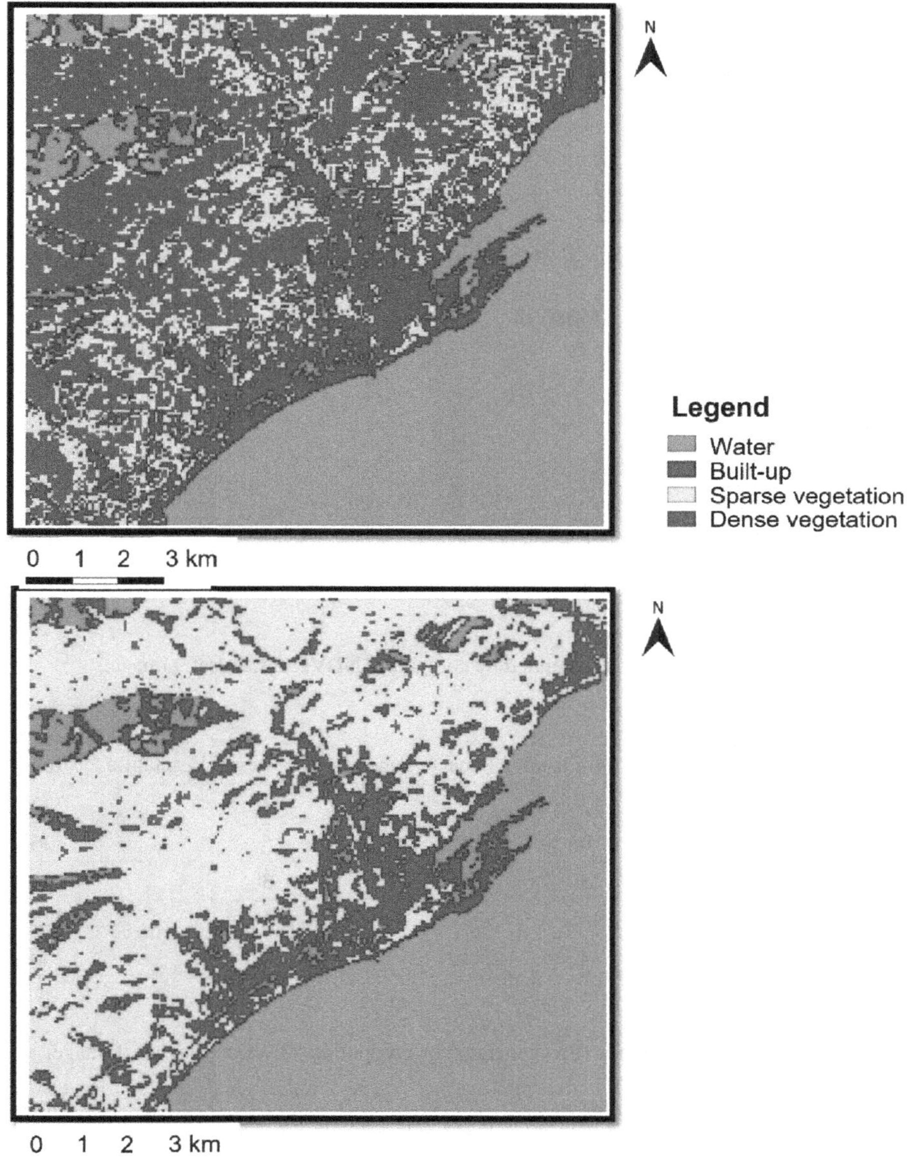

Fig. 3. Land cover maps created by calculating the NDVI (on the top) and MSAVI2 (on the bottom) indices using Landsat 9 images collected in January 2022.

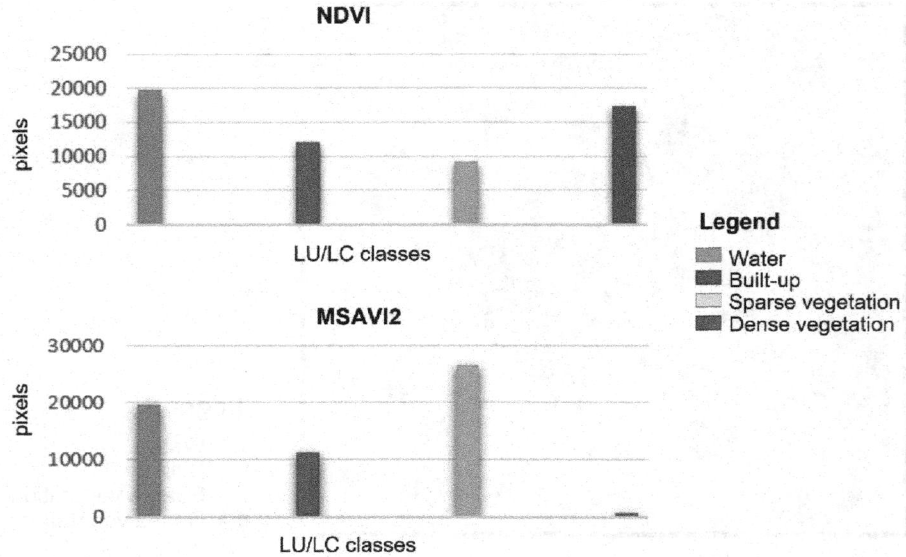

Fig. 4. Histograms of LU/LC classes

Table 1. Error matrix generated by computing NDVI on Landsat 9 image.

NDVI					
	Water	Built-up	Sparse Vegetation	Dense Vegetation	Tot
Water	257	12	2	1	272
Built-up	14	103	14	5	136
Sparse Vegetation	1	23	55	38	117
Dense Vegetation	0	4	39	182	225
Tot	272	142	110	226	750

Table 2. Producer Accuracy (PA) generated by computing NDVI on Landsat 9 image.

	PA		
Water	257/272	0.9449	94.49%
Built-up	103/142	0.7254	72.54%
Sparse Vegetation	55/110	0.5000	50.00%
Dense Vegetation	182/226	0.8053	80.53%

Table 3. User Accuracy (UA) generated by computing NDVI on Landsat 9 image.

	UA		
Water	257/272	0.9449	94.49%
Built-up	103/136	0.7574	75.74%
Sparse Vegetation	55/117	0.4701	47.01%
Dense Vegetation	182/225	0.8089	80.89%

Table 4. Confusion matrix generated by computing MSAVI2 on Landsat 9 image.

MSAVI2					
	Water	*Built-up*	*Sparse Vegetation*	*Dense Vegetation*	*Tot*
Water	249	11	1	0	261
Built-up	15	89	26	0	130
Sparse Vegetation	1	13	322	2	338
Dense Vegetation	0	0	3	6	9
Tot	265	113	352	8	738

Table 5. Producer Accuracy (PA) generated by computing MSAVI2 on Landsat 9 image.

	PA		
Water	249/265	0.9496	93.96%
Built-up	89/113	0.7976	78.76%
Sparse Vegetation	322/352	0.9148	91.48%
Dense Vegetation	6/8	0.7500	75.00%

Table 6. User Accuracy (UA) generated by computing MSAVI2 on Landsat 9 image.

	UA		
Water	249/261	0.9540	95.40%
Built-up	89/130	0.6846	68.46%
Sparse Vegetation	322/338	0.9527	95.27%
Dense Vegetation	6/9	0.6667	66.67%

4 Conclusion

The purpose of this study was to evaluate the feasibility of the index-based approach for extracting LU/LC classes from new optical satellite images given by NASA/USGS: Landsat 9 data. As a result, two of the most often used indicators for retrieving information about the health status and distribution of green spaces were evaluated on the pilot site of Savona city, which was chosen for its specific morphological features, NDVI and MSAVI2. Because of its relationship with biomass, the former is typically used to measure plant phenology, whilst the latter is particular for reducing background soil influence. Although both indices have been shown to be strong predictors of vegetated pixels, MSAVI2 exhibited greater OA and K values in identifying water and sparse and thick vegetation. As a result, it looks to be better suited to investigating green area conditions using medium-resolution satellite data.

Furthermore, by comparing their results to those of earlier studies that used similar indices on Landsat 8 images, it is clear that their results are consistent. Hence, despite the fact that Landsat 9 has higher radiometric resolution, the results obtained did not vary from those obtained with Lansat 8. These observations developed for the research area have the potential to be transferred to other places without any variations. Finally, using the GEE platform allows customers to automate and speed up the entire process, lowering both data collecting and processing time.

References

1. Belward, A.S., Skøien, J.O.: Who launched what, when and why; trends in global land-cover observation capacity from civilian earth observation satellites. ISPRS J. Photogramm. Remote. Sens. **103**, 115–128 (2015)
2. Goward, S.N., Williams, D.L.: Landsat and earth systems science: development of terrestrial monitoring. Photogramm. Eng. Remote Sens. **63**(7), 887–900 (1997)
3. Zhu, Z., et al.: Benefits of the free and open Landsat data policy. Remote Sens. Environ. **224**, 382–385 (2019)
4. Mbow, H.O.P., Reisinger, A., Canadell, J., O'Brien, P.: Special Report on climate change, desertification, land degradation, sustainable land management, food security, and greenhouse gas fluxes in terrestrial ecosystems (SR2). Ginevra, IPCC, vol. 650 (2017)
5. Capolupo, A., Saponaro, M., Fratino, U., Tarantino, E.: Detection of spatio-temporal changes of vegetation in coastal areas subjected to soil erosion issue. Aquat. Ecosyst. Health Manag. **23**(4), 491–499 (2020)
6. Boccia, L., Capolupo, A., Rigillo, M., Russo, V.: Terrace abandonment hazards in a Mediterranean cultural landscape. J. Hazard. Tox. Radioact. Waste **24**(1), 04019034 (2020)
7. Capolupo, A., Boccia, L.: Innovative method for linking anthropisation process to vulnerability. World Rev. Sci. Technol. Sustain. Dev. **17**(1), 4–22 (2021)
8. Lulla, K., Nellis, M.D., Rundquist, B., Srivastava, P.K., Szabo, S.: Mission to earth: LANDSAT 9 will continue to view the world. Geocarto Int. **36**(20), 2261–2263 (2021)
9. Masek, J.G., et al.: Landsat 9: Empowering open science and applications through continuity. Remote Sens. Environ. **248**, 111968 (2020)
10. Potapov, P., Turubanova, S., Hansen, M.C.: Regional-scale boreal forest cover and change mapping using Landsat data composites for European Russia. Remote Sens. Environ. **115**(2), 548–561 (2011)

11. Gorelick, N., Hancher, M., Dixon, M., Ilyushchenko, S., Thau, D., Moore, R.: Google Earth Engine: Planetary-scale geospatial analysis for everyone. Remote Sens. Environ. **202**, 18–27 (2017)
12. Kumar, L., Mutanga, O.: Google earth engine applications since inception: usage, trends, and potential. Remote Sens. **10**, 1509 (2018)
13. Capolupo, A., et al.: An interactive WebGIS framework for coastal erosion risk management. J. Mar. Sci. Eng. **9**(6), 567 (2021)
14. Capolupo, A., Monterisi, C., Tarantino, E.: Development of an open-source 3D WebGIS framework to promote cultural heritage dissemination. in extended reality. In: De Paolis, L.T., Arpaia, P., Sacco, M. (eds.) First International Conference, XR Salento 2022, Lecce, Italy, 6–8 July 2022, Proceedings, Part II, pp. 254–268. Springer, Cham (2022). https://doi.org/10.1007/978-3-031-15553-6_19
15. Capolupo, A., et al.: Workshops: Malaga, Spain, July 4–7, 2022, Proceedings, Part III, pp. 340–353. Springer International Publishing, Cham (2022)
16. Steiniger, S., Hunter, A.J.: Free and open source GIS software for building a spatial data infrastructure. In: OGRS, pp. 247–261 (2009)
17. Chen, Y., Gong, P.: Clustering based on eigenspace transformation–CBEST for efficient classification. ISPRS J. Photogramm. Remote. Sens. **83**, 64–80 (2013)
18. Matsushita, B., Yang, W., Chen, J., Onda, Y., Qiu, G.: Sensitivity of the enhanced vegetation index (EVI) and normalized difference vegetation index (NDVI) to topographic effects: a case study in high-density cypress forest. Sensors **7**(11), 2636–2651 (2007)
19. Abdi, A.M.: Land cover and land use classification performance of machine learning algorithms in a boreal landscape using Sentinel-2 data. GIScience Remote Sens. **57**(1), 1–20 (2020)
20. Ladisa, C., Capolupo, A., Ripa, M.N., Tarantino, E.: Combining OBIA approach and machine learning algorithm to extract photovoltaic panels from Sentinel-2 images automatically. In: Remote Sensing for Agriculture, Ecosystems, and Hydrology XXIV, vol. 12262, pp. 67–76. SPIE (2022)
21. Tarantino, E., Novelli, A., Aquilino, M., Figorito, B., Fratino, U.: Comparing the MLC and JavaNNS approaches in classifying multi-temporal LANDSAT satellite imagery over an ephemeral river area. Int. J. Agric. Environ. Inf. Syst. (IJAEIS) **6**(4), 83–102 (2015)
22. Crocetto, N., Tarantino, E.: A class-oriented strategy for features extraction from multidate ASTER imagery. Remote Sens. **1**(4), 1171–1189 (2009)
23. Novelli, A., Aguilar, M.A., Nemmaoui, A., Aguilar, F.J., Tarantino, E.: Performance evaluation of object based greenhouse detection from Sentinel-2 MSI and Landsat 8 OLI data: A case study from Almería (Spain). Int. J. Appl. Earth Obs. Geoinf. **52**, 403–411 (2016)
24. Breiman, L.: Random forests. Machine learning **45**, 5–32 (2001)
25. Homer, C., Huang, C., Yang, L., Wylie, B.K., Coan, M.: Development of a 2001 national land-cover database for the United States (2004)
26. Anchang, J.Y., Ananga, E.O., Pu, R.: An efficient unsupervised index based approach for mapping urban vegetation from IKONOS imagery. Int. J. Appl. Earth Obs. Geoinf. **50**, 211–220 (2016)
27. Figorito, B., Tarantino, E., Balacco, G., Fratino, U.: An object-based method for mapping ephemeral river areas from WorldView-2 satellite data. In: Remote Sensing for Agriculture, Ecosystems, and Hydrology XIV, vol. 8531, pp. 68–76. SPIE (2012)
28. Capolupo, A., Monterisi, C., Saponaro, M., Tarantino, E.: Multi-temporal analysis of land cover changes using Landsat data through Google Earth Engine platform. In: Eighth International Conference on Remote Sensing and Geoinformation of the Environment (RSCy2020), vol. 11524, pp. 447–458. SPIE (2020)

29. Sangiorgio, V., Capolupo, A., Tarantino, E., Fiorito, F., Santamouris, M.: Evaluation of absolute maximum urban heat island intensity based on a simplified remote sensing approach. Environ. Eng. Sci. **39**(3), 296–307 (2022)
30. Caprioli, M., Figorito, B., Tarantino, E.: Radiometric normalization of Landsat ETM+ data for multitemporal analysis. In: Proceedings of ISPRS Commission VII Mid-Term Symposium on "Remote Sensing: from Pixels to Processes", Enschede (unpaginated CD-ROM) (2006)
31. Tarantino, E., Figorito, B., Caprioli, M.: Comparison of radiometric normalization methods on LANDSAT ETM+ and ASTER data. Bollettino di Geodesia e Scienze Affini **67**(2), 89–106 (2008)
32. Mateo-García, G., Gómez-Chova, L., Amorós-López, J., Muñoz-Marí, J., Camps-Valls, G.: Multitemporal cloud masking in the Google Earth Engine. Remote Sens. **10**, 1079 (2018)
33. Stuhler, S. C., Leiterer, R., Joerg, P. C., Wulf, H., Schaepman, M.E.: Generating a cloud-free, homogeneous Landsat-8 mosaic of Switzerland using Google Earth Engine (2016)
34. Patel, N.N., Angiuli, E., et al.: Multitemporal settlement and population mapping from Landsat using Google Earth Engine. Int. J. Appl. Earth Obs. Geoinf. **35**, 199–208 (2015)
35. Capolupo, A., Kooistra, L., Berendonk, C., Boccia, L., Suomalainen, J.: Estimating plant traits of grasslands from UAV-acquired hyperspectral images: a comparison of statistical approaches. ISPRS Int. J. Geo Inf. **4**(4), 2792–2820 (2015)
36. Kazakis, N., Kougias, I., Patsialis, T.: Assessment of flood hazard areas at a regional scale using an index-based approach and analytical hierarchy process: application in Rhodope-Evros region, Greece. Sci. Total Environ. **538**, 555–563 (2015)
37. Southworth, J.: An assessment of Landsat TM band 6 thermal data for analysing land cover in tropical dry forest regions. Int. J. Remote Sens. **25**(4), 689–706 (2004)
38. Yusuf, B.L., He, Y.: Application of hyperspectral imaging sensor to differentiate between the moisture and reflectance of healthy and infected tobacco leaves. Afr. J. Agric. Res **6**(29), 6267–6280 (2011)
39. Capolupo, A., Monterisi, C., Caporusso, G., Tarantino, E.: Extracting land cover data using GEE: a review of the classification indices. In: Gervasi, O., et al. (eds.) ICCSA 2020. LNCS, vol. 12252, pp. 782–796. Springer, Cham (2020). https://doi.org/10.1007/978-3-030-58811-3_56
40. Sarzana, T., Maltese, A., Capolupo, A., Tarantino, E.: Post-processing of pixel and object-based land cover classifications of very high spatial resolution images. In: Gervasi, O., et al. (eds.) ICCSA 2020. LNCS, vol. 12252, pp. 797–812. Springer, Cham (2020). https://doi.org/10.1007/978-3-030-58811-3_57
41. Rouse, J.W., Haas, R.H., Schell, J.A., Deering, D.W.: Monitoring vegetation systems in the Great Plains with ERTS. NASA Spec. Publ. **351**(1), 309 (1974)
42. Qi, J., Chehbouni, A., Huete, A.R., Kerr, Y.H., Sorooshian, S.: A modified soil adjusted vegetation index. Remote Sens. Environ. **48**(2), 119–126 (1994)
43. Bannari, A., Morin, D., Bonn, F., Huete, A.R.: A review of vegetation indices. Remote Sens. Rev. **13**, 95–120 (1995)
44. Borgogno-Mondino, E., de Palma, L., Novello, V.: Investigating Sentinel 2 multispectral imagery efficiency in describing spectral response of vineyards covered with plastic sheets. Agronomy **10**(12), 1909 (2020)
45. Sidhu, N., Pebesma, E., Câmara, G.: Using Google Earth Engine to detect land cover change: Singapore as a use case. Eur. J. Remote Sens. **51**, 486–500 (2018)
46. Pengra, B., Long, J., Dahal, D., Stehman, S.V., Loveland, T.R.: A global reference database from very high-resolution commercial satellite data and methodology for application to Landsat derived 30 m continuous field tree cover data. Remote Sens. Environ. **165**, 234–248 (2015)

47. Stehman, S.V.; Woodcock, C.E.; Sulla-Menashe, D.; Sibley, A.M.; Newell, J.D.; Friedl, M.A.; Herold, M. A global land-cover validation data set. part I: Fundamental design principles. Int. J. Remote Sens. 2012, 33, 5768–5788
48. Caprioli, M., Tarantino, E.: Accuracy assessment of per-field classification integrating very fine spatial resolution satellite imagery with topographic data. J. Geospat. Eng. **3**, 127–134 (2001)
49. Tarantino, E., Figorito, B.: Mapping rural areas with widespread plastic covered vineyards using true color aerial data. Remote Sens. **4**(7), 1913–1928 (2012)

Collaborative Planning and Designing for the Future with Geospatial Applications (GeoCollab 2023)

Geodesign Education: Case Studies from the US, Brazil and Italy

Ana Clara Mourão Moura[1], Michele Campagna[2], Alenka Poplin[3](✉), Rosanna G. Rivero[4], and Francesco Scorza[5]

[1] Federal University of Minas Gerais, Belo Horizonte, Brazil
anaclara@ufmg.br
[2] University of Cagliari, Cagliari, Italy
campagna@unica.it
[3] Iowa State University, Ames, USA
apoplin@iastate.edu
[4] University of Georgia, Athens, USA
rrivero@uga.edu
[5] University of Basilicata, Potenza, Italy
francesco.scorza@unibas.it

Abstract. This paper focuses on the adoption of the geodesign approach, including methods and tools, in spatial planning and design courses in higher education with an international comparative perspective. The comparative review is based on four case studies developed in the US, Brazil and Italy. They were developed by the authors of this article in order to showcase the differences in the implementation and use of geodesign framework, scenario planning and newly developed web-based tools. The comparison and discussion of case studies demonstrates the possibility and potential of applying geodesign methods at different scales, approaches and variety of participants. The paper concludes with a comparative summary of the presented case studies and a discussion.

Keywords: Geodesign · Scenario planning · Environmental planning · Geospatial technologies

1 Introduction

The main goal of this paper is to comparatively review different case studies in which geodesign framework was used in the process of designing for the future of the studied place. The case studies are coming from US, Brazil and Italy and serve as examples of how geodesign can be taught in studio classes and regular classes at the corresponding universities. Geodesign is generally understood as a a set of techniques and enabling technologies for planning of a sustainable future of built and natural environments. It represents a process that integrates project conceptualization, analysis, design specification, stakeholder participation and collaboration, design creation, simulation, and evaluation (among other stages). The most prominent and widely applied methodology

O. Gervasi et al. (Eds.): ICCSA 2023 Workshops, LNCS 14107, pp. 269–286, 2023.
https://doi.org/10.1007/978-3-031-37114-1_18

in geodesign was suggested by Steinitz (2012). The value of Steinitz' framework for geodesign is arguably in its robustness and flexibility for it can be applied in diverse workflows and technology settings.

The study case of the City of Ames (Iowa, USA) shows a combination of scenario planning (Avin 2012), geodesign framework (Steinitz 2012) and innovations. It concentrates on three systems including energy, transportation and mobility and green infrastructure. The study case of Belo Horizonte (Brazil) proposes an expanded and very innovative version of the geodesign process based on their own research and development (Moura and Freitas 2020, 2021). The goal of their approach is to consider specific conceptual, methodological and technological improvements and advancements aiming to meet the needs of adaptability and flexibility of a geodesign workflow. The study cases of Cagliari and Potenza (Italy) demonstrate the use and implementation of Steinitz's framework (2012) as suggested by the author, without any further adaptation or change. All case studies were implemented in the courses and studios to teach urban planners and designers how to use geospatial tools and data and apply geodesign methodology to design for sustainable future. This paper summarizes the experience gained in these courses.

2 Geodesign in Higher Education: An Overview of International Experiences

Geodesign as a subject in university curricula is novel as, with some notable exceptions, does not have a long tradition. It can be defined as a set of methods, techniques, and enabling geospatial technologies that are well suited to work with multiple stakeholders. Geodesign frameworks can be added to the teaching about planning and design for the future at different scales.

At Iowa State University (ISU), a course on Geodesign was first offered in 2017. It was initially designed as an experimental course to test whether students would enroll and find value in taking the class. The course was appreciated especially because it was included as an elective course in the GIS Minor approved at ISU in 2014. Students are, in general, eager to learn new software skills and this course offered substantial experimentation with geospatial data, the use of GIS software and learning about geodesign as a framework and methodology. Pedagogy in this course is generally based on selecting a study case, studying geodesign as a methodology and process-oriented framework, discuss the framework, and work with geospatial data and software. The experimental course was then changed into a regular elective course. In 2021 it was renamed to Geodesign: Planning for Sustainable Futures and dual listed as an undergraduate and graduate course.

At the University of Georgia, the idea of Geodesign has been embedded in several Urban Planning and Design Studios as well as Landscape Architecture Studios. It has also been applied through a program called NASA Develop, in collaboration with the Department of Geography. Some of these projects with NASA Develop date back to 2014, while the projects in Coastal Georgia were conducted since 2015, in collaboration with the Coastal Regional Commission of Georgia (Rivero et al 2015, 2017, 2018; Smith et al. 2020).

In Brazil, geodesign was applied in urban design teaching, focusing on the process of co-creation in collective reading and planning of a study area. Several studies were developed within the urban planning courses held at the Geoprocessing Laboratory, in the School of Architecture, Federal University of Minas Gerais, Brazil. Between 2016 and 2020, the Geoprocessing Laboratory was involved in 43 geodesign workshops, working on 35 projects. Of these projects, 28 were proposed and conducted by the laboratory coordination, 4 were proposed by other researchers with their support, and in further 3 cases the members of lab acted as participants. Of the 35 experiences, one was developed in analog method, one in ArcGIS (ESRI), one in CityEngine (ESRI), and 32 on Geodesignhub (Ballal 2015). After each workshop, the coordinators applied questionnaires or made notes about performances. Based on the acquired experience, a web-based platform, called GISColab, was developed to apply the principles defined as values to be respected: adaptability, flexibility, and scalability (Moura and Freitas 2020, 2021). From 2020, with the creation of GISColab, 31 more workshops have already been carried out using the newly developed framework on the new platform. Since then, Brazilian studies are putting their efforts in methods and applications to include geo-visualization, in order to enhance the reading of the place. The studies analyze reports based on reality, mental maps, and digital representation. The Geoprocessing Laboratory is constantly working on the improvements of the web-based platform, based on the structure of a Spatial Data Infrastructure (SDI), that can communicate with other web-based applications compliant with the OGC (Open Geospatial Consortium) standards. The main idea is to connect to different tools in a continuum of improvements, respecting interoperability between machines and people. The bibliography produced is available on the website (https://geoproea.arq.ufmg.br/).

In Italy, the implementation of the geodesign approach as defined in the introduction dates back to 2016, although earlier research and education academic experiences in the last two decades or so can be considered earlier examples of the approach, which set the ground for the adoption of a more formal methodology at a later stage. The first pioneering course with a formal denomination as geodesign in Italy was introduced at the Faculty of Engineering and Architecture of University of Cagliari in 2016, and it is currently a major for the BSc students in Architecture and for the MSc Students in Civil and in Environmental Engineering. An account of the evolution of syllabus of the geodesign course at the University of Cagliari was given by Campagna (2017). Since then, extensive international and local research and education projects were carried on, which produced on the one hand research and applied studies and on the other hand BSc, MSc and PhD theses, respectively (Campagna 2016; Campagna and Di Cesare 2016; Campagna et al. 2018; Cocco et al. 2019; Campagna et al. 2020; Campagna 2022). Other examples of geodesign adoption in academic research and education in Italy include the University of Basilicata, and more recently the University of Naples Federico II (Somma et al. 2022). In addition, geodesign tutorials were introduced since 2020 at the PhD winter school on Research methodology in social sciences, urban studies, and spatial, planning (https://researchmethodologyws.org) at the University of Florence. With regards to its implementation in Italy, in the next section, two case studies of application of geodesign in education at the University of Cagliari and at the University of Basilicata are presented.

3 Selected Case Studies Description

3.1 Combining Scenario Planning and Steinitz's Geodesign Framework: Study Case of Ames, Iowa USA

This study case focused on a small college town, the City of Ames in Iowa, USA. The main systems considered in the study were transportation and mobility, energy and green infrastructure. The goal was to apply the existing Geodesign framework (Steinitz 2012) and combine it with Scenario Planning, as proposed by Avin (2012) and Goodspeed (2022). Two groups of students, one from Iowa State University (ISU) and the other one from the University of Georgia (UGA) collaborated on this project. The students were tasked to develop future scenarios for the city of Ames (2035, 2050). In addition, it was also tested how the use of online tools would improve the collaboration of two groups of students: one with local knowledge (ISU) versus a group working remotely with no previous knowledge of the study area (UGA). Both groups had good technical knowledge in urban planning and GIS.

The first part of the analysis used the Generalized Framework for the Futures Planning Process as suggested by Avin (2012, p. 110–111). It is based on identifying issues/trends, values/goals, possible/likely futures and desired futures. In the next step social, technological, economic, political, and environmental Driving Forces were identified. Identification of the Stakeholder Values included values identified for the Government Residents, and Environment. The identified Driving Forces were accompanied with a scenario narrative and basic scenario features as suggested by Avin (2012, p. 120).

Based on this initial analysis, the focus moved to the specifics of each of the selected thematic areas or systems. Three groups of students in Iowa, and three in Georgia were formed to concentrate on the suitability analysis for each of the three systems: transportation and mobility, energy, and green infrastructure. They worked on the acquisition of geospatial data, then they identified criteria for the suitability of newly planned infrastructure, and eventually performed a suitability analysis. The results of the suitability analysis were locations, paths, and areas allocated to the planned developments.

Based on the data integration and analysis (representation and process model) and suitability analysis (evaluation model), the groups developed scenarios of the future development. ESRI's GeoPlanner as a geospatial tool enabled them to sketch the proposed solutions and ideas. The software can integrate geospatial data on different layers and add options for sketching, design, and evaluation of scenario impacts. A new template was created for the project to be able to include the specific features related to the selected systems. The proposed scenario elements were included in the design as GIS objects and used for further analysis in a GIS.

ISU group developed three scenarios in mixed teams. The teams negotiated and ended up with a unique scenario that included the selected features and proposals from all three scenarios (Fig. 1). Central to the final scenario are the following features: greenways interconnected parks and opened spaces, green roofs, green streets, permeable surfaces, green/complete streets, bike sharing and e-bikes stations, photovoltaic bike lanes, electric scooters and charging racks, advanced bus stops, piezoelectric speed bumps and sidewalks, piezoelectric roads/highways/railroads, the geothermal plant, and equitable investment in vulnerable and disadvantaged communities with a focus on environmental justice.

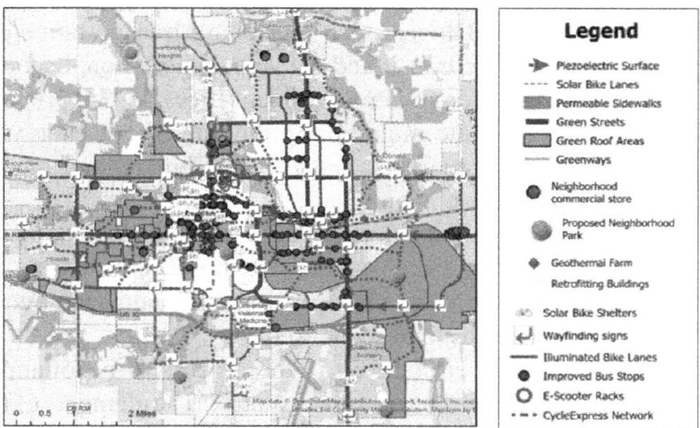

Fig. 1. ISU final scenario

At the UGA, the students developed and documented their process using ArcGIS Hub Geodesign in Ames (arcgis.com). After developing suitability analyses for each of the three systems, two groups were formed, each of them incorporating a collection of innovations and strategies.

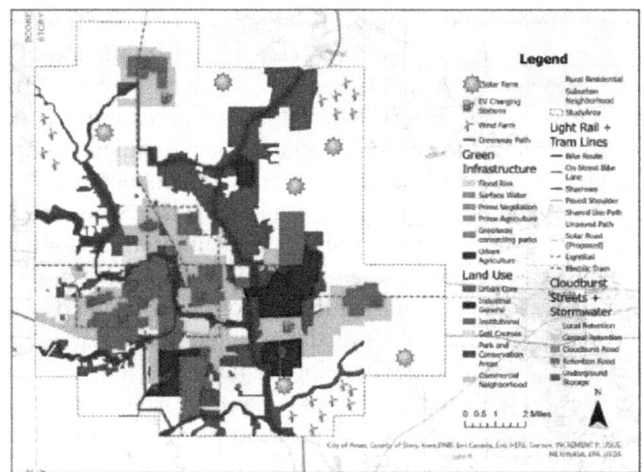

Fig. 2. The UGA final scenario

Group A focused on strategies related to the increase and improvement of public and active transportation, investment in CyRide (local bus), methods for micro-mobility (bikes, scooters, etc.), investments in the existing infrastructure, needs for building retrofitting and road maintenance, and transition to clean energy including natural gas, solar and wind energy. Group B focused on increasing transportation infrastructure connectivity that facilitates public transit and active transportation, encouraging population growth with specific focus on retaining residents ages 25–34, preparing for large population increases due to climate migration, promoting green energy industry and infrastructure through policies, programs, and physical builds, and integrating green infrastructure principles into development.

Both groups used a matrix to conduct negotiations and identify compatibilities and conflicts among them. A synthesis map of their proposal, considering proposals on Land Use, Clean Energy, Mobility and Transportation, Cloudburst Street System and Stormwater Storage is presented as final scenario in Fig. 2.

Both of the final scenarios were derived in the process of negotiation among the groups. The negotiations were based on an impact matrix. The elements of the developed scenarios that had the most positive impacts were then selected to be included in the final scenarios. Both classes presented these final scenarios in the final round of discussion with expert feedback included.

3.2 Geodesign in Urban Design Teaching: The Process of Co-creation in Collective Reading and Planning of the Central Area of Belo Horizonte, Minas Gerais, Brazil

In the Brazilian case study the goal was to teach the role of urban planner as a a) decoder of collective values, doing field capture of data based on cognition and perception, and registering information in a Volunteered Geographic Information (VGI) platform called ViconSaga (which is a VGI application, developed by Marino (2018) at the Rural Federal University of Rio de Janeiro (UFRRJ, https://www.viconsaga.com.br); b) a technical analyst of values related to cultural, social and environmental information using geoprocessing models included in ArcGIS (ESRI); c) a conductor and participant of a co-creation process of ideas, based on ideas, proposals, discussions and votes gathered in a Geodesign workshop (GISColab - UFMG); d) an authorial creator that develops the design respecting the expectations resulted from the co-creation in previous stages.

The challenge addressed in the study is the proposal of integrated actions according to a workflow that included different geospatial technologies. It started with identifying the place by analysis of perception and cognition using a VGI tool, followed by the construction of diagnoses by special analysis using geoprocessing applications. The maps and data produced were organized in a Spatial Data Infrastructure (SDI) using the web-based platform GISColab. Using this platform, a geodesign workshop for co-creation of urban design proposals and measurement of impacts was conducted, including the application of established indicators, and the negotiation of a final design.

The objective of the study was of a didactic nature, for teaching urban design at a local scale, applying the completeness indicator principle, which meets environmental, place and movement values. The novelty was to explore different resources of geospatial technology in an integrated and planned workflow, feeding the Geodesign Platform GISColab, in which the stages of co-creation of ideas were carried out.

Students were initially trained in regulations and legislation related to urban planning and design, and in spatial reading processes through perception and cognition. They did fieldwork and recorded information and images using their cell-phones for feeding VGI in the ViconSaga application. Next, an evaluation of the area was carried out using spatial analysis models by geoprocessing using ArcGIS/ArcMap (ESRI). The information collected in the field, together with the collection of analytical maps, were made available in the web-GIS application GISColab based on an SDI architecture. Students took part in a geodesign workshop using the GISColab platform using the characterization and analytical data.

The workshop itself was conducted in four meetings, in which the participants worked in the stages of reading enrichment (reading the information in an integrated way and recording notes), drawing diagrams of ideas (points, lines and polygons with titles and descriptions), recording debates and comments on the ideas, running impact analysis based on the achievement of established goals (dynamic graphs of compliance with the requested 12 indicators related to completeness indicator principle) and voting (decision for the ideas chosen by the majority).

After the co-creation and co-decision workshop, each student individually developed an individual project, detailing one of the designs from the previous stage. Students learned about the relationship between shared designs, resulting from collective decisions, and individual designs, as a creative response to previously agreed values.

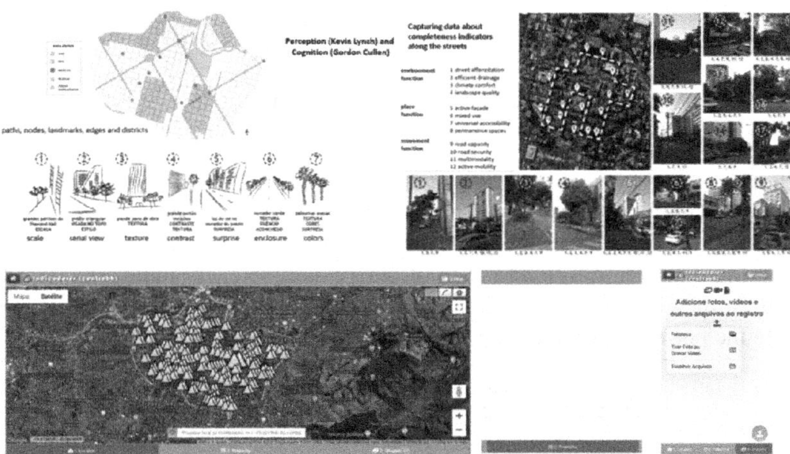

Fig. 3. Field camp – data capture and registering in VGI – ViconSaga

In the first step, in the field camp that enabled them to capture data and read the territory, the students applied the concepts of perception (Lynch 1960) and cognition (Cullen 1961). While capturing the image and the soul of the city, they also registered examples of twelve variables of the completeness indicator index describing qualities of the place according to environment, place, and movement values. They imported the data in the ViconSaga application directly from their mobile phones, or by using the browser of their computers (Fig. 3). As ViconSaga is an excellent example of a resource based on interoperability, data produced were easily organized in GISColab.

In the second step, the students developed a technical analysis of the place, applying geoprocessing models in ArcGIS (ESRI) and carrying on twelve spatial analyses including: 1 street afforestation, 2 efficient drainage, 3 climate comfort, 4 landscape quality, 5 active facade, 6 mixed use, 7 universal accessibility, 8 permanence spaces, 9 road capacity, 10 road security, 11 multimodality, and 12 active mobility. (Fig. 4). The maps were organized in GISColab web-application (Moura and Freitas 2021).

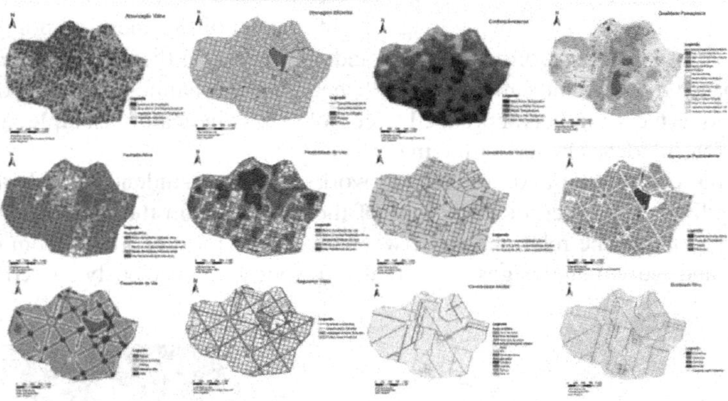

Fig. 4. Spatial Analysis Maps

In the third step, with all data produced organized in GISColab web application, the students took part in the geodesign workshop to learn about the process of co-creation. They proposed ideas in diagrams (points, lines, or polygons) including their descriptions and justifying their contribution to each of the 12 completeness indicators. Ideas were displayed for the discussion. A final design was composed, with the support of a widget to analyze the performance and the achievement of the goals. (Fig. 5).

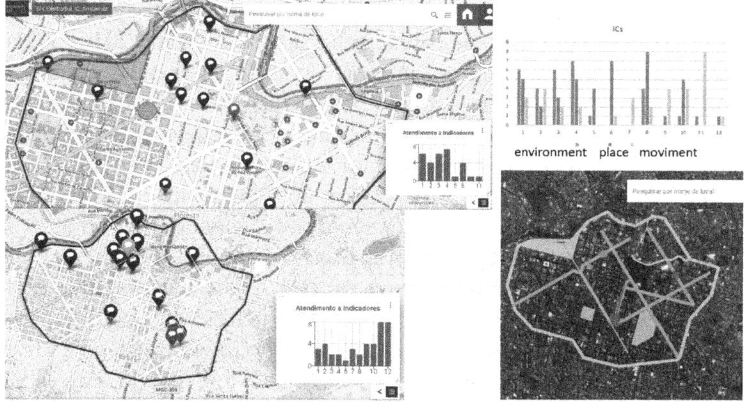

Fig. 5. Geodesign workshop to co-create designs reaching proposed goals

Finally, in the fourth and last step, the students developed authorial drawings as solutions to the negotiated design. In this process they learned about the role of reading the territory, constructing common solutions, and acting as a creative designer. (Fig. 6).

Fig. 6. Examples of authorial drawings

3.3 Geodesign Studio on the Metropolitan City of Cagliari, Italy

The case study of the application of a geodesign studio in education at the University of Cagliari presented here dates back to the autumn 2018. It was developed as a case study of the International Geodesign Collaboration (IGC), following its standards (Fisher et al. 2020). The study area was the Metropolitan City of Cagliari (MCC), including 17 municipalities which host about half-a-million population. The study itself was adapted to an education setting from a previous research study (Campagna 2016; 2022b).

While this case study is presented in more detail in Campagna et al. (2019), the main features of the study are summarized below. It involved two classes of students (i.e., 58 master students in Civil Engineering, and 76 bachelor students in Architecture). They worked in tight coordination on a multiscale design studio. The students in engineering concentrated on an 80 × 80 km area including the whole MCC. The students in architecture worked at a larger scale (i.e., smaller area) on a 20 × 20 km area in the South-East of the MCC. All preparatory data, information, and knowledge (i.e., the Steinitz framework's representation, process, and evaluation models) that supported the design were prepared in advance by the instructors who coordinated the study. Each class worked during 5 sessions, 3 h each, and the final design scenario based on consensus through negotiation was achieved within 15 h. The two classes worked in parallel. The engineering class, working at smaller territorial scale, started first so that the second class could take their recommendations on board when designing at a more detailed scale. This enabled them to make the two designs consistent. The design was organized in the following ten systems (i.e., the nine IGC standard systems, plus one additional system which was locally relevant): Water Infrastructure, Agriculture, Green Infrastructures, Energy, Transport, Industry and Commerce, Residential Lower Density, Mixed-housing, Institutional, and Cultural Heritage. According to the IGC guidelines, the students developed scenarios for 2035 and 2050, with different rates of adoption of technology innovations in the systems design (i.e., non-adopters, late-adopters, early adopters) as shown in the example in Fig. 7. While the data preparation was done in ESRI ArcMap, both of the design workshops were supported by the Geodesignhub planning support system (Ballal 2015).

The workshops produced five scenarios each, consistent within the larger and the smaller areas, and for the two timeframes. Figure 7 shows the maps of the final scenarios, their impact models, and a 3D representation for the MCC South-East study area.

Overall, in a very short time (i.e., 15 class hours) the students who had no previous knowledge of spatial planning and design could learn about territorial planning issues, geodesign methods (i.e., collaboration, negotiation) and technology with a very steep learning curve. They found the collaborative (geo)design experience novel and stimulating. It could raise their knowledge of systems design as well as their awareness on environmental planning issues. This can be considered a very successful teaching experience as the results in terms of learning were above expectations. Limitations included the quality of the final design which left space for improvement; however, the learning focus was purposely on the process methods and technology. In addition, the students were involved only in the framework intervention phase (e.g., change, impact, and decision models). Possible improvements for further development included involving the students in the preparation of the evaluation model, which was eventually implemented in 2019 in a new Geodesign Lab course; and the possibility to involve them in a real-world case study, which is currently under development. Later in 2021, the MCC geodesign study was applied in a real-world planning process, when representatives of the 17 municipalities of the MCC participated in a geodesign workshop within the making of the MCC Strategic Plan, which was adopted a few months later.

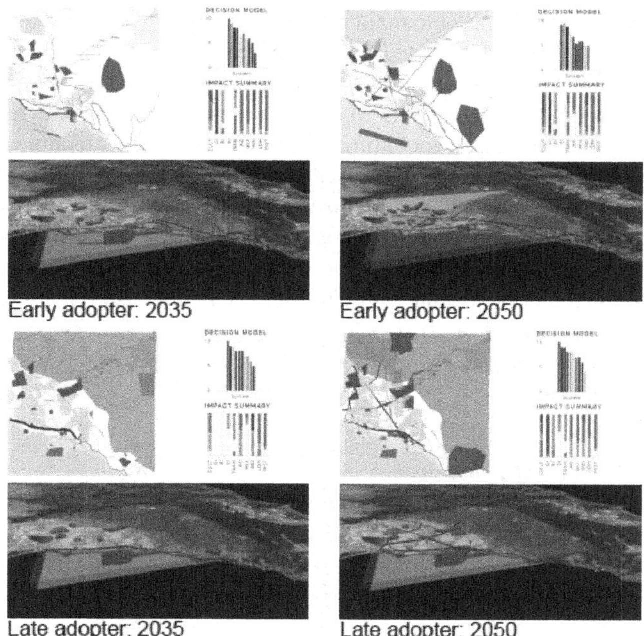

Fig. 7. Scenarios for 2035 and 2050, early adopter and late adopter

3.4 "Political Academy": A Geodesign Case Study at UniBAS

A Geodesign application conducted at University of Basilicata regards the "Potenza 2050 – Political Academy" (Scorza 2020b). The research project was based on two main steps involving different focus group: the first included the students of the "Territorial Engineering" course (Environmental and Civil engineering MSc); the second involved representatives of the Municipality of the City of Potenza.

The Potenza Political Academy Geodesign Workshop, held on 17th January 2020, aimed to deliver components of an urban development strategy in accordance with the EU urban development public investment program of the Integrated Territorial Investment of the City of Potenza (ITI). The ITI was based on a self-defined strategy to implement UE cohesion funds for urban regeneration and development. It represents an innovative procedure of program management that transfers the managing authority responsibility from the Regional Government to the Municipality. The implementation of this program became a critical stage of planning where the Municipality obtained the resources to realize an extensive regeneration program including public infrastructures and services. Such background fits with the geodesign scope to define, through a negotiated approach, a strategic development masterplan on the base of a pre-defined set of intervention areas and budget.

The workshop setup was prepared with students in a studio project where they applied spatial analysis to deliver context knowledge. Then, they acted as stakeholders in the first step of the workshop simulating the main roles characterizing a real urban development interaction: decision makers, developers, environmental activists, SMEs etc.

The second step was organized with real stakeholders, mainly representatives of the Municipality. The invited participants to the workshop were political representatives of the town council of Potenza, including the mayor, as well as technical staff of the main municipal departments dealing with ITI planning and management. Researchers, PhD students, and master students in engineering participated in the workshop as mentors, guiding actors through the methodological steps of the geodesign workflow and explaining technical analyses and the use of the online platform Geodesignhub. Posters in the room documented the evaluation maps and became a base for discussion among technicians and politicians (Fig. 8).

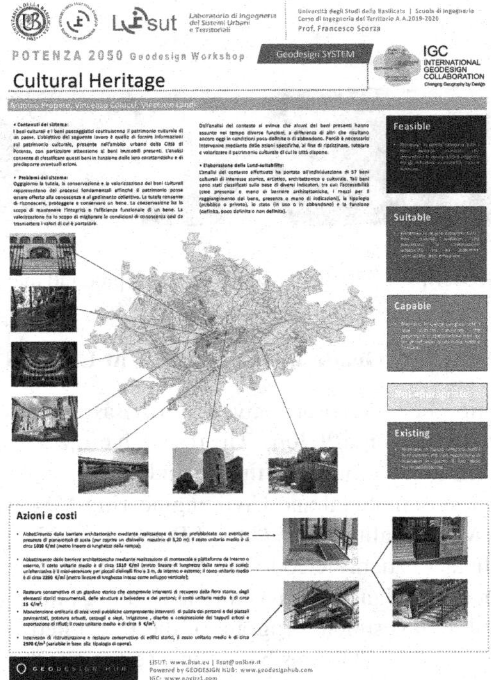

Fig. 8. System evaluation poster supporting stakeholders' interaction

The design phase and change teams' design selection were facilitated by a positive interaction between politicians and technicians. During the presentations of the syntheses, some political conflicts arose between majority and minority groups. Finally, negotiations paid the bill of a simulated discussion delivered in a learning event. The final results of the workshop were not implemented in the ITI implementation process, but participants learned the methodological approach and the effectiveness in defining a shared development scenario for future urban regeneration programs. Additionally, it is relevant to point out how the level of interactions became not effective in terms of conflict resolution and agreement reinforcement among participants, remarking a general situation characterizing geodesign workshop applied in a simulated decision-making context.

Comparing the first step of the workshop led by students with the second one remarked the applicability of the method to a wide scope of planning issues. The approach adopted was organized in learning by doing process. The level of personal learning derived from the participation in the workshop has not been measured by specific survey, but in the final discussion session, several positive remarks were declared by participants (i.e., the politicians). Their appreciation of the experience mainly focused on the applicability of the approach in real-case decision making concerning urban transformations. Participants expressed quite evident understanding of geodesign. The "acceptability" of the geodesign method was demonstrated during the geodesign workshop experience. Participants followed the workshop steps and easily adapted their way to consider the city and its development perspective according to the geodesign process.

4 Comparative Review

The comparison of different geodesign studies is an interesting research challenge as their number continues to grow around the world. Gu et al. (2020) proposed a first analysis in the research and education domain, while Campagna (2022) proposed a comparative review of two main real-world case studies. The latter taxonomy was adapted to this study with regards to geodesign education as shown in Table 1.

Table 1. Comparison of the geodesign teaching case studies

	City of Ames ISU and UGA (USA)	Central area of Belo Horizonte UFMG (Brazil)	Cagliari Metropolitan Area UniCA (Italy)	Potenza 2050 UniBAS (Italy)
Year	2022	2022	2018	2020
Goal	City of Ames: Plan for a Sustainable Future	Requalify the central area according to Completeness Indicators of streets	Metropolitan Strategic Planning	Urban Agenda (integrated investments for urban development)
Students	ISU: 3 undergraduate and 4 graduate planning students UGA: 7 graduate students (Master of Urban Planning and Design)	15 (Urban Planning lectures, BSc Architecture)	58 (MSc Civile engineering) + 72 (BSc Architecture	14 (MSc in Environmental and Civile engineering)

(continued)

Table 1. *(continued)*

	City of Ames ISU and UGA (USA)	Central area of Belo Horizonte UFMG (Brazil)	Cagliari Metropolitan Area UniCA (Italy)	Potenza 2050 UniBAS (Italy)
Stakeholders	City of Ames government officials, ISU Sustainability representatives, and selected community members	Observed and interviewed on streets	N.A: (i.e., Students played the role)	Municipality delegates (including political representatives and technical staff)
Duration	One semester	4 sessions x 4 h along 2 weeks, plus field camp	5 sessions x 3 h along 3 weeks	1 session x 8 h along 1 day
Technology	ESRI's Geoplanner, ArcGIS Pro, ArcGIS Online (ISU and UGA)	ViconSaga, GISColab, ArcGIS	ESRI ArcGIS, Geodesignhub	Geodesignhub, QGis
Systems	Three systems: Transportation and mobility Energy Green infrastructure	12 variables organized in 3 contexts: a) Environment b) Place c) Movement Road	10 systems: Water, Agriculture, Green Infrastructures, Energy, Transport, Industry/ Commerce, Residential, Mixed-housing, Institutional, Cultural Heritage (IGC compliant)	9 Systems: Urban water management, Urban Green Management, Energy infrastructures, Transport infrastructures -Grey mobility, Transport infrastructures -Active mobility, Cultural Heritage, Services supply specialization, Building Stock Renovation, Green Stock Renovation
Live/online/Hybrid	In person and online	Live in class and on streets	Live in class	Live in the town hall
Deliverables	2030 and 2050 Final Scenarios (one for ISU and one for UGA); 5 intermediate scenarios (3 for ISU and 2 for UGA); A collection of Suitability/Evaluation models (3 per system and per university – ISU and UGA, for a total of 6 suitability maps)	Present scenario considering and measuring the goals proposed	2035 and 2050 IGC scenarios (i.e., NA, EA, LA) at 2 scales	2050 scenario of urban development at 1 scale

(continued)

Table 1. (*continued*)

	City of Ames ISU and UGA (USA)	Central area of Belo Horizonte UFMG (Brazil)	Cagliari Metropolitan Area UniCA (Italy)	Potenza 2050 UniBAS (Italy)
Outcomes	Student exchange Learning about the process and geodesign framework Learning how to conduct suitability analysis Focus on innovations Learning how to use ESRI's GeoPlanner online tool Presentation skills Conference presentations by students with stakeholders and national conference	Learning about authorial design and design by co-creation	Fast learning curve in planning and technology	Effective learning on how to manage and interact during the process of scenario building. Effective interaction among students and Municipality delegates
Limitations	Availability of specific data Time and budget constraints Distance and costs for UGA students to visit study area more than once Lack of tools and clear methodology for impact assessment Lack of software that would support impact analysis Lack of proper software documentation (Geoplanner) and relevant tutorials to use with students. Limitations to implement suitability models in GeoPlanner, except Green Infrastructure.Limited software support. Lacks documentation;	Time left to field camp	Quality of design may be improved	The workshop simulated a strategic design for public investments in the city of Potenza, so the level of conflicts among participants was very low

5 Results and Conclusions

From the case studies developed in the United States, Brazil, and Italy, we can conclude that the instructors involved in the implementation of geodesign in their courses already had extensive experience in teaching planning, and that they still innovated their teaching through the inclusion of the geodesign methodology as a reliable way to improve the teaching objectives. Interpreting the geodesign framework proposed by Steinitz (2021) in different ways. Lecturers in Italy based the teaching workflow on the representation, processing, evaluation, change, impact, and decision models. Once the steps were structured, the students expanded their knowledge on how to characterize a study area, according to its potentialities and vulnerabilities, and how to produce these analyses through the use of geospatial technologies as a base to inform design. Other lecturers (for example in the USA) combined parts of Steinitz's geodesign framework with scenario planning and inclusion of innovations. Lecturers in Brazil offered a unique approach of reading, interpretation and an online platform.

Irrespective of whether the students already knew the study area, they expanded their understanding of territorial dynamics and of the way of interpreting and decoding its geography, moving from personal observation to structured quantitative analysis.

In the case study of the United States, the students were from different universities (i.e., ISU and UGA), which favored the understanding of the method in the representation of the study area, so that shared knowledge was built through digital representations, creating maps representing the study area. Thus, it was a way of proving the potential of organized information in representing the problem. In the Brazilian case study, the students worked in an area of their personal experiences, whose knowledge was expanded by the reading enrichment method, using the VGI technique, associated with the concepts of spatial reading proposed by Lynch (1960) and Cullen (1961). In the Cagliari case study (Italy), the students also worked in an area of their personal experiences, and the knowledge about development issues was expanded due to the wide collection of information previously built for the case study. The same workshop took place on more than one occasion, with more than one working group. In the Potenza case study, students actively participated in the creation of knowledge.

The use of different working tools stands out making it clear to prospective geodesign workshop coordinators that the process can be carried out with the support of alternative tools. Either desktop or web-based software were used in the stages of production of representations of the study areas and interpretive analyses (representation, process and evaluation model). To read the place dynamically, in Brazil, the ViconSaga VGI application was used. For the stages of proposing ideas (change, impact, and decision models), the groups used either the web-based resources ESRI GeoPlanner or ArcGis Hub (in the United States), GISColab (in Brazil) and Geodesignhub (in Italy). The choice of possible platforms is flexible, and they can be selected based on the needs and availability at educational organizations. In the future it would be important to consider options that allow greater interoperability, even enabling students to use applications of their preference.

Geodesign workshops can facilitate both decision-making and knowledge building which are considered of great value in every geodesign process. Often, when an academic case study is developed, it may just stay limited to an academic exercise, and it is not meant to be implemented in practice. It has its value in the learning process as it can stimulate developing ideas and learning. Working on real study cases can motivate students and the results can form a basis for some institutional decisions. Such practice-oriented study cases, even though they are just academic studies, can provide opportunities for "transformative learning" (Forester 1999). In all presented geodesign case studies presented in this paper, students and participants went beyond critical thinking, and advanced to the construction and negotiation of proposals, in a collaborative way.

Acknowledgments. Brazilian author thanks FAPEMIG support through the projects PPM-00368–18 and APQ-00779–22. The USA funding came from two university sources: Iowa State University Collaborative Interdisciplinary Fund provided by the Community and Regional Planning Department, and the University of Georgia Graduate School Travel Funding and College of Environment and Design.

References

Avin, U.: Using Scenarios to Make Urban Plans. In: Hopkins, L.D., Zapata, M.A. (eds.) Engaging the Future. Lincoln Institute of Land Policy, Cambridge, Massachusetts (2012)

Ballal, H.: Collaborative Planning with Digital Design Synthesis. Ph. D. thesis, UCL (University College London), London, UK (2015)

Campagna, M.: Metaplanning: about designing the geodesign process. Landscape Urban Plan. (2016). https://doi.org/10.1016/j.landurbplan.2015.08.019

Campagna, M., Di Cesare, E.A.:. Geodesign: lost in regulations (and in practice). In: Papa, R., Fistola, R. (eds.) Smart Energy in the Smart City. Green Energy and Technology. Springer, Cham (2016). https://doi.org/10.1007/978-3-319-31157-9_16

Campagna, M., Steinitz, C., Di Cesare, E., Cocco, C., Ballal, H., Canfield, T.: Collaboration in Planning: the Geodesign approach. Rozwój Regionalny I Polityka Regionalna **35**, 55–72 (2016)

Campagna, M.: Geodesign A-to-Z: evolution of a syllabus for architects and engineers. J. Dig. Landscape Arch. 271–278 (2017). https://doi.org/10.14627/537629028

Campagna, M., Cocco, C., di Cesare, E.: New scenarios for the Metropolitan City of Cagliari, Sardinia, Italy. In: Fisher, T., Orland, B., Steiitz, C. (eds.) The International Geodesign Collaboration: Changing Geography by Design. ESRI Press (2019)

Campagna, M. Di Cesare, E., Matta, A. Serra M.: Bridging the gap between strategic environmental assessment and planning: a geodesign perspective. Int. J. E-Plan. Res. **7**, 34–52 (2018). https://doi.org/10.4018/IJEPR.2018010103

Campagna, M., di Cesare, E.A., Cocco, C.: Integrating Green-infrastructures design in strategic spatial planning with geodesign. Sustainability **12**(5), 1–22 (2020). https://doi.org/10.3390/SU12051820

Campagna, M.: Geodesign in the planning practice: lessons learnt from experience in Italy. J. Dig. Landscape Arch. **2022**(7), 496–503 (2022a). https://doi.org/10.14627/537724048

Campagna, M.: Geodesign iterations: relevance for planning In: Gervasi, O., Murgante, B., Misra, S., Rocha, A.M.A.C., Garau, C. (eds.) Computational Science and Its Applications – ICCSA 2022 Workshops. ICCSA 2022. Lecture Notes in Computer Science, vol. 13379, pp. 181–193. Springer, Cham (2022b). https://doi.org/10.1007/978-3-031-10545-6_13

Cocco, C., Freitas, C. R., Moura, A.C.M., Campagna, M.: Geodesign process analytics: focus on design as a process and its outcomes. Sustainability **12**(1), 119 (2019). https://doi.org/10.3390/SU12010119

Cullen, G.: Townscape. Reinhold Pub. Corp. (1961)

Fisher, T., Orland, B., Steinitz, C. (eds.): The International Geodesign Collaboration: Changing Geography by Design. ESRI Press (2020)

Forester, J.: The Deliberative Practitioner: Encouraging Participatory Planning Processes. MIT Press, Cambridge (1999)

Gu, Y., Deal, B.: Coupling systems thinking and geodesign processes in land-use modelling, design, and planning. J. Digit. Landscape Arch. **2018**(3), 51–59 (2018)

Gu, Y., Deal, B., Orland, B., Campagna, M.: Evaluating practical implementation of geodesign and its impacts on resilience. J. Digit. Landscape Arch. **2020**(5), 467–475 (2020). https://doi.org/10.14627/537690048

Goodspeed, R.: Scenario Planning for Cities and Regions. Managing and Envisioning Uncertain Futures, Lincoln Institute of Land Policy (2020)

Hersperger, A.M., Grădinaru, S., Oliveira, E., Pagliarin, S., Palka, G.: Understanding strategic spatial planning to effectively guide development of urban regions. Cities **94**, 96–105 (2019). https://doi.org/10.1016/J.CITIES.2019.05.032

Hopkins, L.D., Zapata, M.A. (eds.): Using Scenarios to Make Urban Plans, book chapter in the book Engaging the Future, Lincoln Institute of Land Policy, Cambridge, Massachusetts (2012)

Lynch, K.: The Image of the City. MIT Press (1960)

Marino, T., de Campos, M.L.M., Borges, M.R.S., Breslin, J.G., Dabrowski, M.: Architecture for gathering and integrating collaborative information for decision support in emergency situations. Int. J. Inf. Commun. Technol. **12**(3–4), 345–363 (2018). https://doi.org/10.1504/IJICT.2018.090420

Moura, A.C.M., Freitas, C.R.: Brazilian geodesign platform: WebGis & SDI & geodesign as co-creation and geo-collaboration. In: Gervasi, O., et al. (eds.) ICCSA 2020. LNCS, vol. 12252, pp. 332–348. Springer, Cham (2020). https://doi.org/10.1007/978-3-030-58811-3_24

Moura, A.C.M., Freitas, C.R.: Scalability in the application of geodesign in Brazil: expanding the use of the Brazilian Geodesign platform to metropolitan regions in transformative-learning planning. Sustainability **13**(12), 6508 (2021). https://doi.org/10.3390/su13126508

Rivero, R.G., Smith, A., Ballal, H., Steinitz, C.: Promoting collaborative geodesign in a multidisciplinary and multiscale environment: Coastal Georgia 2050, USA. In: Buhmann, E., Ervin, S.M., Pietsch, M. (eds.). Peer Reviewed Proceedings of Digital Landscape Architecture 2015 at Anhalt University of Applied Sciences, pp. 42–58. Dessau, Germany (2015)

Rivero, R.G., et al.: Experiences in geodesign in Georgia, USA. Experiencias en Geodiseño en Georgia, Estados Unidos Disegnarecon **11**(20) (2018)

Rivero, R G., Smith, A.L., Alfonso, M.: Resilience in coastal regions: the case of Georgia, USA. In: Steinberg, S.L., Steinberg, S. (eds.) GIS Applications for Resilience: Across Spatial Geographies. Environmental Systems Research Institute, Inc. (Esri): Redlands, CA (2020)

Smith, A.L., Rivero, R.G., Vick, R.A.: Exploring adaptation challenges and collaborative solutions in a USA Coastal Region through Geodesign. In: Steinitz, Fisher, and Orland (eds.) The International Geodesign Collaboration: Changing Geography by Design. ESRI: Redlands, CA (2020)

Somma, M., Campagna, M., Canfield, T., Cerreta, M., Poli, G., Steinitz, C.: Collaborative and sustainable strategies through geodesign: the case study of Bacoli. In: Gervasi, O., Murgante, B., Misra, S., Rocha, A.M.A.C., Garau, C. (eds.) Computational Science and Its Applications – ICCSA 2022 Workshops. ICCSA 2022. Lecture Notes in Computer Science, vol. 13379, pp. 210–224. Springer, Cham (2022). https://doi.org/10.1007/978-3-031-10545-6_15

Steinitz, C.A.: A Framework for Geodesign. ESRI Press (2012). https://doi.org/10.1007/s13398-014-0173-7.2

Geomatics in Agriculture and Forestry: New Advances and Perspectives (GeoForAgr 2023)

Enhanced Map Composition and Diachronic Land Cover Classification of Landsat Data in Google Earth Engine

Marco Vizzari(✉), Cecilia Parracciani, and Daniela Gigante

Department of Agricultural, Food, and Environmental Sciences, University of Perugia, 06121 Perugia, Italy
{marco.vizzari,cecilia.parracciani,daniela.gigante}@unipg.it

Abstract. Understanding how habitats in the European Natura 2000 network change over time and space is crucial to evaluating the effectiveness of protective measures and developing sustainable management practices. Satellite remote sensing through Earth observation offers a cost-effective, timely, reproducible vegetation analysis. This study aims to analyze the changes in grassland habitats (types 6210 and 6230*, Annex I, European Directive 92/43/EEC) within the Natura 2000 network's areas in Umbria (Central Italy) between 2000 and 2020. The goal is to gather spatial information to develop more sustainable planning and management strategies. In this direction, we selected a three-year time window in two periods (1999–2001 and 2019–2021). We applied an enhanced dataset composition, including cloud-filtering, topography correction, and textural analysis on Landsat 7 and 8 surface reflectance images available in Google Earth Engine (GEE). Additional morphometric features were derived from the digital elevation model of the area. Using machine learning classification (Random Forest – RF), we obtained the land cover maps for the two periods under investigation with high overall accuracy (87 and 88%). Only shrublands showed a lower classification accuracy due to the varied nature of this land cover class and the limited resolution of Landsat data. On this basis, we identified transformations that occurred in the study areas. The results confirmed the effectiveness of enhanced map composition and RF in GEE for diachronic land cover classification. The final spatial information can help identify areas where conservation measures related to the Natura 2000 network have been more or less effective and develop more appropriate management strategies for grasslands of European concern.

Keywords: grasslands dynamics · google earth engine · remote sensing · machine learning · random forest · Landsat 7 · Landsat 8

1 Introduction

Permanent grasslands cover 34% of the European Union's agricultural area and are among Earth's most prominent land cover for human welfare and livestock [1]. Natura 2000 network is by far the most influential EU nature conservation effort implemented

O. Gervasi et al. (Eds.): ICCSA 2023 Workshops, LNCS 14107, pp. 289–299, 2023.
https://doi.org/10.1007/978-3-031-37114-1_19

in Umbria. It is regulated mainly by the Habitat Directive (92/43/EEC, "The Habitats Directive - Environment - European Commission," 1992) [2] and the Birds Directive (2009/147/EC, "The Birds Directive - Environment - European Commission", 2009) [3]. The network includes two types of protected areas: Special Areas of Conservation (SACs) and Special Protection Areas (SPAs). Assessing habitat conservation status is crucial for managing Natura 2000 network according to international conventions such as the Convention on Biological Diversity or the European Biodiversity Strategy [4]. Mapping and monitoring grasslands' habitats are essential for implementing the European Directive 92/43/EEC and protecting and managing the Natura 2000 network [5]. Understanding land cover, landscape, and habitat dynamics in space and time, also considering the spatial gradients [6, 7], is very relevant for the definition of sustainable management practices [8–11] and protecting the ecosystem service flows [12, 13]. Field surveys are needed for collecting ground GIS data [14] and habitat detection and identification [15]; however, analyzing trends and processes requires gathering adequate spatial and temporal information, which is time-consuming and expensive, especially when dealing with large areas. Although its known limitations compared to on-field surveys, Earth observation by satellite remote sensing (RS) offers many possibilities for cost-effective, timely, and reproducible vegetation analysis [16]. Moreover, in the last decade, RS techniques and tools have become very efficient, especially with the advent of easily accessible and open-source data and software [17]. Grassland remote sensing research supports ecology studies because it utilizes multi-platform, multi-sensor, and multi-temporal satellite remote sensing data sources and ground observation data [18–20]. Landsat data have been broadly used for land-use land-cover (LULC) change detection and analysis (see, e.g., [21–23]). Despite its coarser spatial and temporal resolution than other satellites, it provides the most comprehensive free-access remote sensing data globally, thus offering the possibility to gain insights into past trends, which are fundamental for monitoring land cover changes [24, 25].

In recent years, RS data processing has progressively migrated to cloud-based platforms from traditional workstations. Users can rapidly access and analyze pre-processed geospatial data using user-friendly web-based interfaces and powerful scripting languages [26]. Among these technologies, Google Earth Engine (GEE) is a cloud-based geospatial analytic platform that enables users to effectively manage massive amounts of data, storage, processing, and analysis [27].

Machine learning (ML) algorithms generally produce better results than traditional classifiers in the categorization of LULC. Classification and Regression Trees (CART), Random Forest (RF), and Support Vector Machine (SVM) are non-parametric ML classifiers that have been shown to generate exceptionally accurate LULC classification results from remotely sensed imagery [28]. The RF classifier has been widely used in the GEE for RS data classification [29, 30], even in object-based approaches [31–33] due to its non-parametric structure, ability to handle dimensionality and overfitting, and superior performance to other classifiers. However, the unknown splitting rules are one of its most known inherent flaws [22].

This study aims to perform a long-term analysis of vegetation within the Natura 2000 network's areas in Umbria (Central Italy). The analysis focuses on transformations in grassland habitats (Annex I, types 6210 and 6230*) to identify areas where significant degradation phenomena related to reduced green biomass due to erosion or invasion of shrub and tree species can be observed in the last 20 years.

2 Materials and Methods

2.1 Study Areas

The Umbrian Natura 2000 network includes 102 sites: 5 SPAs and 97 SACs. The network protects 41 habitats of Annex I to the Habitats Directive, i.e., habitats of community interest, of which 11 are defined as priorities due to their particular importance, 143 animal species (4 priority), and eight plant species (1 priority). Grassland habitats (Annex I, types 6210 and 6230*, Directive 92/43/EEC) are very relevant to the Umbrian Natura 2000 network sites, especially within the sites falling along the Apennine mountains. Our study area includes the higher altitude (over 700 m a.s.l.) Natura 2000 areas of Umbria. We defined the proper altitude threshold to select the most critical grassland areas in the Natura 2000 network and include all the montane grasslands, traditionally used as pastures and affected in recent decades by a massive decline due to land depopulation [34].

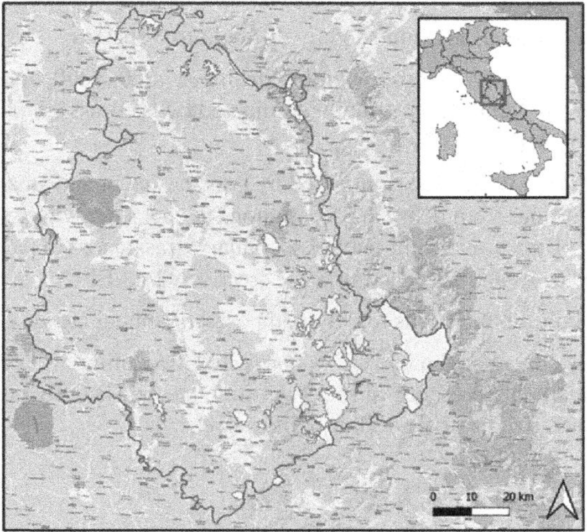

Fig. 1. The geographical location of the study areas.

2.2 Methodology

We tested a diachronic land cover classification in Google Earth Engine (GEE) to assess the main changes in grassland areas between 2000 and 2020, focusing on the sensible decrease of grasslands' biomass and the increase of shrubs and trees. We defined five main land cover classes (Table 1) and spatially compared their extents in the two classifications. As with every typical LULC (Land Use/Land Cover) classification procedure, our workflow includes a) data composition and pre-processing, b) image classification, c) accuracy assessment, and d) LULC transition analysis.

Generating the base composite dataset is a crucial step in every LULC classification. In this regard, GEE offers a vast database of satellite imagery and computational power accessible to all users [35]. We used the Landsat 7 (L7) and the Landsat 8 (L8) data atmospherically corrected at the Surface Reflectance (SR) level in this application, available in GEE. According to Xi et al. [36], we filtered the L7 and L8 GEE datasets considering two sufficiently broad periods of interest (in this case, three years, from 1999 to 2001 and 2019 to 2021) were defined to create a more effective composite image for the subsequent classification. We applied a cloud cover filtering on the resulting dataset using the "pixel_qa" band, which allowed us to almost entirely mask pixels occupied by dense and cirrus clouds and their on-ground shadows [37].

Table 1. Land cover classes used in the classification.

LULC Class	Description
Woodland	Forest vegetation dominated by different tree species
Shrubland	Shrubs and scrublands, including the types 4060, 4090, and 5130 of Annex I, Directive 92/43/EEC (usually dominated by brooms, juniper, blackthorn, and hawthorn)
Grassland	Grassland vegetation dominated by grasses, forbs, and small shrubs in variable proportion, from dense and continuous to sparse and discontinuous, including both primary and semi-natural secondary grasslands (in particular, habitat types 6210 and 6230*, Annex I, Directive 92/43/EEC)
Cropland	Agricultural mosaic is mainly composed of annual crops
Sparse/ No vegetation	Areas characterized by highly sparse and discontinuous vegetation cover, with a remarkable presence of rocky substrate, or persistently non-vegetated areas characterized by bare soil or built-up areas

A topographic correction in mountainous areas is ordinarily necessary to reduce the topographic effect before calculating spectral indices and image classification (Richter et al., 2009). To this aim, using the 30m Shuttle Radar Topography Mission Digital Elevation Model (SRTM DEM), we applied a Sun-Canopy-Sensor + C (SCSc) correction method [38, 39] successfully applied in previous studies [23, 40, 41], already implemented in a GEE script [42]. To correct some noise and aberrations observed on the first SCSc outputs, we smoothed the DEM convolving with a 2-cell radius low-pass filter. Adding spectral indices generally increases the available information and improves the final classification [43, 44]. In this regard, we computed three spectral indices for each image in the period of interest (Table 2).

Textural analysis by GLCM in GEE requires a grey-level 8-bit image as input to generate 18 different textural indices. The algorithm calculates statistical data of texture characteristics by analyzing the distribution of intensity combinations observed at specified positions relative to one another in the image up to the second order [45]. As performed in previous studies [23], we applied a weighted linear combination to median B3, B4, and B5 bands to generate the 8-bit input for the GLCM step in GEE. We selected the first eight metrics for the subsequent classification.

Table 2. Spectral indices and related formulas used in the research.

Index	Formula	Author
BSI	$\frac{(SWIR1+RED)-(NIR+BLUE)}{(SWIR1+RED)+(NIR+BLUE)}$	Rikimaru et al., 2002 [46]
NDVI	$\frac{NIR-RED}{NIR+RED}$	Rouse Jr. et al., 1974 [47]
GARI	$\frac{(NIR-(GREEN-(BLUE-RED)))}{(NIR-(GREEN+(BLUE-RED)))}$	Gitelson et al., 1996 [48]

Table 3. Area of land cover (LC) classes (km^2) in the two analysis periods (2000, 2020) and the increase/decrease percentage within the Natura 2000 sites.

LC classes	2000	2020	Var. %
Woodland	332	359	+ 8.1
Shrubland	44	34	−22.7
Cropland	20	19	−5.0
Grassland	112	98	−12.5
Sparse/No Vegetation	31	30	−3.2

To compose the 30-m resolution base Data Cube (BDC), we calculated the median images for the L8 and the L7 bands and that of the derived spectral indices in GEE. We added the 30m SRTM DEM for altitude and the derived slope and aspect layers to consider the morphological features crucial for an area of interest with complex morphology, such as the Umbria territory.

We computed the land cover classification using the Random Forest (RF) machine learning classifier. RF utilizes bootstrap aggregation (bagging) to build multiple decision trees to combine the results employing a majority voting method to make a more accurate prediction [49, 50].

We collected 1200 randomly distributed points in the two periods, with a reciprocal minimum distance of 200 m, to train the classifier and validate the LULC classification results. These points were classified in QGIS, visually integrating information from high-resolution orthophotos from 2000 and 2020. The classification accuracy was assessed using the confusion matrix method, a widely used approach based on comparing the classification outputs with the ground truth data [51, 52].

3 Results and Discussion

The two final LULC classifications gathered a high overall accuracy (87 and 88%). Classification of shrublands was more problematic due to the varied nature of this land cover class and the limited resolution of Landsat data. Concerning our analysis of changes, the region we examined is situated at high elevations and predominantly composed of natural and semi-natural habitats, with forests and grasslands being the primary land cover types (Table 2). The area covered by forests has increased over the past two decades, while there has been a decrease in the coverage of grasslands. Natural transitional flows from shrubland areas characterized the forests in the area. These phenomena, typical of inner Italian marginal areas, are in counter-tendency compared to those typical of peri-urban areas [53].

Conversely, grasslands have suffered significant losses due to the transition into shrubs or forests, as illustrated (Fig. 2). Shrublands have experienced inflows from grasslands and outflows to forests. Still, despite these transitions, the area covered by shrublands has declined over the past 20 years. Agricultural areas experienced a slight decline in the same period. Non-vegetated and eroded areas decreased only marginally during the analysis period.

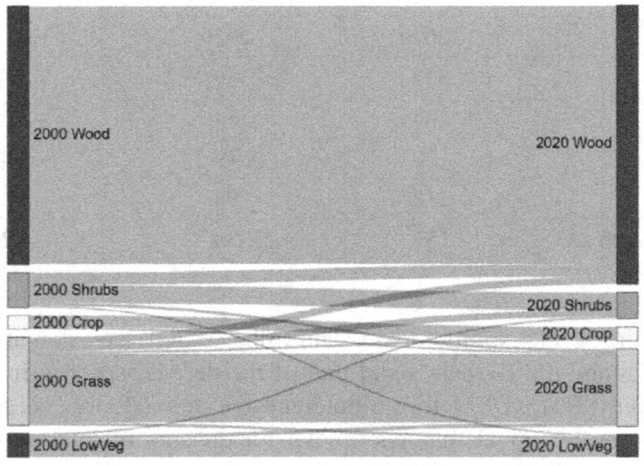

Fig. 2. Sankey's diagram showing the land cover transitions between 2000 and 2020.

The proposed methodology identified the grassland areas in the Umbrian Natura 2000 network where the most relevant degradation phenomena occurred. These phenomena are partly related to biomass reduction (primarily due to the increase of erosion or over-grazing) and partly (the majority) to the invasion of shrubs or trees (Fig. 3). This information helps detect the areas where the conservation measures related to the

Natura 2000 network have been more (or less) effective and address more appropriate management strategies. On the one hand, specific spatially explicit management measures aimed to reduce over-grazing or erosion phenomena and reduce invasion by shrub or tree species (often related to under-grazing) could be defined to increase grassland ecosystem protection.

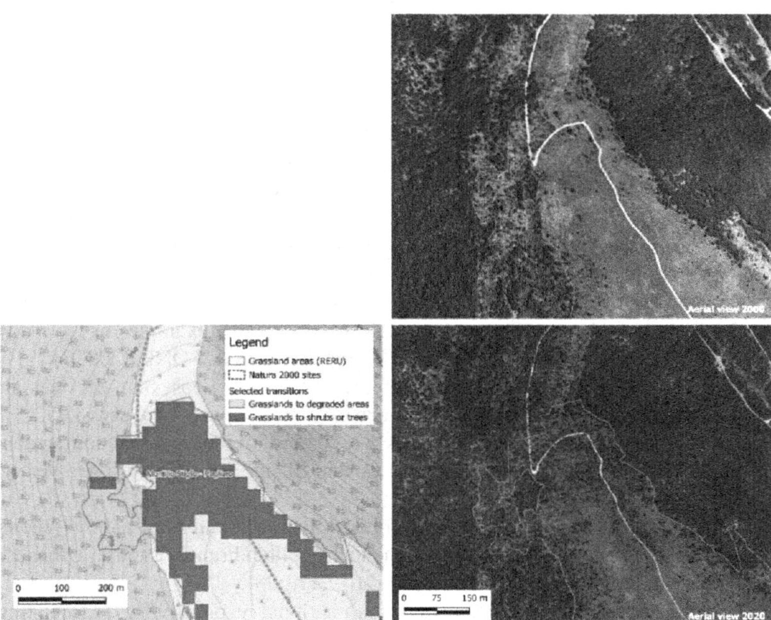

Fig. 3. Example of the diachronic land cover analysis output showing a grassland area occupied progressively by shrubs or trees during the investigated period.

4 Conclusions

This research developed a diachronic land cover analysis of Natura 2000 areas to identify areas where significant degradation phenomena (reduction of the grasslands' biomass or invasion by shrubs or trees) occurred during the 2000–2020 period, generating a loss of grassland areas. The machine learning-based land cover classification in GEE produced high overall accuracy results. However, shrublands classification was more problematic due to the varied nature of this land cover class and the limited resolution of Landsat data. Preliminary results of the diachronic analysis focused on the specific transitions of grassland areas. The green biomass reduced considerably only in a few areas, mainly due to increased erosion phenomena or rarely to over-grazing. The spatial information helps detect the areas where the conservation measures related to the Natura 2000 network have been more (or less) effective and address more appropriate management strategies for protecting grasslands of European concern.

Acknowledgments. This research was developed within the LIFE Project "LIFE IMAGINE UMBRIA" LIFE19 IPE/IT/000015 funded by the European Union.

References

1. Schils, R.L.M., et al.: Permanent grasslands in Europe: Land use change and intensification decrease their multifunctionality. Agric. Ecosyst. Environ. **330**, 107891 (2022). https://doi.org/10.1016/J.AGEE.2022.107891
2. The Habitats Directive - Environment - European Commission. https://ec.europa.eu/environment/nature/legislation/habitatsdirective/index_en.htm. Accessed 27 July 2022
3. The Birds Directive - Environment - European Commission, https://ec.europa.eu/environment/nature/legislation/birdsdirective/index_en.htm. Accessed 27 July 2022
4. Hermoso, V., et al.: The EU biodiversity strategy for 2030: opportunities and challenges on the path towards biodiversity recovery. Environ. Sci. Policy **127**, 263–271 (2022). https://doi.org/10.1016/J.ENVSCI.2021.10.028
5. Friedrichs, M., Hermoso, V., Bremerich, V., Langhans, S.D.: Evaluation of habitat protection under the European Natura 2000 conservation network – the example for Germany. PLoS ONE **13**, e0208264 (2018). https://doi.org/10.1371/JOURNAL.PONE.0208264
6. Vizzari, M., Antognelli, S., Hilal, M., Sigura, M., Joly, D.: Ecosystem services along the urban-rural-natural gradient: a approach for a wide-area mapping. In: Gervasi, O. (ed.) Computational sciences and its applications - ICCSA 2015–15th international conference, Banff, Alberta, Canada, June 22–25 2015, Proceedings, Part III, pp. 745–757. Springer-Verlag, Berlin Heidelberg (2015)
7. Vizzari, M., Hilal, M., Sigura, M., Antognelli, S., Joly, D.: Urban-rural-natural gradient analysis with CORINE data: An application to the metropolitan France. Landsc. Urban Plan. **171** (2018). https://doi.org/10.1016/j.landurbplan.2017.11.005
8. Orsenigo, S., et al.: Red Listing plants under full national responsibility: Extinction risk and threats in the vascular flora endemic to Italy. Biol. Conserv. **224**, (2018). https://doi.org/10.1016/j.biocon.2018.05.030
9. Vizzari, M.: Spatio-temporal analysis using urban-rural gradient modelling and landscape metrics. In: Murgante, B., Gervasi, O., Iglesias, A., Taniar, D., Apduhan, B.O. (eds.) ICCSA 2011. LNCS, vol. 6782, pp. 103–118. Springer, Heidelberg (2011). https://doi.org/10.1007/978-3-642-21928-3_8
10. Neri, M., Menconi, M.E., Vizzari, M., Mennella, V.G.G.: A proposal of a new methodology for best location of environmentally sustainable roads infrastructures. Validation along the Fabriano-Muccia road. Inf. la Constr. **62** (2010). https://doi.org/10.3989/ic.09.043
11. Vizzari, M., Sigura, M.: Urban-rural gradient detection using multivariate spatial analysis and landscape metrics. J. Agric. Eng. 44, (2013). https://doi.org/10.4081/jae.2013.(s1):e91
12. Antognelli, S., Vizzari, M.: Assessing ecosystem and urban services for landscape suitability mapping. Appl. Sci. **11**, 8232 (2021). https://doi.org/10.3390/app11178232
13. Antognelli, S., Vizzari, M., Schulp, C.J.E.: Integrating ecosystem and urban services in policy-making at the local scale: the SOFA framework. Sustainability 10 (2018). https://doi.org/10.3390/su10041017
14. Torquati, B., Vizzari, M., Sportolaro, C.: Participatory GIS for integrating local and expert knowledge in landscape planning. In: Management Association, I.R. (ed.) Agricultural and Environmental Informatics, Governance and Management, pp. 378–396. IGI Global, Hershey, PA (2013). https://doi.org/10.4018/978-1-60960-621-3.ch020

15. Gigante, D., et al.: A methodological protocol for Annex i Habitats monitoring: the contribution of vegetation science. Plant Sociol. **53**, 77–87 (2016). https://doi.org/10.7338/pls2016532/06
16. Lunetta, R.S., Congalton, R.G., Fenstermaker, L.K., Jensen, J.R., McGwire, K.C., Tinney, L.R.: Remote sensing and geographic information system data integration: error sources and research issues. Photogramm. Eng. Remote Sens. (1991)
17. De Luca, G., M. N. Silva, J., Di Fazio, S., Modica, G.: Integrated use of Sentinel-1 and Sentinel-2 data and open-source machine learning algorithms for land cover mapping in a Mediterranean region **55**, 52–70 (2022). https://doi.org/10.1080/22797254.2021.2018667
18. Li, B., Wang, W., Bai, L., Chen, N., Wang, W.: Estimation of aboveground vegetation biomass based on Landsat-8 OLI satellite images in the Guanzhong Basin. China Int. J. Remote Sens. **40**, 3927–3947 (2019). https://doi.org/10.1080/01431161.2018.1553323
19. Royimani, L., Mutanga, O., Dube, T.: Progress in remote sensing of grass senescence: a review on the challenges and opportunities. IEEE J. Sel. Top. Appl. Earth Obs. Remote Sens. **14**, 7714–7723 (2021). https://doi.org/10.1109/JSTARS.2021.3098720
20. Masenyama, A., Mutanga, O., Dube, T., Bangira, T., Sibanda, M., Mabhaudhi, T.: A systematic review on the use of remote sensing technologies in quantifying grasslands ecosystem services. GIScience Remote Sens. **59**, 1000–1025 (2022). https://doi.org/10.1080/15481603.2022.2088652
21. Fichera, C.R., Modica, G., Pollino, M.: Land Cover classification and change-detection analysis using multi-temporal remote sensed imagery and landscape metrics. Eur. J. Remote Sens. **45**, 1–18 (2012). https://doi.org/10.5721/EuJRS20124501
22. Rodriguez-Galiano, V.F., Ghimire, B., Rogan, J., Chica-Olmo, M., Rigol-Sanchez, J.P.: An assessment of the effectiveness of a random forest classifier for land-cover classification. ISPRS J. Photogramm. Remote Sens. (2012). https://doi.org/10.1016/j.isprsjprs.2011.11.002
23. Tassi, A., Gigante, D., Modica, G., Martino, L. Di, Vizzari, M.: Pixel- vs. Object-based landsat 8 data classification in Google earth engine using random forest: the case study of Maiella National Park. Remote Sens. **13**, 2299 (2021). https://doi.org/10.3390/RS13122299
24. Turner, W., et al.: Free and open-access satellite data are key to biodiversity conservation. Biol. Conserv. **182**, 173–176 (2015). https://doi.org/10.1016/j.biocon.2014.11.048
25. Wulder, M.A., et al.: The global Landsat archive: status, consolidation, and direction. Remote Sens. Environ. **185**, 271–283 (2016). https://doi.org/10.1016/j.rse.2015.11.032
26. Shelestov, A., Lavreniuk, M., Kussul, N., Novikov, A., Skakun, S.: Exploring Google earth engine platform for big data processing: classification of multi-temporal satellite imagery for crop mapping. Front. Earth Sci. **5**, 1 (2017). https://doi.org/10.3389/feart.2017.00017
27. Gorelick, N., Hancher, M., Dixon, M., Ilyushchenko, S., Thau, D., Moore, R.: Google earth engine: planetary-scale geospatial analysis for everyone. Remote Sens. Environ. **202**, 18–27 (2017)
28. Vizzari, M.: PlanetScope, Sentinel-2, and Sentinel-1 data integration for object-based land cover classification in Google earth engine. Remote Sens. **14**, 2628 (2022). https://doi.org/10.3390/RS14112628
29. Amani, M., et al.: Google Earth engine cloud computing platform for remote sensing big data applications: a comprehensive review. IEEE J. Sel. Top. Appl. Earth Obs. Remote Sens. **13**, 5326–5350 (2020). https://doi.org/10.1109/JSTARS.2020.3021052
30. Nery, T., Sadler, R., Solis-Aulestia, M., White, B., Polyakov, M., Chalak, M.: Comparing supervised algorithms in land use and land cover classification of a Landsat time-series. In: International Geoscience and Remote Sensing Symposium (IGARSS) (2016). https://doi.org/10.1109/IGARSS.2016.7730346
31. Tassi, A., Vizzari, M.: Object-oriented LULC classification in Google earth engine combining SNIC, GLCM, and machine learning algorithms. Remote Sens. (2020)

32. Matarira, D., Mutanga, O., Naidu, M., Vizzari, M.: Object-based informal settlement mapping in Google earth engine using the integration of Sentinel-1, Sentinel-2, and PlanetScope satellite data. Land **12**, 1–17 (2023). https://doi.org/10.3390/land12010099
33. Matarira, D., Mutanga, O., Naidu, M., Mushore, T.D., Vizzari, M.: Characterizing informal settlement dynamics using Google earth engine and intensity analysis in Durban Metropolitan area, South Africa: linking pattern to process. Sustain. **15** (2023). https://doi.org/10.3390/su15032724
34. Gigante, D., et al.: Habitat conservation in Italy: the state of the art in the light of the first European Red List of Terrestrial and Freshwater Habitats. Rendiconti Lincei. Scienze Fisiche e Naturali **29**(2), 251–265 (2018). https://doi.org/10.1007/s12210-018-0688-5
35. De Luca, G., Silva, J.M.N., Modica, G.: Regional-scale burned area mapping in Mediterranean regions based on the multitemporal composite integration of Sentinel-1 and Sentinel-2 data **59**, 1678–1705 (2022). https://doi.org/10.1080/15481603.2022.2128251
36. Xie, Y., Lark, T.J., Brown, J.F., Gibbs, H.K.: Mapping irrigated cropland extent across the conterminous United States at 30 m resolution using a semi-automatic training approach on Google Earth Engine. ISPRS J. Photogramm. Remote Sens. **155**, 136–149 (2019). https://doi.org/10.1016/j.isprsjprs.2019.07.005
37. Nyland, K.E., Gunn, G.E., Shiklomanov, N.I., Engstrom, R.N., Streletskiy, D.A.: Land cover change in the lower Yenisei River using dense stacking of landsat imagery in Google earth engine. Remote Sens. (2018). https://doi.org/10.3390/rs10081226
38. Soenen, S.A., Peddle, D.R., Coburn, C.A.: SCS+C: a modified sun-canopy-sensor topographic correction in forested terrain. IEEE Trans. Geosci. Remote Sens. (2005). https://doi.org/10.1109/TGRS.2005.852480
39. Vanonckelen, S., Lhermitte, S., Balthazar, V., Van Rompaey, A.: Performance of atmospheric and topographic correction methods on Landsat imagery in mountain areas. Int. J. Remote Sens. **35**, 4952–4972 (2014). https://doi.org/10.1080/01431161.2014.933280
40. Belcore, E., Piras, M., Wozniak, E.: Specific alpine environment land cover classification methodology: Google earth engine processing for sentinel-2 data. Int. Arch. Photogramm. Remote Sens. Spat. Inf. Sci. - ISPRS Arch. (2020). https://doi.org/10.5194/isprs-archives-XLIII-B3-2020-663-2020
41. Shepherd, J.D., Dymond, J.R.: Correcting satellite imagery for the variance of reflectance and illumination with topography. Int. J. Remote Sens. (2003). https://doi.org/10.1080/01431160210154029
42. Burns, P., Macander, M.: Topographic correction in GEE – Open Geo Blog. https://mygeoblog.com/2018/10/17/terrain-correction-in-gee/. Accessed 25 Feb 2021
43. Capolupo, A., Monterisi, C., Tarantino, E.: Landsat Images Classification Algorithm (LICA) to automatically extract land cover information in Google earth engine environment. Remote Sens. **12**, 1201 (2020). https://doi.org/10.3390/rs12071201
44. Singh, R.P., Singh, N., Singh, S., Mukherjee, S.: Normalized Difference Vegetation Index (NDVI) based classification to assess the change in Land Use/Land Cover (LULC) in Lower Assam, India. Int. J. Adv. Remote Sens. GIS. (2016). https://doi.org/10.23953/cloud.ijarsg.74
45. Mohanaiah, P., Sathyanarayana, P., Gurukumar, L.: Image texture feature extraction using GLCM approach. Int. J. Sci. Res. Publ. (2013)
46. Rikimaru, A., Roy, P.S., Miyatake, S.: Tropical forest cover density mapping. Trop. Ecol. (2002)
47. Rouse, W., Haas, R.H., Deering, D.W.: Monitoring vegetation systems in the Great Plains with ERTS, NASA SP-351 (1974)
48. Gitelson, A.A., Kaufman, Y.J., Merzlyak, M.N.: Use of a green channel in remote sensing of global vegetation from EOS-MODIS. Remote Sens. Environ. **58**, 289–298 (1996). https://doi.org/10.1016/S0034-4257(96)00072-7

49. Gislason, P.O., Benediktsson, J.A., Sveinsson, J.R.: Random forests for land cover classification. Pattern Recogn. Lett. (2006). https://doi.org/10.1016/j.patrec.2005.08.011
50. Breiman, L.: Random forests. Mach. Learn. **45**, 5–32 (2001). https://doi.org/10.1023/A:1010933404324
51. Congalton, R.G., Green, K.: Assessing the Accuracy of Remotely Sensed Data: Principles and Practices (1999)
52. Congalton, R.G.: A review of assessing the accuracy of classifications of remotely sensed data. Remote Sens. Environ. **37**, 35–46 (1991). https://doi.org/10.1016/0034-4257(91)90048-B
53. Solano, F., Praticò, S., Piovesan, G., Chiarucci, A., Argentieri, A., Modica, G.: Characterizing historical transformation trajectories of the forest landscape in Rome's metropolitan area (Italy) for effective planning of sustainability goals. L. Degrad. Dev. **32**, 4708–4726 (2021). https://doi.org/10.1002/LDR.4072

Intra-network Analysis Based on Comparison Between Graph Theory Approach and Pathwalker

Giovanni Lumia[1], Samuel Cushman[2], Salvatore Praticò[1], and Giuseppe Modica[3](✉)

[1] Dipartimento di Agraria, Università degli studi 'Mediterranea' di Reggio Calabria, Reggio Calabria, Italy
giovanni.lumia@unirc.it

[2] Wildlife Conservation Research Unit, Department of Biology, University of Oxford, The Recanati-Kaplan Centre, Tubney House, Tubney, Oxon OX13 5QL, UK

[3] Dipartimento di Scienze Veterinarie, Università degli studi di Messina, Messina, Italy
giuseppe.modica@unime.it

Abstract. Today there is increasing investigation of how to succeed in land operations without damaging delicate natural ecosystems. Over the past century, the planning of land interventions operated without following a guideline has led to fragmentation of ecosystems and progressive biodiversity loss. Several strategies have emerged in this regard to identify corridors and protected areas on the territory. It is important to compare the very many strategies in the scientific landscape in order to assess the levels of correlation present among them and to understand how to be able to exploit the products of the analyses in our favor in the planning sphere on a territory threatened by pressing anthropization. The present work compared movement simulations produced by Pathwalker software and corridors identified on the territory by Graphab software. In particular, we took advantage of Pathwalker's ability to evaluate movement predictions by taking into account factors such as mortality risk, attraction and energy in the simulation. This work was important because it allowed to classify predictions according to scales of reliability. In particular, we classified the connectivity indices obtained from the elaborations in Graphab according to 4 levels of reliability ranging from a high degree of consistency to a low degree of consistency. Pathwalker simulations were compared to the above indices to assess similarities and differences. This work is important as it allows to give exploit the combination between different connectivity prediction models provide concrete tool to the planner at decision making time.

Keywords: Graph theory · Pathwalker · Comparison · Ecological network

O. Gervasi et al. (Eds.): ICCSA 2023 Workshops, LNCS 14107, pp. 300–309, 2023.
https://doi.org/10.1007/978-3-031-37114-1_20

1 Introduction

Understanding what techniques and approaches should be followed to protect the environment and habitat loss is one of the hottest topics of scholarly debate in the last century [1–4]. The importance of proper planning of land interventions to avoid fragmentation and loss of biodiversity is now well known. Scientists are questioning what strategies should be followed to give the planner a tool. Numerous approaches based on ecological networks according to single-species or multi-species considerations, graph theory for identifying and weighing network elements, circuit theory, and resistance kernels for simulating animal movements on the land are present in the debate [5–8]. A promising and recent new strategy for simulating movement patterns is Pathwalker [9]; it takes into account in the simulation parameters such as energy, mortality risk, attraction and coefficient that allow the evaluation of an animal's tendency to continue along a direction. Through such additions Pathwalker makes it possible to fill some of the gaps that were often created in more common approaches [10]. In this work we decided to combine graph theory and Pathwalker simulations to evaluate the reliability of the predictions. Initially through graph theory we identified patches, nodes, edges and calculated several connectivity indices commonly used in the literature for evaluating network elements. In a second step we divided according to four levels of consistency values of 3 connectivity indices calculated in Graphab environment. Finally, we divided each connectivity index into 4 consistency levels and used pathwalker motion simulations to evaluate the response of each of the 4 levels.

2 Materials and Methods

2.1 Base Data

The work was carried out on the Reggio Calabria metropolitan area (Fig. 1) over an area covering 47,822.63 ha and including 12 municipalities. The area includes historical buildings [11], cultivated and wooded hilly and mountainous areas and includes beaches and part of the Aspromonte National Park (blue dashed in Fig. 1). The data used in the connectivity simulations come from databases produced in the European context of the Copernicus project (https://land.copernicus.eu/ - last access 30/06/2022). In particular, we have jointly used Corine land Cover data as of 2018 (CLC 2018, which has high level of thematic detail for natural and semi-natural areas) and Urban Atlas as of 2018 (UA 2018, which has high level of thematic and geometric detail for man-made areas). Recent work on the same study area has shown that the combined use of these two data allows for more accurate movement pattern simulations [12].

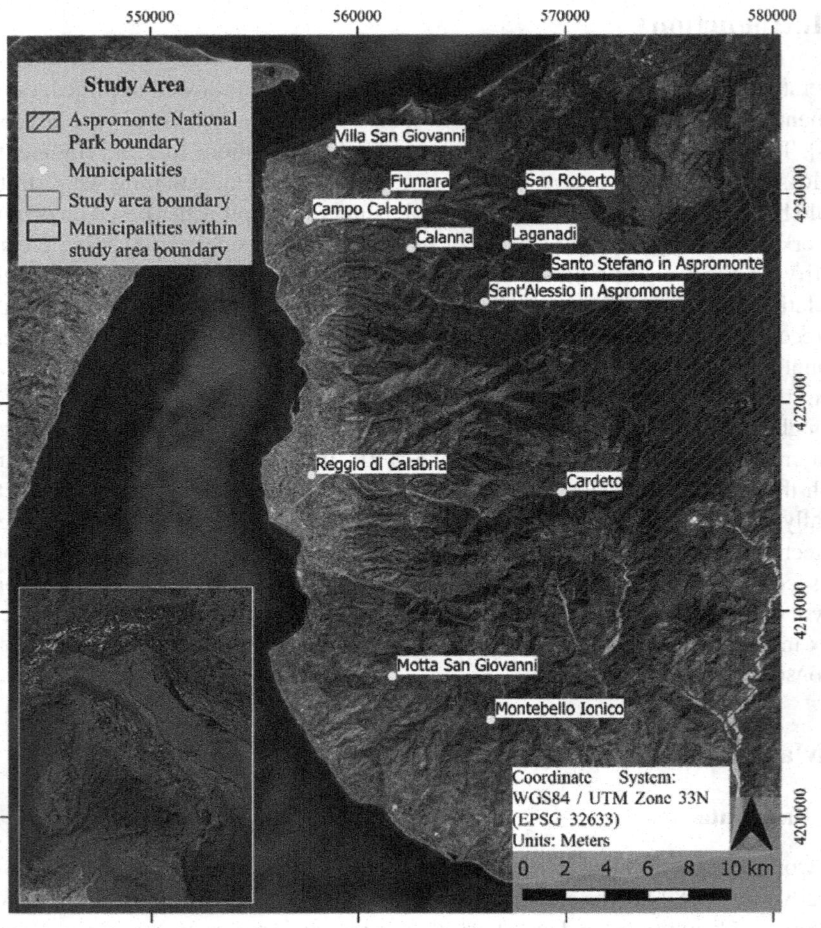

Fig. 1. Geographical location of the study area, in dashed blue the Aspromonte National Park area, in yellow the municipalities within the study area, in red the study area boundary.

The simulations were performed taking into consideration the requirements of 10 selected focal species considering the works in the same area [12–15]. Autoecological information on the species (dispersal distance, home range, habitat suitability) was retrieved from the database on Italic fauna produced by Boitani et al. [16].

2.2 Data Processing

For the first processing done in Graphab, we used the combined map of CLC and UA as the basis on which to perform the simulations. The subsequent considerations that we will list below regarding resistance to movement (understood as the property of the landscape to oppose animal passage with greater or lesser force), home range (understood as the area needed for a species to be able to carry out all primary life functions) and dispersal threshold (understood as the maximum distance an animal can travel to move from one patch to another) were made on the basis of the autecological data collected by Boitani listed in the National Ecological Network (REN) sheets [17].

For each of the different land use codes, we assigned a value indicating the resistance these environments offer to animal movement in the simulation. Specifically, the land use map was rasterized and resistance values were assigned to each pixel corresponding to the respective land use. The raster was initially at a resolution of 2.5×2.5 m later resampled to 10×10 m by a bilinear interpolation function, this operation made it possible to lighten processing without losing information about smaller elements in the map (streets and isolated buildings). The assigned values range from 1 (least resistance to movement) to 100 (greatest resistance to movement). The dispersal threshold was set at 2 km, whereas 2 km is a value that allows each of the 10 focal species to move from patch to patch, as seen in previous work on the same area [12]. The minimum home range extension was set at 2 ha following the same assumption made for dispersal threshold. Patches of area inferior to 2 ha were still considered as suitable areas (stepping stones) for animal movement over the territory [18]. Having set all these parameters within the Graphab software we obtained a graphical visualization of the network, composed of nodes, patches, edges, links, and on it we calculated the Integral Index of Connectivity (IIC) [19], Betweenness Centrality index (BC) [8] and Probability of Connectivity (PC) [20] using the Graphab 2.8 software functions.

At this point, starting from the raster data of land use and, using as source points the graph nodes obtained in the previous elaborations in Graphab [21], we formed the basis for launching the following operations in Pathwalker. In particular Pathwalker allows to simulate movements considering three parameters which are energy (mechanism1), risk (mechanism 2) and attraction (mechanism 3) and four different combinations of them (mechanism 4, 5, 6 and 7). For this work we decided to operate with mechanism 7 which is the combination of all three energy, risk and attraction. In addition, we used a parameter to consider in the simulation the tendency of a moving animal to continue on the same path or to change direction. This parameter ranges from 0 (minimum tendency to change direction) to 1 (maximum tendency to change direction); we set it at 0.25. Operations were produced by setting all of these parmeters within the Pathwalker environment and launched through Anaconda's Powershell Prompt.

We then went on to categorize the values of the connectivity indices calculated in Graphab into four levels of consistency for each of IIC, PC and BC. Subsequently, the level of correlation (using Pearson correlation coefficient) with pathwalker simulations was evaluated for each level using RStudio environment.

3 Results

Here we present results regarding network created by graph theory, obtaining predictions of movement patterns by Pathwalker simulations, and comparing the two methods to identify points of affinity or disagreement.

The network obtained by Graphab consists of 328 nodes that resulted in the same number of patches with an average area of 26 ha. The patches cover 8549.91 ha, and the areas most represented by them are the environments classified as forested areas (76% of the total number of patches). Generally, the largest patches are located in areas far from population centers, hilly and mountainous areas, while the smaller patches with greater distance between each other are near population centers and closer to the coast.

Table 1. Overall connectivity indices calculated on the implemented ecological network. See Lumia et al. [12].

Connectivity Indices	Overall
Integral Index of Connectivity (IIC)	0.032
Probability of Connectivity (PC)	0.033
Betweenness Centrality (BC)	0.25

The connectivity indices analyzed tended to have higher values in mountainous and hilly areas than in flat areas and closer to the coast. The values of the connectivity indices IIC, BC and PC (summarized their overall values in Table 1) were divided into 4 levels raging from lower to higher values (Fig. 2, top right, top center and top left) and correlated with the values and of the Pathwalker simulation (Fig. 2 bottom center).

The correlation values (shown in Fig. 3) showed a negative correlation for thresholds 1, 2 and 3 of BC (BC1, BC2 and BC3), thresholds 1, 2 and 3 of PC (PC1, PC2 and PC3) and threshold 1 of IIC (IIC1). In contrast, a positive correlation was found for threshold 4 of BC (BC4), thresholds 4 of PC (PC4) and thresholds 2, 3 and 4 of IIC (IIC2, IIC3 and IIC4).

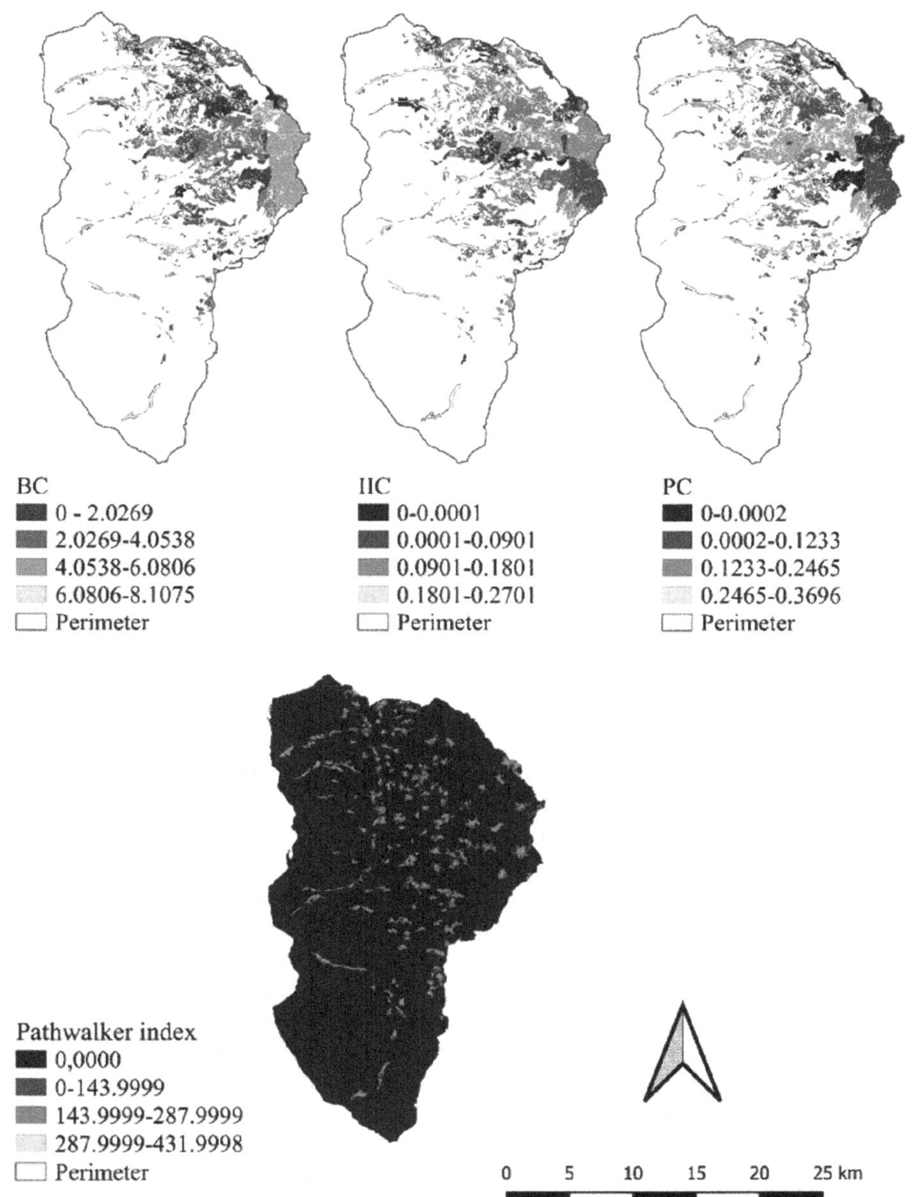

Fig. 2. Pathwalker index (bottom left) and connectivity indices for Betweenness Centrality (top left), Integral Index of Connectivity (top center) and Probability of Connectivity (top right) according to a 4 classes division raging from lower to higher values.

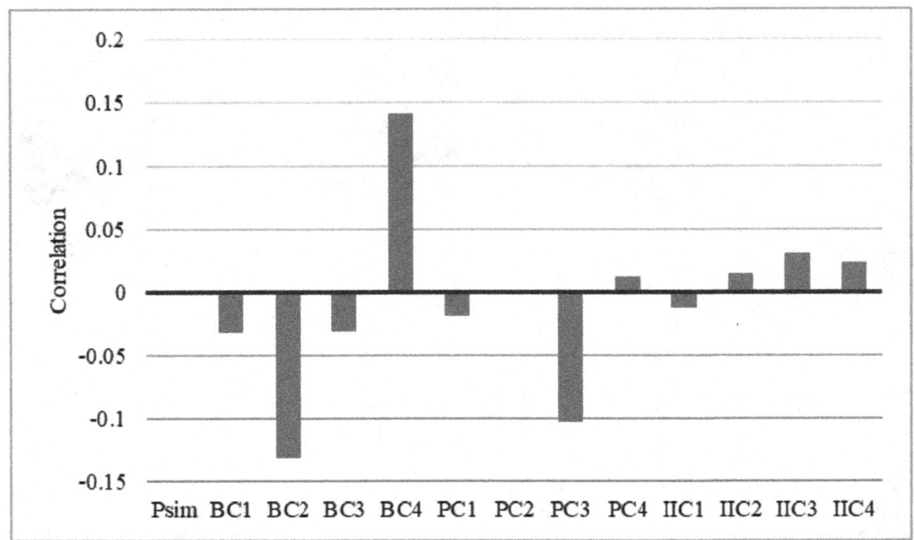

Fig. 3. Correlation values between Pathwalker simulation (Psim) and the 4 thresholds of Betweenness Centrality (BC1, BC2, BC3, BC4), IIC (IIC1, IIC2, IIC3, IIC4) and Probability of Connectivity (PC1, PC2, PC3, PC4).

4 Discussions

A greater number of high area patches in mountainous areas is consistent given the more natural feature of these areas. Indeed, the population centers and areas most occupied by infrastructure and agricultural activities are largely located in the low hill and coastal areas. The trend in the values of the connectivity indices IIC, PC and BC, which were higher near mountainous areas, underscores the greater importance to the network of these areas [12]. Although these results suggest a correct representation of connectivity predictions, correlation analysis with Pathwalker simulations tended to show a negative or slightly positive trend for only a few indices. This was expected. The graphab metrics we used are patch based, and the individual index values refer to the centroids of the patches. In Pathwalker, on the other hand, the movement of the animal is not related to the presence of patches but exploits the mechanism of resistant kernels for simulations. The mechanism of resistant kernels has been shown to be more accurate in predictive terms than the patch-based approach [11–22], this is thus the reason for the general low level of correlation between Graphab and Pathwalker indices. In addition, this phenomenon was expected considering that Graphab does not consider attraction and risk factors. The Pathwalker energy mechanism, understood as the energy budget possessed by an animal that ends its movement when it exhausts it, is the parameter in common with Graphab. The attraction parameter not only evaluates which path is the lowest cost, but also tends to avoid paths where the walker is surrounded by areas of high resistance. The risk parameter, on the other hand, considers the possibility that an animal during a gradually less favorable path will suddenly stop its movement, with a gradually higher probability as the inhospitality of the area increases. The positively trending correlation values for all category 4 levels of the indices underscores the potential in predictive terms of the joint work of the attraction and risk mechanisms. Returning to the B4, PC4 and IIC4 values, the reason why the correlation levels are higher in these areas seems to be related to the presence of large areas with low levels of resistance that do not have a great effect on the risk and attraction mechanisms. A greater effect on the attraction and risk indices occurs instead where patches become smaller and the distances between them increase. In these areas there emerges an underestimation by the IIC, PC and BC indices against the Pathwalker simulations. We next analyze the effect on the simulation (and on the levels of correlation between Graphab and Pathwalker metrics) of using a parameter that indicates the tendency of a walker to continue along its direction or change path. This parameter is intended to make the animal's movement even more faithful to reality. In fact, in nature, animals exploring the territory may not always choose the path that offers the most resources [23]. For this reason, the effect of taking non-ideal paths in highly fragmented areas is more pronounced. The fact that Pathwalker considers this variable as opposed to Graphab further lowers the correlation levels, especially in the level 1, 2 and 3 areas located in the most fragmented areas.

5 Conclusions

In this work, we compared connectivity metrics and motion simulations to identify network weaknesses and, what factors under certain conditions affect the predictions. Specifically, the values of the IIC, BC and PC metrics were divided into 4 levels of consistency, and for each level, the level of correlation with Pathwalker simulations over the same area was analyzed. It was found that Pathwalker's ability to consider factors such as energy, attraction and mortality risk allows it to provide a higher level of detail in predictive terms. Especially the where the natural areas are found to be more fragmented, considering more behavioral factors allows for a more realistic representation of the animal's movements, which is consistent with what is in the literature [10]. The land use resolution used is undoubtedly a limitation that can be overcome in future elaborations. In particular, for the same study area, a habitat map could be used instead of a simple land use map (the implementation of which was planned under the Natura 2000 context: https://www.isprambiente.gov.it/it/servizi/sistema-carta-della-natura - last access 17/05/2023). The use of other statistical analyses could also be considered in the future to highlight other network characteristics [24]. This work has given rise to new insights into the issues of connectivity prediction. We have shown how the reliability of predictions can vary within the same network in dependence on structural factors (of the network), behavioral factors (of the animal species) and the method used (graph theory and Pathwalker).

References

1. Guo, Y., Liu, Y.: Connecting regional landscapes by ecological networks in the Greater Pearl River Delta. Landsc. Ecol. Eng. **13**, 265–278 (2017). https://doi.org/10.1007/S11355-016-0318-2/FIGURES/8

2. Tarabon, S., Godet, C., Coskun, T., Clauzel, C.: Coupling spatial modeling with expert opinion approaches to restore multispecies connectivity of major transportation infrastructure. Landsc. Urban Plan. **221**, 104371 (2022). https://doi.org/10.1016/j.landurbplan.2022.104371
3. Casas, E., et al.: Macroalgae niche modelling: a two-step approach using remote sensing and in situ observations of a native and an invasive Asparagopsis. Biol. Invasions **23**(10), 3215–3230 (2021). https://doi.org/10.1007/s10530-021-02554-z
4. Spatari, G., Lorè, I., Viglianisi, A., Calabrò, F.: Economic feasibility of an integrated program for the enhancement of the Byzantine heritage in the Aspromonte National Park. The Case of Staiti, pp. 313–23 (2022). https://doi.org/10.1007/978-3-031-06825-6_30
5. Kaszta, Ż, Cushman, S.A., Sillero-Zubiri, C., Wolff, E., Marino, J.: Where buffalo and cattle meet: modelling interspecific contact risk using cumulative resistant kernels. Ecography **41**, 1616–1626 (2018). https://doi.org/10.1111/ecog.03039
6. Wang, G., Cushman, S.A., Wan, H.Y., Liu, M., Jombach, S.: Comparison of least-cost path and UNICOR cumulative resistant kernel analyses in mapping ecological connectivity networks in Luohe Region, China. J. Digit. Landsc. Archit., 176–90 (2022). https://doi.org/10.14627/537724018
7. An, Y., Liu, S., Sun, Y., Shi, F., Beazley, R.: Construction and optimization of an ecological network based on morphological spatial pattern analysis and circuit theory. Landsc. Ecol. **36**, 2059–2076 (2021). https://doi.org/10.1007/S10980-020-01027-3/FIGURES/8
8. Foltête, J.-C., Clauzel, C., Vuidel, G., Tournant, P.: Integrating graph-based connectivity metrics into species distribution models. Landsc. Ecol. **27**, 557–69 (2012)
9. Unnithan Kumar, S., Kaszta, Ż., Cushman, S.: Pathwalker: user guide. n.d
10. Unnithan Kumar, S., Cushman, S.A.: Connectivity modelling in conservation science: a comparative evaluation. Sci. Rep. **12**, 16680 (2022). https://doi.org/10.1038/s41598-022-20370-w
11. Calabrò, F., Iannone, L., Pellicanò, R.: The historical and environmental heritage for the attractiveness of cities. the case of the Umbertine forts of Pentimele in Reggio Calabria, Italy. In: Bevilacqua, C., Calabrò, F., Della Spina, L. (eds.) NMP 2020. SIST, vol. 178, pp. 1990–2004. Springer, Cham (2021). https://doi.org/10.1007/978-3-030-48279-4_188
12. Lumia, G., Praticò, S., Di Fazio, S., Cushman, S., Modica, G.: Combined use of urban Atlas and Corine land cover datasets for the implementation of an ecological network using graph theory within a multi-species approach. Ecol. Indic. **148**, 110150 (2023). https://doi.org/10.1016/j.ecolind.2023.110150
13. Modica, G., Praticò, S., Laudari, L., Ledda, A., Di Fazio, S., De Montis, A.: Implementation of multispecies ecological networks at the regional scale: analysis and multi-temporal assessment. J. Environ. Manag. **289** (2021). https://doi.org/10.1016/j.jenvman.2021.112494
14. Lumia, G., Modica, G., Praticò, S., Cusman, S.: Comparison of patch-based and synoptic connectivity algorithms with graph theory metrics (2023). Under review
15. Lumia, G., Modica, G., Unnithan-Kumar, S., Cushman, S.: Using simulation modeling to demonstrate the performance of graph theory metrics and connectivity algorithms (2023). Under review
16. Boitani, L., Falcucci, A., Maiorano, L., Montemaggiori, A.: Italian ecological network: the role of protected areas in the conservation of vertebrates (2003)
17. Boitani, L., Corsi, F., Falcucci, A., Marzetti, I., Masi, M., Montemaggiori, A., et al.: Rete Ecologica Nazionale. Un approccio alla conservazione dei vertebrati Italiani (2002)
18. Saura, S., Bodin, Ö., Fortin, M.-J.: EDITOR'S CHOICE: stepping stones are crucial for species' long-distance dispersal and range expansion through habitat networks. J. Appl. Ecol. **51**, 171–182 (2014). https://doi.org/10.1111/1365-2664.12179
19. Pascual-Hortal, L., Saura, S.: Comparison and development of new graph-based landscape connectivity indices: towards the priorization of habitat patches and corridors for conservation. Landsc. Ecol. **21**, 959–967 (2006). https://doi.org/10.1007/s10980-006-0013-z

20. Saura, S., Pascual-Hortal, L.: A new habitat availability index to integrate connectivity in landscape conservation planning: comparison with existing indices and application to a case study. Landsc. Urban Plan. **83**, 91–103 (2007). https://doi.org/10.1016/j.landurbplan.2007.03.005
21. Foltête, J.-C., Vuidel, G., Savary, P., Clauzel, C., Sahraoui, Y., Girardet, X., et al.: Graphab: an application for modeling and managing ecological habitat networks. Softw. Impacts **8**, 100065 (2021). https://doi.org/10.1016/j.simpa.2021.100065
22. Cushman, S., Lewis, J., Landguth, E.: Why did the bear cross the road? Comparing the performance of multiple resistance surfaces and connectivity modeling methods. Diversity **6**(4), 844–854 (2014). https://doi.org/10.3390/d6040844
23. McGarigal, K., Stafford, S., Cushman, S.: Multivariate Statistics for Wildlife and Ecology Research. Springer, New York (2000). https://doi.org/10.1007/978-1-4612-1288-1
24. Vizzari, M., Sigura, M.: Urban-rural gradient detection using multivariate spatial analysis and landscape metrics. J. Agric. Eng. **44**, 453–459, Article no. e91 (2013). https://doi.org/10.4081/jae.2013.(s1):e91

MEDALUS Model Evolutions and Prospects Case Study Sicily

Rachele Castro[1,4](✉), Simone Lanucara[1], Vincenzo Piccione[2], Giovanni Pioggia[1], Giuseppe Modica[3], and Maria Alessandra Ragusa[4]

[1] Institute for Biomedical Research and Innovation, CNR-IRIB, Messina, Italy
{rachele.castro,simoneluca.lanucara, giovanni.pioggia}@irib.cnr.it

[2] IRSSAT – Institute for Research, Development and Experimentation on the Environment and the Territory, Biancavilla, Italy

[3] Department of Veterinary Sciences, University of Messina, Messina, Italy

[4] Department of Mathematics and Computer Sciences, University of Catania, Catania, Italy

Abstract. Desertification is defined as land degradation in arid, semi-arid, and dry sub-humid areas resulting from various factors, including climatic variations and human activities. The desertification process in the world affects around 200 countries and 2 billion people. It has become a growing threat in the EU due to prolonged drought periods and increasing aridity. The Mediterranean Desertification and Land Use (MEDALUS) method, identify the environmentally sensitive areas (ESAs) through the application of biophysical and socio – economic indicators and relative index (ESAI). The MEDALUS has some limitations, namely the impossibility of reconducting the ESAI results to a single and comparable value, and the need to recalibrate the indices when moving from a regional scale to a local scale. The Environmentally Sensitive Index Patch (ESPI) has been developed to overcome the aforementioned barriers. The ESPI index assigns numerical values to ESAI results on a scale of 0−100. In the present paper, we discuss an experimental application of the MEDALUS method on a local scale and the outcome of the experimentation of the ESPI calculated at different territorial scales. The study was carried out in the Sicily Region. Preliminary results indicate that the ESPI index can be used at all scales on the ESAI and its four constituent qualities. Also, the authors started a critical review of the thematic layers to be adopted for the basin scales.

Keywords: Applied mathematics · Index Sensitive Desertification · MEDALUS · ESA · Ecology · Geological problems · G.I.S. · Spatial analyses

1 Introduction

Land consumption and fertility loss are global issues with serious impacts on the environment, the economy and society. Around 200 countries and 2 billion people are affected by the desertification process in the world [1–3]. 44.44% of EU Member States suffer from soil degradation; the Mediterranean Region is among the most affected by intrinsic

O. Gervasi et al. (Eds.): ICCSA 2023 Workshops, LNCS 14107, pp. 310–326, 2023.
https://doi.org/10.1007/978-3-031-37114-1_21

predisposing factors [4]. The Italian territory is at high risk of desertification, with the most affected territories located in the regions of Basilicata, Calabria, Puglia, Sardinia, and Sicily [5]. Sicily represents the hotspot region of desertification [6]; it is the Italian Region with the greatest risk of desertification [7–14].

The Environmental Sensitive Areas Index (ESAI) is a popular indicator-based methodology that identifies environmentally sensitive areas (ESAs) prone to desertification [15–21]. In Italy, numerous study groups have analyzed desertification processes on a national and regional scale [8, 11, 22–29], producing desertification maps based on only thirty years of climatic data, from 1961 to 1990. These studies did not analyze the situation before and after this period. Also, Sicily's territory has been studied, since the 2000s, with the Mediterranean Desertification and Land Use (MEDALUS) protocol, also known as the ESAI methodology [15–20]. This work aims to share the results of over 20 years of studies dedicated to desertification processes in Sicily, including prospects and opportunities.

This work is organized as follows: first, we describe the study area and the methodology adopted to understand Sicily's susceptibility to desertification. Then, we share the most important results of the last twenty years of study of desertification processes in Sicily, also a local scale, applying the ESAI and the Environmentally Sensitive Patch Index (ESPI). In particular: a) the results of the analyses of the evolution by means of bi-temporal and tri-temporal analysis on the regional and municipal scale; b) the regional Desertification Risk of three periods: 1931–60; 1961–90; 1991–2015; c) the correlation of Desertification Risk with Climate Quality; d) the limits of the ESAI when moving from a regional to a local scale and the possible actions to overcome them, as well as prospects for the study of desertification process; e) the results of a calculation procedure of ESPI, his extension procedure to the four ESAI's qualities and his potential; (f) the regional Desertification Risk of the three periods ESPI-ESAI e ESPI-CQI for the analysis of the trend of Climate Quality. Finally, we describe the conclusions and share the prospects for the study of desertification processes on a local scale.

2 Materials and Methods

2.1 Study Area

The study area of this work is the insular region of Sicily, which is the largest of the Italian and Mediterranean islands, the seventh in Europe [30]. The climate of Sicily is generally dry Mediterranean, with hot and very long summers, mild and rainy winters, and very changeable intermediate seasons. On the coasts, especially the southwestern and south-eastern ones, the climate is more affected by the African currents which cause torrid summers. During the winter season, in inland areas, temperatures are slightly colder, resulting in a Mediterranean climate but with characteristics like those of the continental climate [31].

2.2 Methodology

The original mapping method, ESAI, is applied for the identification and mapping of ESAs exclusively at the regional scale and with a static climate period in regions at risk, allowing the classification of critical, fragile, potentially affected, and non-affected areas [15–20]. The estimation of the soil's ability to resist degradation processes takes place through the combination of the four indices: Vegetation Quality (VQI), Management Quality (MQI), Soil Quality (SQI), and Climate Quality (CQI) using the following formula:

$$ESAI = \sqrt[4]{(SQI \cdot CQI \cdot VQI \cdot MQI)} \quad (1)$$

ESAI is distinguished in four classes of ESAs (see Table 1):

Table 1. ESAs Classification. [https://esdac.jrc.ec.europa.eu/public_path/shared_folder/projects/DIS4ME/esi_jan_05/method.htm].

Sensitivity class	Subclass	Land description
NON-AFFECTED	N	Areas not threatened.
POTENTIAL	P	Areas threatened under significant climate change, if a particular combination of land use is implemented or where off-site impact will produce severe problems elsewhere.
FRAGILE	F1 F2 F3	Areas in which any changes in the delicate balance of natural and human activities are likely to bring. As an example, the impact of predicted climate change could affect vegetation cover, intensify soil erosion and, finally, shift the level of sensitivity of the area to the "critical" class. A land use change (e.g., a shift towards cereal cultivation on sensitive soils) might produce immediate increase in runoff and soil erosion, and perhaps pesticide and fertilizer pollution down-stream.
CRITICAL	C1 C2 C3	Areas already degraded through past misuse, showing a treat to the environment of the surrounding land (e.g., badly eroded areas subjected to severe runoff and sediment loss).

In previous studies [9, 12–14, 32–41], some authors introduced innovations in the application of the canonical ESAI method, including:

- Regional and municipal studies of trends and evolutions of territorial susceptibility to desertification processes through dynamic temporal analysis: bi-temporal, tri-temporal (first and second half of the century, studies using three thirty years of data). Multi-temporal analysis of ESAs allows: a) to detect changes in land use; b) to identify which factors are more predisposing than others in a specific area or period; c) have an information base for spatial planning and the recovery or restoration of areas [9, 14];
- Desertification Sensitivity maps at the municipal scale [12, 13, 32–37]. They are also useful in the perspective of using results for surveys as a basis for spatial planning and land use management procedures.
- The development of the geospatial database that enables the bi-temporal comparison of municipal territories between two ESAI climate periods. The database contains

the following information on all 390 municipalities in the region: municipal limits, ESAI elaborated for two climate periods, 1931–1960 and 1961–1990 [14].

Also, the ESAI method does not allow comparing with a single numerical value the areas. To overcome this limit, some of the authors have developed the ESPI [12, 38–41]. The ESPI provides an estimate a degree of environmental sensitivity and an easy comparison of different plots of land (country, region, province, municipality, river basin, etc.) and periods with a unique value. The ESPI provides a global sensitivity value to desertification on a scale of 0 to 100 for a given territorial context [38–41]. The formula is [38]:

$$ESPI = \frac{\left(\sum I + \sum F\right) \cdot (min + max)}{8} \tag{2}$$

3 Results

In this work, we share the results of previous investigations on desertification processes in the study area: the evolution over time by means of bi-temporal analysis on regional and municipal scale [9, 12, 14, 33, 38–41], and on Regional Parks areas [32, 34–36] (see Fig. 1, 2), the development of a geospatial database that enable the bi-temporal comparison of municipal territories between two ESAI climate periods [14] (see Fig. 3).

From the tri-temporal comparison (see Fig. 4 a, b, c), it has emerged that the characterization of the risk of desertification in the 390 municipalities of the island has the undisputed merit of having equipped the Sicilian Region with an implementation of the knowledge on the course of the phenomenon. In fact, compared to the 17 contributions published in the bulletin of the Accademia Gioenia [14], which gave the bi-temporal comparison of the trend of the risk of desertification (first half of the last century compared to the second half), with the twenty-two IRSSAT notebooks [37, 42] the time comparison is extended to three periods (1931–60, 1961–90, 1991–2015).

The regional Desertification Risk of the three periods (see Fig. 4 a, b, c) [9, 38–41, 43] shows that:

- the Non-Affected Class recorded an increase of 8% in territories from the first to the second period and a loss of about 3.5% in the comparison between the second and third periods [43];
- the Fragile Class suffers a slight increase - about 2% of territories - in the transition between the first and second period, while it increases by almost 10% in the transition from the second to the third period [43];
- the Critical Class improved by 13.6% of territories between the first and second periods, while the increase between the second and third periods was only 1.5% [43].

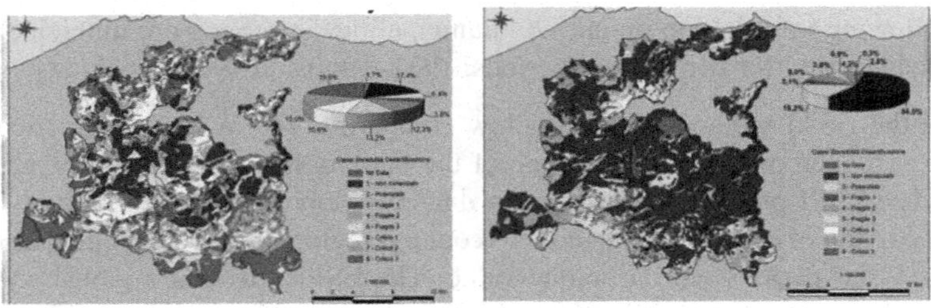

Fig. 1. Result of the comparison between the first and the second half of the century of the ESAs in the territory of the Madonie Regional Park [35]. For the colors of the ESAI classes, see Table 1.

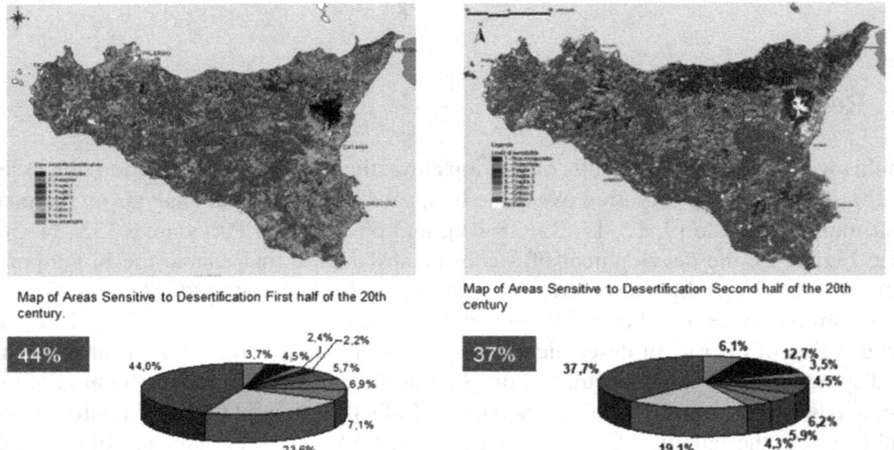

Fig. 2. Sicilian Region ESAs, comparison between first and second half of the 20th century [13].

For the purpose of determining Climate Quality (see Fig. 5 a, b, c) it emerges that [43]:

- High Quality recorded a loss of 6.5% of territories from the first to the second period and a recovery of 4.5% from the second to the third period.
- Average quality is almost constant with a maximum difference between periods of no more than 3% of territories.
- Low Quality shows almost a 9% increase in territories from the first to the second period that are reabsorbed from the second to the third.

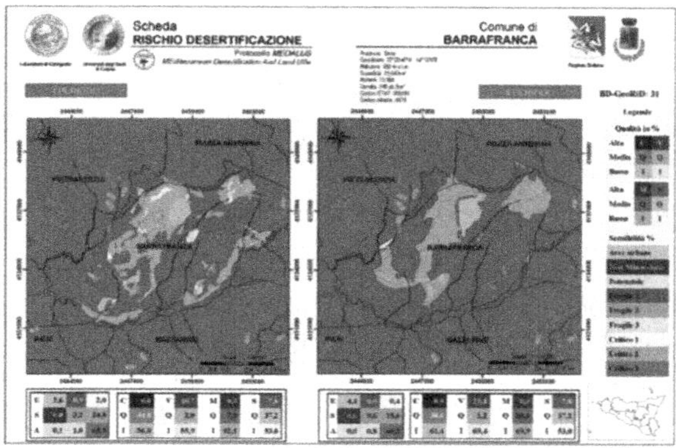

Fig. 3. Example of Georeferenced Database output (Italian language). Project Desertification Risk in Sicily. Bi-temporal characterization of municipal territories in the 9 Sicilian's province [14]. The image shows the comparison between the results of the calculation of the ESA Index on a municipal scale in the first and second half of the twentieth century in the municipality of Barrafranca (EN). The comparison highlights a worsening of the territorial situation. For the colors of the ESAI classes, see Table 1.

The correlation of Desertification Risk with Climate Quality shows that the latter does not seem to have significantly affected the overall trend. The improvement can be attributed to several factors in the second period, such as: reforestation, recovery of degraded environments, establishment of protected areas, reduction of overgrazing, etc. These actions in the second period, compensated for the loss of Climate Quality [43].

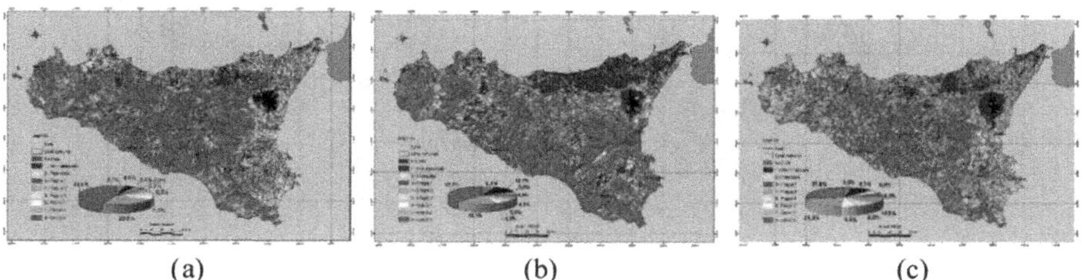

Fig. 4. a, b, c. Tri-temporal ESAI analysis, sensitive areas to desertification period: a) 1931–60, ESAI Critical 3 value 44%; b) 1961–90, ESAI Critical 3 value 37,7%; c) 1991–2015, ESAI Critical 3 value 27,6% [43].

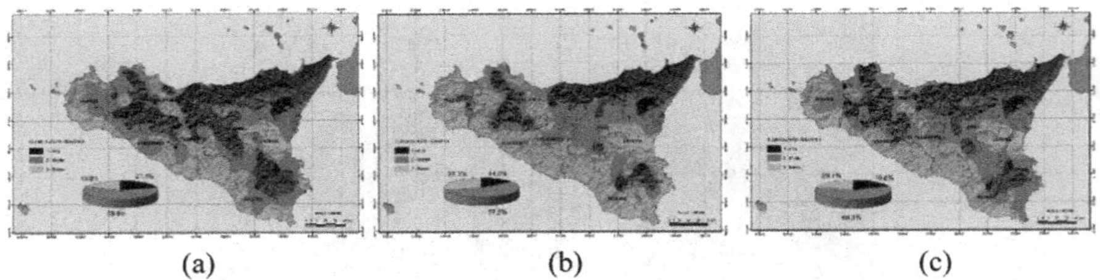

(a) (b) (c)

Fig. 5. a, b, c. Tri-temporal Climatic quality (*sensu* ESAI) relative to the period: a) 1931–1960, CQI high-value 21,1%; b) 1961–1990, CQI high-value 14,6%; c) 1991–2015, CQI high-value19,0% [43].

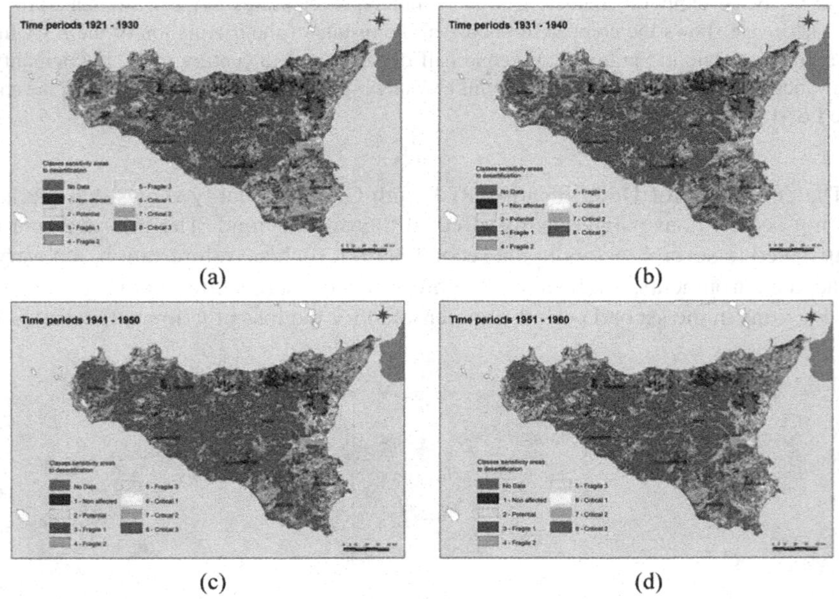

(c) (d)

Fig. 6. a, b, c, d. The validation of the ESPI at the regional scale was obtained by comparing the data and trends with the results of the MEDALUS database developed for the Region of Sicily [12, 13, 38, 43], derived from two scenarios: first half of the 20th century and climate data of four decades 1921–30, 1931–40, 1941–50, 1951–60. The images show the result of querying.

The ESPI was applied, tested, and validated at the municipal scale in districts, provincial, watersheds, and protected areas, comparing the values with the ESAI analysis results (see Fig. 6, 7, 8, 9) [38]. It has also been tested for monitoring the temporal evolution of desertification risk. The ESPI application to the ESAs of the Sicily Region was performed using eight decades of Investigation (1921–2000). By analyzing the annual Desertification Risk of the three periods (see Fig. 10, 11, 12), it is possible to see the substantial difference between the period 1931–1960 and 1961–1990. In the first period, the risk of desertification for all years is in the range of 60–70. In the second period, the risk of desertification fluctuates between 50 and 65 maximum, and in the third, the trend of the previous thirty years is preserved [43].

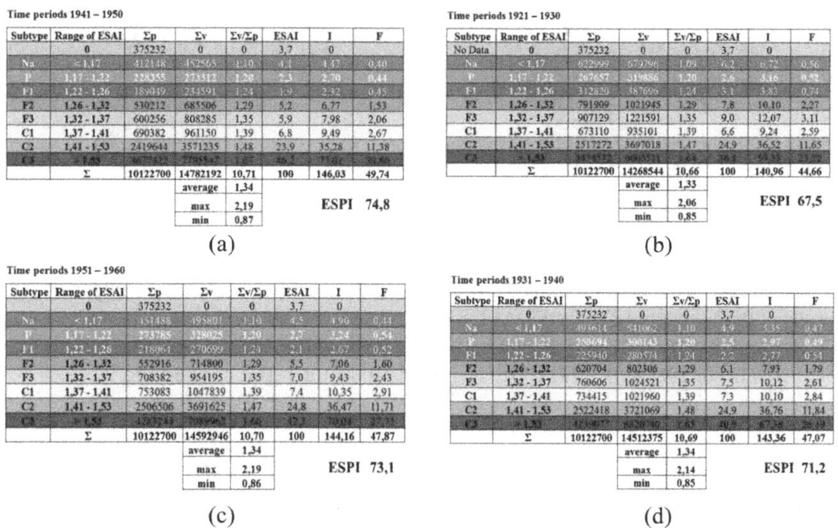

Time periods 1941 – 1950

Subtype	Range of ESAI	Σp	Σv	Σv/Σp	ESAI	I	F
	0	375232	0	0	3,7	0	
Na	< 1,17	412148	452565	1,10	4,1	4,47	0,40
P	1,17 - 1,22	228355	273512	1,20	2,3	2,70	0,44
F1	1,22 - 1,26	189049	234591	1,24	1,9	2,32	0,45
F2	1,26 - 1,32	530212	685506	1,29	5,2	6,77	1,53
F3	1,32 - 1,37	600256	808285	1,35	5,9	7,98	2,06
C1	1,37 - 1,41	690382	961150	1,39	6,8	9,49	2,67
C2	1,41 - 1,53	2419644	3571235	1,48	23,9	35,28	11,38
C3	> 1,53	[illegible]	[illegible]	[illegible]	[illegible]	[illegible]	[illegible]
	Σ	10122700	14782192	10,71	100	146,03	49,74
			average	1,34			
			max	2,19		ESPI	74,8
			min	0,87			

(a)

Time periods 1921 – 1930

Subtype	Range of ESAI	Σp	Σv	Σv/Σp	ESAI	I	F
No Data	0	375232	0	0	3,7	0	
Na	< 1,17	622999	679796	1,09	6,2	6,72	0,56
P	1,17 - 1,22	267657	319886	1,20	2,6	3,16	0,52
F1	1,22 - 1,26	312820	387696	1,24	3,1	3,83	0,74
F2	1,26 - 1,32	791909	1021945	1,29	7,8	10,10	2,27
F3	1,32 - 1,37	907129	1221591	1,35	9,0	12,07	3,11
C1	1,37 - 1,41	673110	935101	1,39	6,6	9,24	2,59
C2	1,41 - 1,53	2517272	3697018	1,47	24,9	36,52	11,65
C3	> 1,53	[illegible]	[illegible]	[illegible]	[illegible]	[illegible]	[illegible]
	Σ	10122700	14268544	10,66	100	140,96	44,66
			average	1,33			
			max	2,06		ESPI	67,5
			min	0,85			

(b)

Time periods 1951 – 1960

Subtype	Range of ESAI	Σp	Σv	Σv/Σp	ESAI	I	F
	0	375232	0	0	3,7	0	
Na	< 1,17	451488	495801	1,10	4,5	4,90	0,44
P	1,17 - 1,22	273785	328025	1,20	2,7	3,24	0,54
F1	1,22 - 1,26	218064	270699	1,24	2,1	2,67	0,52
F2	1,26 - 1,32	552916	714800	1,29	5,5	7,06	1,60
F3	1,32 - 1,37	708382	954195	1,35	7,0	9,43	2,43
C1	1,37 - 1,41	753083	1047839	1,39	7,4	10,35	2,91
C2	1,41 - 1,53	2506506	3691625	1,47	24,8	36,47	11,71
C3	> 1,53	[illegible]	[illegible]	[illegible]	[illegible]	[illegible]	[illegible]
	Σ	10122700	14592946	10,70	100	144,16	47,87
			average	1,34			
			max	2,19		ESPI	73,1
			min	0,86			

(c)

Time periods 1931 – 1940

Subtype	Range of ESAI	Σp	Σv	Σv/Σp	ESAI	I	F
	0	375232	0	0	3,7	0	
Na	< 1,17	493614	541062	1,10	4,9	5,35	0,47
P	1,17 - 1,22	250694	300143	1,20	2,5	2,97	0,49
F1	1,22 - 1,26	225940	280574	1,24	2,2	2,77	0,51
F2	1,26 - 1,32	620704	802306	1,29	6,1	7,93	1,79
F3	1,32 - 1,37	760606	1024521	1,35	7,5	10,12	2,61
C1	1,37 - 1,41	734415	1021960	1,39	7,3	10,10	2,84
C2	1,41 - 1,53	2522418	3721069	1,48	24,9	36,76	11,84
C3	> 1,53	[illegible]	[illegible]	[illegible]	[illegible]	[illegible]	[illegible]
	Σ	10122700	14512375	10,69	100	143,36	47,07
			average	1,34			
			max	2,14		ESPI	71,2
			min	0,85			

(d)

Fig. 7. a, b, c, d. The ESPI procedure in Sicilian ESAs was applied in the first half of the 20th century in the periods 1921–30, 1931–40, 1941–50, 1951–60 [38]. The images show the results of the application of the ESPI on a regional scale.

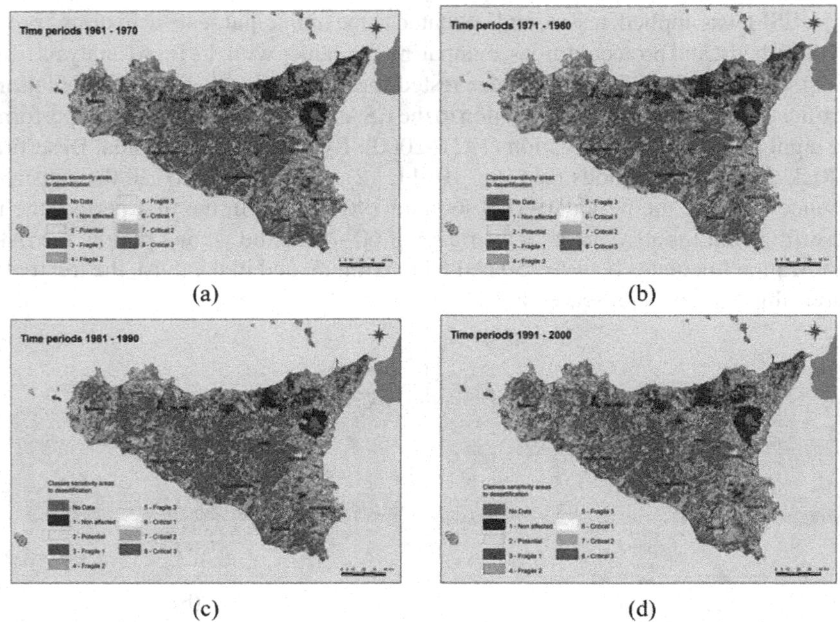

Fig. 8. a, b, c, d. The validation of the ESPI at regional scale was obtained by comparing the data and trends with the results of the MEDALUS database developed for the Region of Sicily [12, 13, 38, 43], derived from two scenarios: first half of the 20th century and climate data of four decades 1961–70, 1971–80, 1981–90, 1991–00. The images show the result of querying.

For the analysis of the trend of Climate Quality (see Fig. 13, 14, 15) emerges [43]:

- in the first period a climatic constant of 60 with ESPI values ranging from 50 to 80;
- in the second, a marked deterioration in the climate from 1961 to 1990, from 60 to 70;
- in the third period, from 1991 to 2015, a condition which seems to be stabilizing, with a range of 60–80 and a single exception in 1996.

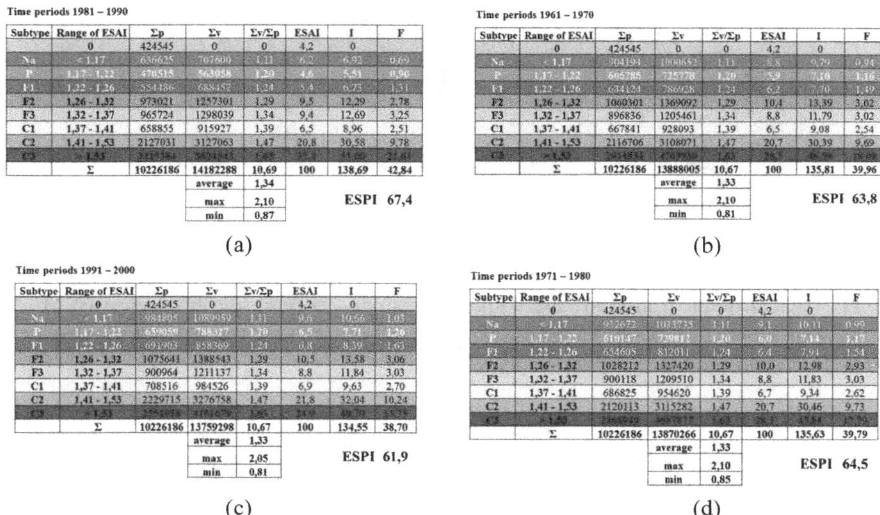

Time periods 1981 – 1990

Subtype	Range of ESAI	Σp	Σv	Σv/Σp	ESAI	I	F
	0	424545	0	0	4,2	0	
Na	< 1,17	636625	707600	1,11	6,2	6,92	0,69
P	1,17 - 1,22	470515	563058	1,20	4,6	5,51	0,90
F1	1,22 - 1,26	554486	688457	1,24	5,4	6,73	1,31
F2	1,26 - 1,32	973021	1257301	1,29	9,5	12,29	2,78
F3	1,32 - 1,37	965724	1298039	1,34	9,4	12,69	3,25
C1	1,37 - 1,41	658855	915927	1,39	6,5	8,96	2,51
C2	1,41 - 1,53	2127031	3127063	1,47	20,8	30,58	9,78
C3	> 1,53	[illegible]	[illegible]	[illegible]	[illegible]	[illegible]	[illegible]
	Σ	10226186	14182288	10,69	100	138,69	42,84
			average	1,34			
			max	2,10			
			min	0,87			

ESPI 67,4

(a)

Time periods 1961 – 1970

Subtype	Range of ESAI	Σp	Σv	Σv/Σp	ESAI	I	F
	0	424545	0	0	4,2	0	
Na	< 1,17	904194	1000652	1,11	8,8	9,79	0,94
P	1,17 - 1,22	606785	725778	1,20	5,9	7,10	1,16
F1	1,22 - 1,26	634124	786928	1,24	6,2	7,70	1,49
F2	1,26 - 1,32	1060301	1369092	1,29	10,4	13,39	3,02
F3	1,32 - 1,37	896836	1205461	1,34	8,8	11,79	3,02
C1	1,37 - 1,41	667841	928093	1,39	6,5	9,08	2,54
C2	1,41 - 1,53	2116706	3108071	1,47	20,7	30,39	9,69
C3	> 1,53	[illegible]	[illegible]	1,63	[illegible]	[illegible]	[illegible]
	Σ	10226186	13888005	10,67	100	135,81	39,96
			average	1,33			
			max	2,10			
			min	0,81			

ESPI 63,8

(b)

Time periods 1991 – 2000

Subtype	Range of ESAI	Σp	Σv	Σv/Σp	ESAI	I	F
	0	424545	0	0	4,2	0	
Na	< 1,17	984805	1089959	1,11	9,6	10,66	1,05
P	1,17 - 1,22	659059	788327	1,20	6,5	7,71	1,26
F1	1,22 - 1,26	691903	858369	1,24	6,8	8,39	1,63
F2	1,26 - 1,32	1075641	1388543	1,29	10,5	13,58	3,06
F3	1,32 - 1,37	900964	1211137	1,34	8,8	11,84	3,03
C1	1,37 - 1,41	708516	984526	1,39	6,9	9,63	2,70
C2	1,41 - 1,53	2229715	3276758	1,47	21,8	32,04	10,24
C3	> 1,53	[illegible]	[illegible]	1,65	[illegible]	[illegible]	[illegible]
	Σ	10226186	13759298	10,67	100	134,55	38,70
			average	1,33			
			max	2,05			
			min	0,81			

ESPI 61,9

(c)

Time periods 1971 – 1980

Subtype	Range of ESAI	Σp	Σv	Σv/Σp	ESAI	I	F
	0	424545	0	0	4,2	0	
Na	< 1,17	932672	1033735	1,11	9,1	10,11	0,99
P	1,17 - 1,22	610147	729812	1,20	6,0	7,14	1,17
F1	1,22 - 1,26	654605	812011	1,24	6,4	7,94	1,54
F2	1,26 - 1,32	1028212	1327420	1,29	10,0	12,98	2,93
F3	1,32 - 1,37	900118	1209510	1,34	8,8	11,83	3,03
C1	1,37 - 1,41	686825	954620	1,39	6,7	9,34	2,62
C2	1,41 - 1,53	2120113	3115282	1,47	20,7	30,46	9,73
C3	> 1,53	[illegible]	[illegible]	1,63	[illegible]	[illegible]	[illegible]
	Σ	10226186	13870266	10,67	100	135,63	39,79
			average	1,33			
			max	2,10			
			min	0,85			

ESPI 64,5

(d)

Fig. 9. a, b, c, d. The ESPI procedure in Sicilian ESAs was applied in the first half of the 20th century in the periods 1961–70, 1971–80, 1981–90, 1991–00 [38]. The images show the results of the application of the ESPI on a regional scale.

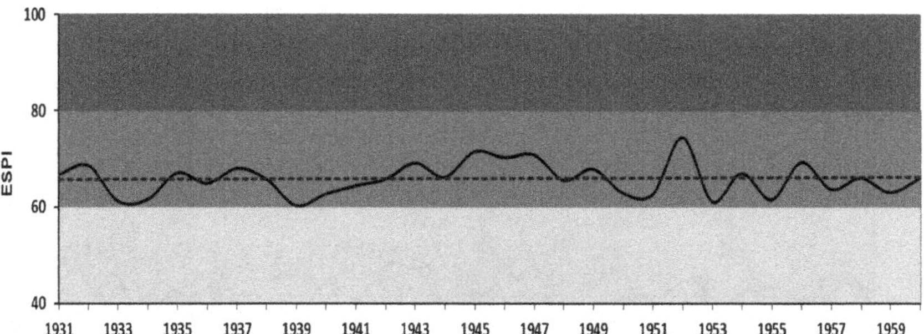

Fig. 10. Annual trend (from 1931 to 1960) of Sensitivity to Desertification sensu ESAI. The abscissa axis shows the time expressed in years. The ordinate axis shows the ESPI ESAI value on a scale from 1 to 100 [43].

4 Conclusions

In areas with a high risk of desertification, such as arid, semi-arid and sub-humid, priority should be given to risk mitigating and enhancing resilient [38]. A first step in planning mitigation actions is the knowledge of the territories, even on a detailed scale. The characterization of desertification risk in the 390 municipal areas of the island has the undisputed merit of having provided the Sicilian Region with an implementation of knowledge on the trend of the phenomenon. However, limitations emerge in the straightforward adoption of the ESAI methodology [12, 33, 37].

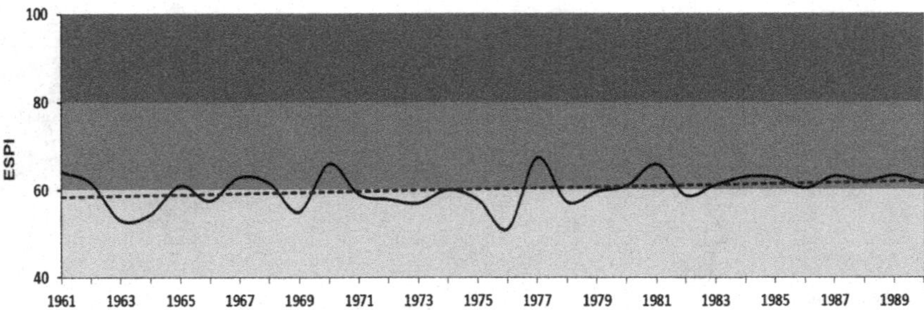

Fig. 11. Annual trend (from 1961 to 1990) of Sensitivity to Desertification sensu ESAI. The abscissa axis shows the time expressed in years. The ordinate axis shows the ESPI ESAI value on a scale from 1 to 100 [43].

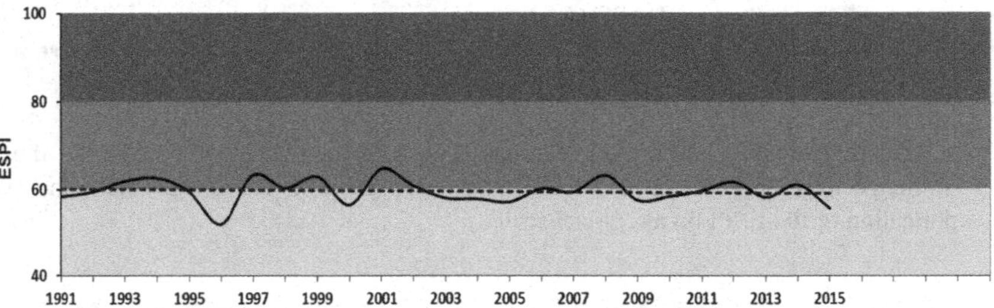

Fig. 12. Annual trend (from 1991 to 2015) of Sensitivity to Desertification sensu ESAI. The abscissa axis shows the time expressed in years. The ordinate axis shows the ESPI ESAI value on a scale from 1 to 100 [43].

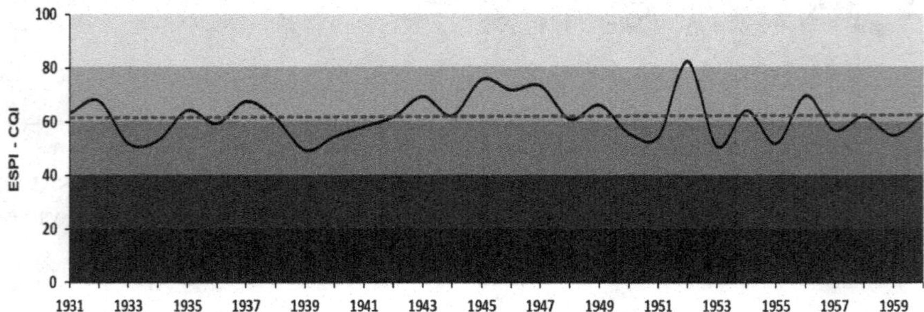

Fig. 13. Annual trend (from 1931 to 1960) of Climatic Quality sensu MEDALUS. The abscissa axis shows the time expressed in years. The ordinate axis shows the ESPI CQI value on a scale from 1 to 100 [43].

The results of the analysis of the new ESPI index tested in Sicily (reference period 1921–2000) are promising for the qualitative and quantitative study of the processes of desertification in space and time. The ESPI applied to ESAI results allows you to produce classifications and comparisons between areas at different scales and periods, and this is advantageous. For example, it can allow stakeholders to control the effectiveness of

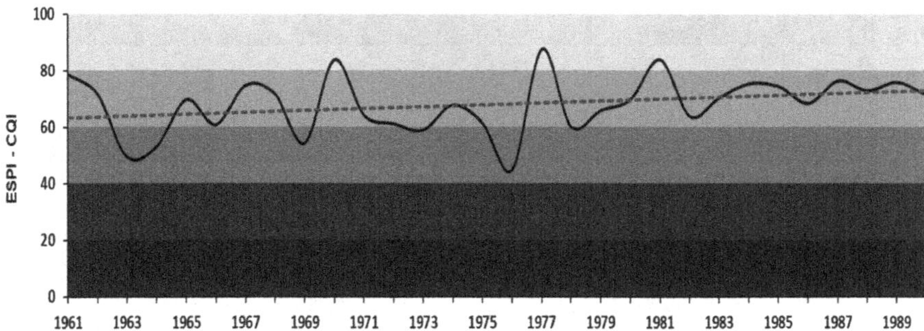

Fig. 14. Annual trend (from 1961 to 1990) of Climatic Quality sensu ESAI. The abscissa axis shows the time expressed in years. The ordinate axis shows the ESPI CQI value on a scale from 1 to 100 [43].

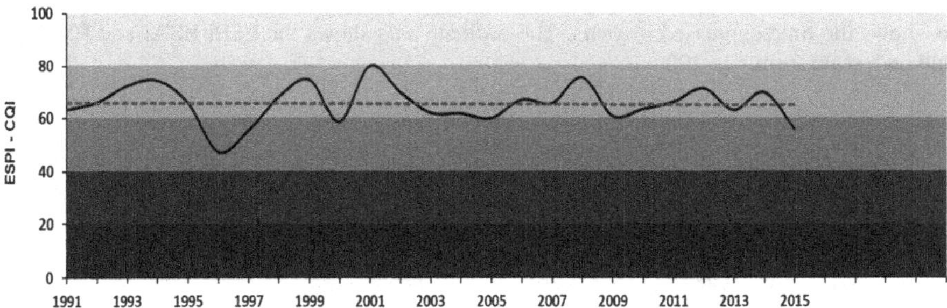

Fig. 15. Annual trend (from 1991 to 2015) of Climatic Quality sensu ESAI. The abscissa axis shows the time expressed in years. The ordinate axis shows the ESPI CQI value on a scale from 1 to 100 [43].

recovery or restoration interventions in a particular territory both from a qualitative and quantitative point of view, with the possibility of developing projections of the evolution of the phenomenon (see Fig. 16, 17, 18). It is very important to monitor the evolution of the risk of desertification in space and time, which is why the ESPI index could be a new environmental standard adopted by public authorities [13, 38].

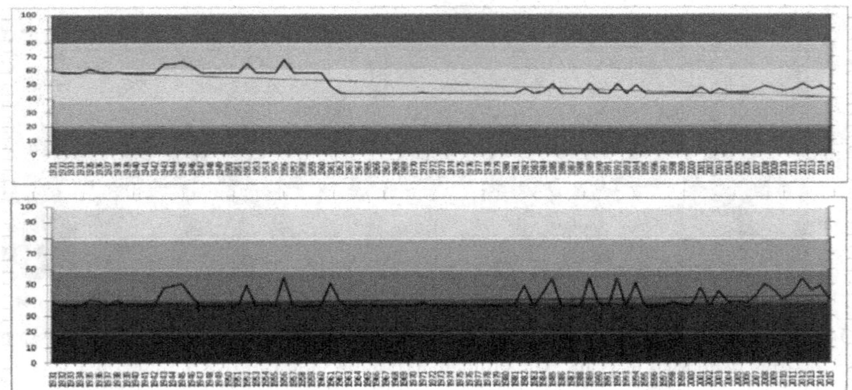

Fig. 16. Annual trend (from 1931 to 2015) Municipality of Sant'Agata di Militello, Messina [42]. The ESPI ESAI and ESPI CQI values indicate a situation of low desertification risk. The abscissa axis shows the time expressed in years. The ordinate axis shows the ESPI ESAI and ESPI CQI value on a scale from 1 to 100.

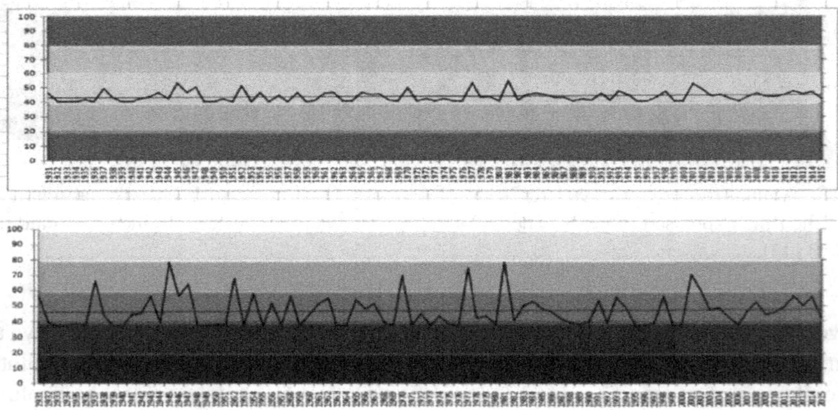

Fig. 17. Annual trend (from 1931 to 2015) Municipality of Castiglione, Catania. The ESPI ESAI and ESPI CQI values indicate potentially stationary situation. The abscissa axis shows the time expressed in years. The ordinate axis shows the ESPI ESAI and ESPI CQI value on a scale from 1 to 100 [42].

ESPI also makes it possible to translate the risk of desertification into opportunities by developing a protocol approach to identify areas irreversibly compromised for soil loss and, therefore, suitable for constructing plants. By doing so, it is possible to valorize those sites which proven the presence of irreversible degradation processes avoiding land take in non-threatened or fragile areas [44].

As part of the investigations carried out, the authors found that some thematic layers of the ESAI methodology need to be revised if we want to study the desertification process at an interregional and local scale. For the study of desertification processes

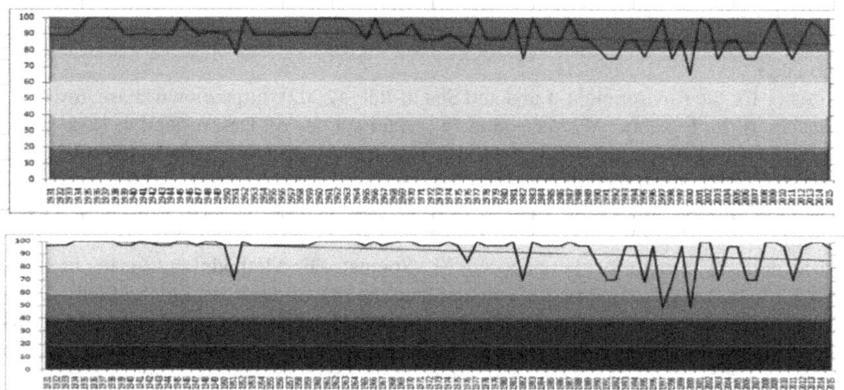

Fig. 18. Annual trend (from 1931 to 2015) Municipality of Portopalo, Siracusa. The ESPI ESAI and ESPI CQI values indicate potentially critical situation. The abscissa axis shows the time expressed in years. The ordinate axis shows the ESPI ESAI and ESPI CQI value on a scale from 1 to 100 [42]. Figures 16, 17 and 18 – ESPI applied on a municipal scale to both ESAI and CQI. Comparison of 3 municipalities with three very different trends [8].

on a local scale, it is necessary [43]: a) to identify new indicators suitable for the local representation scale (1:250,000 - 1:100,000 - 1:50,000) and to establish the relevant criteria, including dedicated guidelines; b) deepening knowledge of the macro indicators that contribute to the characterization of the bioclimatic vulnerability of the territories and the management of the territories also in terms of reducing climate and environmental risks; c) provide the region with detailed classifications of the levels of desertification risk at the municipal administrative level of the extent of the predisposing factors.

Regarding prospects, the authors consider the line of research dedicated to modifying some indices within the MEDALUS procedure to study the territory promising. They also consider integrating machine learning techniques and mathematical models to predict areas at risk of desertification useful for studies. Finally, in the logic of contrasting desertification processes as a participatory process, it is important to evaluate the creation of freely consultable and accessible tools [45–48] that make the research results usable by all the stakeholders [49].

References

1. Ronchi, S., Salata, S., Arcidiacono, A., Piroli, E., Montanarella, L.: Policy instruments for soil protection among the EU member states: a comparative analysis. Land Use Policy **82**, 763–780 (2019)
2. Intergovernmental Panel on Climate Change. Climate Change 2014 Synthesis. In: Summary for Policymakers. IPCC, Geneva (2014)
3. Intergovernmental Panel on Climate Change. Expert Meeting on Communication. https://www.ipcc.ch/site/assets/uploads/2018/08/EMR_COM_full_report.pdf. Accessed 1 July 2016

4. UNCCD: Convention to Combat Desertification. Achieving land degradation neutrality (2017b). https://www.unccd.int/actions/achieving-land-degradation-neutrality. Accessed 16 Feb 2023
5. Ministry for the Environment, Land and Sea of Italy (2007). https://www.mase.gov.it/
6. Cancellieri, F., Piccione, V., Veneziano, V.: Main studies on Desertification Risk in Sicily. Geologia dell'Ambiente, SIGEA, XXV – gennaio-marzo, N. 1/2017, pp. 9–16 (2017). https://www.sigeaweb.it/documenti/gda/gda-1-2017.pdf
7. Arnone, G., et al.: Map of Vulnerability to Desertification in Sicily. Eurografica Palermo (2008)
8. Carnemolla, S., Drago, A., Perciabosco, M., Spinnato, F.: Methodology for the preparation of a 1:250.000 scale map on areas vulnerable to the risk of desertification in Sicily (2001)
9. Duro, A., Piccione, V., Scalia, C., Veneziano, V.: Desertification risk trend in Sicily. Bull. Gioenia Acad. Sc. Nat. **43**(372), 1–13 (2010). https://www.gioenia.unict.it/bollettino/bollettino2010-n372/full_papers/Andamento_del_rischio_desertificazione_in_Sicilia.pdf
10. Ferrara, A., Salvati, L., Sateriano, A., Nolè, A.: Performance evaluation and costs assessment of a key indicator system to monitor desertifcation vulnerability. Ecol. Ind. **23**, 123–129 (2012)
11. Giordano, L., et al.: Identification of areas sensitive to desertification in the Sicilian region, ENEA, Roma (2002)
12. Piccione, V., Veneziano, V., Malacrinó, V.: New aggregate index to calculate and represent the Territorial Incidence of Sensitivity to Desertification (ITSD) in multi-scale according to the MEDALUS protocol. Quad. Bot. Amb. Appl. **19**, 153–160 (2012). https://www.gioenia.unict.it/bollettino/bollettino2012-n374/full_papers/1_Rischio_desertificazione_comuni_provincia_Catania.pdf
13. Piccione, V., Veneziano, V., Malacrinó, V., Campisi, S.: Desertification risk region of Sicily (MEDALUS Protocol). Sensitivity maps and territorial impact on the municipal scale of the ongoing process. Quad. Bot. Amb. Appl. **20**(1), 3–250 (2009). https://www.centroplantapalermo.org/quaderni/20(1)_3-39.pdf
14. Piccione, V., Veneziano, V., Piccione, A.: Georeferenced database project desertification risk in Sicily. Bi-temporal characterization of municipal territories in the Province of Siracusa, Caltanissetta, Enna, Ragusa, Trapani, Agrigento, Catania, Palermo, Messina. Bull. Gioenia Acad. Sc. Nat. **44 e 45**(17) (2011). https://www.gioenia.unict.it/bollettino_anno_2011
15. Kosmas, C., Ferrara, A., Briassouli, H., Imeson, A.: Methodology for mapping Environmentally Sensitive Areas (ESAs) to Desertification. In: Kosmas, C., Kirkby, M., Geeson, N. (eds.) The Medalus Project MEditerranean Desertification and Land USe. Manual on key indicators of desertification and mapping environmentally sensitive areas to desertification, European Union 18882, pp. 31–47 (1999)
16. Kosmas, C., Kirbky, M.: Physically based top-down approaches to sensitive areas. In: Enne, G., Peter, D., Zanolla, C., Zucca, C., Sassari (eds.) The MEDRAP Concerted Action to support the Northern Mediterranean Action Programme to Combat Desertification. Second Workshop on Identification of Sensitive Areas in the northern Mediterranean, Troia, Portugal, pp. 358–374 (2004)
17. Kosmas, C., Kirkby, M., Geeson, N.: The MEDALUS project. Mediterranean Desertification and land use. Manual on key indicators of Desertification and mapping environmentally sensitive areas to desertification. EUR 18882, Bruxelles, Belgium (1999)
18. Kosmas, C., Tsara, M., Moustakas, N., Kosma, D., Yassoglou, N.: Environmentally sensitive areas and indicators of desertification. In: Kepner, W.G., Rubio, J.L., Mouat, D.A., Pedrazzini, F. (eds.) Desertification in the Mediterranean Region. A Security Issue. NATO Security Through Science Series, vol. 3. Springer, Dordrecht (2006). https://doi.org/10.1007/1-4020-3760-0_25

19. Kosmas, C., Tsara, M.: Control of soil crusting. In: Enne, G., Peter, D., Zanolla, C., Zucca, C., Sassari (eds.) The MEDRAP Concerted Action to support the Northern Mediterranean Action Programme to Combat Desertification. First Workshop on Sustainable Management of Soil and Water Resources, Athens, Greece, pp. 88–104 (2004)
20. Kosmas, C.: The desertification issues in the Mediterranean European Countries. According to the DESERTLINKS Project (2004). http://www.kcl.ac.uk/kis/schools/hums/geog/desertlinks/index.htm
21. Bakra, N., Weindorf, D.C., Bahnassy, M.H., El-Badawi, M.M.: Multi-temporal assessment of land sensitivity to desertifcation in a fragile agro-ecosystem: environmental indicators. Ecol. Ind. **15**(1), 271–280 (2012)
22. Barbera, B., Niccoli, R., Piccione, V. (a cura di): Map of Areas Sensitive to Desertification in Calabria. Pubblicazione Calabria. Rubbettino Editore (2005)
23. Calvi, F., et al.: Map of the sensitivity to desertification in Sicily scale 1:250000. Department of Agriculture and Environment, Palermo (2011)
24. Ceccarelli, T., Giordano, F., Luise, A., Perini, L., Salvati, L.: Vulnerability to desertification in Italy: collection, analysis, comparison and verification of mapping procedures and indicators on a national and local scale. APAT, CRA, CNLSD, Manuali e linee guida 40/2006, pp. 1–128 (2006)
25. Ferrara, A., et al.: Map of areas sensitive to desertification in Basilicata. Forest@ **2**(1), 66–73 (2005)
26. Montanarella, L., Baracchini, R., Rusco, E.: Indication of vulnerable areas in Puglia. EUR 19590 IT (2000)
27. Montanarella, L.: Indication of areas vulnerable to desertification in Puglia. In: Documenti del Territorio n. speciale monografico. Il Sistema Informativo Territoriale della Regione Puglia (2001)
28. Motroni, A., Canu, S., Bianco, G., Loj, G.: Map of Areas Sensitive to Desertification (Environmentally Sensitive Areas to Desertification, ESAS) Servizio Agrometeorologico Regionale per La Sardegna, p. 46 (2004)
29. Motroni, A., Canu, S., Bianco, G., Loj, G.: Map of areas sensitive to desertification in Sardinia. N. 16 Fogli in scala 1:100.000, 3 ottobre 2003, Cagliari. Stampa in proprio ERSAT Geoesplora, Roma 27 maggio (2004)
30. Regione Siciliana: Linee guida del piano territoriale paesistico regionale. Assessorato regionale Beni culturali e ambientali e della pubblica istruzione (1996)
31. Drago, A., et al.: Atlante climatologico della Sicilia Seconda edizione. Rivista Italiana di Agrometeorologia **2**, 67–83 (2005)
32. Piccione, V., Castro, R., Duro, A., Piccione, A.: Role of the Regional Natural Park of the Sicani (Sicily) in the mitigation of desertification risk - Bulletin of the Gioenia Academy, vol. 46, no. 376, FP152–FP181 (2013). https://www.gioenia.unict.it/bollettino/bollettino2013/full_papers/Boll_Acc_Gioenia_Sicani_19_02_2014.pdf. ISSN 0393-7143
33. Piccione, V., Veneziano, V., Malacrinò, V., Campisi, S.: Desertification Risk Region of Sicily (MEDALUS Protocol). Maps of sensitivity and territorial incidence at the municipal scale of the process in progress. Quad. Bot. Amb. Appl. **20**(1), 3–250 (2009). https://www.centroplantapalermo.org/quaderni.html
34. Piccione, V., Castro, R., Duro, A., Piccione, A., Rapicavoli, R.V., Veneziano, V.: Role of the Regional Natural Park of Etna (Sicily) in the mitigation of desertification risk - Bulletin of the Gioenia Academy, vol. 46, no. 376, FP62–FP91 (2013). https://www.gioenia.unict.it/bollettino/bollettino2013/full_papers/Boll_Acc_Gioenia_Etna_19_02_2014.pdf. ISSN 0393-7143
35. Piccione, V., Castro, R., Duro, A., Piccione, A.: Role of the Regional Natural Park of the Madonie (Sicily) in the mitigation of desertification risk - Bulletin of the Gioenia Academy, vol. 46, no. 376, FP92–FP121 (2013). https://www.gioenia.unict.it/bollettino/bollettino2013/full_papers/Boll_Acc_Gioenia_Madonie_19_02_2014.pdf. ISSN 0393-7143

36. Piccione, V., Castro, R., Duro, A., Piccione, A.: Role of the Regional Natural Park of the Nebrodi (Sicily) in the mitigation of desertification risk - Bulletin of the Gioenia Academy, vol. 46, no. 376, FP122–FP151 (2013). https://www.gioenia.unict.it/bollettino/bollettino2013/full_papers/Boll_Acc_Gioenia_Nebrodi_19_02_2014.pdf. ISSN 0393–7143
37. Castro, R., Piccione, V., Costa, R., Monforte, P., Seminara, M., Veneziano, V.: DESERTIFICATION IN SICILY. Municipalities of the Province of Agrigento, Caltanissetta, Catania, Enna, Messina versante ionico, Messina versante tirrenico, Palermo est, Palermo ovest, Ragusa, Siracusa, Trapani. 11 notebooks, p. 1880. IRSSAT (2020). http://www.siciliasostenibile.org/collana-desertificazione-sicilia/
38. Duro, A., Piccione, V., Ragusa, M.A., Veneziano, V.: New Environmentally Sensitive Patch Index (ESPI) for MEDALUS protocol. In: AIP Conference Proceedings 1637; (AIP) American Institute of Physics, pp. 305–312 (2014). http://dx.doi.org/10.1063/1.4904593
39. Duro, A., Piccione, V., Ragusa, M.A., Veneziano, V.: The Enviromentally Sensitive Index Patch applied to MEDALUS Climate Quality Index. Additional Information on AIP Conference Proceedings 1738, 480113. su rivista internazionale (AIP) American Institute of Physics, pp. 480113-1–480113-5 (2016). https://dx.doi.org/10.1063/1.4952349
40. Duro, A., Piccione, V., Ragusa, M.A., Rapicavoli, R.V., Veneziano, V.: An index monitoring the sensitivity to desertification: ESPI. In: Seventh Workshop Dynamical Systems Applied to Biology and Natural Sciences, Évora, Portugal, February 2–5, pp. 43–44 (2016)
41. Duro, A., Piccione, V., Ragusa, M.A., Rapicavoli, R.V., Veneziano, V.: Enviromentally Sensitive Patch Index of desertification risk applied to the main habitats of Sicily. In: International Conference of Numerical Analysis and Applied Mathematics (ICNAAM 2016), AIP Conference Proceeding 1863, pp. 510005-1–510005-4. AIP Publishing (2016), 978-0-7354-1538-6/$30.00. https://doi.org/10.1063/1.4992663
42. Castro, R., Piccione, V., Costa, R., Monforte, P., Seminara, M., Veneziano, V.: DESERTIFICATION IN SICILY. Climatic Quality of Municipalities of the Province of Agrigento, Caltanissetta, Catania, Enna, Messina versante ionico, Messina versante tirrenico, Palermo est, Palermo ovest, Ragusa, Siracusa, Trapani. 11 notebooks, p. 1880. IRSSAT (in press, 2023)
43. Castro, R., et al.: Desertification: methodological review of the MEDALUS protocol, Italian Society of Environmental Geology, 4/2021 (2021). https://www.sigeaweb.it/documenti/gda/gda-4-2021.pdf. ISSN 1591-5352
44. Piccione, A.: Proposal for a protocol to identify sites suitable for agriculture by mitigating the risk of desertification. Case study: Sicily. Experimental thesis Master's Degree in Civil Engineering-Structures and Territory. Telematic University "E-Campus" Faculty of Engineering (2023)
45. Von Schoenborn, M.I., Bick, M.: Promises and Challenges Relating to Machine Learning Techniques to Predict Areas at Risk of Desertification: A State-of-the-Art Review. Handbook of Research on Driving Socioeconomic Development with Big Data, pp. 44–75 (2023)
46. Lanucara, S., Praticò, S., Modica, G.: Harmonization and interoperable sharing of multi-temporal geospatial data of rural landscapes. In: Calabrò, F., Della Spina, L., Bevilacqua, C. (eds.) ISHT 2018. SIST, vol. 100, pp. 51–59. Springer, Cham (2019). https://doi.org/10.1007/978-3-319-92099-3_7
47. Lanucara, S., Fugazza, C., Tagliolato, P., Oggioni, A.: Information systems for precision agriculture: monitoring computation of prescription maps. ERCIM NEWS **113**, 24–25 (2018)
48. Lanucara, S., Zilioli, M., Oggioni, A., Carrara, P.: GET-IT, a software suite for easy, interoperable sharing of ecological data in the Long Term Ecological Research Network. In Proceedings of the Conference: EnviroInfo, Luxembourg, pp. 13–15 (2017)
49. Karavitis, C.A., et al.: A desertification risk assessment decision support tool (DRAST). CATENA **187**, 104413 (2020)

Predictive Modelling of Maize Yield Using Sentinel 2 NDVI

Andrea Soccolini and Marco Vizzari(✉)

Department of Agricultural, Food, and Environmental Sciences, University of Perugia, 06121 Perugia, Italy
{andrea.soccolini,marco.vizzari}@unipg.it

Abstract. Accurate yield prediction is essential for precision agriculture as it enables farmers to optimize their inputs and manage their resources more efficiently, ultimately leading to higher profitability and sustainable farming practices. The aim of this research is to verify whether satellite images can be a valid tool for predicting yield in summer maize (*Zea mays* L.). The study was conducted in 2022 in two adjacent fields in Umbria, Italy. The approach adopted is based on the use of NDVI (Normalized Difference Vegetation Index) data from Sentinel 2 (S2) satellites and yield data from combine harvesters to estimate the grain yield of maize. The NDVI data, derived from S2 images acquired at different growth cycle stages, were used for a Principal Component Analysis (PCA). Subsequently, a multiple linear regression (MLR) model was created. The results show a significant correlation between NDVI and grain yield, suggesting that the central stages of the maize phenological cycle are more indicative for this purpose. Further experiments are necessary to confirm the effectiveness of the proposed approach, using more specific vegetation indices or including soil and climate data in the procedure, thus obtaining more comprehensive responses.

Keywords: precision agriculture · yield mapping · NDVI · PCA · multiple regression linear models

1 Introduction

Rational crop management must consider the spatial and temporal variability of the plots, properly modulating the main agronomic practices based on plant and soil needs [1]. Considering this variability, Precision Agriculture (PA) allows for optimizing the distribution of agronomic inputs, reducing costs and environmental impacts, and maximizing crop production. Various technologies are available in PA to ensure timely crop interventions, simplifying their management. These include Global Navigation Satellite Systems (GNSS), Remote Sensing (RS), Variable Rate Technologies (VRT), and yield mapping, which integrate perfectly with Geographic Information Systems (GIS) and predictive models (see, e.g., [2–4]).

Remote sensing represents a readily employable tool for monitoring vegetation, given the ability of sensors to investigate different regions of the electromagnetic spectrum; the most important ones are the red and green bands in the visible region, the red edge,

O. Gervasi et al. (Eds.): ICCSA 2023 Workshops, LNCS 14107, pp. 327–338, 2023.
https://doi.org/10.1007/978-3-031-37114-1_22

and those in the near and mid-infrared. Through algebraic formulas, these bands can be combined to obtain numerous vegetation indices (VI), capable of providing information on vegetation status (see, e.g., [5–8]). Among these, the Normalized Difference Vegetation Index (NDVI) has found the widest diffusion for its simplicity of calculation and interpretation. It represents the normalized difference between red (RED) and near-infrared (NIR) reflectances and has a range of variation between -1 and 1, although in vegetated areas, it is between 0 and 1 [9]. The capacity of this index to estimate some vegetation properties, such as LAI, biomass, and chlorophyll concentration, is widely demonstrated (see, e.g., [10–13]).

The Sentinel-2 satellites (S2) are equipped with a multispectral instrument (MSI) that generates images featuring a spectral resolution of 13 bands, spatial resolutions ranging from 10 to 60 m, a radiometric resolution of 12 bits, and an average temporal resolution of 5 days. They represent a valuable support tool for precision agriculture (see, e.g., [14–17]). The RED (B4) and NIR (B8) S2 bands, used to calculate the NDVI, have a spatial resolution of 10 m.

Yield mapping in PA is carried out by installing GNSS and yield monitoring systems on harvesters. In this way, each yield map can associate the georeferenced grain quantities collected with rectangular areas of different widths. The harvesting surface is expressed as the product of the effective working width of the harvester and the speed of advancement (distance traveled by the harvester/time interval) and is instantly compared to the mass flow of the grain to determine yield [18, 19]. The reliability of a yield map is significantly influenced by the calibration of the numerous sensors mounted on the harvester. Although these operations are sometimes complex and a source of errors [20], the method is effective in providing information on productive variability within plots.

Crop yield prediction is a highly investigated topic, achievable through various methods such as direct field observation during the growing season, crop simulation models, remote sensing, or their combinations [21]. This operation carried out before the end of the growing season, can allow for corrective interventions on crops, improving final yield. However, yield is influenced by multiple crop-specific parameters, climatic conditions, and management choices that complicate the creation of an effective model [22].

Maize is one of the most important cereal crops in the world, providing food, feed, and fuel for millions of people. Accurately forecasting maize yields is, therefore, critical for ensuring food security and economic stability. Remote sensing has been shown to be an effective tool for predicting maize yields, as it allows for the collection of data on various crop parameters, such as plant height, leaf area index, and chlorophyll content [23–25].

In this context, this study aimed to demonstrate the effectiveness of yield prediction in summer corn of a linear model based on the use of Sentinel-2 images.

2 Materials and Methods

2.1 Study Areas

The experimentation was conducted in a single vegetative season (summer 2022) on two adjacent fields belonging to the "Foundation for Agricultural Education in Perugia" (FIA): both plots are located in the Tiber Valley, near Deruta, Umbria, Italy. Field 1 (160 m a.s.l., 42°57′12″ N, 12°22′50″ E) has an area of 21 hectares (Fig. 1, Field 1), while Field 2 (160 m a.s.l., 42°57′08″ N, 12°23′05″ E) has an area of 31 hectares (Fig. 1, Field 2). Both fields are characterized by a texture gradient from east to west, mainly due to the proximity to the Tiber River. The area has a Mediterranean climate, generally alternating between a hot and dry season (May-September) and a cold and rainy season (from October-November to March-April). The experimental crop was summer corn (Zea mays L.) var. P9241, with an FAO maturity class of 300 and a cycle of 95 days, was sown at the end of May. The previous crop was pea (Pisum sativum Asch and Gr.). Both fields were managed using the same cultivation technique, following conservation agriculture principles.

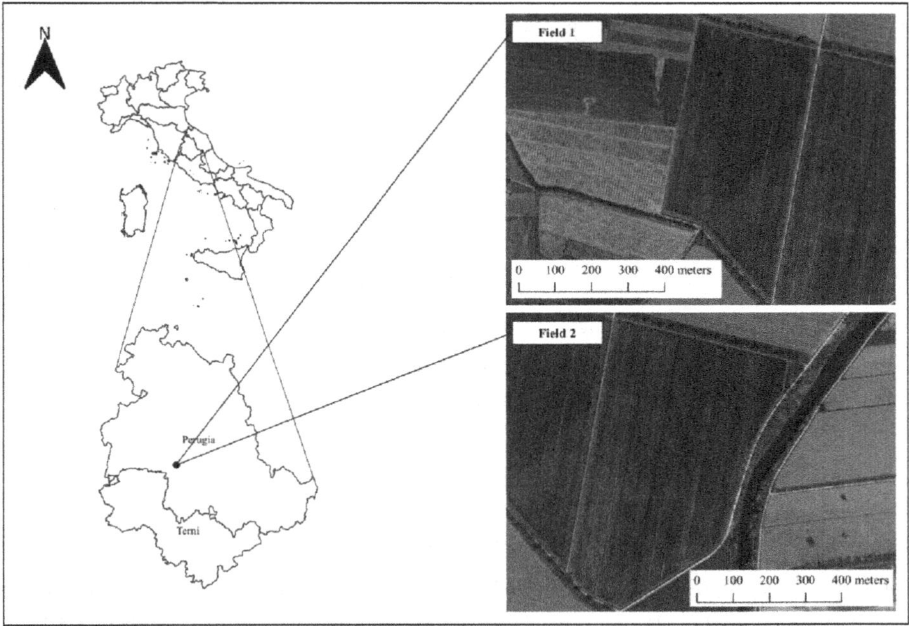

Fig. 1. The geographical location of the study areas.

2.2 NDVI Data

For both plots, 13 Sentinel-2 level 2A images were acquired throughout the entire maize phenological cycle, with a temporal distance between two consecutive images ranging from a minimum of 7 to a maximum of 20 days. The images were downloaded from the Sentinel EO Browser [26]. Using QGIS software version 3.10 64-bit [27], NDVI was calculated from bands 4 and 8 using the "Raster Calculator" tool. For each of the 13 dates, the mean NDVI value for each plot was also calculated within QGIS using the "Statistic for Polygons" tool. A field survey was conducted for each satellite date to observe the crop phenological stage (Table 1).

Table 1. List of 13 images from Sentinel-2 (S2), associated with the relative phenological phase of the corn and the average NDVI value for the two experimental fields (F1 and F2). The days after sowing (DAS) are also reported.

DAS	Date	Phenological phase	F1	F2
0	26 May 2022	Sowing	0.15	0.15
7	02 June 2022	Germination	0.09	0.08
17	12 June 2022	Emergence (VE)	0.12	0.10
24	19 June 2022	4th leaf (V4)	0.13	0.10
32	27 June 2022	6th leaf (V6)	0.31	0.23
39	04 July 2022	9th leaf (V9)	0.44	0.36
54	17 July 2022	Tasseling (Vt)	0.66	0.64
64	27 July 2022	Silking (R1)	0.79	0.77
72	06 August 2022	Blister (R2)	0.80	0.78
89	23 August 2022	Milk (R3)	0.74	0.75
109	12 September 2022	Dough (R4)-Dent (R5)	0.59	0.62
119	22 September 2022	Physiological maturity (R6)	0.41	0.46
132	05 October 2022	Physiological maturity (R6)- Commercial maturity	0.30	0.43

2.3 Yield Data Collection and Pre-processing

For both plots, the harvest was conducted between October 6 and 8, 2022, with the crop in an intermediate stage between physiological and commercial maturity. For the harvest, a Claas Lexion 750 combine harvester was used, equipped with a Topcon YieldTrakk system that processes yield and moisture data through an optical sensor that measures the mass flow of the grain and moisture sensors. Initial calibration was performed in the field on the combine harvester to adjust the effective working width and measure the unit weight of the grain, which was used by the system to convert the measured mass flow (l/s) into Mg. The system produced georeferenced maps in ESRI polygon shapefile format. Only for Field 2, during the harvest, a failure to acquire grain mass and moisture data were found for about 3 ha of surface area, which explains the missing polygons in its yield map.

A data cleaning technique was applied according to the following steps: (1) all values outside the general mean ± 2.5 * standard deviation interval were eliminated, considered statistically anomalous values [28]; (2) all yield monitoring points were removed within 20 m from the plot boundaries, to remove border effects and yield detection errors at the end of the plot [29]. The data is reported in Mg/ha.

To produce a more easily interpretable yield map, the output shapefile containing geo-referenced yield data was converted into a raster with a spatial resolution of 10 m. This step was carried out using the "Multilevel b-spline interpolation" algorithm provided in the QGIS software. Finally, a circular smoothing filter with a radius of three was applied to further reduce the irregularities presented by the surface.

2.4 Yield Predictive Modeling

The methodology proposed in this experiment involves developing a yield prediction model using Multiple Linear Regression (MLR), an algorithm that falls within the class of Supervised Machine Learning. It represents an extension of the linear regression model, whose objective is to predict the values a dependent variable assumes based on the knowledge of those observed on several independent variables. Specifically, the independent variables are represented by all the vigor maps, seeking to evaluate the ability of this factor to predict maize production and understand the most suitable phases of the cycle for this purpose. Considering the two plots as a single study area, a regular grid of points consisting of 1021 samples was created, overlapping it with all NDVI and yield maps to extract the values of the corresponding pixels. After constructing a value table, a Principal Component Analysis (PCA) was applied to eliminate multicollinearity between variables. The most significant principal components were selected as predictors in multiple linear regression (MLR) models. The model's goodness of fit was evaluated using the analysis of the significance and the coefficient of determination (R^2). Training and a validation set were created using 80% and 20% of the initial dataset for MLR, respectively. The comparison analysis between the sets and the model was based on the values provided by the root-mean-square error (RMSE) and the relative root-mean-square error (RRMSE). All statistical analysis was performed using the R statistical software (version 4.2.2) [30].

3 Results and Discussion

3.1 NDVI Trends and Phenological Cycle

The evolution of NDVI for the two plots during the maize growth cycle is shown in Fig. 2. For both plots, the NDVI trend is consistent with maize cultivation in temperate latitudes: a rapid increase in July until reaching the peak around 0.8 in early August, followed by a rather rapid decrease from late August to early October. NDVI is very sensitive to color change caused by the appearance of vegetation cover, but during the first phase of the growth cycle, in the days following crop emergence, maize seedlings do not provide any significant optical response, justifying values ≤ 0.3 in May–June [31]. The rapid and significant increase in NDVI in July is directly related to the height and leaf biomass development of maize, reaching a peak around 0.8 in early August, corresponding to the first reproductive stages. Due to the saturation phenomenon, NDVI cannot detect significant differences in vigor during this phase. The progressive decrease of NDVI from late August to early October is consistent with maize maturity, in which the crop, in addition to a chromatic change of leaves, undergoes drying, varying the response in terms of RED and NIR reflectance. The NDVI trend of the field shows an initial growth phase and a slightly faster maturation phase than field 2, however, the average values considered for each crop stage do not show significant differences.

A more detailed analysis can be conducted by considering the graphical evolution of NDVI from crop emergence to harvest (Fig. 3). In both cases, greater development is observed along the southern slope, but field 2 shows a delay in vegetative growth almost throughout its entire surface compared to field 1. Referring to the date prior to harvest, despite the previously highlighted very limited deviation in NDVI, the crop scenario appears very diversified: while field 1 shows low vigor over the entire surface, field 2 shows a vegetative gradient from east to west, probably due to the greater humidity in the air coming from the Tiber River, which slowed down plant senescence.

3.2 Yield Mapping

The raw yield map of the two plots is shown in Fig. 4a, while the continuous yield map, obtained with the procedure described earlier and used for both visual purposes and predictive analysis, is displayed in Fig. 4b. By visually comparing these maps with the NDVI maps, a possible relationship between yield and vegetative vigor during the central phases of the growth cycle is noted, especially in areas with low NDVI values. In addition, the interpolation applied to the yield data generated maps that tend to overestimate minimum values and underestimate maximum ones.

3.3 Yield Forecasting

The strong correlation between NDVI and yield, especially during the growing stages of plant development, made it necessary to apply PCA to remove collinearity between the considered variables. The first principal component (PC) confirmed a close relationship with the central stages of the cycle, while the second PC demonstrated an inverse relationship between vigor and yield during the maturation phases. The first four PCs were included in the multiple linear regression model, resulting in a high correlation (R^2 0.84) and an extremely low P-value due to many considered samples. A subsequent step was the creation of training and validation sets to develop and test the model based on the selected predictors. The MLR on the training set showed an RMSE of 0.602 t/ha and an RRMSE of 7.169% (Fig. 5a), while these values slightly decreased when MLR was applied on the validation set (Fig. 5b) (RMSE 0.577 t/ha; RRMSE 6.843%).

The results confirm the strong relationship between intermediate phenological stages and maize grain production and the reliability of simple multiple linear regression models for yield prediction. However, more advanced predictive models could be developed and tested by integrating the crop's climatic, pedological, and biophysical data into the vigor index [23, 32]. Additionally, NDVI could be compared with responses provided by more specific indices referring to specific growth stages (e.g., [24, 33–35]).

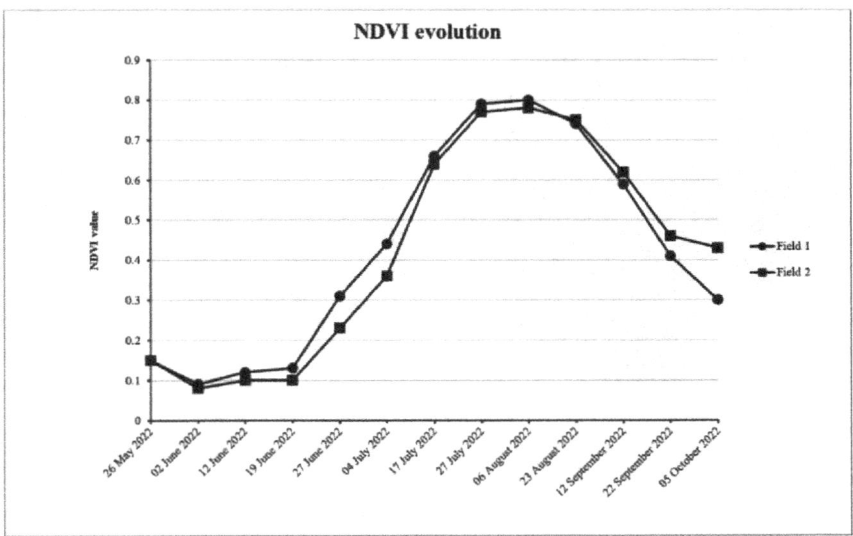

Fig. 2. NDVI's trend of the two experimental fields calculated from Level 2A Sentinel-2 image.

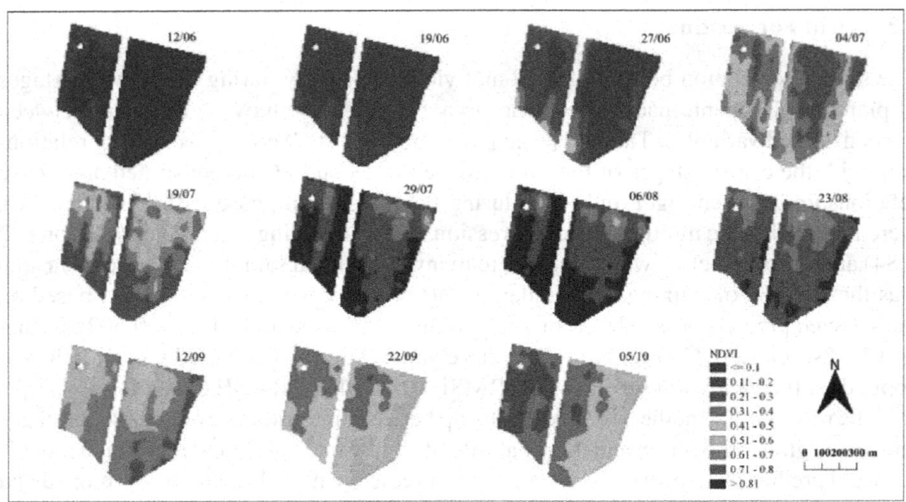

Fig. 3. NDVI's evolution of the two experimental fields, from the crop's emergence to harvest.

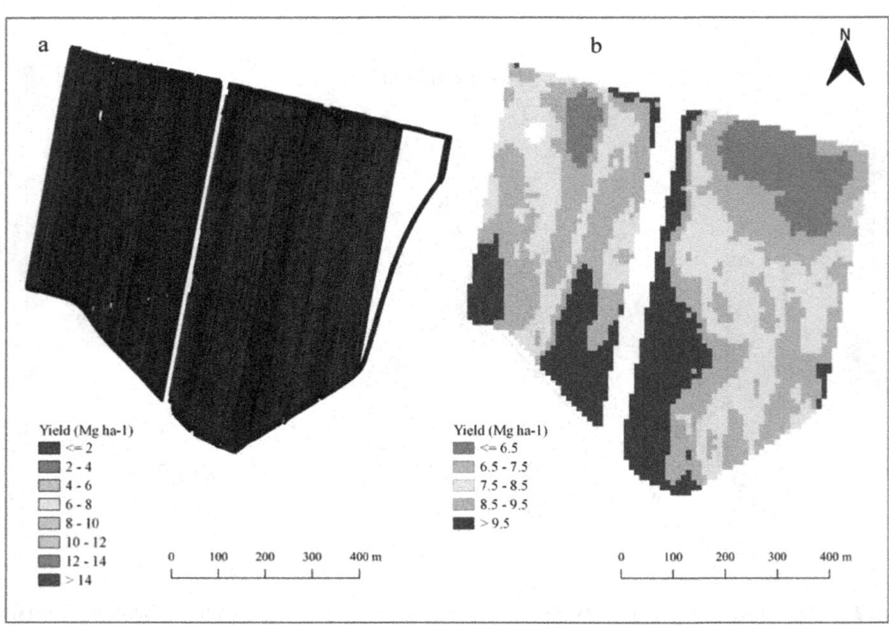

Fig. 4. Yield maps of the two experimental fields, raw (a) and processed data (b).

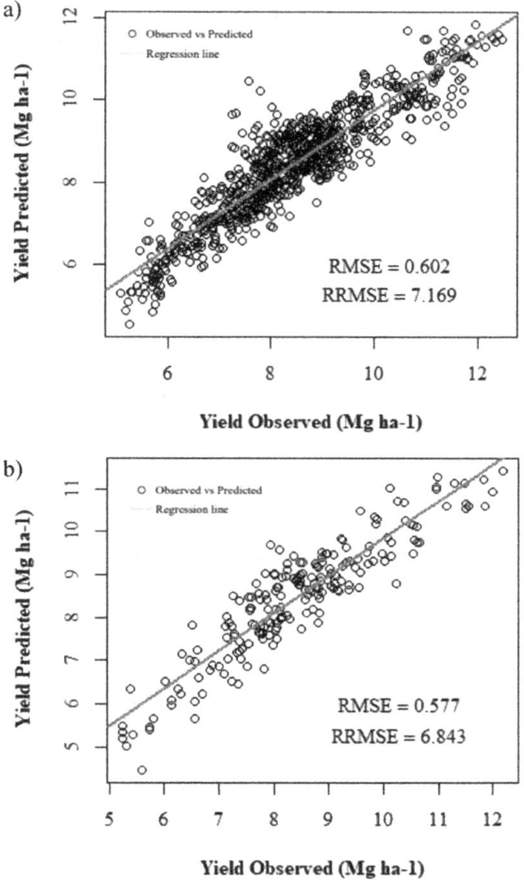

Fig. 5. Comparison graphs between MLR applied on training and validation sets.

4 Conclusions

Our study analyzed the effectiveness of Sentinel 2 images in describing the phenological cycle of maize and their possible use as a predictive model for grain yield. The results confirmed the ability of NDVI to reconstruct the maize growth cycle, showing values consistent with the literature research. Vegetation indices derived from satellite remote sensing can, therefore, successfully identify the spatial variability of plant vigor. However, its causes must necessarily be inferred with a field evaluation. NDVI also proved an effective predictor of maize yield, adapting well to the proposed multiple linear regression model. Specifically, the central phenological stages of maize appeared to be the most representative, in line with bibliographic studies carried out with more complex models for the number and heterogeneity of the variables considered. Further experiments are needed to strengthen the results proposed with this approach, such as including additional parameters in the analysis to obtain more complete responses.

Acknowledgments. The authors wish to thank the farm "Fondazione per l'Istruzione Agraria" (Casalina di Deruta, province of Perugia, Italy) and the farm's Technical Director, Dr. Mauro Brunetti, for its valuable support during all the experimental stages.

References

1. Vecchio, Y., Agnusdei, G.P., Miglietta, P.P., Capitanio, F.: Adoption of precision farming tools: the case of Italian farmers. Int. J. Environ. Res. Public Heal. **17**, 869 (2020). https://doi.org/10.3390/IJERPH17030869
2. Brisco, B., Brown, R.J., Hirose, T., Mc Naim, H., Staenz, K.: Precision agriculture and the role of remote sensing: a review. Can. J. Remote Sens. **24**, 315–327 (2014). https://doi.org/10.1080/07038992.1998.10855254
3. Liaghat, S., Balasundram, S.K.: A review: the role of remote sensing in precision agriculture (2010). http://psasir.upm.edu.my/12390/
4. Yuan, J., Ji, W., Feng, Q., Vrchota, J., Pech, M., Švepešová, I.: Precision agriculture technologies for crop and livestock production in the Czech Republic. Agriculture **12**, 1080 (2022). https://doi.org/10.3390/AGRICULTURE12081080
5. Xue, J., Su, B.: Significant remote sensing vegetation indices: a review of developments and applications. J. Sens. **2017** (2017). https://doi.org/10.1155/2017/1353691
6. Glenn, E.P., Huete, A.R., Nagler, P.L., Nelson, S.G.: Relationship between remotely-sensed vegetation indices, canopy attributes and plant physiological processes: what vegetation indices can and cannot tell us about the landscape. Sensors **8**, 2136–2160 (2008). https://doi.org/10.3390/S8042136
7. Basso, B., Cammarano, D., De Vita, P.: Remotely sensed vegetation indices: theory and applications for crop management. Ital. J. Agrometeorol. **53**, 36–53 (2004)
8. Messina, G., Peña, J.M., Vizzari, M., Modica, G.: A comparison of UAV and satellites multispectral imagery in monitoring onion crop. An application in the 'Cipolla Rossa di Tropea' (Italy). Remote Sens. **12**, 3424 (2020). https://doi.org/10.3390/rs12203424
9. Huang, S., Tang, L., Hupy, J.P., Wang, Y., Shao, G.: A commentary review on the use of normalized difference vegetation index (NDVI) in the era of popular remote sensing. J. For. Res. **32**, 1–6 (2021). https://doi.org/10.1007/S11676-020-01155-1/FIGURES/2
10. Bajocco, S., et al.: On the use of NDVI to estimate LAI in field crops: implementing a conversion equation library. Remote Sens. **14**, 3554 (2022). https://doi.org/10.3390/RS14153554/S1
11. Mihai, H., Florin, S.: Biomass prediction model in maize based on satellite images. AIP Conf. Proc. **1738**, 350009 (2016). https://doi.org/10.1063/1.4952132
12. Gitelson, A.A., Merzlyak, M.N.: Remote sensing of chlorophyll concentration in higher plant leaves. Adv. Sp. Res. **22**, 689–692 (1998). https://doi.org/10.1016/S0273-1177(97)01133-2
13. Benincasa, P., et al.: Reliability of NDVI derived by high resolution satellite and UAV compared to in-field methods for the evaluation of early crop N status and grain yield in wheat. Exp. Agric. **54**, 1–19 (2017). https://doi.org/10.1017/S0014479717000278
14. Segarra, J., Buchaillot, M.L., Araus, J.L., Kefauver, S.C.: Remote sensing for precision agriculture: Sentinel-2 improved features and applications **10**, 641 (2020)
15. Vizzari, M.: PlanetScope, Sentinel-2, and Sentinel-1 data integration for object-based land cover classification in google earth engine. Remote Sens. **14**, 2628 (2022). https://doi.org/10.3390/RS14112628
16. Santaga, F.S., Agnelli, A., Leccese, A., Vizzari, M.: Using Sentinel-2 for simplifying soil sampling and mapping: two case studies in Umbria, Italy. Remote Sens. **13**, 3379 (2021). https://doi.org/10.3390/RS13173379

17. Santaga, F., Benincasa, P., Vizzari, M.: Using Sentinel 2 data to guide nitrogen fertilization in central Italy: comparison between flat, low VRT and high VRT rates application in wheat. In: Gervasi, O., et al. (eds.) ICCSA 2020. LNCS, vol. 12253, pp. 78–89. Springer, Cham (2020). https://doi.org/10.1007/978-3-030-58814-4_6
18. Arslan, S., Colvin, T.S.: Grain yield mapping: yield sensing, yield reconstruction, and errors. Precis. Agric. **3**, 135–154 (2002). https://doi.org/10.1023/A:1013819502827
19. Santaga, F.S., Benincasa, P., Toscano, P., Antognelli, S., Ranieri, E., Vizzari, M.: Simplified and advanced Sentinel-2-based precision nitrogen management of wheat. Agronomy **11**, 1156 (2021). https://doi.org/10.3390/agronomy11061156
20. Colvin, T.S., Arslan, S.: A review of yield reconstruction and sources of errors in yield maps. In: Proceedings of the 5th International Conference on Precision Agriculture, Bloomington, Minnesota, USA, 16–19 July 2000, pp. 1–13 (2000)
21. Basso, B., Cammarano, D., Carfagna, E.: Review of crop yield forecasting methods and early warning systems. In: Proceedings of the First Meeting of the Scientific Advisory Committee of the Global Strategy to Improve Agricultural and Rural Statistics (2013)
22. Paudel, D., et al.: Machine learning for large-scale crop yield forecasting. Agric. Syst. **187** (2021). https://doi.org/10.1016/j.agsy.2020.103016
23. Meng, L., Liu, H., Ustin, S.L., Zhang, X.: Predicting maize yield at the plot scale of different fertilizer systems by multi-source data and machine learning methods. Remote Sens. **13**, 3760 (2021). https://doi.org/10.3390/RS13183760
24. Yang, B., Zhu, W., Rezaei, E.E., Li, J., Sun, Z., Zhang, J.: The optimal phenological phase of maize for yield prediction with high-frequency UAV remote sensing. Remote Sens. **14**, 1559 (2022). https://doi.org/10.3390/RS14071559
25. Bonciarelli, U., et al.: Long-term evaluation of productivity, stability and sustainability for cropping systems in Mediterranean rainfed conditions. Eur. J. Agron. **77**, 146–155 (2016). https://doi.org/10.1016/j.eja.2016.02.006
26. Sentinel Hub EO Browser. https://apps.sentinel-hub.com/eo-browser/?zoom=10&lat=41.9&lng=12.5&themeId=DEFAULT-THEME&toTime=2023-04-12T11%3A42%3A50.129Z. Accessed 12 Apr 2023
27. Quantum GIS Development Team: Quantum GIS Geographic Information System (2020). http://qgis.osgeo.org
28. Vizzari, M., Santaga, F., Benincasa, P.: Sentinel 2-based nitrogen VRT fertilization in wheat: comparison between traditional and simple precision practices. Agronomy **9**, 278 (2019). https://doi.org/10.3390/agronomy9060278
29. Vega, A., Córdoba, M., Castro-Franco, M., Balzarini, M.: Protocol for automating error removal from yield maps. Precis. Agric. **20**(5), 1030–1044 (2019). https://doi.org/10.1007/s11119-018-09632-8
30. R Development Core Team: R: A language and environment for statistical computing. R Foundation for Statistical Computing, Vienna, Austria (2020)
31. Rolle, M., Tamea, S., Claps, P., Ayari, E., Baghdadi, N., Zribi, M.: Analysis of maize sowing periods and cycle phases using Sentinel 1&2 data synergy. Remote Sens. **14**, 3712 (2022). https://doi.org/10.3390/RS14153712/S1
32. Baez-Gonzalez, A.D., et al.: Large-area maize yield forecasting using leaf area index based yield model. Agron. J. **97**, 418–425 (2005). https://doi.org/10.2134/AGRONJ2005.0418
33. Barzin, R., Pathak, R., Lotfi, H., Varco, J., Bora, G.C.: Use of UAS multispectral imagery at different physiological stages for yield prediction and input resource optimization in corn. Remote Sens. **12**, 2392 (2020). https://doi.org/10.3390/RS12152392

34. Croci, M., Impollonia, G., Meroni, M., Amaducci, S.: Dynamic maize yield predictions using machine learning on multi-source data. Remote Sens. **15**, 100 (2023). https://doi.org/10.3390/RS15010100/S1
35. Kayad, A., Sozzi, M., Gatto, S., Marinello, F., Pirotti, F.: Monitoring within-field variability of corn yield using Sentinel-2 and machine learning techniques. Remote Sens. **11**, 2873 (2019). https://doi.org/10.3390/RS11232873

UAV LiDAR Survey for Forest Structure Metrics Estimation in Planning Scenario. A Case Study on a Laricio Pine Forest in the Sila Mountains (Southern Italy)

Giandomenico De Luca[1,2], Salvatore Praticò[2], Gaetano Messina[2], Enrico Borgogno-Mondino[3], and Giuseppe Modica[2,4](✉)

[1] Istituto Per La BioEconomia (IBE), Consiglio Nazionale Delle Ricerche (CNR), Via Madonna del Piano 10, 50145 Sesto Fiorentino, Italy
giandomenico.deluca@unirc.it

[2] Dipartimento Di Agraria, Università Mediterranea Di Reggio Calabria, Località Feo Di Vito, 89122 Reggio Calabria, Italy
{salvatore.pratico,gaetano.messina}@unirc.it

[3] Dipartimento Di Scienze Agrarie Forestali E Alimentari, Università Di Torino, Largo Paolo Braccini 2, 10095 Grugliasco, Italy
enrico.borgogno@unito.it

[4] Dipartimento Di Scienze Veterinarie, Università Degli Studi Di Messina, Viale G. Palatucci S.N, 98168 Messina, Italy
giuseppe.modica@unime.it

Abstract. LiDAR (light detection and ranging) sensors, mounted on UAVs (unmanned aerial vehicles), are a consolidated technology for the remote sensing of the urban and/or natural structural parameters. This study investigates a practical aspect of the advantages of drone UAV LiDAR systems in estimating the main dendrometric parameters in a Calabrian laricio pine forest. In particular, the criteria of hypsometric dendrometry were applied, in which, unlike the classic criteria based on field surveys only, the variable to be determined is the diameter of the individual trees rather than the height. In fact, this last variable is definitely more available for more shafts than the diameter, thanks to LiDAR surveys. Dendrometric variables, such as trees' density, diameter and height, were measured adopting classic field-based methods for all the trees within some survey sample areas (SSAs), and other mean parameters were then obtained (e.g., mean basal area, mean diameter, mean Lorey's height, above ground trees' volume). The same parameters, retrieved by integrating hypsometric dendrometry and LiDAR data, were thus compared, and the degree of correlation/error was calculated. The error degree, obtained by comparing the field-measured diameters with the respective ones predicted using the LiDAR-based hypsometric model ($R^2 = 0.62$; $RMSE =$ 11.30 cm; $Bias = 0.48$ cm), confirmed the reliability of LiDAR systems for their practical application in the professional forestry sector.

Keywords: airborne laser scanning (ALS) · forest management · above-ground biomass (AGB) · dendrometry · remote sensing · drone · image processing

O. Gervasi et al. (Eds.): ICCSA 2023 Workshops, LNCS 14107, pp. 339–349, 2023.
https://doi.org/10.1007/978-3-031-37114-1_23

1 Introduction

1.1 A Subsection Sample

The well-known hypsometric models, adopted in the forestry planning common practice, are based on the principles of diametric dendrometry, as defined by Abramo et al. [1], for which the unknown structural variable to be predicted is constituted by the height of the individual trees. In fact, the forestry volumetric models use two specific dendrometric variables for the estimation of the volume of the above-ground structural parts of the single trees (trunk and great branches): the diameter at breast height (*D*) of the trunk and the tree's height from the ground to the highest point (*H*). During field survey campaigns, both variables are measured for a sample part of individual trees, grouped in sample survey areas (SSAs) to represent the entire forest. Although the simplification, *D* is still easier to retrieve than *H* of all the trees in the SSAs. Consequently, tree heights must be estimated using a hypsometric relationship.

With the introduction of remote sensing (RS) and light detection and ranging (LiDAR) sensors mounted on board an unmanned aerial vehicle (UAV) in forest structure parameters survey [2–8], the height of individual trees became more easily obtainable than *D*. In fact, in a single flight survey, the UAV LiDAR system can detect a very larger amount of the heights.

This reversal perspective has allowed the introduction of hypsometric dendrometry principles [1]. These are based on the inverting of hypsometric models, assuming that the *H* variable can be used as the known independent variable while *D* would be set as the variable to be determined.

Although new airborne laser scanning (ALS) systems have been introduced in the commercial market, reducing their costs, as well as more efficient software has been developed for easier processing of LiDAR data, the professional sector still seems to be wary of their full adoption as support in forestry surveys.

The purpose of the present study was to adopt and evaluate the criteria of hypsometric dendrometry for estimating the main dendrometric parameters, within a *laricio* pine monoplane forest, through the integration and comparison of structural trees variables measured by field and UAV LiDAR surveys. A hypsometric relationship was constructed between LiDAR-based trees' height and field-measured trees' diameters falling in the SSAs. This relationship was subsequently employed to predict the diameter values of all the trees located outside the SSAs in the study area. Integrating these two structural variables, different dendrometric parameters were estimated, including the trees' above-ground volume by applying two different volumetric models, and compared to those retrieved by field surveys only.

2 Study Site

The study area was located on the Sila (Southern Italy) mountain territory (39° 21'N; 16° 54'E), in the valley of Ampollino Lake, between 1250 and 1640 m a.s.l. In particular, the study area occupied 4.60 ha (Fig. 1), characterized by an average slope of 22%, involving a monoplane forest of *laricio* pine (*Pinus nigra* Arn. Spp *laricio* Poiret var. *Calabrica* Delamare), interspersed with small and young sparse groups of beech (*Fagus sylvatica* L.).

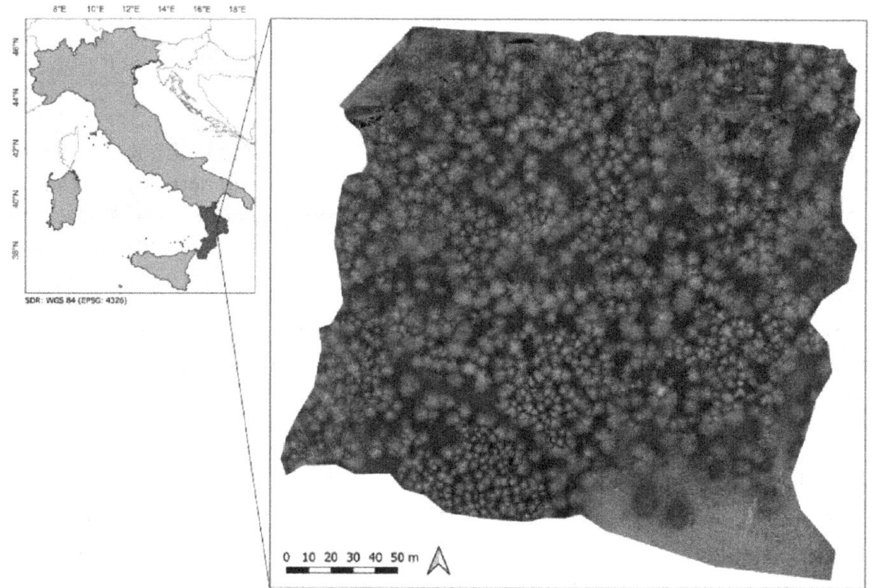

Fig. 1. Study area: location within the national territory (on the left); overview of the study area represented by the RGB orthophoto processed from the images acquired during the UAV survey.

3 Materials and Methods

3.1 Surveys and Datasets

Field Dendrometric Measurements

The dendrometric variables were measured during a site-survey campaign conducted in seven circular SSAs ($r = 10$ m or 20 m), randomly distributed and representative of the entire study site. In each SSA, D was measured for all the alive-standing trees. H was also measured using a Vertex IV hypsometer for the same trees. Only the trees having $D \geq 12.5$ cm were considered for the subsequent analyses.

On the basis of the acquired data, and for each SSA, various dendrometric parameters were calculated, such as the number of plants (N), the total basal area (G; Eq. 1), the average basal area (g; Eq. 2), the mean diameter of mean basal area (d_g; Eq. 3); and the mean Lorey's height (Eq. 4), defined as the mean height of the trees weighted by their basal area (H_{Lorey}):

$$G = \frac{\pi}{4} \cdot \sum_{(i=1)}^{N} D_i^2 \tag{1}$$

$$g = \frac{G}{N} \tag{2}$$

$$d_g = \sqrt{\frac{4 \cdot g}{\pi}} \tag{3}$$

$$\text{H}_{\text{Lorey}} = \frac{\sum_{i=1}^{N} \frac{\pi}{4} \cdot D_i^2 H_i}{\sum_{i=1}^{N} \frac{\pi}{4} \cdot D_i^2} \tag{4}$$

where *i* represents the single generic tree.

The volume of the single trees was estimated by the use of two different volumetric models: the first one is represented by a local single-entry (*D*) volumetric model (V_{PEBSP}; Eq. 5); the second one, was developed by the *Istituto Sperimentale per l'Assestamento Forestale e per l'Alpicoltura* (ISAFA) during the Italian national forest inventory (IFNI) [9] (V_{IFNI}; Eq. 6):

$$\begin{aligned} V_{PEBSP} = {} & 0.000000000122989 \cdot D^6 - 0.000000038608516 \cdot D^5 + 0.000004839988707 \\ & \cdot D^4 - 0.000314196719082 \cdot D^3 + 0.012222419503339 \cdot D^2 - 0.197600010896784 \\ & \cdot D + 1.219706133402030) \end{aligned} \tag{5}$$

$$\begin{aligned} V_{IFNI} = {} & 0.000457023 + 0.0000380346 \cdot D^2 \cdot H - 0.0000423133 \cdot D + 0.00160308 \cdot H \\ & - 0.000112508 \cdot D \cdot H + 0.0000210093 \cdot D^2 + 0.0000132827 \cdot H^2 + 0.00000000337571 \\ & \cdot D^2 \cdot H^2 - 0.000000177836 \cdot D^3 - 0.000000000491192 \cdot D^3 \cdot H^2 \end{aligned} \tag{6}$$

In order to relate the dendrometric parameters of each tree detected within the SSAs to the remotely sensed digital information, all the plants were progressively numbered, and the corresponding geographical coordinates detected by in-field visual inspection, supported by the use of the RGB orthophoto provided by the UAV survey. The semi-thick canopy cover prevented the use of GNSS receivers.

UAV Survey and Pre-processing of LiDAR Data

The drone surveys were performed using the Zenmuse L1 multi-sensor module mounted on a DJI Matrice 300 RTK drone. Specifically, the L1 module is formed by 3 different sensors: i) a Livox LiDAR sensor with a class 1 laser and a field of view (FOV) of 70.4° x 77.2° (horizontal x vertical), 480,000 points emitted per second up to a maximum distance of 450 m; ii) a 1-inch 20 megapixel CMOS sensor RGB camera, synchronized to LiDAR capture; and iii) a high precision inertial measurement unit (IMU) able to constantly monitor the flight parameters (pitch, roll, and yaw). The use of the high-precision GNSS D-RTK mobile station guaranteed the correct georeferencing of the data. In order to obtain the RGB-colored point clouds, the raw data have been processed using the proprietary software DJI Terra because no other alternative software solution is available [10]. The point cloud returned by the survey had an average density of 379 points/m^2.

A fundamental step in the LiDAR data pre-processing workflow is correctly identifying what in the point-clouds represents the ground and what represents the above-ground forest structure [11]. The cloud points were classified using the automatic *point cloud classification* algorithm implemented in eCognition Developer 10.3 software [12] (Fig. 2).

Once classified, the point clouds were used to construct the digital surface -models (DSM) and the digital terrain model (DTM). After having set the *Z* parameter value

Fig. 2. DJI Matrice 300 RTK drone with DJI L1 module mounted (top); At the bottom, the RGB orthophoto (left) and the LiDAR point clouds (right).

(elevation) of each output pixel as the maximum value of the points falling in and the interpolation kernel size equal to 3 for empty pixels filling, the *rasterize point cloud* algorithm was separately applied to the points classified as ground and as above ground objects to retrieve the DTM and the DSM, respectively. The spatial resolution of the final output was 0.1 m × 0.1 m. Finally, the canopy height model (CHM) was calculated by subtracting the DTM from the DSM.

3.2 Hypsometric Model Construction

As a first step, the relationship between field-measured H values (reference) and the respective LiDAR-based tree heights (H_L), directly retrieved from the CHM, was investigated. The coefficient R^2 (Eq. 7), root mean squared error (*RMSE*) (Eq. 8), and the *Bias* (Eq. 9) were calculated as indicators of the degree of correlation and error:

$$R2 = 1 - \sum_{j=1}^{n} \frac{(H_{Li_j} - H_j)^2}{(H_j - \mu_H)^2} \tag{7}$$

$$RMSE = \sqrt{\frac{\sum_{j=1}^{n} (H_{Li_j} - H_j)^2}{n}} \tag{8}$$

$$Bias = \frac{\sum_{i=1}^{n} (H_{Li_j} - H_j)}{n} \tag{9}$$

where H_{Lij} represents the height of tree j measured by LiDAR; Hj represents the field-measured reference height of the tree j; μH represents the average of all the reference heights measured for the comparison; *n* represents the number of trees used in the comparison.

A part (66%) of the individual dendrometric variables (H_L and D) measured within the SSAs were used for the calibration of the hypsometric model (Eq. 10). Inversely from what commonly happens in diametric dendrometry, the variable to be determined (y) is represented by the tree's diameter (D_L), while the known variable (x) is the respective H_L:

$$y(D_L) = a \cdot e^{x \cdot b} \tag{10}$$

Having available both the D_L and the H_L values, these were employed to calculate the dendrometric parameters *G*, *g* and *dg* in each SSAs, and, apply the two volumetric models to estimate the volume of standing trees.

The accuracy of the model was assessed by comparing the remaining part (34%) of field-measured *D* values to the corresponding values predicted with the exponential equation in Eq. 10. The R^2, *RMSE* and *Bias* metrics were used as analytical accuracy descriptors.

3.3 Estimation and Mapping of Dendrometric Parameters on the Entire Study Area

In order to calculate the main dendrometric parameters for each individual pine tree in the entire study area and map their spatial distribution, the hypsometric relationship expressed by Eq. 10 was initially applied to each pixel of the CHM image to obtain the distribution map of D_L (diameter map). In turn, having both the H_L (CHM) and *DL* values in raster format, these were involved in implementing Eqs. 5 and 6 to obtain the respective volume maps. After that, the unique value of the respective dendrometric parameter for the specific canopy, reported on each map described above, was finally obtained by calculating the *majority* zonal statistic for each group of pixels belonging to a single canopy. Subsequently, the fundamental dendrometric parameters *N*, *G*, *g*, d_g and *V* were calculated for all the trees in the study area.

4 Results and Discussions

4.1 Field-Measured Dendrometric Parameters

The dendrometric parameters obtained from the seven SSAs, occupying a compressive area of 4089.20 m^2, are shown in Table 1.

It is noticeable as the mean diameter (d_g) mainly falls into two "diametric classes": around 40 cm (SSAs 1,2 and 4) and around 52 cm (SSAs 3,5 and 7), with the only exception represented by the SSA 6, which is slightly over 56 cm. Consequently, the mean basal area (g) remains constant between 0.12–0.13 m^2 and 0.21–0.25 m^2. The mean Lorey's height (H_{Lorey}) is similar in all SSAs, between 28.2 m and 32.8 m. This was predictable, considering the monoplane structure of the analyzed pine forest. The above-ground structure volume calculated from the two different volumetric models was co-consistent, with the V_{PEBSP} returning slightly lower values (never exceeding 12%).

Table 1. Field-measured dendrometric parameters for each of the seven survey sample areas (SSA), referred both to one hectare (ha) and to the entire study area (4.60 ha).

	r [m]	N [n]	G [m²]	g [m²]	d_g [cm]	H_{Lorey} [m]	V_{PEBSP} [m³]	V_{INFI} [m³]
SSA 1	10	22	2.74	0.12	39.09	30.00	36.87	38.05
SSA 2	10	27	3.48	0.13	40.68	29.80	47.00	48.13
SSA 3	20	45	10.04	0.22	52.93	32.30	137.12	155.31
SSA4	10	24	3.20	0.13	40.68	30.50	45.35	46.95
SSA 5	10	15	3.18	0.21	51.71	28.20	43.52	46.16
SSA 6	10	13	3.23	0.25	56.42	32.80	44.03	48.66
SSA 7	20	53	11.74	0.22	52.93	33.00	161.65	178.42
ha		487	92.09	0.19	49.18	31.70	1255.82	1373.54
TOT study site		2240	423.06				5799.38	6318.28

4.2 LiDAR-Vertex Height Correlation

Figure 3 shows the scatter plot in which the linear relationship between field-measured H values and LiDAR-based H_L is reported. Observing the R^2 value (0.61), the correlation between the two data is relatively good, with a higher degree of linearity observable between 28 m and 38 m (considering H). However, some outliers are visibly present, significantly below 28 m (H), bringing the *RMSE* and *Bias* values to 2.16 m and 1.11 m, respectively.

Neglecting the intrinsic error to which the LiDAR sensor may be subject, the most sensitive error step comprises the estimation phases by interpolating the DTM and DSM. Future studies will aim to optimize this step, trying to understand and reduce the source of the errors.

4.3 Hypsometric Model and Its Validation

Observing Fig. 4, the relationship between H_L and D appears to be exponential. The model allowed the estimation of the diameters D_L of the individual pine trees falling within the entire study area. This was possible thanks to the availability of a datum such as the CHM. A single drone flight mission, in fact, allows the rapid survey of a greater number of tree heights than could be done by field surveys. The SSAs were used to have comparative information between traditional and Lidar-based data, besides a group of data for training and validating the hypsometric model.

The accuracy assessment of the model revealed that the R^2, *RMSE* and *Bias* reached values equal to 0.62, 11.30 cm and 0.48 cm. Considering the preliminary nature of these experiments, a good result aimed at optimizing the process for more substantial future applications. This is further confirmed by comparing the LiDAR-based dendrometric parameters shown in Table 2 with those field-measured presented in Table 1.

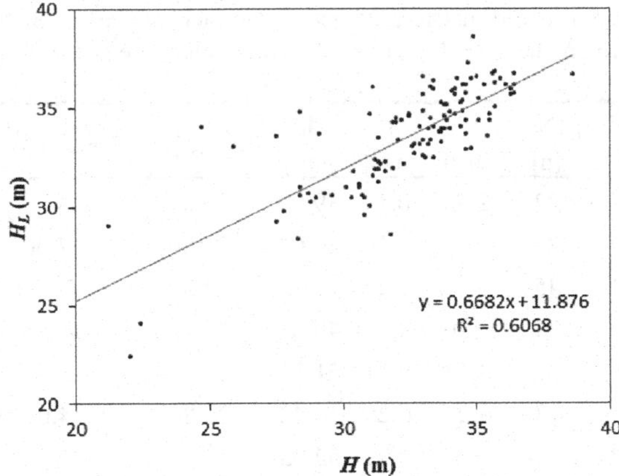

Fig. 3. Scatterplot showing the linear correlation between the field-measured trees height values (H) and the corresponding reference values measured by the LiDAR (H_L).

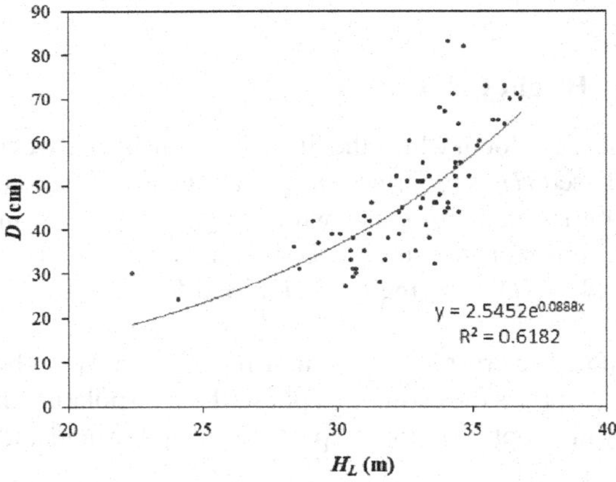

Fig. 4. Ipso-diametric relationship, from which the exponential trend curve (red line) was interpolated between the heights extracted from the CHM obtained from the LiDAR survey and the diameters measured on the ground.

4.4 Estimation and Mapping of Dendrometric Parameters on the Entire Study Area

In Fig. 5, the maps report the spatial distribution of the main dendrometric parameters obtained directly (CHM) or indirectly (diameters and volumes maps) from the LiDAR surveys.

Comparing the dendrometric parameters (Table 3) retrieved starting from the maps mentioned above for the entire study area and comparing them with those of Table 2 calculated for the SSAs, the only noticeable difference is the number of plants: 256 *N*/ha, against the 487 *N*/ha estimated through SSAs. This is due to the heterogeneity of habitats and natural systems that the SSAs-based surveys fail to catch: the density of the trees

Table 2. Dendrometric parameters based on the HL and DL parameters obtained from LiDAR surveys for each of the seven survey sample areas (SSA), referred to as hectare (ha) and for the entire study area (4.60 ha).

	r [m]	N [n]	G [m^2]	g [m^2]	d_g [cm]	H_{Lorey} [m]	V_{PEBSP} [m^3]	V_{INFI} [m^3]
SSA 1	10	22	3.04	0.14	42.22	31.90	35.90	38.97
SSA 2	10	27	4.09	0.15	43.70	32.50	49.23	53.85
SSA 3	20	45	8.64	0.19	49.18	34.10	114.66	131.01
SSA4	10	24	3.58	0.15	43.70	32.30	45.31	49.34
SSA 5	10	15	3.10	0.21	51.70	34.40	35.25	40.42
SSA 6	10	13	3.32	0.26	57.54	35.40	44.30	51.78
SSA 7	20	53	11.77	0.22	52.93	35.00	155.53	180.96
ha		487	91.97	0.19	49.18	34.00	1174.26	1336.03
TOT study site		2240	423.06				5401.60	6145.74

varies unpredictably along the study area. However, the remaining dendrometric parameters remain consistent. Even the volume can be considered proportionally consistent. This demonstrated, on the one hand, the reliability of the method. On the other hand, the problem of the SSAs remains mainly the exact population density estimate.

Table 3. Dendrometric parameters obtained from dendrometric parameter maps (CHM, diameter map and volume maps), referred to hectare (ha) and for the entire study area (4.60 ha).

	N [n]	G [m^2]	g [m^2]	dg [cm]	H_{Lorey} [m]	V_{PEBSP} [m^3]	V_{INFI} [m^3]
ha	256	49.16	0.19	49.18	34.00	672.80	775.03
TOT study site	1176	226.13				3094.90	3565.16

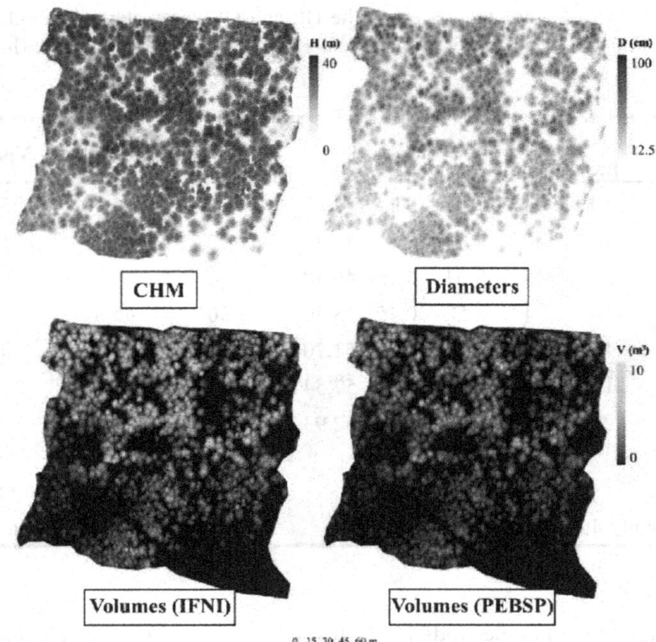

Fig. 5. Maps reporting the spatial distribution of Lidar-based heights (CHM), diameters (diameters map), and volumes (volumes map). The latter is represented by those calculated with the VIFNI and the V_{PEBSP}.

5 Conclusions

The present study showed the reliability of LiDAR for measuring fundamental dendrometric and forest structure parameters in a monoplane conifer forest. The remote measurement of tree heights, on a larger scale and in a short time, allows the reduction of the time-onerous amount of forest field surveys and the increase of detected territory portions. Consider that the increasing availability of open-source, user-friendly applications based on artificial intelligence might significantly help improve the reliability of these processes and practical applications.

A limit to the present approach could be modeling the trees belonging to the secondary vertical forest planes. In future analyses, it will be necessary to evaluate the capability of the DJI L1 module for measuring the heights of those trees in more heterogeneous forest environments.

References

1. Abramo, E., Barilotti, A., Sepic, F.: From a diameter-based to a height-based dendrometry: estimate of tree volume from laser scanning measurements. Forest@ - Rivista di Selvicoltura ed Ecologia Forestale **4**(4), 373–385 (2007). https://doi.org/10.3832/efor0481-0040373

2. Solano, F., Modica, G., Praticò, S., Box, O.F., Piovesan, G.: Unveiling the complex canopy spatial structure of a Mediterranean old-growth beech (Fagus sylvatica L.) forest from UAV observations. Ecol. Indic. **138**, 108807 (2022). https://doi.org/10.1016/j.ecolind.2022.108807
3. Bartholomeus, H., et al.: Evaluating Data Inter-Operability of Multiple UAV–LiDAR Systems for Measuring the 3D Structure of Savanna Woodland. Remote Sensing **14**(23), 5992 (2022). https://doi.org/10.3390/rs14235992
4. Jin, C., Oh, C., Shin, S., Njungwi, N.W., Choi, C.: A comparative study to evaluate accuracy on canopy height and density using UAV, ALS, and fieldwork. Forests **11**(2), 241 (2020). https://doi.org/10.3390/f11020241
5. Cao, L., Liu, H., Fu, X., Zhang, Z., Shen, X., Ruan, H.: Comparison of UAV LiDAR and digital aerial photogrammetry point clouds for estimating forest structural attributes in subtropical planted forests. Forests **10**(2), 145 (2019). https://doi.org/10.3390/f10020145
6. Hu, T., et al.: Development and performance evaluation of a very low-cost UAV-lidar system for forestry applications. Rem. Sens. **13**(1), 77 (2020). https://doi.org/10.3390/rs13010077
7. Wallace, L., Lucieer, A., Watson, C., Turner, D.: Development of a UAV-LiDAR system with application to forest inventory. Rem. Sens. **4**(6), 1519–1543 (2012)
8. Wallace, L., Lucieer, A., Malenovsky, Z., Turner, D., Vopenka, P.: Assessment of forest structure using two UAV techniques: a comparison of airborne laser scanning and structure from motion (SfM) point clouds. Forests **7**(12), 62 (2016). https://doi.org/10.3390/f7030062
9. Abramo, E., Barilotti, A., Sepic, F.: From a diameter-based to a height-based dendrometry: estimate of tree volume from laser scanning measurements. Forest@ - Rivista di Selvicoltura ed Ecologia Forestale **4**(4), 373–385 (2007). https://doi.org/10.3832/efor0481-0040373
10. Štroner, M., Urban, R., Línková, L.: A new method for UAV Lidar precision testing used for the evaluation of an affordable DJI ZENMUSE L1 scanner. Rem. Sens. **13**(23), 4811 (2021). https://doi.org/10.3390/rs13234811
11. Neuville, R., Bates, J.S., Jonard, F.: Estimating forest structure from uav-mounted lidar point cloud using machine learning. Remote Sensing **13**(3), 352 (2021). https://doi.org/10.3390/rs13030352
12. Trimble Germany GmbH. Trimble Documentation eCognition Developer 10.1 User Guide. Trimble Germany GmbH, Munich, Germany (2021)

Palm Tree Dataset Construction with Plant Height Estimation and Plant Counting Tasks

Phisit Srijan and Chantana Chantraporncha(✉)

Faculty of Engineering, Kasetsart University, Bangkok, Thailand
phisit.srij@ku.th, fengcnc@ku.ac.th

Abstract. In this paper, we present the methodology to construct the palm tree dataset from drone images. The two analysis tasks are demonstrated from the derived dataset: Plant height estimation using point cloud processing and tree counting. Open-source software is utilized. WebODM is used to process the drone image data set to construct the orthomosaic image. The 3D point cloud data asset is also derived. We focus on the use of 3D point cloud data and 2D images for further analysis tasks. The data set is located at https://github.com/MambaClaw/Palm-Tree-Height-Estimation-and-Counting-Tasks.git. We demonstrate the use of data sets in two tasks. For plant counting, a 2D image with a template matching can easily be done directly from the orthoimage. For a tree height estimation task, we utilize the 3D dataset. The 3D point clouds of the area are manually selected for each tree, and the tree height in meters is estimated from the measurement tool in WebODM. It is used as a ground truth for the height estimation. On the other hand, Open3D is utilized to remove noises and find the tree bounding box. Linear regression is used to construct the model to estimate the tree height. From the experiments, the accuracy can be up to 97%.

Keywords: Plant height estimation · Plant counting · Drone image processing · WebODM · Open3D · CloudCompare

1 Introduction

In agriculture, a drone is usually utilized for field surveying and data collection. The image data obtained from each flying are used to analyze the plant growth and field yield. After the drone images are collected, they are processed to create orthomosaic photos. The orthomosiac photo stitches all small images obtained from flying in a specified route based on the collected georeference points.

In this paper, we demonstrate the pipeline of drone image analysis with two tasks: tree counting and tree height estimation. The analysis from raw drone images is done using open-source tools. First, we construct the dataset from our field trip, palm trees. The open-source tools are utilized for all the steps. First, the orothomosaic image is created using WebODM [8]. With this software, the other

O. Gervasi et al. (Eds.): ICCSA 2023 Workshops, LNCS 14107, pp. 350–367, 2023.
https://doi.org/10.1007/978-3-031-37114-1_24

related GPS data are extracted. The software can generate 3D point clouds. The point clouds can be exported to be further analyzed. Secondly, the 3D point clouds of trees are cut using CloudCompare [5] while the measurements are performed. The point cloud data are then processed using Open3D [20] to eliminate outlined before using them as training data. At last, OpenCV [4] is used for 2D image processing, i.e., for transforming image channels, binarization, contour finding, etc., for the template matching purpose, for the tree counting task.

2 Backgrounds

WebODM [8]is one of the software for drone image processing. Since it is an open-sourced software, it has a large user community. The processing results include 2D orthophotos and 3D point cloud data created by Structure from Motion (SFM). 2D orthophotos can be used to calculate Normalized Difference Vegetation Index (NVDI) images, and Digital Elevation Model (DEM), contour. 3D point cloud data includes features such as measurement and volume estimation.

An unmanned aerial vehicle (UAV), commonly known as a drone, is an aircraft without any human pilot, crew, or passengers on board. UAVs were originally developed through the twentieth century for military missions too "dull, dirty or dangerous" for humans. A drone using a photogrammetry camera system can assemble a point cloud as one of the outputs from the resulting three-dimensional image. In either case, the resulting cloud is a detailed and accurate picture of the scanned area.

Template Matching is a method for searching and finding the location of a template image in a larger image. OpenCV comes with a function cv.matchTemplate() for this purpose. It simply slides the template image over the input image (as in 2D convolution) and compares the template and patch of the input image under the template image. It returns a grayscale image, where each pixel denotes how much the neighborhood of that pixel match with the template.

Linear regression is a supervised machine learning approach. Linear regression analysis is used to predict the value of a variable based on the value of another variable. The variable to predict is called the dependent variable. The other variable used to predict is called the independent variable. The analysis estimates the coefficients of the linear equation involving one or more independent variables that will predict the best value of the dependent variable. Linear regression tries to fit a straight line or a surface which minimizes the error between predicted and actual output values. The simple linear regression measurement is the "least squares" method to find the best-fit line for a set of paired data: the estimated value of dependent variable from the independent variables. Equation (1) presents the example equation where Y is the estimated of dependent variable, β_0 is Y-intercept, β_1 is the gradient of the line, X is the independent variable, and u is an error term.

$$Y = \beta_0 + \beta_1 X + u \tag{1}$$

From the processed images and 3D point clouds, there is much possible analytics to improve precision agriculture. The simplest ones would be tree height estimation, volume estimation, and plant counting. These are common on many commercial drone image processing platforms [7,15] since they imply the growth and resulting yields in the field.

In this work, we focus on utilizing the drone image data set and constructing analytic services, which help improve future agricultural yields and can be extended to support WebODM extension. The methodology from obtaining the data, preprocessing, and cleaning, and the model construction is described. The dataset can be shared for further studies.

First, we studied the works for drone image analysis. Li et al. proposed a method for estimating crop height for rice based on moving surface and point clouds [11]. The acquired data are from GNSS, IMU, and LiDAR. The data were captured in Jingkou District, Zhenjiang, Jiangsu Province, China. The sampling area was 1m $\times$ 1m divided into 100 grids in a pattern of 10$\times$10 using a soft rope. The moving surface fitting elevation approach is used to classify the ground and crop point clouds.

Sun et al. estimated the plant height from the point clouds from RGB images since RGB camera is low-cost compared to LiDAR[17]. The RGB images were transformed into point clouds using SFM. Then, the point clouds were segmented into the ground layer and plant layer. The ground layers were removed, and the plants were segmented based on orthophotos. The height was computed by inverse distance weighting. Ground height estimation achieves sub-10 cm accuracy.

Valente et al. utilized machine vision and convolutional neural network to do plant counting with high-resolution images[19]. The approach has counted ten weeks old spinach plants in an experimental field with a surface area of 3.2 ha. Validation data of plant counts were available for 1/8 of the surface area. The approach can count plants with an accuracy of 95%

David et al. performed plant detection and counting from high-resolution RGB images [6]. The comparison between deep-learning and handcrafted methods with application to plants: maize, sugar beet, and sunflower was done. The data set contains a total of 16,247 plants. Faster RCNN was used to create ROI for each plant. The dataset was cleaned manually to remove weeds on the ground. RMSE below 5% was obtained.

Mushar et al. applied the machine learning approach for tree volume estimation [12]. The work uses the real tree data that had been gathered from Compartment 37 in the Cherul Forest Reserve, Terengganu, Malaysia. The ground truth data were measured from both the standing and felled trees. The volume is calculated based on Huber's formula. The total number of trees used is 241. The data set was divided into train and test sets at the ratio of 70:30. Three estimation methods were done: regression, SVR, and ANN.

Sreeram utilized OpenCV library to count the number of palm trees [16]. The work counts the number of palm trees in the top-view picture. One palm tree was cropped from a top view and used as a template. After preprocessing, the work utilized the OpenCV function matchTemplate() to search for a matching between a top view picture that has many palm trees and an input image and used the OpenCV function findContour() that helps in extracting the contours from the image and counted palm trees those matched the condition.

3 Materials and Method

Our process starts from dataset constructions, preprocessing, and model construction.

3.1 Dataset Collection

The data set was obtained by flying the drone (DJI Maverick III) on the private area of the oil palm owned by the Faculty of Agriculture, Kasetsart University (14.26156, 10.90700). The selected area covers 20,000 square meters in this work.

First, the drone was flying at a speed of 4.0 m per second and 100 m in height from the ground. The pictures were collected by CMOS camera sensor from multiple angles. The realistic 3D model point cloud was auto-generated by combining pictures using the overlapping images by WebODM.

WebODM was utilized to process the raw drone images. WebODM has many processing steps as in [18]. Figure 1 is the steps extracted from the software. The user can also start from any step to reprocess the data. These are the typical steps in most software such as ArcGIS [1]. After loading the data set, the structure from motion (SFM) is processed. Next is point filtering, meshing, and georeferencing. At steps 8 and 9, DEM and orthophoto were constructed. The orthophotos and point clouds from meshing are the ones we utilized.

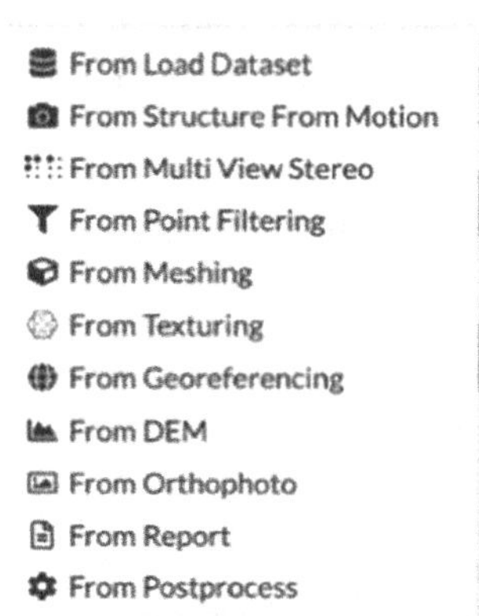

Fig. 1. WebODM processing steps.

Figure 2(a) presents an example orthophoto obtained in 2D from WebODM. For plant height estimation, we view the mesh in 3D as in Fig. 2(b). The point clouds are extracted as a ply file. From the dataset, the annotation can be done depending on the task goal.

(a) (b)

Fig. 2. (a) Orthophoto example (palm fields). (b) 3D point clouds.

3.2 Tree Height Estimation Task

The first goal is to find the relationship between the actual tree height and the tree height from 3D point cloud geometry. As a prototype, we selected a linear regression model to use the 3D point cloud tree height to predict the tree height.

To estimate the tree height, we utilize the tree point clouds obtained from WebODM. First, the ground truth must be constructed. In WebODM, there is a measurement tool on the left side panel of Fig. 3. Zooming in on the point clouds, we use the measurement tools for measuring the height as shown in Fig. 3 The height of each palm tree is collected as ground truth in a meter unit.

On the other hand, the saved *ply* file was edited using CloudCompare [5]. The corresponding tree point clouds from Fig. 3 are selected and cut using the software. Totally, 30 palm trees were manually extracted. The cut tree point clouds may embed the grounds or pixels of neighbors as in Fig. 4(a). The noise reduction process was performed. We utilized Open3D for processing the point cloud data [20]. The Open3D statistical outlier removal was performed as in Fig. 4(b).

On the other hand, the bounding box of the palm tree in pixels was collected using the Open3D function as ground truth. Figure 5(a) shows two kinds of bounding boxes: AxisAlignedBoundingBox (red) and OrientedBoundingBox (green). We used OrientedBoundingBox in our dataset. The bounding box has eight coordinates.

Table 1 shows the measurement from WebODM and from Open3D.

Once obtained both pixel height and meter height, we constructed the linear regression model to estimate the transformation in pixels to meters. We divide the train set: test set as 70:30. Figure 5(b) shows the model constructed for the

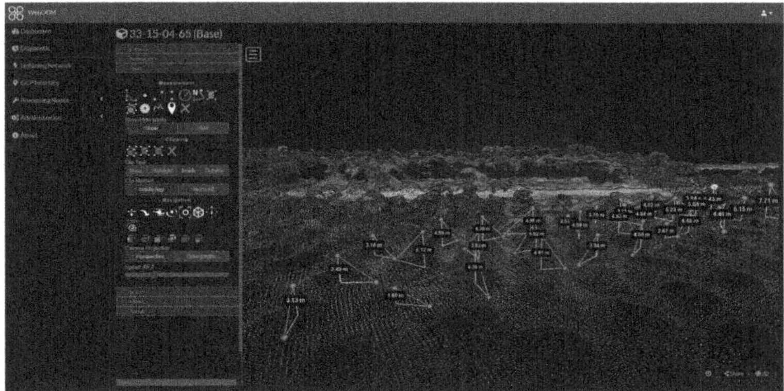

Fig. 3. Height measurement tool in WebODM.

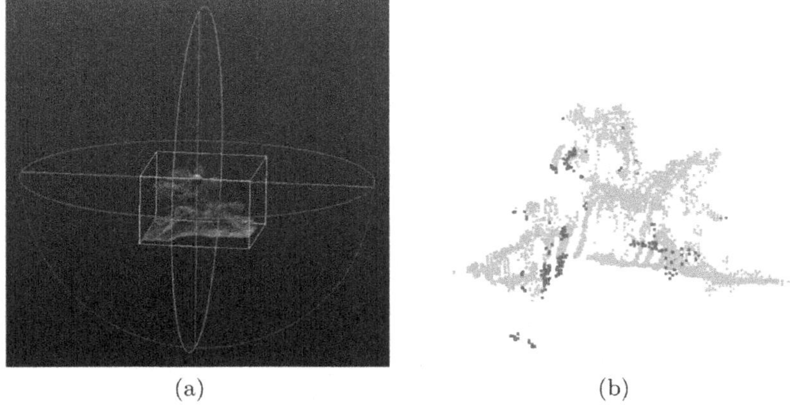

(a) (b)

Fig. 4. (a) Example tree on CloudCompare. (b) Noise reduction in Open3D.

Table 1. Ground truth from WebODM and Open3D.

Plant ID	Real Height (Meters)	Pixel Height (Pixels)
1	3.95	3.99
2	6.47	6.57
3	7.71	7.99
4	5.58	5.71
5	5.15	5.17
6	4.46	4.54
7	4.52	4.46
8	5.23	5.24
9	3.23	3.25
10	4.84	4.97
11	4.48	4.8
12	3.7	3.72
13	6.63	7.05
14	2.67	2.93
15	4.99	5.16
16	4.5	4.73
17	4.98	5.27
18	5.02	5.12
19	3.34	3.6
20	4.39	4.44
21	3.93	4.27
22	4.81	4.92
23	4.59	4.89
24	5.12	5.19
25	4.35	4.57
26	2.53	2.78
27	3.14	3.18
28	3.49	3.49
29	1.8	1.89
30	3.13	3.17

test data. With the test data, the model can estimate with 97.431% accuracy maximum and 93.507% minimum. In effect, the error estimation is about 18.4, as shown in Table 2.

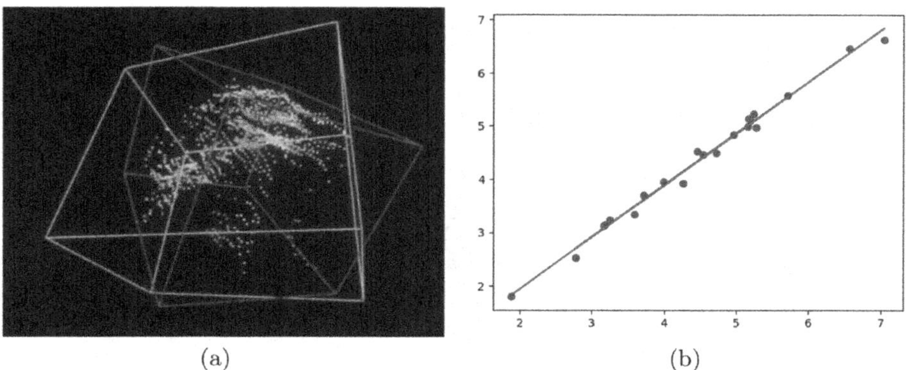

(a) (b)

Fig. 5. (a) Bounding box finding (Open3D). (b) Linear regression model.

Table 2. Error comparison for test set.

Plant ID	Real Height(Meters)	Predict Height(Meters)	Accuracy(%)	Error(Meters)
3	7.71	7.76	99.34	0.05
11	4.48	4.66	95.89	0.18
14	2.67	2.84	93.51	0.17
18	5.02	4.97	98.99	–0.05
20	4.39	4.31	98.21	–0.08
22	4.81	4.78	99.41	–0.03
23	4.59	4.75	96.42	0.16
25	4.35	4.46	98.03	0.09
28	3.49	3.39	97.09	–0.10

3.3 Palm Trees Counting Tasks

We implemented the palm tree counting process on our dataset. For counting the number of trees, it is easy to work with 2D data, which is orthophoto. The 2D palm image was exported from WebODM.

Most approaches utilize a machine vision approach with the OpenCV library. We tested the approach in [16]. The step begins with choosing proper HSV thresholds for color filtering [14]. Figure 6 shows a part of the orthophoto we worked on. Figure 7(a) shows the template of the selected palm tree. Figure 7(a) is the template before adjusting, and Fig. 7(b) shows the HSV after the adjustment. We adjusted the HSV so that the color filtering threshold is easy to select. In Fig. 9, the HSV filtering threshold can be varied with the scrollbar. Afterward,

Fig. 6. Top view of palm trees.

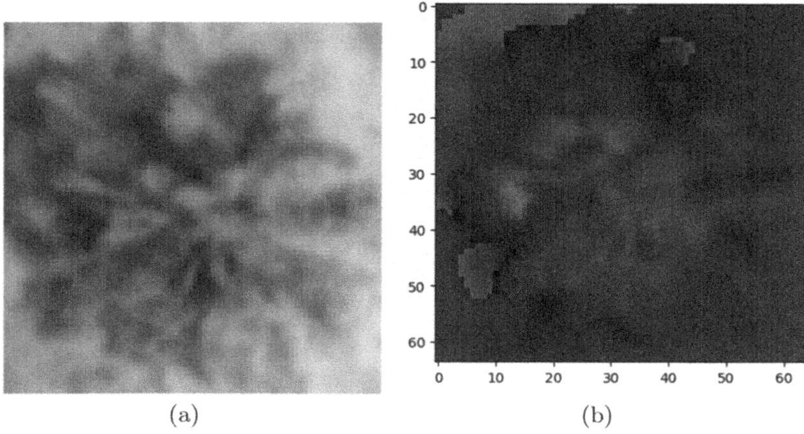

(a) (b)

Fig. 7. (a) Template of palm tree (b) HSV palm tree template

the ground and the grasses can easily be seen. Figure 9 is the setting we chose to remove grounds from palm trees. For this area, we particularly selected Hmin = 42, Smin = 41, Vmin = 90, Hmax = 81, Smax = 240 and Vmax = 233.

After we did the same for the binary template in Fig. 8(a), we denoised it to reduce the hole inside or the noise outside and add a border. The denoised binary template is shown in Fig. 8(b). Then, we used the distance transform from the template in Fig. 8(c).

We applied the same process to the palm image set but added the morphological transformations before doing the distance transform to make the edges sharpen to reduce some connected contours, which may accidentally combine 2 or 3 palm trees into one tree. After that, we did template matching, and the proper threshold to make it the binary image was found. Figure 10 and Fig. 11 show the matching template in greyscale and in binary which is used to find the contours, respectively. Those with more than 1,000 contour areas were selected as the trees.

Figure 12 presents the resulting output. The template matches near perfectly in our images. This setting results in 312 trees out of 317 trees in the picture (98.42% accuracy). This is because two uncounted trees are too small, and three uncounted trees were cropped to make this photo not too long, making 5 of them have less than 1,000 contourArea. We may reduce the parameter contourArea to 600 to make the perfect match, but in the large field, it will be sensitive to small trees or noises.

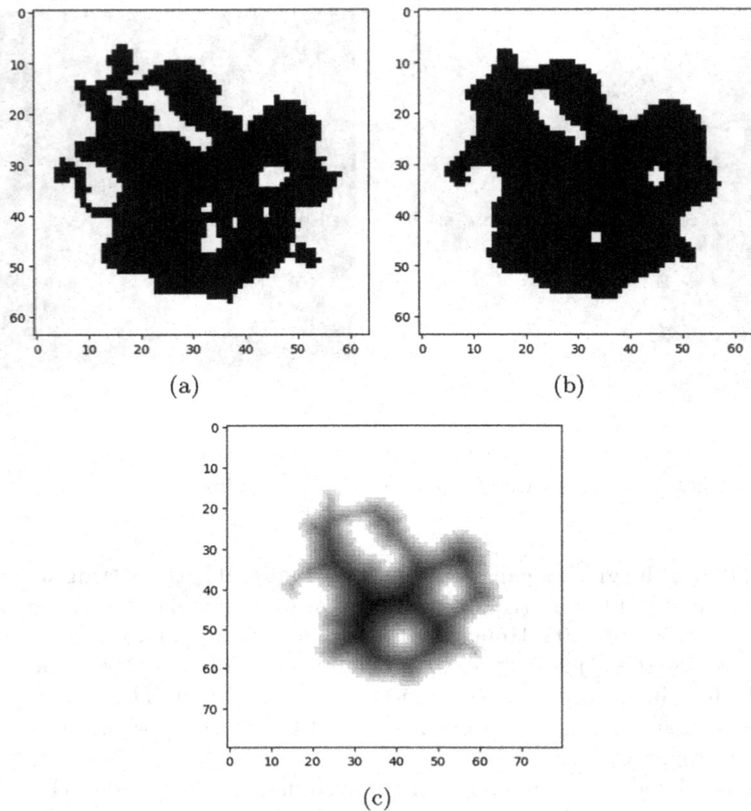

Fig. 8. (a) Binary palm tree template (b) Denoised binary palm tree template (c) Distance transform palm tree template.

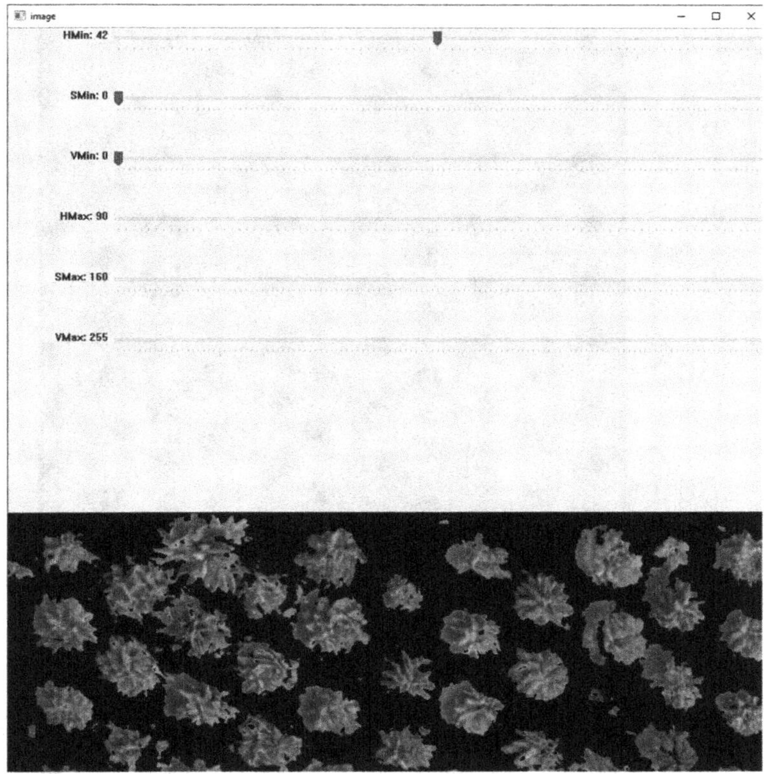

Fig. 9. HSV color filtering.

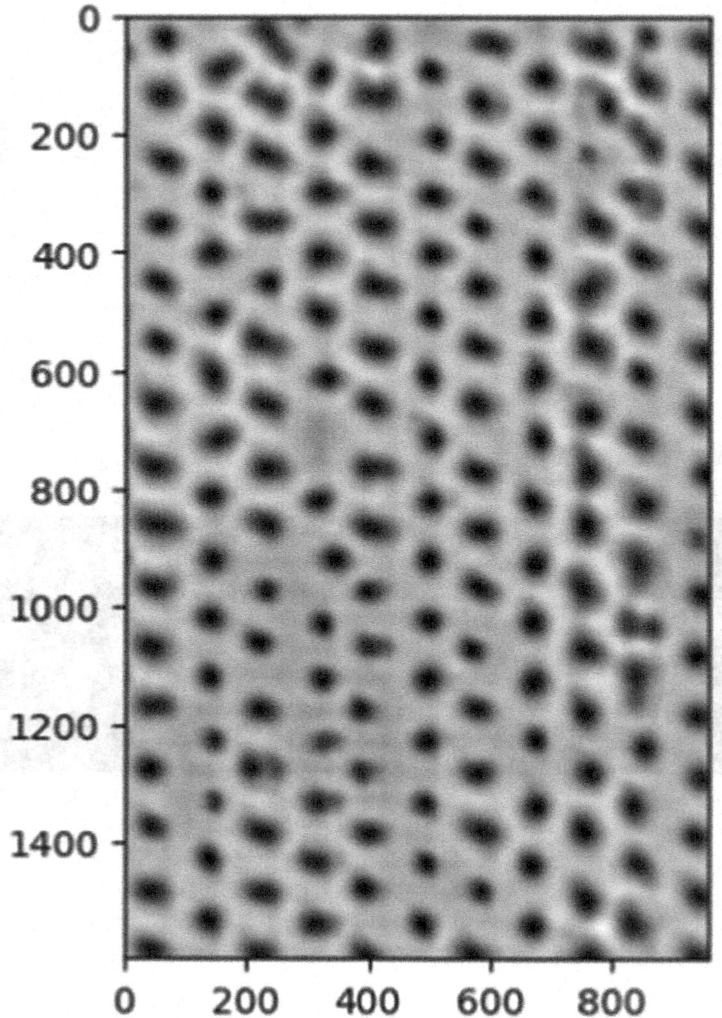

Fig. 10. matchingTemplate()'s output.

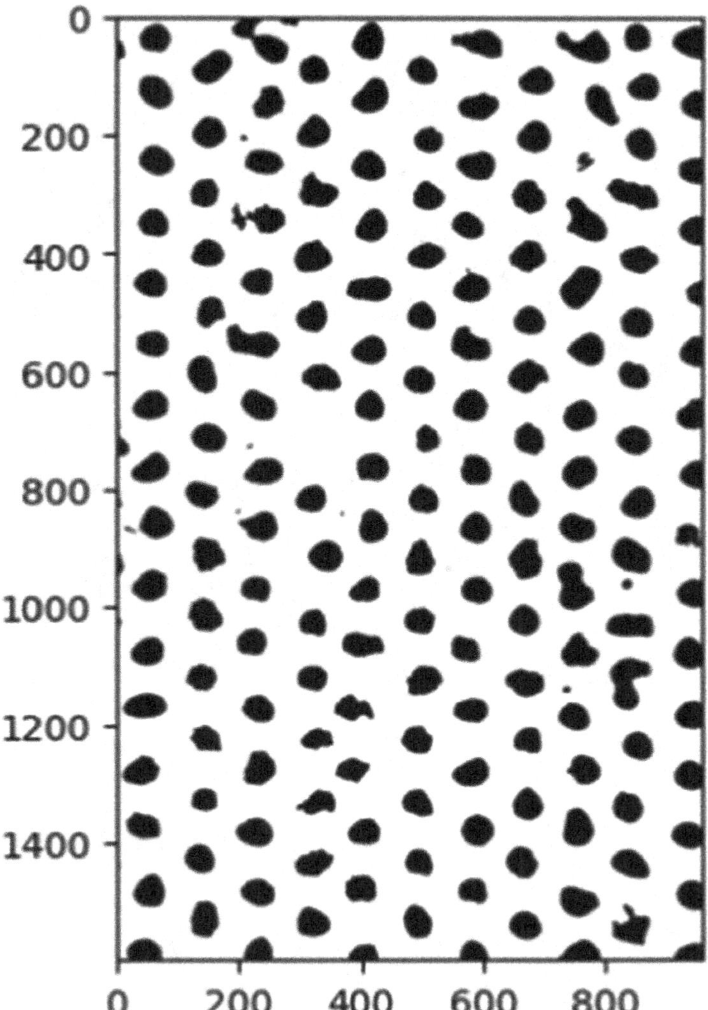

Fig. 11. matchingTemplate()'s binary output.

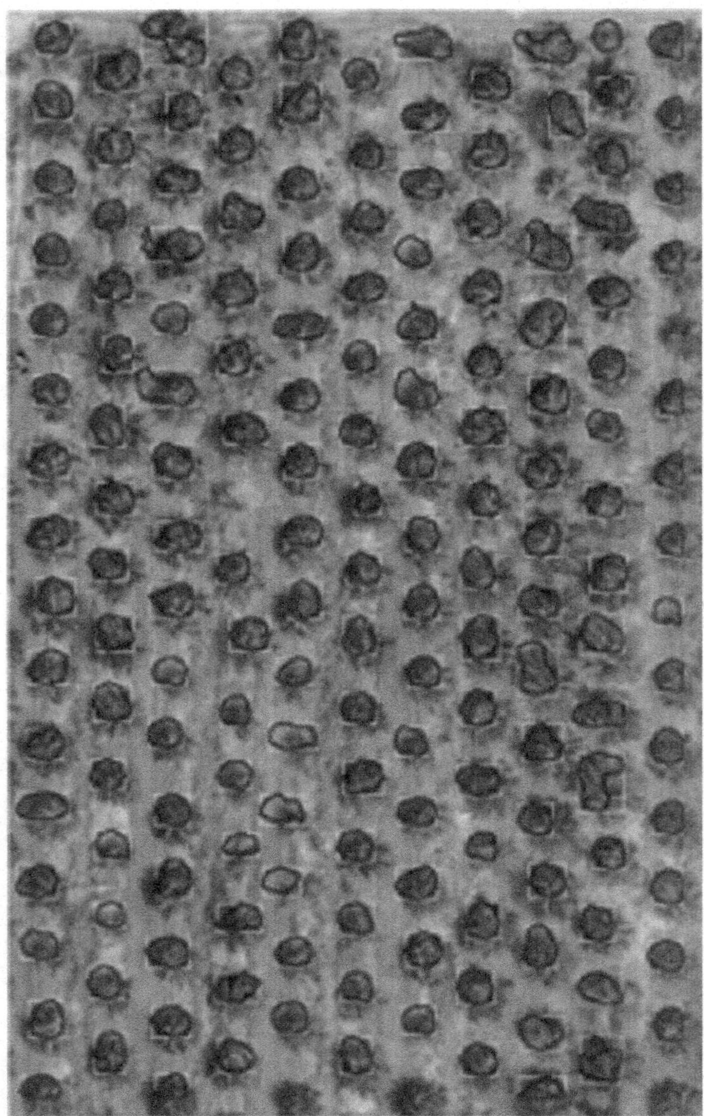

Fig. 12. Counting output.

4 Related Datasets and Discussion

There are not many raw orthophoto datasets available for studying yet. Most of them are the datasets from urban area such as [2] which proposed dataset for car detection. The downloaded photos are preprocessed orthophotos. For [3], the raw images from drone flying are available for Mymar urban area (https://smithsonian.figshare.com/articles/dataset/Orthomosaic_of_drone_image_in_12_locations_in_Myanmar/12780041) from the survey.

In agriculture area, Vélez et.al. presented a complete dataset for photogrammetric reconstruction over a Pistachio Orchard in Spain. The dataset contains the raw images as well as 3D point clouds and others such as DEM, GCPs etc. Kumar et.al. presented the dataset for detecting maize growth and tassel detection [9,10]. No public dataset avaiable for this work. Simiarly, Monteiro et.al. presented the work for weed segmentation with UAV images[13]. The paper does not provide raw public dataset avaiable

In our case, we intend to provide the case study of processing flows from raw images until preprocessed images and cloud points for further analysis. The 3D point cloud dataset is still small since it takes time to manually annotate from the software. Further automatic annotation is during investigation.

For the tree height estimation, the important part is measuring the tree height in WebODM software, because in choosing a point that we will refer to as a ground point, we want to find the lowest point from the surrounding ground that is uneven in height and has grass that makes the point high. Therefore, we must choose a good angle to view the point to choose. And make sure that the point is not noise.

For the tree counting task, The important part is choosing proper HSV thresholds for color filtering and it's difficult when a canopy of trees were overlapped and includes the shadow from one tree that overlaps another tree, making it look like they are connected to a big tree, this forces us to filter HSV thresholds narrower. We can get rid of shadowing from the start. The improvement will be to fly a drone at 11AM to 1PM. so that the sunlight is at a straight angle which will cause minimum shadows.

5 Data Availability

The dataset can be downloaded at located at https://github.com/MambaClaw/Palm-Tree-Height-Estimation-and-Counting-Tasks.git The first folder is `3D Point Clouds` storing point clouds of each palm tree in a ply file, and the second folder `2D Orthophoto` contains the 2D orthophotos of the palm field. There are two Jupyter notebooks (`.ipynb` extension) containing the sample Jupyter notebook for tree height estimation and tree counting tasks with a regression model. The code for noise removal and computing the bounding box of point clouds using Open3D is also included in the notebook. The template tree is included in the folder. The CSV file for tree height data as well `data_tree.csv`. The installation instruction for the required library is described in README.md. Also, the raw palm images are in folder `Raw`.

6 Conclusion

We proposed the palm tree data drone dataset. We described the protocol steps to construct the data set and tools used to manipulate data. All open-sourced tools are utilized. WebODM is the starting software to stitch the drone images and then SFM construction. From the derived assets, CloudCompare is utilized to point cloud cutting and noise-cleaning. Next, the 30 palm tree point clouds were extracted and can be further used in the Open3D library for deriving tree properties. We demonstrated two tasks based on our dataset: three height estimation and tree counting. More datasets will be extracted from other types of trees, and other tree properties will be explored from point cloud data.

Acknowledgements. This work is supported in part by Kasetsart University Research and Development Institute, Thailand, KURDI FF (KU) 33.65.

References

1. 10.8, A.: Ortho mapping with mosaic datasets (2021). https://desktop.arcgis.com/en/arcmap/latest/manage-data/raster-and-images/ortho-mapping-overview.htm
2. Ballesteros, J.R., Sanchez-Torres, G., Branch-Bedoya, J.W.: Hagdavs: Height-augmented geo-located dataset for detection and semantic segmentation of vehicles in drone aerial orthomosaics. Data **7**(4) (2022). https://www.mdpi.com/2306-5729/7/4/50
3. Biswas, S., Huang, Q., Leimgruber, P.: Orthomosaic of drone image in 12 locations in Myanmar (August 2020). https://doi.org/10.25573/data.12780041.v4
4. Bradski, G.: The OpenCV Library. Dr. Dobb's J. Softw. Tools **120**, 122–125 (2000)
5. CloudCompare: CloudCompare 3D point cloud and mesh processing software Open Source Project. https://www.danielgm.net/cc/
6. David, E., et al.: Plant detection and counting from high-resolution RGB images acquired from UAVs: comparison between deep-learning and handcrafted methods with application to maize, sugar beet, and sunflower. bioRxiv (2023). https://doi.org/10.1101/2021.04.27.441631, https://www.biorxiv.org/content/early/2023/01/17/2021.04.27.441631
7. DroneDeploy: Full Reality Capture. https://www.dronedeploy.com/
8. GNU Affero General Public License v3.0.: WebODM (2022). https://github.com/OpenDroneMap/WebODM
9. Kumar, A., et al.: Efficient maize tassel-detection method using UAV based remote sensing. Remote Sens. Appl. Soc. Environ. **23**, 100549 (2021). https://doi.org/10.1016/j.rsase.2021.100549, https://www.sciencedirect.com/science/article/pii/S2352938521000859
10. Kumar, A., et al.: UAV based remote sensing for tassel detection and growth stage estimation of maize crop using multispectral images. In: IGARSS 2020 - 2020 IEEE International Geoscience and Remote Sensing Symposium, pp. 1588–1591 (September 2020). https://doi.org/10.1109/IGARSS39084.2020.9323266
11. Li, X., et al.: High-throughput plant height estimation from RGB Images acquired with Aerial platforms: a 3D point cloud based approach. In: 2019 Digital Image Computing: Techniques and Applications (DICTA). pp. 1–8 (2019)
12. Mohd Mushar, S.H., Syed Ahmad, S.S., Kasmin, F., Zamah Shari, N.H.: Machine learning approach for estimating tree volume. J. Phys. Conf. Ser. **1502**, 012039 (2020). https://doi.org/10.1088/1742-6596/1502/1/012039
13. Monteiro, A., von Wangenheim, A.: Orthomosaic dataset of RGB aerial images for weed mapping (2019). http://www.lapix.ufsc.br/weed-mapping-sugar-cane)

14. nathancy: OpenCV: Choosing HSV thresholds for color filtering (2013). https://stackoverflow.com/questions/10948589/choosing-the-correct-upper-and-lower-hsv-boundaries-for-color-detection-withcv
15. PrecisionHawk: Automated Plant Counts with Drones for Precision Agriculture. https://www.precisionhawk.com/blog/media/topic/understanding-your-aerial-data-plant-counting
16. Sreeram: Count-the-number-of-Palm-Trees (2018). https://github.com/sreeram004/Count-the-number-of-Palm-Trees
17. Sun, Y., Luo, Y., Zhang, Q., Xu, L., Wang, L., Zhang, P.: Estimation of crop height distribution for mature rice based on a moving surface and 3D point cloud elevation. Agronomy **12**(4) (2022). https://www.mdpi.com/2073-4395/12/4/836
18. Toffanin, P.: OpenDroneMap: The Missing Guide, 1st edn. UAV4GEO (2019)
19. Valente, J., Sari, B., Kooistra, L., Kramer, H., Mücher, S.: Automated crop plant counting from very high-resolution aerial imagery. Precis. Agric. **21**, 1366–1384 (2020)
20. Zhou, Q.Y., Park, J., Koltun, V.: Open3D: a modern library for 3d data processing (2018). http://arxiv.org/abs/1801.09847

Geographical Analysis, Urban Modeling, Spatial Statistics (Geog-An-Mod 2023)

Grid-Based Generalisation of Area Polygons for Automated Application in Small-Scale Statistical Maps

Marion D. Simon[1(✉)] and Hartmut Asche[2]

[1] Faculty of Science, University of Potsdam, Karl-Liebknecht-Street 24-25, 14476 Potsdam, Germany
marion.simon@uni-potsdam.de
[2] Computer Graphics System Group, Hasso Plattner Institute, University of Potsdam, Prof.-Dr.-Helmert-Street 2-3, 14482 Potsdam, Germany
hartmut.asche@hpi.de

Abstract. The added value of map representations of statistical mass data is now highly appreciated in big business. Most statistical maps are produced by non-experts using to GIS technologies or mapping functions embedded in statistical programmes. However, the range of semi-automated tools offered does not exploit the full potential of cartographic visualisation. Most map representations of statistical data colour administrative units resulting in area cartograms or choropleth maps. Visualisation of these area-related data need to focus on correct representation of the area rather than on the topographic elaboration boundary polygons. Hence the simplification or generalisation of the polygon lines becomes important for visual communication and perception. Up to date, no generally accepted rules exist for the generalisation of the polygon lines of area cartograms in which presentation scales. This paper deals with solution approaches in line generalisation using square grids. As well as an answer to the question, if square grids could be an option for fully automated map generalization in small scaled statistical maps.

Keywords: Geovisualisation · raster · generalisation · simplification · statistical maps · small-scale maps · business maps · cartographic generalisation · automated generalisation · raster grids

1 Description of the Problem

Most statistical map representations visualising quantitative enterprise (geo)data are areal representations, since the data provided usually refer to a defined area. Areas are differentiated by area colouring (e.g., choropleth) or map symbols (e.g., diagrams) placed in the respective areas (see Fig. 1). Administrative boundaries are most frequently used to delineate the areas in question. This line network of area boundaries is the basic element of this simple map type. Alternatively, quantitative data with area reference can also be plotted on artificial line networks in addition to the administrative reference area.

O. Gervasi et al. (Eds.): ICCSA 2023 Workshops, LNCS 14107, pp. 371–383, 2023.
https://doi.org/10.1007/978-3-031-37114-1_25

Applying this so-called field principle results in the field cartogram map type. Administrative boundary lines and area units are freely available on the internet for defined scales. On its GISCO platform [1], Eurostat of the European Commission offers, among other data, linear and areal representations (lines and polygons) of administrative boundaries (worldwide) for representations at scales of 1:1 million, 1:3 million, 1:10 million, 1:20 million, 1:60 million. For small-scale statistical maps, the geometric precision of boundary polygons contained in these data sets needs to be reduced. That is because the unwanted level of detail of boundary line representations affects processing time, computing power, memory requirements. Moreover, simplification (or generalisation) is mandatory for map representation in a frequently reduced output scale to and the amount of generalisation appropriate to the output scale to ensure readability of the respective map.

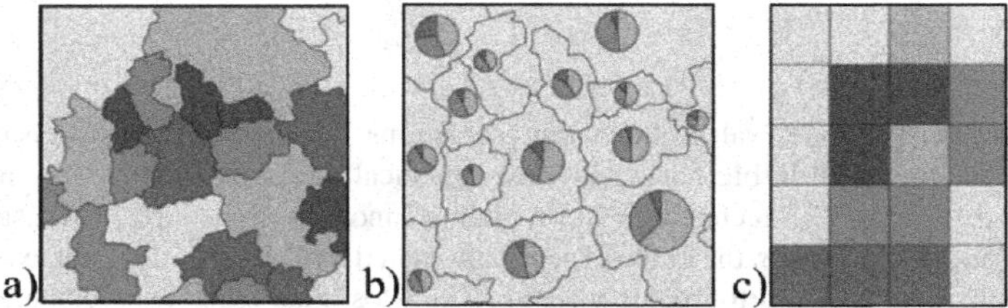

Fig. 1. Mapping principle of a) choropleth maps, b) area diagram maps and c) grid net maps (source: [2])

A range of software tools, such as Mapshaper, are available for the generalisation of boundary lines. These tools offer various mathematical algorithms with an individually adjustable degree of line generalisation [3]. The assessment whether the results generated meet the requirements of the base map lies exclusively with the user. Buttenfield [4] segments line elements for ordering into hierarchical tree structure with subsequent statistical examination of the geometries of the line segments. Lay and Weber [5] deal with the generalisation of mosaic maps (specifically forest areas) on a raster basis considering the automated generalisation of screen maps whose raster cells are used as a measure of the mesh size of the grid. However, no definition can be found how simple "highly simplified" line polygon generalisation is. The Eurostat national borders polygon datasets mentioned are provided for a scale of map provision. Specific recommendations for the usability in concrete application-related map types and the necessary generalisation requirements per scale are not given.

This work is intended to contribute to the research of line generalisation by grids with a view to increase the degree of automation in the research field of automated map construction. The aim is to define scale ranges and to assign them degrees of generalisation for administrative units which enable a standardisation for thematic map representations. An acceptable generalisation solution for an island representation adapted to the output scale range is provided in this work for a specific scale range. Zooming in or out of the screen display is effected with the determined degree of generalisation within the scale window to be defined. The objectives of the study are to assess the degree of automation, speed, correctness, and effectiveness of the resulting map representation. For this purpose, the following parameters are assessed:

Recognisability of chosen administrative unit (yes/no),
Ease of map exploration (high, medium, low),
Correctness of boundary depiction (yes/no),
Data maintenance effort (high, medium, low),
Performance assessment (good, medium, poor),
Usability rating (good, medium, poor),
Degree of automation (high, medium, low).

2 Solution Approach

The generalisation of a linear polygon delimiting an administrative area unit is tested in this work by using grids of various cell size in combination with different line generalisation approaches. First, approaches for base point reduction will be carried out on the basis of vector data. This is followed by a generalisation approach on a so-called raster basis. Based on the "raster", which originally refers to non-vector pictorial information, square grids will be used for line generalisation solutions.

1. The first vector-based approach (area-area) assumes a minimum overlap of grid cell area and underlying area unit (polygon), after which relevant contour components of the area ring are to be generalised (line generalisation). Further runs are to be made with a variation of the mesh size and the minimum coverage.
2. The second vector-based approach (line-line) considers only line intersections of boundary lines of the grid cells and polygon boundary lines (area perimeter, e.g., national boundary line).
3. The third line generalisation approach is the grid-based approach. Similar to the quadtree principle it pursues the division of a grid cell (grid cell as square) into exactly four daughter cells, if the grid field (areal) lies over a section of the linear area ring (area-line). After a defined number of iterations the smallest square is depicted by means of colour filling to delimit the area.

The results of these three line generalisation approaches will be compared with a generalised reference at a certain scale.

This conceptual approach results in following work packages:

Select reference map

- Definition of a generalised base map for statistical map representation consisting of administrative units.
- Adoption of the scale used in the reference map to derive a display scale range based on this base map.
- If necessary, digitalisation of the reference if available in analog form and determination of the number of base points (coordinate pairs) used.

Compile investigation material

- Geodata research and, if necessary, data extraction of the spatial section that occurs in the reference.

- Description of the data set elected regarding the map projection and accuracy (provision scale, number of support points used).

Develop implementation concept

- Set up the investigation procedures for each grid-based line generalisation approach.
- Requirements formulation for the evaluation of the results.

Application

- Implementation of the concepts developed for a defined scale range on extracted examination material.
- Presentation of results.
- Comparison of the graphical and numerical results with the reference.
- Validation based on at least two further administrative units for mapping in the same scale window.

The polygon generalised as an administrative unit is covered with a network of regular square grids of a certain mesh size. The reduction of polygon support points, each located with x and y coordinates, is to take place at those partial lines whose surrounding cuboids are "filled" to more than 60% by the polygon. A line segment is cut at the entry and exit point of a raster cell. Two new coordinate pairs are created at the intersection points. In order to avoid an increase in memory instead of reduction, the intersect conditions need to be described. To ensure reduction it is required that only cells that containing more than three grid points are allowed to intersect.

The results of this approach are generated for different square grid sizes. After these passes, a mean result is extracted from each scale range as a standard. This scale-dependent cascade can be used in the automated construction of thematic map representations.

3 Implementation

First, the scale range is defined starting from the initial data set for maps at a scale of 1:1 million. Since the next data set from the same data source is available for the scale 1:3 million, a scale range from 1:1 million to 1:3 million is defined for which the results are to be produced.

Various grid shapes (hexagon, triangle, rectangle, square, trapezoid) are available with their respective advantages and disadvantages for mesh formation. For this work, a grid shape is chosen and its origin superimposed on the origin of the map grid (bottom left). This facilitates localisation or geocoding, if necessary. Following this procedure, a square grid is preferable to a rectangular grid because sides are of equal length.

3.1 Initial Data Set and Reference Map

For users of the EU member states, the geographical data of the European Commission from the geographic information system (GISCO) [1] managed by Eurostat can be used. Selected country sections are extracted from the data set "NUTS_RG_01M_2021_3035" covering Europe. These data from the year 2021 can be mapped in high detail for a scale of 1:1 million in Lambert's areal azimuthal projection (ETRS_1989_LAEA, EPSG-code 3035). For this purpose, the land area of Albania (27,398 km^2 – [6]) is extracted from the presented dataset. The land area ring of this original dataset comprises 785 points.

As a reference and for the evaluation of the results, the country polygon of Albania generalised for statistical maps from the Albanian National Atlas [7] is used. The map, which is available in analogue form, was digitised for this purpose at the working scale of 1:500,000.

This scale ensures the recognition of each line segment and the precise positioning of support points. This digitised national polygon is described by 181 support points. As has been mentioned, the projection used for the atlas is not known. Georeferencing is hence necessary for a direct comparison of the results. If the result is positive, the solution approach can be validated on countries with about 10,000 km^2 larger and smaller areas (Switzerland 41,285 km^2, Slovenia 20,151 km^2), [6], as these can be mapped in the same target scale range.

3.2 Vector-Based Grid Generalisation

The first vector-based generalisation approach (area-area) presented in Sect. 2 is aimed at reducing existing line support points. A square grid of different mesh size is placed on the area unit to be generalised. Subsequently, coverage percentages of the land area (x) are set in relation to the area of the grid squares (100%). All grid squares where the coverage by the land area is between 60% and 99.9% are generalised in the following. The following steps are carried out (see Fig. 2):

- Base point generation at grid edge and country ring intersections,
- Deletion of the intervening original support points

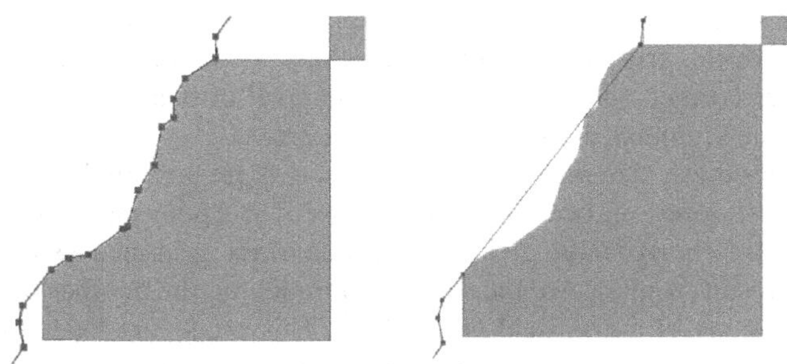

Fig. 2. Left: before, right: after line generalisation through grid-cell based generalisation with partly filled grid cell by underlying polygon (own source)

In this way, sections of the country's perimeter will remain in the original and other line sections will be represented as straight lines.

The second vector-based generalisation approach presented (line line), uses a square grid of a defined size placed on the polygon of the area unit to be generalised. This way a new linear feature is created. It consists of pairs of coordinates, defined at the intersections of the grid edges (or nodes) and the area boundary line. This is done by setting vertices and connecting them with a line. The original vertices of the area perimeter remain unaffected.

3.3 Raster-Based Grid Generalisation

The grid-based solution approach is suitable for scales ranging from 1:1 million to 1:2.5 million. The country area to be generalised is covered with a square grid dimensioned according to the map grid design used. Starting with a mesh size of 7,500 m, the overlap of a grid field with the line segment is checked. In case of overlap of a line segment, the grid cells are further divided by a number of iterations following to the quadtree approach. An iteration step means a further subdivision of a grid field into exactly four equal squares. The final step consists of filling the smallest squares. In this application, the colouring is used to represent the polygon ring. With this approach all area polygons are scanned first and thus no island of relevant size is deleted from the map display.

4 Application

4.1 Vector-Based Grid Generalization

The bay of Vlora with the island of Sazanit is strongly distorted when applying a mesh size of 15,000 m (see Fig. 3, b). When using a smaller mesh size of 10,000 m the topographic features are retained (see Fig. 3, a, left circle). The recognition of the southern tip of the country is also more likely with the smaller mesh size than the result with 15,000 m mesh size allows. The grid calculation refers to a bounding box surrounding the land area with the grid origin at the bottom left. Variant a) (Fig. 3) appears to be graphically more correct, since the differences in level of detail of generalised versus ungeneralised line segments are visually more apparent.

Despite larger mesh size and, as a consequence, a greater number of interpolation point reductions, the opposite occurred. The number of grid points generated and retained is 376 in a) and 424 in b). Thus, doubling the area of the grid meshes is not an option for halving the result from a). Another option for reducing the number of grid points is to halve the coverage of a grid field (10,000 m). This procedure leads to the fact that the entire national boundary polygon becomes relevant for generalisation (see Fig. 4) and would have to be generalised completely according to the approach described in Sect. 3.2.

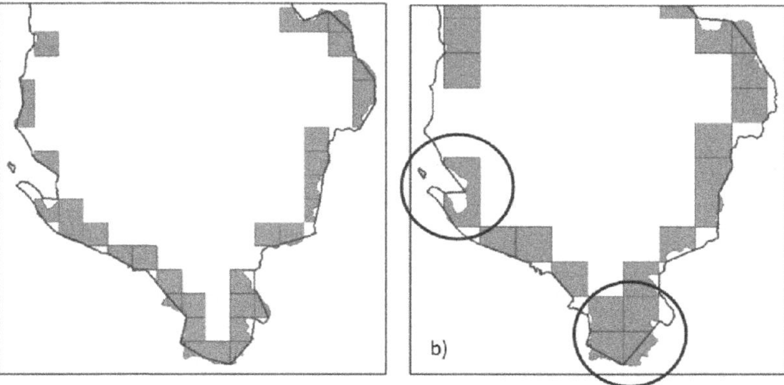

Fig. 3. Comparison of the border polygon of South Albania with grid-based line generalisation using mesh sizes of a) 10,000 m, b) 15,000 m and grid fillings of 60–99.9%, respectively. (own source)

As a consequence, the coverage parameter in the approach is replaced to generate a new line element (country polygon). The modified procedure is to first place a square grid a with mesh size of 7,500 m on the country polygon of the initial data set for Albania. In a second step a support point is placed at each intersection of the grid and the country polygon and subsequently connected them by open polygon lines. The result is shown in Fig. 5 in combination with the underlying reference data set. The reference data set is described by 181 vertices, the generalised original data set of the output data with 176 interpolation points. A visually pleasing appearance is also guaranteed.

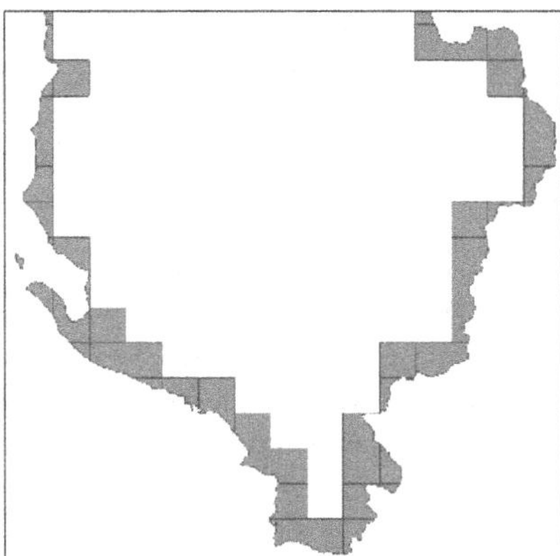

Fig. 4. Reduction of vertices halving the area overlap 30–99.9% (own source)

The result presented has been verified by an adaptation of Salistščev's nomogram, which systematically arranges recommendations for scales or scale ranges for mapping defined countries or continents onto a given mapping surface [8]. This procedure raises

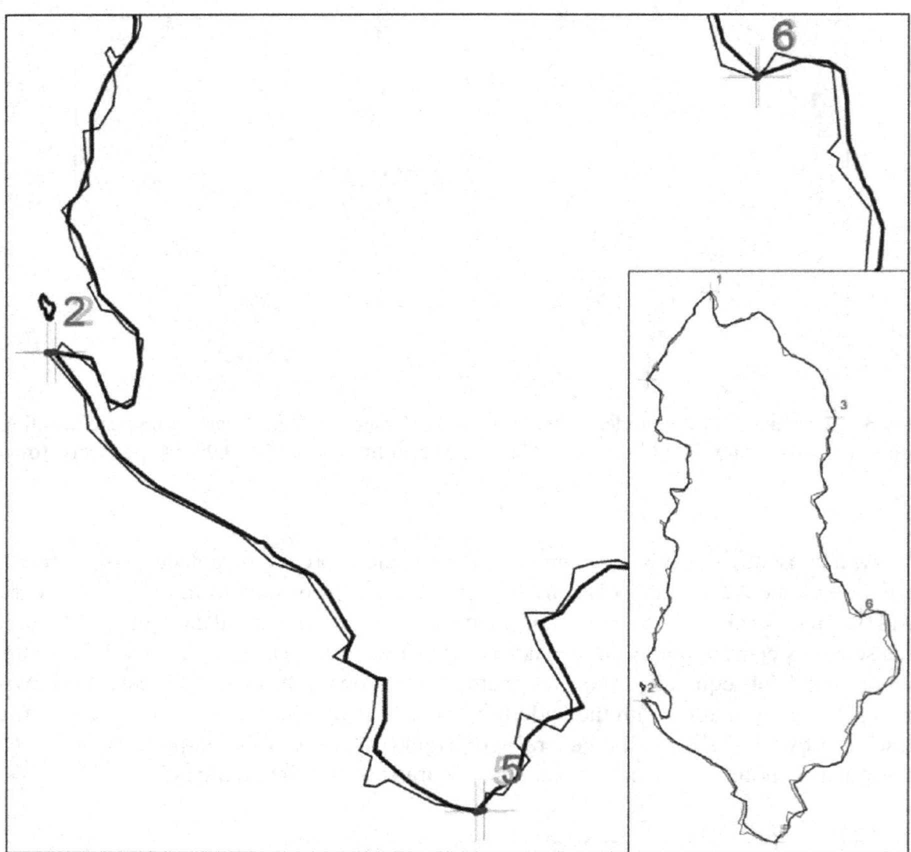

Fig. 5. Georeferenced national boundary polygon of Albania 1:1,750,000: thin line shows borderline generalised for statistical map (Albania atlas) (181 control points), thick line shows georeferenced result with 6 control points according to vector-based grid generalisation approach with grid size of 7,500 m (own source)

the question whether the underlying methodology is generic and can be applied to other countries in a similar scale range (1:1,000,000 to 1:2,500,000) as well. For this purpose, countries with a land area of approximately 10,000 km^2 smaller and larger than Albania were used as an example (Slovenia < Albania < Switzerland) (Figs. 6 and 7).

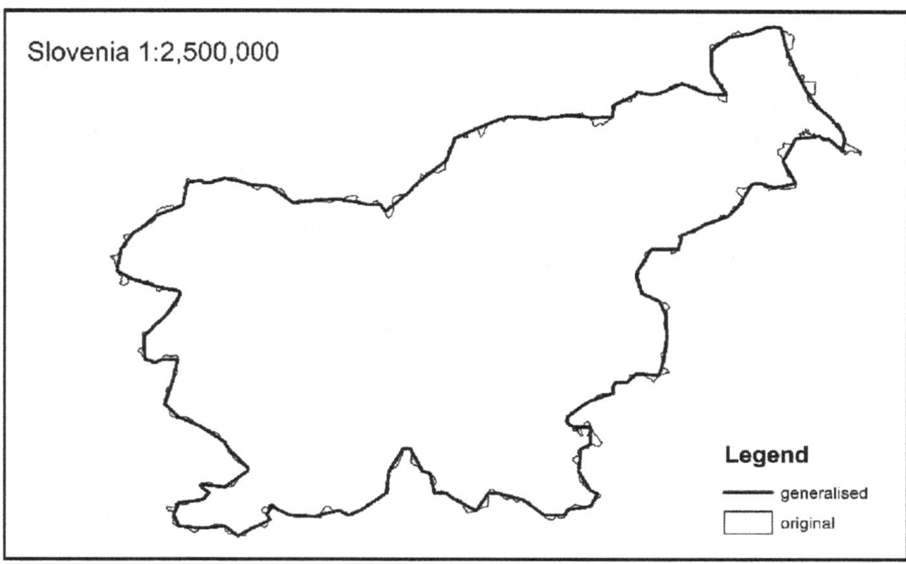

Fig. 6. Slovenia 1:2,500,000 generalised by pure grid-based line generalisation (own source)

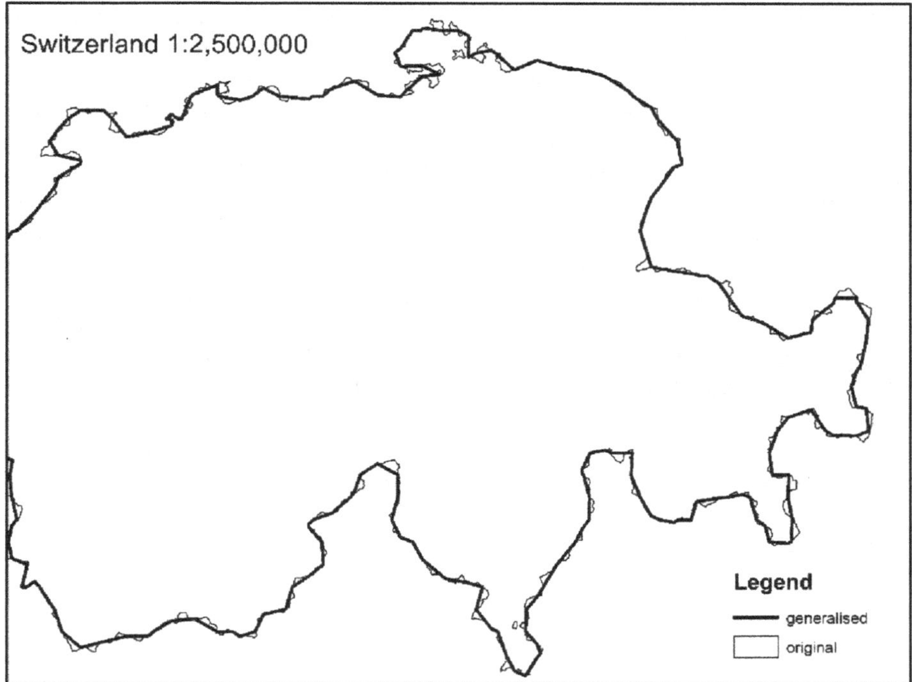

Fig. 7. Switzerland 1:2,500,000 generalised by pure grid-based line generalisation (own source)

4.2 Raster-Based Grid Generalisation

To start the process, the initial mesh size was set to 7,500 m. This figure is based both on the positive results from the second vector-based line generalisation and considering the relationship with the reference map scale. Koch and Stams [9] emphasise the "close interdependence" of "field size and scale". Based on this initial mesh size, the grid-based line generalisation approach presented in Sect. 3.2 is then iteratively processed using a square grid. The grid field division is a halving of the grid edge lengths and a re-check of the overlap of new grid patches and the line from the area outline (Fig. 8).

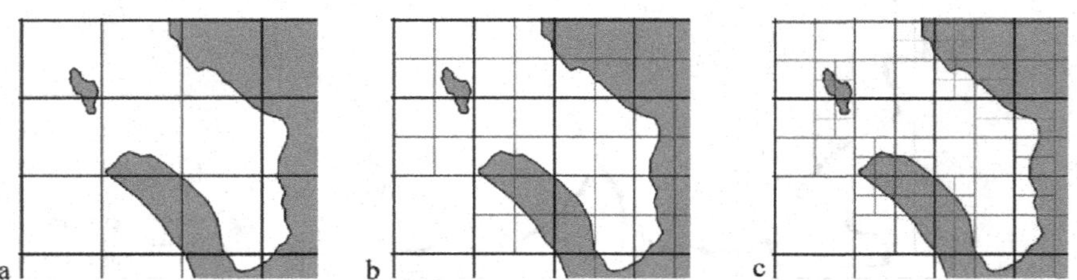

Fig. 8. Quadtree approach of grid field reduction when covered with polygonal ring; mesh sizes: a) 7,500 m, b) 3,750 m, c) 1,875 m (own source)

The number of iterations is performed up to a defined mesh size. This depends on the application or the type of map to be created (see Fig. 9). For an area cartogram based on administrative units, a linear representation and thus a smaller mesh size is required than a cartogram produced following the field principle. The latter is characteristically created using semantically coloured/filled raster cells. The result is a map of the field cartogram type. This automatically generated map representation is optimally suited to provide an easy-to-perceive overview of the geographical distribution of the statistical data in small scales. It is apparent that the defined cell size controls the number of iterations required to generate the delineation of the country's area.

Code is necessary for automation. A possible code could be explained as follows:

/* Function to load the shapefile CNTR.shp, project it in EPSGcode 3035, overlays a rectangular gridnet with cellsize 7,500 m, divide each cell in 4 rectangles, if cell overlies polygon line of the loaded polygon, the iteration of cell splitting continues until cell size reaches 468.75 m. */

Using the example of the grid-based approach, the content of a suitable code, here based on the programming language C, could have the following structure:

```
Int main (void);
int loadShapefileAndDivideCells(...) {
    // Initialize GDAL
    // Open the shapefile
    // Get the layer
    // Get the spatial reference
    // Set the EPSG code
    // Create a rectangular grid
    // Iterate over the cells
            // Check if the cell overlaps the border of the polygon
            // Divide the cell into 4 rectangles
                 // Check if the rectangles overlap the border of the
                    polygon
                      // Decrease the cell size
            // Destroy the feature
    // Destroy the rectangle
    // Close the shapefile
    return 0;
}
```

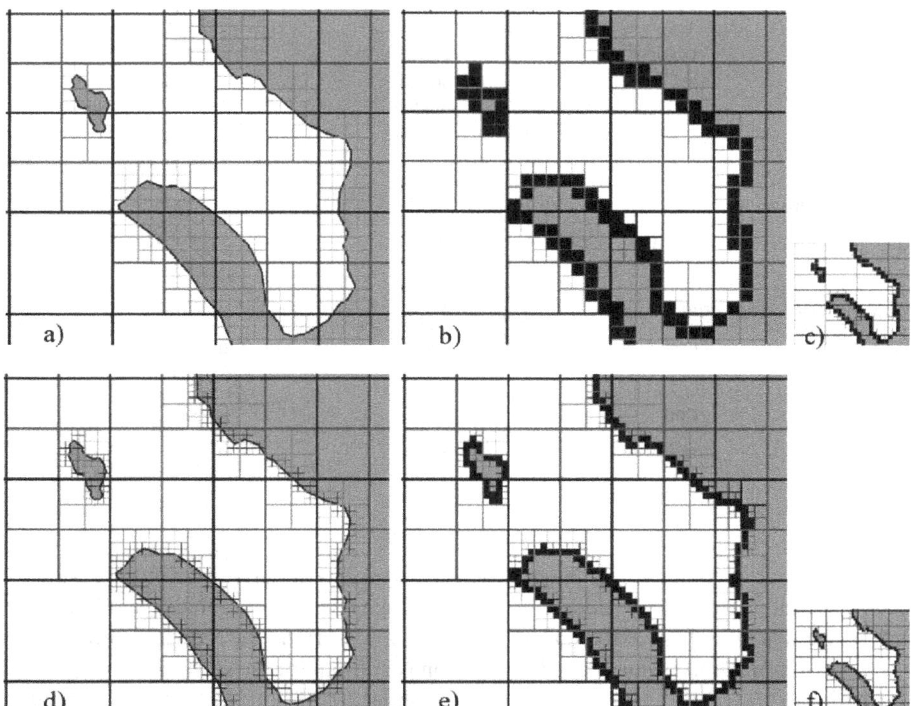

Fig. 9. Quadtree approach of grid field reduction with closed polygon coverage; mesh sizes: a-c 937.5 m; d-f 468.75 m; a), b), d), e) at working scale 1:150,000; c) and f) at target scale 1:1,750,000 (own source)

5 Concluding Remarks

The quality of the various grid-based line generalisation approaches are assessed against the objectives listed at the beginning (Table 1). In detail, the following results have been found: Both vector-based approaches (area-area; line-line) include island polygons off the sea-land border polygon only if a vector or grid cell intersects with or covers the topographic form of an island (polygon or line). Otherwise it is excluded from generalisation and subsequent map representation. The vector-based generalisation approach for area boundary lines described in Sect. 3.2 can be neglected in the form of the area coverage-dependent generalisation approach because of the high data maintenance effort (compared with the original data set) and the comparatively high computational effort. It also emerged that a correct and speedy perception of the administrative units and a visually pleasing appearance of the latter is strongly dependent on the selected mesh size and the original data set.

Table 1. Evaluation of the investigation objectives per grid-based line generalisation method

	Vector-based area – area (meshes: 10,000 x 10,000 m, coverage: 60%)	Vector-based line - line (meshes: 7,500 m x 7,500 m)	Raster-based area - line (initial mesh width: 7,500 m)
Recognisability	yes	yes	yes
Interpretation speed	medium	fast	very fast
Data storage effort	high	low	medium
Performance assessment	poor	good	good
Usability	good	good	good
Degree of automation	medium	high	high

The variant of the pure line intersection-based solution derived from the results of the above, but neglecting the degree of area coverage, is computationally less intensive. This is due to a high degree of data reduction while preserving the recognisability of the country polygons at the same time. The solution is optimal for the scale range mentioned (1:1 million to 1:2.5 million) and area sizes from about 20,000 km^2 to 40,000 km^2 because it keeps the usual vector-based procedure of base point reduction and shifting in line generalisation.

Depending on the chosen map type (field cartogram, choropleth/area diagram map), the new, raster-based line generalisation approach is extremely well suited for line generalisation for area delineation for the scale range being processed. A significant advantage of this generalisation approach is that several cartographic steps can be combined in a single operation. The production of statistical maps and their cartographic generalisation of the base map are processed together using square grids.

When used to create a field cartogram, the map content can be perceived and analysed easily and quickly. This map type with its boundary generalisation proves to be particularly efficient in communication area-related statistical information to a wide audience. One reason is that the focus of attention is directed a to the map topic, and not to topographic details of the delimitation of the respective administrative units. Furthermore, in contrast to vector-based approaches, a fast combination with raster-based information from satellite data is possible.

In summary, grid-based line generalisation can be a useful option for the production of statistical maps. It simplifies the initial input data, reduces file size and processing time, and allows the production of maps at different scales. For these reasons, an extension of the grid-based line generalisation approach to other scale ranges and area sizes is conceivable. The results provide an efficient, easily automated generalisation component for area delineation in the base map. In a broad sense, grid-based line generalisation can be considered one of the most effective statistical map representation. It thus significantly contributes to the full automation of the map construction process for statistical representations.

References

1. Gisco, Europäische Kommission: Geobasisdaten. https://ec.europa.eu/eurostat/de/web/gisco/geodata/reference-data. Accessed 17 April 2023
2. Bollmann J., Koch, W. G. (Hrsg.): Lexikon der Kartographie und Geomatik. In two volumes, vol. 1, p. 118, 248, 250. Spektrum Akademischer Verlag. Heidelberg, Berlin (2001)
3. Mapshaper: Liniengeneralisierungswerkzeug. https://mapshaper.org/. Accessed 17 Apr 2023
4. Buttenfield, B. P.: Digital Definitions of Scale-Dependent Line Structure. 1986. https://www.researchgate.net/publication/245928529_Digital_Definitions_of_Scale-Dependent_Line_Structure
5. Lay, H.-G.; Weber, W.: Waldgeneralisierung durch digitale rasterdatenverarbeitung. In: Institut für Angewandte Geodäsie. Bundesamt für Kartographie und Geodäsie (Hrsg.): Nachrichten aus dem Karten- und Vermessungswesen. Reihe 1: Originalbeiträge. Heft Nr. 91., p.61–71. Verlag des Instituts für Angewandte Geodäsie. Frankfurt am Main (1983). ISSN 0469–4236
6. CIA: Worldfactbook. https://www.cia.gov/the-world-factbook/countries/albania/. Accessed 17 Apr 2023
7. Bërxholi, A.: (Hrsg.). Stability Pact for South Eastern Europe (Hrsg. Organ): Atlas of Albania. Demographic Atlas of Albania. Tiranë: Shtypshkronja Ilar (2003)
8. Sališčev, K.A.: Nationalatlanten. Vorschläge zu ihrer Vervollkommnung. In: Neef, E. (Hrsg.): Petermanns Geographische Mitteilungen. 104. Jahrg. pp.77–88. VEB Hermann Haack. Geographisch-Kartographische Anstalt. Gotha (1960)
9. Koch, W.G., Stams, W.: Felderprinzip. In: Bollmann J., Koch, W.G. (Hrsg.): Lexikon der Kartographie und Geomatik. In two volumes, vol. 1, p. 241. Spektrum Akademischer Verlag. Heidelberg, Berlin (2001)

Natural Fracture Network Model Using Machine Learning Approach

Timur Merembayev and Yerlan Amanbek(✉)

Department of Mathematics, School of Sciences and Humanities, Nazarbayev University, Kabanbay batyr 53, Astana, Kazakhstan
yerlan.amanbek@nu.edu.kz

Abstract. A fracture network model is a powerful tool for characterizing fractured rock systems. In this paper, we present the fracture network model by integrating a machine learning algorithm in two-dimensional setting to predict the natural fracture topology in porous media. We also use a machine learning algorithm to predict the fracture azimuth angle for the natural fault data from Kazakhstan. The results indicate that the fracture network model with LightGBM performs better in designing a fracture network parameter for hidden areas based on data from the known area. In addition, the numerical result of the machine learning algorithm shows a good result for randomly selected data of the fracture azimuth.

Keywords: Fracture characterization · Machine learning · LightGBM

1 Introduction

The mapping of natural fracture networks plays a significant role in predicting the hydrocarbon production of reservoir, flow and transport problems in oil and gas production. Due to insufficient data on the subsurface characteristic, predicting the fracture network is still a challenge.

The current literature contains numerous publications that explore the fracture model in the subsurface by utilizing geomechanical conditions that necessitate significant computational power. In recent years, several publications have been published documenting the fracture model in porous media. These works focus on analyzing the fracture behavior in the coupled system and give insights into complex mechanics [1,2,19,24]. However, the complexity of geomechanical models can lead to challenges in verifying simulation results because the model's inputs, including physical properties, boundary conditions, and others, exhibit significant uncertainty and spatial variations.

Considering the problem of mapping fracture network from a geomechanical point of view, the direction of fractures depends on the properties of the subsoil, such as geomechanical features, intersections of fractures, and others [6]. The stress field near fracture nodes is critical in modeling fracture propagation. The research [19,24] showed that energy minimization is important in systematically

O. Gervasi et al. (Eds.): ICCSA 2023 Workshops, LNCS 14107, pp. 384–397, 2023.
https://doi.org/10.1007/978-3-031-37114-1_26

modeling the fracture path using the phase field model. Therefore, the influence of adjacent fractures should be considered when modeling the direction of the fracture.

To overcome these challenges, recent research has focused on developing fracture models that can effectively model complex fracture networks. These models aim to provide a faster and more realistic simulation process that can be used in real-time decision making for reservoir management. One of the effective tools for reducing uncertainty in porous media is stochastic simulation algorithms [8]. These methods incorporate geological data of the fracture network, including fracture azimuth distributions, location and length. While the fracture network model may not always generate the exact topology of porous media, it still provides a suitable configuration for the flow and transport process [3,4,12]. The application of such tasks can be useful for ground remediation, CO2 sequestration, hydrocarbon production, and others. Data collected near a wellbore, or preliminary seismic process from a specific location is a good candidate for training geostatistical models to simulate geological configuration for unknown near locations. These stochastic approaches have gained considerable attention from researchers in their ability to reduce uncertainty in geological modeling.

The Fracture Network model is a powerful tool for simulating fluid flow in fractured porous media. The accuracy of the model depends on the ability to represent the geometry of fractures in the subsurface accurately. There are several approaches that can be used to create the geometry of fractures, including geostatistical analysis, numerical modeling, and field observations. A hybrid approach that combines these methods can provide the most accurate representation of the subsurface while minimizing uncertainties.

Machine learning solves the problems of developing learning algorithms, including unsupervised learning, supervised learning, data dimensionality reduction methods, and feature evaluation. Unsupervised learning allows the identification of stable and rare states of systems; regression and classification are used to predict and identify the state of objects. The use of classical or modern machine learning methods is determined by the amount of data at the disposal of researchers [10,20].

In the literature, some works have shown the application of machine learning methods to reduce uncertainty in geoscience applications [5,16,17]. The well log data is also used by machine learning algorithms such as KNN, Decision Tree, Random Forest, XGBoost, and LightGBM in order to detect multilabel lithofacies classification in [18].

The authors of the paper [15] proposed geostatistical modeling of the fracture system using pattern statistics. The images used multiple-point statistics (MPS) to model the fracture network and its propagation. The authors of [9] used the same MPS for simulating a fracture network; the authors trained the model on satellite images to build fractures on the surface and deep into the earth. This approach is closest to machine learning algorithms. MPS is a popular method for constructing a fracture network if fracture images are available. The MPS method is used in studies [7,13] to model the fracture network system. The MPS method considers the available data around fractures. It builds statistical histograms of known zones to model a network of fractures for unknown zones while maintaining properties from the known zone. This method has limitations for the problem under consideration, building a network of fractures underground. Tasks contain a significant amount of uncertainty, and obtaining images is difficult. Training the MPS method requires a large number of images for quality training. In this regard, this approach for subsurface construction of a fractured network will not be considered.

In this paper, we extend the fracture network model [3] by incorporating with machine learning algorithm in 2D to predict the parameters of fractures in the porous media. We also used machine learning algorithms to generate the parameters of fracture topology, including azimuth angle and compared them with the proposed fracture network model. The natural fault data from Kazakhstan (North of Balkhash Lake) was used to verify the proposed model.

2 Methodology

We consider the fractures for the algorithm and use the digitized data from the geological fault zone. In the fracture network model, the fracture is a collection of segments, which is the line between nodes. In other words, the fracture is a graph containing nodes and branches(fracture segments). Segment's midpoint is used to define the segment location in a domain. In Fig. 1, nodes are presented in black circles, and the midpoint of segments is in the blue circle. Based on the defined location of segments we calculate the azimuth angle of each of them. The azimuth angle of the segment is measured between the fracture segment direction and the north vector, see Fig. 1.

2.1 Fracture Network Algorithm

We use machine learning approaches for the probabilistic classification of azimuth fractures. The input data is the 2D fracture network, which contains the coordinates of each fracture segment. Based on the coordinates, we calculated the azimuth of the fracture segment and the distance between the closest fracture segments, see Fig. 2.

Generated features from the known region fracture networks describing fracture geometries and positions are used to predict the azimuth of the fracture network in the unknown region. The key goal of the classification model is to predict the 8 classes of azimuth of the fracture segment. Below, detailed information about the classification of azimuth angle is presented. The steps of generation features from the fracture network are presented below, and as an example, it is for one initial fracture:

- The azimuth of the closest 6 fractures segment in the fracture network (6 parameters);
- The coordinates of the closest 6 fractures segment: X coordinates are 6 features, and Y coordinates are 6 features;

- The distance of the closest 6 fractures segment (polar coordinates);
- The azimuth for the closest 6 fractures segment (polar coordinates).

In Fig. 3, there is a flowchart of the proposed steps of the algorithm. We prepared a training and validation dataset from the fracture network. The target of the training model is an azimuth angle. In the algorithm, the prediction of azimuth angle segments in machine learning model proceeds as follows:

1. We define the 6 neighbor fractures for each fracture segment. From each fracture, we got true azimuth fractures for the training model.
2. We calculate two types of azimuth: First, the azimuth angle of the 6 closest fractures segment, and second, the azimuth angles from the initial fracture to the 6 closest fractures segment. Also, we define distances from the initial fracture to the 6 closest fractures.
3. The azimuth fracture angles range from 0 to 360 and are divided into 8 equal sectors of angle 45 centered at the fracture. The angle ranges related to each azimuth class are provided in Table 2.
4. Preparing the dataset for training and validation is performed in two ways:
   (a) split the dataset randomly;
   (b) split the dataset by known and hidden areas of interest.
5. Training the LightGBM models and validating the result of the models on the validation dataset.

After training, the ML model can forecast the class azimuth of a fracture network for the location where the model has been trained.

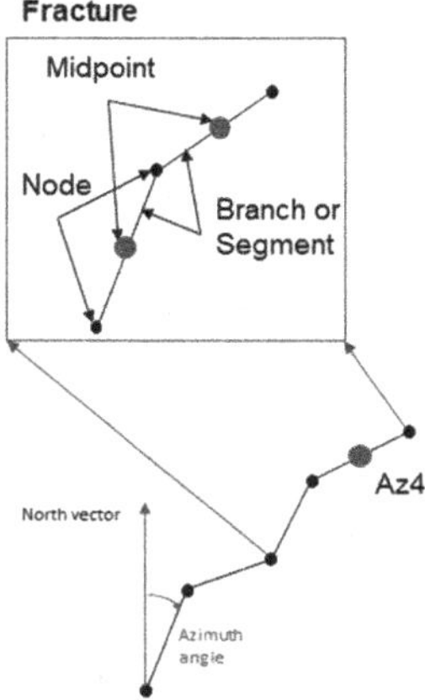

Fig. 1. The fracture network illustrates different node and segment types.

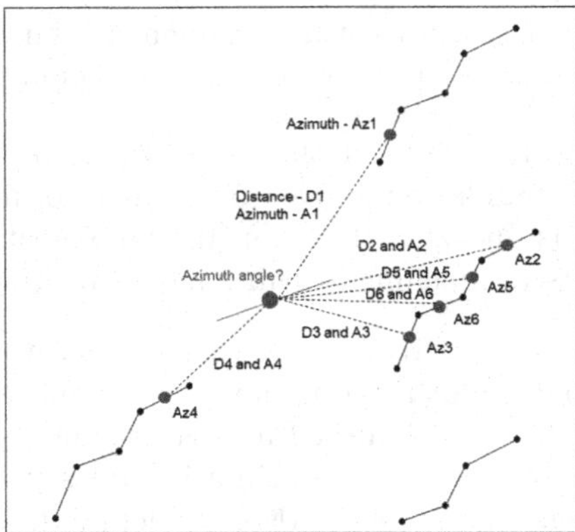

Fig. 2. The searching closest fracture segments.

2.2 Machine Learning Algorithm

Now there are separate machine learning algorithms, each with pros and cons for resolving various problems. In the study, we chose one machine learning algorithm - LightGBM, to verify our hypothesis and classify fracture characterization. The LightGBM algorithm is an open-source framework used for almost tabular data, and our dataset is also tabular. This approach is decision-tree-based, an improved variant of the gradient boosting decision tree (GBDT) algorithm [14].

Another reason is the boosting ensemble algorithms can provide good performance for multi-class imbalanced data. The various problems are multi-class imbalanced data, which have been managed by applying ensemble learning techniques. It is one of the main reasons why we chose LightGBM for this task [23]

The aim of LightGBM algorithm is to obtain an estimate $\widehat{F(X)}$, of the function $F(X)$ mapping X to Y with minimization of the loss function $L(Y, F(X))$.

In gradient boosting, each new b_i algorithm (tree) is added to the already built composition:

$$a_i(x) = a_{i-1}(x) + b_i(x) \tag{1}$$

Such an algorithm corrects the answers of the algorithm $a_i(x)$ to correct answers on the training set. If we consider several algorithms, the algorithm is:

$$a_n(x) = \sum_{i=1}^{N} b_t(x) \tag{2}$$

For the classification task, the loss function has several options, one of option is:

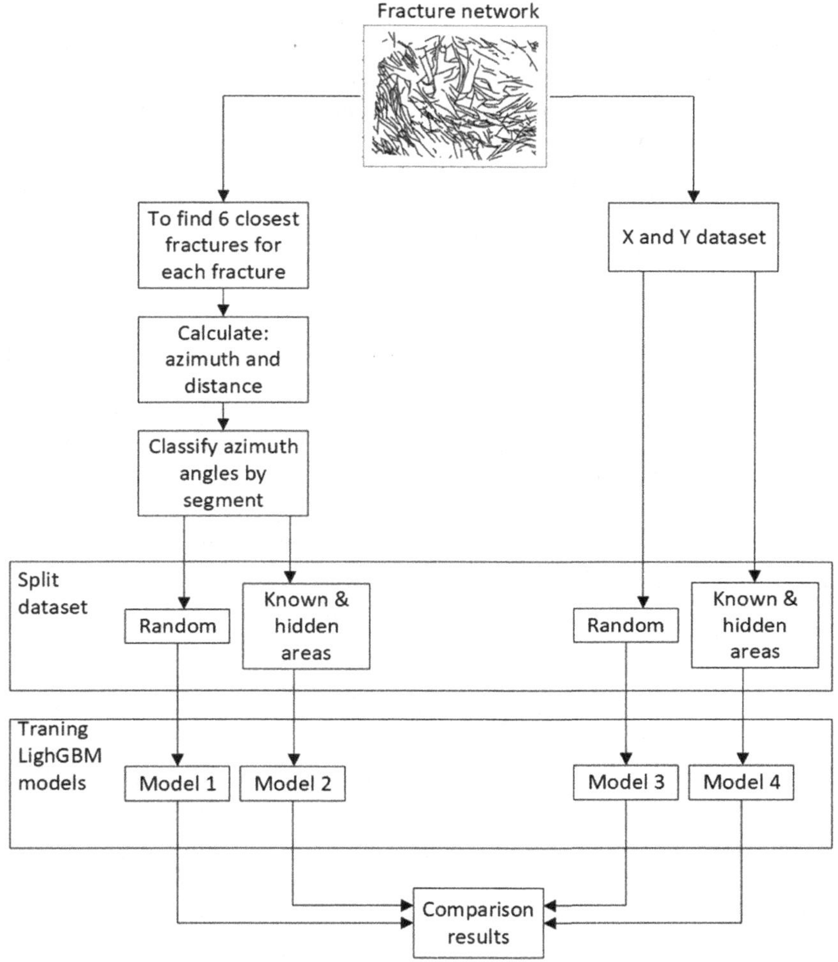

Fig. 3. Flow-chart of the fracture algorithms.

$$L(Y, F(x)) = log(1 + exp(-YF(x))) \tag{3}$$

where $F(x) = a_n(x) + s_i$, $s = (s_1, ..., s_l)$ - vector of shift (correction). Our loss function is:

$$L(Y, F(x)) = log(1 + exp(-YF(x))) \tag{4}$$

$$\sum_{i=1}^{l} log(1 + exp(-y_i * (a_n(x_i) + s_i))) \rightarrow \min_s \tag{5}$$

The forecasting performance of the machine learning models is estimated by one statistical indicator - f1 score [11]. The f1 score has a balance between precision and recall. This metric is used when the class distribution has irregular. The f1 metric is a good scoring metric for imbalanced data when a model needs to classify the positives [21].

$$F1 = 2 * \frac{(precision * recall)}{(precision + recall)} \tag{6}$$

2.3 Data Analysis

We train and validate the algorithm in a 31701 km^2 area north of Balkhash lake, Kazakhstan. The area of interest is near several gold, silver, and copper mines [22]. In addition, there are several actual and possibility mines in the area, see Fig. 4 and Fig. 5. We made digit data of geology and faults for the study area to train and evaluate fracture characterization.

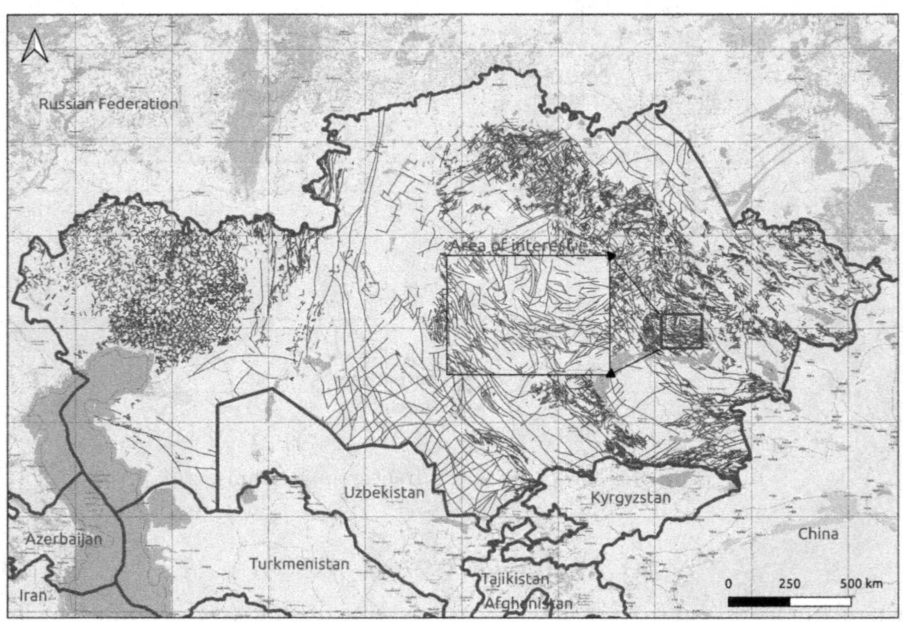

Fig. 4. Area of interest in Kazakhstan [22].

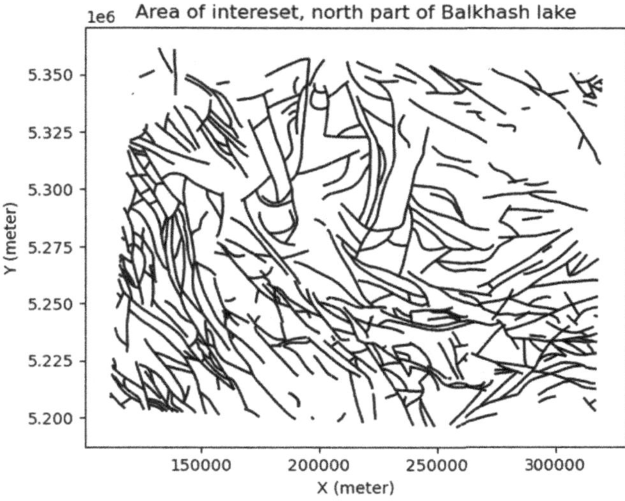

Fig. 5. The geological faults data of Central Kazakhstan.

Figure 6 shows histograms of the azimuth of geology faults. Azimuth angle presented from 0 until 360. The histogram is non-normal distribution because there are several groups of azimuth. Table 1 gives a descriptive statistic of azimuth.

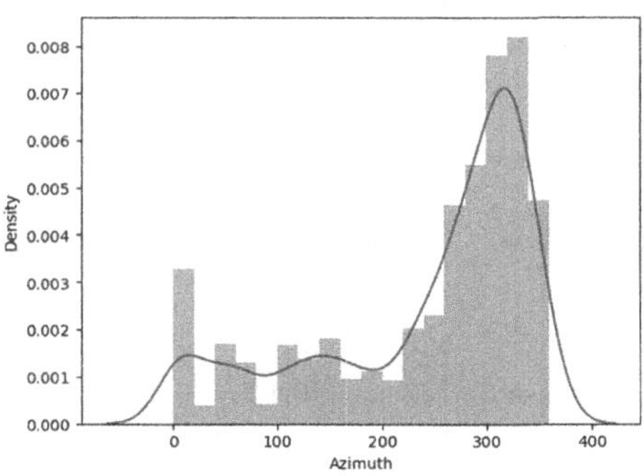

Fig. 6. Histograms of azimuth.

Table 1. The descriptions of azimuth.

Statistics parameter	Value
Count	3087
Mean	241.4
Mode	351.0
Std	104.5
Min	0
25%	173.4
50%	284.9
75%	320.0
Max	359.0

The histogram showed that some segments have a small number of azimuth angles. We classified azimuth by segments. In table 2, azimuth is classified by segments. The 4 segments [0,45), [45,90), [135,180), and [180,225) have not enough account azimuth for training. Therefore we do not use these segments for the training model because a model can not be trained on these segments.

3 Numerical Results

We applied LightGBM to real geological fracture networks to classify the azimuth of fractures. We provide a comparison of the result LightGBM for two cases of splitting dataset and two cases of input dataset:

Table 2. The angle ranges related to each azimuth class for Balkhash dataset.

Class	Count	Azimuth (Degree)
0	7	[0,45)
0	5	[45,90)
class 0	122	[90,135)
0	3	[135,180)
0	8	[180,225)
class 1	98	[225,270)
class 2	231	[270,315)
class 3	92	[315,360)

- Split training and validation datasets are performed randomly by 80% and 20%, respectively. The dataset contains just locations X and Y; secondly, the input dataset all information about the 6 closest fractures;
- Split training and validation datasets are performed by known and hidden areas, see Fig. 7.

For each prepared dataset, we trained LightGBM models, as mentioned in the flow-chart of the fracture algorithms Fig. 3. Models 1 and 2 used data for 6 closest fractures, with random and known and hidden areas splitting, respectively. Models 3 and 4 used data for location data just X and Y features, with random and known and hidden areas splitting, respectively

3.1 Case with Random Selection

The total dataset for the 6 closest fractures is 535 rows and 30 features. We randomly split the dataset into the training dataset contains 428 rows and 30 features, and the validation dataset contains 117 rows and 30 features. The total dataset for the X and Y fractures is 2961 rows and 2 features. We randomly split the dataset into the training dataset contains 2368 rows and 2 features, and the validation dataset contains 593 rows and 2 features.

The result has been compared on X and Y and by 6 closest fractures datasets by the f1 metrics. The classification report of the models are provided in Table 3 and 4. By considering the score information from the tables, we highlighted that model 3 showed better results for a dataset with X and Y, and every 4 classes have more than 0.64 f1 scores. For the 6 closest fractures, model 1 got less f1 score, but for class 0, it is 0.87, other classes f1 scores are less.

3.2 Case with Known and Hidden Areas

To validate the model for this case, we hide some areas of the fracture network in the center area (cropped from the original domain). In Fig. 7, the red color line is the limit of the crop domain from the original fractures. The black color lines are the original fractures or fractures from the known area.

The total dataset for the 6 closest fractures is 553 rows and 30 features. We took data from a known area containing 461 rows and 30 features, and the validation dataset, the hidden area, contains 92 rows and 30 features. The total

Table 3. Classification report of LightGBM result for X and Y.

Class	Precision	Recall	F1	Count
0	0.63	0.64	0.64	147
1	0.71	0.60	0.65	93
2	0.69	0.68	0.69	165
3	0.69	0.74	0.71	188

Table 4. Classification report of LightGBM result for 6 closest fractures.

Class	Precision	Recall	F1	Count
0	0.82	0.92	0.87	25
1	0.46	0.35	0.40	17
2	0.45	0.48	0.47	31
3	0.45	0.44	0.45	34

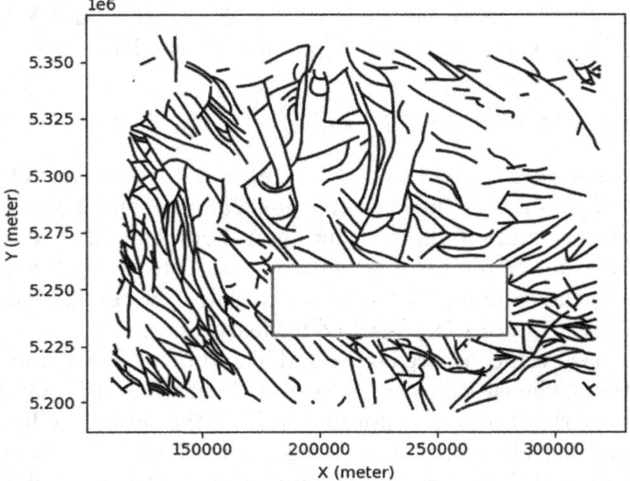

Fig. 7. Hidden zone of fractures from the geological faults data from Kazakhstan.

dataset for the X and Y fractures is 2961 rows and 2 features. We took data from a known area containing 2434 rows and 2 features, and the validation dataset, the hidden area, contains 442 rows and 2 features.

The classification report of the models are provided in Table 5 and 6 for cases with known and hidden areas. The model showed 2 better results for a dataset with 6 closest fractures, each of 4 classes having more than 0.46 f1 scores, and it is better than X and Y datasets (model 4).

Table 5. Classification report of LightGBM result for X and Y.

Class	Precision	Recall	F1	Count
0	0.24	0.20	0.22	107
1	0.30	0.26	0.28	86
2	0.26	0.25	0.25	122
3	0.32	0.42	0.36	127

Table 6. Classification report of LightGBM result for 6 closest fractures.

Class	Precision	Recall	F1	Count
0	0.40	0.55	0.46	14
1	0.65	0.65	0.65	20
2	0.59	0.80	0.62	29
3	0.47	0.79	0.59	29

4 Discussion

Using the natural fault data from Kazakhstan, we established that a machine learning algorithm could be used for the problem of recreation of a fracture network for a zone with uncertainty. We considered machine learning approaches for the probabilistic classification of azimuth fractures. This approach contains two limitations.

Firstly, machine learning approaches require a lot of data to get a reasonable result. In our case, we have the same problem with an imbalanced dataset, and some classes do not have enough data to train a model. We excluded some classes from the process due to the amount of data that is not reasonable to catch a pattern of fracture in these classes. Therefore, the selected dataset should contain enough data to train and validate a model of machine learning.

Secondly, we concentrated on the fixed length of the fracture segment. The length of the fracture segment defines the fracture propagation from the initial point to the neighbor fracture segment. We set the length of the segment as an average fracture length distribution from a known fracture network. In further research, we will study fracture length, anisotropy, and connectivity available of fractures, it should enable better prediction of fracture network.

5 Conclusion

This paper analyzes the numerical models integrated with LightGBM to classify fracture network azimuth from the Kazakhstan geological data in different scenarios. The findings suggest that the fracture network model with LightGBM shows better results in creating fracture geometry parameters for the unknown area based on known area features. The real fault data from Kazakhstan was applied to different models. The direct model, which uses coordinates with azimuth angles, has a good result in F1 measurement for the randomly selected subset of data.

When comparing the classification results by machine learning algorithm for two datasets with features of only fracture segment coordinates and 6 nearest neighbors, we observed that the model 3 has a good result for the dataset with coordinates in randomly splitting the dataset for training and validation dataset. In the case of hidden zone problem, model 2 predicts better for a dataset containing features with 6 neighbors. This suggests that model 2 captures the key knowledge of fault patterns in the known zone and applies it to the hidden zone successfully.

In our further research, we intend to concentrate on the regression of azimuth fracture; also, we will apply deep learning algorithms such as LSTM to predict azimuth.

Acknowledgement. The authors wish to acknowledge the support of the research grant, no. AP19575428, from the Ministry of Science and Higher Education of the Republic of Kazakhstan. Authors gratefully acknowledge the support of the Nazarbayev University Faculty Development Competitive Research Grant (NUFDCRG), Grant No. 20122022FD4141.

References

1. Almani, T., Kumar, K.: Convergence of single rate and multirate undrained split iterative schemes for a fractured biot model. Comput. Geosci. 1–20 (2022). https://doi.org/10.1007/s10596-021-10119-1
2. Almani, T., Lee, S., Wheeler, M.F., Wick, T.: Multirate coupling for flow and geomechanics applied to hydraulic fracturing using an adaptive phase-field technique. In: SPE Reservoir Simulation Conference. OnePetro (2017)
3. Amanbek, Y., Merembayev, T., Srinivasan, S.: Framework of fracture network modeling using conditioned data with sequential gaussian simulation. Arab. J. Geosci. **16**(3), 219 (2023)
4. Andrianov, N., Nick, H.M.: Modeling of waterflood efficiency using outcrop-based fractured models. J. Petrol. Sci. Eng. **183**, 106350 (2019)
5. Andrianov, N., Nick, H.M.: Machine learning of dual porosity model closures from discrete fracture simulations. Adv. Water Resour. **147**, 103810 (2021)
6. Berrone, S., Della Santa, F., Pieraccini, S., Vaccarino, F.: Machine learning for flux regression in discrete fracture networks. GEM - Int. J. Geomath. **12**(1), 1–33 (2021). https://doi.org/10.1007/s13137-021-00176-0
7. Chandna, A., Srinivasan, S.: Modeling natural fracture networks using improved geostatistical inferences. Energy Proc. **158**, 6073–6078 (2019)
8. Chandna, A., Srinivasan, S.: Probabilistic integration of geomechanical and geostatistical inferences for mapping natural fracture networks. Math. Geosci. 1–27 (2023)
9. Chugunova, T., Corpel, V., Gomez, J.P.: Explicit fracture network modelling: from multiple point statistics to dynamic simulation. Math. Geosci. **49**(4), 541–553 (2017)
10. Esteban, A., Zafra, A., Ventura, S.: Data mining in predictive maintenance systems: a taxonomy and systematic review. Wiley Interdiscip. Rev. Data Mining Knowl. Disc. **12**(5), e1471 (2022)
11. Grandini, M., Bagli, E., Visani, G.: Metrics for multi-class classification: an overview. arXiv preprint arXiv:2008.05756 (2020)
12. Hyman, J.D., Karra, S., Makedonska, N., Gable, C.W., Painter, S.L., Viswanathan, H.S.: DFNworks: a discrete fracture network framework for modeling subsurface flow and transport. Comput. Geosci. **84**, 10–19 (2015)
13. Jung, A., Fenwick, D.H., Caers, J.: Training image-based scenario modeling of fractured reservoirs for flow uncertainty quantification. Comput. Geosci. **17**(6), 1015–1031 (2013). https://doi.org/10.1007/s10596-013-9372-0

14. Ke, G., et al.: Lightgbm: A highly efficient gradient boosting decision tree. In: Advances in Neural Information Processing Systems, vol. 30 (2017)
15. Liu, X., Srinivasan, S., Wong, D.: Geological characterization of naturally fractured reservoirs using multiple point geostatistics. In: SPE/DOE Improved Oil Recovery Symposium. OnePetro (2002)
16. Merembayev, T., Amanbek, Y.: Time-series event prediction for the uranium production wells using machine learning algorithms. In: 56th US Rock Mechanics/Geomechanics Symposium. OnePetro (2022)
17. Merembayev, T., Bekkarnayev, K., Amanbek, Y.: The identification models of the copper recovery using supervised machine learning algorithms for the geochemical data. In: 55th US Rock Mechanics/Geomechanics Symposium. OnePetro (2021)
18. Merembayev, T., Yunussov, R., Yedilkhan, A.: Machine learning algorithms for stratigraphy classification on uranium deposits. Proc. Comput. Sci. **150**, 46–52 (2019)
19. Mikelic, A., Wheeler, M.F., Wick, T.: A phase-field method for propagating fluid-filled fractures coupled to a surrounding porous medium. Multiscale Model. Simul. **13**(1), 367–398 (2015)
20. Nguyen, G., et al.: Machine learning and deep learning frameworks and libraries for large-scale data mining: a survey. Artif. Intell. Rev. **52**, 77–124 (2019)
21. Opitz, J., Burst, S.: Macro f1 and macro f1. arXiv preprint arXiv:1911.03347 (2019)
22. Syusyura, B., Box, S.E., Wallis, J.C.: Spatial databases of geological, geophysical, and mineral resource data relevant to sandstone-hosted copper deposits in central Kazakhstan. Technical report, US Geological Survey (2010)
23. Tanha, J., Abdi, Y., Samadi, N., Razzaghi, N., Asadpour, M.: Boosting methods for multi-class imbalanced data classification: an experimental (2020)
24. Wick, T., Singh, G., Wheeler, M.F.: Pressurized-fracture propagation using a phase-field approach coupled to a reservoir simulator. In: SPE Hydraulic Fracturing Technology Conference. OnePetro (2014)

Indicators Engineering for Land Use Changes Analysis. A Study on the Mediterranean Coastal Strip

Francesco Zullo, Cristina Montaldi(✉), Lorena Fiorini, Alessandro Marucci, and Bernardino Romano

University of L'Aquila, 67100 L'Aquila, Italy
{francesco.zullo,lorena.fiorini,alessandro.marucci, bernardino.romano}@univaq.it, cristina.montaldi@graduate.univaq.it

Abstract. Since historical times, coastal areas have been the most extensively transformed territories worldwide. Even today they are subject to strong transformational pressure due to various reasons, mainly tied to climate, greater accessibility to infrastructure networks and services, and mass tourism, which is one of the main sources of income and anthropogenic impact. Landscapes and ecosystems are now largely impacted, especially in the Mediterranean area, due to the better climatic conditions. In recent years, the significant transformative drive that marked the last decades of the past century has decreased in intensity as a result of the growing awareness of environmental issues. The aim of our paper is to analyze land use transformations between 1990 and 2018 in the 500-m shoreline strip, paying special attention to settlement development. This helps gear possible actions/strategies aimed at improving current environmental conditions within the framework of territorial policies to achieve sustainability.

Keywords: Coastal urbanization · Mediterranean Coast · Urbanization impact

1 Introduction

Dualism is the noun that describes the condition of almost all of the world's coastal areas. Although they are an important source of resources, economies and ecosystem services, they are subject to increasing anthropogenic pressure that undermines their integrity and conservation [1–4]. This is even more evident in closed or semi-closed seas, such as the Mediterranean Sea, where an increase in the intensity and frequency of man-made changes, together with ongoing climate change, have led over time to coastal degradation and loss of environmental quality [5–11]. The distinctive morphological and geological conformation of the Mediterranean basin, together with its particular biogeographical characteristics, make it unique in the world [12–14]. This area has always been an important crossroads for the civilizations that followed one another in different historical eras [15], when the sea was the main communication route to establish

O. Gervasi et al. (Eds.): ICCSA 2023 Workshops, LNCS 14107, pp. 398–410, 2023.
https://doi.org/10.1007/978-3-031-37114-1_27

trade relations between peoples, but also the scene of battles for political and military dominance. In the age of geographical discoveries, with the opening of new trade routes across oceans, the center of gravity of international relations and trade began to gradually shift beyond the Strait of Gibraltar, resulting in a decrease in internal trade. The opening of the Suez Canal in 1869 led to a further decline in trade traffic importance with major consequences for local economies [16]. From this period onwards, mass tourism became one of the main economic activities in these places [17–19]. In recent decades, urban transformation related to activities of this type is starting to encroach more and more intensely on various coastal areas along the over 16,600 km coastline [20–22]. This system affects 6 of the 27 States of the European Community which, together with the coastal areas of Albania, Turkey and Montenegro, have been investigated in this study. All the various islands in the Mediterranean basin have been excluded. This paper focuses on a strip of 500 m from the shoreline, dividing it among the different administrative units considered at the third level (NUTS - Nomenclature of territorial units for statistics), excluding all the various islands. The total expanse amounts to about 8,000 km^2, divided into 123 administrative units having an average size of 65 km^2 (Median: 50 km^2 – IQR: 61 km^2). No information is available on demographic density in this strip. The analysis of global population distribution maps having a 1 km/pixel resolution (https://landscan.ornl.gov/), available from 2000 to 2018, shows a population increase of about 2,500,000, equivalent to 140,000 new residents each year. The average population density is just over 1,000 inhabitants/km^2 with values ranging between 4,000 and 5,000 in some Italian areas and over 10,000 inhabitants/km^2 in the Istanbul area. There are large stretches of the Greek coast with population densities below 100 inhabitants/km^2. As mentioned earlier, this area is extremely abundant in habitats: there are about 700 sites of the Natura 2000 network for a total of 2,300 km^2, equal to over 25% of the area surveyed. Maintaining, restoring, and safeguarding these habitats are the key points of several policies adopted at European level since 1976 through the Mediterranean Action Plan (MAP), an offshoot of the United Nations Environment Program (UNEP) through which various programs are implemented addressing the scientific, socio-economic, cultural and legal aspects of the protection of the Mediterranean environment. Signed also by non-European countries, this Convention is a regulatory tool to plan measures for the sustainable management of all activities that may have significant adverse effects on the coastal environment. The protection of the marine environment is taken up by the subsequent Marine Strategy Framework Directive adopted by the European Union in June 2008 (2008/56/EC) updated in 2017, and later followed by the EU Recommendation on Integrated Coastal Zone Management (ICZM). The ICZM is a dynamic, interdisciplinary and interactive process to aggregate all policies that have an impact on European coastal regions, planning appropriately both the management of resources and coastal space. Another interesting initiative is the one adopted in 2013, namely a draft Directive, to establish a framework for maritime spatial planning and integrated coastal management in EU Member States, with a view to promoting the sustainable growth of maritime and coastal activities and the sustainable use of coastal and marine resources. It is essential to understand and monitor anthropogenic and natural transformations taking place in these fragile environments. Hence, this paper aims to assess land cover transitions along the coastal arc of the European part of the Mediterranean Sea from 1990 to 2018.

We have conducted our analysis using the NUTS3 administrative level to appropriately assess conditions in each coastal area. This understanding is a fundamental prerogative to guide possible actions/strategies to improve current environmental conditions within the framework of territorial policies to achieve sustainability.

2 Materials and Methods

Land cover maps [23], are derived from the European portal Copernicus (https://www.copernicus.eu/en). The minimum mapping unit (MMU) is 25 ha for areal phenomena and a minimum width of 100 m for linear phenomena. This database covers a 30-year time span (data acquired in the following years: 1990, 2000, 2006, 2012, 2018), with essentially unchanged data genesis. Land cover changes were analyzed through change layers also available in the same repository (MMU 5 ha). Data on the geography of European countries were derived from the EUROSTAT website (updated at 2019 - https://ec.europa.eu/eurostat/web/gisco/geodata/reference-data/administrative-units-statistical-units/nuts). The coastline was then extracted from this database. All data used are projected in the ETRS89 LAEA Europe (EPSG: 3035) reference system. The coastal strip was subdivided into 143 plots derived from the geographical and administrative location of the boundaries of the 123 units (Provinces/Districts) in the study area. Each of these plots was assigned an ordinal value (from 1 to 143) from West to East in order to analyze changes in geographical and spatial continuity. Therefore, the value 1 was attributed to the Province of Cadiz in Spain (City of Tàrifa) and 143 to the province of Hatay in Turkey on the border with Syria. The first part of this research focuses on assessing the development of settlements by analyzing urbanization density index and on the changes in surfaces transformed to urban use in the period considered. By urbanized surfaces we mean those intended for urban functions, with the replacement or retention of natural land. This type of surface includes built-up land and areas used for settlement ancillary functions, such as public and private gardens, sports facilities, unpaved roads and other service areas. Suburban roads are excluded from the calculation. These surfaces are the same as those recorded under item 1 in the CLC nomenclature. Settlement pressure, both in its diachronic and synchronic form, was analyzed using the urbanization density index and the urban variation ratio, whose formulas are shown below:

$$\mathrm{UD} = \left(\sum \mathrm{Us}\right)/\mathrm{Au}(\%) \tag{1}$$

$$\mathrm{UVR(Urban\ Variation\ Ratio)} = (\mathrm{Aurbt}_1 - \mathrm{Aurbt}_0)/\mathrm{Aurbt}_0(\%) \tag{2}$$

where:

Us = Urbanized surface
Au = Reference territorial surface

Both indices were calculated in two 2 specific time periods: 1990 and 2018. Index (a) provides information on the degree of existing anthropic pressure while index (b) is linked to settlement behavior adopted by individual administrative units. The latter provides information on the percentage increase of urbanized surfaces between two distinct time periods compared to the initial condition. In the second part of our research, we analyzed the entire range of land use transitions. We investigated, in particular, land use transformations between two successive time periods (1990–2000; 2000–2006; 2006–2012; 2012–2018). The different types of possible land use transitions are listed below:

Natural - semi-natural - Artificial (from 3 to 1; from 4 to 1; from 5 to 1): change from natural to artificial use (e.g., a wetland converted to urban use);

Natural-semi-natural - Agricultural Use (from 3 to 2; from 4 to 2; from 5 to 2): transition from natural to semi-natural use (e.g., a forest converted to agricultural use);

Agricultural Use - Artificial (from 2 to 1): change from a semi-natural to an artificial use (e.g., conversion of an agricultural area to urban use);

Agricultural use - Natural (from 2 to 3; from 2 to 4; from 2 to 5): this type of transition is tied to the abandonment of farmed areas for example;

Natural - Natural (from 3 to 4; from 3 to 5; from 4 to 3; from 4 to 5; from 5 to 3; from 5 to 4): transition from a natural use to another natural use of a different category (e.g.: from wetland to water body).

Artificial - (Agricultural - Semi-natural - Natural) (from1 to 2 or 3 or 4 or 5): these transitions usually involve the use of de-sealing techniques.

Lastly there are the transitions within the same macroclass. Added to this, we need to consider whatever remains unchanged and the ensuing increases/decreases in surface for each of the different land use classes. All transitions to artificial land use take away fertile soil, are often irreversible, and have additional direct negative impacts in terms of environmental fragmentation, loss of ecosystem services, climate and hydrogeological effects as well as a range of indirect impacts (increased air and noise pollution, increased energy consumption and transport demand…). Conversely, changes from anthropogenic to natural uses obviously have several positive impacts on multiple aspects and help mitigate several risks: increase in vegetation cover, decrease in surface runoff and creation of new habitats for animal and plant species, just to name a few. This type of analysis therefore provides information from both a geographical and a statistical point of view, in order to interpret dynamics and identify the drivers that have modified land use [24–26]. There is a lack of data for Albania for the 1990 period.

3 Results

3.1 Urban Coastal Dynamics

The condition observed in 1990 (hatched grey in Fig. 1) appears distinctly different from that of the present day. In 1990 urbanized areas along the coastal strip amounted to about 1,570 km^2, equivalent to a UD of just over 19%, with areas lacking urbanization concentrated mainly along the northern part of the Italian Adriatic coast and in some parts of Central Macedonia in Greece. There are 18 areas with a UD above 50% (12% of the total) involving a stretch of the Spanish coast (Malaga) and most of the French coastal area, up to and including the entire Ligurian arc in Italy. Similar conditions are also found along large stretches of the Adriatic coastline. In Greece and Turkey, these urbanization rates are reached in the districts of respective capitals. Furthermore, 75% of investigated areas have a UD below 38%.

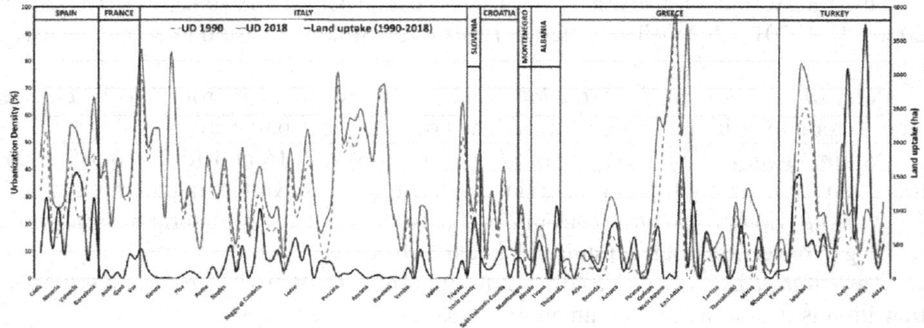

Fig. 1. UD index trend in 1990 (dotted gray) and 2018 (red). Land uptake is also shown (black) as measured over the period considered in each coastal area

Between 1990 and 2018, major urbanization processes affected most of the Greek coastline and some parts of the Turkish coast. The mean value of the UVR index of the entire Mediterranean coast is 35%, while the one of these 2 countries is approximately twofold. In Italy and France this value is much lower than the average. In the case of Italy, this is due to different initial settlement conditions, compared to Greece and Turkey. The transformative drive that substantially changed the appearance of the Italian coastline reached very high values between the early 60's and the late 80's, when settlements eroded significant parts of the coastal system (Romano et al., 2017, 2014). The French coasts already had a significant degree of urbanization back in 1990 (UD > 30%), with the exception of some stretches where settlement processes were limited by morphology. Spain is the only country with an index value in line with that of the Mediterranean area. Among the 12 provinces administering the over 1,500 km coastline, Valencia and Castellón have doubled their urbanized areas, reaching a UD of around 50%. This makes them among the most intensely urbanized areas along the Spanish coast. Among the countries in the Balkan area, Croatia has a UVR value of 20%. Along this coastline, the Split-Dalmatian region has the greatest urbanization, owing to regions with important historical settlements at national level, such as the cities of Split, Solin and Kastel. The northern part of the coast is where the highest values of the UVR index are found: 36% in the Istrian Region, where the flourishing tourist activity has transformed large stretches of the coastline, and 65% in the Lika and Senj Region, but in the latter case transformations are less intense and more localized, due also to the rugged coastal morphology (Fig. 2).

Furthermore, transition matrices were created and analyzed using land cover change data provided by the Copernicus Land Project (Fig. 3).

Between 1990 and 2000 over 12,000 ha of agricultural land were converted to urban use, 70% of which in Turkey and 15% in Spain. As a result, 5.2% of agricultural land present in 1990 was permanently lost. Turkey is the country with the highest conversion rate (1,200 ha/year), followed by Spain (270 ha/year), while Italy and Greece transform their coastal territories at a substantially identical rate (approximately 130 ha/year).

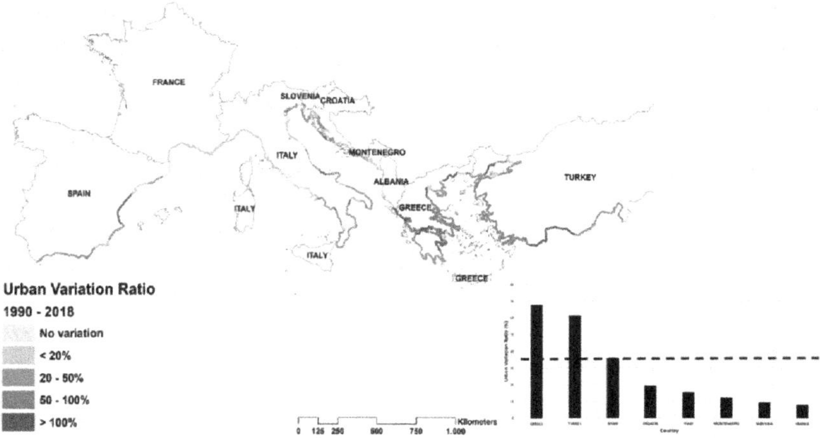

Fig. 2. UVR index values between 1990 and 2018. The dashed black line shows the observed value for the entire Mediterranean coast

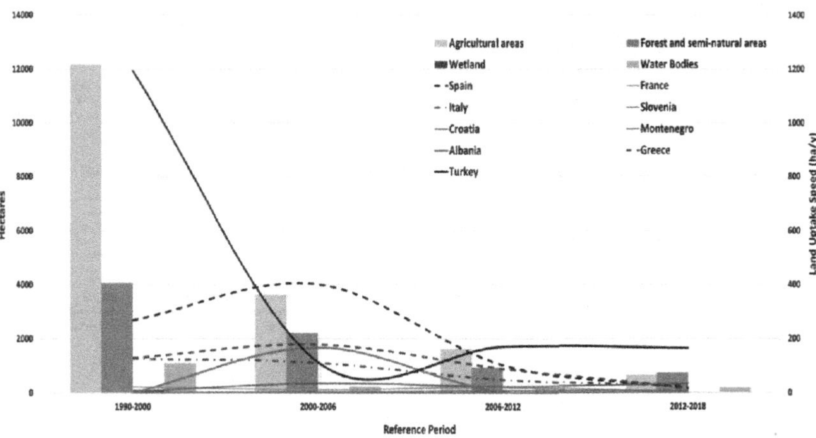

Fig. 3. Land-to-Urban conversion matrix (bars) in the two distinct time periods and land uptake rate trends (ha/year) along the coastlines in the countries considered (lines)

Forests and semi-natural areas are also affected by settlement-related phenomena: 40 km^2 are converted to urban use. Grasslands (21%), sclerophyllous vegetation areas (23%) and, to a slightly greater extent, transitional woodland-scrub areas (25%) are the most commonly transformed. In this case too, most of the transformations have occurred in Turkey (58%), and to a lesser extent in Spain (20%) and Greece (16%). The highest rate of urban transformation of land occurred in this period: 17.5 km^2 irreversibly lost each year. Between 2000 and 2006, there was a slowdown in the transformation drive, with 10 km^2 of land converted to urban use each year. In this period, Spain had the highest rate (4 km^2/year) followed by Greece and Albania (2 km^2/year). Agricultural areas are still the most commonly affected (60%). The downward trend is also confirmed by data in the following period (2006–2012): approximately 30 km^2 converted to urban use, 60% of which was farmland previously. The yearly uptake rate has dropped further and is halved compared to the previous period. Almost 80% of transformations concerns the coastal areas of only 3 countries (Turkey, Spain and Greece). However, despite the decline, Turkey is the only country where transformation has picked up again since 2006 and where as much as 60% of total forest classes, transformed from 2012 to 2018, have been converted to urban use, followed by Croatia with an alarming 20%. Moreover, maquis is most commonly converted to urban use. Another important aspect is the low rate of land uptake in France (maximum 20 ha/year between 2006 and 2012) with very limited overall land uptake, entirely unlike other Western European countries.

3.2 Land Cover Transitions

Figure 4 shows all possible transitions (analyzed at the first CLC level) together with the number of hectares in the area concerned for each of the countries investigated. The bar chart shows the percentage of transformed land through each transition, compared to total areas undergoing a change in class in each of the countries considered.

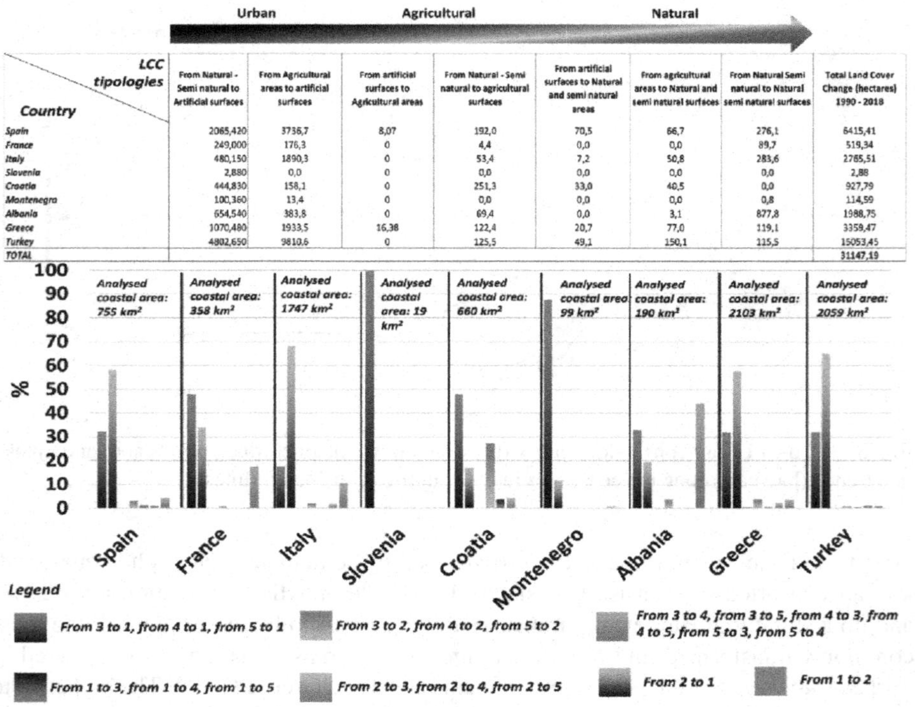

Country \ LCC tipologies	From Natural - Semi natural to Artificial surfaces	From Agricultural areas to artificial surfaces	From artificial surfaces to Agricultural areas	From Natural - Semi natural to agricultural surfaces	From artificial surfaces to Natural and semi natural areas	From agricultural areas to Natural and semi natural surfaces	From Natural Semi natural to Natural semi natural surfaces	Total Land Cover Change (hectares) 1990 - 2018
Spain	2065,420	3736,7	8,07	192,0	70,5	66,7	276,1	6415,41
France	249,000	176,3	0	4,4	0,0	0,0	89,7	519,34
Italy	480,150	1890,3	0	53,4	7,2	50,8	283,6	2765,51
Slovenia	2,880	0,0	0	0,0	0,0	0,0	0,0	2,88
Croatia	444,830	158,1	0	251,3	33,0	40,5	0,0	927,79
Montenegro	100,360	13,4	0	0,0	0,0	0,0	0,8	114,59
Albania	654,540	383,8	0	69,4	0,0	3,1	877,8	1988,75
Greece	1070,480	1933,5	16,38	122,4	20,7	77,0	119,1	3359,47
Turkey	4802,650	9810,6	0	125,5	49,1	150,1	115,5	15053,45
TOTAL								31147,19

Fig. 4. 1990–2018 transition matrix for Mediterranean coastal areas broken down per country

The table shows that, between 1990 and 2018, 90% of transitions are to artificial land use types, further emphasizing the strategic importance of coasts for settlements.

The country with the lowest figure is Albania (52%), followed by Croatia with 65%. All other countries exceed 80% and Turkey, Montenegro and Slovenia had only transitions to artificial land. Additional anthropic transitions include those to agricultural classes. These transformations certainly have a greater degree of reversibility compared to the former, but the areas affected are still subject to significant anthropic pressure that could further exacerbate water supply-related issues. 900 ha are affected by this type of transformation, most of which in Croatia (30%) and Spain (22%). Abandoned farmland and pastures or transitional natural vegetation are what characterize transitions from any type of land cover to a natural one. This type of transition has concerned only 7.5% of total transformations, most of which were concentrated in Albania (about 880 ha), a very high figure if compared to Italy (340 ha), Spain (413 ha) and Turkey (312 ha) that have vaster coastal expanses. This is mainly due to consolidated economies linked to the tourist industry in Italy and Spain and the significant growth of this sector in Turkey since the early 2000s linked to strong public and private investment [27–29] stimulated by the steady increase in the number of tourists. In order to provide a more detailed territorial picture, this system of transitions has been analyzed at the NUTS3 level (Fig. 5).

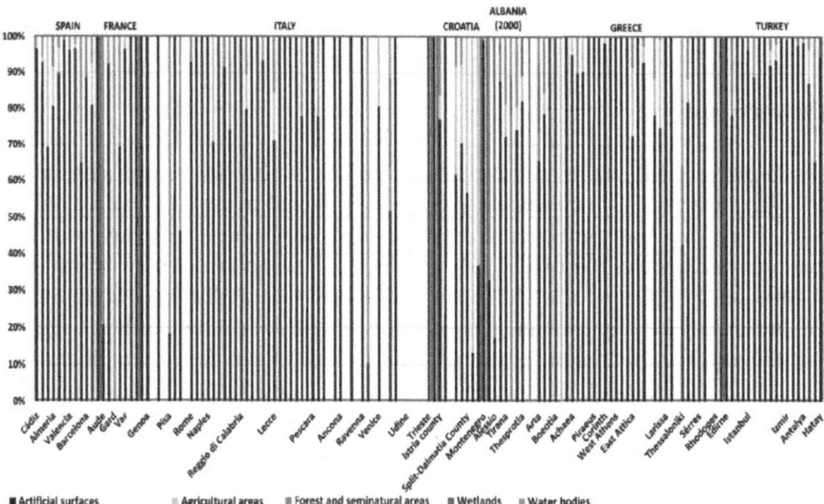

Fig. 5. Land cover transitions expressed as percentages of total transformed areas between 1990 and 2018 for each of the NUTS3 levels analyzed

In all Spanish coastal areas, the prevailing transition is towards artificial land uses, whose percentage is never below 65% of the total. Significant transitions to other types of land use may be found in the provinces of Granada (31% farmland) and Tarragona (33% water bodies). As far as French coastal areas are concerned, the important transitions to natural land uses in the Departments of Aude and Gard are due to Natural Parks (Narbonnaise en Méditerranée Natural Regional Park) and Natura 2000 sites which have curbed the less intense transformation drive affecting other areas. Of the 54 areas analyzed along the Italian coastline, 26 (approximately 50%) have transitioned to urban uses only, while few areas have been converted to farmland, mainly in the provinces of Salerno and Lecce. Important transitions to natural land uses can be found in the Province of Catanzaro and in the previously mentioned Salento region. The coastal areas in the Croatian regions are marked by a higher percentage of changes to agricultural use of land. Most of these are concentrated in the Dubrovnik-Neretva County, an area scarcely affected by mass tourism, which instead is mostly concentrated in the northern part of the country and its islands. The situation in Albania is more intricate: major transitions to artificial land uses may be found in the counties of Shkodër (87%), Tirana (73%) and Korcë (75%), while significant transitions to natural land uses concern the coastal territories of Gjirokastër (79%) and Durrës (41%). The Greek coastal areas have similar dynamics to the Italian ones, although the settlement process drive is greater. Indeed, 700 ha of land have been converted to urban use in Greece, with 18 of the 37 areas analyzed transitioning only to CLC class 1. Transitions to natural land are not very significant and are found only in the Aetolia-Acarnania region (15% of the total) and in the Chalkidiki region (12%). Transitions to agricultural uses are slightly more significant, accounting for the only transition in the West Attica territories (100%) and for 20% of transitions in the areas of East Attica and Magnesia Prefecture. Turkey does not differ much from the country with which it borders on the Thracian Sea. Transitions to natural land uses reach at least 20% of the total only in a couple of areas (Çanakkale and Adana).

4 Discussion

Our research has analyzed land cover transitions in the Mediterranean coastal system over the last 30 years. The entire analysis was conducted using CLC data available for the entire European continent over several time periods. However, the methods used for the cartographic acquisition of CLC data (MMU 25 ha and minimum width of linear elements equal to 100 m) do not make it possible to detect all dispersed settlements [30] present in some of the countries analyzed, such as Italy, Spain, Albania and Greece. Many new settlements (residential or tourist accommodation) have the typical characteristics of sprawl [31, 32] (particularly evident along the Turkish coast), due to obvious reasons tied to economic return, but in many coastal areas, settlements can be ascribed to the sprinkling model owing to their building density and extremely low coverage ratios [33–36]. This type of settlement is often developed spontaneously or subject to poor land-use planning control, compounded by the lack of underlying urban planning, making it extremely impactful from the standpoint of landscape, energy, land consumption and management costs.

Our work shows that in approximately 30 years over 550 km^2 have been urbanized with a linear land uptake rate equal to 40 km/year. However, based on our previous remarks, this figure could be significantly higher. It is therefore clear that given the different geographic, typological-functional and morphological characteristics of settlements in some European countries, data having greater cartographic detail would be needed in order to properly monitor urban development. Clearly even change layers, whose MMU is equal to 5 ha, are unable to detect these changes because this pervasive form of settlement has the size of a single building or of aggregates of a few units (Fig. 6). The analysis has also highlighted that coastal areas are subject to intense and

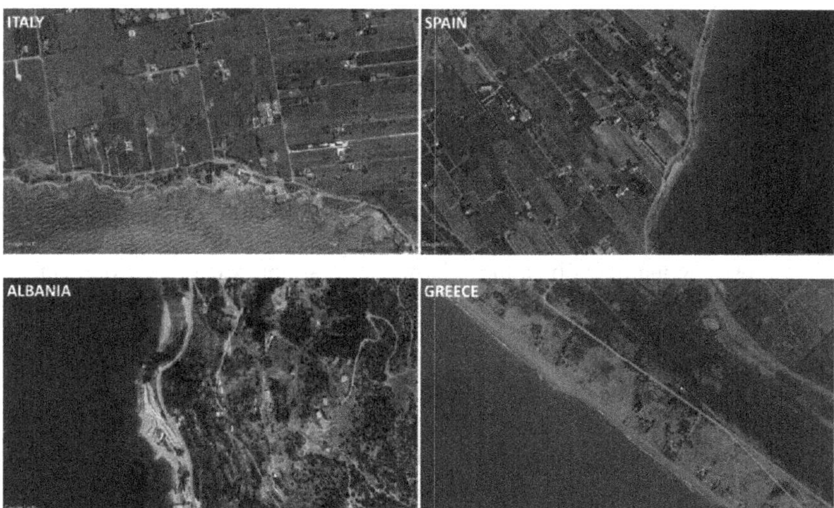

Fig. 6. Examples of sprinkling along the coastline in some countries in the investigated area

continuous anthropic pressure over time. The significant tourist attractiveness of places together with one of the most favorable climates globally (mild winters, long summers and an ideal atmospheric temperature range) have intensified settlement and agricultural transformations largely altering extensive coastal areas. These 2 types of transitions account for over 90% of transformations in countries such as Spain, Croatia, Greece and Turkey where this figure nears 98%. Italy and France are just below this threshold with 88% and 82% respectively, while Albania is the only country where transitions to natural land cover have reached high values (45%). Coastal areas with strong urban dominance (DU > 40%) account for 31% of the total. These are areas undermined by urban development where nature is often relegated to residual interstitial spaces between buildings and infrastructure. They are found along almost the entire Spanish coastline, in the coastal arc that goes from Var (France) to Liguria (Italy) and along the Tyrrhenian Sea in the areas of the coast of Rome and the Gulf of Naples. Calabrian coastal areas, both Tyrrhenian and Ionian, also share the same characteristics, while along the Adriatic it is the western part that is in more critical conditions, especially the area from upper Abruzzo to the coast of Romagna. Along the eastern part, similar conditions are found only in the Primorje-Gorski Kotar county and Split-Dalmatia County. Although Greece and Turkey are the countries with the greatest land uptake for urban use during the period analyzed, they have few areas in these conditions: the Athens-Piraeus area, in the case of the former and the Istanbul and Balikesir area, in the case of the latter. Many of the settlements found today along the Turkish coast are of recent construction, linked to the growing tourist attractiveness of these places [37] and have affected many of the coastal forest areas [38, 39]. Unlike what has happened in other countries in the Mediterranean area, these settlements are entirely designed in accordance with appropriate regulations that limit the maximum height of buildings and protect archaeological areas and natural habitats.

5 Conclusion

This research work is the first, at international level, to investigate natural and anthropogenic transitions affecting over 16,600 km of Mediterranean coastline in the past 30 years. Despite limitations tied to CLC data acquisition techniques for urbanized areas, our research highlights the strong transformational pressure that coastal territories are subject to, due to their important role in both local and national economies. Moreover, the use of NUTS3 administrative boundaries has helped us understand which coastal areas are mostly jeopardized by anthropic transformations, where environmental rehabilitation and habitat restoration are very difficult to implement due to the considerable pervasiveness of settlements. This could help foster more detailed studies on these areas to investigate the actual distribution of built-up areas and their function in the broader geographical context, in order to implement appropriate policies and targeted actions. In this regard, correct Integrated Coastal Zone Management (ICZM) depends greatly on an efficient monitoring system capable of detecting in real time any transformative processes threatening coastal areas. Satellite imagery already help us obtain data with the necessary geometric accuracy, while available technologies help process huge amounts of data very quickly. It is therefore appropriate to implement a console of indicators (environmental, urban, ecological and demographic) capable of providing quick feedback on the actual conditions in each of the European coastal areas, connected to an early warning system for any potential risks caused by incorrectly planned transformations.

References

1. Zheng, Z., Wu, Z., Chen, Y., Yang, Z., Marinello, F.: Exploration of eco-environment and urbanization changes in coastal zones: a case study in China over the past 20 years. Ecol. Indic. **119**, 106847 (2020)
2. Parravicini, V., Rovere, A., Vassallo, P., et al.: Understanding relationships between conflicting human uses and coastal ecosystems status: a geospatial modeling approach. Ecol. Indic. **19**, 253–263 (2012)
3. McDonald, R.I., Green, P., Balk, D., et al.: Urban growth, climate change, and freshwater availability. Proc. Natl. Acad. Sci. **108**(15), 6312–6317 (2011)
4. Defeo, O., McLachlan, A., Schoeman, D.S., et al.: Threats to sandy beach ecosystems: a review. Estuar. Coast Shelf Sci. **81**(1), 1–12 (2009)
5. Haddad, N.M., Brudvig, L.A., Clobert, J., et al.: Habitat fragmentation and its lasting impact on Earth's ecosystems. Sci. Adv. **1**(2), e1500052 (2015). https://doi.org/10.1126/sciadv.1500052
6. Verburg, P.H., Crossman, N., Ellis, E.C., et al.: Land system science and sustainable development of the earth system: a global land project perspective. Anthropocene **12**, 29–41 (2015)
7. Micheli, F., Halpern, B.S., Walbridge, S., et al.: Cumulative human impacts on Mediterranean and Black Sea marine ecosystems: assessing current pressures and opportunities. PloS One **8**(12), e79889 (2013)
8. Bajocco, S., De Angelis, A., Perini, L., Ferrara, A., Salvati, L.: The impact of land use/land cover changes on land degradation dynamics: a Mediterranean case study. Environ. Manag. **49**(5), 980–989 (2012). https://doi.org/10.1007/s00267-012-9831-8

9. Ciscar, J.C., Iglesias, A., Feyen, L., et al.: Physical and economic consequences of climate change in Europe. Proc. Natl. Acad. Sci. **108**(7), 2678–2683 (2011). https://doi.org/10.1073/pnas.1011612108
10. Garcia-Ruiz, J.M., Lòpez-Moreno, J.I., Vicente-Serrano, S.M., Lasanta–Martìnez, T., Beguerìa, S.: Mediterranean water resources in a global change scenario. Earth-Sci. Rev. **105**(3–4), 121–139 (2011)
11. Fischer, E.M., Schar, C.: Consistent geographical patterns of changes in high-impact European heatwaves. Nat. Geosci. **3**(6), 398–403 (2010)
12. Coll, M., Piroddi, C., Steenbeek, J., et al.: The biodiversity of the Mediterranean Sea: estimates, patterns, and threats. PloS One **5**(8), e11842 (2010)
13. Abdulla, A., Gomei, M., Hyrenbach, D., Notarbartolo-di-Sciara, G., Agardy, T.: Challenges facing a network of representative marine protected areas in the Mediterranean: prioritizing the protection of underrepresented habitats. ICES J. Mar. Sci. **66**(1), 22–28 (2009). https://doi.org/10.1093/icesjms/fsn164
14. Zeder, M.A.: Domestication and early agriculture in the Mediterranean Basin: origins, diffusion, and impact. Proc. Natl. Acad. Sci. **105**(33), 11597–11604 (2008)
15. Pounds, N.J.G.: The urbanization of the classical word. Ann. Assoc. Am. Geogr. **59**(1), 135–157 (1969)
16. Abulafia, D.: The Great Sea: A Human History of the Mediterranean. Penguin Books, London (2014). Ed. publ. with updates
17. Segreto, L., Manera, C., Pohl, M.: Europe at the Seaside: The Economic History of Mass Tourism in the Mediterranean. Berghahn Books, New York (2009)
18. Pons, P.O., Crang, M., Travlou, P.: Cultures of Mass Tourism: Doing the Mediterranean in the Age of Banal Mobilities. Ashgate Publishing, Ltd., Farnham (2009)
19. Bramwell, B.: Coastal Mass Tourism: Diversification and Sustainable Development in Southern Europe. Channel View Publications, Bristol (2004)
20. Anthony, E.J., Marriner, N., Morhange, C.: Human influence and the changing geomorphology of Mediterranean deltas and coasts over the last 6000 years: from progradation to destruction phase? Earth-Sci. Rev. **139**, 336–361 (2014). https://doi.org/10.1016/j.earscirev.2014.10.003
21. Malavasi, M., Santoro, R., Cutini, M., Acosta, A., Carranza, M.L.: What has happened to coastal dunes in the last half century? A multitemporal coastal landscape analysis in Central Italy. Landsc. Urban Plan. **119**, 54–63 (2013)
22. Van Der Maarel, E.: Some remarks on the functions of European coastal ecosystems. Phytocoenologia **33**, 187–202 (2003). Published online
23. Büttner, G.: CORINE land cover and land cover change products. In: Manakos, I., Braun, M., (eds.) Land Use and Land Cover Mapping in Europe. RDIP, vol. 18, pp. 55–74. Springer, Dordrecht (2014). https://doi.org/10.1007/978-94-007-7969-3_5
24. Lambin, E.F., Meyfroidt, P.: Land use transitions: socio-ecological feedback versus socio-economic change. Land Use Policy **27**(2), 108–118 (2010)
25. Lambin, E.F., Meyfroidt, P.: Global land use change, economic globalization, and the looming land scarcity. Proc. Natl. Acad. Sci. **108**(9), 3465–3472 (2011)
26. Feranec, J.: European Landscape Dynamics CORINE Land Cover Data (2016). https://www.taylorfrancis.com/books/9781315372860. Accessed 26 July 2022
27. Demiroz, D.M., Ongan, S.: The contribution of tourism to the long-run Turkish economic growth. Ekon. Cas. **9**, 880–894 (2005)
28. Tosun, C.: Challenges of sustainable tourism development in the developing world: the case of Turkey. Tour. Manag. **22**(3), 289–303 (2001)
29. Buckley, P., Geyikdagi, N.V.: Explaining foreign direct investment in Turkey's tourism industry. Transnatl. Corp. **5**, 99–110 (1996)

30. Romano, B., Zullo, F.: Models of urban land use in Europe: assessment tools and criticalities. Int. J. Agric. Environ. Inf. Syst. **4**(3), 80–97 (2013). https://doi.org/10.4018/ijaeis.2013070105
31. Egidi, G., Cividino, S., Vinci, S., Sateriano, A., Salvia, R.: Towards local forms of sprawl: a brief reflection on Mediterranean urbanization. Sustainability **12**(2), 582 (2020)
32. Hennig, E.I., Schwick, C., Soukup, T., Orlitova, E., Kienast, F., Jaeger, J.A.: Multi-scale analysis of urban sprawl in Europe: towards a European de-sprawling strategy. Land Use Policy **49**, 483–498 (2015)
33. Dutta, I., Das, A.: Exploring the dynamics of urban sprawl using geo-spatial indices: a study of English Bazar Urban Agglomeration, West Bengal. Appl. Geomat. **11**(3), 259–276 (2019)
34. Urbieta, P., Fernandez, E., Ramos, L., Méndez Martínez, G., Bento, R.: A land-cover based urban dispersion indicator suitable for highly dispersed, discontinuously artificialized territories: the case of continental Portugal. Land Use Policy **85**, 92–103 (2019). https://doi.org/10.1016/j.landusepol.2019.03.048
35. Saganeiti, L., Favale, A., Pilogallo, A., Scorza, F., Murgante, B.: Assessing urban fragmentation at regional scale using sprinkling indexes. Sustainability **10**(9), 3274 (2018). https://doi.org/10.3390/su10093274
36. Romano, B., Zullo, F., Fiorini, L., Ciabò, S., Marucci, A.: Sprinkling: an approach to describe urbanization dynamics in Italy. Sustainability **9**(1), 97 (2017). https://doi.org/10.3390/su9010097
37. Burak, S., Doğan, E., Gazioğlu, C.: Impact of urbanization and tourism on coastal environment. Ocean Coast. Manag. **47**(9–10), 515–527 (2004). https://doi.org/10.1016/j.ocecoaman.2004.07.007
38. Başkent, E.Z., Kadioğullari, A.I.: Spatial and temporal dynamics of land use pattern in Turkey: a case study in İnegöl. Landsc. Urban Plan. **81**(4), 316–327 (2007). https://doi.org/10.1016/j.landurbplan.2007.01.007
39. Atmics, E., Ozden, S., Lise, W.: Urbanization pressures on the natural forests in Turkey: an overview. Urban For. Urban Green. **6**(2), 83–92 (2007)

Agricultural Crops and Spatial Distribution of Migrants: Case Studies in Campania Region (Southern Italy)

Giovanni Mauro[1(✉)], Maria Ronza[2], and Claudio Sossio De Simone[3]

[1] Department of Humanities, Vanvitelli University, Caserta, Italy
giovanni.mauro@unicampania.it
[2] Department of Humanities, University of Naples Federico II, Naples, Italy
mronza@unina.it
[3] Department of Humanities, University of Roma Tor Vergata, Rome, Italy
claudiosossio.desimone@students.uniroma2.eu

Abstract. In the current context of increasing stabilization of migrants permanently residing in the Campania region (southern Italy), this paper aims to investigate the relationship between the spatial distribution of migrants and the work opportunities in the agricultural sector. We analyse data in the agriculture and population censuses currently available at the municipality level (referring to 2011) and we apply spatial autocorrelation techniques, using the Local Indicator of Spatial Association (LISA) and Getis-Ord Gi* statistic. The maps clusters of migrants (classified by continent) and agricultural crops or breeding (horticulture, orchards and citrus, buffalo and poultry farms), highlight a positive spatial correspondence between resulting hot spots. Finally, we overlay the resulting cluster maps to understand the significance of any external factors, such as the employment opportunities in the areas where migrants have settled.

Keywords: Migrations · Agriculture · Campania Region · Spatial autocorrelation · Cluster analysis

1 Introduction

Italy's booming economy began attracting workers from surrounding countries during the early 1970's. Over the next fifty years, migration has become a significant component of the Italian population: according to official sources[1], in Italy there are now more than five million migrants, about 8.5% of the total population. This percentage is in line with that of the European Union (currently home to 37.5 million migrates[2]), often dubbed

[1] *Immigrati.stat*, http://stra-dati.istat.it/, last accessed 2023/04/15.

[2] Statistics on migration in Europe, https://commission.europa.eu/strategy-and-policy/priorities-2019-2024/promoting-our-european-way-life/statistics-migration-europe_en, last accessed 2023/04/18.

O. Gervasi et al. (Eds.): ICCSA 2023 Workshops, LNCS 14107, pp. 411–426, 2023.
https://doi.org/10.1007/978-3-031-37114-1_28

Fortress Europe [1] to describe the way in which legal immigration is controlled[3]. These, often underestimated, numbers concern a heterogeneous collection of illegal immigrants who very frequently consider Italy as only a transit territory to other European countries.

Due to the different job opportunities, their distribution in Italy is uneven: nearly 60% live in the North, 25% in the Centre, while only 12% in the South[4] [2]. They represent about 10% of the current workforce in Italy, mainly employed in the services (64.1%) and manufacturing (28.6%) sectors. The remaining 7.3% (about 165,000 people) work in agriculture; these are mainly Romanians (about a quarter, but this number has declined in recent years), Moroccans (10%), Albanians (10%) and Indians (10%). Conversely, African (e.g., Senegalese, Nigerian, Malian, etc.) and South Asian (e.g., Pakistani and Bangladeshi) groups have rapidly increased in recent years [3].

Their presence is today a structural factor for the agricultural sector and their ratio in relation to the Italian farmers is constantly increasing [4]. Despite this, their working conditions are frequently characterized by precariousness; illegal exploitation, undeclared work, and earnings below allowable limits [5], so much so as to be referred to as a *new slavery*. This situation, frequently conditioned by short-term employment, has created a so-called *disposable* form of slavery [6]. This is a widespread trend throughout the entire country from Friuli to Sicily, but it is most prevalent in the South, where the proportion of migrants employed in the agricultural sector (about 40%) [7] is much higher. Hired as herdsmen, fruit and vegetable pickers, shepherds, woodcutters, etc. the migrants are agricultural workers willing to do any job. This *cost-cutting* migrant labor force [8] is composed of invisible people, scattered across farmland, often occupying abandoned or disused farmhouses or creating new ghettos [9].

A prevailing uncertainty about the data makes any research about migration more difficult. In fact, even though it is a highly relevant geographical topic, the bibliography concerning the use of GIS technology in this field is rather scarce. There are, however, several studies investigating the spatial distribution of migrants using geo-statistics. For instance, spatial autocorrelation techniques are used to analyze migration flows in Italy [10, 11] and in other European cities [12]. Some research to evaluate the potential of spatial network analysis to analyze migration patterns such as research by Di Mario [13] in the case of Libya has been undertaken. Other research, conducted by Rashid [14] considers the capability of a GIS-based multicriteria decision analysis approach in formulating a spatial migration mode.

The spatial distribution of immigrants in a territory, considered sometimes as a key integration indicator [15], may be random and scattered, mixed (mainly in the urban areas) or in isolated enclaves. Although theoretically the reasons for this choice could be individual, the studies in this area highlight that it is often not a free choice at all. According to *Spatial Assimilation Theory*, «immigrants will concentrate in the same ethnic area, not only to overcome disadvantages associated with language barriers, information uncertainty, and low socioeconomic status, but also to make the best use of employment and welfare conditions attributable to being in a community of immigrants» (see Murayama and Nagayasu, 2021, 3849) [16]. Instead, the *Differential Incorporation*

[3] Since 1988, *Fortress Europe* is also a press review remembering the victims of the European border, http://fortresseurope.blogspot.com/, last accessed 2023/04/15.

[4] The residual 4% live in the main islands (Sicily and Sardinia).

Theory emphasizes how this process depends mainly on external factors, closely linked to the host population (the dominant group), which often discriminates against migrants based on ethnicity and skin colour [17].

Without being exhaustive, this paper aims to investigate the relationship between the spatial distribution of migrants in the Campania Region (southern Italy) and the work opportunities in the agricultural sector. We will briefly describe the regional context, mainly with reference to agriculture and the current presence of migrants. Then, we will analyse Census data from the Italian National Institute of Statistics (ISTAT) of 2011. Unfortunately, we had to choose this old data because these are the only figures currently available on agriculture at the municipal scale. Upon this dataset, we can apply spatial autocorrelation techniques to map significant clusters of municipalities characterized by: 1) migrant groups, classified by continent; 2) some agricultural crops or breeding activities, in which migrants are usually involved. Finally, we will discuss our results to understand the significance of these external factors (i.e. work opportunities) on the spatial distribution of migrants.

2 The Regional Context: Agriculture and Migrants in Campania

Campania is a predominantly hilly (more than 40%) and mountainous Region, traversed by the Apennine chain with some particularly prominent mountain groups, such as Matese, Partenio, Picentini and Alburni. The remaining plains (Caserta, Sarno and Sele) account for about a quarter of this territory and are generally very densely populated (Fig. 1). Despite very strong urban growth in the last fifty years, this territory maintains a very high biodiversity. The contraction of agricultural land and traditional farming systems in favor of natural reforestation (especially in internal areas) and an increase in arable land are some of the most significant transformations in recent decades [18]. The cultivation of the so-called *Mediterranean triad* (wheat, olives, and wine) has always characterized agriculture in this area. There are, however, other excellent agri-food products, some known internationally, the most famous of which being the Buffalo Mozzarella.

The European quality labels, such as the protected designation of origin (PDO) or the protected geographical indication (PGI), promote and protect these products by banding them to the territory and landscape in which they are made[5].

The number of farms in the region, sharply declining over the last twenty years, is still quite relevant (almost 80,000). Usually, these are family farms (about 97%) of small size (about 6.5 ha) [19] in which more than 65,000 people (the 4.1% of regional employed) find employment [20]. Although the trend in the average farm area is growing (in 2000 the average size was 2.5 ha), it is still an *atomized* agricultural structure; the largest average farm sizes are mainly located along the Apennine ridge (Roccamonfina, Matese, Picentini, etc.) and in the Caserta and Sele Plains [21, 22]. Areas cultivated with cereals (wheat and maize) are predominant (about 25%), but the fruit and vegetable sector also remain very important (more than 10%). The number of farms with livestock

[5] Other famous examples of typical products from the Campania Region are the Sorrento lemon (PGI) or the Amalfi Coast lemon (PGI), the Cilento extra virgin olive oil (PDO), the Vesuvius Piennolo tomato (PDO), etc.

Fig. 1. Overview of principal regional rural landscapes.

and livestock-only farms is also significant, accounting for more than 6% of the national total. Buffalo breeding remains a Campanian brand; the farms involved total nearly 1,100, more than 70% of total livestock nationwide [19, 23].

Officially, the current number of migrant residents in Campania is approximately 240,000 (4.8% of residents in Italy). Although the presence of irregular and illegal migrants has always been a significant component, this number has increased in recent decades whenever there is an amnesty [24]. Until the early 2000s, this region was often considered a transit area for migrants, who usually later moved on to northern Italy or other European countries. However, over the last two decades, Campania has become a stable settlement area for migrants [25], so their numbers have consistently grown.

Naples has always been the region's main area of attraction, where about half of the migrants live, while approximately 20% inhabit the coastal provinces of Caserta and Salerno. The remaining 10% live in the inland provinces of Avellino and Benevento. This situation is very similar to that of 2011, the year to which the data analyzed in this research paper refers to. Ten years ago, the migrants were almost 150,000, with the same spatial distribution within the Region. They were mostly Europeans (almost 60%), while Asians and Africans were equally proportionate (about 17%).

In addition to better job opportunities than in the country of origin, currently the main reasons for migration are family reunification and asylum seeking, while in the past migrants were predominantly middle-aged women, they are now young men. The migrant community is becoming larger (in absolute terms) and at the same time, more diverse by place of origin: the most prominent groups are Ukrainians and Romanians, followed by Moroccans, Sinhalese and Chinese. These first five communities account for more than 50% of the migrants in Campania, although there has been a strong growth of South Asian (e.g., Bangladeshi and Pakistani) and sub-Saharan (e.g., Nigerian, Senegalese, and Ghanaian) communities since 2000 [26]. The 2021 ISTAT data [19] estimates that migrants employed in the agriculture sector in Campania number more than 25,000 people, almost a quarter of all people working in this sector. They are equally divided between EU and non-EU in origin, and over 80% are employed on fixed-term contracts.

3 Data and Methodology

3.1 Source of Data

ISTAT Censuses data were considered for analysis at the municipal level to evaluate the potential relationships between job opportunities and the spatial distribution of migrants. We analyzed the data of the 6th General Census of Agriculture (2011) and the 15th General Census of Population and Housing (2011). We had to consider these old data because the first results of the current Census of Agriculture (2021) are available only at a regional level [19].

Regarding the census data on agriculture [27, 28], we have considered variables closely related to employment opportunities in which migrants are generally involved. For this reason, we analyzed data on horticultural cultivations and orchards (also including the citrus class). Usually, as is well known, migrant labor is favored for harvesting because of its extremely low costs. This is seasonal work, but nevertheless quite prolonged and, therefore, different from the decidedly more occasional grape or olive harvest. We evaluated the total acreage (Ha) of horticultural and fruit crops at the municipal level, expressed as percentage of *utilized agricultural acreage*. For similar reasons, buffalo and poultry number were also examined; in this case migrant labor is often required for the routine management (feeding, milking, dung cleaning, etc.) of these animals. In this case, we considered the absolute value of animal heads for each municipality of the Campania region.

We also observed the number of migrants per municipality. The population Census of 2011 [29] provided these data by classifying migrants by continent (European, Africans, Asians, etc.). Also in this case, the figures were expressed as a percentage of the total number of inhabitants per municipality.

3.2 Theoretical Overview

In order to map the sharper boundaries between wealth and poverty or the unexpectedly high rates of cancer in a specific area, the analysis will need to employ a growing collection of spatial and nonspatial information [30]. According to this consideration, this research aims to integrate analytical geo-computation and modelling practices to place events and facets of human society in the analytical space, a framework typical of GIScience [31, 32].

For these reasons, it has been decided to employ a specific model of classification, a cluster analysis workflow, to highlight whether there were units with similar values clustered, randomly distributed, or dispersed [33]. Indeed, as it is such a fruitful method to analyse and examine events, patterns, and relationships in space and time they are employed in various geographic research projects. For example, in physical geography it has been used to select regions based on their climatic parameters or to identify patterns of regional climate change. In social and economic geography, clustering is used to identify crime hotspots or study spatio-temporal patterns of socio-economic change. Moreover, in a multidisciplinary project, it is also utilised to identify the variables representing the social, economic, agriculture, and health sectors as the main resilience indicators [34].

The purpose of cluster analysis is to create groups of statistical units as a collective, so that the units included in the same group are as similar to each other as possible and there is maximum dissimilarity to the units comprising the opposing groups [35]. The cluster analysis, related on geographical objects has been utilised as the principal aspect of spatial autocorrelation, that elaborate on the first law of geography [36].

According to Goodchild (1986) [37], spatial autocorrelation is defined as a descriptive index, which measures how a set of units are correlated and distributed in space. The measurement of the indices is at a global or local level. Global measures of spatial autocorrelation estimate a single measure of the relationship between observations. However, local measures provide a value at each location, considering the relationship between both its neighbouring sites and the entire dataset [38]. It must also be noted that this measure can be expressed in the positive or negative. Positive spatial autocorrelation results when nearby locations have correlated attribute values. In turn, negative spatial autocorrelation occurs when dissimilar values are correlated [39, 40].

The most common GIS software utilises specific tools for calculating indices of Spatial autocorrelation, like the Global Moran's and Geary's c or Local Indicator of Spatial Association (LISA), that help in statistically validating the representation of identified clusters [41][6].

3.3 Spatial Autocorrelation: Techniques on GIS

We used the Local Indicator of Spatial Association (LISA) to define the highest values of foreigners in our study area in relationship with the highest level of similarity with neighboring municipalities. We did the same to check the correlation to spatial distribution of foreign people and the work opportunity in the primary sector. In particular, the indices used are local Moran's I (LISA) and Gi* statistic measures.

Starting from the described database (see Sect. 3.1), spatial clusters of features with high or low values were identified. In the GIS toolset, it is computed a value for the local index, a z score, a pseudo p value, and a code representing the type of cluster for each statistically significant feature. The z scores and pseudo p values represent the statistical significance of the calculated index values [42][7].

In particular, the Local Moran's Ii is defined in compliance with the hypothesis of Anselin (1995) [43] and it allows, for each location, to evaluate the similarity of each

[6] Regarding the mathematical properties of the above-mentioned indices see Serra-Sogas *et al.* [38].

[7] The p-value is a probability that the observed spatial cluster was created by some random process while z-scores are standard deviations, see Mitchell 2005 [42].

observation to the surrounding elements in four scenarios [11]: distinguishes between statistically significant clusters of high values (HH), clusters of low values (LL), clusters in which a high value is surrounded mainly by low values (HL), and clusters in which a low value is surrounded mainly by high values (LH). Statistical significance is given by features with p-values and z-values. In the specific case, the p-value results less than 0.05 are considered statistically significant, while a low z-score (e.g., less than −3.96) indicates a statistically significant cluster of spatial data[8]. Instead, The Gi* statistic, in according to the Getis and Ord (1992, 1996) [44, 45], measures the degree of this association that results from the concentration of weighted points (or the area represented by a weighted point) and all other weighted points within a distance radius of the original weighted point [46]. The Getis-Ord Gi* map was constructed based on z-values. At statistically significant positive z scores, the higher the z score, the greater the clustering of high values (named hot spot). Moreover, significant negative z scores, the lower the z score, the most intense is the clustering of low values (named cold spot) [38][9].

In summary, the cluster analysis workflow of research is the following.

i. Collecting and analysed the data of ISTAT about foreigners from 15th General Census of Population and Housing and about 6th General Census of Italian Agriculture (2011).
ii. Designed a spatial dataset about the foreign people and some variable of the primary sector at regional level (Campania region) in GIS-platform. In this case, in addition to the data in (i), the Regional Land Use Plan (Campania) is also integrated.
iii. LISA and Getis-Ord Gi* cluster maps of foreign people (total foreign values; Europeans; Asians; Africans) can be constructed in Mapping Clusters toolset (ArcGIS pro software). The LISA maps are developed in the Cluster and Outlier Analysis (Anselin Local Moran's I) tool, instead, the Getis-Ord Gi* cluster maps in Hot Spot Analysis tool.
iv. Analyzed the data from the LISA and Getis-Ord Gi* cluster maps in computational software and selected the best cluster maps, specifically the Getis-Ord Gi* cluster maps.
v. Overlayed, in GIS-platform, the cluster analysis data of foreigners with those of agricultural classes. The overlay algorithm used combines features from the *input layer* and the *intersect layer*, resulting in features that cover both layers' features. The *overlay maps* symbology are setting colours based on discrete groups of attribute value, in detail the sum of the *GIN_bin* values of the hot spots (see Sect. 4).

[8] In this research it is not taken into account The FDR correction, that reduces the p-value threshold from 0.05 to a value that better reflects the 95% confidence level given, https://pro.arcgis.com/en/pro-app/latest/tool-reference/spatial-statistics/h-how-cluster-and-outlier-analysis-anselin-local-m.htm, last accessed 2023/04/24.

[9] https://pro.arcgis.com/en/pro-app/latest/tool-reference/spatial-statistics/h-how-hot-spot-analysis-getis-ord-gi-spatial-stati.htm, last accessed 2023/04/24.

4 Results

The presence of migrants in Italy and their contribution to the country's economy, and thus to agriculture, must be framed in the broader perspective of the demographic and structural changes of the country. By using the available data from the recent agricultural and population censuses at the municipal level (source ISTAT), the cluster analysis aims to understand to what degree the variables involved (e.g., horticultural areas, presence of foreign men, etc.) are connected.

By comparing the clusters obtained from the two cluster analysis indices, local Moran's I (LISA) and Getis-Ord Gi * statistic measures, it can then be decided which are the most significant clusters for the study area. In particular, the Getis-Ord Gi* index is more suitable for the research's dataset and is able to track an increasing number of clusters at the opposite end of a smaller number of elements that are un-clustered (Fig. 2) Indeed, among the 550 units consider (municipalities in the Campania region) 386 units were detected with high cluster values (hot spot clusters) compared with 187 (HH and HL clusters) concerning the LISA index.

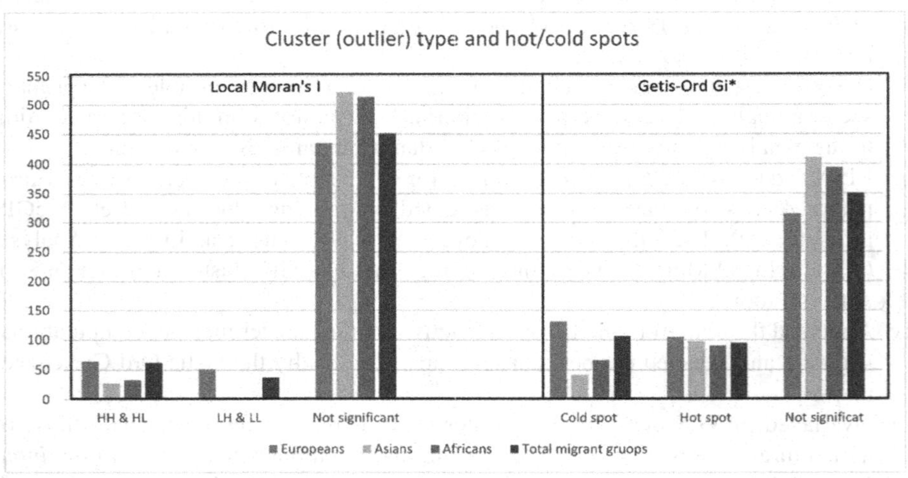

Fig. 2. Comparison of local Moran's I (LISA) and Getis-Ord Gi * statistic measures: number and type of clusters.

The Getis-Ord Gi*'s map clusters (Fig. 3), identified the different spatial distribution of each group of migrants assessed by continent (Europeans, Asians, Africans) and the cluster of total migrants.

It should also be noted that the Getis-Ord Gi*'s maps have a set of fixed, statistically significant ranges[10]. The features, therefore, adhere to the following structural ranges; organized in a 99%–95% confidence, a 95%–90% confidence and a 90% and lower confidence threshold. In addition, the maps utilize a color gradient scale based on that

[10] Statistical significance can be expressed as a percentage degree of significance.

regions' confidence level[11]. The degree of percent significance of hot and cold spots offers a more uniform outlook on the location of migrants in different areas of Campania. It is certainly a possibility that migrants are present in large numbers in one or two municipalities, but their location can be characterized as nucleated or dispersed on a regional scale (see Sect. 2).

The largest number of migrant hot spot clusters are in the western area of Caserta province (around the Volturno littoral cost area) and in the central area of the Salerno province at the border of Salerno city. In contrast, the cold spot clusters are in Benevento province and in the Naples area. By examining the individual groups, it can be observed that the Europeans have a denser population in the Salerno province; the Asians groups occupy the Phlegrean Fields near Naples and Sele Plain (Salerno); whilst the African population is clustered in the Caserta province.

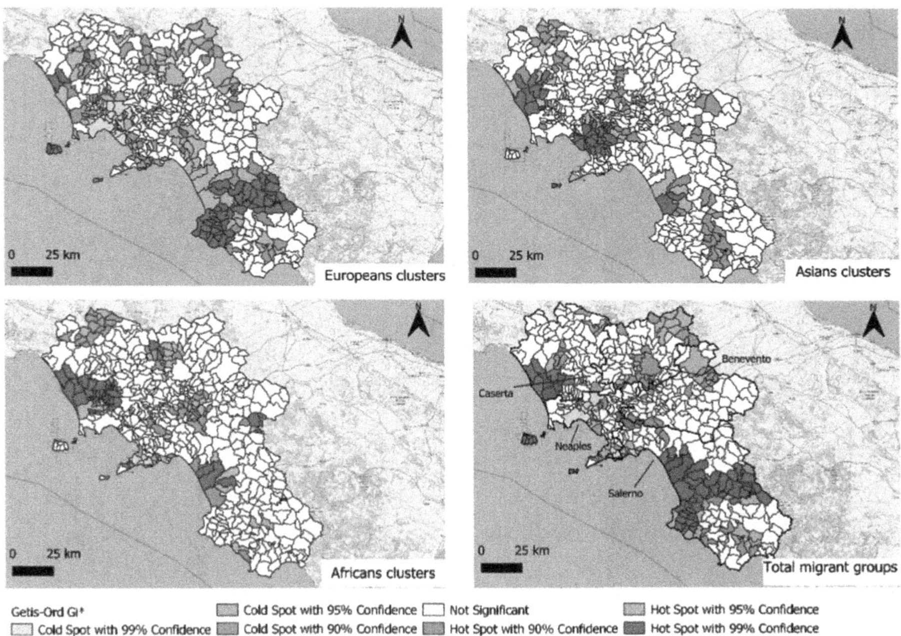

Fig. 3. Getis-Ord Gi*'s map clusters of migrant groups in the Campania region.

We applied the same algorithm (Getis-Ord Gi* index) to define the significant clusters related to the agricultural variables (horticulture and orchard areas, number of buffalo and poultry).

The Getis-Ord Gi* cluster map generated from official data highlighted a specific cluster system centered around the principal agricultural production area (Fig. 4). The main cluster hot spot of horticulture value is centrally placed in the Plain Systems,

[11] The red colour scale concerning the hot spot records and blue colour scale concerning the cold spot records.

between the Volturno Plain and the Sele Plain. In addition, according to the 6th Census, the hot spot cluster of citrus and orchards values is located around the Phlegraean Hills and the Sorrento area. However, in the Benevento area this production area is represented by cold spots. Furthermore, regarding buffalo farms, clusters have been established in the traditional production areas, Volturno Plain, Volturno littoral cost area and Sele Plain.

Finally, an overlap analysis was carried out between the cluster analysis data of migrants and the agricultural classes. We combine features from migrant hot spots layer (Fig. 3) and the agricultural hot spots layer (Fig. 4). Their intersection resulted in a new feature that covered both layers. If the input feature(s) only partially lie within the other layer's feature(s), they are split along the boundary of the other layer's feature(s). Then, we sum the *GIN_bin* values of the hot spots[12] (see Sect. 3.3); the *overlay maps* utilize a color gradient scale based on discrete grouping of the final attribute values (Fig. 5).

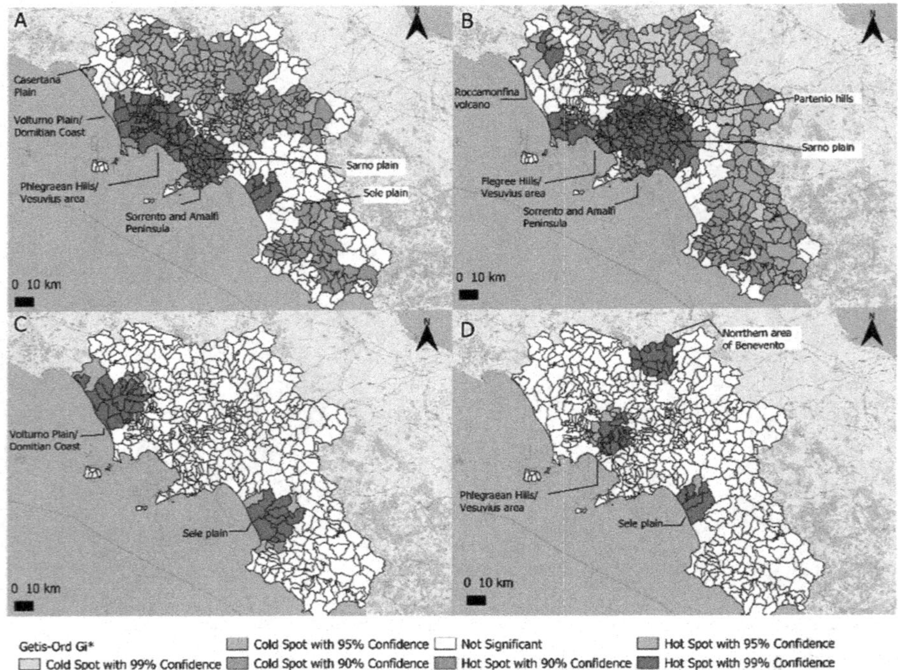

Fig. 4. Getis-Ord Gi*'s maps clusters of agriculture dataset at region scale: A horticulture; B) Citrus and horchards: C) buffalo farm D); poultry farm.

[12] The value is equal to *GIN_bin* hot spot foreign records added to *GIN_bin* hot spot agricultural records.

5 Discussion and Final Remarks

The uncertainty of data about migrants and the relevance of their workforce in a specific sector are difficulties in defining a geographic relationship between the job opportunities and the spatial distribution of migrants. The uncertainty of data concerning migrants and the relevance of their workforce in a specific sector demonstrate the difficulties in defining a geographic relationship between the job opportunities and the spatial distribution of migrants. This is especially true in agriculture, a sector where illegality and migrant labor often coexist for lower production costs. In a field employing only a marginal share of immigrant workers (less than 8%), the reasons behind their residential choice may be obscured. Employment in the manufacturing or services sectors, lower rental costs, a concentration of the same ethnicity in the same geographic area could all be factors, so any associations between the type of work and the resident population can only indicate a general trend, and not necessarily the rule. It is equally difficult to define precisely in which areas of agriculture (i.e., horticulture, livestock, etc.) a national or ethnic group is involved, since migrants working in the agricultural sector are *transversal* [8], namely they adapt well to any task. In view of this, we can analyze the overlap maps between migrant residents and agricultural activities (Fig. 5).

Urban concentration of migrants in the metropolitan area of Naples and conspicuous migratory flows towards the rural areas in the Phlegrean Fields, Caserta, Sele and Sarno plains have characterized the migration in Campania since the 1980s [24]. While being a dynamic and complex phenomenon, our results highlight how much recent changes in the agricultural sector have weighed on the different migration components. In fact, in a regional context, characterized by a pulverized agricultural structure (Sect. 2), the farms in the Caserta and Sele low plains were an exception even ten years ago [27]. This implies the development of a more organized, modern, and competitive agricultural sector capable of stabilizing its workforce, even for seasonal activities. Although undergoing a strong restructuring of the agri-food system (with a contraction, for example, of tomato production), in these areas horticultural production and buffalo breeding (flanked by other forms of breeding such as poultry breeding) remain very important (Fig. 4). And this is probably why the presence of African migrants (especially Maghrebi and sub-Saharan), like Asian migrants (mainly Indians and Pakistanis) in the Caserta and Sele plains, acquires more of a residency characteristic over time [8]. During the early 1990s, this situation generated some precarious agglomerations in the Province of Caserta, such as the ghetto of Villa Literno (where several hundred Senegalese, Ivorians, etc. lived) or the African enclave of Castel Volturno[13], or in the ghetto of the San Nicola Varco in the Province of Salerno close to Eboli (created in the first decade of the 2000s). Caserta remains one of the *blackest* provinces in Italy, but now the presence of African immigrants, although concentrated along the coastal area, is certainly more scattered within its territory (Fig. 3). In this context, the presence of Europeans is

[13] Castel Volturno is small town on the mouth of the Volturno River in the province of Caserta. In the late 1980s, the collapse in the cost of real estate, mainly due to the presence of local displaced people from the 1982 earthquake, attracts many sub-Saharan migrants (often farm workers in the surrounding areas), transforming in a short time this seaside resort into an *ethnoburb* [47].

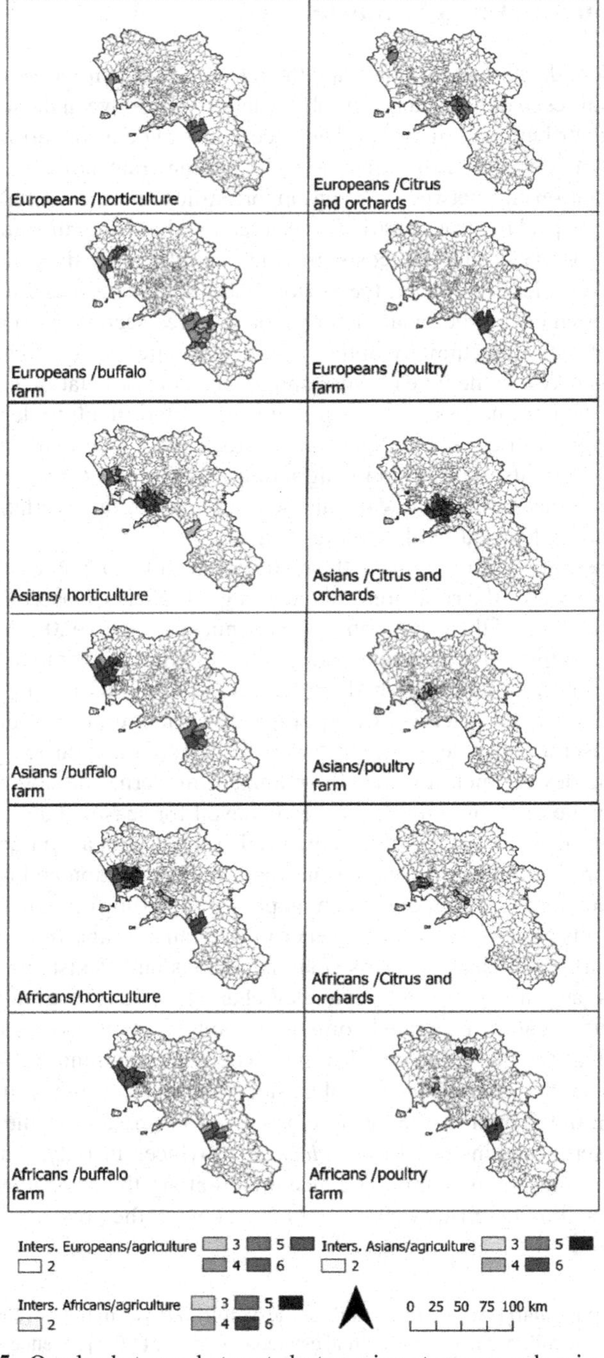

Fig. 5. Overlap between hot spot cluster: migrant groups and agriculture.

also quite important: these are mainly Albanians, Bulgarians, Romanians, and Ukrainians, mostly engaged in other crops (e.g. Albanians with tobacco). Additionally, in the province of Salerno, Eastern European migrants are often employed in valuable horticulture such as that practiced in greenhouses [48], as well as in the livestock sector. They are also involved in fruit-picking and pruning activities in the orchards of the Salerno hills, between the Sarno plain and the Picentini mountains. More difficult to define, due to its complexity, is the relationship between Asian groups and horticultural and citrus fruit-related work in the Vesuvius area. In addition to their involvement in the agricultural sector, this cluster is probably also due to the significant presence in these territories of the Chinese community, which participates extensively in the manufacturing of textiles and clothing [24].

In a Region that until a few years ago was only a transit territory, the process of stabilization and integration of migrants is slowly progressing. However, the proposed methodology, which uses 2011 data, shows that ten years ago there were clusters of migrants, partially connected to agricultural sector activities. Sometimes, these rural concentrations of migrants induced territorialization processes with negative outcomes, triggering social and territorial tensions. But migration is dynamic and complex by nature. For this reason, to understand how much the spatial permeability of migrants residing in Campania has now taken on post-migration characteristics [49], it will be necessary to update this research using current data on immigration in Campania and the forthcoming data from the recently concluded 2021 Census of Agriculture. Acquiring greater awareness of the increasing role of migrants in our society and the reasons driving their settlement choices can help normalize, even in Italy, this demographic process. Migration has always been experienced as a constant emergency from which the country seems unable to escape, but conscious national and EU policies could turn this phenomenon into a structural reality that can be governed [50].

Author Contribution. This paper is a result of the full collaboration of all the authors. However, G. Mauro wrote Sects. 1 and 5, M. Ronza wrote Sects. 2 and 3.1, while C.S. De Simone wrote Sects. 3.2, 3.3 and 4. The figures layout is edited by C.S. De Simone.

References

1. Fassman, H., Haller, M., Lane, D.: Migration and Mobility in Europe: Trends, Patterns and Control. Edward Elgar, Cheltenham (UK) (2009)
2. ISTAT: Statistiche, Report Stranieri residenti. ISTAT, Roma (2023)
3. Centro Studi e Ricerche IDOS: Dossier Statistico Immigrazione 2022. IDOS, Roma (2022)
4. Macrì, M.C.: Gli stranieri nella popolazione e nell'economia italiana. Analisi multi-temporale dal 2008 al 2017. In: Macrì, M.C. (a cura di) Il contributo dei lavoratori stranieri all'agricoltura italiana, pp. 9–13. CREA, Roma (2019)
5. Longo, A.: Immigrazione e lavoro nero in Italia: attualità di un fenomeno socioeconomico. Geotema **43**, 158–164 (2012)
6. Bales, K.: I nuovi schiavi. La merce umana nell'economia globale. Feltrinelli, Milano (2002)
7. De Leo, S., Vanino, S.: Immigrati in agricoltura in Italia: chi sono e da dove vengono. In: Macrì, M.C. (a cura di) Il contributo dei lavoratori stranieri all'agricoltura italiana, pp. 21–36. CREA, Roma (2019)
8. Amato, F.: Atlante delle migrazioni in Italia. Carocci Editore, Roma (2008)

9. Cristaldi, F.: I nuovi schiavi: gli immigrati del gran ghetto di San Severo. Rivista Geografica Italiana **122**, 119–142 (2015)
10. Scardaccione, G., Scorza, F., Casas, G.L., Murgante, B.: Spatial autocorrelation analysis for the evaluation of migration flows: the Italian case. In: Taniar, D., Gervasi, O., Murgante, B., Pardede, E., Apduhan, B.O. (eds.) ICCSA 2010. LNCS, vol. 6016, pp. 62–76. Springer, Heidelberg (2010). https://doi.org/10.1007/978-3-642-12156-2_5
11. Murgante, B., Borruso, G.: Analyzing migration phenomena with spatial autocorrelation techniques. In: Murgante, B., et al. (eds.) ICCSA 2012. LNCS, vol. 7334, pp. 670–685. Springer, Heidelberg (2012). https://doi.org/10.1007/978-3-642-31075-1_50
12. Antczak, E., Lewandowska-Gwarda, K.: Migration processes in European cities: a spatio-temporal analysis using different spatial weights matrices. Estudios de economía aplicada **33**(1), 53–80 (2015)
13. Di Maio, M., Leone Sciabolazza, V., Molini, V.: Migration in Libya: a spatial network analysis. World Bank Policy Research Working Paper, vol. 9110, pp. 2–38 (2020)
14. Rashid, M.F.A.: Capabilities of a GIS-based multi-criteria decision analysis approach in modelling migration. GeoJournal **84**(2), 483–496 (2019)
15. Alba, R.D., Foner, N.: Strangers No More: Immigration and the Challenges of Integration in North America and Western Europe. Princeton University Press, Princeton (USA) (2015)
16. Murayama, K., Nagayasu, J.: Toward coexistence of immigrants and local people in Japan: implications from spatial assimilation theory. Sustainability **13**(7), 3849 (2021)
17. Darden, J.T., Cristaldi, F.: Immigrants and residential segregation. In: Gold, S.J., Nawyn, S.J. (eds.) International Handbook of Migration Studies, pp. 202–214. Routledge, London (2012)
18. Di Gennaro, A.: Il territorio rurale della Campania nelle nuove politiche regionali per l'agricoltura e il paesaggio. In: Del Prete, R., Leone, A.P. (a cura di) Paesaggi rurali. Percezione, promozione, gestione, sviluppo sostenibile, pp. 159–175. Regione Campania, Napoli (2017)
19. ISTAT: 7° Censimento generale dell'agricoltura: primi risultati. ISTAT, Roma (2022)
20. Centro di ricerca Politiche e Bioeconomia: L'agricoltura nella Campania in cifre 2021. CREA, Roma (2021)
21. Ciaravino, R., Salato, N., Chiara, S.: Analisi degli scenari agricoli in Campania. Interpretazione dei territori attraverso una diversa chiave di lettura. CREA, Roma (2021)
22. Ronza, M., Lapiccirella, V., Giglio, A.: Aziende agricole tra diversificazione e innovazione. Resistenze e prospettive per il Mezzogiorno. In: Amato, V. (a cura di) Innovazione, impresa e competitività nel Mezzogiorno, pp. 203–216. Aracne editrice, Roma (2013)
23. Ronza, M.: Buffalo breeding in the Volturno plains between identifying perseverance and prospect for development. In: Bryant, C., Grillotti Di Giacomo, M.G. (eds.) Quality Agriculture: Historical Heritage and Environmental Resources for the Integrated Development of Territories, pp. 741–752. Brigati editore, Genova (2007)
24. Amato, F., D'Alessandro, L., Spagnuolo, D.: Gli immigrati in Campania. In: Amato, F., Coppola, P. (a cura di) Da migranti ad abitanti. Gli spazi insediativi degli stranieri nell'area insediativa di Napoli, pp. 97–146. Alfredo Guida Editore, Napoli (2009)
25. Russo Krauss, D.: Geografia dell'immigrazione. Spazi multietnici nelle città: in Italia. Liguori Editore, Napoli (2005)
26. Strozza, S., Gabrielli, G.: Gli stranieri in Campania: dimensioni e caratteristiche di un collettivo in evoluzione. In: Bruno, G.C. (a cura di) Lavoratori stranieri in agricoltura in Campania. Una ricerca sui fenomeni discriminatori. CNR Edizioni, Roma (2018)
27. ISTAT: 6° Censimento Generale dell'Agricoltura. Atlante dell'agricoltura italiana. ISTAT, Roma (2013)
28. Regione Campania: Il territorio rurale della Campania. Un viaggio nei sistemi agroforestali della regione attraverso i dati del 6° Censimento Generale dell'Agricoltura. Imago Editrice, Dragoni (CE) (2013)

29. ISTAT: 15° Censimento Generale della Popolazione e delle Abitazioni 2011. Il censimento della popolazione straniera. ISTAT, Roma (2012)
30. Gimond, M.: Intro to GIS and Spatial Analysis. https://mgimond.github.io/Spatial/index.html. Accessed 20 Apr 2023
31. Goodchild, M.F.: Geography and the information society. In: Kolosov, V., García-Álvarez, J., Heffernan, M., Schelhaas, B. (eds.) A Geographical Century, pp. 225–234. Springer, Cham (2022). https://doi.org/10.1007/978-3-031-05419-8_16
32. Yuan, M.: From representation to geocomputation: some theoretical accounts of geographic information science. In: Li, B., Shi, X., Zhu, AX., Wang, C., Lin, H. (eds.) New Thinking in GIScience, pp. 1–10. Springer, Singapore (2022). https://doi.org/10.1007/978-981-19-3816-0_1
33. Fotheringham, A.S., Brunsdon, C., Charlton, M.: Quantitative Geography: Perspectives on Spatial Data Analysis. Sage, London (2000)
34. Opach, T., Scherzer, S., Lujala, P., Ketil Rød, J.: Seeking commonalities of community resilience to natural hazards: a cluster analysis approach. J. Geogr. **74**(3), 181–199 (2020)
35. Cerutti, S., De Falco, S., Graziano, T.: Geografia della marginalità dei Comuni italiani: esiti di un'indagine multifattoriale mediante cluster analysis. Bollettino della Associazione Italiana di Cartografia **174**, 49–70 (2022)
36. Grasland, C.: Spatial analysis of social facts. In: Bavaud, F., Mager, C. (eds.) Handbook of Theoretical and Quantitative Geography, pp. 1–39. FGSE, Lausanne (2010)
37. Goodchild, M.F.: Spatial Autocorrelation Concepts and Techniques. Geo Books, Norwich (1986)
38. Serra-Sogas, N., O'Hara, P., Canessa, R., Bertazzon, S., Gavrilova, M.: Exploratory spatial analysis of illegal oil discharges detected off Canada's Pacific Coast. In: Gavrilova, M.L., Tan, C.J.K. (eds.) Transactions on Computational Science VI. LNCS, vol. 5730, pp. 219–233. Springer, Heidelberg (2009). https://doi.org/10.1007/978-3-642-10649-1_13
39. Kumari, M., Sarma, K., Sharma, R.: Using Moran's I and GIS to study the spatial pattern of land surface temperature in relation to land use/cover around a thermal power plant in Singrauli district, Madhya Pradesh, India. Remote Sens. Appl.: Soc. Environ. **15**, 100239 (2019)
40. Mathur, M.: Spatial autocorrelation analysis in plant population: an overview. J. Appl. Nat. Sci. **7**(1), 501–513 (2015)
41. Fu, W.J., Jiang, P.K., Zhou, G.M., Zhao, K.L.: Using Moran's I and GIS to study the spatial pattern of forest litter carbon density in a subtropical region of Southeastern China. Biogeosciences **11**(8), 2401–2409 (2014)
42. Mitchell, A.: The ESRI Guide to GIS Analysis, vol. 2. ESRI Press, London (2005)
43. Anselin, L.: Local indicators of spatial association—LISA. Geograph. Anal. **27**(2), 93–115 (1995)
44. Getis, A., Ord, J.-K.: Local spatial statistics: an overview. In: Longley, P., Batty, M. (eds.) Spatial Analysis: Modelling in a GIS Environment, pp. 261–282. Wiley, New York (1996)
45. Getis, A., Ord, J.-K.: The analysis of spatial association by use of distance statistics. Geograph. Anal. **24**(3), 189–206 (1992)
46. Kalinic, M., Krisp, J.M.: Kernel density estimation (KDE) vs. hot-spot analysis–detecting criminal hot spots in the City of San Francisco. In: Mansourian, A., Pilesjö, P., Harrie, L., Van Lammeren, R. (eds.) Geospatial Technologies for All: Selected Papers of the 21st AGILE Conference on Geographic Information Science, pp. 12–15. Springer, Lund (2018)
47. D'Ascenzo, F.: Disfunzioni migratorie e territorio: gli africani di Castel Volturno. Meridione **XVI**(3), 109–148 (2016)
48. Carchedi, F.: Campania: il caso della Piana del Sele (Salerno). In: Carchedi, F., Bilongo, J.-R. (a cura di) Agromafie e capolarato. Quinto rapporto, pp. 291–320. Osservatorio Placido Rizzotto FLAI-CGIL, Futura, Roma (2022)

49. Meini, M.: Verso una governance interculturale in Italia? Questioni aperte tra migrazione e postmigrazione. Geotema **61**, 25–33 (2019)
50. Aru, S.: Spazi d'asilo. Il sistema di accoglienza in Italia tra norme e politiche alle diverse scale territoriali. Geotema **61**, 34–40 (2019)

Simulation of Total Phosphorus in Biscayne Bay, USA

Vladimir J. Alarcon[1(✉)], Paul F. Mickle[1], Christopher R. Kelble[2], Anna C. Linhoss[3], and Alexandra Fine[2]

[1] Northern Gulf Institute, MSU Science and Technology Center, 1021 Balch Blvd, NASA Stennis Space Center, Starkville, MS 39529, USA
{valarcon,pmickle}@ngi.msstate.edu

[2] NOAA Atlantic Oceanographic and Meteorological Laboratory, 4301 Rickenbacker Causeway, Miami, FL 33149, USA
{chris.kelble,alexandra.fine}@noaa.gov

[3] Department of Biosystems Engineering, Auburn University, 3101 Shelby Center Auburn, Auburn, AL 36849, USA
acl0089@auburn.edu

Abstract. This research presents a preliminary water quality model for Biscayne Bay (Florida, USA). During the month of December 2018, water quality monitoring stations located in central Biscayne Bay reported total phosphorous concentration (TP) peaks ranging from 0.03 to 0.052 mg/L. Median TP concentrations range between 0.003 to 0.004 mg/L. The water quality simulations presented in this research show that the observed TP peaks were most probably caused by a surge in TP in the Atlantic Ocean waters close to the ocean boundary of Biscayne Bay. Analysis of observed chlorophyll-a concentrations showed that high TP concentrations during December 2018 were not related to algae or phytoplankton bloom. Computational experiments showed that the observed TP peaks are not likely caused by the transport of a sudden release of a high-concentration TP pulse at the coast. Dilution of TP concentration by ocean water limits the spatial reach of coastal contaminant plumes. In testing the TP ocean-surge-origin hypothesis, pulses of 0.044 and 0.024 mg/L were applied to the ocean boundary. The latter pulse generated TP concentrations of around 0.03 mg/L in most of central Biscayne Bay. This estimated concentration is very similar to the TP peaks observed in December 2018. Therefore, those concentration peaks could have originated by a TP pulse of magnitude similar to 0.024 mg/L that occurred in the Atlantic Ocean waters close to the ocean boundary of Biscayne Bay.

Keywords: Water quality modeling · Biscayne Bay · total phosphorus · boundary conditions

1 Introduction

Biscayne Bay is an estuary located on Florida's Atlantic coast. Rapid urban growth in the last decades and human activities (agriculture, etc.) have increased runoff and nutrient transport from inland watersheds to the Bay. Recent studies have identified

O. Gervasi et al. (Eds.): ICCSA 2023 Workshops, LNCS 14107, pp. 427–438, 2023.
https://doi.org/10.1007/978-3-031-37114-1_29

increased chlorophyll-a and phosphate concentrations within the bay, which is more evident throughout the northern area and in nearshore areas of central Biscayne Bay, suggesting an urgent need for land use and land cover management to reduce local nutrient wash-off from the watershed to the Bay [1–3]. Santos et al. [4] established that freshwater discharges into nearshore areas (contaminated by anthropogenic disturbances) have resulted in the fragmentation of the spatial patterning of submerged aquatic vegetation, which is thought to influence the distribution, community composition, and behavior of marine fauna. Man-made canals and waterways carry excess run-off and contaminants, from inland watersheds to Biscayne Bay.

Biscayne Bay has experienced considerable environmental changes due to a century of extensive regional population growth that accelerated coastal and watershed development. Documented changes include periods of hypersalinity, algal blooms, seagrass die-offs, loss of some fish species, localized pollution problems, among others [5]. These changes have been attributed to extensive urbanization agricultural activities and changes in water management practices.

During the month of December 2018, water quality monitoring stations located in central Biscayne Bay reported total phosphorous concentration (TP) peaks ranging from 0.03 to 0.052 mg/L. These high concentrations are fourteen times the observed TP median concentration at an offshore water quality station (BB 37), and nine times the observed TP median concentration at a coastal station (BISC 101) (Fig. 1).

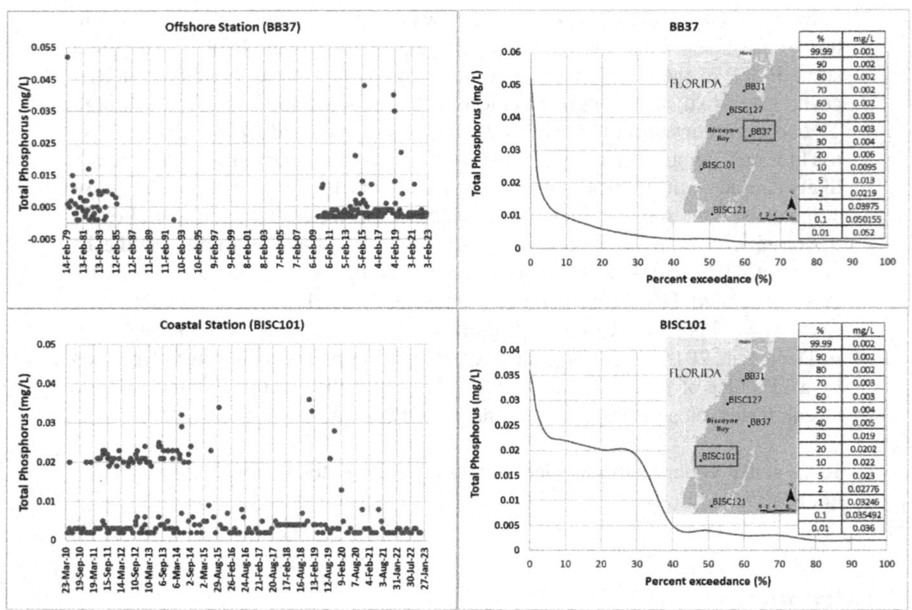

Fig. 1. Total phosphorous (TP) historical data for two water quality monitoring stations located in central Biscayne. Data for offshore station BB 37 corresponds to February 1979 through February 2023, and for coastal station BISC 101 to March 2010–January 2023. Probability of exceedance curves for total phosphorous concentrations are also shown.

Preliminary analysis of historical TP data (Fig. 1) shows that at the offshore station (BB 37) concentrations greater than 0.03 mg/L have a probability of exceedance of only 1.5%. TP concentrations greater than 0.04 mg/L have a probability of exceedance smaller than 0.8%. At the coastal station (BISC 101), with 12-year TP data records, concentrations greater than 0.03 mg/L have a probability of exceedance of only 2%. Interestingly, TP concentrations greater than 0.04 mg/L have a probability of exceedance smaller than 0.01%, at station BISC 101.

Figure 1 shows that TP concentrations at the coastal station (BISC 101) are greater than at the offshore station (BB37), since 80% of TP concentrations observed at the BISC 101 are smaller than 0.02 mg/L while 95% of TP concentrations observed at BB37 (offshore station) are smaller than 0.02 mg/L. Contaminants coming from inland watersheds are most probably degrading consistently the water quality of coastal waters. However, the greatest TP concentrations were observed at the offshore station (BB37): 0.052 mg/L on 19-March-1979, 0.043 mg/L on 3-June-2015, and 0.04 mg/L on 5-Dec-18.

The latter December-2018 TP concentration peak was observed at all stations in Biscayne Bay. The TP source is uncertain and for water quality modeling purposes it is important to ascertain where TP originated: inland watersheds or the ocean. As will be shown in next sections of this paper, meteorology does not play a role since observed precipitation was very low compared to rainfall observed in the wet season.

In this research, three hypotheses explaining these peaks are tested: 1) TP peaks come from algae or phytoplankton blooms, 2) TP peaks come from a sudden release of a high concentration TP pulse at the coast that is transported to most of the Bay, and 3) TP peaks come from the nearby ocean through the Biscayne Bay's ocean boundary. TP peaks could also be explained by data acquisition or instrument calibration issues, but the multiple days observed, and the standardization of the NOAA protocols for data collection suggest that this hypothesis is not valid. The computational experiments designed to test the hypotheses were performed via a 3-D water quality model developed in this research. The period of analysis was 2012–2022.

2 Methods

2.1 Study Area

Biscayne Bay (Fig. 2) is located on the southern Florida Atlantic coast, USA. It is a shallow estuary (average depth is around 3 m) characterized by having diurnal tides (average tidal range 0.48 m), short flushing rate (residence time less than one week), and well-mixed waters [6]. It receives freshwater inputs from several man/made canals and natural creeks and streams. The watersheds that drain to the bay are mostly covered by agricultural land in southern sectors and urban land cover in central and north Biscayne Bay.

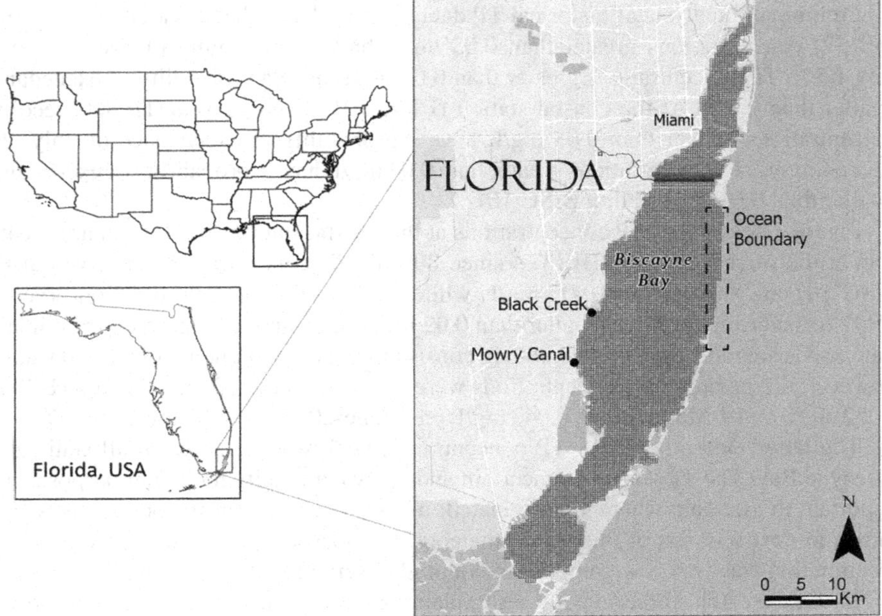

Fig. 2. Biscayne Bay. Computational grid, ocean boundary, Black Creek and Mowry Canal.

2.2 Water Quality Modeling

The estimation of water quality constituents in Biscayne Bay (total phosphorus, TP, and total nitrogen, TN) was performed by extending an existing hydrodynamic and salinity model of Biscayne Bay [7, 8]. The existing hydrodynamic model (Fig. 2) consists of 9,434 grid cells, two vertical layers, nine freshwater input cells (main streams draining to Biscayne Bay), and three open-ocean boundaries that represent the connection of the Bay with the Atlantic Ocean. The computational model was developed using the EFDC+ software [9]. To implement water quality, TP and TN boundary conditions were set up at the ocean water entrance to the estuary (Fig. 2). Three-dimensional salinity transport was calculated using the water quality module available in EFDC+.

2.3 Water Quality Data

This research used public domain water quality data from the following databases: South Florida Water Management District's environmental database DBHYDRO [10], and Miami Dade County Groundwater and Surface Water Quality Viewer, available through the Division of Environmental Resource Management [11]. Preprocessing and postprocessing of the observed water quality data available through these portals was performed using standard statistical software.

2.4 Data Analysis and Simulation Scenarios

Hypothesis 1 was tested through analysis of historical data for monitoring stations BB37 (an offshore station located close to the ocean boundary), and BISC101 (a station located near the central Biscayne Bay shoreline).

Hypotheses 2 and 3 were tested using the water quality model presented in this research. Since the TP peaks observed in December 2018 were preceded and followed by low TP concentrations, it was assumed (hypothesis 2) that they were caused by sudden TP peaks at the outfall of Black Creek or Mowry Canal. The Black Creek outfall is located close to a wastewater treatment plant; therefore, it is feasible that a 1.0 mg/L peak could have occurred during a short period of time. Mowry Canal is one of the main freshwater contributors to Central Biscayne Bay and the occurrence of a 0.084 mg/L TP peak is also possible since its watershed catchment covers urban areas which main wastewater management disposal treatment are septic tanks. To test hypothesis 3, pulses of 0.044 mg/L and 0.024 pulse mg/L were applied to the ocean boundary.

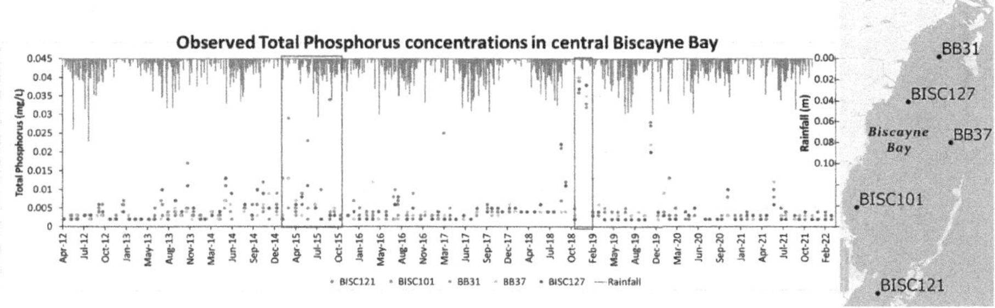

Fig. 3. Observed Total Phosphorus (TP) concentrations at water quality monitoring stations in central Biscayne Bay.

3 Results

3.1 High Concentrations of TP Originate from Algal or Phytoplankton Blooms

Figure 3 shows observed Total Phosphorus (TP) concentrations at water quality monitoring stations in central Biscayne Bay. The figure also shows precipitation at the top of the figure.

As shown in Fig. 3, most of observed TP concentrations are below 0.02 mg/L. There are some peak concentrations in the 2012/2022 period but the most noticeably peak occurs in December 2018, in which all monitoring stations show TP concentrations above 0.03 mg/L, reaching up to 0.04 mg/L. For water quality modeling purposes, it is important to understand the source of this TP peak. Observed precipitation was very low compared to rainfall observed in the rainy season.

One of the main causes of TP in estuaries and lakes is algal blooms. Algal growth causes a drastic change in aquatic conditions over a diel cycle, which may induce sensitive feedback systems in sediments, causing P release [12]. Release of TP from dead algae is an important nutrient source that will support continuous algal blooms in lakes and estuaries [13]. However, if algal blooms are the source of the reported 2018 TP peaks, chlorophyll-a (an indicator of algal biomass) during or before their occurrence should also be observed. Moreover, if algal blooms were present, light attenuation in the estuary should be more efficient than when water is clear. As increased suspended matter (algae, suspended solids, etc.) occurs in the water column, light attenuation increases as well. When turbidity is high in the water column, light attenuation is also increased, and the absolute value of the attenuation coefficient K is also high.

Figure 4 shows charts corresponding to observed chlorophyll-a concentrations and light attenuation (represented by the attenuation coefficient K) for monitoring stations BISC101 and BB37. These stations were chosen because they are representative of the coastal region and the offshore locations that are close to the ocean boundary.

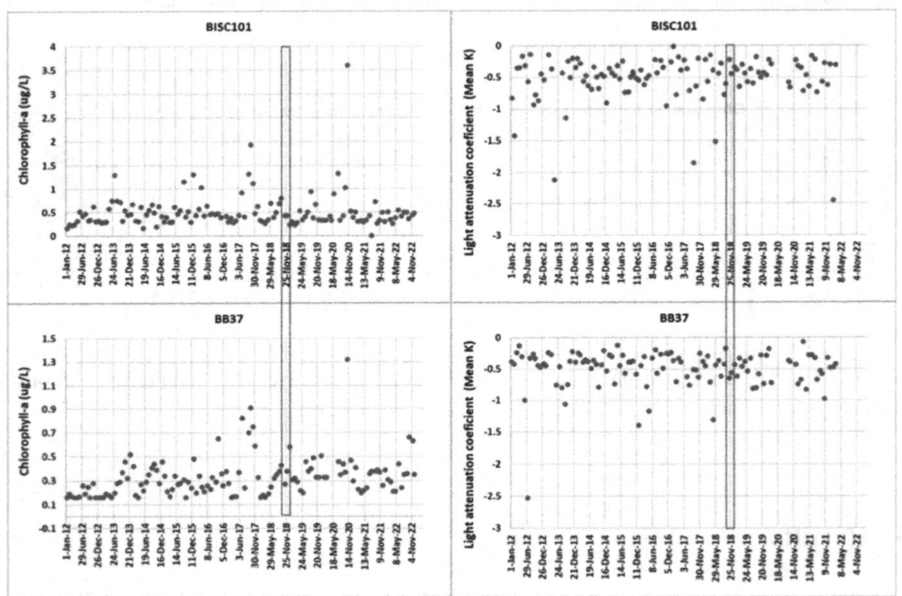

Fig. 4. Observed chlorophyll-a concentrations and light attenuation coefficient K for monitoring stations BISC101 and BB37. As the water gets more turbid, light attenuation is more effective and the absolute value of the light attenuation coefficient K is higher.

As shown in Fig. 4, observed chlorophyll-a concentrations from November 2018 to January 2019 were below 0.7 μg/L which indicates that algal presence was not particularly high during those months. Similarly, observed light attenuation coefficient values for the same months ranged between 0 and −0.7, showing that ocean water at those locations was within normal turbidity range. This leads to the conclusion that high TP concentrations during December 2018 are not directly connected to algae or phytoplankton bloom.

3.2 High Concentrations of TP Come from High TP Pulses Occurring at the Outfall of Streams that Feed Biscayne Bay

In order to test the second hypothesis, a computational experiment was performed using the hydrodynamic model of Biscayne Bay. Two phosphate pulses (Fig. 5) were implemented at two coastal locations (Mowry Canal, Black Creek) to see if those pulses would produce a TP response in Biscayne Bay similar to what was observed in December 2018. The principal dissolved phosphorus species in natural waters is the inorganic phosphate anion, orthophosphate. Orthophosphate is the form of phosphorus preferred by algae and free-living micro-organisms, including the phytoplankton.

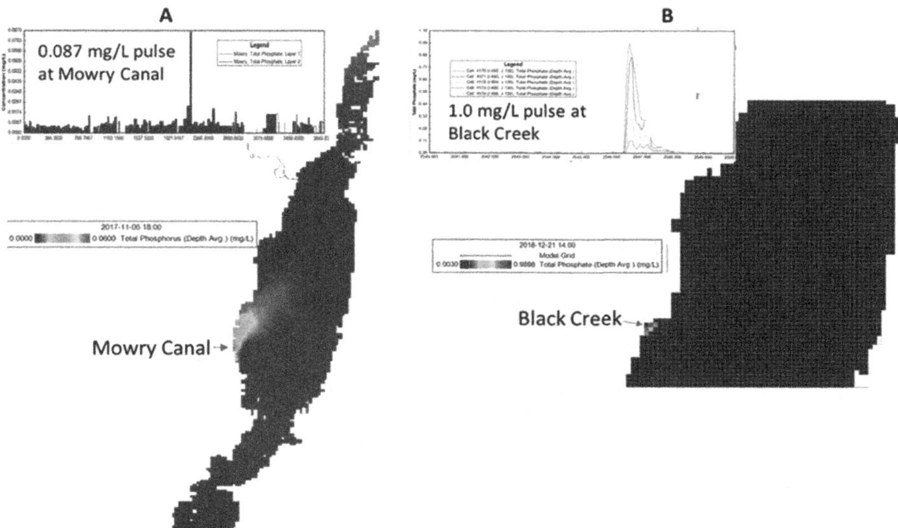

Fig. 5. Application of a pulse of 0.087 mg/L at Mowry canal (A), and 1.0 mg/L pulse at Black Creek (B). Mowry canal is one of the most important freshwater contributors to central Biscayne Bay. Black Creek is a stream located near a wastewater treatment plant.

Figure 5A shows the results of applying a sustained pulse of 0.087 mg/L of phosphate at Mowry canal. Mowry canal is one of the most important freshwater contributors to central Biscayne Bay. Notice that this concentration is twice the TP concentration that was observed during December 2018 throughout the Bay.

As shown in Fig. 5A, at its maximum spatial coverage the spatial distribution of TP concentration is shown to rapidly decrease for offshore locations. The dilution of the high pulse concentration by ocean water is shown to be very effective. The simulation shows that a pulse of these characteristics would not produce the 0.03–0.04 mg/L concentrations observed during December 2018.

Figure 5B shows the effect of implementing a 1.0 mg/L pulse at Black Creek. Since this stream contributes lower flowrate than Mowry Canal, a much higher concentration pulse was applied. Similar to what was simulated for Mowry Canal, even this high concentration pulse has limited spatial reach within Biscayne Bay. Figure 5B also shows TP time-series plots corresponding to consecutive 300-m grid cells going from Black Creek towards the ocean boundary, horizontally. In 1500 m, the 1.0 mg/L pulse is damped to concentrations smaller than 0.05 mg/L. At 2500 m from Black Creek outfall, concentrations reduce to 0.003 mg/L.

Although it is unlikely that a high contaminant pulse would occur at two locations at the same time, Fig. 6 shows the effects of a simultaneous 0.5 mg/L phosphate pulse at Black Creek and Mowry Canal. As shown, the spatial extent of the contaminant plume is also limited.

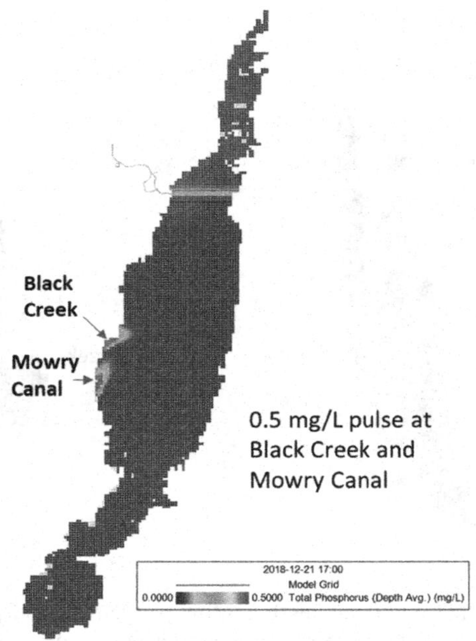

Fig. 6. Application of a simultaneous 0.5 mg/L phosphate pulse at Black Creek and Mowry Canal. The spatial extent of the contaminant plume at both locations is not large.

The computational experiments (summarized in Figs. 5 and 6) show that the observed December 2018 TP peaks are not caused by hydrodynamic transport of a high-concentration TP pulse applied at coastal streams. Dilution of TP concentrations by ocean water limits the spatial reach of the contaminant plume and the pulse cannot reach all water quality station's locations as observed in December 2018.

3.3 High Concentrations of TP Originate in the Ocean

In testing of the third hypothesis, a pulse of 0.044 mg/L pulse (twentieth of the pulse applied to Mowry Canal) was applied to the ocean boundary (Fig. 7A). As shown in the figure, such a pulse would raise TP concentrations to 0.04 mg/L in regions close to the ocean boundary, 0.03 mg/L in mid-bay, and 0.01 mg/L at central Biscayne Bay shoreline. Figures 7B and 7C show simulation results for a 0.024 mg/L pulse applied on 12-18-2012 that is decreased to 0.022 a week later (12-25-2018). By the end of the day on 12-18-2018, 0.03 mg/L concentrations are estimated in regions close to the ocean boundary, 0.025 mg/L in mid-bay, and 0.012 mg/L at central Biscayne Bay shoreline (Fig. 7B). Twenty-five days later (on 01-19-2019, Fig. 7C) the simulation shows that concentrations in most of central Biscayne Bay are around 0.03 mg/L. This estimated concentration is very similar to what was observed in December 2018 Fig. 3.

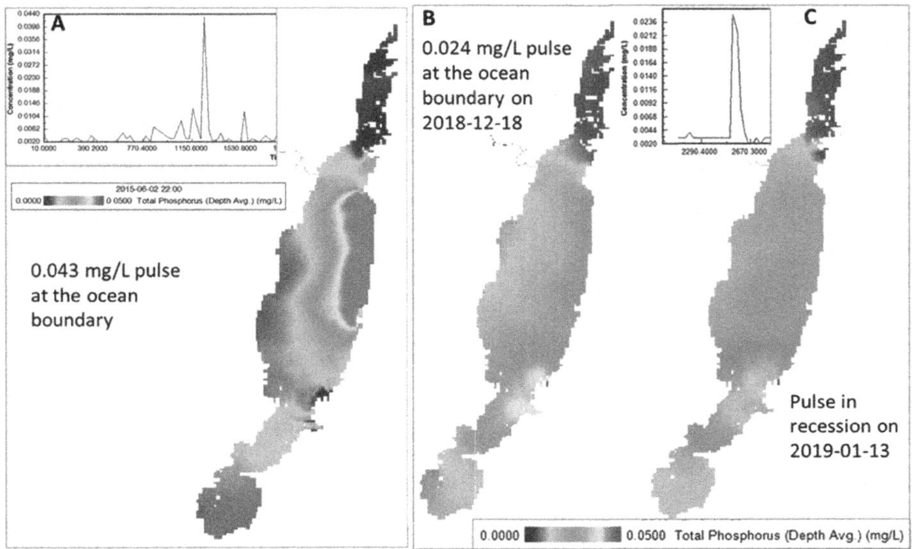

Fig. 7. TP concentration pulses at the ocean boundary. A) Simulation results for a pulse of 0.044 mg/L applied to the ocean boundary. B) Simulation results for a 0.024 mg/L pulse applied on 12-18-2012, decreased to 0.022 a week later. C) Simulation results after 25 days from the pulse application.

The rapid hydrodynamic dispersion of TP observed in Figs. 7B and C is a consequence of the efficient circulation of ocean water in the Bay. Figure 8 shows velocity vectors for 12-18-2018, at 8 AM (ebb tide), and 4 PM (flood tide). During ebb tide (Fig. 8A), water exits Biscayne Bay through the ocean boundary. Velocity vectors have higher magnitudes at the ocean boundary (up to 0.5 m/s approximately) than at the shoreline. Throughout the bay water moves towards the ocean boundary: southeast wards from northern sectors and northeast wards from southern zones. During flood tide (Fig. 8B), water vectors reach up to 0.7 m/s at the ocean boundary, and consequently water velocities towards the shoreline are greater than during ebb tide. Therefore, ocean water quality constituents will be hydrodynamically transported more efficiently towards the shoreline during flood tide, than contaminated freshwater will travel towards the ocean during ebb tide.

The velocity vectors shown in Fig. 8 show that water circulation imposed by the ocean boundary dominates water and water quality constituents transport in central Biscayne Bay. This is consistent with other research that explored the effects of ocean boundaries in enclosed estuaries [14, 15].

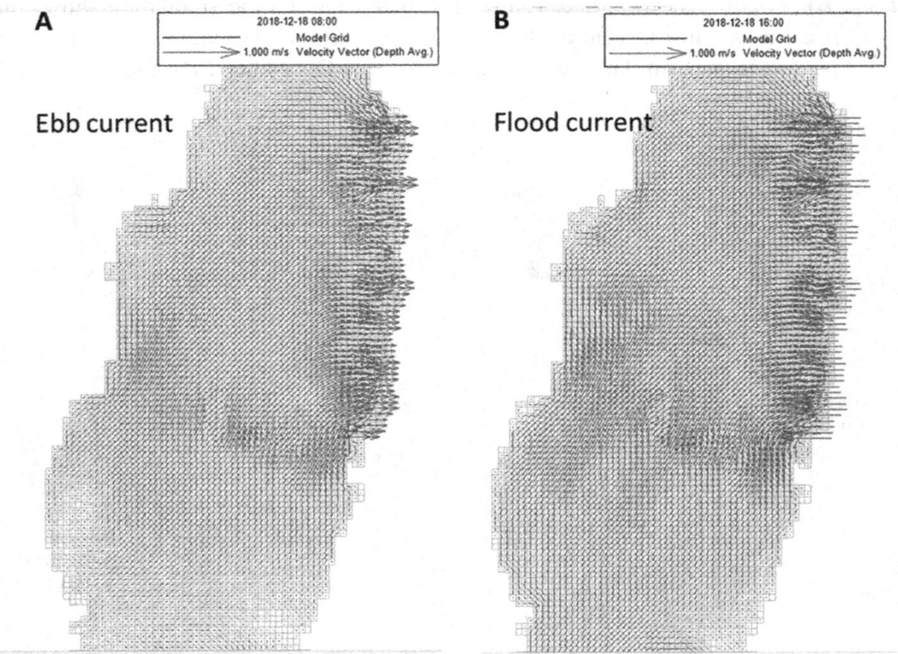

Fig. 8. Velocity vectors during ebb and flood current for December 18, 2018. A) Ebb current at 8 AM. B) Flood current at 4 PM. Vectors show that ocean water quality constituents would be hydrodynamically transported towards the shoreline more efficiently during flood tide, than contaminated freshwater would travel towards the ocean during ebb tide.

4 Conclusions

The water quality simulations generated in this research show that the observed total phosphorus (TP) peaks observed throughout Biscayne Bay during December 2018 were most probably caused by a surge in TP in the Atlantic Ocean waters close to the ocean boundary of Biscayne Bay. Analysis of observed chlorophyll-a concentrations from November 2018 to January 2019 showed that algal presence was not particularly high during those months (<0.7 μg/). Similarly, observed light attenuation coefficient values for the same months ranged between 0 and −0.7, showing that ocean water at those locations was within normal turbidity range. This leads to the conclusion that high TP concentrations during December 2018 were not directly connected to algae or phytoplankton blooms.

Computational experiments showed that the observed December 2018 TP peaks are not likely caused by the transport of a sudden release of a high-concentration TP pulse at the coast. Pulses of several magnitudes (0.088, 0.5, and 1.0 mg/L) were implemented at Black Creek and Mowry Canal (independent and concurrent pulses). Dilution of TP concentration by ocean water limits the spatial reach of the contaminant plume and the pulses did reach all monitoring stations as observed in December 2018.

In testing the TP ocean-surge-origin hypothesis, a pulse of 0.044 mg/L pulse was applied to the ocean boundary. This pulse raised TP concentrations to 0.04 mg/L in regions close to the ocean boundary, 0.03 mg/L in mid-bay, and 0.01 mg/L at central Biscayne Bay shoreline. Similarly, a 1-week duration 0.024 mg/L pulse applied to the ocean boundary generated TP concentrations of around 0.03 mg/L in most of central Biscayne Bay. This estimated concentration is very similar to the TP peaks observed in December 2018. Therefore, those peaks were most probably caused by a surge in TP in Atlantic Ocean waters close to the ocean boundary of Biscayne Bay.

Acknowledgements. This research was funded by a NOAA/Atlantic Oceanographic and Meteorological Laboratory grant to the Northern Gulf Institute (award number NA160AR4320199). The authors thank Jennifer Green for improving the quality of figures in the paper.

References

1. Millette, N.C., Kelble, C., Linhoss, A., Ashby, S., Visser, L.: Using spatial variability in the rate of change of chlorophyll a to improve water quality management in a subtropical oligotrophic estuary. Estuaries Coasts **42**(7), 1792–1803 (2019). https://doi.org/10.1007/s12237-019-00610-5
2. Swart, P.K., Anderson, W.T., Altabet, M.A., Drayer, C., Bellmund, S.: Sources of dissolved inorganic nitrogen in a coastal lagoon adjacent to a major metropolitan area, Miami Florida (USA). Appl. Geochem. **38**, 134–146 (2013)
3. Caccia, V.G., Boyer, J.N.: A nutrient loading budget for Biscayne Bay, Florida. Mar. Pollut. Bull. **54**(7), 994–1008 (2007). Epub 2007 Apr 5, PMID: 17418240. https://doi.org/10.1016/j.marpolbul.2007.02.009
4. Santos, R.O., Lirman, D., Pittman, S.J., Serafy, J.E.: Spatial patterns of seagrasses and salinity regimes interact to structure marine faunal assemblages in a subtropical bay. Mar. Ecol. Progr. Ser. **594**, 21–38 (2018). https://doi.org/10.3354/meps12499
5. SFWMD, South Florida Water Management District: South Florida Environmental Report (2021). https://www.sfwmd.gov/sites/default/files/documents/2021_sfer_highlights_hr.pdf
6. Wang, J.D., Luo, J., Ault, J.S.: Flows, salinity, and some implications for larval transport in South Biscayne Bay. Florida. Bull. Mar. Sci. **72**(3), 695–723 (2003)
7. Alarcon, V.J., et al.: Coastal inundation under concurrent mean and extreme sea-level rise in Coral Gables. Nat. Hazards **2022**, 1 (2022). https://doi.org/10.1007/s11069-021-05163-0
8. Alarcon, V.J., Linhoss, A.C., Mickle, P.F., Kelble, C.R., Fine, A.: Estimation of groundwater and salinity for the Central Biscayne Bay Coast, Florida, USA. In: Gervasi, O., Murgante, B., Misra, S., Rocha, A.M.A.C., Garau, C. (eds.) ICCSA 2022. LNCS, vol. 13379, 594–606. Springer, Cham (2022). https://doi.org/10.1007/978-3-031-10545-6_40
9. DSI: The Environmental Fluid Dynamics Code: Theoretical & Computational Aspects of EFDC+, Dynamic Solutions - International, LLC, Edmonds, WA, USA (2017)

10. SFWMD, South Florida Water Management District: DBHYDRO (Environmental Data) (2020). https://www.sfwmd.gov/science-data/dbhydro
11. DERM, Division of Environmental Resource Management: Miami Dade County Groundwater and Surface Water Quality Viewer (2023). https://mdc.maps.arcgis.com/apps/webappviewer/index.html?id=3fd24515ee614f5db63924d7323a4ea7
12. Chen, M., et al.: Mechanisms driving phosphorus release during algal blooms based on hourly changes in iron and phosphorus concentrations in sediments. Water Res. **133**, 153–164 (2018). https://doi.org/10.1016/j.watres.2018.01.040
13. Feng, W., Li, C., Zhang, C., et al.: Characterization of phosphorus in algae from a eutrophic lake by solution 31P nuclear magnetic resonance spectroscopy. Limnology **20**, 163–171 (2019). https://doi.org/10.1007/s10201-018-0562-2
14. Alarcon, V.J.: Using gridded multi-mission sea surface height data to estimate tidal heights at Columbia River Estuary. In: Misra, S., et al. (eds.) ICCSA 2019. LNCS, vol. 11621, pp. 602–611. Springer, Cham (2019). https://doi.org/10.1007/978-3-030-24302-9_43
15. Alarcon, V.J.: The role of boundary conditions in water quality modeling. In: Murgante, B., et al. (eds.) ICCSA 2014. LNCS, vol. 8581, pp. 721–733. Springer, Cham (2014). https://doi.org/10.1007/978-3-319-09150-1_53

Mapping Political Extremism on Twitter in Brazil

Geisa Tamara Bugs[1(✉)], Agnes Silva de Araujo[1], Diego Saez-Trumper[2], and Rodrigo Firmino[1]

[1] Pontifícia Universidade Católica do Paraná (PUCPR), Curitiba PR, Brazil
gestaourbana@pucpr.br
http://www.pucpr.br
[2] Universitat Pompeu Fabra, Barcelona, Spain
dsaez-trumper@acm.org

Abstract. Data from Social Media Networks may contain individual level information that is rarely available in institutional databases. It can reveal subjective and immaterial aspects that can help us to understand social behavior and, when geolocated, it may also enable understanding of spatial patterns and relationships. There is a wide range of studies that address the relationships between Twitter use and political campaigns and how it has been used in several countries to drive debates, news agenda and influence public opinion. This paper focuses on analyzing the relationship between Brazil's 2022 election results, the most polarized in recent years, and Twitter geolocated data regarding the January 8th events in Brazil, when the invasion of the National Congress and the Supreme Court in Brasília took place. The goal was to understand what the territory might reveal about this relationship. The state of Paraná was selected because it is from where many demonstrators left for Brasilia. We performed visual exploratory data analysis and spatial data analysis at municipality scale. As a result, we can cite a strong relationship between the municipalities that have more votes in each of the candidates and the number of tweets in favor or against the far-right extremist activities, and that a significant number of individuals turned against the act, especially after the media showed the damage caused to public property.

Keywords: location based social networks · Brazilian elections · January 8th

1 Introduction

The omnipresence of digital technologies, the ubiquity of geolocated urban data, and media activism of social movements, among other phenomena have emerged from the age of information and the network society along with the geospatial

Supported by Pontifícia Universidade Católica do Paraná (PUCPR).

O. Gervasi et al. (Eds.): ICCSA 2023 Workshops, LNCS 14107, pp. 439–454, 2023.
https://doi.org/10.1007/978-3-031-37114-1_30

revolution. For a while now we have been experiencing a massive use of new information and communication technologies as digital social networks in which geographic localization plays a central role in the context of dynamic data production and appropriation [1].

On digital social networks users share all sorts of information and professionals from different fields are paying great attention to them [2]. From these data treatment and modeling, besides visualizing the users' manifestations, it is possible to make several inferences about them, such as: what identity elements they carry, what they are posting about, what keywords they use, what their positions are on certain controversies, with which other users they interact, or even how they articulate themselves in a network to consume and pass on the news or other updates [3,4].

The information transmitted in online platforms is often attached to a geolocation related component, which in most cases means the physical locale where we are sending information from [5]. Digital geographical footprints left on the so-called Location Based Social Networks - LBSN [6] bring locative information allowing other readings about the indirect relationships that are formed [3]. A broad definition of LBSN includes any social media services with geo tagged media content, such as Twitter for geo tagged Tweets, or Flickr for geo tagged photos [7]. Places become informational layers by connecting different actors, allowing computational processes to generate inferences about profiles and behaviors [3].

But according to Martí et al. [8] obtaining meaningful information from these sources represents both a challenge and an opportunity. On one hand, the amount, quality, and usability of data are growing, and automatic retrieval represents a technological advance. Moreover, the information contained in LBSN data enables the exploration of intangible aspects of urban life, offering a multi-perspective approach to the study of cities. On the other hand, there is a lack of consistency in providing acceptable amounts of geolocated data, and LBSN data retrieved about specific locations may not be transferable to other studies. Also, no personal details are retrieved, and some users are not private and the data in this case is driven by public relations.

Nevertheless, online social networks such as Twitter have been the subject of scientific investigation with respect to citizen-government interactions, spatial convergence and segregation, modes of individual and collective performativity, urban analysis, social activity, and other approaches [7,9–14]. Twitter offers particularly attractive conditions as it makes its metadata bank public through the principle of anonymity. The set of variables provided by the Twitter API includes user IDs along with the timestamp and geographical coordinates of each tweet [10]. Besides being a popular service in terms of political content postings [9,10].

There are several studies on how political demonstrations can happen in line with the use of social networks, especially Twitter. These studies aim to understand how manifestations of political inclination are expressed in social networks, as well as to understand the strategies used by political and social agents to mobilize and influence public opinion. One of the main approaches used in these studies aims to identify the emotions and attitudes expressed by users on social networks in relation to certain topics, which makes it possible to understand how public opinion is divided in relation to political issues, and to identify sources of polarization and conflict. Another common approach seeks to understand how people relate on social networks through the measurement of hubs and connections in the spread of information or opinions.

These understandings of social behavior on social networks have been heavily used by political campaigns in majoritarian elections in several countries, the most recent examples being the US presidential elections in 2016 and the plebiscite for the Brexit in the UK in the same year, as well as the general elections in Brazil in 2018 [15–19]. Most of these studies highlight the polarization and partisan orientation of users, with emphasis on the role of emotions in the expression of opinions.

There is, however, an important gap in studies on political engagement through social media, including Twitter, which concerns the possibility of understanding the spatial relationships between the use of networks and political positions, as well as the cultural and social context of users. Spatializing engagement data with geotagging may help to understand layers of network behavior, linking geographic position and positioning on policy issues.

In this context, the present article uses part of the Twitter database to analyze the posts about the January 8th events in Brazil, when the invasion of the National Congress and the Supreme Court (STF) in Brasília took place, and the repercussions compared to the result of the presidential elections. The objective is to verify if there is a relationship between the political positioning of the event, the votes for each candidate and the geolocation of Twitter users in the state of Paraná, located in the southern region of the country (Fig. 1). In terms of demographic, economic and social data, Paraná stands out as an interesting case because it is sometimes homogeneous and stands out clearly from the rest of the country, and at other times presents internal contrasts that resemble part of its territory to other regions of Brazil [20]. This state is commonly referred to as the land of one of the most politically conservative populations in the country. Paraná was also one of the states of origin of most of the demonstrators arrested after the antidemocratic acts. According to Agência Pública [21], most coaches hired to transport demonstrators to Brasilia came from the states of São Paulo and Paraná, thirty-one and twenty-three respectively, followed by fourteen from Minas Gerais, and less than four from each of the other twenty-three states. Therefore, proportionally to their populations (44 million people live in São Paulo and 11 million in Paraná) Paraná was the most prominent state in the acts of January 8th.

The acts occurred 8 days after the inauguration of President-elect Luiz Inácio Lula da Silva. The 2022 presidential election was one of the most polarized in recent decades in Brazil. The candidates Lula (PT) and Bolsonaro (PL) finished the second round with a very narrow margin of votes: 50.90% percent and 49.10%, respectively. According to Nagy and Thal's [22] study a geographical polarization can be observed, with each of the two candidates having strengths where they were particularly strong and areas of weakness where the other dominated. Lula won in fourteen states, mostly in the Northeast, and Bolsonaro won in twelve states and the Federal District. In the state of Paraná Lula received 37.60% of the valid votes and Bolsonaro 62.40%.

It was the first time in Brazil's history that an incumbent President was not re-elected. The result generated strong complaints from supporters of the defeated candidate, for not accepting the results. Many people took to the streets in Brazilian cities in protest, voicing against Lula's victory and alleging electoral fraud in the electronic voting system [23]. Others have camped out in front of headquarters, calling for military intervention [24]. Everything leads one to believe that the attack on democratic powers was organized by alleged supporters of former President Jair Bolsonaro - with the former President himself flashing doubts about the electoral process through his social media accounts.

Although he claims to have no responsibility over the attacks and yet defended the attackers [25], for 58 percent of Brazilian voters [26] Bolsonaro had some degree of responsibility. Bolsonaro's campaign admittedly made use of digital social media to disseminate his ideas and interact with voters, being regularly associated with fake news dissemination [27,28]. The association between Bolsonaro's political performance with the production and distribution of misinformation is not a novelty in the Brazilian electoral scenario. According to [29]:102, the "strategy of spreading misinformation through social media is a powerful tool, used by Bolsonaro's supporters during and following the 2018 general election". Among the tools, WhatsApp and Telegram groups stand out, in which messages circulated with calls for anti-democratic acts in Brasilia [30].

2 Methodology

2.1 Data Collection

In this study we focused on Twitter information about the invasion of the Brazilian National Congress and Supreme Court, generated within the state of Paraná (Fig. 1). Our goal was to obtain geo located tweets, looking for a municipality level granularity.

There are two main channels to obtain Twitter's data: the Application Programming Interface - API [31] and the User Interface - UI. The former allows programmers to hit the Twitter database and receive information in machine readable format (JSON). However, the type and number of queries are limited. Moreover, its free access has been cut since February 2023. On the other hand, the UI is built for humans that access Twitter through phone or desktop frontends. One interesting feature on the UI, that does not exist on the API, is the ability to query tweets using an approximate location, that Twitter infers using a set of heuristics [32], while the API considers only tweets that have an explicit location (through the phone's GPS location).

Considering that just around 1% of the tweets contain exact coordinates [33], the approximated location becomes a powerful tool to perform location-aware

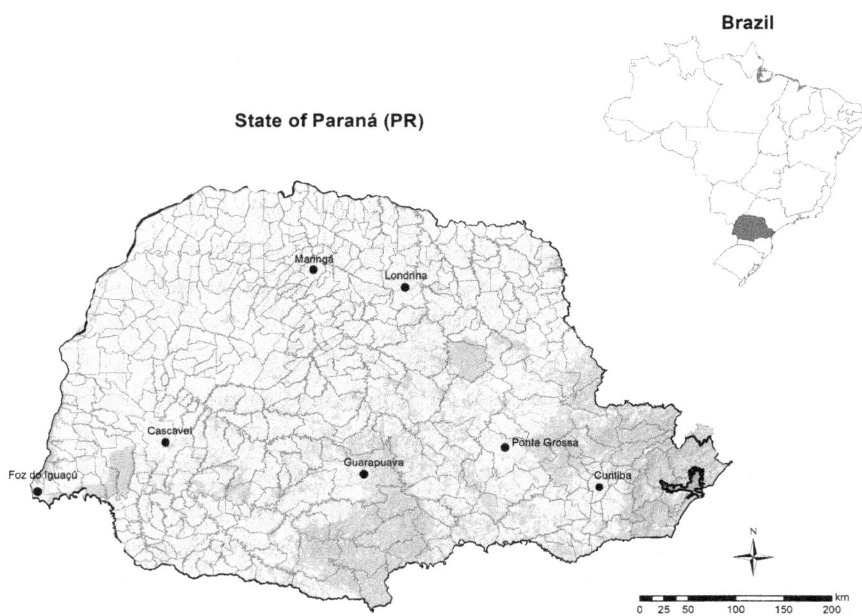

Fig. 1. Parana state municipalities

studies. The main limitation of Twitter UI is its format, coming in HTML that is easy to read for humans, but not directly readable for machines. In order to overcome these problems, there are a set of efforts to build wrappers. In this context, wrappers refer to a piece of code used to gather human-readable data and transform it into structured data. In this study, we have used the popular Python scraper package [34] that allows us to perform approximate location searches and transform them into JSON, CSV, or Excel readable files.

Our data collection process was built by searching for a set of keywords and hashtags (see Figs. 2 and 3) and limiting the search space by location. Specifically, we took the geo center coordinates of all 401 Parana state municipalities, using a radius of 20km. We also temporarily restricted our search, looking for tweets produced between 7 to 11 of January 2023. A total number of 3299 tweets compose the initial dataset.

This query returns several fields, including the Tweet content, the approximate geolocation computed by Twitter, tweet ID, and the author's username. Given that the 20km produces some overlaps between regions, we removed all the duplicated data from our dataset, and used the location assigned by Twitter. Also, to preserve users' privacy, we anonymize the username, using a hashing function [35]. This technique allows us to assign a random identification number of each user in our dataset, as exemplified in Fig. 4.

'Eleição OR Democracia OR "Forças armadas" OR "Atos antidemocráticos" OR "Três poderes" OR "Ataque" OR Armas OR Golpistas OR "Palácio do planalto" OR Invasão OR Terrorista OR Povo OR Poder OR Direita OR Esquerda OR Comunista OR Acampamento OR Bolsonarista OR Militares OR Exército OR "Bolsonaro é culpado" OR semanistiaparagolpista OR "Estado democrático de direito" OR "pátria e família" OR "3 poderes" OR "Faz o B" until:2023-01-15 since:2023-01-07 near:" -23.7358, -53.5920," within:20km'

Fig. 2. Query Example for the "Xambrê" municipality (in Portuguese)

Eleição , Democracia , "Forças armadas" , "Atos antidemocráticos" , "Três poderes" , "Ataque" , Armas , Golpistas , "Palácio do planalto" , Invasão , Terrorista , Povo , Poder , Direita , Esquerda, Comunista, Acampamento , Bolsonarista , Militares , Exército , "Bolsonaro é culpado" , semanistiaparagolpista, "Estado democrático de direito", "pátria e família", "3 poderes", "Faz o B"

Fig. 3. Keywords used for Search (in Portuguese)

Next, we manually evaluate each tweet, classifying them with three labels: "Support the act", "Reject the act" and "Not sure". During this process, some tweets were removed because they were out of context (such as the use of the word 'povo', which means people in Portuguese, to other issues). Our final dataset has 2.968 tweets.

2.2 Data Limitations

Our dataset has some limitations. First, the list of keywords was built by reviewing the trending topics for the selected day, and might be biased towards popular trends, ignoring other - less popular, but relevant - keywords. This is an intrinsic limitation of this kind of study. However, the number of tweets not considered in our search should be small in comparison with the analyzed dataset. Unfortunately, it is not possible to estimate the coverage of the analyzed dataset. This limitation should be considered when analyzing our results.

The second limitation is the potential errors in the Twitter approximate location estimation. This process is usually based on an IP address that does not have some precision from GPS coordinates. Anyhow, we opted for using this approximation to capture as many tweets as possible, focusing on recall instead of the precision for our data.

	username_anon	renderedContent	lat	lon	clean_place
91	500518638337186926	eu queria ver bolsonarista sendo tratado igual...	-25.993234	-48.995433	Guaratuba
899	-6271232442799670818	@eas_info_br @exercitooficial @NBCNews @cbstv ...	-25.644752	-49.391643	Curitiba
0	-3021135016698098404	Os caras não conhecem história e querem tomar ...	-23.375411	-50.812575	Cornélio Procópio
241	8257822057118756708	Deixou 2 salários minimos em uma peixaria, iss...	-25.644752	-49.391643	Curitiba
40	3178254838579307705	@rafaelsatie Por quê o impeachment do luladrao...	-25.709038	-53.990943	Capanema

Fig. 4. Dataset sample

A third problem was the stacking of tweets in the Centroid of the Municipality. To overcome this limitation, a technique of random distribution of points within the municipal limits was applied. This distribution was later validated manually, comparing whether the data referring to a tweet in the city of "Curitiba", for example, was within the limits of the municipality.

Another relevant aspect refers to the classification of Tweet content. This process cannot be performed automatically, due to the use of the same words in positive (in favor of the act) and negative (against the act) contexts. To get around this limitation, the points were classified manually by the authors based on the content analysis of the Tweets.

2.3 Data Analysis

Three main methodologies are used in this paper: 1st) analysis of the statistical relationship between the number of tweets in favor and against the act of January 8th and the number of votes for Lula and Bolsonaro in the second round of the 2022 elections by municipality, obtained in the Superior Electoral Court (2023); 2nd) spatial analysis between the clusters of municipalities that most voted for each of the candidates and the density of points of tweets for and against the act and 3rd) statistical bivariate maps to display of association between the variables of the most voted candidate and number of Tweets.

Regarding statistical analysis, a simple linear regression model was applied. It determines the relationship between two variables: the dependent (y) and the independent or explanatory (x) variables. Equation 1 describes the statistical relationship between the variables in this study:

$$Y = \beta\theta + \beta_1 X + \epsilon \tag{1}$$

where: Y represents the number of Tweets in favor or against the act (independent variable); β are the intercept and slope parameters of the regression model; X represents the number of votes for Bolsonaro or Lula in the second round of the 2022 elections (explanatory variables); ϵ is the sum of the residuals in the model. It is important to mention that the variables were analyzed in pairs: number of votes for Lula and Tweets against the act and number of votes for Bolsonaro and Tweets in favor of the act.

Regarding the spatial analysis, a kernel density estimator (k) was used to transform the tweets point data into a density surface which allows the analysis of the locations where there were more tweets in favor or against the act. The density surface was then visually compared to hotspot maps of votes concentration in Bolsonaro or Lula, prepared using the Getis-Ord (Gi*) algorithm. The Getis-Ord (Gi*) algorithm allows spatial analysis of hotspots in area vector layers, which is not possible using a kernel density estimator. Nonetheless, Manepalli et al. [36] discuss that both methods can be used comparatively since they present similar spatial results.

To analyze and demonstrate the spatial relationship between two variables (votes for each candidate and number of tweets in favor or against the act) in a single map, we adopted bivariate maps. The idea was to analyze where the two variables tend to be in agreement or disagreement. To develop a bivariate map, we counted the number of tweets per municipality which allowed both variables to be aggregated in the same vector data of municipalities, then we broke the variables into 3 classes each and we based the choice of color scheme on Tumbo's [37] recommendations.

3 Results and Discussion

Almost 43% of the tweets were in favor of the act. However, there is an increase in the Tweets with disapproval content over time (Fig. 5). It is inferred that as the media presented the damage caused to public property during the act, part of the population changed its opinion, even of individuals who can be considered extreme right. Most of the far-rightist disinformation and extreme opinions are focused on the fact that "there were leftists infiltrated in the act" and this was the reason for the destructive result (Fig. 6).

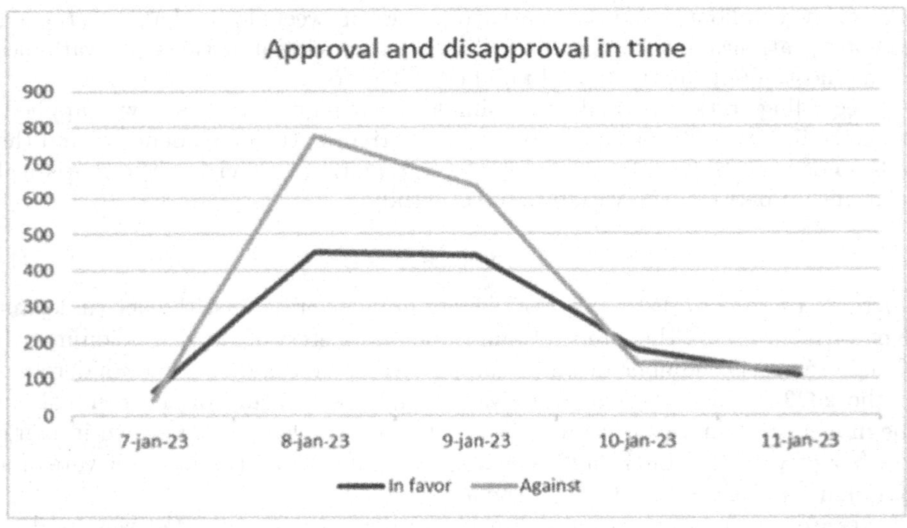

Fig. 5. Analysis of Tweet content over time

Content analysis shows that extreme rightist opinions are centered on the opinion that "there were leftists infiltrated in the act". The second most used word in tweets in favor of the act is "esquerda" (the original in Portuguese, means "left") and the word "infiltrados" (the original in Portuguese, means "infiltrators") is the one that appears more frequently (right corner of the word cloud). The second most used word in tweets against the act is "golpista" (the original in Portuguese, means "scammer"). What's more interesting, however, is the fact that for both categories of tweets (in favor and against) the word "terrorist" appears more frequently (Fig. 6). It reflects a position change of the left and the extreme right in the legal debate around the term. Since 2016 (on the occasion of the Olympic Games) there has been a specific law in Brazil that classifies certain crimes as terrorism and the STF Minister classified the 8th of January acts as terrorism against democracy and the Brazilian institutions. While the left has previously mobilized to exclude political motivation from the characterization of terrorism, the extreme right is now using the law to prevent the attacks perpetrators from being punished as such.

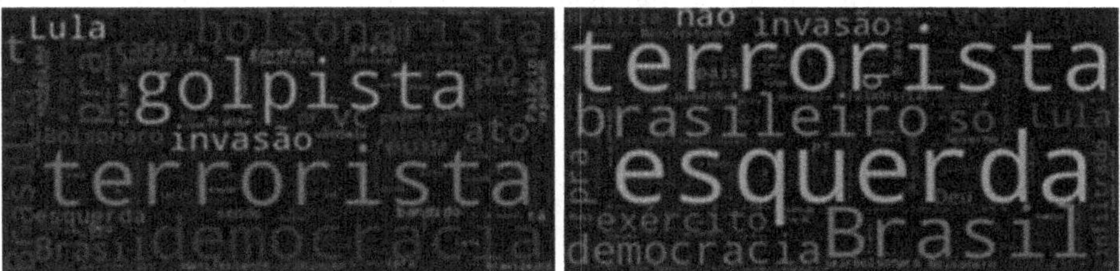

Fig. 6. Content analysis of Tweets (against on left side and in favor on right side)

The results of the linear regression are presented in Table 1. The statistical analysis showed R^2 greater than 0.85 for both pairs of variables with a positive and statistically significant relationship (p-value = 0.0000). In this case, it demonstrates a relationship between the political opinion displayed in Social Media Networks and election results. Two recent examples of this type of social media influence are the Facebook/Cambridge Analytica scandal in 2018 and the invasion of the US Capitol building in 2021.

Table 1. Linear regression results

Regression outputs	Votes for Bolsonaro and teet in favor	Votes for Lula and tweets against
R^2	0.867443	0.870003
R^2 adjusted	0.867111	0.869678
F-statistics	2611.03	2670.31
AIC	2966.28	3282.45

The Facebook/Cambridge Analytica case involves the power of large corporations to change political opinions and behavior. Cambridge Analytica used data from Facebook users' clicks and likes to produce political messages tailored to the interests and beliefs detected by users' behavior. This allowed them to manipulate people's political opinions, often without their prior knowledge or consent. The case was particularly worrying because it demonstrated the ease with which large organizations can manipulate public opinion and influence election results [38].

Similarly, in the case of the invasion of the Capitol building, social media platforms such as Facebook, Twitter, and YouTube played a critical role in organizing and disseminating the message of the people and groups involved [39,40]. Social networks were used to plan and publicize the event, using false information that fueled the anger and frustration of the participants. This type of use of networks also allowed everything to be documented and shared in real time, further amplifying the impact of the event, and contributing to inciting violence and encouraging others to participate in the insurrection. Ironically, both in the US and in Brazil, the publicized material also allowed prosecutors and the courts to form proof against the demonstrators, facilitating their indictment.

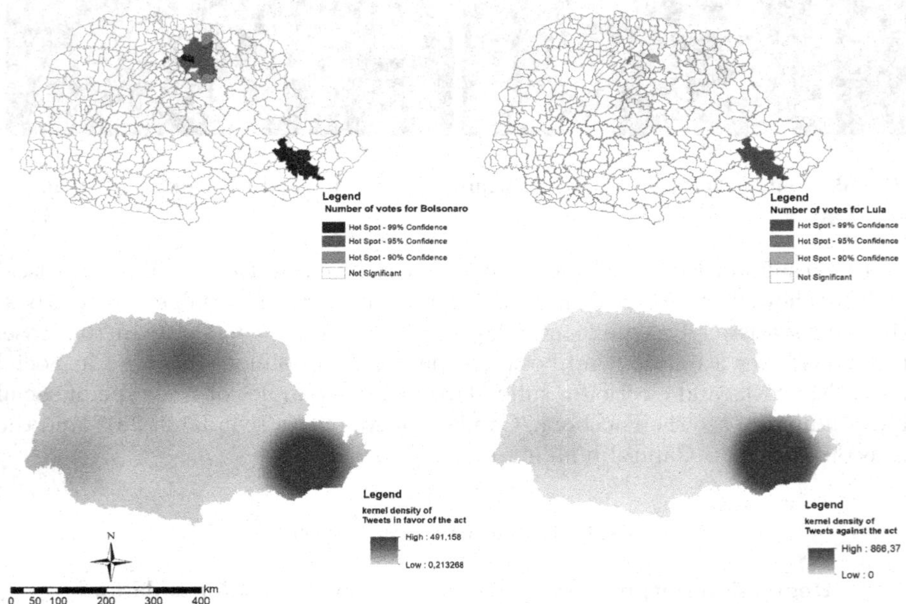

Fig. 7. Spatial patterns between municipalities with the highest number of votes for Bolsonaro and Lula and number of Tweets in favor and against the act

In addition to quantitative data, we sought to understand the spatial relationship between variables. According to Théry et al. [20] in Paraná there are two main population concentrations, one coastal around Curitiba (the state capital, and the only city with more than one million inhabitants in the state), and another in the north around Maringá and Londrina, although pole-cities and medium-sized cities, such as Guarapuava and Cascavel, stand out in the interior of the state, and in the far west Foz do Iguaçu (Fig. 1). As expected, the number of tweets collected per city follows the demography distribution. The top 5 cities with the most tweets collected are Curitiba (1288), Maringá (214), Londrina (158), Cascavel (82) and Foz do Iguaçu (77). In other words, one can observe clusters of tweets in municipalities with a larger number of inhabitants. Both the Metropolitan Region of Curitiba and the axis in the northeast of Paraná (Londrina and Maringá) had the highest number of Tweets in favor and against the act (Fig. 7).

The capital and its surroundings have a high industrial concentration, the center of the state and part of the north are dominated by agriculture, while the secondary cities depend mainly on services. The state has more than a third of the land with priority use for agriculture. Within this activity, in the southern part family labor predominates and in the northern part hired labor, as it is the main agribusiness territory [20]. The highest Human Development Index - HDI of the state is concentrated in the regions of greater industrial activity and agribusiness-oriented agricultural activities in the western and northwestern portions, also marked by social inequality, whereas the central region of Paraná is the least developed [20]. The HDI of the smaller municipalities tends to be lower than that of the municipalities in the Metropolitan Region of Curitiba and the medium-sized cities in northern Paraná (Londrina and Maringá) [40].

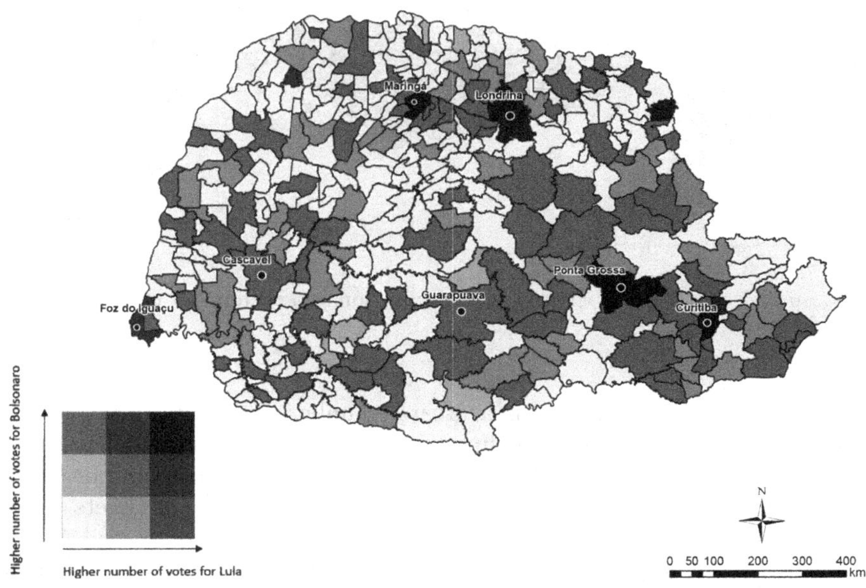

Fig. 8. Results of the second round of the 2022 elections

The voting results in the second round (Fig. 8) can be read considering socioeconomic characteristics. The map clearly demonstrates the polarization of these elections. Bolsonaro won in large cities in the interior with positive indicators, a result of the good performance of the countryside in recent years. Lula won in a much smaller number of cities and in the smallest towns in Paraná, a state considered politically conservative, as mentioned earlier.

Figures 9 and 10 show the relationship between the number of tweets in favor and against the act and the number of votes for Bolsonaro or Lula. One aspect that must be considered when analyzing these maps is that in small municipalities, the number of tweets was very small or non-existent, for this reason, only the variables of the result of the second-round elections stand out. Despite this limitation, spatial relationships can be observed.

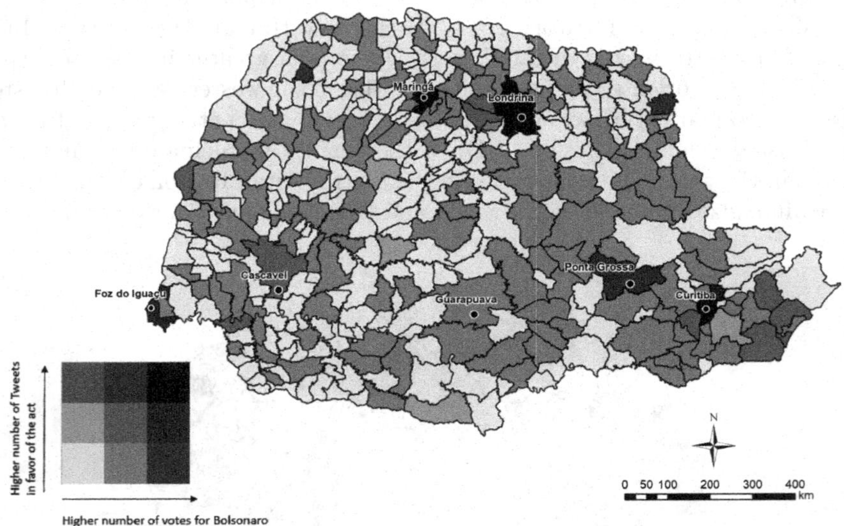

Fig. 9. Spatial relationship between votes for Bolsonaro and number of tweets in favor of the act.

One can observe that there is a greater number of Tweets in favor of the act in Londrina and Maringá, in line with the election results in those cities that had the highest number of votes for Bolsonaro. The Metropolitan Region, on the other hand, stands out for the greater concentration of tweets against the act, despite having a higher number of votes for Bolsonaro as well. Smaller municipalities did not show significant results, even though it was in smaller municipalities where the percentage of votes for candidate Lula was higher. This fact highlights the problem of representativeness of the social media data which is exacerbated when spatial patterns are discussed.

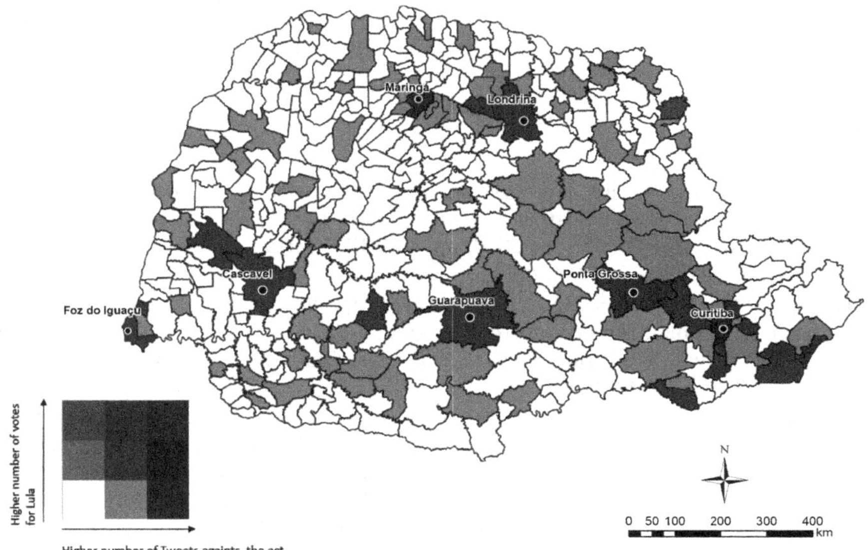

Fig. 10. Spatial relationship between votes for Lula and number of tweets against the act

4 Final Remarks

The results revealed a strong relationship ($R^2 = 0.86$) between the municipalities that have more votes in each of the candidates (Bolsonaro or Lula) and the number of tweets in favor or against the act, respectively. As expected, some municipalities that had more votes for Bolsonaro, also had a greater number of tweets in favor of the act. That is the case of the municipalities in the north of the state such as Londrina and Maringá, agribusiness territory. On the other hand, the Metropolitan Region, in which the capital Curitiba is inserted, had a greater number of tweets against the act and a greater number of votes for Bolsonaro as well. In the municipalities where the votes in favor of Lula prevailed, smaller ones, the number of tweets, both in favor of the act and against it, were very small or non-existent.

The results show that, firstly, a significant number of individuals were against the act, even rightists, especially after the media showed the damage caused by demonstrators to public property and, second, emphasizes the problem of representativeness of the social media data which is exacerbated when spatial patterns are discussed because we have big voids with no tweets related to small towns and rural areas, this does not mean that this population has no opinion on the subject, just that they do not use social media.

A contribution that should be highlighted is that this article is part of a range of research that seeks to assess the use of Location Based Social Networks data to analyze their concurrence or divergence from established methodologies and thereby increase our understanding regarding the use of this kind of data.

References

1. Florentino, P.V., Pereira, G.C.: Structures of interactions and data in urban networks: the case of PortoAlegre.cc. In: Oliveira, J., Farias, C.M., Pacitti, E., Fortino, G. (eds.) BiDU 2018. CCIS, vol. 926, pp. 156–170. Springer, Cham (2019). https://doi.org/10.1007/978-3-030-11238-7_10
2. Rocha, M.C.F., Pereira, G.C., Loiola, E., Murgante, B.: Conversation about the city: urban commons and connected citizenship. In: Gervasi, O., et al. (eds.) ICCSA 2016. LNCS, vol. 9790, pp. 608–623. Springer, Cham (2016). https://doi.org/10.1007/978-3-319-42092-9_46
3. Sousa, P.V., Florentino, P.V.: Rastreamento e visualização de redes sociais: Investigando redes indiretas a partir de dados georreferenciais. In: 3o Simpósio Internacional LAVITS: Vigilância, Tecnopolíticas, Territórios (2015)
4. Quercia, D., Saez, D.: Mining urban deprivation from foursquare: implicit crowdsourcing of city land use. IEEE Pervasive Comput. **13**(2), 30–36 (2014)
5. Lemos, A., Firmino, R.: I connect, therefore I am!: places, locales, locations and informational territorialization. Revista Estudos do Século XX **15**, 17–34 (2015)
6. Zheng, Y.: Tutorial on Location-Based Social Networks. In: Proceedings of the 21st international conference on World Wide Web, p. 1078. ACM (2012)
7. Yang, D., Qu, B., Cudre-Mauroux, P.: Location-centric social media analytics: challenges and opportunities for smart cities. IEEE Intell. Syst. **36**(5), 3–10 (2021)
8. Martí, P., Serrano-Estrada, L., Nolasco-Cirugeda, A.: Social media data: challenges, opportunities and limitations in urban studies. Comput. Environ. Urban Syst. **74**, 161–174 (2019)
9. Flores, C.C., Rezende, D.A.: Twitter information for contributing to the strategic digital city: towards citizens as co-managers. Telemat. Inform. **35**(5), 1082–1096 (2018)
10. Rosales Sánchez, C., Craglia, M., Bregt, A.K.: New data sources for social indicators: the case study of contacting politicians by Twitter. Int. J. Digit Earth **10**(8), 829–845 (2017)
11. Netto, V.M., Pinheiro, J.M., Meirelles, J.V., Leite, H.: Digital footprints in the cityscape. In: International Conference on Social Networks on Proceedings, Publisher, Athens, USA (2015)
12. Matzner, T.: Beyond data as representation: the performativity of big data in surveillance. Surveill. Soc. **14**(2), 197–210 (2016)
13. Bernabeu-Bautista, A., Serrano-Estrada, L., Perez-Sanchez, V.R., Martí, P.: The geography of social media data in urban areas: representativeness and complementarity. ISPRS Int. J. Geo Inf. **10**(11), 747 (2021)
14. Adelfio, M., Serrano-Estrada, L., Martí-Ciriquián, P., Kain, J.H., Stenberg, J.: Social activity in Gothenburg's intermediate city: mapping third places through social media data. Appl. Spat. Anal. Policy **13**(4), 985–1017 (2020)
15. Waisbord, S., Amado, A.: Populist communication by digital means: presidential Twitter in Latin America. Inf. Commun. Soc. **20**(9), 1330–1346 (2017)
16. Wignell, P., Tan, S., O'Halloran, K.L., Chai, K.: The twittering presidents. J. Language Polit. **20**(2), 197–225 (2021)

17. Tromble, R.: The great leveler? Comparing citizen-politician Twitter engagement across three Western democracies. Eur. Polit. Sci. **17**(2), 223–239 (2018)
18. Jungherr, R.: Twitter use in election campaigns: a systematic literature review. J. Inf. Technol. Polit. **13**(1), 72–91 (2016)
19. Vergeer, M.: Twitter and political campaigning. Sociol. Compass **9**(9), 745–760 (2016)
20. Théry, H., Nagy, A., Junior, R. N.: O Paraná no Brasil: uma contextualização em treze imagens (e meia), Confins 27 (2016)
21. Agência Pública Homepage. https://apublica.org/2023/01/maioria-dos-onibus-que-transportaram-terroristas-sao-do-parana-e-sao-paulo/. Accessed 11 Apr 2023
22. Nagy, A., Thal, F.: Geografia das eleições de 2022: o Brasil cortado em quatro, Confins **57** (2022)
23. Correia, E.F.C.R.D., Tavares, F., Soares, A.M., Assis, I.B., Eleições presidenciais no Brasil. Polis **26** (2022)
24. The Guardian Homepage. https://www.theguardian.com/world/2022/dec/22/brazil-bolsonaro-militants-lefist-lula-president. Accessed 09 Apr 2023
25. O Globo Homepage. https://oglobo.globo.com/politica/noticia/2023/02/nos-eua-bolsonaro-defende-presos-no-dia-8-de-janeiro-chefes-de-familia.ghtml. Accessed 09 Apr 2023
26. Datafolha Homepage. https://www1.folha.uol.com.br/poder/2023/04/datafolha-58-veem-alguma-responsabilidade-de-bolsonaro-no-ataque-de-81.shtml. Accessed 09 Apr 2023
27. Viscardi, J.M.: Fake news, true and lie according to Jair Bolsonaro's twitter account. Trabalhos em Linguística Aplicada **592**, 1134–1157 (2020)
28. Lisbôa, J.P., Oliveira, V.: Fake News enquanto Instrumento de Política Externa: Uma Perspectiva Construtivista do Caso Bolsonaro. Trabalhos em Linguística Aplicada **592**, 1134–1157 (2020)
29. Evangelista, R., Firmino, R.: Modes of pandemic existence: territory, inequality, and technology. In: Data Justice and COVID-19: Global Perspectives, pp. 100–107, Meatspace Press (2020)
30. G1 Homepage. https://g1.globo.com/politica/noticia/2023/01/08/mensagens-bolsonaristas-terroristas-brasilia.ghtml. Accessed 09 Apr 2023
31. Twitter API Developer Platform. https://developer.twitter.com/en/docs/twitter-api. Accessed 09 Apr 2023
32. Filtering Tweets by location - API Developer Platform. https://developer.twitter.com/en/docs/tutorials/filtering-tweets-by-location. Accessed 09 Apr 2023
33. Hoang, T.B.N., Mothe, J.: Location extraction from tweets. Inf. Process. Manag. **54**(2), 129–144 (2018)
34. Snscrape Github Homepage. https://github.com/JustAnotherArchivist/snscrape. Accessed 09 Apr 2023
35. Hash function Wikipedia Homepage. https://en.wikipedia.org/wiki/Hashfunction. Accessed 09 Apr 2023
36. Manepalli, U.R.R., Bham, G.H., Kandada, S.: Evaluation of hotspots identification using kernel density estimation (K) and Getis-Ord (Gi*) on I-630. In: 3rd International Conference on Road Safety and Simulation on Proceedings, pp. 14–16 (2011)
37. Tumbo, B.E.: A theory for coloring bivariate statistical maps. Am. Stat. **35**(4), 220–226 (1981)
38. Isaak, J., Hanna, M.J.: User data privacy: Facebook, Cambridge Analytica, and Privacy Protection. Comput. (Long Beach Calif.) **51**(8), 56–59 (2018)

39. Chirwa, C., Manyana, Z.: The rise of Fake news: surveying the effects of social media on informed democracy. The Thinker **88**(3), 59–66 (2021)
40. Calderón, C. et al.: Relatório do Desenvolvimento Humano 2021–2022: Tempos incertos, vidas instáveis: A construir o nosso futuro num mundo em transformação. Report UN, Brazil (2022)

Increasing Urban Sustainability Designing Vertical Garden: The Experience of Pisticci Municipality (Southern Italy)

Beniamino Murgante[1(✉)], Giuseppe Trabace[2], Veronica Vespe[2], and Domenico Laviola[1,2,3]

[1] School of Engineering, University of Basilicata, Viale dell'Ateneo Lucano 10, 85100 Potenza, Italy
beniamino.murgante@unibas.it
[2] Studio Tecnico Giuseppe Trabace, Via San Francesco, 7, 75019 Tricarico, Matera, Italy
[3] Studio Geologo Domenico Laviola, Corso Metaponto 13, 75015 Pisticci, Matera, Italy

Abstract. Climate change is one of the significant challenges and risks for the environment, economy, and society. It is a phenomenon that involves a persistent alteration of global or regional weather patterns, leading to variations in temperature, precipitation, and extreme weather events. This transformation is primarily caused by human actions such as burning fossil fuels and deforestation, which produce greenhouse gases that trap heat in the atmosphere, causing global warming. This problem can be addressed by reducing urban fragmentation, land take, soil sealing, urban sprawl, urban sprinkling, and loss of ecosystem services. These phenomena can be tackled on various levels. On a larger scale, it involves implementing urban strategies and regulations that can mitigate these trends. At a local scale, realizing green spaces and infrastructure could reduce this trend. Vertical gardens have the potential to increase green space in several situations.

1 Introduction

Today, climate change is one most important challenges of humanity. It poses significant challenges and threats to our environment, economy, and society. Climate change refers to a long-term shift in global or regional weather patterns, often resulting in changes in temperature, precipitation, and weather extremes. This shift is caused by human activities, such as burning fossil fuels and deforestation, which release greenhouse gases into the atmosphere and trap heat, leading to global warming.

Climate change is primarily caused by the release of greenhouse gases into the atmosphere. These emissions are mainly the result of human activities, such as burning fossil fuels, deforestation, heavy industry, traffic, and agriculture.

The effects of this phenomenon can be detected in terms of global temperature increase over the past century leading to heat waves, droughts, and wildfires; fluctuations in precipitation patterns, and more frequent and intense rainfall occurring in some regions in others arise droughts; the rise of global temperatures produces glaciers and ice sheets melt, causing sea levels to rise also leading to flooding and erosion of coastlines; impact

O. Gervasi et al. (Eds.): ICCSA 2023 Workshops, LNCS 14107, pp. 455–467, 2023.
https://doi.org/10.1007/978-3-031-37114-1_31

on ecosystems and biodiversity and significant economic effects, such as loss of crops and fisheries, property damage due to extreme weather events, and increased healthcare costs.

Tackling climate change requires immediate and sustained action to reduce greenhouse gas emissions and adapt to its impacts. This involves taking measures such as transitioning to renewable energy sources, improving energy efficiency, protecting and restoring natural ecosystems, and promoting sustainable land use and transportation practices. Greenhouse gas emissions (GHG) could be significantly reduced by adopting renewable energy sources, such as wind, solar, and geothermal, carbon pricing, and emissions reduction targets.

Climate change mitigation could be implemented by reducing greenhouse gas (GHG) emissions and stabilizing or reducing the concentration of GHGs in the atmosphere, thereby slowing down or preventing the negative impacts of climate change.

The main actions to mitigate climate change could be summarized in the following steps:

- Energy transition: Transitioning to renewable energy sources, such as wind, solar, and geothermal, can significantly reduce greenhouse gas emissions and mitigate climate change. This involves phasing out fossil fuels, the primary carbon emissions source.
- Energy efficiency: Improving energy efficiency in buildings, transportation, and industry can also help to reduce GHG emissions. This involves implementing energy-saving technologies and practices, such as using LED light bulbs, insulating buildings, and optimizing transportation routes.
- Sustainable land use: Sustainable land use practices, such as agroforestry and conservation agriculture, can help to reduce GHG emissions by sequestering carbon in soil and vegetation.
- Carbon capture and storage: Carbon capture and storage (CCS) technologies can capture carbon dioxide (CO2) emissions from industrial processes and store them underground, preventing them from entering the atmosphere.
- Climate-friendly consumer choices: Individuals can make choices in their everyday lives, such as reducing meat consumption, driving less, and choosing energy-efficient appliances.
- International cooperation: International cooperation and commitments, such as the Paris Agreement, are crucial for mitigating climate change on a global scale. This involves countries working together to set emissions reduction targets, share knowledge and technology, and provide financial support to developing countries.

Climate change mitigation requires a comprehensive approach involving government policies, private sector actions, and individual behavior changes. Reducing GHG emissions and stabilizing the climate can prevent the worst impacts of climate change and build a more sustainable future for everybody.

International cooperation and commitments, such as the Paris Agreement, are also crucial for addressing climate change on a global scale. Also, pursuing Sustainable Development Goals (SDGs) [1] could be essential in mitigating GHG emissions.

More particularly, Sustainable Development Goal 13, "take urgent action to combat climate change and its impacts," suggests to integrate climate change measures into national policies, strategies, and planning, and SDG 7, "ensure access to affordable, reliable, sustainable and modern energy" to ensure access to modern, affordable, reliable, and sustainable energy for all people, also promoting investments in the use of renewable energy sources, in energy infrastructure and clean energy technologies and improving energy efficiency.

2 Natural Solutions for Climate Change Mitigation

The primary measure to reduce climate change impacts is related to environmental depletion reduction. This impoverishment is generated by urban fragmentation, land take, soil sealing, urban sprawl, urban sprinkling, and loss of ecosystem services.

Urban fragmentation [2–5] refers to breaking up and dividing urban areas into smaller, disconnected, or isolated patches, often resulting in a discontinuous and scattered development pattern. This phenomenon typically occurs due to rapid urbanization and sprawl, where urban areas expand outward in a low-density and haphazard manner.

Urban sprawl [6–14] refers to the unplanned, uncontrolled, and often rapid expansion of urban areas into previously undeveloped or rural land, resulting in low-density, spread-out, and car-dependent development patterns. Urban sprawl typically involves the outward growth of cities, often fragmented and disconnected, resulting in converting agricultural land, natural habitats, or other open spaces into urbanized areas.

Land take [15–19] refers to converting land previously classified as non-built-up or non-urban land into built-up or urban land. It involves the transformation of natural or agricultural land into land used for residential, commercial, industrial, or infrastructural purposes, such as roads, highways, and urban development.

Land take is a phenomenon associated with urbanization and land development, and it can significantly impact the environment, society, and economy. The process of land take can result in the loss of natural habitats, agricultural land, and open spaces, leading to biodiversity loss, soil degradation, and reduced ecosystem services. It can also contribute to climate change by increasing the loss of carbon-sequestering vegetation and promoting urban heat island effects.

Soil sealing [20–23] refers to covering the natural soil surface with impermeable materials, such as pavement, concrete, buildings, or other artificial structures, resulting in the loss of its natural functions and properties. Soil sealing is a form of land degradation that occurs when the natural soil surface is covered with impervious materials, preventing water infiltration, air exchange, and nutrient cycling and altering the natural hydrological and ecological processes.

Soil sealing is often associated with urbanization and land development, as it is commonly used for constructing roads, buildings, parking lots, and other infrastructure in urban and suburban areas. It can also occur in different land use types, such as industrial, commercial, and agricultural areas, where natural soils are covered with impermeable materials for various purposes.

Urban sprinkling [24–30] occurs in very low population density and is characterized by territorial pulverization due to small settlements.

Ecosystem services [31–36] refer to the wide range of benefits that people receive from nature or ecosystems. These services result from natural ecological processes that support human well-being, provide goods and services essential for human survival and prosperity, and contribute to economic, social, and cultural values.

These phenomena can be addressed at different scales. At a broader scale adopting urban plans and policies able to reduce these trends, and at a local scale, implementing programs for increasing green areas and infrastructures.

Green infrastructure [37–42] refers to a planned network of natural and semi-natural areas, such as forests, wetlands, parks, green roofs, and green walls, designed to provide multiple environmental, social, and economic benefits to communities and ecosystems. Green infrastructure is an approach to urban and regional planning that seeks to integrate nature-based solutions into the design, development, and management of built environments to promote sustainability, resilience, and well-being.

The concept of green infrastructure recognizes that natural systems can provide valuable services essential for human well-being and environmental health, such as stormwater management, air purification, climate regulation, biodiversity conservation, and recreational opportunities. Green infrastructure can also enhance the aesthetic value of urban and rural landscapes, create habitats for wildlife, and provide cultural and educational opportunities for communities.

Green infrastructure can be implemented at different scales, from small-scale interventions, such as green roofs on individual buildings, to large-scale regional planning, such as green corridors or greenbelts that connect different natural areas. Green infrastructure can be designed to be multifunctional, meaning it can provide multiple benefits. It can be integrated into other land uses, such as residential, commercial, and transportation corridors.

It is crucial to strengthen urban green areas to improve the impact of anthropization on the environment. Using vast space to include green places in urban spaces is essential. In several cases, vertical gardens could be a solution to increasing green areas.

3 Vertical Gardens

Vertical gardens are green walls that can be created inside or outside a building, using plants and flowers to create a green area in a limited space. Vertical gardens, also known as green walls, have been proposed as a potential solution for mitigating the effects of climate change. The climate crisis reminds us to design more environmentally sustainable urban areas immediately. Vertical gardens can reduce CO2 emissions and, at the same time, produce oxygen. It is an innovative approach to designing our cities without remaining an experience related to a few projects. Although they are not a complete solution to climate change, they can be an effective tool for mitigating its effects in urban areas.

Here are some ways in which they can help:

- Temperature regulation: Green walls can help regulate temperature by reducing the heat buildings absorb. This can help reduce the urban heat island effect when cities are significantly warmer than surrounding rural areas.
- Carbon sequestration: Plants absorb carbon dioxide from the atmosphere and store it in their tissues. By increasing the amount of vegetation in urban areas, green walls can help sequester carbon and reduce greenhouse gas emissions.

- Air quality improvement: Plants absorb pollutants from the air, including volatile organic compounds (VOCs) and particulate matter. By adding green walls to urban areas, we can improve air quality and reduce the risk of respiratory problems.
- Water management: Green walls can help manage stormwater runoff by absorbing and filtering rainwater. This can help reduce the risk of flooding and improve water quality.
- Biodiversity promotion: Green walls can provide habitat for birds, insects, and other animals, which can help promote biodiversity in urban areas.

Vertical gardens can be categorized into typologies based on design and installation methods. Here are some common typologies of vertical gardens:

1. Green Facade: This type of vertical garden is installed on the exterior facade of a building, covering the walls with plants. Green facades can be installed using different systems, such as trellis, cable, wire, or modular panel systems.
2. Panel System: In this typology, pre-fabricated panels with built-in pockets or trays are attached to the walls to hold the plants. These panels are often made of metal, plastic, or composite materials and can be installed with irrigation and drainage systems.
3. Modular System: Modular systems involve individual modules or modules with pockets attached to the wall, forming a grid or matrix. Plants are then inserted into these pockets, creating a living wall. Modular systems offer flexibility in design and installation and can be easily replaced or modified as needed.
4. Tray System: Tray systems consist of trays or containers attached to the wall, each containing plants and a growing medium. These trays can be removed and replaced, allowing easy maintenance and plant replacement.
5. Pocket System: Pocket systems involve pockets or sleeves attached to the wall where plants are inserted. These pockets can be made of fabric, felt, or other materials and arranged in different patterns or configurations.
6. Hydroponic System: Hydroponic systems use a soilless growing medium and a nutrient-rich water solution to deliver nutrients directly to the plants. These systems are typically used for indoor vertical gardens and offer precise control over plant nutrition and water uptake.
7. Indoor Systems: Vertical gardens can also be installed indoors, using artificial lighting, irrigation, and climate control systems to create optimal growing conditions for the plants. Indoor vertical gardens are often used in commercial or residential buildings and retail or public spaces.

It is fundamental to consider the following good practices for designing, installing, and maintaining vertical gardens:

1. Plant Selection: Choose appropriate plant species suitable for vertical growth and the local climate. Consider sunlight exposure, temperature, wind, and humidity levels when selecting plants for the vertical garden. Opt for plants with low water requirements that thrive in vertical growing conditions.
2. Irrigation and Drainage: Install an efficient irrigation system that provides adequate water to the plants without causing waterlogging or over-irrigation. Use a drip irrigation system that delivers water directly to the root zone of the plants, minimizing water waste. Ensure proper drainage to prevent water accumulation and root rot.

3. Growing Medium: Use a high-quality growing medium that provides adequate nutrients, water retention, and plant aeration. The growing medium should be lightweight to prevent excessive weight on the vertical structure, and it should be able to support plant growth without compacting over time.
4. Structural Considerations: Ensure that the vertical structure or wall is structurally sound and can support the weight of the plants, growing medium, and irrigation system. Consult with a structural engineer or a qualified professional to ensure the vertical garden system's proper installation and load-bearing capacity.
5. Maintenance: Regular maintenance is essential for the health and longevity of the vertical garden. This may include pruning, fertilizing, pest and disease control, and monitoring the irrigation system. Inspect the vertical garden periodically for any signs of plant stress, nutrient deficiencies, or structural issues.
6. Sustainability: Consider sustainable practices in the design and maintenance of the vertical garden. Use organic or slow-release fertilizers, avoid chemical pesticides, and minimize water use through efficient irrigation and rainwater harvesting. Consider using native or drought-tolerant plant species that require less maintenance and resources.
7. Education and Engagement: Use the vertical garden as an educational tool to raise awareness about the benefits of green spaces, biodiversity, and environmental conservation. Engage the local community and stakeholders in the vertical garden's planning, installation, and maintenance to promote a sense of ownership and stewardship.

There are numerous examples of vertical gardens around the world. Here are a few notable ones:

1. One Central Park, Sydney, Australia: Designed by Patrick Blanc, One Central Park features two towers covered in vertical gardens with over 38,000 plants from 383 species. The gardens are irrigated with recycled water and combine native and exotic plants to create a lush and sustainable living wall.
2. The Bosco Verticale (Vertical Forest), Milan, Italy: Designed by Stefano Boeri Architects, the Bosco Verticale is a pair of residential towers covered by 94 different plant species, 59 of which are helpful for birds, 60 are tree species, and 33 are evergreens. The project aims to increase greenery in urban areas and promote biodiversity while improving air quality and reducing energy consumption.
3. Gardens by the Bay, Singapore: The Supertree Grove at Gardens by the Bay in Singapore features towering vertical gardens in the form of iconic tree-like structures. These vertical gardens are covered in various plant species and serve as a visual focal point of the park while providing shade, improving air quality, and capturing rainwater for irrigation.
4. Green Oasis at Bikini Berlin, Germany: Located in Berlin, the Green Oasis is a large vertical garden covering the facade of the Bikini Berlin building. It features a mix of plant species, including ferns, mosses, and other shade-loving plants, creating a lush and vibrant green wall.
5. Sky Garden, London, United Kingdom: Sky Garden is a public garden on the top of the Walkie-Talkie building in London. It features a large vertical garden covering the interior walls of the building, with a variety of plant species and stunning views of the city.

4 The Case Study

The experience of vertical gardens has been developed with a project in Pisticci Municipality in Southern Italy's Basilicata region (Fig. 1).

Basilicata region is characterized by a low population density (536.659 people distributed over 9,992 km^2, or 53.5 people per km^2) that, partly due to poor policy and partially due to a lack of significant private investors, has not been able to capitalize on its highly valuable landscape in the past decades to develop tourism. Pisticci municipality could represent a typical example of this trend.

Pisticci has a population of 16.836 inhabitants and is the fifth-bigger municipality in Basilicata. It is between the Cavone and Basento rivers and connected with S.S. Basentana and S.S. Jonica motorways. Ridges and uplands characterize the northern portion of the city, whereas the region near the Ionian Sea is primarily flat in shape.

The problem of land take affects the coastline region due to the considerable tourism demand. The territory has a different morphology which leads to the location of settlements along the main ridge.

The history of Pisticci is strongly linked to the landslides that changed its urban structure, morphology, toponymy, and history several times. This is due to the clayey nature of the soil on the Pisticci hillside. The recognized main cause of such events in Pisticci is a small torrent, called "La Salsa," of brackish water flowing under the districts of the town center most affected by the landslides and blamed for the destabilization of the terrain.

Fig. 1. Location of Pisticci Municipality.

Fig. 2. Shotcrete intervention in Pisticci Municipality.

In 1976, after three centuries without significant events, a part of the 'Croci' district collapsed following the November rains. The affected area was evacuated in time, so there were no victims or injuries. The landslide affected an area about 250 m wide and 800 m long. The landslide was reclaimed by regularising the escarpment and landslide body, deep and surface drainage, pile bulkheads, and lining the prominent escarpment with shotcrete (Fig. 2). The intervention is located where the landslide occurred in November 1976, which caused much of the Croci district to collapse. The project's strategic goal is to improve urban spaces' quality and usability by intervening in public green areas. The goal is to develop multifunctional networks: green infrastructure, ecological values, identity, cultural and social values. The idea of urban regeneration is part of a reorientation for urban development to contrast processes of physical and social degradation in the city by intervening in an area, which despite its historical and scenic values, now appears as an urban void. The project aims to promote interaction between areas affected by de-qualification and the public areas below it, which are considered marginal, with the center of the town of Pisticci. The two areas are not entirely disconnected; small actions and a few interventions can improve their connectivity.

4.1 Pisticci's Vertical Garden

The project is based on several interventions linked together to improve the area's quality and make this place more livable. The overall project is based on the following interventions: Green Wall, Photovoltaic panels, designed to ensure the energy independence of the whole project, a terraced garden through naturalistic engineering interventions, and regeneration of the parking area (Fig. 3).

The main project goal is to transform urban environments into places suitable for well-being by integrating urban structures with the environment. Plants can be crucial in merging the anthropized with nature, eliminating the typical sharp separation between the built and natural environments. This can allow to observe and live the nature even in an urban environment, conveying the more relaxed atmosphere of the rural environment even in cities. In this case, technology no longer represents an element of disconnection

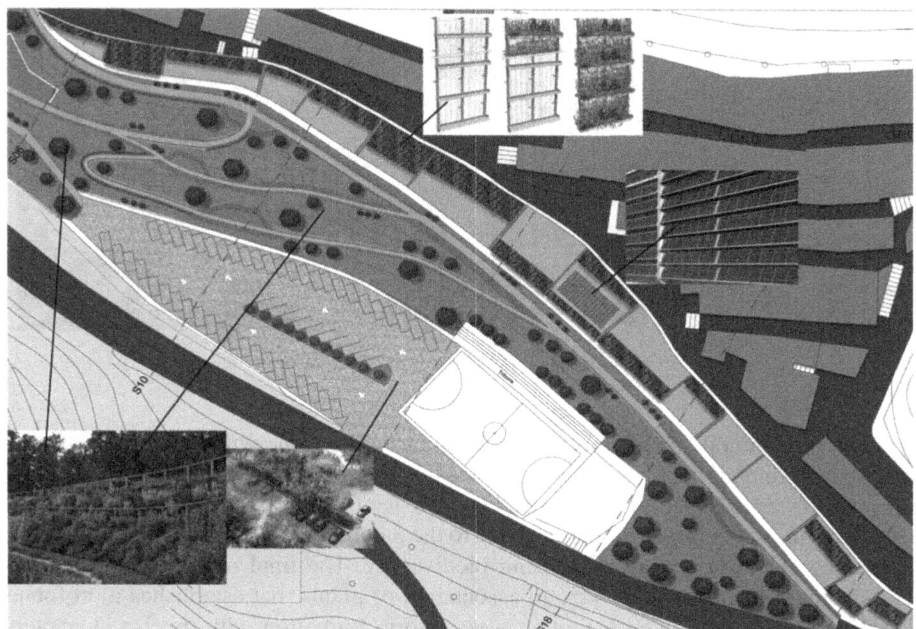

Fig. 3. Project scheme of Pisticci's vertical garden.

from nature, of environmental depletion, but can be the bridge between worlds that have always been considered antithetical. Vertical gardens can symbolize this union, offering the possibility of including and propagating greenery in the most anthropized and degraded areas. This is the reason that led to the hypothesis of the project of a vertical garden measuring 4,000 m^2, the largest green wall in Europe, to mask "the scar" of Pisticci, due to shotcrete intervention, with an integrated system of hanging green.

The perfect exposure for solar panels is when facing directly towards the sun with no shading, which means the panels should be oriented towards the south in the northern hemisphere or the north in the southern hemisphere. It is essential to avoid shading the panels from trees, buildings, or other obstructions, as it can significantly reduce their efficiency. Pisticci's vertical garden is well-oriented and has no obstacles that can produce shadows. In order to make the whole project independent from the energetic point of view, several modules of photovoltaic panels will be included along the shotcrete wall, alternating them with green elements. Energy efficiency will be pursued, making the project's irrigation and lighting systems independent (Fig. 4).

The terraced garden involves landscaping the slope just below the shotcrete wall. Today it appears as a large area of uncultivated greenery, which will be transformed into a livable space where it will be possible to walk comfortably among the greenery and reach the historic center of Pisticci in a pleasant and reasonably fast way.

Fig. 4. Project of Pisticci's vertical garden.

Applying naturalistic engineering techniques on the slope will ensure the environmental upgrading of the intervention area, leading to a significant reduction in the visual impact. Only native species will be used for revegetation works and in the vertical garden. The aim is to achieve a situation close to the natural one, contributing to improving morphological diversity and increasing biodiversity. The final results should lead to reproducing a phytocoenosis, i.e., an association of plants that establishes a profound interdependence relation, constituting a vegetation formation with precise characters correctly inserted into the environmental context. In this way, technical functionality is combined with perfect ecological-landscape integration of the project.

The regeneration of the parking area involves implementing measures that minimize the environmental impact while meeting visitors' parking needs. The project includes green infrastructure elements such as permeable pavements, rain gardens, and bioswales to manage stormwater runoff. These features help reduce the burden on the local drainage system, improve water quality, and promote groundwater recharge. It also integrates trees, shrubs, and native plantings within and around the parking area. Vegetation enhances the aesthetics, provides shade, reduces the heat island effect, and supports biodiversity by attracting pollinators and other wildlife.

By implementing these sustainable measures, the regeneration of a parking area can contribute to environmental conservation, promote sustainable transportation options, and enhance the overall visitor experience while minimizing the facility's ecological footprint.

5 Conclusions

In conclusion, the project combining a Green Wall, Photovoltaic panels, a terraced garden, and the regeneration of a parking area offers numerous benefits and opportunities.

The Green Wall provides a vertical garden that enhances the aesthetic appeal of the structure, while also improving air quality and biodiversity. The living vegetation helps to purify the air by filtering out pollutants and producing oxygen. Moreover, the presence of greenery promotes a sense of well-being and connection with nature.

Integrating Photovoltaic panels in the design allows for generating clean and renewable energy. The project reduces greenhouse gas emissions and reliance on traditional energy sources by harnessing solar power. This benefits the environment and demonstrates a commitment to sustainability and energy efficiency.

The inclusion of a terraced garden adds a functional and beautiful green space. The terraces can be utilized for recreational purposes, such as outdoor seating areas or community gardens, providing opportunities for social interaction and leisure activities. Additionally, the terraced garden can help manage rainwater runoff, reducing the strain on drainage systems and minimizing the risk of flooding.

Renewing a parking area into a green space is a significant improvement in urban sustainability. Converting an underutilized or environmentally damaging space into a vibrant and eco-friendly area contributes to the overall livability and attractiveness of the urban environment.

In summary, integrating a Green Wall, Photovoltaic panels, a terraced garden, and the regeneration of a parking area in a project showcases a holistic approach to sustainable development. It combines environmental benefits, such as improved air quality and energy generation, with social advantages, such as creating green spaces for community engagement. This type of project demonstrates a commitment to sustainable practices and contributes to urban areas' overall well-being and resilience.

Acknowledgments. The authors are grateful to Pisticci Municipality Administration and the technical staff for supporting the project's development.

References

1. United Nations: Sustainable Development Goals (SDGs), New York (2015)
2. De Montis, A., Martín, B., Ortega, E., Ledda, A., Serra, V.: Landscape fragmentation in Mediterranean Europe: a comparative approach. Land Use Policy **64**, 83–94 (2017). https://doi.org/10.1016/j.landusepol.2017.02.028
3. You, H.: Quantifying urban fragmentation under economic transition in Shanghai City, China. Sustainability **8**, 21 (2015). https://doi.org/10.3390/SU8010021
4. Nagendra, H., Munroe, D.K., Southworth, J.: From pattern to process: landscape fragmentation and the analysis of land use/land cover change. Agric. Ecosyst. Environ. **101**, 111–115 (2004). https://doi.org/10.1016/J.AGEE.2003.09.003
5. Saganeiti, L., Pilogallo, A., Scorza, F., Mussuto, G., Murgante, B.: Spatial indicators to evaluate urban fragmentation in Basilicata region. In: Gervasi, O., et al. (eds.) ICCSA 2018. LNCS, vol. 10964, pp. 100–112. Springer, Cham (2018). https://doi.org/10.1007/978-3-319-95174-4_8
6. Merriam-Webster: Urban sprawl Definition & Meaning. https://www.merriam-webster.com/dictionary/urbansprawl. Accessed 21 Apr 2023
7. Hasse, J.E., Lathrop, R.G.: Land resource impact indicators of urban sprawl. Appl. Geogr. **23**, 159–175 (2003). https://doi.org/10.1016/J.APGEOG.2003.08.002
8. Molaei Qelichi, M., Murgante, B., Yousefi Feshki, M., Zarghamfard, M.: Urbanization patterns in Iran visualized through spatial auto-correlation analysis. Spat. Inf. Res. **25**, 627–633 (2017). https://doi.org/10.1007/s41324-017-0128-0
9. Galster, G., Hanson, R., Ratcliffe, M.R., Wolman, H., Coleman, S., Freihage, J.: Wrestling Sprawl to the Ground: Defining and Measuring an Elusive Concept (2001)

10. Brueckner, J.K.: Urban sprawl: diagnosis and remedies. Int. Reg. Sci. Rev. **23**, 160–171 (2000). https://doi.org/10.1177/016001700761012710
11. Hennig, E.I., Schwick, C., Soukup, T., Orlitová, E., Kienast, F., Jaeger, J.A.G.: Multi-scale analysis of urban sprawl in Europe: towards a European de-sprawling strategy. Land Use Policy **49**, 483–498 (2015). https://doi.org/10.1016/J.LANDUSEPOL.2015.08.001
12. Amato, F., Pontrandolfi, P., Murgante, B.: Supporting planning activities with the assessment and the prediction of urban sprawl using spatio-temporal analysis. Ecol. Inform. **30**, 365–378 (2015). https://doi.org/10.1016/j.ecoinf.2015.07.004
13. Amato, F., Pontrandolfi, P., Murgante, B.: Using spatiotemporal analysis in urban sprawl assessment and prediction. In: Murgante, B., et al. (eds.) ICCSA 2014. LNCS, vol. 8580, pp. 758–773. Springer, Cham (2014). https://doi.org/10.1007/978-3-319-09129-7_55/COVER
14. Di Palma, F., Amato, F., Nolè, G., Martellozzo, F., Murgante, B.: A SMAP supervised classification of landsat images for urban sprawl evaluation. ISPRS Int. J. Geo-Inf. **5**, 109 (2016). https://doi.org/10.3390/IJGI5070109
15. Geneletti, D., Biasiolli, A., Morrison-Saunders, A.: Land take and the effectiveness of project screening in Environmental Impact Assessment: findings from an empirical study. Environ. Impact Assess. Rev. **67**, 117–123 (2017). https://doi.org/10.1016/j.eiar.2017.08.008
16. Fiorini, L., Zullo, F., Marucci, A., Romano, B.: Land take and landscape loss: effect of uncontrolled urbanization in Southern Italy. J. Urban Manag. **8**, 42–56 (2019). https://doi.org/10.1016/J.JUM.2018.09.003
17. Science for Environment Policy: Future Brief: No net land take by 2050? European Commission DG Environment, Bristol (2016)
18. Sallustio, L., Quatrini, V., Geneletti, D., Corona, P., Marchetti, M.: Assessing land take by urban development and its impact on carbon storage: findings from two case studies in Italy. Environ. Impact Assess. Rev. **54**, 80–90 (2015). https://doi.org/10.1016/j.eiar.2015.05.006
19. Fiorini, L., Marucci, A., Zullo, F., Romano, B.: Indicator engineering for land take control and settlement sustainability. WIT Trans. Ecol. Environ. **217**, 437–446 (2018). https://doi.org/10.2495/SDP180391
20. European Commission: Guidelines on best practice to limit, mitigate or compensate soil sealing (2012). https://doi.org/10.2779/75498
21. Munafò, M., Salvati, L., Zitti, M.: Estimating soil sealing rate at national level - Italy as a case study. Ecol. Indic. **26**, 137–140 (2013). https://doi.org/10.1016/j.ecolind.2012.11.001
22. Calzolari, C., Tarocco, P., Lombardo, N., Marchi, N., Ungaro, F.: Assessing soil ecosystem services in urban and peri-urban areas: from urban soils survey to providing support tool for urban planning. Land Use Policy **99**, 105037 (2020). https://doi.org/10.1016/j.landusepol.2020.105037
23. Artmann, M.: Institutional efficiency of urban soil sealing management – from raising awareness to better implementation of sustainable development in Germany. Landsc. Urban Plan. **131**, 83–95 (2014). https://doi.org/10.1016/J.LANDURBPLAN.2014.07.015
24. Romano, B., Zullo, F., Fiorini, L., Ciabò, S., Marucci, A.: Sprinkling: an approach to describe urbanization dynamics in Italy. Sustainability **9**, 97 (2017). https://doi.org/10.3390/su9010097
25. Saganeiti, L., Favale, A., Pilogallo, A., Scorza, F., Murgante, B.: Assessing urban fragmentation at regional scale using sprinkling indexes. Sustainability **10**, 3274 (2018). https://doi.org/10.3390/su10093274
26. Saganeiti, L., Pilogallo, A., Faruolo, G., Scorza, F., Murgante, B.: Territorial fragmentation and renewable energy source plants: which relationship? Sustainability **12**, 1828 (2020). https://doi.org/10.3390/SU12051828
27. Scorza, F., Saganeiti, L., Pilogallo, A., Murgante, B.: Ghost planning: the inefficiency of energy sector policies in a low population density region. Arch. di Stud. Urbani e Reg. **127**, 34–55 (2020). https://doi.org/10.3280/ASUR2020-127-S1003

28. Romano, B., Fiorini, L., Marucci, A.: Italy without urban "sprinkling". A Uchronia for a country that needs a retrofit of its urban and landscape planning. Sustainability **11**, 3469 (2019). https://doi.org/10.3390/SU11123469
29. Romano, B., Fiorini, L., Zullo, F., Marucci, A.: Urban growth control DSS techniques for de-sprinkling process in Italy. Sustainability **9**, 1852 (2017). https://doi.org/10.3390/su9101852
30. Manganelli, B., Murgante, B., Saganeiti, L.: The social cost of urban sprinkling. Sustainability **12**, 2236 (2020). https://doi.org/10.3390/SU12062236
31. Costanza, R., et al.: Modelling and measuring sustainable wellbeing in connection with the UN Sustainable Development Goals. Ecol. Econ. **130**, 350–355 (2016). https://doi.org/10.1016/j.ecolecon.2016.07.009
32. Sallustio, L., et al.: Assessing habitat quality in relation to the spatial distribution of protected areas in Italy. J. Environ. Manag. **201**, 129–137 (2017). https://doi.org/10.1016/J.JENVMAN.2017.06.031
33. Salata, S., Ronchi, S., Arcidiacono, A., Ghirardelli, F.: Mapping habitat quality in the Lombardy region, Italy. One Ecosyst. **2**, e11402 (2017). https://doi.org/10.3897/oneeco.2.e11402
34. Ronchi, S., Arcidiacono, A., Pogliani, L.: Integrating green infrastructure into spatial planning regulations to improve the performance of urban ecosystems. Insights from an Italian case study. Sustain. Cities Soc. **53**, 101907 (2020). https://doi.org/10.1016/j.scs.2019.101907
35. Cannas, I., Lai, S., Leone, F., Zoppi, C.: Green infrastructure and ecological corridors: a regional study concerning Sardinia. Sustainability **10**, 1265 (2018). https://doi.org/10.3390/su10041265
36. Scorza, F., Pilogallo, A., Saganeiti, L., Murgante, B., Pontrandolfi, P.: Comparing the territorial performances of renewable energy sources' plants with an integrated ecosystem services loss assessment: a case study from the Basilicata region (Italy). Sustain. Cities Soc. **56**, 102082 (2020). https://doi.org/10.1016/j.scs.2020.102082
37. Lai, S., Leone, F., Zoppi, C.: Implementing green infrastructures beyond protected areas. Sustainability **10**, 3544 (2018). https://doi.org/10.3390/su10103544
38. Lai, S., Isola, F., Leone, F., Zoppi, C.: Assessing the potential of green infrastructure to mitigate hydrogeological hazard, pp. 109–133 (2021). https://doi.org/10.6092/1970-9870/7411
39. Zoppi, C.: Ecosystem services, green infrastructure and spatial planning. Sustainability **12**, 4396 (2020). https://doi.org/10.3390/su12114396
40. Venter, Z.S., Barton, D.N., Martinez-Izquierdo, L., Langemeyer, J., Baró, F., McPhearson, T.: Interactive spatial planning of urban green infrastructure – retrofitting green roofs where ecosystem services are most needed in Oslo. Ecosyst. Serv. **50**, 101314 (2021). https://doi.org/10.1016/J.ECOSER.2021.101314
41. Meerow, S., Newell, J.P.: Spatial planning for multifunctional green infrastructure: growing resilience in Detroit. Landsc. Urban Plan. **159**, 62–75 (2017). https://doi.org/10.1016/j.landurbplan.2016.10.005
42. Zhang, S., Muñoz Ramírez, F.: Assessing and mapping ecosystem services to support urban green infrastructure: the case of Barcelona, Spain. Cities **92**, 59–70 (2019). https://doi.org/10.1016/j.cities.2019.03.016

The 15-minute City Model: Assessment of the Socio-Economic and Environmental Impacts Associated with the Location of Essential Amenities

Dino Molinaro[1], Valentina Santarsiero[1,2], Lucia Saganeiti[3](✉), and Beniamino Murgante[1]

[1] School of Engineering, University of Basilicata, Viale dell'Ateneo Lucano 10, 85100 Potenza, Italy

[2] CNR IGAG, Area della ricerca di Roma 1, strada provinciale 35d, 9, 00010 Montelibretti (RM), Italy

[3] Department of Civil, Construction-Architectural and Environmental Engineering – DICEAA, University of L'Aquila, Via G. Gronchi, 18, 67100 L'Aquila, Italy

lucia.saganeiti@univaq.it

Abstract. The 15-minute city is a way of strategically and ecologically planning the amenities and spaces of an urban area. This model based on sustainable urban planning, built on the concept of proximity of amenities, facilitates the commuting and brings an environmental advantage in terms of reduction of greenhouse gas emissions from vehicular traffic. The application of this city model becomes critical in areas characterized by settlement dispersion.

In fact, there are several socio-economic and environmental impacts linked to a dispersed location of essential amenities in non-compact urban contexts. For example, the economic cost of travelling, the time taken to reach essential amenities which are often decentralized in peripheral districts of cities, the pollution generated by the widespread use of private means of transport, determined by inefficient mass transport systems. This research aims to analyze the socio-economic and environmental impact of context characterized by peripherality, settlement dispersion and lack of essential amenities. The study area focuses on the Italian Municipalities of Terni, Matera, Pisa and Trento where the 15-minute city model has not been pursued in the urban planning process. The work carried out highlights the distinction that exists between the different cities, showing how the provision and location of essential amenities, considered as a fundamental parameter for the study, improves the quality of life.

Keywords: Sustainable City · Urban Sprawl · Accessibility · 15-minute city

1 Introduction

The concept of the 15-minute city was introduced in 2016 by Carlos Moreno [1–3], who proposes a new idea of proximity within cities, oriented towards sustainable development and referring to the theory of chrono-urbanism, which takes into account not only space

O. Gervasi et al. (Eds.): ICCSA 2023 Workshops, LNCS 14107, pp. 468–479, 2023.
https://doi.org/10.1007/978-3-031-37114-1_32

but also the temporal dimension when designing cities. According to this model, an urban context with a high degree of liveability is one in which all different types of amenities and socializing places are ideally within a 15-min walk or cycle ride from their residence. The aim of this innovative approach to planning is to positively influence the pace of life in cities, reconnecting people with their surroundings and eliminating unnecessary travel by polluting and energy-intensive means.

The positive effects of the 15-minute city model were tested and adopted during the pandemic, due to smart working and total lockdown rules to control and contain the spread of the virus. What it proposes, in fact, is a sort of return to the vitality of neighborhoods, promoting the frequenting of the streets 'down home' with many benefits, starting from a re-appropriation of one's own vital time, thanks to the drastic reduction of hours wasted in long journeys, traffic jams within the metropolis [4, 5].

In this context, the model of the 15-minute city could represent a long-term objective for cities in post-pandemic recovery. The solutions linked to cycle-pedestrian mobility and the redevelopment of open spaces should, however, be evaluated not only from a purely quantitative point of view, but also by the presence of amenities (already existing or to be built) that guarantee an attractiveness and a level of use appropriate to the places, linked to the temporality of the functions they can accommodate.

The implementation of this city model becomes problematic in areas characterized by urban sprawl and settlement dispersion [6, 7]. The spread of sprawl, in areas already affected by demographic and social imbalances, determines high costs for the population. There are several elements that characterize the impact in socio-economic and environmental terms; socio-economic impacts refer both to the economic cost of travel, and to the time taken to reach essential amenities often concentrated in central districts. In environmental terms, however, reference is made to the pollution generated by the extensive use of private means of transport, in turn determined by the difficulty of articulate functional mass transport systems in areas where the low population density generates weak demand [8]. Currently, compact development remains the most sustainable form of the high-density city [9]. From a spatial point of view, the level of peripherality of territories with respect to urban centers, home to a wide range of amenities, profoundly influences the quality of life of citizens and the level of social inclusion. Peripheral areas force the people living in them to bear high time and monetary costs to access central ones [8]. When describing the distribution of travel determined by the demand for the use of basic amenities, it also emerges that the terms accessibility and mobility are used interchangeably. It is necessary, however, to distinguish the two notions, pointing out, in particular, how the concept of accessibility, with reference to a service, is declined in the possibility of reaching it and in the manner in which this is reached by the user [10]. The objective of this research concerns the evaluation of costs resulting from the effects of the urban sprinkling phenomenon, i.e. the dispersed and low-density city. By classifying the amenities of primary necessity and assessing the demand for amenities through the division into travel isochrones, the case studies of the cities of Matera, Terni, Pisa and Trento will be compared.

2 Material and Method

2.1 Study Area

The research focused on the study of four Italian municipalities with similar socio-demographic and morphological characteristics: Matera, Terni, Pisa and Trento (Fig. 1).

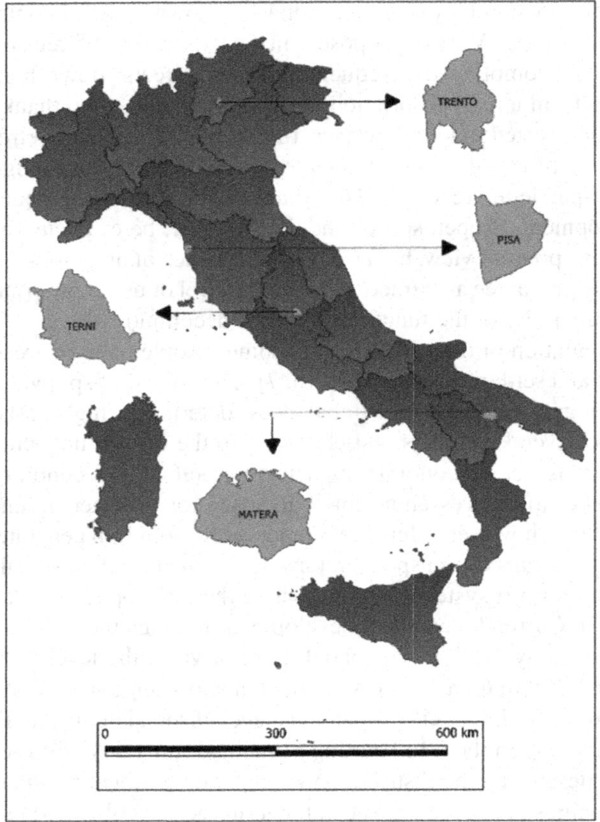

Fig. 1. Territorial Framework.

The city of Matera is located in the eastern part of the Basilicata region at 401 m above sea level and is the largest municipality in the region with its 392.09 km^2. It is the second most populous municipality in the region with its 59824 inhabitants, 4.9% of whom are foreigners, and a population density of 152.58 inhabitants/km^2. It is also known as the 'City of the Sassi', precisely because of the peculiarity and uniqueness of its historical center, characterized by ancient settlements excavated in calcarenite, close to the gorge carved by the Gravina stream. Since 1993, UNESCO has declared the Sassi district a World Heritage Site. In 1952, the law for the displacement of the Sassi was passed and the city began to expand into new neighborhoods; the neighborhoods created in the 1950s had as their main characteristics large common green spaces and buildings with few floors, to reproduce the Sassi's social life models as much as possible. An initial phase of orderly expansion that perfectly followed Piccinato's first urban planning instrument was followed, in the 1990s, by a phase of disorderly expansion, resulting in neighborhoods characterized by the morphological and typological inhomogeneity of the built fabric, a lack of green spaces, undersized roadways and an absence of urbanization works [11]. Terni is located 130 m above sea level in the region of Umbria with a large land area of 212.43 km^2, the resident population is about 106844 inhabitants of which 12.2% are foreigners. The population density is 502.96 inhabitants/km^2. The territory is mainly mountainous, the hilly areas cover an area of about 31.6%. The city of Terni has a modern structure, due to post-war reconstruction; it has had a strong urban expansion, developing on four axes arranged radially around the central core. One of the city's problems is the poor connection of the suburbs with the urban center. The city of Pisa lies a few kilometers from the mouth of the river Arno, in the north of the region of Tuscany, in a flat area called Valdarno Inferiore, at 4 m above sea level, and extends over an area of 185.18 km^2, with a population density of 485.08 inhabitants/km^2 and a total of 89828 inhabitants; 14% of these are foreigners. The urban fabric has an 'oil spot' configuration, in which the settlement system expands uniformly around the compact historical center, delimited by the city walls. A peculiar characteristic of the city is the presence of the so-called 'Pisan gardens', private green areas that are quite extensive but not very accessible as they are separated from the urban fabric by stone walls. As they are separated from the urban fabric by brick or stone walls. The greatest modern urban revolution took place in the 1970s when the suburbs began to develop to the west and in the early 1980s when they began to develop to the east, taking the modern suburbs of foreign cities as a model.

Trento, with an area of 157.88 km^2, is located in the central part of Trentino-Alto Adige at 194 m above sea level. It has a population of approximately 118632 inhabitants and a population density that is not characteristic of compact cities due to its vastness extension, amounting to 751.41 inhabitants/km^2. The municipal population is mainly concentrated in the city, but there are numerous scattered centers or suburbs, which are quite different from one another and still retain their own rural and cultural identity. The four study cities are classified differently in the mapping of the SNAI (National Strategy for Inner Areas) [12]. The Map of Inner Areas updated to 2020 classifies the cities of Pisa, Trento and Terni as a Pole and Matera as an Intermediate Municipality. This classification system defines service poles as those municipalities with an articulated upper secondary school offer (at least one high school - scientific or classical - and at least one technical and professional institute), at least one hospital with an emergency room and intensive care units, a railway station of at least silver type. Neighboring municipalities are defined according to the distance from the municipalities service pole. The Municipality of Matera is considered an intermediate municipality as it does not have a silver category station.

2.2 Methodology

The dataset used for the analysis of population movements, in relation to the amenities available in all cities, consists of open data, including information on resident population, location of amenities and reason and mode of travel. Resident population data were obtained from the European Copernicus website by accessing the Urban Atlas project in the Land Monitoring Service section [13].

Spatial information in vector format dating back to 2018 was used, taking into account the polygons falling within the surveyed territory. The vector files were processed using the opensource software QGIS, filtering out geometries with a population value greater than zero; they were then switched from areal to point information, generating the centroid of each polygon. The data concerning the essential amenities present in the various territorial contexts were obtained from the information present within the OpenStreetMap map using the QuickOSM plugin. Only amenities belonging to the categories health, economy and finance, education and sport and leisure were selected. The database obtained was supplemented with other amenities obtained from geolocation by photointerpretation on Google Maps. Data from the 18th Audimob Report on the Mobility of Italians [14] were used for the analysis of trips, in particular information on the distribution of trips by motivation and the percentage of transport used according to the size of cities by number of residents.

The endowment of essential amenities is a fundamental parameter against which to assess the quality of life in a specific territory. It can also be understood as a deficit assessment, i.e. the absence of minimum requirements for the supply of essential amenities with reference to the urban functions exercised by each territorial unit [15, 16]. The main categories of amenities examined for each study area were extracted from Google My Maps using the Points of Interest export function. The service points were imported into the GIS environment and reclassified into 10 main categories, each consisting of subcategories as follows (Table 1):

Table 1. List of amenities and equipment.

REFERNCE CODE	TYPE OF SERVICE
CM	Commerce
CU	Culture and Art
ED	Education
HE	Health
S	Services
FS	Financial Services
PS	Public Services
SA	Safety
SF	Sport and free time
TR	Tourism

The analysis of the road traffic in the four territories was carried out using the ORS Tools plugin (openrouteservice routing, isochrones and matrix calculations for QGIS), which is able to generate isochrones, i.e. the location of points having equal distance, spatial or temporal, with respect to a fixed point entered as input. The distance between the initial point of departure and the points of arrival is not linear but, by setting a value in metres or minutes in the plugin, is calculated as a function of the possible real routes that can be travelled within the OpenStreetMap road network. In this research it was chosen to use as a starting point, a point belonging to the center of each individual city, symbolically identifying it with the town hall. A spatial interval between two consecutive isochrones of 2000 m was set, with the option of selecting the fastest route. Starting from the information available in the dataset, the elements of the vector files of population and amenities were re-processed by associating to each element the information relative to the isochronous band to which it belongs. This operation made it possible to obtain the total population and amenities data in each band.

The analysis of the movements for each portion of the population was carried out using the statistical data on mobility for the year 2018 [14]. From the available statistical data, the trips made by the population residing in the band under consideration were evaluated. In a corresponding approach, the distribution of amenities across the territory was determined by calculating the number of amenities located in each isochronous range.

It was assumed that 5.1% of all trips were for study purposes and 32.7% for sport and leisure. For the categories health and economy and finance, the percentage value of trips for family management (34.4%) was taken into account. The remaining part of work-related trips (30.8%) was not taken into account in the study-related trips because it is considered that work-related trips are influenced by different factors than the other amenities considered.

In order to obtain the movements of the population to reach amenities, a demand model was used to derive the population data from URBAN ATLAS [13], amenities and displacement referred to each isochrone.

In each isochrone band the satisfaction of the demand for the service considered was verified, if the demand was not considered satisfied according to the presence of at least one element belonging to the category of service requested, for example in the case of the absence of amenities, the hypothesis of a displacement towards the contiguous isochrone band closest to the center was assumed, iterating the procedure until the condition was verified by proceeding towards the city center.

Subsequently, in order to estimate the costs and the production of C02 resulting from trips from one isochrone to another, generated by the absence of amenities, and in order to analyses the consumption resulting from these trips, the total distance travelled was analyzed using the number of trips that occur with the passage between two adjacent isochrones whose distance is fixed at 2 km.

The total distance travelled on a daily basis is thus the sum of the number of trips made by each inhabitant as a function of the number of isochrones crossed. The analysis of the CO2 production estimate was carried out by multiplying the total distance travelled, determined for each city, by the coefficient of CO2 emissions expressed in Kg/Km, taken from the *terraup.it* website [17], choosing as the route a mixed path, entering the best-selling car models in Italy (Fiat Panda, Fiat 500, Fiat Punto, Jeep Renegade and Volkswagen Golf) [18]. The fuel price was set at the average price for the month of July/August 2022 of €1.859/liter for diesel and €1.869/liter for petrol, choosing an urban route. The evaluation of the management costs of a private car was carried out using the ACI 2022 Tables [19] which provide, for each car model, a mileage reimbursement coefficient which takes into account all management costs (fuel costs, wear mechanics, ordinary and extraordinary maintenance, insurance costs and ownership tax). The coefficient relating to each of the 5 car models taken into consideration was chosen by multiplying it by the distance traveled in both cities. The values of CO2 production, fuel consumption and running costs, obtained for each car model, were averaged to obtain the daily value and, subsequently, the monthly and annual value.

3 Results and Discussions

The reconstruction of the essential amenities has made it possible to create a complete database of all the essential amenities present in the investigated municipalities. This database and the related Service Charters provide an initial overview of the location and distribution of amenities in the investigated cities. Comparing the demographic trends of the Italian resident population from 2009 to 2019, the cities of Matera and Terni show a slight decrease in population, while the cities of Trento and Pisa show an opposite trend and show a small increase in the resident population (Fig. 2).

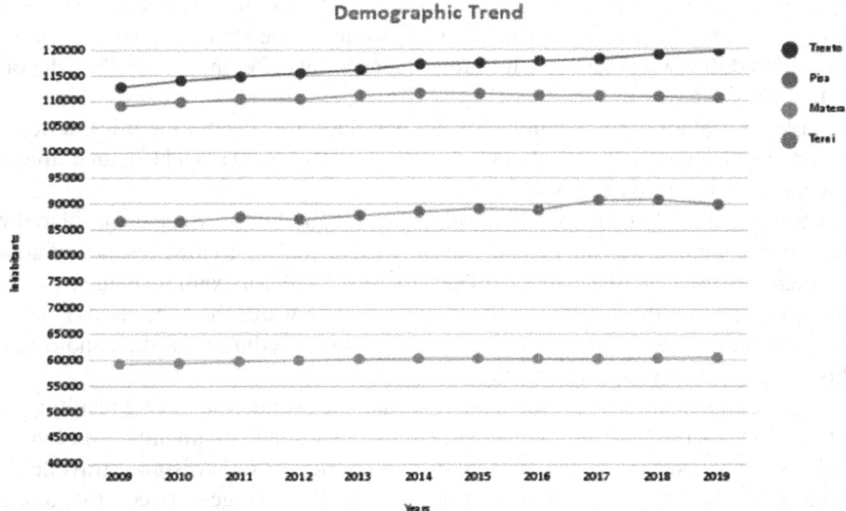

Fig. 2. Demographic trend.

The identification of the amenities has highlighted, in addition to the difference in positioning on the territory, a different assortment in the different isochrone bands. The data relating to the first band (0–2000 m) are substantially similar for all categories of amenities (Fig. 3).

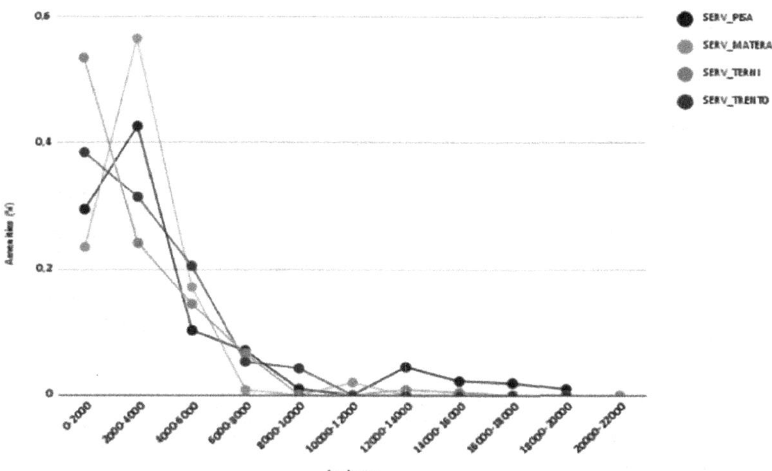

Fig. 3. Distribution of amenities divided into ranges of isochrones.

The analysis of the displacements was carried out for each isochronous band starting from the contained population value. For each type of service, the fraction of the total movements that take place to reach that category of service was calculated and, subsequently, the methods with which the movement takes place were specified.

The evaluation of journeys with private vehicles was possible by knowing the value of total kilometers travelled, and the percentages of the methods with which journeys with own means of transport take place on average, i.e. with cars and motorcycle.

There is a clear correlation between the kilometers traveled and the number of users moving between the cities of Trento and Terni. Completely different scenarios emerge for the cities of Matera and Pisa.

For the city of Matera we note a large number of people who need to move to access amenities, but traveling shorter distances, because the kilometric data obtained is not high, otherwise it happens in the city of Pisa, because the number of population it moves does not differ much from that of Matera, but the kilometers traveled are about three times (Fig. 4).

Using the online service offered by the terraup.it site and the ACI tables, the CO2 production value in kg, the cost of fuel consumption and the cost of car management were obtained from the kilometers travelled. Obtained the results relating to the calculation of the kilometers traveled in each city, the monetary cost of the journeys and the production of CO2 were calculated. These two variables are considered the main consequences of the demand for mobility determined by the imbalances in the distribution of amenities and which produce the more significant externalities, in economic and environmental terms, for the resident population.

The results obtained from the experimented methodology refer only to travel to reach amenities, as the purpose of this analysis is to highlight in which city the environmental and monetary costs referable to the travel demand generated by the distribution of population and amenities are higher.

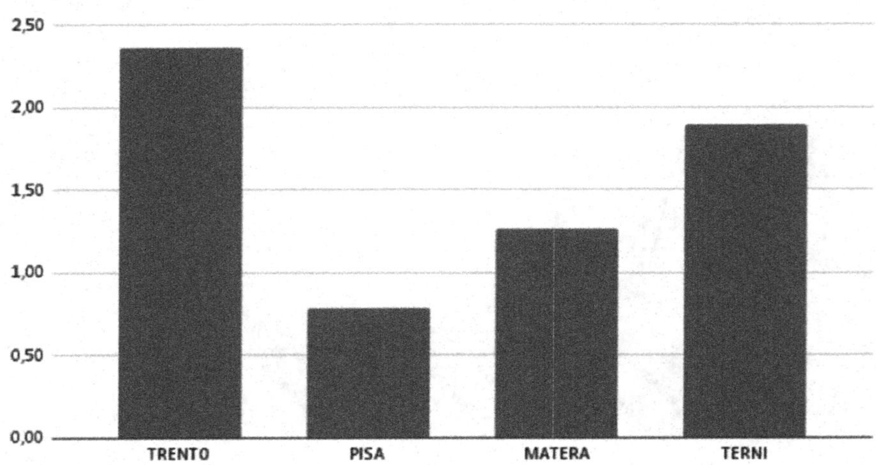

Fig. 4. Percentage of displacement.

In Fig. 4, it can be seen, in percentage terms, the population that moves to reach amenities, it is noted that only 0.20% of the population of Trento needs to move to reach an essential service. For Pisa and Matera, the percentage of the population that moves is similar, while in the case of the Municipality of Terni, 7.52% of the population has to move to reach a service.

The small percentage of the population that travels by car to reach amenities in the city of Trento is the result of a constant revision of planning tools, starting from the master plan drawn up in the 1960s up to the most recent one updated to 2022. Conformation of the territory has constituted a fundamental determinant of the planning action, orienting the concentration of the urban settlement along the valleys, where the amenities are also located, limiting the urban settlements on the slopes of the surrounding mountains and in particular by equipping the industrial area of amenities.

In clear contrast Terni: one of the first industrial cities in Italy, whose industrial revolution has distorted the appearance of the city. In fact, it expands by relocating the city center, in fact it emerges that most of the amenities present in the area are located in the city center, to the south-east of the territory, while a large number of the population resides in the peripheral areas without essential amenities.

The city of Matera has had an evolution from an urban point of view from the second half of the twentieth century, when the Sassi were declared unusable due to poor sanitary conditions and consequently displaced, the city was planned with the limitations due to Gravina. In the nineties the scenario changes, new built-up areas are born which expand the city in a very disorderly way. The city center has a good range of amenities, lacking instead in the northern part of the city where, however, part of the population is concentrated; therefore 3.54% of the population is destined to move towards the city center to reach essential amenities. Data similar to that of the city of Matera, we have for Pisa, the amenities are more present in the center of the city, in this case in the upper

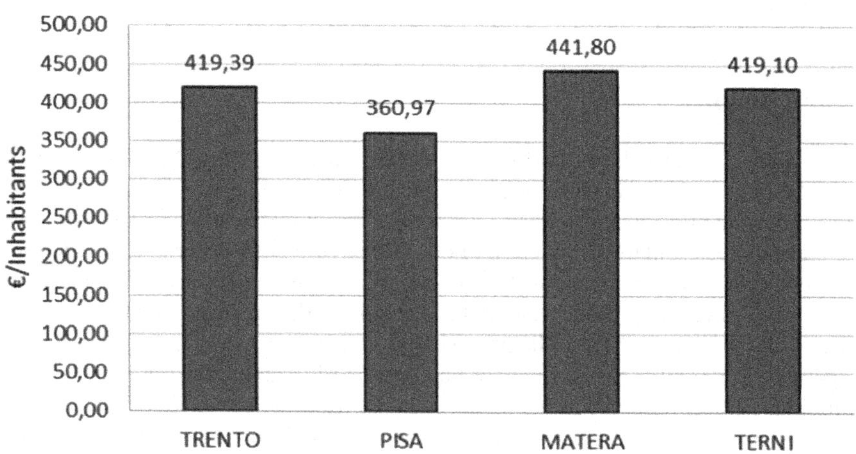

Fig. 5. Average annual cost in euro.

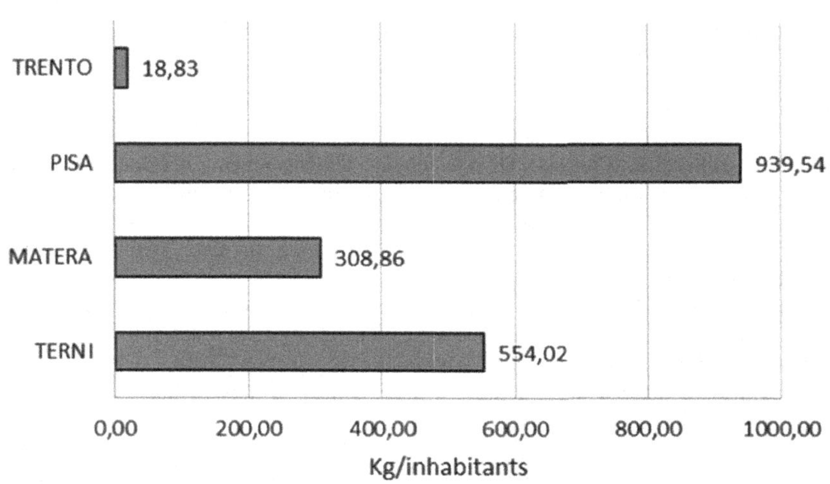

Fig. 6. Average annual production of CO2 per inhabitant.

part, while the area of the Pisan coast records a scarcity of amenities, but a high presence of population; a similar scenario can be found in the southern quadrant of the city.

Examining the costs distributed over the entire population, it can be seen that the city of Terni has the highest cost and emission values. On the contrary, by dividing the costs only on the portion of the population that travels to access basic amenities, we note that in the Municipality of Pisa, a user who travels to access a basic service spends around 240 euros a year and produces about 815 kg of CO2; these data are closely linked to the percentage of the population that moves (Fig. 6), for this reason the per capita consumption and production of CO2 for the city of Terni are low, because the population that moves is high (Fig. 5).

4 Conclusions

This research represents the main elements of a first experiment based on the study of four cities. The first goal of this work was to create a methodology to link the two localized data, through displacements; secondly, however, the objective has shifted towards the calculation of costs and the production of CO2 due to travel; in order to mark the impact that poor territorial planning causes both economically and on the environment; with the future goal of integrating processing and improving traditional methodologies.

The cities of Trento, Pisa, Matera and Terni, referring to the definition of livable city, defined in the introduction, cannot be considered livable cities, due to the lack of essential amenities in the isochrone zones furthest from the city center. The 15-minute city model loses its validity due to the low population density and the fragmentation of the peripheral areas; these characteristics limit the possibility of a reconfiguration of the service system that satisfies the requirement of proximity, and that favors the use of alternative forms of mobility to the car to access the functions.

The work carried out highlights the distinction that exists between the different cities, showing how the provision and location of essential services, considered as a fundamental parameter for the study, improves the quality of life.

References

1. Allam, Z., Bibri, S.E., Chabaud, D., Moreno, C.: The theoretical, practical, and technological foundations of the 15-minute city model: proximity and its environmental, social and economic benefits for sustainability. Energies **15**, 6042 (2022)
2. Caragliu, A.A.: La città dei 15 minuti: Una moda di gran richiamo mediatico? ARCIPELAGOMILANO **17**, 1–8 (2022)
3. Balletto, G., Ladu, M., Milesi, A., Borruso, G.: A methodological approach on disused public properties in the 15-minute city perspective. Sustainability **13**, 593 (2021)
4. Roberts, D.: How to make a city livable during lockdown. Vox (2020)
5. Abdelfattah, L., Deponte, D., Fossa, G.: The 15-minute city: interpreting the model to bring out urban resiliencies. Transp. Res. Proc. **60**, 330–337 (2022)
6. Saganeiti, L., Favale, A., Pilogallo, A., Scorza, F., Murgante, B.: Assessing urban fragmentation at regional scale using sprinkling indexes. Sustainability **10**, 3274 (2018). https://doi.org/10.3390/su10093274
7. Saganeiti, L., Mustafa, A., Teller, J., Murgante, B.: Modeling urban sprinkling with cellular automata. Sustain. Cities Soc. **65**, 102586 (2021). https://doi.org/10.1016/J.SCS.2020.102586
8. Manganelli, B., Murgante, B., Saganeiti, L.: The social cost of urban sprinkling. Sustainability **12**, 2236 (2020). https://doi.org/10.3390/su12062236
9. Thomas, L., Cousins, W.: A new compact city form: concepts in practice. In: Compact City: A Sustainable Urban Form, pp. 328–338 (1996)
10. Ferrario, M.: L'accessibilità alle opportunità urbane: uffici postali e altri servizi della città di Milano (2019)

11. Santarsiero, V., Nolè, G., Lanorte, A., Tucci, B., Cillis, G., Murgante, B.: Remote Sensing and Spatial Analysis for Land-Take Assessment in Basilicata Region (Southern Italy) (2022). https://doi.org/10.3390/rs14071692
12. Bacci, E., Cotella, G., Vitale Brovarone, E.: La sfida dell'accessibilità nelle aree interne: riflessioni a partire dalla Valle Arroscia. TERRITORIO, pp. 77–85 (2021). https://doi.org/10.3280/TR2021-096007
13. Urban Atlas 2018 - Copernicus Land Monitoring Services. https://land.copernicus.eu/local/urban-atlas/urban-atlas-2018
14. 17° Rapporto sulla mobilità degli Italiani. https://www.isfort.it/progetti/17-rapporto-audimob-sullamobilita-%0Adegli-italiani/
15. Santarsiero, V., Nolè, G., Scorza, F., Murgante, B.: Geographic information and socio-economic indicators: a reading of recent territorial processes in the test area of Basilicata region. In: Calabrò, F., Della Spina, L., Piñeira Mantiñán, M.J. (eds.) NMP 2022. LNNS, vol. 482, pp. 2104–2111. Springer, Cham (2022). https://doi.org/10.1007/978-3-031-06825-6_202
16. Santarsiero, V., Nolè, G., Scorza, F., Murgante, B.: Evaluation of spatial variables related to the provision of essential services in the Basilicata region. In: Gervasi, O., Murgante, B., Hendrix, E.M.T., Taniar, D., Apduhan, B.O. (eds.) ICCSA 2022. LNCS, vol. 13376, pp. 344–353. Springer, Cham (2022). https://doi.org/10.1007/978-3-031-10450-3_29
17. Terraup. https://terraup.it/confronta_auto
18. Al Volante. https://www.alvolante.it/
19. Tabelle Aci. https://www.missionline.it/mission-fleet-post/tabelle-aci-2022/

Spatial Multi-criteria Analysis for Identifying Suitable Locations for Green Hydrogen Infrastructure

Rossella Scorzelli[1(✉)], Shiva Rahmani[1], Annamaria Telesca[1], Grazia Fattoruso[2], and Beniamino Murgante[1]

[1] School of Engineering, University of Basilicata, Viale dell'Ateneo Lucano 10, 85100 Potenza, Italy
rossella.scorzelli@unibas.it
[2] Photovoltaic and Sensor Applications Laboratory, ENEA RC Portici, P.le E. Fermi 1, 80055 Naples, Italy

Abstract. The paper proposes a Spatial Multi-Criteria Analysis for identifying suitable locations for green hydrogen infrastructure. The production and use of hydrogen as a renewable energy carrier can play a critical role in reducing carbon footprint and increasing energy security in cities worldwide. The approach considers multiple criteria, such as demand, accessibility, environmental impact, and cost, to identify optimal locations for hydrogen production, storage, and distribution facilities. The GIS component enables spatial analysis, allowing visualization and analysis of spatial relationships between potential locations and other relevant factors. The research claims that green hydrogen can significantly improve energy resilience and transform energy systems. The method is applied to a case study, an energy-intensive industry in the city of Potenza (Italy). The result is the map identifying suitable areas where hydrogen production facilities can be located. The approach suggests that urban planners, decision-makers, and stakeholders develop and use green hydrogen as a sustainable energy source.

Keywords: Green Hydrogen Infrastructure (GHI) · Analytic Hierarchy Process (AHP) · Geographic Information System (GIS)

1 Introduction

Green energy is generated by minimizing all possible negative environmental impacts. In other words, it is a renewable energy source. Green energy sources such as solar, wind, geothermal, and hydro energy are being created and promoted as alternatives with minor contributions to climate change. These energy sources are usually called "green" since they do not generate dangerous pollutants or greenhouse gases (GHGs). Switching to green energy is critical for combating climate change and lowering GHG emissions. It is also vital to realize that using green energy alone will not address the climate change problem. Additional measures, such as energy efficiency, conservation,

O. Gervasi et al. (Eds.): ICCSA 2023 Workshops, LNCS 14107, pp. 480–494, 2023.
https://doi.org/10.1007/978-3-031-37114-1_33

and behavioral and lifestyle adjustments that lower demand for natural gas, coal, or oil-burning power plants, are required to cut emissions and address climate change issues. Rational environmental and urban planning [1, 2] based on sustainable development [3] is necessary in this respect. Hydropower and geothermal energy are clean sources with zero GHG emissions.

Furthermore, green hydrogen derived from water electrolysis (an electrolytic process in which the passage of an electric current causes the dissociation of water into oxygen and hydrogen gas) has the potential to play a significant role in the transition to a low-carbon energy system and help mitigate climate change [4]. Nevertheless, widespread acceptance will depend on cost competitiveness, technology developments, and advantageous laws and regulations. In this way, water electrolysis yields only around 5% of the hydrogen produced annually.

However, green hydrogen is now the hydrogen production system of most significant interest for two main reasons: a) the process of dissociating the water molecule into oxygen and hydrogen in the gaseous state does not result in greenhouse gas emissions; b) the electricity that is used to separate oxygen from hydrogen can be produced from renewable energy sources, and the entire process is environmentally sustainable. The first benefit is more of an environmental nature, and the second is more of a strategy in that green hydrogen production can be a tool to reduce the need to import oil, methane gas, and coal. The most significant advantage of hydrogen is that in its use the energy, it does not emit greenhouse gases and polluting factors, but the only by-product of its use is water. Thus, provided it is produced through electricity from renewable sources and is sustainable (therefore using low-impact plant and transportation solutions), green hydrogen can be considered concretely as a green fuel. The main disadvantage of hydrogen, mainly green hydrogen, has always been its cost, which is much higher than other fossil fuels. Before the start of the Ukraine War, as of early 2021, the cost alone of producing renewable hydrogen was approx. 6.5 euros/kg, while the cost of producing fossil-derived hydrogen (from the reforming of gas methane) was approx. 1.50 euros/kg, and for this reason, without an adequate incentive system, green hydrogen was not competitive against fossil alternatives. With the European energy crisis brought about by the conflict above, the scenario has changed considerably, and today hydrogen is already positioned itself as competitive with traditional fossil fuels such as gasoline, diesel, and gasoil; this is also thanks to the policy of incentives activated by the Italian government through the Plan National Restoration and Resilience plan (PNRR) [5], which provides a financial allocation of 3.2 billion euros for the "main action" called "Hydrogen." As for the 2050 horizon, on the other hand, the goal is to achieve a more robust use of hydrogen in the industries of chemicals and transportation (up to 80% of long-haul trucks) and especially in "hard-to-abate" sectors (such as energy-intensive manufacturing processes energy, aviation or the maritime sector. These emissions are in sectors and applications for which electricity is not currently the form of energy at the point of end-use and for which direct electricity-based solutions come with high costs or technical drawbacks), as well as for heating residential and commercial, with the goal of up to 20% penetration of hydrogen in final demand. This target, at least in the maximum, is more ambitious than the EU Strategy for Hydrogen (2020), which calls for a 13–14% penetration of hydrogen with low-carbon emissions.

This paper aims to investigate and identify the ideal case for establishing a green hydrogen infrastructure. We will employ a spatial multicriteria analysis technique that integrates the Analytic Hierarchy Process (AHP) method with Geographic Information Systems to accomplish this (GIS). Spatial analysis approaches have grown into a low-cost, rapid, and reliable tool for evaluating the potential of renewable energy sources. Many studies [6–12] have used spatial analytic tools to examine the possibility of renewable sources such as solar, wind, hydropower, and biomass. We will be able to consider a range of criteria and components by using these methodologies, such as the availability of renewable energy sources, present infrastructure, population density, and transportation systems. We are seeking the most feasible and desired place for creating green hydrogen infrastructure by studying and contrasting various scenarios based on these principles.

Additionally, by promoting green hydrogen as a viable alternative to traditional fossil fuels, our study will help to establish a more sustainable, low-carbon energy system. Choosing the best scenario for constructing green hydrogen infrastructure is a sophisticated and broad task that requires considering various geographical, environmental, and economic factors. We plan to build a comprehensive framework that considers these variables and helps us make informed and data-driven decisions by using the capabilities of GIS and AHP techniques. GIS allows us to see and analyze geographical data such as renewable energy potential, population density, and infrastructure. Still, AHP gives an orderly and logical way of determining the relative importance of various criteria factors and the best option. When these techniques are integrated, we will have a strong tool for analyzing and comparing alternative scenarios, such as building green hydrogen production facilities, transportation networks, and distribution systems.

The paper is divided into three sections. First, the methodology is analyzed: spatial Multi-Criteria Analysis. In the second section, these techniques are applied to identify the best site for producing green hydrogen to serve the "Siderpotenza" industry in Potenza (Basilicata, Italy). Finally, the third section discusses the study's results, outlining research perspectives.

2 Methodology

Land suitability analysis is among the main challenges for the Green Hydrogen Infrastructure (GHI) location, as multiple criteria need to be considered. Multi-Criteria Decision Making (MCDM) methods are used in several studies to solve complex decision-making problems involving both qualitative and quantitative criteria [13–15].

The literature shows that the most commonly used multi-criteria methods are [16]: Analytic Hierarchy Process (AHP), ELimination Et Choix Traduisant la REalité (ELECTRE), Technique for Order Preference by Similarity to Ideal Solution (TOPSIS), and VlseKriterijumska Optimizacija I Kompromisno Resenje (VIKOR).

AHP is the most popular sustainable energy management technique [17]. The choice of using the spatial multi-criteria analysis integrating the AHP method in the Geographic Information System (GIS) environment as a methodology is legitimized by the scientific literature that connotes this tool as powerful and established [18] to assess the suitability of various sites for the installation of RES plants [19–23]. This integrated approach makes it possible to (i) consider multiple and different criteria; (ii) assess and manage multiple spatial information; (iii) involve different stakeholders in the decision-making process. Few studies concern the GHI location [4, 24–27], highlighting that identifying the criteria necessary to evaluate the different alternatives represents a complex step in implementing the methodology. This paper aims to develop land suitability maps to determine the best site for producing green hydrogen to serve the Siderpotenza industry in Potenza (Basilicata, Italy). Figure 1 shows the methodology developed in this study for selecting suitable green hydrogen production sites.

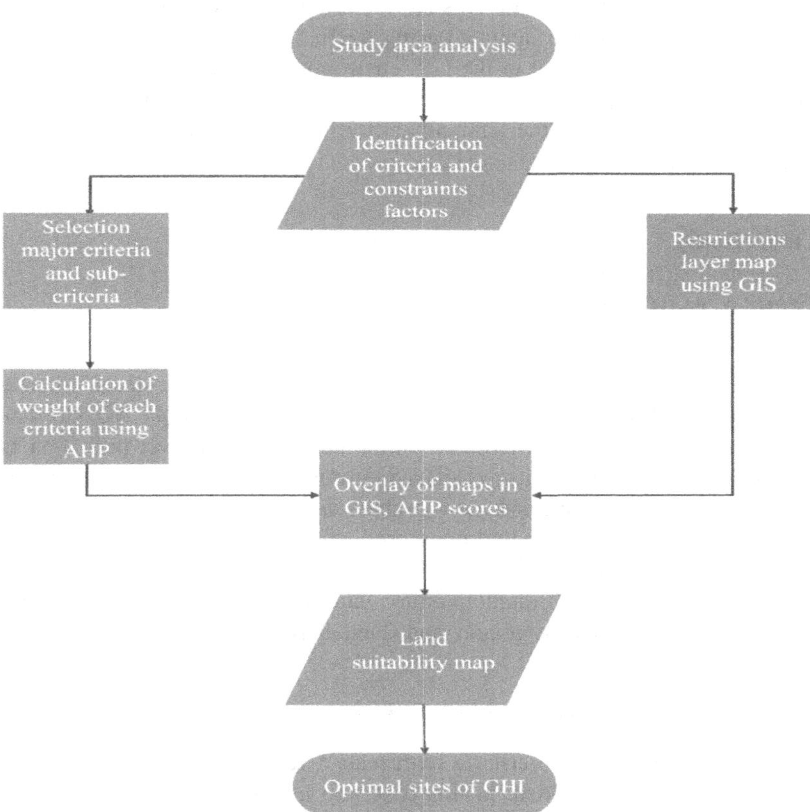

Fig. 1. Flowchart of methodology.

In the "Case Study" section, the description of the study area centered on the "Siderpotenza" industry and the surrounding area is illustrated. The first step is the identification of criteria and constraints factors. Within the GIS environment, two types of criteria are distinguished:

1) constraints criteria;
2) weighting criteria (same as those used in the AHP).

The constraints criteria were identified through a literature review [10, 24, 26, 28, 29] and an analysis of the constraints already present in the territory. The result of the analysis is the restrictions layer map. Next, the criteria and sub-criteria are identified, and for each one, a weight is calculated using AHP. After reclassifying the criteria, the individual weights are reported in the GIS environment. The Overlay tool in ArcGIS allows Map Algebra expressions to be performed in order to obtain the output of the methodological process, i.e., the land suitability map. The suitable sites for the GHI location are then identified.

3 Case Study

3.1 Study Area Analysis

The implemented case study concerns Siderpotenza, an industry belonging to the Pittini Group. The latter is configured as the first Italian producer of "long steels" intended for the construction and mechanical industry. The plant is located in the industrial area of Potenza (Basilicata, Italy). It is bordered on the northeast by a river park area and on the remaining sides by other industrial sites. Siderpotenza has been identified as three of Italy's largest energy-intensive and hard-to-abate industries and, therefore, particularly suitable for establishing a green hydrogen production plant. The study area, shown in Fig. 2, covers 728 km^2 and includes the municipality of Potenza, in which the Siderpotenza falls, and the first belt municipalities: Vaglio, Picerno, Pietragalla, Ruoti, Tito, Brindisi Montagna, Pignola, Avigliano, and Cancellara.

3.2 Identification of Criteria and Sub-criteria

The choice of criteria and sub-criteria represents a fundamental and decisive step in elaborating the final result. Also, in this case, the identification of the main criteria comes from a literature review and discussions with experts in the field. Our choice fell on three main criteria, as shown in Table 1: technical, economic, and environmental. The description of the sub-criteria is in Sect. 3.4.

Fig. 2. Study area.

Table 1. Identification of criteria and sub-criteria.

Main Criteria	Sub-Criteria
Technical	Slope
	Solar radiation
Economic	Distance of roads
	Distance of industry
	Distance of RES
	Distance of GAS pipelines
Environmental	Land use

3.3 Calculation of Criteria's Weight Using AHP

Thomas Saaty introduced AHP as a measurement method with ratio scales that allows different options to be evaluated and ranked according to specific criteria and sub-criteria [30]. AHP can reduce the complexity of decision-making problems by using a pairwise comparison technique to determine the relative importance of the criteria involved. The criteria selected depend on the research objective, which in this study is the search for a suitable area for GHI location. The first step concerns the hierarchical articulation of the decision problem's elements: goal, criteria, sub-criteria, and alternatives. It is necessary to point out that in the case of spatial AHP, the hierarchy is made up of several more or less extensive levels. Generally, [31] the alternatives are spatially characterized and represented on each criteria map as a point, linear, or polygonal vector layer. In the case study proposed here, the alternative sites are represented as the square cells of a vector grid.

Then the AHP is, therefore, to perform a pairwise comparison of the criteria and sub-criteria. The pairwise comparison of criteria was developed using a scale defined by Saaty, shown in Table 1. This semantic scale allows qualitative judgments to be made concerning the elements compared. A value of 1 indicates that the two elements have equal weight, while a value of 9 emphasizes the extreme importance of one element over the other.

Table 2. Saaty semantic scale.

Score	Definition	Explanation
1	Equal importance	Two activities contribute equally to the objective
3	Moderate importance	Judgment slightly favors one activity over another
5	Strong importance	Judgment strongly favors one activity over another
7	Very strong importance	An activity is favored very strongly over another
9	Extreme importance	Favoring one activity over another is of the highest affirmation
2, 4, 6, 8	Intermediate values	A compromise is needed

The comparison results in the C_x matrix are shown in Eq. 1.

$$C_x = \begin{bmatrix} C_{11} & \cdots & C_{1n} \\ \vdots & \ddots & \vdots \\ C_{n1} & \cdots & C_{nn} \end{bmatrix} \tag{1}$$

The matrix is organized into a *n* x *n*, where *n* represents the rank of the matrix, i.e. the number of elements compared. $C_x = |C_{ij}| \forall i,\ j = 1, 2, \ldots, n$ for *n* criteria that influence the ultimate objective of the study, where C_{ij} demonstrates the relative importance of the criteria C_i over C_j. The matrix is:

- square: with size equal to the number n of sub-criteria compared;
- positive: ($C_{ij} > 0 \, \forall \, i, j$ and with $i, j = 1, 2 \ldots n$) with elements equal to 1 on the main diagonal ($C_{ii} = C_{jj} = 1 \, \forall \, i, j$ and with $i, j = 1, 2 \ldots n$);
- reciprocal: ($C_{ij} = 1/C_{ji}$).

The matrix of the direct comparison of all sub-criteria is illustrated in Table 2. The second step is to calculate the vector of weights. For this purpose, its i-th element is obtained by calculating the arithmetic mean of each row of the normalized matrix C_x [32]. The normalisation is done through the ratio of each matrix element to the sum of all those in the same column. The vector of weight expressed in % is represented in Table 3.

Table 3. Pairwise comparison matrix and weights of sub-criteria.

	C_1	C_2	C_3	C_4	C_5	C_6	C_7	w_i (%)
C_1	1,00	0,25	0,25	0,20	0,20	0,50	0,33	4
C_2	4,00	1,00	3,00	0,50	0,33	3,00	0,50	14
C_3	4,00	0,33	1,00	0,33	0,50	3,00	0,33	10
C_4	5,00	2,00	3,00	1,00	3,00	3,00	2,00	28
C_5	5,00	3,00	2,00	0,33	1,00	3,00	0,50	18
C_6	2,00	0,33	0,33	0,33	0,33	1,00	0,33	6
C_7	3,00	2,00	3,00	0,50	2,00	3,00	1,00	20

In attributing weights through pairwise comparison, i.e., through the formulation of judgments, decision makers, or the experts they use to express priorities, may unintentionally provide some degree of inconsistency. In the AHP, one must therefore verify the level of consistency concerning the priorities expressed through the Consistency Ratio (CR) calculation. The check is satisfied if: CR $< 5\%$ ($n = 3$); CR $< 9\%$ ($n = 4$); CR $< 10\%$ ($n > 4$). CR is given by the ratio between the Consistency Index (CI) and the Random Consistency Index (RCI). CI is obtained with Eq. 2:

$$CI = \frac{\lambda\text{max} - n}{n - 1} \tag{2}$$

While RCI depends on the number n of variables according to Table 4.

Table 4. RCI values.

n	1	2	3	4	5	6	7	8	9
RCI	0	0	0,58	0,90	1,12	1,24	1,32	1,41	1,45

The consistency check is satisfied, as shown in Table 5.

Table 5. Consistency check.

λmax	n	CI	RCI	CR	CR (%)
7,68	7	0,11	1,32	0,09	8,59

3.4 Elaboration of Criteria's Maps

In order to identify optimal sites for the implementation of green hydrogen infrastructure, a spatial assessment was performed. This was accomplished using GIS software to overlay normalized data related to the project goals and criteria. Each sub-criterion was represented in a distinct map layer, resulting in nine layers of spatial data analysis. These layers included assessments of the solar radiation, slope, distance from roads, proximity to Industry (Pittini), availability of renewable energy sources (RES) in the area, distance from gas pipelines, and land usage. Table 6 shows the type of layer used with description and source for each sub-criteria.

Table 6. Data collection and their sources.

Sub-Criteria	Data	Type of layer	Source
Slope	Digital Terrain Model (DTM)	Raster	Regional Spatial Data Infrastructure of Basilicata (RSDI)
Solar radiation	Digital Terrain Model (DTM)	Raster	RSDI
Distance of roads	Road network	Vector	RSDI
Distance of industry	Industrial lots	Vector	RSDI
Distance of RES	Industrial lots	Vector	RSDI
Distance of GAS pipelines	GAS distribution network	Vector	RSDI
Land use	Corine Land Cover	Vector	European Union, Copernicus Land Monitoring Service 2018, European Environment Agency (EEA)

The following parts will give us more details about processing each map. Solar radiation is a key criterion in determining the suitability of a particular area for implementing green hydrogen. Green hydrogen is produced using renewable energy sources, particularly solar power, which converts sunlight into electricity through photovoltaic panels. The amount and intensity of solar radiation in a given area directly affect the efficiency and viability of solar power generation, which impacts green hydrogen production. Therefore, analyzing the solar radiation levels in a potential location can provide valuable insight into the amount of renewable energy that can be harnessed and subsequently used to produce green hydrogen. Additionally, considering solar radiation levels along with other factors such as topography, land use, and infrastructure can aid in identifying the most suitable locations for green hydrogen implementation. The ArcGIS Spatial Analyst extension's solar radiation analysis tools facilitate the cartographic and analytical assessment of the sun's impact on a specific geographical area.

Slope assessment (Fig. 3. a) is crucial to consider in technical criteria in terms of determining the viability of implementing green hydrogen infrastructure in a particular area.

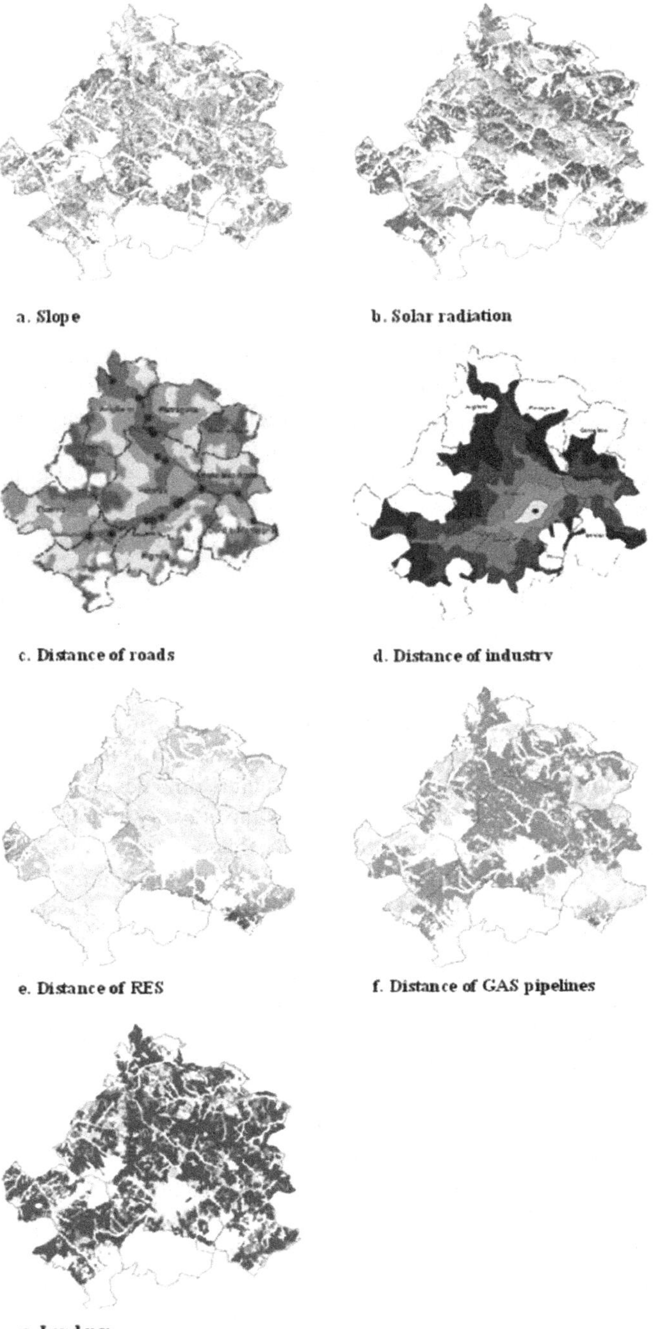

Fig. 3. Criteria's maps.

Regarding the study area's solar radiation map (Fig. 3. b), the region's high proportion of solar radiation is a positive characteristic. This is because most of the area receives a substantial amount of sunlight, depicted by the darker red hue on the map. The gradient and steepness of the terrain can affect the placement, orientation, and stability of solar panels used to generate renewable energy to produce green hydrogen. As shown in the map, steep slopes can pose challenges in terms of the installation and maintenance of solar panels in the study area; we can see a few sites with low slopes (dark red), which consequently can impact the efficiency of solar power systems due to shading and limited exposure to sunlight. Therefore, areas with gentle slopes are typically more favorable for installing solar arrays, as they allow for greater flexibility in the design and placement of solar panels and maximum exposure to sunlight throughout the day. Furthermore, the slope assessment is also relevant for constructing other infrastructure necessary for green hydrogen production, such as hydrogen storage facilities and transportation systems, as steep slopes may pose challenges to safe and efficient hydrogen transport.

For proximity maps, we applied two different methods. To calculate distance from roads (Fig. 3. c) and industrial sites (Fig. 3. d), we use the Isochrone tool because it calculates based on time, so we will have the fastest road to transforming the green hydrogen. On the other hand, the second tool which is used is NEAR.

There is a relevance between proximity to roads and producing green hydrogen, as the transportation of hydrogen from the point of production to its point of use can be a significant factor in the cost and efficiency of the process. Suppose a production facility for green hydrogen is located near a major road or highway. In that case, it can significantly reduce transportation costs and increase the efficiency of the process. This is because it becomes easier and cheaper to transport the hydrogen by truck to its point of use or to connect the production facility to the existing pipeline.

Here we calculate the isochrone distance, which is time dependence method to calculate proximity to intersections of main roads in the area of study by ORS tool in GIS. The distance is calculated from 5 min by heavy cars and trucks until 25 min. The map shows that heavy car reaches the vast study area in less than 30 min.

As Pittini is an end user of green hydrogen, it is essential to do it faster, so we applied the same method that we used for roads from 5 min to 25 min to have time dependence distance, which is crucial to transport hydrogen more sustainably. Regarding the map, it shows that not all the area is in the fast transport zone in Pittini destination.

Going to the second group of distance maps, the availability and reliability of RES can significantly impact the production process. For instance, fluctuations in solar or wind energy production can lead to variations in the availability of electricity for the electrolysis process. To ensure a consistent and reliable energy supply, choosing a location where renewable energy sources are abundant and where energy storage solutions can be integrated effectively is important. To measure the distance from RES (Fig. 3. e), we used the NEAR function in GIS to determine the proportion of nearest sites where intervention is possible.

We used the same method for proximity to gas pipelines (Fig. 3. f).

Furthermore, the use of the land is one of the main criteria to consider because the aim is to produce green hydrogen most sustainably, so in addition to excluding the map area that we did at the beginning, we classified the use of land into five different classes

(Fig. 3. g). The most suitable use for us is brownfield and industrial areas; on the other hand, the green areas are less important and get a five value.

3.5 Land Suitability Map

The final results of the spatial multi-criteria analysis how shown in Fig. 4, which integrated GIS and AHP methods to identify the most feasible and desirable location for establishing a green hydrogen infrastructure to serve the Siderpotenza industry, suggest that there are limited high-suitability lands for the construction of green hydrogen production facilities and distribution systems in the study area. The second level of suitable land, most of the land in the study area, falls under the medium-high suitability level, with the most favorable location near the center and close to the Pittini facility. The highest percentage of free lands is considered medium or medium-low. These findings suggest that the potential for renewable energy sources, existing infrastructure, transportation systems, and population density are significant factors in determining the suitability of a location for green hydrogen infrastructure.

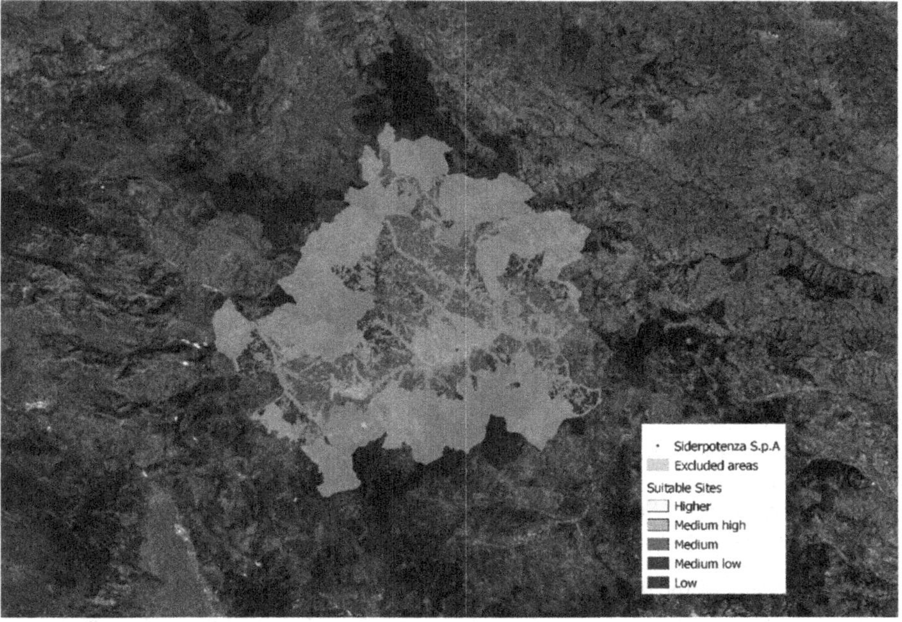

Fig. 4. Land suitability map.

4 Conclusion

In conclusion, the article aims to identify the most feasible and desirable location for establishing a green hydrogen infrastructure to promote sustainable and low-carbon energy systems. By integrating GIS and AHP techniques, the authors have developed a comprehensive framework for spatial multi-criteria analysis that considers various geographical, environmental, and economic factors. This methodology can evaluate and compare scenarios for constructing green hydrogen production facilities, transportation networks, and distribution systems. The study's results, presented in the third section, will provide valuable insights and research perspectives for policymakers, energy companies, and stakeholders interested in promoting green hydrogen as an alternative to traditional fossil fuels. Ultimately, this research contributes to the global effort to reduce greenhouse gas emissions and combat climate change.

The methodology developed in this article for identifying the best site for establishing a green hydrogen infrastructure can be applied to other sites beyond Potenza, Italy. In particular, the goal is to identify other case studies to use different criteria to obtain different scenarios. Using the spatial multi-criteria analysis technique that integrates GIS and AHP methods, policymakers, energy companies, and stakeholders can evaluate and compare different locations based on various criteria, such as renewable energy potential, existing infrastructure, population density, and transportation systems. This approach can be adapted to various regions and industries interested in transitioning to low-carbon energy systems. It can provide valuable insights into the feasibility and effectiveness of using green hydrogen as an alternative to traditional fossil fuels.

Acknowledgements. The authors would like to thank ENEA. This research is funded by the ongoing Project POR H2 - RICERCA E SVILUPPO DI TECNOLOGIE PER LA FILIERA DELL'IDROGENO. Accordo di Programma MiTE - ENEA, PNRR Investimento 3.5 - Ricerca e Sviluppo sull'Idrogeno.

The authors would like to thank the Pittini Group for their willingness and for providing the necessary data to implement the case study through the Sustainability Report (2021).

References

1. Las Casas, G., Scorza, F., Murgante, B.: Razionalità a-priori: una proposta verso una pianificazione antifragile. Scienze Regionali **18**, 329–338 (2019). https://doi.org/10.14650/93656
2. Scorza, F., Pilogallo, A., Saganeiti, L., Murgante, B.: Natura 2000 areas and sites of national interest (SNI): measuring (un)integration between naturalness preservation and environmental remediation policies. Sustainability **12**, 2928 (2020). https://doi.org/10.3390/su12072928
3. Murgante, B., Borruso, G., Lapucci, A.: Sustainable development: concepts and methods for its application in urban and environmental planning. Stud. Comput. Intell. **348**, 1–15 (2011). https://doi.org/10.1007/978-3-642-19733-8_1
4. Dagdougui, H., Ouammi, A., Sacile, R.: A regional decision support system for onsite renewable hydrogen production from solar and wind energy sources. Int. J. Hydrog. Energy **36**, 14324–14334 (2011). https://doi.org/10.1016/j.ijhydene.2011.08.050
5. Consigli dei Ministri: Piano nazionale di ripresa e resilienza #nextgenerationitalia, Italy (2021)
6. Sánchez-Lozano, J.M., Teruel-Solano, J., Soto-Elvira, P.L., Socorro García-Cascales, M.: Geographical information systems (GIS) and multi-criteria decision making (MCDM) methods for the evaluation of solar farms locations: case study in south-eastern Spain. Renew. Sustain. Energy Rev. **24**, 544–556 (2013). https://doi.org/10.1016/J.RSER.2013.03.019
7. Janke, J.R.: Multicriteria GIS modeling of wind and solar farms in Colorado. Renew. Energy **35**, 2228–2234 (2010). https://doi.org/10.1016/J.RENENE.2010.03.014

8. Giamalaki, M., Tsoutsos, T.: Sustainable siting of solar power installations in mediterranean using a GIS/AHP approach. Renew. Energy **141**, 64–75 (2019). https://doi.org/10.1016/J.RENENE.2019.03.100
9. Uyan, M.: GIS-based solar farms site selection using analytic hierarchy process (AHP) in Karapinar region, Konya/Turkey. Renew. Sustain. Energy Rev. **28**, 11–17 (2013). https://doi.org/10.1016/J.RSER.2013.07.042
10. Al Garni, H.Z., Awasthi, A.: Solar PV power plant site selection using a GIS-AHP based approach with application in Saudi Arabia. Appl. Energy **206**, 1225–1240 (2017). https://doi.org/10.1016/J.APENERGY.2017.10.024
11. Doorga, J.R.S., Rughooputh, S.D.D.V., Boojhawon, R.: Multi-criteria GIS-based modelling technique for identifying potential solar farm sites: a case study in Mauritius. Renew. Energy, 1201–1219 (2019). https://doi.org/10.1016/j.renene.2018.08.105
12. Georgiou, A., Skarlatos, D.: Optimal site selection for sitting a solar park using multi-criteria decision analysis and geographical information systems. Geosci. Instrum. Methods Data Syst. **5**, 321–332 (2016). https://doi.org/10.5194/gi-5-321-2016
13. Al-Shalabi, M.A., Mansor, S.B., Ahmed, N.B., Shiriff, R.: GIS Based Multicriteria Approaches to Housing Site Suitability Assessment. Shaping the Change XXIII FIG Congress Munich, Germany (2006)
14. Kornyshova, E., Salinesi, C.: Proceedings of the 2007 IEEE Symposium on Computational Intelligence in Multicriteria Decision Making (MCDM 2007) MCDM Techniques Selection Approaches: State of the Art
15. Caylor, J.P., Hanratty, T.P.: Survey of Multi-Criteria Decision-Making Methods for Complex Environments
16. Nesticò, A., Passaro, R., Maselli, G., Somma, P.: Multi-criteria methods for the optimal localization of urban green areas. J. Clean. Prod. **374** (2022). https://doi.org/10.1016/j.jclepro.2022.133690
17. Pohekar, S.D., Ramachandran, M.: Application of multi-criteria decision making to sustainable energy planning - a review (2004). https://doi.org/10.1016/j.rser.2003.12.007
18. Ghasempour, R., Nazari, M.A., Ebrahimi, M., Ahmadi, M.H., Hadiyanto, H.: Multi-criteria decision making (MCDM) approach for selecting solar plants site and technology: a review (2019). https://doi.org/10.14710/ijred.8.1.15-25
19. Rapal, B.K.A.L., Sumabat, A.K.R., Lopez, N.S.A.: Analytic hierarchy process for multi-criteria site selection of utility-scale solar and wind projects. Chem. Eng. Trans. **61**, 1255–1260 (2017). https://doi.org/10.3303/CET1761207
20. Villacreses, G., Gaona, G., Martínez-Gómez, J., Jijón, D.J.: Wind farms suitability location using geographical information system (GIS), based on multi-criteria decision making (MCDM) methods: the case of continental Ecuador. Renew. Energy **109**, 275–286 (2017). https://doi.org/10.1016/J.RENENE.2017.03.041
21. Koc, A., Turk, S., Şahin, G.: Multi-criteria of wind-solar site selection problem using a GIS-AHP-based approach with an application in Igdir Province/Turkey. https://doi.org/10.1007/s11356-019-06260-1/Published
22. Alhammad, A., Sun, Q., Tao, Y.: Optimal solar plant site identification using GIS and remote sensing: framework and case study. Energies **15** (2022). https://doi.org/10.3390/en15010312
23. Alqaderi, M.B., Emar, W., Saraereh, O.A.: Concentrated solar power site suitability using GIS-MCDM technique taken UAE as a case study. Int. J. Adv. Comput. Sci. Appl. **9**, 261–268 (2018). https://doi.org/10.14569/IJACSA.2018.090440
24. Messaoudi, D., Settou, N., Negrou, B., Settou, B.: GIS based multi-criteria decision making for solar hydrogen production sites selection in Algeria. Int. J. Hydrog. Energy **44**, 31808–31831 (2019). https://doi.org/10.1016/J.IJHYDENE.2019.10.099

25. Ali, F., Bennui, A., Chowdhury, S., Techato, K.: Suitable site selection for solar-based green hydrogen in southern Thailand using GIS-MCDM approach. Sustainability **14** (2022). https://doi.org/10.3390/su14116597
26. Taoufik, M., Fekri, A.: A GIS-based multi-criteria decision-making approach for site suitability analysis of solar-powered hydrogen production in the Souss-Massa Region, Morocco
27. Esteves, N.B., Sigal, A., Leiva, E.P.M., Rodríguez, C.R., Cavalcante, F.S.A., De Lima, L.C.: Wind and solar hydrogen for the potential production of ammonia in the state of Ceará – Brazil. Int. J. Hydrog. Energy **40**, 9917–9923 (2015). https://doi.org/10.1016/J.IJHYDENE.2015.06.044
28. Wang, G., Qin, L., Li, G., Chen, L.: Landfill site selection using spatial information technologies and AHP: a case study in Beijing, China. J. Environ. Manag. **90**, 2414–2421 (2009). https://doi.org/10.1016/J.JENVMAN.2008.12.008
29. Höfer, T., Sunak, Y., Siddique, H., Madlener, R.: Wind farm siting using a spatial analytic hierarchy process approach: a case study of the Städteregion Aachen. Appl. Energy **163**, 222–243 (2016). https://doi.org/10.1016/J.APENERGY.2015.10.138
30. Saaty, T.L.: A scaling method for priorities in hierarchical structures. J. Math. Psychol. **15**, 234–281 (1977). https://doi.org/10.1016/0022-2496(77)90033-5
31. Siddiqui, M.Z.: Everett: terms and conditions privacy policy landfill siting using geographic information systems: a demonstration. J. Environ. Eng. **122**, 515–523 (1996). https://doi.org/10.1061/(asce)0733-9372(1996)122
32. Fishburn, P.C.: Letter to the editor—additive utilities with incomplete product sets: application to priorities and assignments. Oper. Res. **15**, 537–542 (1967). https://doi.org/10.1287/opre.15.3.537

Urban Regeneration in the Age of Transitions

Celestina Fazia[1(✉)], Dora Bellamacina[2], Giulia Fernanda Grazia Catania[1], and Federica Sortino[1]

[1] Faculty of Engineering and Architecture, University of Enna Kore, Cittadella Universitaria, 94100 Enna, Italy
celestina.fazia@unikore.it, {giuliafernandagrazia.catania, federica.sortino}@unikorestudent.it
[2] Mediterranea University, 89 100 Reggio Calabria, Italy
dora.bellamacina@unirc.it

Abstract. Joint Programming Initiatives (JPI) - designed to fund research projects on Europe 2020 and sustainable development - target the challenge of cities to lead the urban transition towards a sustainable future. Ecological and environmental, social and demographic, technological and digital transformations are understood as prerogatives of the third millennium.

Although European guidelines are clear, in line with the challenge of climate change, the question arises as to whether cities are sufficiently prepared (in terms of urban planning tools and in terms of administration, organization and social awareness) to manage the changes taking place.

Through an analysis of current regeneration programs and projects, it will be possible to determine how urban transformations are being managed. Are the various ongoing urban regeneration initiatives succeeding in achieving the goals set by European recommendations? Comparison with good practice in operational terms is necessary. It is indeed imperative to monitor the implementation of urban regeneration interventions.

The aim of this dissertation is to conduct a survey, through current initiatives, of successful experiments in terms of urban regeneration in order to constitute a virtuous index.

Keywords: Ecological Transition · Resilience · Social Justice

1 Introduction

Resilience is far from a new concept, but it enjoys marked versatility today, especially in urban settings. New, however, is the role that the current need is giving it, confirming the broadening range of areas of use of the term. Today, however, it is no longer enough to speak of a resilient city; our cities need to be fast, safe, high-performing and respond perfectly to the model of the new Smart city.

The interplay between these two needs, however, is not always obvious [1].

Many of our cities have been conformed to an urban planning model that evolved in an era when fossil fuel energy was the undisputed base, the expansion of cities and the

O. Gervasi et al. (Eds.): ICCSA 2023 Workshops, LNCS 14107, pp. 495–509, 2023.
https://doi.org/10.1007/978-3-031-37114-1_34

gradual abundance of the historic center created numerous chasms in the urban grid and drove land consumption rates to unprecedented levels.

For today's times, these cities appear rigid, having at best "structural resilience" and not ecological.

A "smart" and "resilient" approach is therefore expected from the design of new cities and their infrastructure.

2 Regenerate: The New City Between Smart and Green

Cities are getting bigger and bigger and more complex, and within them there are more and more "machines," generators and energy sinks.

As much as talking about "green city" and "smart city" may seem an oxymoron in reality, technology has shown us that it can fulfill in an egregious way to improve the offerings of cities, adjusting them to higher and higher parameters of resilience and performance, making itself an active and indispensable component in aiming for the regeneration of neighborhoods and cities [2].

Technological evolution is leading us to the achievement of new frontiers that are coming to fruition, especially in the field of transportation. Created for military needs, self-driving vehicles are becoming more established and widespread, but while self-driving cars represent an increasingly near future, less information is available on self-driving ships that actually already count some concrete examples.

Although they are still in the embryonic stage of development, the United States, on April 7, 2016, already christened the Sea Hunter, one of the first autonomous surface vehicles, a military vessel with the function of scanning the Pacific seabed for enemy submarines.

The outlook is also rosy for civilian uses, especially in the business sector, which sees the future of self-driving ships engaged as cargo transport.

Indeed, Norway has christened the Yara Birkeland, the world's first fully electric, autonomous, zero-emission container ship. Yara promises to reduce diesel truck transport by 40,000 trips per year.

In the regenerative perspective, we cannot rely only on the vanguards in terms of transportation. These, in fact, represent only one of the building blocks capable of mitigating the ecological traumas we are facing. Urban resilience must have the capacity to deal with the cataclysms and difficulties that dominate our age.

The land-sea relationship has always been complex, even more so today with the growing concerns regarding climate change and the consequent rise in sea level.

Scientific studies show that the average sea level has risen by more than 20 cm since 1880, and is predicted to worsen unstoppably, rising a further 30 cm by 2050.

This is just one of the catastrophic consequences of our reckless behavior.

The only implementation that can be considered lies in "Nature based solutions" to a reinvestment and rethinking of the city as an organic structure closely tied to nature and respect for the environment, eliminating the uses and abuses perpetuated to date (Fig. 1).

Many countries, intimidated by the predictions are running for cover.

According to forecasts by the New York City Panel on Climate Change by 2050, tidal growth will inundate the financial district and the Lower Manhattan Seaport monthly, reaching a daily cadence by 2080.

Fig. 1. Yara Birkeland is the world's first fully electric and autonomous container vessel with zero emissions. Source: https://www.yara.com/news-and-media/media-library/press-kits/yara-birkeland-press-kit/.

The new project includes a nearly one-mile multi-level waterfront that includes the construction of floodwalls well camouflaged in the landscape.

Resilient green infrastructure and stormwater storage and pumping stations that not only act as a lightning rod for calamitous eventualities but also provide new green public spaces for socializing.

A new Jagged Coastline that will allow for the emergence of new inlets is the restoration of natural habitat and biodiversity.

This example certainly provides us with food for thought on how human actions today must increasingly draw on and blend in with nature. The gradual removal and brutalization from the landscape and natural environment brings problems of no small magnitude, and only experiments that as close as possible to it can be the solution [3] (Fig. 2).

Fig. 2. Masterplan Financial District e SeaPort New York. Credit: NYCEDC. Source: https://www.rinnovabili.it/greenbuilding/smart-city/gli-effetti-mortali-del-cambiamento-climatico-new-york-si-prepara-a-difendersi/.

Another American gimmick that combines well technological sophistication and the demand for urban greenery is the Pop Up parking lot, which proposes a functional solution to two different problems: the lack of parking spaces and the need for green areas.

According to recent studies, 30% of roadblocks are caused by motorists looking for parking. The increase in population has led to an obvious increase in means of locomotion making the present services insufficient.

This has led to the need to find new spaces to be used for parking spaces or garages, often at the expense of green areas.

An innovative proposal comes from Denmark, the architectural firm THIRD NATURE has developed a contrivance called POP-UP, which by exploiting Archimedes' principle manages to solve 3 problems with a single "smart" solution: lack of parking spaces, protection from flooding events, and provision of new green areas.

Thus, was born the Pop Up floating parking lot: a tank that serves as a water reservoir and floating space where cars can be parked with green covering to crown the structure.

If the day is sunny, the parking lot is underground and the green space will result ground height; if, on the other hand, the day is rainy, the reservoir will be opened to allow rainwater collection and consequently the garage structure will rise above ground (Fig. 3).

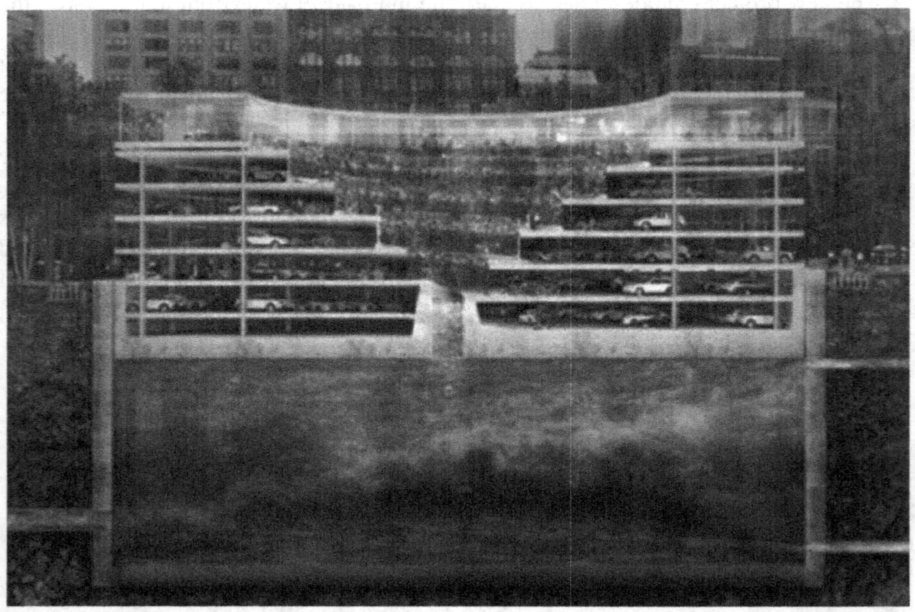

Fig. 3. Reander of the POP-UP parking project. Source: https://www.abitare.it/it/gallery/habitat/urban-design/inondazioni-new-york-parcheggio-gallery/?ref=319993#gallery.

Another example demonstrating that by investing in the pursuit of sustainable urbanism, the problems due to climate change can be addressed and mitigated.

The new city will have to be informed and informing, have the capacity to accommodate and interact well with the technologies that are being experimented and commercialized in so many countries, but at the same time treasure past.

3 What is the Status of Project Implementation and Results Achieved?

Much of the future of cities lies in the hands of administrations, whose task would be to halt the use of "new" land for the benefit of primordial environmental identity through the regeneration of existing heritage. This change of perspective, where the planner no longer intervenes only on a building, but on a portion of land, is the key to achieving more environmentally functional projects while preserving what has not yet been used. From this perspective, urban regeneration is opposed to land transformation in that the aim is to protect and restore the soil and its ecosystem functions while ensuring the quality of the urban fabric and social security.

In order to attract a diverse population that contributes to the realization of a new identity related to regenerated areas, the key is to prepare a range of services assessed on the dimensional character of the plan. So what is the status of project implementation? While attention must be paid to the personal and social dimensions of the citizen's daily life on the other hand, it is necessary to refer to all those ecosystemic and sustainable aspects that conform to new lifestyles. In Italy, for example, regeneration acquires a certain urgency and a large part of the resources must be focused on the rehabilitation of existing structures while limiting land consumption to a minimum. To date, there are significant examples of implementation of the projects, which are having a positive feedback in the enhancement of the city's real estate heritage, among them we find Milan and Rome Capital as well as many small municipalities. For example, in Lombardy the results obtained in reference to this issue are relevant, although the area redeveloped is significantly down compared to 2014, 70% of this is covered by urban regeneration areas (221 km^2), while 30% pertains to land transformation interventions (90.5 km^2). (Source Real Estate Scenarios).

And what are the results achieved? As Fabiana Megliola, Tecnocasa Group Research Office Manager, confirms, "In Milan in the last ten years prices have increased by 19.3%, but from 2017 to 2022 houses have increased their value by 43.2%. These interventions, - such as the extension of the subway or the rehabilitation of brownfield sites - are enhancing the value of real estate. Such urban regeneration is a strategic choice in order to restore capacity and grandeur to the already urbanized areas of cities such as are degraded, unused, unplanned, and with random functional mixes - former rail infrastructure, former industrial settlements - that are no longer being used and left to their own decline of collapse and abrupt decline [4] (Figs. 4, 5, 6 and 7).

Another example is the social and cultural redevelopment of the Casali neighborhood area in the historic center of Cosenza through interventions of various kinds, from the care of greenery and street furniture to new forms of animation in the area, from the safety of the area to cultural integration, from the usability of sports facilities and cultural services to assistance intended for the vulnerable or marginalized. The project has been focused on three areas of intervention, innovation, culture and sociality, where each

Fig. 4. Regeneration Business District of Santa Giulia building Spark One. Source: https://www.infobuildenergia.it/approfondimenti/rigenerazione-urbana-citta/#Nord_%E2%80%93_Milano.

Fig. 5. Regeneration of Porta Naviglio Grande (MI). Source: https://www.infobuildenergia.it/approfondimenti/rigenerazione-urbana-citta/#Nord_%E2%80%93_Milano.

area provides a physical place in what are the basic structures of the neighborhood: the Sports Hall, the Vallone di Rovito under the archway of an ancient aqueduct, and the Museums of the area on the history and archeology of the territory. They become spaces of socialization, through which the urban and social regeneration of the entire neighborhood passes, nerve centers of the redevelopment action, from which the renewal spreads to the whole city (Fig. 8).

Fig. 6. MoLeCoLa (Mobility's Bovisa neighborhood fabric mending masterplan (Mobility Learning Community Lab) (MI). Source: https://www.infobuildenergia.it/approfondimenti/rigenerazione-urbanacitta/#Nord_%E2%80%93_Milano.

Fig. 7. Redevelopment of San Cristoforo district, Boscanavigli (MI). Source: https://www.infobuildenergia.it/approfondimenti/rigenerazione-urbanacitta/#Nord_%E2%80%93_Milano.

In Padua, a prison facility in the city center, in Piazza Castello, was decommissioned in favor of a cultural center. In reality it was born as a Castle-Reggia, completely frescoed inside and out, only to become the prison of Padua, thus shedding its identity as a Castle, just as it had lost it in the memory of the citizens. This regeneration, which aims to transform it into a major cultural center, brings a rebirth for the city of Padua and to revive the forgotten place. Three distinct excerpts are planned, giving rise to exhibition spaces for design and contemporary art: one relating to the south side, another to the east side, and finally, a third, to the north side. With the transformation of the Castle into a

Fig. 8. The Museum of Brettii and Enotri in the heart of Cosenza. Source: https://cosenza.italiani.it/scopricitta/il-museo-dei-brettii-e-degli-enotri/.

large cultural space, Padua will not only recover significant pieces of its lost identity but will come to have one of the most significant spaces, in the Northeast, for the languages of contemporary Art and design (Fig. 9).

Fig. 9. From Padua prison to a great design hub. Source: https://mattinopadova.gelocal.it/padova/cronaca/2021/02/27/news/da-carcere-a-grande-polo-del-design-al-castello-carrarese-nasce-il-pad-1.39961093.

San Paolo 2030 is the physical and intangible urban regeneration plan developed by the Bari municipal administration for the San Paolo neighborhood. This neighborhood was born in the late 1950s as an isolated neighborhood being outside the SS 16 belt enclosing the consolidated city. This isolation, together with the lack of services and connections and the low assortment of the social mix, made this place unsafe, socially vulnerable and with high crime. Therefore, a process of social and material redemption has begun with the aim of improving the quality of life for the inhabitants that has recently used culture and cultural processes as an element of transformation [5] (Fig. 10).

Fig. 10. Bari, the 10 murals of San Paolo. Source: https://www.borderline24.com/2021/09/01/bari-i-10-murales-del-san-paolo-saranno-scelti-dai-condomini-artisti-anche-da-australia-e-cile/.

The presence of the subway, the neighborhood's infrastructural endowment, and cultural services have connected the neighborhood to the city center within minutes, thus regenerating the neighborhood. The driving intervention that has been at the heart of the neighborhood's regeneration through urban art.

4 Strategies to Combat Climate Change and Urban Regeneration Plans and Programmes: A Winning Link

The issue of combating climate change is closely connected to that of urban regeneration for many and many reasons. This, in particular, plays a fundamental role in terms of reuse of existing buildings, energy conversion and risk mitigation [6].

In fact, urban regeneration was born in contrast to the expansive urban planning model of second generation plans in Italy, which have indeed contributed to producing a significant disciplinary evolution, but which have been regulated by an excessive culture of expansion. The advent of the transformation plans, then, has come to demonstrate the reflections and the disciplinary debate on the climate crisis and urban planning, as a matter that manages and organizes territorial and social functions [7, 8] (Fig. 11).

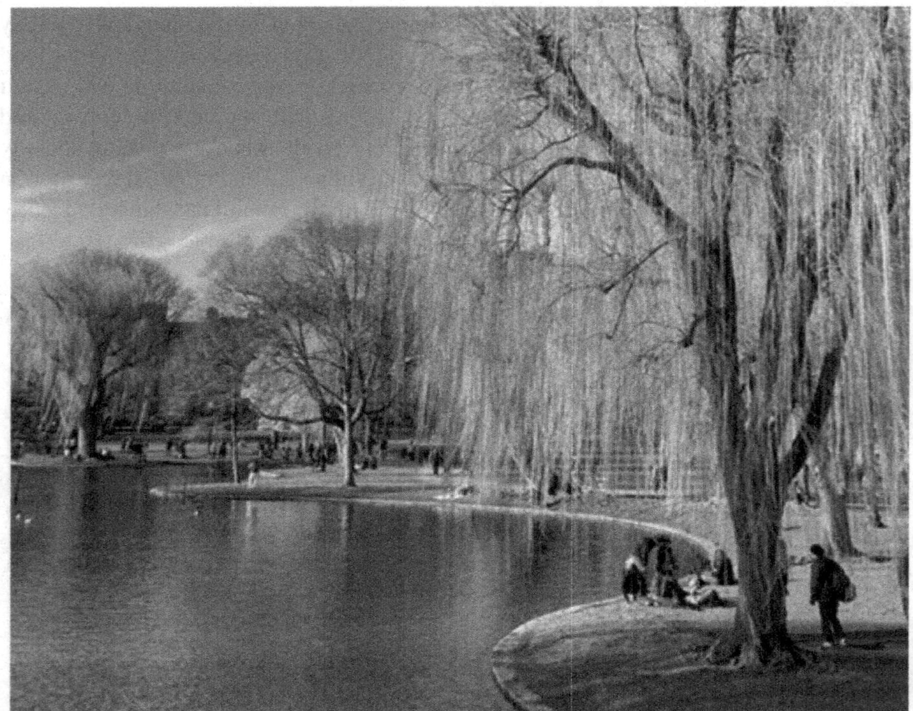

Fig. 11. Boston Common, Boston, MA. Source: Photographic processing by Dora Bellamacina.

European strategies on urban regeneration are based on the concept known as DUT - Driving Urban Transition - in guiding cities in the transformation towards a sustainable future. This transformation is applied according to three fundamental macro themes:

- the transition path of circular urban economies - Circular Urban Economies, CUE - aimed at promoting urban regeneration projects by making neighborhoods and urban communities sustainable, inclusive and green. It is also intended to specify that the term "urban sustainability" means a process that is both from a natural and from an economic point of view; in the latter case, in fact, a community is said to be sustainable if it manages to trigger circular processes that feed on the flows of its own resources;
- the transition path of positive energy districts - Positive Energy Districts, PED - which aims to optimize the local energy system through energy efficiency, flexibility and local generation of energy from renewable sources in actions towards the (urban) energy transition and climate neutrality and the integration of these actions into urban planning processes;
- the 15 min city -, particularly developed after the Covid19 pandemic, which is based on a concept by the academic Carlos Moreno and then taken up by the former mayor of Paris Anne Hidalgo, is based on the concept of rethinking the system of existing mobility and of the urban morphology to encourage soft and sustainable mobility

choices, such as the use of bicycles or zero-emission urban public transport, redistributing the urban space to organize its sharing by the social community, not only as a place of passage but as a public space that joins the personal private one, in the general reorganization of urban daily activities aimed at making cities more neutral from a climate point of view, liveable and inclusive. It refers to the concept of proximity of urban plans, on a practical model that is widely discussed starting from 2020 [9].

The theme of the reuse of the existing, in the macro challenge to climate change, is part of the objectives of the Community orientation which provides for the zeroing of land consumption by 2050 (also in line with the regional urban planning laws on zero land consumption or tending to In particular, ISPRA has defined soil consumption as a phenomenon associated with the loss of a fundamental environmental resource, such as the territory, the landscape, due to the overbuilding of green surfaces, linked to settlement dynamics. at the expense of the natural one.

The natural soil is in fact home to biological organisms useful for the correct procedure of the climatic and temporal phases. Woods, beaches, agricultural fields, but also places capable of hosting wild fauna and flora are protagonists of the natural life process of planet earth. In the past, dense urbanization risked and still risks conditioning the correct performance of vital natural functions. Just think of the overbuilding of hectares of green land, the deforestation for the necessary replacement of the existing natural territory with artificial one and the anthropic densification (Fig. 12).

The urban plans dealt with regulating the expansion - although providing for an organization into zones, which was never fully implemented and thus causing discontent in terms of proximity services - however they envisaged growth patterns which then turned out to be "excessive". A correct review of what has been done is only possible through the transformation of the areas, in view of the European directives.

Education, training in non-wasteful attitudes must be taken away from people from an early age, so that these strategies do not take the form of an obligation imposed by far-sighted programming, but as a shared modus operandi [10].

Also, that of energy conversion, with the ambivalent environmental and economic function, given the relationship between the quality of the environment and of life. The urban development indices of the last decade place countries such as Norway, Iceland, Australia at the top of the rankings for quality of life, whose score is above 95% for the satisfaction of the established indicators. At the same time, with the exception of Australia, the other two European countries do not appear in the top 50 for carbon dioxide emissions. One wonders if the two themes are connected. If environmental policies go hand in hand with the increase in people's quality of life.

From the study of all data, the binomial energy-economy is closely connected. Regenerating cities from an energy point of view translates into enrichment from an economic point of view, in terms of avoiding the dispersion of resources, attracting investments and intercepting community contributions.

Last but not least – it is in fact the most widely debated topic in common opinion, almost to the detriment of other urban regeneration policies – that of risk mitigation in the context of climate change (Fig. 13).

Although such mitigation policies are primarily connected to a non-waste lifestyle and the resilient capacity of communities, they are also developed in the context of

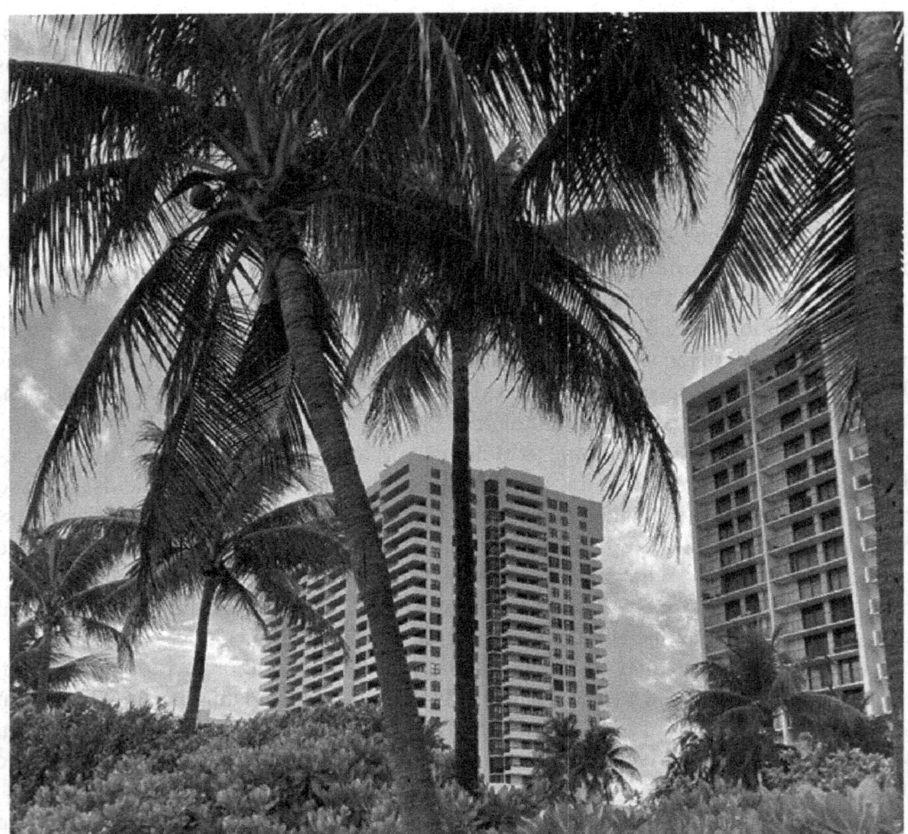

Fig. 12. Promenade_-Miami-beach_-Miami_-FL. Source: Photographic processing by Dora Bellamacina.

the transformation of cities, in support of the environmental cause. In fact, it is in this perspective that strategies for the redevelopment of public space are placed, as bearers of well-being as an example for communities [11].

In particular, the Italian territory is characterized by a complex morphological structure, as well as a central geographical location with respect to the Mediterranean context and the presence of an exceptional multitude of historical and cultural references, thanks above all to the numerous UNESCO sites present in the area. In risk mitigation, in fact, it is necessary to consider the urban structure of Italian cities, which in addition to some large centers is peculiar to the small communities that inhabit historic centers scattered throughout the territory.

Intervening in the urban regeneration of the aforementioned fabric is therefore an almost more difficult operation than what could happen by reasoning on the concept of tabula rasa. In fact, from a legislative point of view, the mixing of more and more entities for the protection of the territory is foreseen, in addition to local administrations and the ability of the designer but also of those who launch tenders for transformation projects.

Fig. 13. Promenade, Miami beach, Miami, FL. Source: Photographic processing by Dora Bellamacina.

The concept of urban regeneration referring to climate change therefore appears as the mixture of several themes. The main ones are connected to each other and the approach must be logical and mathematical, capable of combining the needs of the communities, the adequate reading of the territory and of the legislations on the guidelines of the European strategies.

The urban planner thus presents himself as a forward-looking figure, not a mere enforcer of the laws drawn on paper, but a far-sighted environmental philosopher who in the twenty-first century dusts off the aesthetic garments of thought to transform them into a vision that accords with the 'environment.

5 Conclusions

The diverse and multi-sectoral case studies presented offer food for thought on of ways and means to contain environmental pollution, for urban circular metabolism, for climate change and resilience, for urban regeneration and social. The Yara Birkeland (Norway) the world's first fully electric, autonomous and zero-emission container ship. The POP-UP (Third Nature, Padua) designed by exploiting the Archimedes principle manages to solve the city's problems with a single 'intelligent' solution. Also in Padua, a prison structure in the city centre, in Piazza Castello, has been decommissioned in favour of a cultural centre; the San Paolo 2030 project is the physical and immaterial urban regeneration plan developed by the municipal administration of Bari for the transition of circular urban economies; the Circular Urban Economies, CUE to promote urban regeneration projects by making neighbourhoods and urban communities sustainable, inclusive and green; the 15-min city based on an idea by Carlos Moreno and applied in Paris, is current and can be proposed at different scales. Other interventions, both recent and in progress, are urged by the new programming, the measures provided by the PNRR and the interventions for the reorganization of services, for inclusion and territorial cohesion from the Next Generation Eu funds [1]. The challenge is an opportunity to give impetus to the creation of models and strategies with a start-up effect also with respect to the themes and sectors indirectly involved. The opportunities offered are endless. At the Italian level, the country's relaunch is based on three strategic axes: digitalization and innovation, ecological transition and social inclusion [12]. They are instrumental in radically improving the competitiveness of the economy, the quality of work, and people's lives, and in making Italy, through its cities and activities, a protagonist in the global technological challenge [13]. The ecological transition will be the basis of the new economic and social model of development on a global scale, in line with the UN's 2030 Agenda for Sustainable Development. The missions include investments and reforms for the circular economy and to improve waste management, energy efficiency by strengthening existing infrastructures, modernizing existing ones or developing new facilities in all sectors involved, to reach ambitious targets [14]. One of the intangible infrastructures for the recovery of cities in transition is undoubtedly 'the city', which becomes an incubator for experimentation and at the same time a vehicle and recipient of specific and varied measures of intervention intercepting the sectors of services, urban endowments, urban welfare, mobility and infrastructure, energy and cultural heritage. An open laboratory of experimentation and contamination [15].

Contribution. Attributions: although the research is the result of the work carried out jointly by all the authors, the drafting of the essay is to be attributed differently to each of them, although many references and the setting of the project are attributed to Celestina Fazia:

The Abstract and introduction by Celestina Fazia; § 2 by Federica Sortino; § 3 by Giulia Fernanda Grazia Catania; § 4 by Dora Bellamacina; § 5 Conclusions by Celestina Fazia.

Dora Bellamacina took care of the graphics of the images and took the photos of Boston and Miami.

References

1. Moraci, F.: Territory and resilient infrastructures, report in the online conference public works and territory: the importance of monitoring systems and their maintenance, CNI, National Council of Engineers, May 2020
2. Bogunovich, D.: Eco-tech cities: smart metabolism for a green urbanism. J.F. Martin-Dunque & LC Wadhwa (2022)

3. Meyer, H.: City and port: the transformation of port cities, Londra, Barcellona, New York, Rotterdam. International Books, Utrecht (1999)
4. https://www.infobuildenergia.it/approfondimenti/rigenerazione-urbana-citta/#Nord_%E2%80%93_Milano
5. https://www.interno.gov.it/it/notizie/contributi-comuni-progetti-rigenerazione-urbana-firmato-decreto-interministeriale
6. Pavia, R.: Tra suolo e clima. La terra come infrastruttura ambientale, Donzelli Editore, Roma (2019)
7. Maragno, D.: Ict, resilienza e pianificazione urbanistica. Per adattare le città al clima, Franco Angeli Edizioni, Milano (2019)
8. Baliestreri, M.: Pianificazione e clima, Franco Angeli Edizioni, Milano (2022)
9. Marino, M.: Governare la transizione. Il Piano urbanistico locale tra sperimentazione e innovazione climate-proof, Franco Angeli Edizioni, Milano (2023)
10. Zanchini, E., Musco, F.: Il clima cambia le città. Strategie di adattamento e mitigazione nella pianificazione urbanistica, Franco Angeli Edizioni, Milano (2014)
11. Magni, F.: Climate proof planning. L'adattamento in Italia tra sperimentazioni e innovazioni, Franco Angeli Edizioni, Milano (2019)
12. Colantonio, A., Dixon, T.: Measuring Socially Sustainable Urban Regeneration in Europe: Final Report. Oxford Institute for Sustainable Development (OISD). Oxford Brookes University, Oxford (2009)
13. Macchi Cassia, C.: Il grande progetto urbano. The shape of the city and the desires of citizens, La Nuova Italia Scientifica, Rome (1991)
14. Dixon, T., Raco, M., Catney, P., Lerner, D.N. (eds.): Sustainable Brownfield Regeneration: Liveable Places from Problem Spaces. Blackwell, Oxford (2007)
15. Barton, H., Grant, M., Guise, R.: Shaping Neighbourhoods: A Guide for Health, Sustainability and Vitality. Spon, London (2003)

Emerging Technology Trends in Geocomputation Methods: A Literature Review

Simone Corrado and Francesco Scorza(✉)

School of Engineering, Laboratory of Urban and Regional Systems Engineering (LISUT), University of Basilicata, Potenza, Italy
{simone.corrado,francesco.scorza}@unibas.it

Abstract. The main focus of this paper is to present a systematic literature review on the emerging technology trends in geocomputation methods. The tools supporting planning have always been influenced by scientific and technological developments in other sectors. Actually, geospatial scientific research is advancing rapidly due to the development of new Machine Learning algorithms, increased in computing power and the size of geospatial Big-data. This has led to renewed interest in this line of research and the importance to have reliable techniques for SDI's analysis and avoiding potential data biases in decision-making process. The paper analyzes the evolution of topics covered in the literature and highlights new research trends in geocomputation, including spatially explicit AI, GeoAI and Geographic Knowledge Graph. The results highlight that even though the geoAI topic is emerging, it already has a significant impact on the urban and regional planning discipline and the related scientific production. In conclusion, scientific mapping was discussed in order to assess the evolution of main research topics, identifying also the main research lab and the relevant active authors.

Keywords: geoAI · Geographic Knowledge Graph · spatially explicit AI · science mapping · Bibliometrix

1 Introduction

The integration of geocomputation and innovative modeling techniques to support the design and evaluation of decision alternatives has emerged as one of the major applications of GIS in the planning, design, and management of territories and in the recent years for smart cities [1, 2]. This has led to the development of a wide range of new or revamped tools in step with technological developments known as Space Decision Support Systems (SDSS) or Planning Support Systems (PSS) [3]. While the latter relates to the platforms used to handle long-term, strategic planning objectives, the former concept refers to the instruments used to address short-term spatial challenges [4].

Thus, the ability to synthesize the context into a short- or long-term vision turns out to be a key skill to make a choice among all the possible scenarios for spatial development of a context. Moreover, the planners' aim is to measure in details how

O. Gervasi et al. (Eds.): ICCSA 2023 Workshops, LNCS 14107, pp. 510–520, 2023.
https://doi.org/10.1007/978-3-031-37114-1_35

space and location affect process and trying to anticipate outcomes. This skill identified in the literature as Geographical Thinking is fundamental for planning activity [5]. This perspective requires planner advanced competences in using and managing data and mining information and knowledge that often are obfuscated in the noise of data flows [6].

It is commonly accepted that a substantial amount of data has a geographic component or a geographical potential. It means that the spatial dimension of information can be easily exploited through geo-coding or geo-referencing algorithms, we are talking about percentages as high as 80% [7]. This statement is true especially when analyzing all the location-based services, sensors, and mobile devices that produce huge amounts of geospatial data. Moreover, it is recognized in the literature that social science and all scientific research can benefit from this heterogeneity of database [8].

As a result of these considerations, scientific research is moving toward the fourth paradigm: "data-driven science" [9], which heavily uses Artificial Intelligence (AI) to produce novel scientific discoveries, methods and approaches. This strand is not accepted by some authors that are concerned about the exponential growth of data and information to this revolution as the end of the theoretical approach to many disciplines in favor of data-driven theories [10]. Other authors, however, point out that the need to be able to interpret, understand, and finalize the insights gained from data. These ability that are based on disciplinary theories, must remain essential [11].

Data interpretation is always influenced by personal know-how and sometimes hunch, and working with big data is not an exception [12]. Thus, is important to be aware of potential data biases and ensure that conclusions drawn from the data are sound reasoning [13]. The tools supporting planning research have always been influenced by scientific and technological developments in other sectors [14]. Actually, geospatial scientific research is advancing rapidly due to the development of new machine learning algorithms, to the improved computing power and renewed interest in this line of research [15, 16].

New research trends result in:

- Spatially explicit AI refers to AI techniques that explicitly consider spatial relationships and patterns in the data. The spatially explicit models substantially outperform data science AI general models when applied to spatial data. Primarily, designing neural architectures for spatially explicit models can also be regarded as introducing an inductive bias [17];
- GeoAI is the integration of AI with geospatial data and technologies. It involves the use of AI techniques such as machine learning, deep learning, and computer vision to analyze and interpret geospatial data. Specifically GeoAI, is an interdisciplinary field that draws on a variety of disciplines, including geography, mathematics and computer science that enables the finalization of plan choices and maximization of positive impacts on territories without any simplification or loss of information [18].

- Geographic Knowledge Graph is a type of knowledge graph designed specifically for geospatial data. This type of Knowledge Graphs aimed at providing rich semantic representations, i.e. ontologies, of real-world entities by mainly emphasizing topological relationships between different geometric feature.

These improved GIS and Geocomputation methods help to better analyze geospatial data, to get a better insight about the fine spatio-temporal dynamics and enhance the SDIs [19].

The aim of this paper is to propose the evidences of an extended literature review to evaluate the thematic evolutions of the previous mentioned topics in scientific literature with a specific focus on geoAI and new data sciences in planning. The principal research topics and the research labs engaged with the development of advanced research on spatial explicit AI are identified in order to support researchers and planning practitioners in mining relevant references and arguments.

2 Methods

The input data for the literature review are the results of a combination of multiple queries carried out on Scopus. Indeed, Scopus is a freely accessible online bibliographic database of scientific references that allows structured and dynamic query [20]. In the following, detailed description of query building is explained. The first query, the most general ones, ensured that the scientific mapping is carried out as comprehensively as possible and that the intellectual structure of the scientific domain is fully covered. The query is as follows:

ALL ("geoai" OR "geographic knowledge graph" OR "spatially explicit ai" OR "spatial data mining" OR "spatial ml") AND (LIMIT-TO (LANGUAGE, "english")) AND (LIMIT-TO (SRCTYPE, "j") OR LIMIT-TO (SRCTYPE, "p")) AND (LIMIT-TO (PUBSTAGE, "final")) AND (LIMIT-TO (OA, "all")).

The dataset was analyzed with the software Bibliometrix an open source tool for quantitative scientific research [21]. Indeed, Bibliometrix is an R statistical package that provides useful scientometrics tool for science mapping providing the conceptual, the intellectual and the social structure of the analyzed discipline [22]. Thus, the application is not limited for measuring academic publication and scientific productivity but through a robust statistical analysis it establishes a systematic, transparent and reproducible review process.

Since the aim of this research is to identify the new research trends in geocomputation domain, by examining the "trend topic graph" and dividing the analysis into different time span, it was possible to study the evolution of topics and refine the query. Therefore, the second and final query focused on the topic of "geoAI" because looking at the distribution of publication per year, a burst in the research is evident in the year 2017, which corresponds with the year this term appeared for the first time in the literature [23], (see Fig. 1).

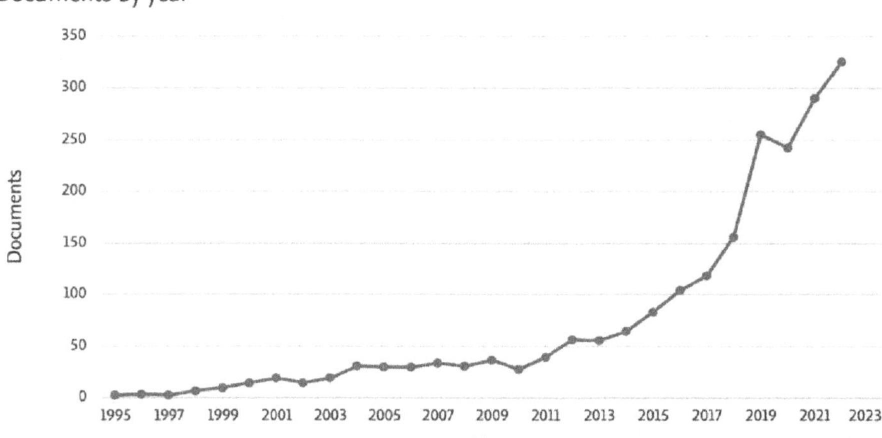

Fig. 1. The annual scientific production of the first query on Scopus.

3 Results and Discussion

This section shows the results of the two queries. The first section quickly focuses on describing the results of the first query and the need for refining the query and limiting the search to the topic "geoAI". The result of the first query leads to 2,190 articles by 5709 different authors and within a period of time between 1995 and 2023.

The figures below show the author's mostly used keywords in two different time intervals and also highlight the connections between different topics. The first image highlights the trending topics before 2017, and it is evident that the most used technique to get information from spatial data was data mining algorithm, see Fig. 2. The motor themes of these group of articles are density-based clustering, spatial relationship, information retrieval, outlier detection, and visual analytics.

The analysis of the second group of articles, i.e., those published from 2017 to 2023, highlights the tendency of some topics to merge together and shows that some topics split into multiple themes. In particular, three compact groups by both density characters and cluster centrality are shown in the figure below [24], see Fig. 3.

New techniques for geospatial domain such as random forest, support vector machine and artificial neural network gaining momentum while spatial data mining is set as a basic topic. The methods described above all refer to AI and data science and specifically to machine learning models [16]. Moreover, analyzing this cluster in detail showed that the trend themes that occur most frequently are precisely geoAI, Knowledge graph and geospatial data with a term frequency of 31, 10 and 9 respectively.

Then, once we assessed the evolution of the topics, we focused on identifying the main research laboratories and the most influential authors on the discipline by restricting our focus to the topic of geoAI. Thus, the second database consists of 686 resources spanning from 2017 to 2023 with an annual growth rate of 25.88% and an average citation per document of 8.68. These data highlight that even though the topic is emerging

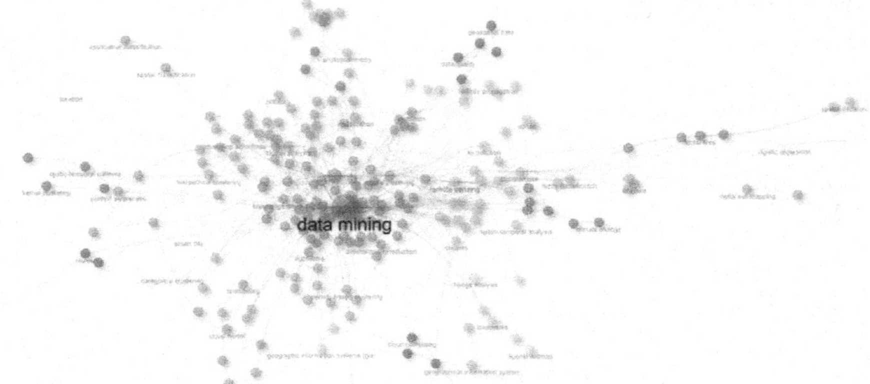

Fig. 2. Author's keywords Co-occurrence network before year 2017, the size of node is the topic relevance and the colors represent the clusters to which each word belongs.

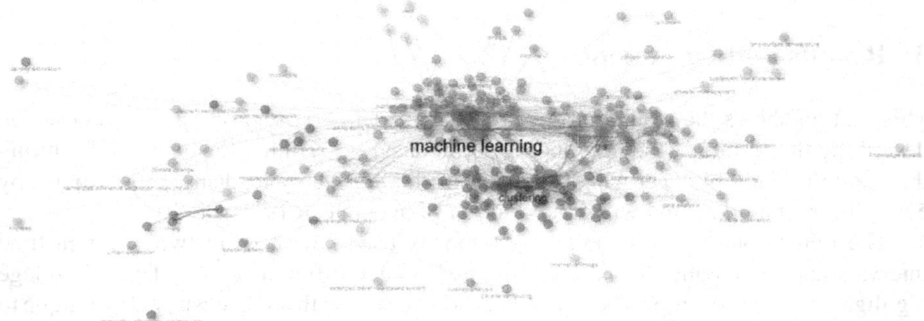

Fig. 3. Author's keywords Co-occurrence network after year 2017, the size of node is the topic relevance and the colors represent the clusters to which each word belongs.

it has a significant impact on the discipline and the related scientific production. The most relevant authors are represented below through Bibliometrix's fractional authorship indicator, which allows the individual author's contribution to published papers to be assessed, see Fig. 4.

As depicted by the graph, Wenwen li who is Professor of Geographic Information Science at the Arizona State University and director of the Cyberinfrastructure and Computational Intelligence Lab (CICI), with a score of 7 is the author with the greatest impact on the field. She is followed by Assistant Professor Filip Biljecki from the National University of Singapore and Professor Song Gao from the University of Wisconsin, Madison, where he leads the Geospatial Data Science Lab (GeoDS@UW). Moreover, the co-authorship network, shown in Fig. 5, which represents the collaborations between various research labs, confirm the importance of those institutions in the emerging field of geoAI .

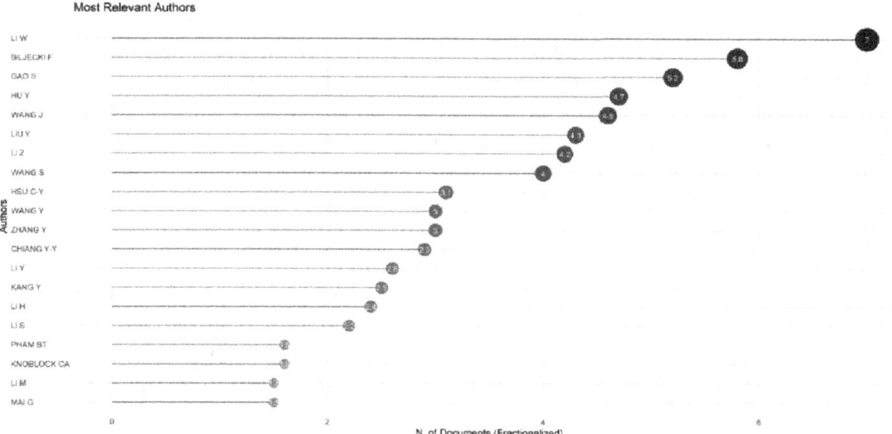

Fig. 4. The 20 most relevant authors per n. of authored documents in the field of geoAI.

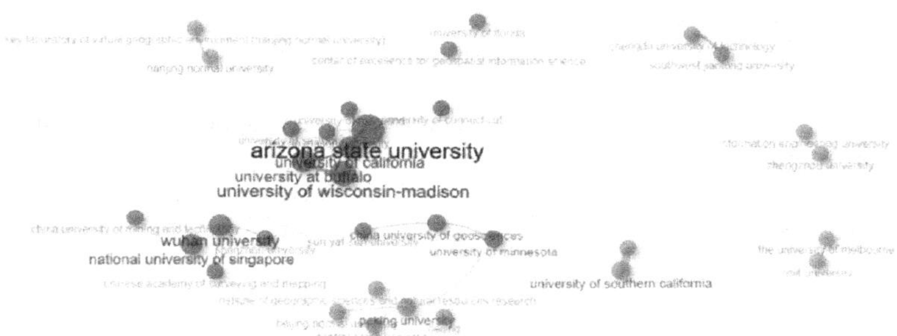

Fig. 5. The co-authorship network representing collaborations among various institutions, the size of node indicates the centrality of the research lab.

4 Conclusions

The literature review proposed in this paper is useful in assessing the rapid advancement of geospatial scientific research in the last years. Indeed, the mapping of the discipline, although still in a preliminary form, has identified emerging trend topic for geocomputational methods. In particular three key topics represent the most promising research area where advances in the short term will be available:

- Spatially explicit AI,
- geoAI
- Geographic Knowledge Graph.

This work benefitted from the robust support in science mapping of the Bibliometrix software. It represents an outstanding tool for analyzing the scientific literature in a specific field of research and inferring the evolution of trends over time, the most researched topics, identifying the most relevant authors and the relationships between different research laboratories. More generally, it was possible to highlight the "big picture" of a discipline and identify themes that are intertwined among various disciplines [21].

Indeed, we know that planning has always been a bridging discipline that seeks to make synthesis from the scientific advancement of other fields [25] through an integrated approach that links thematic knowledge [26–34], lessons learned [35–41], normative references and collaborative approaches [42–51]. Especially planning tools have always been influenced by technological developments and in the last decade by the rapid advances in Computer Science [52, 53].

The present work focused on understanding the contribution that innovative geo-computational methods already delivered to improve planning discipline and what we expect in the short term. The approach of this work primarily analyzed the evolution of author's keywords on 2,190 scientific articles by 5709 different authors. It emerged that from a broader analysis of the literature, issues related to clustering and data mining have been influencing the discipline for the longest time. Since the identification of a burst in the literature production around 2017, the query was refined to the geoAI theme because it was considered as the motor trend in the last years.

In conclusion, these improved Geocomputation methods, that refer to AI and specifically ML techniques, seems to be used by planner to better analyze geospatial big-data, to get a better insight about the fine spatio-temporal dynamics and enhance the SDIs [54, 55]. Furthermore, accurate measurement and synthesis of context dynamics, made possible by geoAI techniques, could play a crucial role in supporting sustainable development of the urban and territorial context especially regarding environmental issue [56, 57], for defining better climate change actions and policies [58], and to include in planning practice the emerging topics [32, 33, 59–65] for better cities of the future.

References

1. Murgante, B., Borruso, G., Lapucci, A.: Geocomputation and urban planning. Stud. Comput. Intell. **176**, 1–17 (2009)
2. Keenan, P.B., Jankowski, P.: Spatial decision support systems: three decades on. Decis. Support Syst. **116**, 64–76 (2019). https://doi.org/10.1016/j.dss.2018.10.010
3. Casas, G.L., Scorza, F.: Sustainable planning: a methodological toolkit. In: Gervasi, O., et al. (eds.) ICCSA 2016. LNCS, vol. 9786, pp. 627–635. Springer, Cham (2016). https://doi.org/10.1007/978-3-319-42085-1_53
4. Geertman, S., Ferreira, J., Goodspeed, R., Stillwell, J.: Planning Support Systems and Smart Cities, vol. 213. Springer, Cham (2015). ISBN 9783319183671. https://doi.org/10.1007/978-3-319-18368-8
5. Golledge, R.G.: The nature of geographic knowledge. Ann. Assoc. Am. Geogr. **92**, 1–14 (2002). https://doi.org/10.1111/1467-8306.00276
6. Goldberg, L.R.: The Signal and the Noise: Why So Many Predictions Fail – but Some Don't , by Nate Silver, Penguin, vol. 14 (2014)
7. Hahmann, S., Burghardt, D.: How much information is geospatially referenced? Networks and cognition. Int. J. Geogr. Inf. Sci. **27**, 1171–1189 (2013). https://doi.org/10.1080/13658816.2012.743664
8. Lazer, D., et al.: Computational social. Science (1979) **323**, 721–723 (2009)
9. Hey, T., Tansley, S., Tolle, K.: The Fourth Paradigm: Data-Intensive Scientific Discovery, 287 p. Microsoft Research, Redmond, Washington (2009)

10. Anderson, C.: The end of theory: the data deluge makes the scientific method obsolete. Wired Mag. **16**, 7–16 (2008)
11. Varian, H.: Hal Varian on How the Web Challenges Managers. https://www.mckinsey.com/industries/technology-media-and-telecommunications/our-insights/hal-varian-on-how-the-web-challenges-managers. Accessed 20 Apr 2023
12. Smith, J., Noble, H.: Bias in research. Evid. Based Nurs. **17**, 100–101 (2014). https://doi.org/10.1136/eb-2014-101946
13. Seely-Gant, K., Frehill, L.M.: Exploring bias and error in big data research. J. Wash. Acad. Sci. **101**, 29 (2015)
14. Arribas-Bel, D., Reades, J.: Geography and computers: past, present, and future. Geogr. Compass **12**, e12403 (2018)
15. Rey, S.J., Arribas-Bel, D., Wolf, L.J.: Geographic data science with python (2020)
16. Hastie, T., Tibshirani, R., James, G., Witten, D.: An Introduction to Statistical Learning. Springer Texts, 2nd edn., vol. 102, p. 618 (2021). https://doi.org/10.1007/978-1-0716-1418-1
17. Janowicz, K., Gao, S., McKenzie, G., Hu, Y., Bhaduri, B.: GeoAI: spatially explicit artificial intelligence techniques for geographic knowledge discovery and beyond. Int. J. Geogr. Inf. Sci. **34**, 625–636 (2020)
18. Li, W.: GeoAI: where machine learning and big data converge in GIScience. J. Spat. Inf. Sci. **20**, 71–77 (2020). https://doi.org/10.5311/JOSIS.2020.20.658
19. Amato, F., Guignard, F., Robert, S., Kanevski, M.: A novel framework for spatio-temporal prediction of environmental data using deep learning. Sci. Rep. **10**(1), 1–11 (2020). https://doi.org/10.1038/s41598-020-79148-7
20. Ballew, B.S.: Elsevier's Scopus®database. J. Electron. Resour. Med. Libr. **6**, 245–252 (2009)
21. Aria, M., Cuccurullo, C.: Bibliometrix: an R-tool for comprehensive science mapping analysis. J. Informetr. **11**, 959–975 (2017). https://doi.org/10.1016/j.joi.2017.08.007
22. Aria, M., Misuraca, M., Spano, M.: Mapping the evolution of social research and data science on 30 years of social indicators research. Soc. Indic. Res. **149**, 803–831 (2020). https://doi.org/10.1007/s11205-020-02281-3
23. Hu, Y., Gao, S., Lunga, D., Li, W., Newsam, S., Bhaduri, B.: GeoAI at ACM SIGSPATIAL. SIGSPATIAL Spec. **11**, 5–15 (2019). https://doi.org/10.1145/3377000.3377002
24. Oldham, S., Fulcher, B., Parkes, L., Arnatkevic̆iūtė, A., Suo, C., Fornito, A.: Consistency and differences between centrality measures across distinct classes of networks. PLoS ONE **14**, e0220061 (2019). https://doi.org/10.1371/journal.pone.0220061
25. Wolf, L.J., et al.: Quantitative geography III: future challenges and challenging futures. Prog. Hum. Geogr. **45**, 596–608 (2021). https://doi.org/10.1177/0309132520924722
26. Saganeiti, L., Pilogallo, A., Faruolo, G., Scorza, F., Murgante, B.: Energy landscape fragmentation: Basilicata region (Italy) Study case. In: Misra, S., et al. (eds.) ICCSA 2019. LNCS, vol. 11621, pp. 692–700. Springer, Cham (2019). ISBN 9783030243012. https://doi.org/10.1007/978-3-030-24302-9_50
27. Scorza, F., Pilogallo, A., Las Casas, G.: Investigating tourism attractiveness in Inland areas: ecosystem services, open data and smart specializations. In: Calabrò, F., Della Spina, L., Bevilacqua, C. (eds.) ISHT 2018. SIST, vol. 100, pp. 30–38. Springer, Cham (2019). https://doi.org/10.1007/978-3-319-92099-3_4
28. Scorza, F., Gatto, R.V.: Identifying territorial values for tourism development: the case study of Calabrian Greek area. Sustainability **15**, 5501 (2023). https://doi.org/10.3390/SU15065501
29. Gatto, R., Santopietro, L., Scorza, F.: Tourism and abandoned inland areas development demand: a critical appraisal. In: Gervasi, O., Murgante, B., Misra, S., Rocha, A.M.A.C., Garau, C. (eds.). ICCSA 2022. LNCS, vol. 13382, pp. 40–47. Springer, Cham (2022). https://doi.org/10.1007/978-3-031-10592-0_4

30. Scorza, F., Santopietro, L.: A systemic perspective for the sustainable energy and climate action plan (SECAP). Eur. Plan. Stud., 1–21 (2021). https://doi.org/10.1080/09654313.2021.1954603
31. Santopietro, L., Scorza, F., Murgante, B.: Multiple components in GHG stock of transport sector: technical improvements for SECAP baseline emissions inventory assessment. TeMA J. Land Use Mobil. Environ. **15**, 5–24 (2022). https://doi.org/10.6092/1970-9870/8391
32. Scorza, F., Fortunato, G.: Cyclable cities: building feasible scenario through urban space morphology assessment. J. Urban Plan. Dev. **147**, 05021039 (2021). https://doi.org/10.1061/(ASCE)UP.1943-5444.0000713
33. Scorza, F., Fortunato, G.: Active mobility-oriented urban development: a morpho-syntactic scenario for a mid-sized town. Eur. Plan. Stud., 1–25 (2022). https://doi.org/10.1080/09654313.2022.2077094
34. Scorza, F.: Improving EU cohesion policy: the spatial distribution analysis of regional development investments funded by EU structural funds 2007/2013 in Italy. In: Murgante, B., et al. (eds.) ICCSA 2013. LNCS, vol. 7973, pp. 582–593. Springer, Heidelberg (2013). ISBN 9783642396458. https://doi.org/10.1007/978-3-642-39646-5_42
35. Gatto, R., Santopietro, L., Scorza, F.: Roghudi: developing knowledge of the places in an abandoned Inland municipality. In: Gervasi, O., Murgante, B., Misra, S., Rocha, A.M.A.C., Garau, C. (eds.) ICCSA 2022, pp. 48–53. LNCS, vol. 13382. Springer, Cham (2022). https://doi.org/10.1007/978-3-031-10592-0_5
36. Corrado, S., Gatto, R.V., Scorza, F.: The European digital decade and the tourism ecosystem: a methodological approach to improve tourism analytics. In: Proceedings of the 18th International Forum on Knowledge Asset Dynamics (IFKAD) - Managing Knowledge for Sustainability, Matera (2023)
37. Gatto, R.V., Corrado, S., Scorza, F.: Towards a definition of tourism ecosystem. In: Proceedings of the 18th International Forum on Knowledge Asset Dynamics (IFKAD) - Managing Knowledge for Sustainability (2023)
38. Capodiferro, M., et al.: "University equity": students' facilities in major tourism destination towns. In: Gervasi, O. (ed.) Computational Science and Its Applications - ICCSA 2023 (2023)
39. Lagonigro, D., et al.: Downscaling NUA: matera new urban structure. In: Gervasi, O. (ed.) Computational Science and Its Applications - ICCSA 2023, pp. 14–24. Springer, Cham (2023)
40. Florio, E., et al.: SuperABLE: matera accessible for all. In: Gervasi, O. (ed.) Computational Science and Its Applications - ICCSA 2023, pp. 152–161. Springer, Cham (2023)
41. Esposito Loscavo, B., et al.: Innovation ecosystem: the added value in a unique UNESCO city. In: Gervasi, O. (ed.) Computational Science and Its Applications - ICCSA 2023, pp. 129–137. Springer, Cham (2023)
42. Las Casas, G., Scorza, F., Murgante, B.: Conflicts and sustainable planning: peculiar instances coming from Val D'agri structural inter-municipal plan. In: Papa, R., Fistola, R., Gargiulo, C. (eds.) Smart Planning: Sustainability and Mobility in the Age of Change. Green Energy and Technology, pp. 163–177. Springer, Cham (2018). https://doi.org/10.1007/978-3-319-77682-8_10
43. Scorza, F., Santopietro, L., Giuzio, B., Amato, F., Murgante, B., Casas, G.L.: Conflicts between environmental protection and energy regeneration of the historic heritage in the case of the city of matera: tools for assessing and dimensioning of sustainable energy action plans (SEAP). In: Gervasi, O., et al. (eds.) ICCSA 2017. LNCS, vol. 10409, pp. 527–539. Springer, Cham (2017). ISBN 9783319624068. https://doi.org/10.1007/978-3-319-62407-5_37
44. Soligno, R., Scorza, F., Amato, F., Casas, G.L., Murgante, B.: Citizens participation in improving rural communities quality of life. In: Gervasi, O., et al. (eds.) ICCSA 2015. LNCS, vol. 9156, pp. 731–746. Springer, Cham (2015). ISBN 978-3-319-21406-1. https://doi.org/10.1007/978-3-319-21407-8_52

45. Scorza, F., Pontrandolfi, P.: Citizen participation and technologies: the C.A.S.T. architecture. In: Gervasi, O., et al. (eds.) ICCSA 2015. LNCS, vol. 9156, pp. 747–755. Springer, Cham (2015). https://doi.org/10.1007/978-3-319-21407-8_53
46. Steinitz, C.: A Frame Work for Geodesign. Changing Geography by Design; ESRI, Ed. ESRI Press (2012)
47. Steinitz, C., Orland, B., Fisher, T., Campagna, M.: Geodesign to address global change. Intell. Environ., 193–242 (2023). https://doi.org/10.1016/B978-0-12-820247-0.00016-3
48. Scorza, F.: Sustainable urban regeneration in Gravina in Puglia, Italy. In: Fisher, T., Orland, B., Steinitz, C. (eds.) The International Geodesign Collaboration. Changing Geography by Design, pp. 112–113. ESRI Press, Redlands, California (2020). ISBN 978-1-58948-613-3
49. Dastoli, P.S., Pontrandolfi, P., Scorza, F., Corrado, S., Azzato, A.: Applying geodesign towards an integrated local development strategy: the Val d'Agri case (Italy). In: Gervasi, O., Murgante, B., Misra, S., Rocha, A.M.A.C., Garau, C. (eds.) ICCSA 2022. LNCS, vol. 13379, pp. 253–262. Springer, Cham (2022). https://doi.org/10.1007/978-3-031-10545-6_18
50. Scorza, F., et al.: Training for territorial sustainable development design in Basilicata remote areas: geodesign workshop. In: Gervasi, O., Murgante, B., Misra, S., Rocha, A.M.A.C., Garau, C. (eds.) ICCSA 2022. LNCS, vol. 13379, pp. 242–252. Springer, Cham (2022). https://doi.org/10.1007/978-3-031-10545-6_17
51. Scorza, F.: Training decision-makers: geodesign workshop paving the way for new urban agenda. In: Gervasi, O., et al. (eds.) ICCSA 2020. LNCS, vol. 12252, pp. 310–316. Springer, Cham (2020). ISBN 9783030588106. https://doi.org/10.1007/978-3-030-58811-3_22
52. Dangermond, J., Goodchild, M.F.: Building geospatial infrastructure. Geo-Spat. Inf. Sci. **23**, 1–9 (2020). https://doi.org/10.1080/10095020.2019.1698274
53. Arribas-Bel, D., Rey, S.J., Wolf, L.J.: Geographic data science with Python (2020)
54. Liu, X., et al.: Geographic information science in the era of geospatial big data: a cyberspace perspective. Innovation **3**, 4–5 (2022). https://doi.org/10.1016/j.xinn.2022.100279
55. Corrado, S., Scorza, F.: Machine learning based approach to assess territorial marginality. In: Gervasi, O., Murgante, B., Hendrix, E.M.T., Taniar, D., Apduhan, B.O. (eds.) ICCSA 2022. LNCS, vol. 13376, pp. 292–302. Springer, Cham (2022). https://doi.org/10.1007/978-3-031-10450-3_25
56. Corrado, S., Santopietro, L., Scorza, F.: Municipal climate adaptation plans: an assessment of the benefit of nature-based solutions for urban local flooding mitigation **2021** (2022). https://doi.org/10.31428/10317/10497
57. Corrado, S., Giannini, B., Santopietro, L., Oliveto, G., Scorza, F.: Water management and municipal climate adaptation plans: a preliminary assessment for flood risks management at urban scale. In: Gervasi, O., et al. (eds.) ICCSA 2020. LNCS, vol. 12255, pp. 184–192. Springer, Cham (2020). ISBN 9783030588199. https://doi.org/10.1007/978-3-030-58820-5_14
58. Santopietro, L., Scorza, F.: The Italian experience of the covenant of mayors: a territorial evaluation. Sustainability **13**, 1289 (2021). https://doi.org/10.3390/su13031289
59. Fortunato, G., Scorza, F., Murgante, B.: Hybrid oriented sustainable urban development: a pattern of low-carbon access to schools in the City of Potenza. In: Gervasi, O., et al. (eds.) ICCSA 2020. LNCS, vol. 12255, pp. 193–205. Springer, Cham (2020). ISBN 9783030588199. https://doi.org/10.1007/978-3-030-58820-5_15
60. Fortunato, G., Scorza, F., Murgante, B.: Cyclable city: a territorial assessment procedure for disruptive policy-making on urban mobility. In: Misra, S., et al. (eds.) ICCSA 2019. LNCS, vol. 11624, pp. 291–307. Springer, Cham (2019). https://doi.org/10.1007/978-3-030-24311-1_21
61. Scorza, F., Fortunato, G., Carbone, R., Murgante, B., Pontrandolfi, P.: Increasing urban walkability through citizens' participation processes. Sustainability **13**, 5835 (2021). https://doi.org/10.3390/su13115835

62. Scorza, F., Saganeiti, L., Pilogallo, A., Murgante, B.: Ghost planning: the inefficiency of energy sector policies in a low population density region. Archivio di Studi Urbani e Regionali, 34–55 (2020). https://doi.org/10.3280/ASUR2020-127-S1003
63. Scorza, F., Pilogallo, A., Saganeiti, L., Murgante, B., Pontrandolfi, P.: Comparing the territorial performances of renewable energy sources' plants with an integrated ecosystem services loss assessment: a case study from the Basilicata region (Italy). Sustain. Cities Soc. **56**, 102082 (2020). https://doi.org/10.1016/j.scs.2020.102082
64. Pilogallo, A., Scorza, F.: Ecosystem services multifunctionality: an analytical framework to support sustainable spatial planning in Italy. Sustainability **14**, 3346 (2022). https://doi.org/10.3390/SU14063346
65. Isola, F., Lai, S., Leone, F., Zoppi, C.: Strengthening a regional green infrastructure through improved multifunctionality and connectedness: policy suggestions from Sardinia, Italy. Sustainability **14**, 9788 (2022). https://doi.org/10.3390/SU14159788

Optimising a Virtual 3D City Model for Citizen-Based Urban Development in East Jerusalem

Andreas Fricke[1](✉), Jürgen Döllner[1], Hartmut Asche[1], and Fadi Isaac[2]

[1] Hasso Plattner Institute, Digital Engineering Faculty, University of Potsdam, Prof.-Dr.-Helmert-Str. 2-3, 14482 Potsdam, Germany
{andreas.fricke,juergen.doellner,hartmut.asche}@hpi.uni-potsdam.de

[2] The Applied Research Institute - Jerusalem (ARIJ), Karm Mu'ammar- Karkafeh Street, Bethlehem, Palestine
fadi@arij.org

Abstract. This contribution presents the use of a newly developed approach for the generation and modelling of spatially referenced, multidimensional virtual city models from remote sensing data, exemplified by the case of East Jerusalem. The focus is on the effective application of the entire process from data acquisition, pre-processing and management to spatial analysis and applications. Using East Jerusalem as a study area, the contribution demonstrates how high-resolution stereo aerial imagery and semantic data from various sources can be integrated to form a fully referenced virtual multidimensional spatial model. The resulting digital city model offers user-specific functions for spatial exploration. It thus facilitates a range of applications in the context of urban planning, community development, decision-making as well as, e.g., education or tourism. The work presented shows that a common database must be established, consolidated, and maintained prior to the appropriate use of these models. The modular design of interchangeable components for individual functionalities, workflow segments and applications, along with effective presentation capabilities, are crucial factors to provide ease of use for the user as well as straightforward communication. Practical use cases of the approach discussed are the integration of data on health and education infrastructure, wastewater, and waste management, as well as transport infrastructure and usage, coupled with socio-demographic and socio-economic indicators. These cases demonstrate the scope and, at the same time, hint at the built-in generic capabilities allowing to transfer the methodology to different fields of applications. In summary, the approach presented here allows for the generation of diverse virtual city models which in many regional and thematic contexts constitute an appropriate starting point for sustainable and efficient urban development. It can be shown that the range of use cases can easily be extended to accommodate for new applications and different regional settings. The presentation highlights some methodical, technological, and content limitations that had to be overcome to adequately build, visualise and utilise 3D virtual city models to help foster sustainable and efficient urban development.

O. Gervasi et al. (Eds.): ICCSA 2023 Workshops, LNCS 14107, pp. 521–535, 2023.
https://doi.org/10.1007/978-3-031-37114-1_36

Keywords: virtual city models · urban planning · data integration · modular workflow design

1 Overview and Context

This contribution discusses the application of a newly developed process for the generation and modelling of spatially referenced, multi-dimensional virtual city models from remote sensing data for the urban area of East Jerusalem. This approach has been developed and applied within the framework of an EU R&D project (ENI/2018/397-546). The overall objective of this project was to strengthen the political, economic, and environmental participation and self-determination of the city's Palestinian communities and organisations. One important aspect of the project was the creation of a comprehensive database on East Jerusalem for civil society, including local communities, national/international state and non-state actors and Palestinian businesses. In this project, a specially developed generic workflow has been used to cover the entire process chain from data collection to appropriate visualisation in order to communicate information effectively. The preparatory work is described in detail in [6–8]. Using this generic workflow, the project has set up a comprehensive geodatabase through the acquisition and processing of high-resolution stereoscopic remote sensing imagery. The geodatabase contains up-to-date 3D geospatial and thematic data of unprecedented scope and depth, allowing for detailed analysis of the social, economic and environmental conditions of East Jerusalem communities. To facilitate the use and dissemination of this data, the ALQUDS.INFO digital platform has been developed and made available. This platform is used for decision-making, education, and research by civil society, community stakeholders and the general public.

2 Problem Statement and Challenges

Creating meaningful and accurate 3D city models for urban planning and decision-making is a challenging task, especially in regions with limited or no reference data at all [1,5]. East Jerusalem is a paradigmatic example of such a case, as it lacks an adequate database for a variety of reasons. The area of East Jerusalem is therefore a suitable study area to analyse the problem resulting from a lack of reference data. East Jerusalem is a complex and historically significant urban agglomeration with political and cultural tensions. Due to the Israeli-Palestinian conflict, information and data on the entire city is often difficult to access or non-existent. This is particularly true for geospatial data, which is essential for the creation of 3D city models. The limited availability of basic geo-topographic data, topographic maps and detailed urban information makes it difficult to develop accurate and comprehensive 3D city models. A special feature of the highly nested structure of the oriental city type is not only a visual but also a technical challenge of distinguishing objects in the complex urban fabric, as shown in Fig. 1. This situation results in a lack of reference data required for accurate modelling and visualisation of East Jerusalem.

Fig. 1. Representation of the oriental city type with highly nested urban structures. The nadir image creates a visual effect similar to an aerial photograph, but is a highly accurate model that allows detailed representation of building complexes and structures.

Given these challenges, it is important to develop a comprehensive workflow that is specifically adapted to the characteristics and constraints of East Jerusalem. This workflow is to enable the collection of data from different sources, the integration of existing information and the processing of the data into a coherent and accurate 3D city model. Developing such an effective workflow for East Jerusalem has far-reaching implications for urban planning and decision-making. It allows for an improved data base to make informed decisions and promote citizen participation. It can also serve as a model for other regions where lack of reference data is also a major challenge.

3D virtual city models in general are important tools for urban planning and development, as they allow an accurate representation of urban structures and characteristics [13]. To build them, one is frequently faced with the problem of limited or non-existent data, making it difficult to implement urban planning policies and decisions [15]. This is particularly true in conflict areas, such as East Jerusalem, where political conflicts may limit or restrict access to data sources [13]. As a prerequisite for the creation of an up-to-date 3D city model geospatial data were acquired by a flight campaign capturing high resolution stereo imagery. The mass of geodata was then processed with photogrammetric methods including image analysis, geometric object definition and semantic enrichment through supplementary household survey data.

This contribution focuses on both workflow and optimisation of the existing 3D model of East Jerusalem, in order to make it more useful for citizen participation and urban planning activities. The optimisation of the 3D model must take into account not only the technical aspects, but also the ease of use. One challenge in optimising the 3D model is to improve its efficiency and its usability. In addition, easy communication of information plays a crucial role. Citizen participation is an important factor in the success of urban development processes and should be considered when optimising the 3D model for East Jerusalem. Citizen participation leads to better acceptance of urban planning measures, thus increasing the overall chances of success [2,17]. Another important factor in the creation of 3D virtual city models is the integration of data from different sources. There are a variety of data sources that can be used to create 3D city models, such as remote sensing data, especially LiDAR data, geodatabases, and crowdsourcing platforms such as Open Street Map [10,11,19]. However, these data need to be consolidated, harmonised and provided in a uniform way to create a complete and consistent 3D model [13]. Another issue in the creation of 3D virtual city models is the complexity of the underlying technologies. The creation of 3D models requires some expertise in geoinformatics, computer graphics, geometry and statistics. Hence it is important that experts from different disciplines work together to create and optimise 3D models [11,19].

3 Process Implementation

The creation of such a 3D virtual city model requires a functional process of data acquisition, processing and integration to achieve a detailed and accurate representation of the urban environment. The development and implementation has been discussed in [6–8]. Due to the lack of reference data, it was necessary to start the data collection from scratch. Point clouds are uniquely suited for this purpose due to their structural properties. Their ability to capture precise geometric information and represent realistic surfaces enables a detailed and accurate representation of objects and scenes in 3D as shown in Fig. 2. This makes it a preferred format for applications such as 3D modelling, virtual reality, visualisation and simulation. The high accuracy and detail of point clouds allows complex geometry and fine surface detail to be faithfully represented in 3D. This makes them a powerful tool for capturing, analysing and displaying spatial information across a wide range of disciplines.

Data Acquisition: To construct the 3D city model of East Jerusalem, an aerial survey was conducted in September 2019, collecting a total of 571 RGBI aerial

Fig. 2. Representation of a high-resolution point cloud model of the Old City of Jerusalem with real aerial photographs integrated as sections on the left and right. The quality of the point cloud is so high that it is almost indistinguishable from photographic images.

images. These aerial images had a resolution of 10cm GSD, with an overlap of 80% in the longitudinal direction and 60% in the transverse direction. In addition, approximately 3500 households were interviewed to collect semantic information such as income, demographics, etc. No reference data were available, except for the photogrammetric analysis for which GCPS (Ground Control Points) were used.

Data Processing and Integration: The process of data processing and integration to create the 3D virtual city model of East Jerusalem involved several steps to ensure that the various data sets were efficiently merged and harmonised.

Data Acquisition: The database for the 3D city model consists of a variety of sources, including aerial imagery and semantic information from household surveys. The aerial imagery was acquired through an aerial survey in September 2019, using 571 RGBI aerial images. These high-resolution aerial images, with a ground sampling distance (GSD) of 10 cm, allowed for detailed coverage of the urban environment. In parallel, a household survey was carried out to collect statistical information on different areas such as income, demographics and type of use.

Integration of Semantic Information: Further semantic and spatial data were provided by partner organisations (NGOs) or collected during the project period. These data covered different aspects such as environmental services, access to water, sanitation, waste management, transport network and land use. The semantic information was integrated into the different steps of the process (see here [6–8]) by assigning additional attributes and properties to the objects in the 3D city model. For example, information such as type of use, height, number of residents was assigned to the buildings.

Data Integration: Integrating the various data sources was critical to creating a consistent and meaningful 3D city model. A key step in this process was the harmonised integration of aerial imagery derived 3D data and semantic information. Open source geographic information systems such as QGIS were used to import, transform and merge the data into a single coordinate system and to transfer it into a common database with a custom data model. By combining the aerial imagery derived 3D data with the semantic information, it was possible to create a accurate and detailed 3D model of the region of East Jerusalem.

Data Processing: Specialist software solutions were used to process the data. In particular, Bentley ContextCapture software was used to process the aerial imagery and reconstruct the 3D geometry of the region. Advanced algorithms were used to extract spatial information from the aerial imagery to create a high-resolution and realistic 3D model of the city. In addition, QGIS and custom software were used for further data processing and analysis, particularly for object formation, extraction, and creation. The semantic information from the household surveys was imported and linked to the 3D objects in the virtual model. QGIS provided a range of functions and tools to process, filter and analyse the data. This included assigning attributes such as building use type, height, and number of residents to semantically enrich the 3D city model for further analysis.

Hardware and Software Infrastructure: The 3D city model of East Jerusalem required a specialised hardware and software infrastructure to create, manage and deploy. High-resolution multispectral cameras and RGBI aerial stereo imagery were used for data acquisition to accurately assess and reconstruct the three-dimensional information. Data processing used powerful workstations and Bentley ContextCapture software, QGIS and custom software to generate 3D point clouds and textured meshes. Mapping and spatial calculations were performed using QGIS and custom software to convert the imagery into high-resolution 3D data and extract object information. GeoServer managed the geodatabase, while a custom database schema efficiently stored and managed the georeferenced data and models. The resulting 3D city model of East Jerusalem was made available through an online platform by combining high quality hardware and specialised software infrastructure.

Features of the 3D City Model: The 3D virtual city model of East Jerusalem incorporates several features to provide a comprehensive representation of the urban environment. These include detailed representation of buildings, streets and public facilities. The model contains semantic information such as the type of use, height, year of construction and owner associated with the buildings. It also enables the visualisation of the road network and transport infrastructure, including bridges, junctions and traffic signs. In addition, information on public facilities such as schools, hospitals, parks and government buildings can be displayed. These features support civic participation and urban planning by enabling accurate analysis and visualisation of the urban environment. For example, city planners or architects can use the model to assess the accessibility of schools or hospitals in specific areas and make better urban planning decisions.

Web Publication of the 3D City Model: The 3D model of East Jerusalem was published on an online platform. The data was transferred and backed up by connecting the extensive geodatabase to the publisher Virtual City Systems. The data was hosted on a server in Bethlehem. For web publishing, web technologies such as HTML, CSS and JavaScript were used to provide an interactive user interface. Users were able to explore the 3D city model online, navigate and use certain features such as overlaying specific information or switching between different layers and display modes. The final 3D model with the web platform is shown in Fig. 3.

Data Quality Assurance: Data quality assurance measures were implemented to ensure accurate and high quality 3D urban modelling of East Jerusalem. This included verifying the accuracy of aerial imagery and validating semantic information from household surveys. Quality control procedures and metrics were applied to address data errors. Extensive data processing and integration resulted in an accurate 3D virtual city model. Specialist software such as Bentley ContextCapture and QGIS played a vital role in processing and analysing the data. Data quality assurance validated aerial imagery and semantic information to ensure reliability.

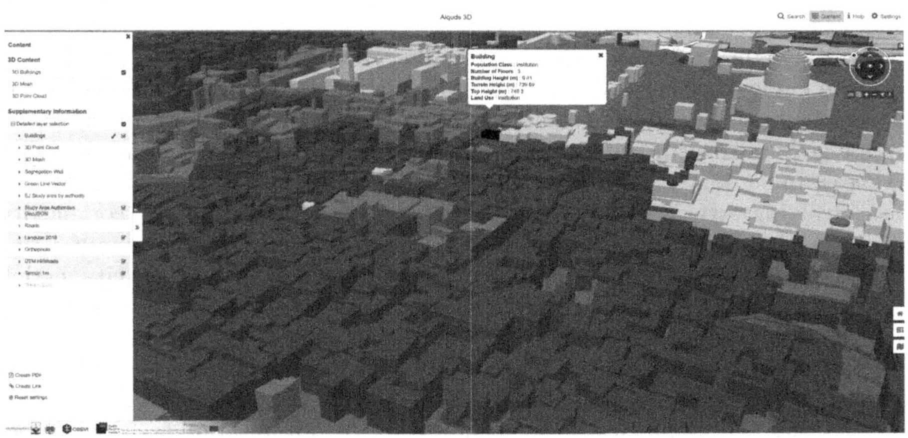

Fig. 3. Representation of the virtual 3D city model of East Jerusalem on the web platform described. The model shows detailed 3D buildings of the Old City of Jerusalem, coloured according to their function. It is a dedicated visualisation system that statically displays the pre-processed data.

4 Optimisation

A 3D virtual city model plays a crucial role in urban planning and development, providing an accurate and detailed representation of the urban fabric. It serves as a valuable tool for decision making and finding effective solutions to urban challenges. However, several factors need to be considered in order to create a functional and effective model. One important factor is data integration, which involves the consolidation of different data sources to ensure a comprehensive and cohesive representation of the city. Another factor is the abstraction of reality, where the model is required to strike a balance between capturing sufficient depth of information and enabling easy communication and understanding. The complexity of the model is also an important consideration [11,19]. It encompasses the granularity of the urban environment, such as the variety of structures, landscapes and infrastructure. Creating an optimised 3D city model requires a holistic approach that considers technical, design and user factors. Geometric simplification is a key technique for optimising the model, allowing efficient representation without compromising essential detail. The integration of heterogeneous data sources is another aspect, ensuring that different types of data are seamlessly incorporated into the model. Cartographic visualisation techniques enhance the visual appeal and usability of the model, facilitating effective communication. User interaction is essential for a user-friendly experience, allowing stakeholders to explore and interact with the model intuitively. In addition, adapting the model to specific use cases, such as virtual reality, enhances its applicability and utility. However, implementing 3D city models can be challenging. Integrating independent components and harmonising different data sources and types can be complex and require careful coordination [11,19]. Adapting proprietary visualisation platforms can have limitations, particularly in terms of dynamic capabilities and on-the-fly processing of user requests. Efforts must be made to ensure that the model is valuable for citizen participation and urban planning. Despite the challenges, maximising the usefulness of the model by integrating relevant information and analysis can greatly enhance its effectiveness. In summary, the optimisation of 3D city models is a multidisciplinary task involving various aspects such as data integration, abstraction, complexity, geometry simplification, data source integration, visualisation, user interaction and adaptation to specific use cases. By addressing these factors, 3D city models can be improved to provide realistic, efficient and user-friendly representations that benefit urban planning and development processes [20].

Optimisation of 3D city models is a vast area of research focused on improving the performance and usability of these models. Numerous scientific papers address different approaches and techniques for the optimisation of 3D city models, providing valuable insights. Santhanavanich & Coors (2020) [16] discuss dynamic 3D city models, highlighting their concepts, methods and applications. Dynamic models enable the capture and tracking of urban development changes in real time, supporting responsive decision making. The authors highlight the importance of open standards and open source software for the efficient development and updating of dynamic models. Ledoux et al. (2021) [14] explore various optimisation techniques for 3D urban models, including geometric simplification, model size reduction and performance improvement. They find that open source software provides a cost-effective and flexible alternative to proprietary software. Girindran et al. (2020) [9] investigate the use of OpenStreetMap (OSM) to create 3D city models. They show how OSM data can be used to derive building geometries and generate models. This open source approach allows for broad participation and collaborative development of 3D city models. Xie et al. (2012) [21] address dynamic simplification of 3D city models and present techniques for adapting models to changes in urban development. Efficient algorithms and techniques are crucial to ensure real-time performance of dynamic models. Döllner & Hagedorn (2007) [3] explore the seamless integration of heterogeneous data sources for 3D city models. They discuss different approaches to achieve comprehensive and consistent modelling, highlighting the importance of efficient algorithms and techniques for the integration process. Julin et al. (2018) [12] focus on optimising the visualisation and communication of 3D city models. They emphasise the application of cartographic principles such as shape simplification, colour coding and visual hierarchies to improve the readability and comprehension of the models. Ledoux et al. (2021) [14] discuss the optimisation of user interaction in 3D city models and present methods to improve navigation, information access and interaction with the model. They highlight the importance of intuitive user interfaces and user-centric features. Sugihara et al. (2015) [18] investigate the automatic generalisation of 3D building models and present methods for simplifying complex models and adapting them to different scales. The aim is to improve readability and efficiency, especially for larger spatial domains. Döllner & Buchholz (2005) [4] specifically address the optimisation of 3D city models for virtual reality (VR) applications. They discuss techniques to reduce model complexity, improve visual quality, and integrate real-time data to create an immersive and realistic VR experience. This is particularly important for architectural visualisation and urban planning applications.

In order to improve the performance, usability and applicability of 3D city models, several important aspects should be considered during the optimisation process. The main aspects are discussed below:

- Simplify geometry: Reduce the complexity of 3D geometry using techniques such as polygon reduction and level of detail (LOD) to improve performance and visual quality.
- Data integration: Integrate disparate data sources to create comprehensive 3D city models, resolve conflicts and ensure data quality.
- Cartographic visualisation: Apply cartographic design principles to improve the readability and aesthetics of 3D city models, such as colour coding, visual hierarchies and contrasts.

- User interaction: Designing user-friendly interfaces and integrating interaction tools to improve user experience and usability.
- Quality assessment: Implementing mechanisms to assess the accuracy and reliability of 3D city models.
- Performance optimisation: Using optimised algorithms and techniques to improve the performance and real-time visualisation of 3D city models.
- Interoperability: Promoting interoperability between different systems and data sources using open standards and interfaces.
- User-centred design: Designing the user interface based on user-centred principles to enable easy and intuitive use of 3D city models.
- Data accuracy and validation: Conducting quality assessments to ensure data accuracy and validity in 3D city models.
- Semantic enrichment: Integrate semantic information to enrich 3D city models with additional contextual data.
- Multi-scale representation: Developing techniques to represent 3D city models at different scales for a comprehensive understanding.
- Real-time updates: Implementing mechanisms for real-time updating of 3D city models based on the latest developments.
- Collaborative and participatory modelling: Encouraging collaboration and participation of different stakeholders in the development and updating of 3D city models.
- Accessibility and inclusivity: Designing 3D city models to be accessible to all user groups.

Fig. 4. Representation of the virtual city model with 3D buildings, underlying land use classes and static spatial units.

In future efforts to optimise the 3D city model of East Jerusalem, an important and transformative step is to move away from the proprietary and static system provided by Virtual City Systems. As shown in Fig. 5, the 3D city model in VCS can only be displayed using a predefined style. This means that the user is severely restricted and unable to change the way the map is displayed, such as changing the layer hierarchy or making simple colour changes to objects or data. Figure 4 shows that the resulting model has some limitations. It requires the programming of certain declarative styles in the backend and does not provide any interaction or manipulation capabilities on-the-fly within the final visualisation. For example, the third dimension of buildings is little used or not used at all, although it could be used effectively as a communication medium.

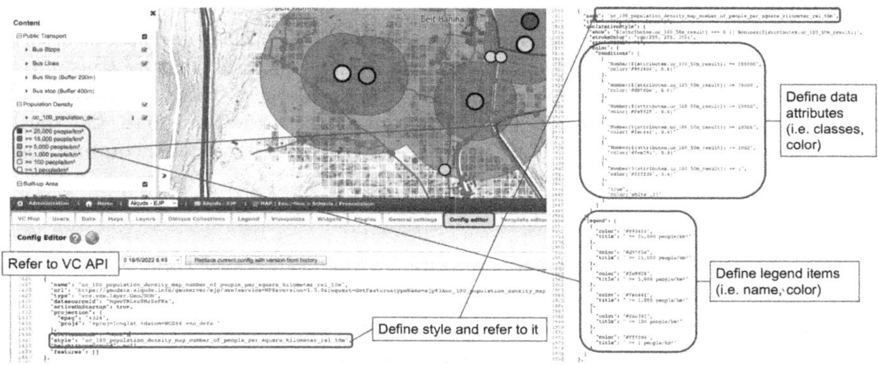

Fig. 5. Overview of the backend and map display illustrating the required elements of the declarative style.

The adoption of an open source alternative that is specifically tailored to the unique needs and challenges of the East Jerusalem region is critical. As a static system VCS system is also unable to make dynamic changes to scene content. Only previously created scenarios can be played and activated or deactivated. Due to the lack of a link to 3D data, the 3D display does not seem to make sense and in most cases a 2D map is the better communication medium as shown in Fig. 6.

This shift to open source components will allow for greater flexibility, customisation and adaptability, enabling the model to effectively capture the complex dynamics and nuances of the area. A primary goal of the optimisation process is to prioritise usability, making the 3D city model of East Jerusalem intuitively simple and easy to use. This user-centred approach is essential to ensure that a wide range of stakeholders, including non-experts and laypersons, can easily navigate and interact with the model. By improving accessibility and the overall user experience, the model will become a powerful tool for effective urban

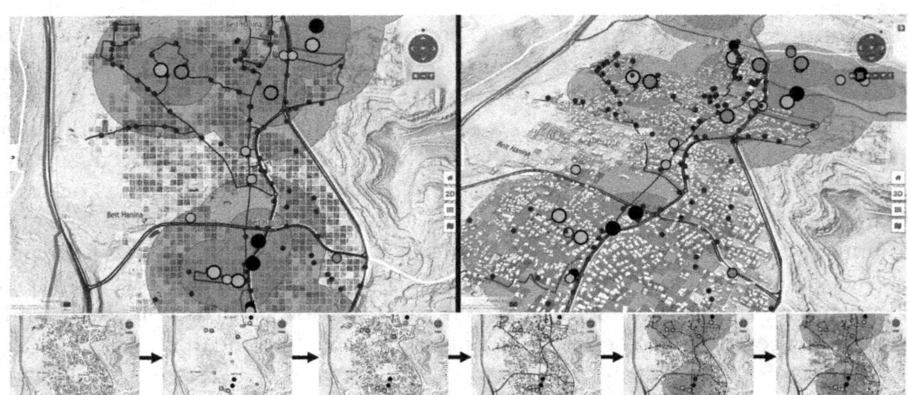

Fig. 6. Map representation of an application example with classified school locations and their catchment areas according to distance, transport infrastructure (bus network and bus stops) and underlying population density on a static spatial unit (grid). The process of merging different layers of information leads to the final map. On the left, the 2D view; on the right, the 3D view. There is a clear difference in communication and readability, with the 2D view being superior.

planning and development decision-making in the context of East Jerusalem. In addition, the implementation phase has provided invaluable lessons that will guide future improvement efforts. These lessons shed light on the specific challenges and obstacles encountered during the implementation process, such as data integration, system coordination and visualisation limitations. The optimised system should present different use cases according to their purpose in an automated and user-friendly way, make them usable accordingly and provide them automatically "on the fly", as shown in Fig. 7.

By leveraging this knowledge, future efforts can address the above challenges and develop strategies to mitigate potential roadblocks, resulting in a more efficient and successful 3D city model optimisation process. By using open source solutions and focusing on usability, the optimised 3D city model of East Jerusalem will provide a comprehensive and customised platform for stakeholders to explore, analyse and make informed decisions about urban planning and development. The model will facilitate collaboration and engagement between different stakeholders, including citizens, government officials and urban planners, promoting a participatory approach to decision-making. This will ultimately contribute to the sustainable growth, development and preservation of the unique cultural, historical and geopolitical aspects of East Jerusalem.

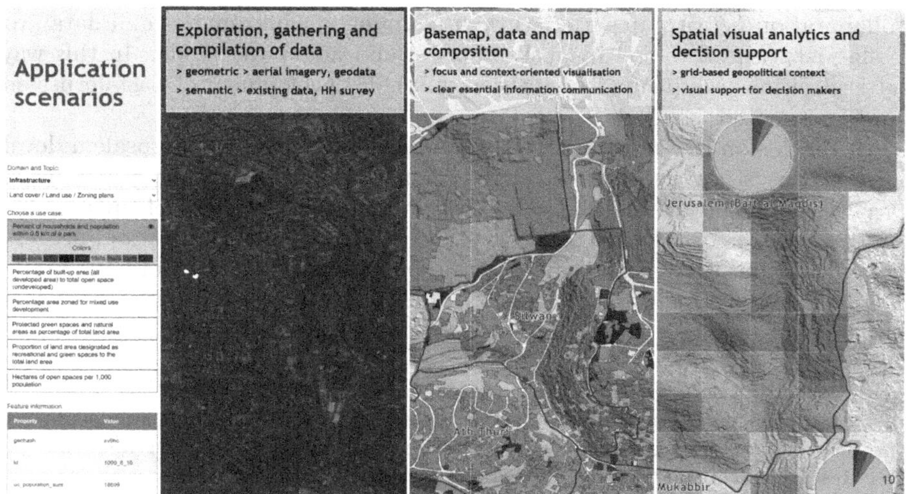

Fig. 7. Different uses for East Jerusalem, illustrated in three scenarios. Left: Simple 2D and 3D presentation for realistic exploration, data collection and orientation. Middle: Thematic map display, e.g. land use, for focus and context to enable clear communication of information. Right: Static spatial unit as a basis for complex geostatistical analysis and data enrichment for visual analysis and decision support.

5 Concluding Remarks

In conclusion, this study has presented a comprehensive workflow for optimising the 3D virtual city model of East Jerusalem to facilitate community-based urban development. By applying various methods such as data processing, integration and validation, the quality, accuracy and efficiency of the model were improved. The use of open source software played a key role in providing a cost-effective and flexible solution. The optimised 3D city model of East Jerusalem offers numerous benefits for urban planning and decision-making. It enables the analysis of urban planning challenges, supports decision-making processes, engages citizens and stakeholders, and predicts the impact of urban development policies. It serves as a valuable tool for creating sustainable and effective planning policies in the region.

However, it is important to recognise the challenges and limitations associated with optimising the 3D city model. Technical limitations, privacy and security requirements, and stakeholder engagement and participation need to be carefully considered to achieve the desired outcomes. Ongoing maintenance, updating and adaptation of the model is essential to ensure its optimal performance and usability. Future research in 3D city model optimisation should focus on further improving the methods and technologies used. This includes the development of open source software, the integration of real-time data and artificial intelligence, and the consideration of stakeholder requirements and needs.

Collaboration between experts in urban planning, geoinformatics and data processing is essential to continuously improve and adapt the model. In this way, better decisions can be made and the sustainable development of East Jerusalem can be promoted.

In conclusion, the optimised 3D virtual city model of East Jerusalem developed in this study provides a robust framework for community-based urban development. The transferability of the workflow and the use of open source software enable cost-effective and efficient solutions for data collection, processing and visualisation. This contribution improves the availability of high quality 2D/3D databases for urban planning, ultimately promoting sustainable urban development not only in East Jerusalem, but also in other urban regions.

Acknowledgements. The work discussed here is part of a larger R+D project on East Jerusalem with Palestinian, East Jerusalem, and NGO partners funded by the European Union. Part of this research work is supported by a PhD grant from the HPI Research School and the Chair of the Computer Graphics Systems department for Service-Oriented Systems Engineering at the Hasso Plattner Institute for Digital Engineering, University of Potsdam. The funding of both institutions is gratefully acknowledged.

References

1. Batty, M.: The New Science of Cities. The MIT Press, Cambridge (2013). https://doi.org/10.7551/mitpress/9399.001.0001
2. Bryn, A., der Wal, R.V., Norton, L., Hofmeester, T.: Citizen science: data collection by volunteers. In: Monitoring Biodiversity, pp. 108–121. Routledge, March 2023. https://doi.org/10.4324/9781003179245-6
3. Döllner, J., Hagedorn, B.: Integrating urban GIS, CAD, and BIM data by servicebased virtual 3d city models. In: Urban and Regional Data Management, pp. 169–182. CRC Press, October 2007. https://doi.org/10.4324/9780203931042-15
4. Döllner, J., Buchholz, H.: Continuous level-of-detail modeling of buildings in 3D city models. In: Proceedings of the 13th Annual ACM International Workshop on Geographic Information Systems. ACM, November 2005. https://doi.org/10.1145/1097064.1097089
5. Ehlers, M., Woodgate, P., Annoni, A., Schade, S.: Digital earth reloaded - beyond the next generation. IOP Conf. Ser. Earth Environ. Sci. **18**, 012005 (2014). https://doi.org/10.1088/1755-1315/18/1/012005
6. Fricke, A., Asche, H.: Geospatial database for the generation of multidimensional virtual city models dedicated to urban analysis and decision-making. In: Misra, S., et al. (eds.) ICCSA 2019. LNCS, vol. 11621, pp. 711–726. Springer, Cham (2019). https://doi.org/10.1007/978-3-030-24302-9_52
7. Fricke, A., Asche, H.: Constructing geo-referenced virtual city models from point cloud primitives. In: Gervasi, O., et al. (eds.) ICCSA 2020. LNCS, vol. 12252, pp. 448–462. Springer, Cham (2020). https://doi.org/10.1007/978-3-030-58811-3_33
8. Fricke, A., Döllner, J., Asche, H.: A virtual 3D city model for urban planning and decision-making - the east jerusalem case. In: Gervasi, O., Murgante, B., Hendrix, E.M.T., Taniar, D., Apduhan, B.O. (eds.) Computational Science and Its Applications - ICCSA 2022, vol. 13376, pp. 144–159. Springer, Cham (2022). https://doi.org/10.1007/978-3-031-10450-3_11

9. Girindran, R., Boyd, D.S., Rosser, J., Vijayan, D., Long, G., Robinson, D.: On the reliable generation of 3D city models from open data. Urban Sci. **4**(4), 47 (2020). https://doi.org/10.3390/urbansci4040047
10. Haklay, M.: Citizen science and volunteered geographic information: overview and typology of participation. In: Sui, D., Elwood, S., Goodchild, M. (eds.) Crowdsourcing Geographic Knowledge, pp. 105–122. Springer, Dordrecht (2012). https://doi.org/10.1007/978-94-007-4587-2_7
11. Jovanović, D., et al.: Building virtual 3D city model for smart cities applications: a case study on campus area of the university of Novi sad. ISPRS Int. J. Geo-Inf. **9**(8), 476 (2020). https://doi.org/10.3390/ijgi9080476
12. Julin, A., et al.: Characterizing 3D city modeling projects: towards a harmonized interoperable system. ISPRS Int. J. Geo-Inf. **7**(2), 55 (2018). https://doi.org/10.3390/ijgi7020055
13. Ketzler, B., Naserentin, V., Latino, F., Zangelidis, C., Thuvander, L., Logg, A.: Digital twins for cities: a state of the art review. Built Environ. **46**(4), 547–573 (2020). https://doi.org/10.2148/benv.46.4.547
14. Ledoux, H., et al.: 3dfier: automatic reconstruction of 3D city models. J. Open Source Softw. **6**(57), 2866 (2021). https://doi.org/10.21105/joss.02866
15. Sagl, G., Resch, B., Hawelka, B., Beinat, E.: From social sensor data to collective human behaviour patterns: analysing and visualising spatio-temporal dynamics in urban environments. In: Proceedings of the GI-Forum, pp. 54–63. Herbert Wichmann Verlag Berlin (2012)
16. Santhanavanich, T., Coors, V.: CityThings: an integration of the dynamic sensor data to the 3D city model. Environ. Plan. B: Urban Anal. City Sci. **48**(3), 417–432 (2020). https://doi.org/10.1177/2399808320983000
17. Saßmannshausen, S.M., Radtke, J., Bohn, N., Hussein, H., Randall, D., Pipek, V.: Citizen-centered design in urban planning: How augmented reality can be used in citizen participation processes. In: Designing Interactive Systems Conference 2021. ACM, Jun 2021. https://doi.org/10.1145/3461778.3462130
18. Sugihara, K., Murase, T., Zhou, X.: Automatic generation of 3D building models from building polygons on digital maps. In: 2015 International Conference on 3D Imaging (IC3D). IEEE, December 2015. https://doi.org/10.1109/ic3d.2015.7391817
19. Wang, H., Pan, Y., Luo, X.: Integration of BIM and GIS in sustainable built environment: a review and bibliometric analysis. Autom. Constr. **103**, 41–52 (2019). https://doi.org/10.1016/j.autcon.2019.03.005
20. Wentz, E.A., et al.: Six fundamental aspects for conceptualizing multidimensional urban form: a spatial mapping perspective. Landscape Urban Plann. **179**, 55–62 (2018). https://doi.org/10.1016/j.landurbplan.2018.07.007
21. Xie, J., Zhang, L., Li, J., Wang, H., Yang, L.: Automatic simplification and visualization of 3D urban building models. Int. J. Appl. Earth Observ. Geoinf. **18**, 222–231 (2012). https://doi.org/10.1016/j.jag.2012.01.014

Transport and Logistics Performance Assessment: Beyond the Conventional Approach

Francesco Bruzzone[1,2], Federico Cavallaro[1], and Silvio Nocera[1(✉)]

[1] IUAV University of Venice, Santa Croce 191 Tolentini, 30100 Venice, Italy
nocera@iuav.it

[2] Polytechnic University of Turin, Viale Mattioli 39, 10125 Turin, Italy

Abstract. Assessment of transport projects and policies is traditionally performed by means of conventional approaches, such as the cost-benefit or multicriteria analyses. However, these methods are complex and unable to incorporate the multifaceted perspectives that transport planning and governance require. For this reason, simpler and more tailored methods to evaluate specific transport solutions are being pursued. This paper explores the potential of index-based methods to assess sectorial transport policy and innovations. The focus is put on the environmental, social, and operational performances. The distribution of goods using public transport means, also known as freight-on-transit (FOT), is used as a case study, to be assessed by means of appropriate indexes. Benefits and trade-offs compared to traditional evaluation methods are highlighted. Moreover, generalized guidelines for the definition of appropriate sets of indexes are provided, starting from the application within the FOT framework.

Keywords: Performance Assessment · Freight-on-Transit · Index-Based Method · Transportation Decision-Making

1 Introduction

Transport researchers and practitioners are acquainted with the need to assess the impacts and implication of each transport choice, at all stages of the decision-making process: *ex-ante* (before the choice is made), *in itinere* (while the decision is being implemented), and *ex-post* (when the project/policy is delivered and operational) [1]. In practice, transport projects appraisal is normally based on the cost-benefit analysis (CBA), as required by laws and regulations in most European countries [2, 3]. In few cases, the CBA is integrated or substituted by other appraisal methods. Among them, the most commons belong to the family of multicriteria analyses (MCA). Both CBA and MCA, however, present several issues that can affect the transportation decision making process, making it less effective and transparent. The CBA is based on welfare economics and is often regarded as excessively efficiency-oriented, incapable of capturing social, ethical, equity and fairness issues [4]. Furthermore, several discretional aspects in the monetization process may lead to distorted results. The MCA, instead, is very much discretional and its validity depends on the competences and priorities of the stakeholders involved in

O. Gervasi et al. (Eds.): ICCSA 2023 Workshops, LNCS 14107, pp. 536–546, 2023.
https://doi.org/10.1007/978-3-031-37114-1_37

the decision-making process, from political authorities to technical experts, to citizens. The risk is to propose assessments based on superficial qualitative inputs and limited quantitative support, or to evaluate alternatives based on weights that are not representative of the multi-faceted framework of actors [5]. Hence, traditional appraisal methods are at the same time excessively complicated and only partially effective for smaller-scale transport policy and decision-making. For these reasons, scholars and practitioners explore other possible solutions to evaluate business models and process improvements. These approaches involve simpler processes and have greater focus on desired appraisal components, rather than seeking an overarching -but often incomplete- approach.

In this paper, we debate the use of index-based methods (IM) as an integration to traditional appraisal tool (mainly based on CBA and MCA), for achieving a more comprehensive and effective decision-making process. In this analysis, we consider operational, environmental, and social impacts, by discussing advantages of index-based methods, as well as inevitable trade-offs compared to more complex assessments. We present the evaluation of freight-on-transit (FOT) schemes as a subfield of transport policy where performance evaluation by means of indicators can be consistently adopted.

The remainder of this paper is structured as follows: Sect. 2, starting from existing literature, discusses more in detail the main drawbacks of conventional appraisal in the transport sector; furthermore, it introduces IM as a possible integrative solution to improve the reliability of the assessment. Section 3 describes IM from a conceptual and methodological perspective. Section 4 introduces FOT as a transport policy innovation and explores the use of IM within FOT assessment. Finally, Sect. 5 draws some guiding principles and concludes the paper.

2 Conventional Appraisal Tools and Index-Based Methods

2.1 Conventional Appraisal Tools

The CBA is the most widely adopted appraisal tool within the transport sector in the Western world [2, 3]. Being prescribed by norms and European guidelines, and taking advantage of a standardized process, the CBA gained broad acceptance. Its outcomes are often taken as dominant criteria for decision-making. A large body of literature is available on the CBA, going beyond the scope of this article: for methodological and content details, readers may refer to Mishan and Quah [6]. Synthetically, the CBA measures the desirability of a transport option based on welfare economics [7], following an efficiency criterion that leads to recommending projects in which monetary gains outweigh the sum of monetary losses [8]. This process requires the conversion of each impact into monetary values, using discounted values to acknowledge people's attitude towards present and future consequences [10]. Yet, there is increasing awareness that the CBA cannot provide a comprehensive aid to transportation decision-making, as its efficiency-oriented approach fails to address sustainability, (intergenerational) justice, and fairness issues [4]. According to Vassallo and Bueno [11], the arbitrary assignment of monetary values to "priceless goods", such as most of the social and environmental ones, is a main limitation of the CBA, also considering that these "priceless goods" are at the very base of the concept of sustainability, a priority in contemporary transportation decision-making. Being aware of this, scholars and practitioners have explored other solutions. In the last decade, the MCA has gained some attention as an alternative or complementary method to the CBA. It consists of a multi-objective decision-making technique useful for *ex-ante* appraisal, particularly suitable to situations in which single criteria (e.g., economic efficiency) do not fully satisfy the scope of the analysis [12]. Within the MCA, the assessment criteria are chosen by the decision-makers. At a later stage, criteria are weighted according to target groups and stakeholders' preferences. The ability to capture multiple perspectives is also regarded as the main drawback of the method, given the excessive discretional power of involved experts. Because of this, the MCA is often mentioned by European institutions as a valid complement to transportation decision-making, but it is not part of official appraisal processes [13].

In short, traditional appraisal methods offer valuable insights into the effectiveness of transport projects and long-term policies, but the efficiency-oriented focus of the CBA and the discretionary aspects of the MCA hinder their capacity of providing comprehensive outcomes. Moreover, the complexity of these methods complicates their use by transport decision-makers and practitioners working for smaller entities and/or dealing with limited data. Indeed, the availability of vast and reliable information to both policymakers and involved stakeholders is fundamental for an effective appraisal process through the CBA and MCA. An additional element of complexity of these methods is the need for extensive and adequate stakeholders' involvement. Ignoring the perspective of some concerned groups can mislead the planning process, leading to suboptimal decisions. Within this context, several alternatives have been proposed and, in few cases, integrated as a support to conventional appraisal tools.

2.2 Beyond the Cost-Benefit Analysis: Towards an Index-Based Assessment

Vassallo and Bueno [11] proposed a method for the intertemporal aggregation of environmental, social, and economic impacts of transport projects, called STAR. STAR weights criteria through Rembrandt pairwise comparison, based on previous real-life application. This overcomes the mono-objective limit of the CBA while obtaining a comparable and quantifiable multi-objective evaluation. Alternatively, the family of Life Cycle Analyses can be adapted to assess social, territorial, or other categories of transport-related impacts. These methods, however, present similar complexities to that of the CBA. A consensus on the impacts to be included has not yet been reached, thus limiting the practicality of the tool [11]. According to the specific subject of evaluation, other tools have also been developed, such as the Wider Economic Impacts assessment [4, 14], Spatial Impacts Analysis, and partial or general equilibrium models [15]. Rather than replacing, they can support conventional appraisal to cover some of the fields that are left unassessed by them, with particular reference to social goals and objectives not pertaining to the concept of efficiency.

To evaluate impacts of transportation choices while reducing the overall procedural complexity, several authors and practitioners have opted for the use of performance indexes (or indicators). These can be supported by spatial analyses by means of Geographic Information Systems (GIS). Indexes can be both qualitative and quantitative, although the latter are more frequent as they allow for more comparable results [16, 17].

The main advantage of IM is that they simplify the assessment to straightforward formulas, clearly expressing the data input and the significance and interpretation of output values. Like more conventional and overarching assessment methods, index-based evaluation presents some challenges. First, the definition of the appropriate set of metrics for each context is complex. For this reason, it is important that transportation decision makers receive adequate education and that they can rely on extensive guidelines and manuals. Second, IM necessarily compare different scenarios: typically, they assess the difference between an *ex-ante* situation, where the transport project or policy is not in place, and one or more *ex-post* conditions, that must be adequately described and simulated. However, the completeness of the assessment can be enhanced by providing a scenario analysis, with several varying conditions [18].

Overall, IM can improve the efficacy and reliability of transportation decision-making by simplifying several steps of the process, from data acquisition and elaboration to the overview of different scenarios and varying conditions. The assessment through IM, then, is more manageable by means of professionals that are less expert in assessment techniques, but still are faced with the need to make the right decisions. Still, IM have some drawbacks: unlike more comprehensive analyses, they generally do not include a public engagement phase; their main advantage of being focused on selected aspects can also be a limit; and, mostly, they are only effective if they are carefully chosen and thoroughly calculated.

3 Performance Indexes in Transportation Decision-Making

Indicators have been used in the field of transport since the 1992 United Nations Conference on Environment and Development. Their adoption is traditionally linked to the study of sustainability within the transport sector [19]. Indexes are defined as "selected, targeted, and compressed variables that reflect public concerns and are of use to [transportation] decision makers" [20]. Whereas consensus on a universal methodology for the assessment of transport performances through IM has not yet been reached, several criteria that indicators must follow have been stated [21]. They include consistency with assessment goals, conciseness and appropriateness (based on needed detail), availability, measurability, robustness, comprehensibility, sensitivity and reciprocity. Sinha and Labi [1] say that performance metrics for transportation decision making must satisfy five properties:

- Suitability: the indicator should be influent and appropriate for the purpose at-stake;
- Measurableness: the indicator must be easily and objectively measurable. Results, moreover, must satisfy certain standards of reliability and accuracy;
- Realism: collecting, generating and extracting relevant data relating to the indicator should be possible without investing excessive resources;
- Defensibility: the indicator must be defined and developed in a clear and concise manner. Moreover, its assessment and interpretation should be clearly communicable to decision makers and public;
- Universality: IM should be generalizable and applicable to individual or combined modes. In this sense, the use of dimensionless quantities is a valid opportunity.

Performance measures are fundamental in assessing transportation decisions in relation to community objectives and resource allocation. More in detail, IM are particularly suitable for comparing trends and impacts across communities and territories, for understanding impacts of different decisions, and to evaluate progress towards or away from defined transport or society goals and targets [22]. Meyer [23] classifies indexes in general performance metrics (including population, mobility indicators, vehicle kilometers and hours), effectiveness measures (availability, quality, and supply of transport services), and efficiency measures (cost efficiency, occupancy ratio and vehicle utilization, productivity, energy use, financial sustainability). A different three-tier classification, based on service quality, outcomes, and cost efficiency, is proposed by several authors, including Carter and Lomax [24], Litman [25], and Vuchic [26].

Recently, IM have been adopted for the assessment of several impacts within the wider context of transportation decision-making. Relevant applications are those regarding urban resilience [27], accessibility [28, 29], sustainability performance [30, 31], safety [32], and energy use [33]. Notably, IM have been recently used to approach the assessment of innovative processes in urban logistics and first-last mile transportation of passengers and goods, which are among the most challenging aspects of contemporary transport operations and planning [22].

4 A Case Application of Index-Based Assessment

4.1 Freight-on-Transit

FOT (i.e., the integration of passengers and cargo flows on the same vehicles (typically, buses) is among the innovative solutions that are studied to reduce the significant impacts of the passenger-freight first-last mile [34, 35]. The discussion of first-last mile issues is not in the scope of this paper: interested readers can refer to Arvidsson et al. [36] and Cavallaro and Nocera [37] for a broad overview. FOT aims at increasing efficiency and efficacy (or reliability) of passenger and freight transport, resulting in more financially viable operations in both dense urban cores and rural, low demand areas [36, 38]. According to FOT studies, this implies lower direct and generated costs for all involved stakeholders, more care for environmental issues, and higher social value [22]. The concept mainly represents a conceptual, normative, and procedural innovation. Some physical modifications to the mobility system are needed (such as operating consolidation hubs and adapting transit fleets and stations to goods transport and deposit), but most assets, including the transport infrastructure, the natural and anthropic environments where the system operates, and the vehicles themselves, receive no or minor modifications. Yet, the business models, routing schemes, and priorities of both passenger and freight carriers change significantly. Other stakeholders of the passenger transport and supply chain fields are also impacted, from shopkeepers to planning agencies [39].

Assessing the effects of such an impactful transport measure, requiring limited initial investment and minimal structural modifications, is challenging. Traditional appraisal is not suitable for the objective, being unable to capture the benefits and drawbacks of locally developed transport policies [9]. This is exacerbated by the fact that FOT contributes to the social and environmental goals of the transport sector through operational innovation rather than through technological development or investment in sustainable infrastructure. The operational aspect of the FOT has indeed received a fair amount of attention from researchers. Several studies have developed or adapted routing problems to correctly model FOT in both urban and rural settings [40–43]. In most cases, scholars developed variants of metaheuristic approaches to routing and pickup-delivery problems with varying constraints. The mathematical solution of these problems, though, does not provide guidance to transportation decision makers to understand under which circumstances it is convenient from the perspective of the main involved stakeholders to switch to FOT rather than performing freight and passenger transport independently. Moreover, effective assessment should determine if FOT provides more frequent and cheaper services at comparable costs for both the funding authorities and customers, and if FOT contributes to increasing the social acceptability of transport and logistics. To address this issue, a few national and EU-funded projects have tested FOT applications in real life [44, 45], developing both a conceptual framework for FOT operations and an evaluation framework. Within this context, IM have been identified as a promising evaluation method, especially for assessing the sustainability, financial viability, and social impacts of the system.

4.2 Index-Based Assessment for Freight-on-Transit

Within transportation decision-making, IM are used to evaluate performances both at the network level (to program, set priority, and estimate funding) and project level (to select the best policy and design). Chosen indexes should respect the overall properties of indicators in order to be effective, as discussed in Sect. 3. Moreover, the set of indicators should be restricted and targeted to FOT and to the specific setting under evaluation, avoiding the risks of redundancy and inconsistency [46]. In accordance with Trentini and Mahlene [35], FOT on buses and other transit vehicles is particularly suitable for indicator-based assessment. Other types of passenger-freight integration, such as cargo trams on shared tracks and infrastructural and nodal sharing more in general, require more specific and technical evaluations. To effectively assess FOT and successfully substitute conventional appraisal methods, providing simpler and more thorough results in support to decision-makers, the selected set of indicators must be able to include the multiple perspectives of involved stakeholders (including transit operators and logistics companies, transit users, clients, residents, and retailers). Additionally, they must provide an organic synthesis of the passenger and freight components, safeguarding their peculiarities while evaluating a unified framework [22, 47].

Literature is not abundant when discussing the use of IM to assess FOT settings. However, scholars have recently taken some steps forward, following a framework based on literature [22, 48–51], also tested and validated within some EU-funded and national projects specific for FOT. Among them, NOVELOG [45] and COCKPIT [52] are notable. The focus is put on four main assessment categories (financial, operational, environmental, and social) [25, 48, 52] within the wider context of transport Efficiency, Effectiveness, and Equity (the "3E" of transport planning) [47]. Table 1 shows the categories of indexes for FOT evaluation proposed by different authors in up-to-date literature and the total number of suggested indicators.

Each of the categories presented in Table 1 can be assessed by means of a limited set of indexes, describing in detail the system's performance compared to the *status quo*. Referring to Bruzzone et al. [47], for instance, financial indicators include the transport cost per unit of passenger or freight and the affordability of the same movement for

Table 1. Indexes for assessing the performance of Freight-on-Transit: categories and set abundance.

Source	Categories of indexes	Suggested no of indexes
Ali et al. [53]	Strategic determinants, Information systems, Infrastructure management systems, City logistics	33
Anderson et al. [54]	Financial, Operational, Environmental	11
Behrends et al. [55]	Actors' involvement, Transport intensity, Traffic intensity, Technical capability	17
Bruzzone et al. [47]	Financial, Operational, Environmental, Social	11
Bruzzone et al. [22]	Operational, Environmental, Social	7
Cavallaro and Nocera [51]	Financial, Operational, Environmental, Social	8
Lindholm and Behrends [56]	Planning principles, Land use, Accessibility, Transport, Traffic	n.a
Litman [25]	Service quality, Outcomes, Cost efficiency	64[b]
Mazzarino and Rubini [49]	Transport supply, Transport availability, Spare capacity	4
Muriel et al. [57]	Livability, Operational	5
NOVELOG [45]	Economy and energy, Environment, Transport and mobility, Society, Policy and measure maturity, Social acceptance, User uptake	137[a]
Pietrzak et al. [58]	Service, Infrastructure, Impact, Quality of Life, Profit	9
Posset et al. [52]	Operational, Service quality, Environmental, Financial	96[a]
Shah et al. [59]	Demand and context, Affordability and accessibility, Mobility, Economic development, Quality of life, Operational efficiency, Environmental and resource conservation, Safety, Infrastructure condition and performance	20
Teychenne et al. [60]	Financial, Social	9
Van Duin et al. [61]	Jobs, Emissions, Safety, Operations	5

[a]Comprehensive lists from which decision-makers are expected to choose according to policy objectives and context characteristics.
[b] Selection made by the authors on more extended set designed for all transport modes.

customers. Operational indicators refer to overall distances, traffic, frequency, fuel and energy consumption, as well as to reliability and punctuality. Environmental indicators deal with the various types of pollution and with the impact on land use and, finally, social indicators include both internal aspects (i.e., the impact on the labor sector) and exogenous aspects (i.e., the stakeholders and public acceptance of transport and logistics operations).

5 Conclusions

In addition to conventional appraisal methods, IM are considered effective tools to assess operational innovation and transport policy. Yet, they aid transportation decision makers thanks to their simplicity but, meanwhile, great capacity to incorporate multiple perspectives and objectives, even in absence of relevant infrastructural or service investments. Simple does not mean trivial. The ability of IM to assess potential impacts of transport policies while reducing the complexity of the assessment process and its discretion is one of the main drivers for the promotion of index-based assessment. However, the definition of the set of indicators, of the timeframe to consider when performing the assessment, and the incorporation of index-based appraisal in consequent decision-making process is still challenging. To address this last issue, it is important to follow a scalable approach, starting with small-scale applications (including real-life tests and pilots, but also incremental application of fully developed policies), and continuously monitoring the coherence of observed impacts with the results of the appraisal process. Monitoring and adaptation, which are essential steps of any decision-making process, remain vital also following decisions aided by index-based appraisal.

When referring to freight on transport, the need for tools assisting transport planners and practitioners in choosing the most suitable indexes has been scarcely addressed. Still, future efforts should be expected by scholars and institutions to provide more comprehensive and standardized guidelines. These are needed to ensure that the index-based assessment is effectively chosen to aid transportation decision-making, substituting or in complement to conventional appraisal, and reducing the risk of unsupported decisions, overcomplexity, or incapacity to capture all relevant components to be assessed. The institutionalization of index-based assessment and its inclusion within transportation decision-making tools and plans (here including Sustainable Urban Mobility Plans), could be a relevant driver for the diffusion and perfection of the methodology.

References

1. Sinha, K.C., Labi, S.: Transportation Decision Making: Principles of Project Evaluation and Programming. Wiley, Hoboken (2011)
2. European Commission: Guide to cost-benefit analysis of investment projects: economic appraisal tool for cohesion policy 2014–2020. European Union (2015)
3. European Commission: Economic appraisal Vademecum. General principles and sector applications. European Union (2021)
4. Rothengatter, W.: Approaches to measure the wider economic impacts of high-speed rail and experiences from Europe. In: ADBI Working Paper. Asian Development Bank Institute, Tokyo (2019)

5. CEPS: Study on social impact assessment as a tool for mainstreaming social inclusion and social protection concerns in public policy in EU member states. London: Published Reports of the European Commission. http://csdle.lex.unict.it/docs/labourweb/Study-on-Social-Impact-Assessment-asa-tool-formainstreaming-social-inclusion-and-social-protection/2459.aspx. Accessed 09 Apr 23
6. Mishan, E.J., Quah, E.: Cost-Benefit Analysis. Routledge, Milton Park (2020)
7. Mouter, N.: Chapter one—standard transport appraisal methods. In: Mouter, N. (ed.) Advances in Transport Policy and Planning, vol. 7. Academic Press (2021)
8. Mackie, P., Nellthorp, J.: Cost–benefit analysis in transport. In: Handbook of Transport Systems and Traffic Control. Emerald Group Publishing Limited (2001)
9. Cappelli, A., Nocera, S.: Freight modal split models: data base, calibration problem and urban application. WIT Trans. Built Environ. **89**, 369–375 (2006)
10. Mouter, N.: A critical assessment of discounting policies for transport cost-benefit analysis in five European practices. Eur. J. Transp. Infrastruct. (2018)
11. Vassallo, J.M., Bueno, P.C.: Sustainability assessment of transport policies, plans and projects. In: Advances in Transport Policy and Planning, vol. 7. Elsevier (2021)
12. Thomopoulos, N., Grant-Muller, S., Tight, M.R.: Incorporating equity considerations in transport infrastructure evaluation: current practice and a proposed methodology. Eval. Prog. Plan. **32**(4), 351–359 (2009)
13. European Commission: Social issues (2021). https://transport.ec.europa.eu/transport-themes/social-issues_en
14. Cavallaro, F., Bruzzone, F., Nocera, S.: Effects of high-speed rail on regional accessibility. Transportation (2022). https://doi.org/10.1007/s11116-022-10291-y
15. The World Bank: Regional economic impact analysis of high-speed rail in China—main report: The World Bank - China and Mongolia Sustainable Development Sector Unit (2014)
16. Monzon, A., Ortega, E., Lopez, E.: Efficiency and spatial equity impacts of high-speed rail extensions in urban areas. Cities **30**, 18–30 (2013)
17. Pagliara, F.: Consumer's surplus: an equity measure of high speed rail investments. Sustainability **13**(8), 4537 (2021)
18. Bruzzone, F., Cavallaro, F., Nocera, S.: The effects of high-speed rail on accessibility and equity: evidence from the Turin-Lyon case-study. Socio-Econ. Plan. Sci., 101379 (2022)
19. JRC: Joint Research Centre Institute for Environment and Sustainability. Indicators to Assess Sustainability of Transport Activities. Office for Official Publications of the European Communities. Luxembourg: Office for Official Publications of the European Communities, Luxembourg (2009)
20. Gudmundsson, H.: Sustainable transport and performance indicators. Issues Environ. Sci. Technol. **20**, 35–63 (2004)
21. Seco, A.J.M., Gonçalves, J.H.G.: The quality of public transport: relative importance of different performance indicators and their potential to explain modal choice. In: Urban Transport XIII: Urban Transport and the Environment in the 21st Century, pp. 313–325 (2007)
22. Bruzzone, F., Cavallaro, F., Nocera, S.: The integration of passenger and freight transport for first-last mile operations. Transp. Policy **100**, 31–48 (2021)
23. Meyer, M.: Measuring that which cannot be measured at least according to conventional wisdom. In: Transportation Research Board. Proceedings from the 26th Annual Meeting on Performance Measures to Improve Transportation Systems and Agency Operations, Irvine, 29 October–1 November (2000)
24. Carter, D.N., Lomax, T.J.: Development and application of performance measures for rural public transportation operators. Transp. Res. Rec. **1338**, 28–36 (1992)
25. Litman, T.: A Good Example of Bad Transportation Performance Evaluation. Victoria Transport Policy Institute (2009)

26. Vuchic, V.R.: Urban Transit: Systems and Technology. Wiley, New York (2007)
27. Da Mata Martins, M.C., Rodrigues da Silva, A.N., Pinto, N.: An indicator-based methodology for assessing resilience in urban mobility. Transp. Res. Part D Transp. Environ. **77**, 352–363 (2019)
28. Vasconcelos, A.S., Farias, T.L.: Evaluation of urban accessibility indicators based on internal and external environmental costs. Transp. Res. Part D Transp. Environ. **17**, 433–441 (2012)
29. Lessa, D.A., Lobo, C., Cardoso, L.: Accessibility and urban mobility by bus in Belo Horizonte/Minas Gerais – Brazil. J. Transp. Geogr. **77**, 1–10 (2019)
30. Munira, S., San Santoso, D.: Examining public perception over outcome indicators of sustainable urban transport in Dhaka city. Case Stud. Transp. Policy **2**, 169–178 (2017)
31. Diez, J.M., Lopez-Lambas, M.E., Gonzalo, H., Rojo, M., Garcia-Martinez, A.: Methodology for assessing the cost effectiveness of sustainable urban mobility plans (SUMPs). J. Transp. Geogr. **68**, 22–30 (2018)
32. Castro-Nuno, M., Arevalo-Quijada, M.T.: Assessing urban road safety through multidimensional indexes: application of multicriteria decision making analysis to rank the Spanish provinces. Transp. Policy **68**, 118–129 (2018)
33. Gustaffsson, M., Svensson, N., Anderberg, S.: Energy performance indicators as policy support for public bus transport – the case of Sweden. Transp. Res. Part D Transp. Environ. **65**, 697–709 (2018)
34. European Commission: Green Paper - Towards a new culture for urban mobility (2007)
35. Trentini, A., Mahene, N.: Towards a shared urban transport system ensuring passengers & goods cohabitation. In: Working Paper, Trimestrale del Laboratorio Territorio Mobilità e Ambiente, Dipartimento di Pianificazione e Scienza del Territorio, Università degli Studi di Napoli Federico II (2010)
36. Arvidsson, N., Givoni, M., Woxenius, J.: Exploring last mile synergies in passenger and freight transport. Built Environ. **42**, 523–538 (2016)
37. Cavallaro, F., Nocera, S.: Integration of passenger and freight transport: a concept-centric literature review. Res. Transp. Bus. Manag. **43**, 100178 (2022)
38. Monios, J.: Geographies of governance in the freight transport sector: the British case. Transp. Res. Part A Policy Pract. **121**, 295–308 (2019)
39. Fatnassi, E., Chaouachi, J., Klibi, W.: Planning and operating a shared goods and passengers on-demand rapid transit system for sustainable city logistics. Transp. Res. Part B **81**, 440–460 (2015)
40. Ghilas, V., Demir, E., Van Woensel, T.: Integrating passenger and freight transportation: model formulation and insights. In: Working Paper. TU/e Eindhoven (2013)
41. Ghilas, V., Demir, E., Van Woensel, T.: The pickup and delivery problem with time windows and scheduled lines. Inf. Syst. Oper. Res. **54**(2), 147–167 (2016)
42. Jansen, T.A.M.: Development of a design model for integrated passengers and freight transportation system. Master thesis. TU/e School of Industrial Engineering (2014)
43. Spoor, J.M.: Replenishing nanostores in megacities for a consumer packaged goods company. Master thesis. TU/e School of Industrial Engineering (2015)
44. TKI, Dinalog: Cargo hitching. https://www.dinalog.nl/en/project/cargo-hitching/. Accessed 08 Apr 23
45. NOVELOG: NOVELOG Deliverable D.3.1 "Evaluation Framework" (Project report), NOVELOG Project (2016)
46. Hope, J., Fraser, R.: Beyond Budgeting: How Managers Can Break Free from the Annual Performance Trap. Harvard Business School Press, Boston (2003)
47. Bruzzone, F., Cavallaro, F., Nocera, S.: Appropriate key performance indicators for evaluating integrated passenger-freight transport. In: Nathanail, E.G., Gavanas, N., Adamos, G. (eds.) CSUM 2022. LNITI, pp. 1278–1290. Springer, Cham (2023). https://doi.org/10.1007/978-3-031-23721-8_103

48. Eboli, L., Mazzulla, G.: Performance indicators for an objective measure of public transport service quality (2012)
49. Mazzarino, M., Rubini, L.: Smart urban planning: evaluating urban logistics performance of innovative solutions and sustainable policies in the Venice Lagoon—the results of a case study. Sustainability **11**, 4580 (2019)
50. Litman, T.: Developing indicators for comprehensive and sustainable transport planning. Transp. Res. Rec. **2017**, 10–15 (2007)
51. Cavallaro, F., Nocera, S.: Flexible-route integrated passenger–freight transport in rural areas. Transp. Res. Part A Policy Pract. **169**, 103604 (2023)
52. Posset, M., Haeuslmayer, H., Gronalt, M.: Clear, operable and comparable key performance indicators for intermodal transportation. www2.ffg.at/verkehr/file.php?id=340. Accessed 07 Apr 2023
53. Ali, N., Javid, M.A., Hussain, S.A., Abdullah, M.: Key performance indicators for sustainable freight transport and scenario-based impediments in Pakistan freight industry. IPTEK J. Proc. Ser., 1–8 (2020)
54. Anderson, S., Allen, J., Browne, M.: Urban logistics—how can it meet policy makers' sustainability objectives? J. Transp. Geogr. Sustain. Interact. Between Extern. Eff. Transp. (Part Spec. Issue, 23–99) **13**, 71–81 (2005)
55. Behrends, S., Lindholm, M., Woxenius, J.: The impact of urban freight transport: a definition of sustainability from an actor's perspective. Transp. Plan. Technol. **31**, 693–713 (2008)
56. Lindholm, M., Behrends, S.: Challenges in urban freight transport planning – a review in the Baltic Sea Region. J. Transp. Geogr. Spec. Sect. Rail Transit Syst. High Speed Rail **22**, 129–136 (2012)
57. Muriel, J.E., Zhang, L., Fransoo, J.C., Perez-Franco, R.: Assessing the impacts of last mile delivery strategies on delivery vehicles and traffic network performance. Transp. Res. Part C Emerg. Technol. **144**, 103915 (2022)
58. Pietrzak, K., Pietrzak, O., Montwiłł, A.: Light freight railway (LFR) as an innovative solution for sustainable urban freight transport. Sustain. Cities Soc. **66**, 102663 (2021)
59. Shah, Y., Manaugh, K., Badami, M., El-Geneidy, A.: Diagnosing transportation: developing key performance indicators to assess urban transportation systems. Transp. Res. Rec. **2357**, 1–12 (2013)
60. Bly, P.H., Teychenne, P.: Three financial and socio-economic assessments of a personal rapid transit system. In: Automated People Movers 2005: Moving to Mainstream (2005)
61. Van Duin, R., Wiegmans, B., Tavasszy, L., Hendriks, B., He, Y.: Evaluating new participative city logistics concepts: the case of cargo hitching. Transp. Res. Procedia (2019). 3rd International Conference "Green Cities – Green Logistics for Greener Cities"

Agrovoltaic as an Answer to the Difficult Relationship Between Land Use and Photovoltaics. A Case Study from Apulia Region

Andrea Gallo[1(✉)] and Claudio Sossio De Simone[2]

[1] Univesity of Trieste, Piazzale Europa 1, 34127 Trieste, Italy
andrea.gallo3@phd.units.it

[2] University of Rome "TorVergata", Via Columbia 1, 00133 Rome, Italy

Abstract. Decarbonization in the electricity production sector represents a fundamental step for reducing greenhouse gas emissions and achieving the objectives set by the Paris Agreements for 2050. Reflecting on the use of rural areas in the 21st century is an extremely central topic in the debate on the long-term development of renewable energies. While cities show a model of energy consumption in constant growth, rural areas assume a significant role in terms of potential development regarding renewable energy sources. This new specialization of these areas could represent both an effective response to climate change and a reduction in dependence on fossil fuels to mitigate respective economic and environmental impacts. The proposed contribution aims, as a first step, to describe the different impacts caused by the implementation of renewable energy sources in rural areas with reference to the Tavoliere della Puglia study area. This research will take into account the economic, energy, and geographic factors underlying the localization of some photovoltaic parks. In addition, the experience of some companies in the sector, active for several years in designing, building and managing innovative plants for the production of electricity from renewable sources, will also be considered. By analyzing the official cartography (e.g. Regional Territorial Landscape Plan) and participatory cartography (e.g. OpenStreetMap) at the municipal scale in a GIS-based approach, the main changes in land use and the impact of photovoltaic parks will be estimated, also in relation to a dimension of planning and environmental management. The first results obtained would finally highlight a clear contrast between the conservation of land with strong agricultural potential and the massive expansion of renewable energy production in rural areas.

Keywords: Agrivoltaic system · Land Use · Renewable energy · Apulia

The paper is the result of the joint work of the two authors. However, Claudio Sossio de Simone wrote paragraphs 2–3, while Andrea Gallo wrote paragraphs 4–5. The paragraph 1 was written togheter.

O. Gervasi et al. (Eds.): ICCSA 2023 Workshops, LNCS 14107, pp. 547–559, 2023.
https://doi.org/10.1007/978-3-031-37114-1_38

1 Introduction

By definition, fossil fuels are non-renewable sources [1]. The excessive consumption of these energy sources is producing negative externalities both for the environment [2], in reference to climate change, and for the problem of resource scarcity and the inevitable economic impact on the energy resource market. This has highlighted the importance of decarbonization through the transition to renewable and clean energy sources, in which solar energy represents the primary resource [3]. Photovoltaic technologies have experienced a rapid technological upswing in recent years, improving their efficiency and significantly lowering production and installation costs [4]. Today, photovoltaic energy represents the best possible tool for meeting the constantly increasing global energy demand. The IEA estimates that, to meet the energy demand, by 2050 over 16% of the energy produced will need to come from photovoltaic sources [5]. However, the photovoltaic technology poses a concrete problem that we will try to analyze in this contribution: due to the relatively widespread nature of solar energy, large surfaces are needed to be covered with photovoltaic panels. Part of this demand can be met by integrating photovoltaic modules into traditional buildings and through photovoltaic roofs. However, to achieve the set goals, the key role that ground-based plants will assume appears fundamental. The use of large tracts of land for solar power plants will increase competition for land resources, as food production demand and energy demand are growing and competing for limited land resources [6]. These coupled land challenges can be mitigated by using the concept of agrivoltaics, that is, the joint development on the same surface of a photovoltaic solar power plant integrated with conventional agriculture [7].

Land consumption continues to transform the Italian territory at high speed. In the last year, new artificial covers affected 69.1 km^2, or an average of about 19 ha per day. This increase shows a clear acceleration compared to the data collected in the recent past, sharply reversing the trend of reduction in recent years and causing our country to lose 2.2 m^2 of land every second. More precisely, at the national level, the artificial cover of the land can now be estimated at about 21,500 km^2 (86% of which are located on useful soil), to which another 624 km^2 of areas subject to other forms of direct alteration due to artificial land cover (such as non-paved greenhouses and bridges) must be added, which are not considered as causing land consumption [8]. The relationship between land consumption and population dynamics confirms that the link between demography and processes of urbanization and infrastructure is not direct, and there is an increase in artificial surfaces even in the presence of stabilization or, in many cases, a decrease in the resident population, with an increase in land consumed per capita from 2020 to 2021 of 3.46 m^2/person and 5.46 m^2/person in two years (Fig. 1).

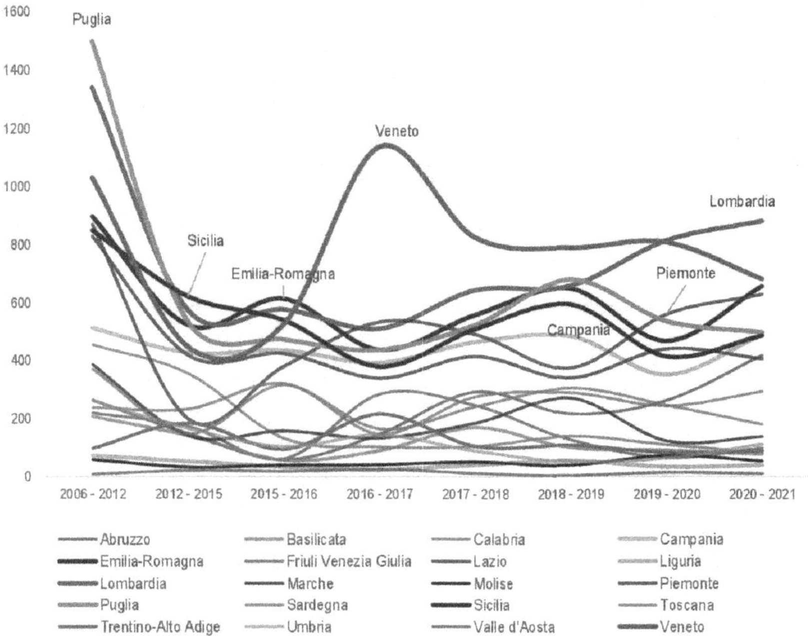

Fig. 1. Regional net annual land consumption trend from 2006 to 2021. Source: ISPRA elaborations on SNPA cartography (Source: ISPRA, 2022)

2 Solar Power Plants and Land Consumption in Italy: A Complex Relationship

Among the causes of land consumption in our country, according to what is reported by Superior Institute for Environmental Protection and Research [8], photovoltaic installations can be considered. It should be noted that according to the data collected in the National Land Consumption Map, a distinction is made between ground-mounted installations, which are identified in a specific class, and those present on non-ground surfaces (buildings, warehouses, sheds, greenhouses, etc.) which fall into other classes. Focusing on ground-mounted installations, according to the Photovoltaic Solar Statistics Report [9], the factors that determine the incidence of ground-mounted photovoltaic installations are multiple, including geographic location, morphological characteristics of the territory, weather conditions, and availability of suitable areas. As a result, the distribution of installed photovoltaic panel power by location among the different regions is highly heterogeneous. Indeed, according to GSE data (2021) [9], at the national level, only 36% of the 22,594 MW installed at the end of 2021 is located on the ground, while the remaining 64% is distributed on non-ground surfaces.

The greater penetration of ground-mounted photovoltaic panels is observed in the southern regions, and in particular in Puglia and Basilicata, where there is a relatively high incidence of ground-mounted installations (respectively, 72% and 64% of the regional total). In contrast, in the northern regions, there is widespread penetration of the capacity of non-ground installations, with maximum values observed well beyond 90% in Liguria, Lombardy, Valle d'Aosta, and in the provinces of Trento and Bolzano. In general, considering the ISPRA [8] data and the GSE report (2021) [9], the new ground-mounted photovoltaic installations (detected between 2020 and 2021) will have a total of 70 ha of land consumption corresponding to a power of about 37 MW. Indeed, in 2022 the total area occupied by ground-mounted photovoltaic panels is 644,9 ha corresponding to a power of 365 MW [10]. Overall, at the national level, ground-mounted PV occupies between 15,200 and 17,560 ha, for a total power output greater than 25 GW [10] (Fig. 2).

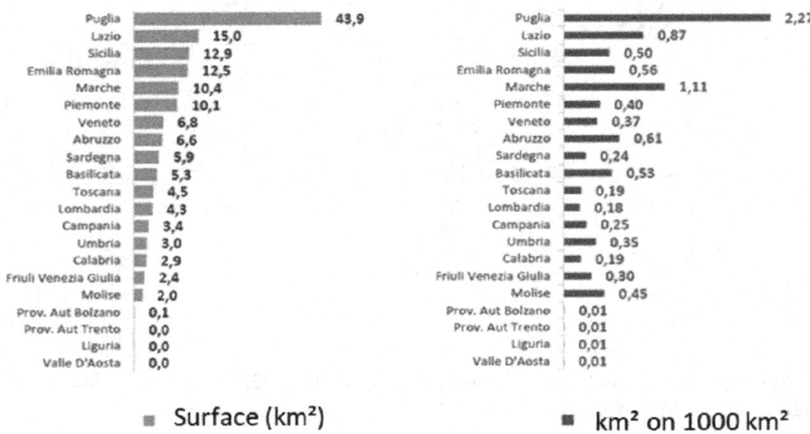

Fig. 2. Distribution of the ground-mounted PV in the Italian regions at the end of 2021 (Source: GSE, 2021).

On the other hand, the obsessive focus on renewable energy and the growing need for decarbonization is profoundly changing energy policies both internationally and nationally [11]. In line with the European Energy Plan (Repower EU)[1], Italy's Ecological Transition Plan (PTE)[2] envisages that by 2030, 70% of electricity will come from renewable sources, mainly from photovoltaic solar energy. This goal is already partly outlined in the Integrated National Plan for Energy and Climate (Pniec)[3], which in 2019 hoped to add about 30 GW of capacity to the national photovoltaic capacity of 22 GW, to exceed a capacity of 50 GW [12]. According to some estimates by ISPRA [15], this direction would lead to an 8-fold increase in total net annual land take (Fig. 3).

[1] https://commission.europa.eu/strategy-and-policy/priorities-2019-2024/european-green-deal/repowereu-affordable-secure-and-sustainable-energy-europe_en. Last accessed 24/03/2023.

[2] https://www.italiadomani.gov.it/en/il-piano/missioni-pnrr/rivoluzione-verde-transizione-ecologica.html. Last accessed 24/03/2023.

[3] https://www.mise.gov.it/images/stories/documenti/it_final_necp_main_en.pdf. Last accessed 24/03/2023.

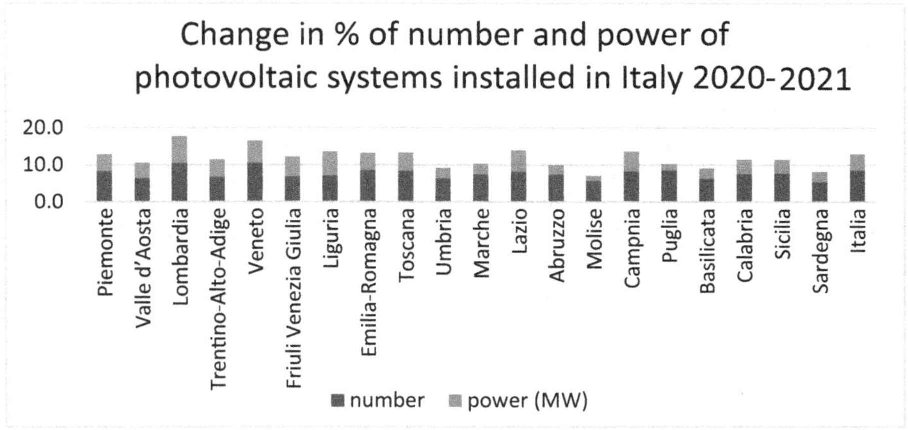

Fig. 3. Change in % of number and power of photovoltaic systems installed in Italy 2020–2021 (Source: GSE, 2021; by Author).

3 Observation and Analysis From Apulia Region: The Case of Foggia Area

An exemplary case of this challenging relationship, between renewable energy installations and land consumption is Apulia and in particular the Foggia administrative province.

It is to be recalled, that in the area is located the Tavoliere, one of the symbols of Southern Italy's rural identity. Indeed, between the sixteenth and eighteenth centuries, this area was one of the protagonists of the "great transhumance" between Abruzzo and Puglia [13]. In addition, the area is among the main intervention zones of the land reform of the early 1950s, which strengthened the supremacy of arable land and woody crops. In today's Tavoliere, traces of these processes can still be seen, remnants of a heritage not entirely lost [14]. This heritage contributes to vitalizing the richness and variety of the agricultural and productive structures of the region, which stand out from the rest of Italy [16].

Within the framework of the Regional Territorial Landscape Plan[4], the region has defined particular measures for the location and installation of plants powered by renewable sources, including photovoltaic plants, in ecological safeguards of the rural heritage [17, 18]. On the other hand, Apulia with reference to the regional distribution of the number and power of photovoltaic plants (at the end of 2020) takes the Italian leadership in terms of installed capacity. A total of 2,900 MW is produced here, accounting for 13.4% of the national photovoltaic capacity. In the region is registering, moreover, the highest average size of installations (53.4 kW), of which 72% of these are on the ground (GSE, 2021). However, in 2022 Italy produced 28.161 GWh, which 4.194 GWh from the Apulia region [10]. Moreover, to consider that between 2006 and 2021, there are an estimated 13,000 ha of land consumed in the region, and there are about 5,000 ha occupied by ground-mounted PV installations [8],

[4] https://www.sit.puglia.it/portal/portale_pianificazione_regionale/Piano%20Paesaggistico%20Territoriale.

On observing the trend at a local scale, this is even more exemplified. According to Aretano *et al.* (2022) [19], it is evaluated in relative terms (in thousandths, ‰) the loss of land taken to ground-mounted photovoltaic installations compared to the total area of municipalities in the province of Foggia. Indeed, on the geographical distribution of PV farms of Tavoliere area, using a GIS approach [35][5], we created the land take map (Fig. 4) of the municipalities of Foggia.

The range of estimated land take across the entire set of municipalities is between 0.18‰ and 10.53‰. Considering only municipalities (28 on the 64) with PV farms, the average of loss in soil is 0.82 ‰ and an average of 33 ha of PV in each municipality. Conversely, the average Pv size is 3.8 ha, and most plants do not outgrow the size 1.8 ha.

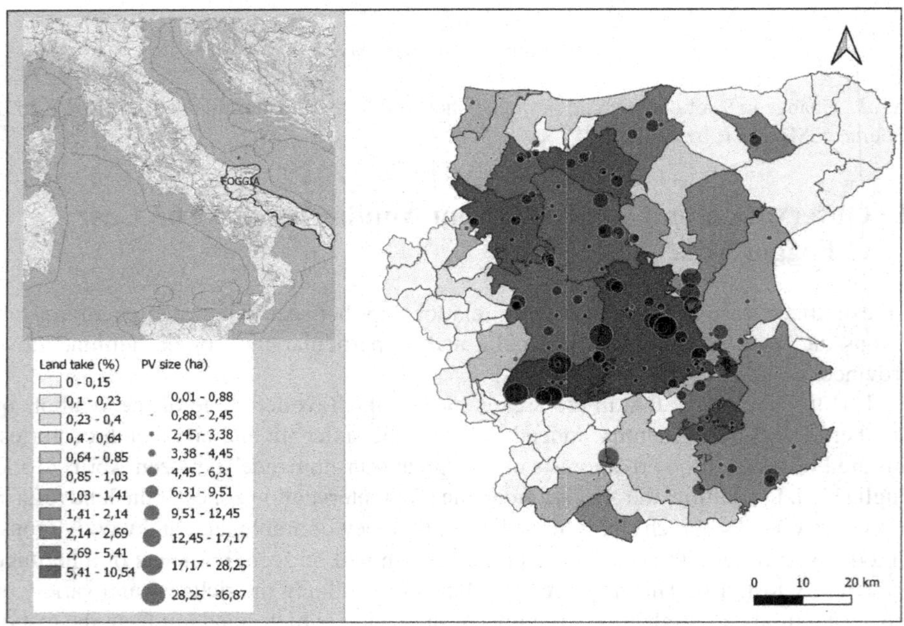

Fig. 4. Change The Land take (‰) at municipality level (Author: De Simone).

In this scenario, a remarkable transformation of the rural landscape is clearly evident. As reported by Arpa Puglia, moreover, in the Foggia area 830 ha of agricultural land has been lost [19]. The overlaying information layers of ground-mounted photovoltaic (National Land Use Map, 2021) and map of agricultural land (Land use map SIT Puglia, 2011) confirmed the prevision. Indeed, out of about 1,000 registered hectares of PV 541 of them are on agricultural land which means that on average 43% of each individual plant is located on agricultural land (Fig. 5)[6].

[5] In QGIS software (3.28), the tools of Map Algebra and Raster Analysis were used both to geolocalisation data from the National Land Use Map (2021) about ground-mounted photovoltaic installations both to extract the municipal level share of land take.

[6] The projection is taking into account the period 2011–2021.

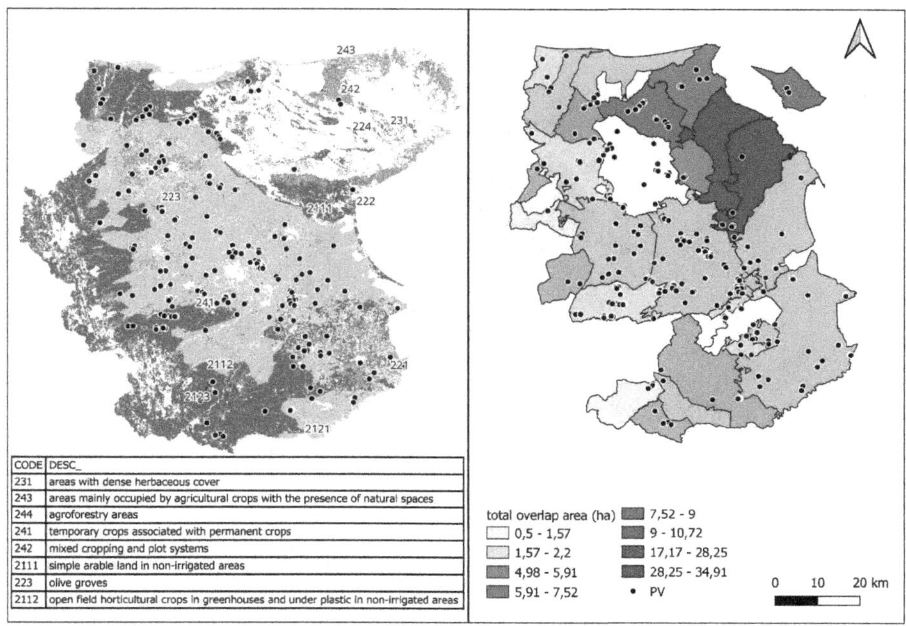

Fig. 5. The overlaying of ground-mounted photovoltaic (National Land Use Map, 2021) on map of agricultural land (Land use map SIT Puglia, 2011) (Author: De Simone).

With regard to agricultural landscape, in addition, it is favorable to compare the location of ground-mounted photovoltaic with the land use capacity map of the Regional (LCC), aimed at assessing the productivity of soils for agro-sylvo-pastoral uses. Also in according to Arpa Puglia prevision, the 44% o PV fall in the Apulia are classified as having no limitation for agricultural use and that would have required greater attention to the agronomic characteristics of the soils favorable to silvo-agro-pastoral activities [19]. Moreover, at municipality level, more than 70% of PVs are located on arable and arboreal land (II s class on LCC Map) (Fig. 6).

On that basis, rural areas assume a relevant role in terms of potential development with regard to renewable energy sources. This new specialization of such areas could be an effective response in the fight against climate change and a reduction of energy dependence on fossil sources. In this perspective, they can take a key rule to mitigate the economic and environmental impacts on a national scale. What is the price, however, in terms of land take and loss of identity heritage of our country's rural areas?

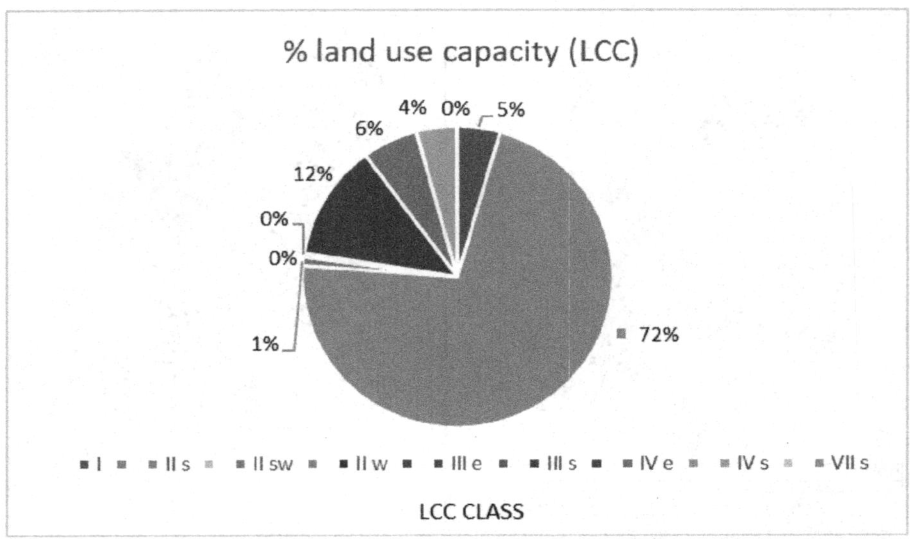

Fig. 6. Proportion of Land Use Capacity data (LCC) of research area (Author: De Simone)

4 Agrovoltaics Practice-Techniques and Classification

Agrovoltaics is a system that combines agricultural production with that of renewable energy. This is done through the installation of modular solar panels placed on raised supports, using the space below for traditional cultivation of plants, vegetables, fruits and vegetables [20]. The fundamental aspect of agrovoltaics derives from the maximization of the potential of the soil used, as the same area will be allocated ambiguously to the production of renewable electricity and agricultural production [32]. The replacement of traditional agricultural activity and the introduction of photovoltaic systems are motivated by several competitive advantages: firstly, the use of photovoltaic panels can be useful in providing shade to crops, which subsequently translates into a reduction in water consumption, with savings that can reach up to 20% [21]; photovoltaic panels can also protect the crops underneath from adverse weather conditions such as heat waves, strong winds, or torrential rains and hail [31]. In light of these benefits for the agricultural sector, it should be emphasized that the renewable energy generated by photovoltaic panels can be used to power irrigation systems, agricultural equipment and lighting systems, reducing dependence on fossil fuels, lowering greenhouse gas emissions and generating positive economic impact, not only in terms of energy cost savings but also as a source of profit from self-produced energy not consumed and fed into the distribution network [22].

However, in light of these numerous advantageous aspects, it is also necessary to consider some critical issues associated with the use of agrovoltaics: the installation of photovoltaic panels mounted on mobile trackers at various heights would cause shading of the agricultural land, reducing the amount of solar radiation received by the crops [23, 34]. The photovoltaic system will therefore require careful and accurate planning in the inclination of the panels in order to find the combination capable of maximizing energy and agricultural productivity [21]. The second aspect to consider is the management and maintenance costs of the photovoltaic systems, and finally the most significant problem is the installation costs of the systems, which can be up to 40% higher than common ground-based photovoltaic systems. Agrovoltaic systems commonly used can be classified based on their different characteristics and applications. A first distinction is that of open or closed systems: a closed system refers to photovoltaic modules installed on the roofs of greenhouses. In contrast, open systems are those in which the photovoltaic system is positioned in an open area [24]. There are then three different structural possibilities for agrovoltaic systems: the construction of a tensile structure between 3 and 5 m in height, under which traditional agricultural practices are adopted; the insertion of ground-mounted photovoltaic panels, increasing the distance between different rows of vegetables, and finally, the installation of vertically inserted photovoltaic panels between rows [25]. While the dual use of the land will lead to economic and productive benefits, it must be considered that these installations will inevitably have a significant visual environmental impact [26, 33]. Regarding photovoltaic systems mounted on a raised structure, it should be noted that these will usually be mounted on mobile trackers, capable of adapting their angle to obtain the best possible exposure for both electricity production and agricultural needs [24].

Another classification of agrovoltaic systems is based on the different agricultural practices adopted: field crops, referring to traditional field crops following a highly mechanized supply chain, or orchards, which refer to fruit tree cultivation planted in a specific arrangement based on rows and requiring some protection from adverse weather conditions.

To evaluate the efficiency of different agrovoltaic systems, it is possible to use some indicaTo evaluate the efficiency of different agrovoltaic systems, it is possible to use some indicators, which we will now proceed to present [27].

The first indicator under analysis is the Ground Coverage Ratio (GCR): the ratio of the area covered by photovoltaic panels to the cultivated agricultural land. This indicator can be expressed by the following formula: $GCR = \frac{A_{PV}}{A_{Agr}}$.

The second indicator is the energy and agricultural yield of the land. The energy produced Y_{el} (expressed in MWh/hectare) represents the amount of solar energy produced during a year per hectare. Y_{Agr} on the other hand, indicates agricultural production expressed in kg per hectare (kg/ha).

The third key indicator for evaluating the efficiency of photovoltaic systems is the so-called "spatial efficiency," a measure that was created to measure the increase in land efficiency by installing a photovoltaic system and allocating the land for agricultural use at the same time. The indicator used to measure land efficiency is the Land Equivalent Ratio (LER). This index is constructed from the following formula: $LER = \frac{Y_{Agr,AGR}}{Y_{Agr,N}} + \frac{Y_{el,AGR}}{Y_{el,N}}$.

In this indicator, Y_{Agr} denotes traditional agricultural production (N) or using an agrovoltaic system (AGR), while Y_{el} represents electricity production using agrovoltaic particles compared to traditional production. If the LER index is greater than 1 then the use of agrovoltaics will imply an increase in overall land productivity, otherwise this practice will be inefficient [27].

4.1 Contextualization of the Regulatory Framework in Italy

The recent GUIDELINES (2022) from the Ministry of Ecological Transition and Sustainable Development (MITE) regarding agrovoltaic installations attempt to provide a unique definition and describe the characteristics of such installations, with the aim of experimenting with new practices and new design solutions. The Simplification Bis Decree (Decree-Law 77/2021) and the corresponding Law (108/2021) passed in the same year have already been important in this regard.

Moreover, the National Recovery and Resilience Plan (PNRR) includes a mission called "Green Revolution and Ecological Transition" which aims to incorporate this legislation and allocate 1.1 billion euros to achieve a production capacity from agrovoltaic installations of 1.04 GW.

According to the available data, the MITE predicts a cost of around 750 €/kW for traditional type installations (800 €/kW with single-axis tracking) and up to about 1,200 €/kW for systems with seed crops (with a variability of about 375 €/kW) and 950 €/kW for systems with permanent crops (with a variability of about 270 €/kW). On average, there is a 60% increase compared to a traditional installation for a seed crop system, and a 25% increase for a permanent crop system. On average, there is a 13% reduction in O&M costs compared to a traditional installation for an agrovoltaic system. As for the cost of generating electricity (LCOE), starting from 55–69 €/MWh for ground-mounted single-axis tracking installations, there is a range of 73–93 €/MWh for agrovoltaic systems with seed crops and 60–76 €/MWh for systems with permanent crops. These values also include a variability of about 25 €/MWh for systems with seed crops and 15 €/MWh for systems with permanent crops due to possible variations in investment costs. It should be noted that, while the cost difference with ground-mounted installations is quite significant for systems with seed crops (on average around 35%), it is rather moderate for systems with permanent crops (10%). Finally, the monitoring system for the production of electricity from agrovoltaic installations, as evaluated in paragraph 3.3, does not involve any extra costs compared to those associated with monitoring a photovoltaic installation. This monitoring system involves the collection of data already widely shared in real-time by thousands of installations throughout the country through a portal managed by the GSE.

5 Conclusions and Final Consideration

Meeting the constantly increasing global energy demand, assisted by a growing push towards an ecological transition and the search for renewable energy sources [25], represents one of the most daring and pressing challenges to face, with the awareness that this process can only happen by moving away from the use of non-renewable fossil energy sources in favor of sustainable energy production. In the current economic and social landscape (from the current war in Ukraine, to the pandemic, etc.), market uncertainty and the high volatility of commodity and energy prices have highlighted the need and urgency to try to pursue the goal of independence from non-renewable energy sources. For these reasons, we have decided to present this contribution on an innovative practice such as agrovoltaics [28]. Common solar photovoltaic systems require large areas due to the relatively dispersed nature of solar energy. Part of this demand can be met by using photovoltaic systems integrated into buildings and roofs, but ground-mounted photovoltaic parks are the primary driver of growth and development in the widespread use of these renewable energy sources. The use of large plots of land for the construction of solar parks generates, as a direct consequence, a decision-making process in the land-use destination, as food production and energy production currently compete for the limited resources of the land. To address this important debate, this decision-making process could be overcome by using the emerging concept of agrovoltaics: developing a photovoltaic park on the same area of land, built on a tensile structure at a significant height above the ground (from 2.5 to 5 m), to allow traditional agriculture to develop in the underlying soil [29]. This technological solution thus allows sharing agricultural land with photovoltaic energy production, enabling the farmer to continue producing crops using commonly used techniques (such as tractors, harvesters, etc.) and allowing the same area to be used for a photovoltaic system as well. Photovoltaic panels mounted on mobile trackers that follow the daily course in order to modulate shading and favor crop growth. Through the first applications of the agrovoltaic production model, an initial measurement of the technical potential has suggested that the value of energy production combined with shade-tolerant crop production has generated an increase in value that ranges between 30% and 60% of the economic value of farming businesses that implement such agrovoltaic systems instead of conventional agriculture. The use of shade-tolerant crops allows minimizing crop yield losses and thus maintaining crop price stability. Furthermore, this dual use of agricultural land can have a significant effect on national photovoltaic production.

Agrovoltaic systems therefore incorporate efficient dual use of agricultural land resources, namely arable land for agricultural and photovoltaic production, or pasture for animal breeding and photovoltaic production. There are various test sites and some commercial installations around the world to reduce pressure on agricultural spaces. This combined use would allow a reduction in conflicts regarding land use between the energy and agricultural sectors. It is expected that total soil productivity could increase significantly due to the effects of shading and altered water availability. This could even develop beneficial effects for all, such as reducing heat stress and providing more consistent water supply to plants during the summer to improve the resilience of agricultural systems in a changing climate [30]. Agrovoltaic systems could contribute to promoting regional development in the agricultural and energy sectors. By making the agricultural sector more attractive (ensuring higher profits per hectare), the younger generation can be encouraged to stay in rural areas, thereby strengthening infrastructure and the economy. In the EU, urbanization and energy dependence can be combated while supporting the transition towards decentralized energy supply. The potential of these dual production systems for both the agricultural and photovoltaic sectors has resulted in the inclusion of agrovoltaics in the PNRR, with an investment of 2.6 billion euros in the sector. This once again highlights how such practices can represent a fundamental driver of sustainable development for the future.

References

1. Droege, P.: Renewable energy and the city: urban life in an age of fossil fuel depletion and climate change. Bull. Sci. Technol. Soc. **22**(2), 87–99 (2002)
2. El Fadel, M., Rachid, G., El-Samra, R., Boutros, G.B., Hashisho, J.: Emissions reduction and economic implications of renewable energy market penetration of power generation for residential consumption in the MENA region. Energy Policy **52**, 618–627 (2013)
3. Granovskii, M., Dincer, I., Rosen, M.: Greenhouse gas emissions reduction by use of wind and solar energies for hydrogen and electricity production: economic factors. Int. J. Hydrog. Energy **32**(8), 927–931 (2007)
4. Pearce, J.M.: Photovoltaics–a path to sustainable futures. Futures **34**(7), 663–674 (2002)
5. IEA: Technology Roadmap: Solar Photovoltaic Energy (2014)
6. Nonhebel, S.: Renewable energy and food supply: will there be enough land? Renew. Sustain. Energy Reviewsa **9**(2), 191–201 (2005)
7. Calvert, K., Mabee, W.: More solar farms or more bioenergy crops? Mapping and assessing potential land-use conflicts among renewable energy technologies in eastern Ontario. Appl. Geogr. **56**, 209–221 (2015)
8. Munafò, M.: Consumo di suolo, dinamiche territoriali e servizi ecosistemici. Istituto Superiore per la Protezione e la Ricerca Ambientale, Roma (2022)
9. Gestore dei Servizi Energetici (GSE): Solare Fotovoltaico - Rapporto Statistico 2021 (2021). https://www.gse.it/Dati-e-Scenari_site/statistiche_site. Accessed 26 Mar 2023
10. Gestore dei Servizi Energetici: Infotovoltaico. Statistiche trimestrali sul settore fotovoltaico in italia (GSE 2022) (2022). https://www.gse.it/documenti_site/Documenti%20GSE/Rapporti%20statistici/GSE%20-%20Nota%20trimestrale%20FTV%20-%20quarto%20trimestre%202022.pdf. Accessed 26 Mar 2023
11. Battisti, G.: La questione energetica nel terzo millennio. Geotema **65**, 24–34 (2021)
12. Sesana, I.: Fotovoltaico a terra: tra rischi e benefici per il (fragile) suolo. Altreconomia **248**, 1–10 (2022)
13. Di Cicco P.: La transumanza e gli antichi tratturi del Tavoliere. In: «Civiltà della transumanza». Atti della Giornata di Studi (Castel del Monte, 4 agosto 1990), Cosmo Iannone Editore, Isernia, pp. 107–103 (1992)
14. Rinella, A., Rinella, F.: Il Tavoliere della transumanza tra iconemi relitti e rizomi resilienti. Geotema, 166–177 (2021)
15. Sistema Nazionale per la Protezione dell'Ambiente (SNPA), Consumo di suolo e servizi ecosistemici. Edizione 2022. Report tecnico SNPA (2022)
16. Varraso, I., Cesari, O.: Concentrazione delle coltivazioni ortive e produzione del carciofo in provincia di Foggia (Puglia). In: L'apporto della Geografia tra rivoluzioni e riforme, pp. 1879–1889 (2019)
17. Legambiente: Scacco matto alle Fonti Rinnovabili (2021). https://www.legambiente.it/wp-content/uploads/2021/11/Scacco-matto-alle-rinnovabili_report-2022.pdf. Accessed 26 Mar 2023
18. Labianca, M.: Towards the new common agricultural policy for biodiversity: custodian farmers for sustainable agricultural practices in the Apulia region (South of Italy). Belgeo **4**, 1–21 (2021)
19. Aretano, R., La Ghezza,V., Radicchio, B., Rotolo, C., Ungaro, N., Campanaro, V.: Impianti fotovoltaici in Puglia: valutazione integrata degli impatti sulle aree agricole. In: Munafò, M. (eds.) Istituto Superiore per la Protezione e la Ricerca Ambientale, Roma, pp. 421–426 (2022)
20. Amaducci, S., Yin, X., Colauzzi, M.: Agrivoltaic systems to optimise land use for electric energy production. Appl. Energy **220**, 545–561 (2018)

21. Trommsdorff, M., et al.: Combining food and energy production: design of an agrivoltaic system applied in arable and vegetable farming in Germany. Renew. Sustain. Energy Rev. **140**, 110694 (2021)
22. Dinesh, H., Pearce, J.M.: The potential of agrivoltaic systems. Renew. Sustain. Energy Rev. **54**, 299–308 (2016)
23. Agostini, A., Colauzzi, M., Amaducci, S.: Innovative agrivoltaic systems to produce sustainable energy: an economic and environmental assessment. Appl. Energy **281**, 116102 (2021)
24. Sekiyama, T., Nagashima, A.: Solar sharing for both food and clean energy production: Performance of agrivoltaic systems for corn, a typical shade-intolerant crop. Environments **6**(6), 65 (2019)
25. Dupraz, C., Marrou, H., Talbot, G., Dufour, L., Ferard, Y.: Combining solar photovoltaic panels and food crops for optimising land use: towards new agrivoltaic schemes. Renew. Energy **36**(10), 2725–2732 (2011)
26. Willockx, B., Herteleer, B., Ronsijn, B., Uytterhaegen, B., Cappelle, J.: A standardized classification and performance indicators of agrivoltaic systems. In: EU PVSEC Proceedings (2020)
27. Willockx, B., Lavaert, C., Cappelle, J.: Geospatial assessment of elevated agrivoltaics on arable land in Europe to highlight the implications on design, land use and economic level. Energy Rep. **8**, 8736–8751 (2022)
28. European Commission, Joint Research Centre: Horizon Scanning Alert: Agrivoltaics, Shielding Crops with PV Panels; European Commission, Brussels, Belgium (2020)
29. Jain, P., Raina, G., Sinha, S., Malik, P., Mathur, S.: Agrovoltaics: step towards sustainable energy-food combination. Bioresour. Technol. Rep. **15**, 100766 (2021)
30. Ott, E.M., Kabus, C.A., Baxter, B.D., Hannon, B., Celik, I.: Environmental analysis of agrivoltaic systems. In: Reference Module in Earth Systems and Environmental Sciences (2020)
31. Alsema, E.A., Nieuwlaar, E.: Energy viability of photovoltaic systems. Energy Policy **28**(14), 999–1010 (2000)
32. Schindele, S., et al.: Implementation of agrophotovoltaics: techno-economic analysis of the price-performance ratio and its policy implications. Appl. Energy **265**, 114737 (2020)
33. Toledo, C., Scognamiglio, A.: Agrivoltaic systems design and assessment: a critical review, and a descriptive model towards a sustainable landscape vision (three-dimensional agrivoltaic patterns). Sustainability **13**, 6871 (2021)
34. Momtazur, M.D., Khan, I., Field, D.L., Techato, K., Alameh, K.: Powering agriculture: present status, future potential, and challenges of renewable energy applications. Renew. Energy **188**, 731–749 (2022)
35. Mauro, G., Lunghi, V.: Mapping land use impact of photovoltaic farms via crowdsourcing in the Province of Lecce (Southeastern Italy). Sol. Energy **155**, 434–444 (2017)

Implementing a Development Strategy for Revitalizing Industrial Areas in Crisis. The Experience of the Tito Industrial Area in the Basilicata Region (Southern Italy)

Beniamino Murgante[1](✉), Luigi Vergari[2], Canio Alfieri Sabia[3], Giuseppina Lo Vecchio[4], Michele Micucci[5], and Francesco Scorza[1]

[1] School of Engineering, University of Basilicata, Viale dell'Ateneo Lucano 10, 85100 Potenza, Italy
{beniamino.murgante,francesco.scorza}@unibas.it
[2] Society of Industrial Production Areas of Basilicata (Api-Bas), Largo Azzarà 1, 85100 Potenza, Italy
[3] Consiglio Nazionale delle Ricerche, Institute of Heritage Science (ISPC), Tito Scalo, Potenza, Italy
canioalfieri.sabia@cnr.it
[4] PhD School in Engineering for Innovation and Sustainable Development, University of Basilicata, Viale dell'Ateneo Lucano 10, 85100 Potenza, Italy
giuseppina.lovecchio@unibas.it
[5] Teseo Consult, S.r.l. - Via Monginevro 7, 75028 Policoro, Matera, Italy

Abstract. This paper reports an experience of a development strategy for the industrial area of Tito (PZ) in the Basilicata Region in southern Italy, which represents a primary node of the industrial infrastructure of Basilicata. The main actor in this activity is represented by the Society of Industrial Production Areas of Basilicata (Api-Bas), which organized extensive and inclusive consultations with all possible stakeholders. This strategy is based on a combination of many factors that can entice entrepreneurs to invest resources in the Tito industrial area. The main elements of this strategy can be synthesized into tax incentives, special economic zones (ZES) resources, Next-generation Eu funding, and the Italian national recovery and resilience plan (PNRR). The project aims to digitize all aspects of contracting completely. The Api-Bas Territorial Information System has been fully realized in a GIS (Geographic Information System) environment, enabling the quick implementation of all procedures.

Keywords: First Keyword · Second Keyword · Third Keyword

1 Introduction

One of the main problems in industrialized countries is the crisis in several areas due to the production localization in Asia to reduce labor costs. In many cases, national and local governments offer support for reducing the impacts on the populations of these areas.

O. Gervasi et al. (Eds.): ICCSA 2023 Workshops, LNCS 14107, pp. 560–574, 2023.
https://doi.org/10.1007/978-3-031-37114-1_39

There are several ways that governments and international organizations can support underdeveloped areas, both in developing countries and in economically disadvantaged regions of developed countries. It is essential to take a comprehensive and coordinated approach that addresses a range of economic, social, and political factors [1]. This approach can be implemented by adopting several measures:

- Infrastructure investments: Governments can invest in infrastructure projects, such as transportation networks, energy systems, and water and sanitation facilities, to improve the economic and social conditions in underdeveloped areas.
- Education and skills training: Providing access to education and skills training can help improve the employability and earning potential of people living in underdeveloped areas and promote economic growth and social mobility.
- Healthcare services: Providing access to healthcare services, including preventative care, primary care, and emergency services, can help to improve health outcomes and reduce the burden of disease in underdeveloped areas.
- Microfinance and small business support: Providing access to microfinance and other forms of small business support can help stimulate economic growth and job creation in underdeveloped areas and promote entrepreneurship and innovation.
- Foreign aid and development assistance: Governments and international organizations can provide aid and development assistance to support underdeveloped areas, including funding for infrastructure, education, healthcare, and other critical needs.
- Tax and other economic incentives: Governments can offer tax incentives and other incentives to encourage businesses to invest in underdeveloped areas, promoting economic growth and job creation.

It is common for governments to offer tax incentives to attract new businesses to their jurisdiction. Tax incentives can take many forms, such as tax credits, tax exemptions, or tax deductions, and they are often designed to encourage specific types of investment or job creation. While tax incentives can effectively attract new business investment, they can also be controversial. Some critics argue that tax incentives create a race-to-the-bottom dynamic where jurisdictions compete to offer the most generous tax breaks, leading to a loss of revenue and a lack of accountability for businesses. Others argue that tax incentives can be a necessary tool for promoting economic growth and job creation in underserved areas. Governments may offer tax incentives for a variety of reasons, including:

- Economic development: Tax incentives can stimulate economic growth in specific industries or geographic areas. By offering tax breaks, governments can encourage businesses to invest in new facilities, hire more workers, and expand their operations.
- Competition: In some cases, tax incentives may be offered to compete with other jurisdictions for new business investments. Governments can attract businesses that might otherwise locate elsewhere by providing lower tax rates or more generous incentives.

- Public policy goals: Tax incentives can also be used to achieve specific public policy goals, such as promoting renewable energy development or supporting affordable housing.

On the other side, companies could pursue localization strategies to lower their overall tax burden. This may involve relocating their operations to a jurisdiction with lower tax rates or taking advantage of tax incentives offered by local governments. The goal is to increase profits by reducing taxes paid on income, property, or other business-related expenses. There are several factors that companies may consider when choosing a location to reduce their taxes. Companies may consider jurisdictions with lower tax rates, such as states or countries with low corporate income or no sales tax [2]. Local governments may offer tax incentives to attract new businesses, such as tax credits for hiring employees, property tax abatements, or reduced sales tax rates. Companies may also consider factors such as access to transportation, availability of skilled labor, and quality of life when choosing a location.

2 Tax Incentives for Economic Development

Governments commonly use tax incentives to encourage economic development, particularly in areas struggling economically or seeking to attract new industries or businesses. Tax incentives for economic growth are often designed to encourage companies to invest in new facilities or equipment, hire more workers, or increase their spending on research and development. These incentives can be targeted toward specific industries or geographic areas and can be structured in various ways to achieve policy goals.

These incentives can take many forms, such as tax credits, property tax abatements, sales tax exemptions, and research and development tax credits.

Tax credits are a tax incentive that reduces a taxpayer's tax liability by reducing the amount of taxes owed. This means the same amount reduces the taxpayer's overall tax bill for every volume of tax credit claimed.

Tax credits can be either refundable or non-refundable. Refundable tax credits can reduce a taxpayer's tax liability below zero, refunding the excess amount. On the other hand, non-refundable tax credits can only reduce a taxpayer's tax liability to zero and cannot result in a refund. Tax credits can be targeted toward various policy goals, such as promoting renewable energy, encouraging research and development, or supporting low-income households.

Property tax abatements are tax incentives that reduce the property taxes a property owner owes. Governments often use property tax abatements to encourage investment in new facilities or equipment, particularly in areas seeking to attract new industries or businesses. Property tax abatements can be structured differently, but they typically involve a temporary reduction in property taxes for a specified period. This reduction may be partial or total, and it may be phased in or out over time. Property tax abatements may sometimes be conditional upon specific requirements, such as job creation or investment levels.

There are several typologies of property tax abatements:

- Targeted to specific areas or industries: Property tax abatements are often designed to encourage investment in specific geographic areas or enterprises that need economic development.
- Temporary: Property tax abatements are usually temporary and are designed to provide a short-term boost to investment. The abatement period may be anywhere from a few years to several decades.
- Conditional: In some cases, property tax abatements may depend on specific requirements, such as job creation, investment levels, or the use of particular types of equipment.
- Proportional: The amount of the property tax abatement is usually proportional to the level of investment or job creation, with more significant investments or jobs resulting in a more considerable abatement.

Sales tax exemptions are tax incentives that exempt certain products or services from the state or local sales tax. Governments often use sales tax exemptions to incentivize certain behaviors or industries, such as promoting renewable energy or supporting charitable organizations [3]. Sales tax exemptions are usually designed to target specific products or services deemed in the public interest. For example, some countries offer sales tax exemptions for food, clothing, or medical supplies. Depending on policy goals and political considerations, sales tax exemptions can be temporary or permanent.

Sometimes, sales tax exemptions may be conditional upon specific requirements, such as using renewable energy sources or providing certain services. The amount of the sales tax exemption is usually proportional to the value of the product or service being purchased. The Research and Development Tax Credit is a tax incentive encouraging businesses to invest in research and development activities. The credit incentivizes firms to engage in these activities, leading to innovation, increased competitiveness, and economic growth.

3 Next-Generation EU Funding and Italian National Recovery and Resilience Plan

Next Generation EU is a European Union (EU) recovery instrument created in response to the economic and social impacts of the COVID-19 pandemic. The tool provides significant funding to support the EU's economic recovery and promote long-term resilience and sustainability. The Next Generation EU program provides financing over seven years, from 2021 to 2026. The budget is allocated to EU member states through grants and loans, with a focus on supporting investments in critical areas such as:

- Green transition: Funding supports the transition to a sustainable, low-carbon economy, with investments in renewable energy, sustainable transportation, and energy efficiency.
- Digital transformation: Funding is provided to promote the digitalization of the economy and society, with investments in digital infrastructure, digital skills, and e-government services.

- Economic resilience: Funding is provided to support economic recovery and resilience, with investments in infrastructure, innovation, and job creation.
- Social inclusion: Funding is provided to address social and economic inequalities, with investments in affordable housing, social services, and healthcare.

The Next Generation EU program is a significant initiative that reflects the EU's commitment to promoting economic recovery and long-term sustainability during the pandemic. The program is expected to impact the economies and societies of EU member states significantly and will likely be a key driver of growth and innovation in the future.

The Italian National Recovery and Resilience Plan is a government-led initiative to support the country's economic recovery from the COVID-19 pandemic and promote long-term economic growth and sustainability. The plan is part of the European Union's Recovery and Resilience Facility, which provides financial support to member states to help them address the economic and social impacts of the pandemic.

The Italian plan includes a wide range of measures and investments across several key areas, including:

- Digital transformation: The plan aims to promote the digitalization of the Italian economy and society, including investments in digital infrastructure, developing e-government services, and support for digital education and skills training.
- Climate transition: The plan includes measures to promote the transition to a low-carbon economy and address the challenges of climate change, including investments in renewable energy, sustainable transportation, and energy efficiency.
- Infrastructure: The plan includes significant investments in transportation infrastructure, including railways, highways, and ports, as well as investments in social infrastructure, such as schools and hospitals.
- Education and training: The plan aims to promote the development of skills and education across all age groups, including investments in early childhood education, vocational training, and higher education.
- Social inclusion: The plan includes measures to address poverty and social exclusion, including investments in affordable housing, social services, and healthcare.

The Italian National Recovery and Resilience Plan is a comprehensive and ambitious initiative that reflects the government's commitment to promoting economic growth and sustainability during the pandemic. The plan is expected to receive significant funding from the EU's Recovery and Resilience Facility. It will likely significantly impact the Italian economy and society in the coming years.

Within these measures, several funding has been considered for Special Economic Zones.

4 Special Economic Zones (ZES)

Special Economic Zones (ZES) are a tool used by many countries to promote economic development and attract foreign investments. Special Economic Zones are geographical areas where governments provide special financial and regulatory incentives to encourage businesses to invest and operate. ZES are typically designed to promote economic growth and development in underdeveloped or disadvantaged regions by attracting domestic and foreign investment, creating jobs, and promoting technology transfer. The specific incentives offered to businesses operating in ZES vary by country but typically include tax breaks, customs duty exemptions, streamlined regulatory procedures, and access to infrastructure and other government services. The goal is to create a business-friendly environment encouraging investment and economic growth.

The term ZES refers to a geographically delimited and clearly identified area located within the borders of the State, also consisting of non-territorially adjacent areas, provided that they have a functional economic connection and that includes at least one port area with the characteristics established by Regulation (EU) No. 1315 of 11 December 2013 of the European Parliament and the Council, on Union guidelines for the development of the trans-European transport network (TEN-T). For the exercise of economic and entrepreneurial activities, companies already operating and those that will settle in the ZES can benefit from special conditions concerning the incremental nature of investments and business development activities.

ZES are often established in areas with unique advantages for specific industries, such as access to natural resources, strategic geographic location, or a skilled workforce. Examples of ZES include the Shenzhen Special Economic Zone in China, the Dubai International Financial Centre in the United Arab Emirates, and the Colombo Port City in Sri Lanka.

Critics of ZES argue that they can be a form of corporate welfare that benefits large corporations at the expense of smaller businesses and local communities. Additionally, they may not always deliver the promised economic benefits and can sometimes exacerbate social and environmental problems in the surrounding areas.

Despite these criticisms, ZES remain a popular tool for governments seeking to attract investment and promote economic development in underdeveloped areas.

In Italy, ZES was introduced in 2017 following the approval of a law regulating their establishment and operation. The Italian approach to developing ZESs is based on a strategy that combines tax incentives, regulatory simplification, and infrastructure development. The Italian government has established a program called "Zones of Economic and Social Development" (ZES) to promote the development of ZES in Italy. The ZES program aims to attract foreign investments, boost exports, and stimulate economic growth in disadvantaged areas of the country. The program is designed to support creation of new businesses and job opportunities, especially in the regions affected by economic decline and unemployment.

The ZES program is managed by the Ministry of Economic Development, which has established a set of guidelines and criteria to identify the areas eligible for ZES. The criteria include factors such as the infrastructure level, access to transportation, skilled labor, and the potential for economic growth. Once an area is identified as eligible, the government will work with local authorities to create a development plan that meets the area's specific needs. The ZES program provides a range of incentives and benefits to companies that operate within the ZESs. These include tax breaks, streamlined bureaucratic procedures, and access to financing and investment opportunities. The program also supports infrastructure development, including transportation networks, energy supply, and telecommunications.

The ZES program was created as a national policy to relaunch Southern Italy. Unfortunately, the context contribution of the beneficiary regions changed profoundly in the short term, with a succession of economic and social circumstances complicated to predict: the pandemic crisis, the first post-pandemic recovery, and the energy crisis linked to the Russo-Ukrainian conflict.

This situation, directly and indirectly, impacts the regional economic and industrial sector with unpredictable effects, whose statistical evidence will surely not be timely. Therefore, governance actions in the system will be complex. As a result of this situation, the ZES Program was refinanced with PNRR resources.

4.1 Special Economic Zones in Basilicata Region

Basilicata Region is located in southern Italy, bordering Campania to the west, Apulia to the north and east, and Calabria to the south (Fig. 1). The Region covers an area of 9,995 square kilometers (3,859 square miles) and has a population of around 570,000 people. The regional capital is Potenza, located in the region's central part. Historically, Basilicata has been one of the poorest regions in Italy, with a largely agrarian economy. However, in recent years, the region has seen some growth in tourism, renewable energy, and the service industry.

The region also has extensive industrial plants, particularly in the chemical and petrochemical sectors. Considering this situation, European Union included Basilicata Region in the Objective 1 regional development program. This program addresses the economic and social disparities between regions within the EU. The program aimed to support economic development and promote job creation in the EU's most economically disadvantaged regions, designated as "Objective 1 areas." Objective 1 areas were identified based on their low levels of economic development, high rates of unemployment, and other social and economic indicators. These regions were typically located in rural or urban areas affected by industrial decline, population loss, or other factors contributing to economic underdevelopment. The Objective 1 program provided financial support to these regions through various mechanisms, including grants, loans, and technical assistance. The program was designed to promote investment in infrastructure, education and training, research and development, and other activities deemed essential for promoting economic growth and job creation.

Referring specifically to the pandemic crisis's effects [4–6], Basilicata's regional economy, according to the Bank of Italy report of 2020, is heavily conditioned with an impact that has affected all productive sectors. Significant effects are recorded in all sectors: industry in the strict sense, with a generalized drop in turnover and working hours and a decline in investments. This occurred in the automotive industry, with a significant decrease in FCA production. The market of companies operating in the construction and real estate markets, with a substantial drop in real estate transactions and a reduction in prices in the residential sector. Private non-financial services show a significant decrease in activity as a consequence of the restrictions due to the pandemic, with substantial impacts partially balanced by extraordinary state support.

The Regional Administration in Basilicata has contributed to the Strategic Development Plan (PSS) of the "Puglia-Basilicata Interregional Ionian ZES," established by DPCM on June 6, 2019.

Fig. 1. Basilicata Region location.

The PSS (Special Economic Zone Plan) of the ZES recognizes the natural function of the Basilicata region's territorial system as a hinterland to the logistical infrastructure of the Port of Taranto, with the identification of a series of regional logistical polarities. The PSS highlights the aim of removing a structural condition of territorial isolation that affects industrial logistics by defining a development direction for the productive system capable of attracting investments. The ZES represents a condition of competitive advantage for established and future companies and therefore defines an instrumental condition for achieving the development objectives identified by the Basilicata region. The ZES represents a platform for enhancing the competitiveness of Basilicata's industrial and productive system, which includes a dimension of intangible facilitations for the development of new investments and the organization of entrepreneurial activities, combined with actions to strengthen the infrastructure of production settlements.

The formation of the PSS was developed through numerous political, technical, and administrative acts that provided for a comprehensive phase of involvement of territorial stakeholders in the agreement of strategic and operational requirements on which to structure the proposal of the ZES. At this regional level, an interregional consultation action was added, linked to the nature of the overall proposal, which concerns a large territorial platform straddling Puglia and Basilicata.

5 The Experience of Special Economic Zones of Tito-Potenza in the Basilicata Region

The industrial area of Tito (PZ) represents an internal node of the industrial system that SVIMEZ (Association for the Development of Industry in Southern Italy) identifies as the 'Continental Quadrilateral' Naples, Bari, Taranto, Gioia Tauro concerning which to define the logistic-productive reorganization and territorial reconnection policy. These four poles have to be considered cornerstones in reorganizing the logistical-productive and territorial reconnection policy.

This factor, coherently with the strategy of the PPS of the Ionian ZES, makes the infrastructure project of the Tito ZES area a node in a broader network connected to the continental dimension of Southern Italy.

ZES actions will be integrated with the massive PNRR investment and regional programming, considering the development and cohesion policies supported by the Structural Funds. Implementing all these complementary actions leads to realizing a broader economic development process that will have to coordinate different functions and management models.

The industrial area of Tito had its significant development following the financing aimed at industrial strengthening, provided after the earthquake that hit the areas of Irpinia and Basilicata in 1980. It is located close to Basentana Highway 407, which guarantees good accessibility.

Two factors have led to a slowdown in the area's industrial development. The economic stagnation recorded in Italy starting from the early 2000s, emphasized by the Lehman Brothers bankruptcy caused in 2008 by the subprime mortgage crisis, which on the one hand, did not have direct implications for entrepreneurs in the area, has represented an incentive to relocate to countries in Eastern Europe and Asia, causing the closure of Western European plants. The other element slowing down the development of the industrial nucleus has been the identification, within its perimeter, of large areas subject to land reclamation of national interest (SIN) delimited by the Ministry of the Environment decree of 8 July 2002. Still today, these areas are affected by environmental reclamation procedures" [7].

Its proximity to the regional capital and the contiguity with 407 Highway ensures excellent connection to the main road routes of the region. It allows access to the A2 Highway in about 30 min. It is also located near the railway line that connects the Tyrrhenian coast with the Ionian coast, passing through the regional capital. The area is located in the municipality of Tito and is close to Picerno. The southern part of the industrial area borders the municipality of Pignola and is a short distance from the WWF oasis of Pantano Lake. The site has national and international manufacturing companies, particularly in the engineering and automotive sectors (not only related to the Stellantis pole in San Nicola di Melfi). Industries in the agro-food sector should be highlighted. There are also some services and scientific research (CNR) activities (Fig. 2).

Fig. 2. Industrial area of Tito location.

5.1 Special Economic Zones of Tito-Potenza Project

The Z.E.S. area project comes after a careful and deep discussion with the stakeholders. In particular, thanks to a discussion table promoted by Api-Bas (Society of Industrial Production Areas of Basilicata) and the Basilicata Region, numerous meetings were held at the latter with the Municipality of Tito, with the regional offices involved in the project, and with the old Industrial Consortium in liquidation.

The project is aimed at the total digitization of contracting activities. It has been fully realized in a GIS (Geographic Information System) environment, effectively building a solid basis for implementing the Api-Bas Territorial Information System and allowing rapid implementation of all procedures.

The ZES intervention in the industrial area of Tito (PZ) configures the infrastructural intervention as an enhancement of the industrial site by referring to organizational criteria of the settlement fabric oriented to maximize:

- the re-use of existing road infrastructure as a basis for the construction of the subdivision scheme;
- the integration of sub-service networks with the existing infrastructure;
- a rationalization of spaces for activities settlement based on a modular approach of lots with a minimum surface area of 5000 square meters
- an internal and service road scheme for the area that guarantees suitable access options to the lots and adequate maneuvering spaces for industrial vehicles and articulated trucks;
- the subdivision of the areas considering the morphological elements and slopes compatible with industrial allotment operations.

The location of the Z.E.S. areas is particularly favorable for reusing existing infrastructure, which in most cases only requires adaptation. The territorial extension of the area interested by the Z.E.S. intervention is a function of specific components explained in the following equation:

$$A_{tot} = A_a + A_r + A_e + A_g = 373557 \text{ mq} \quad (1)$$

Where:
Aa = Allotment Area = 245,325 sqm
Ar = Road infrastructure Area = 59893 sqm
Ae = Elisurface Area = 7000 sqm
Ag = Green Areas = 61339 sqm

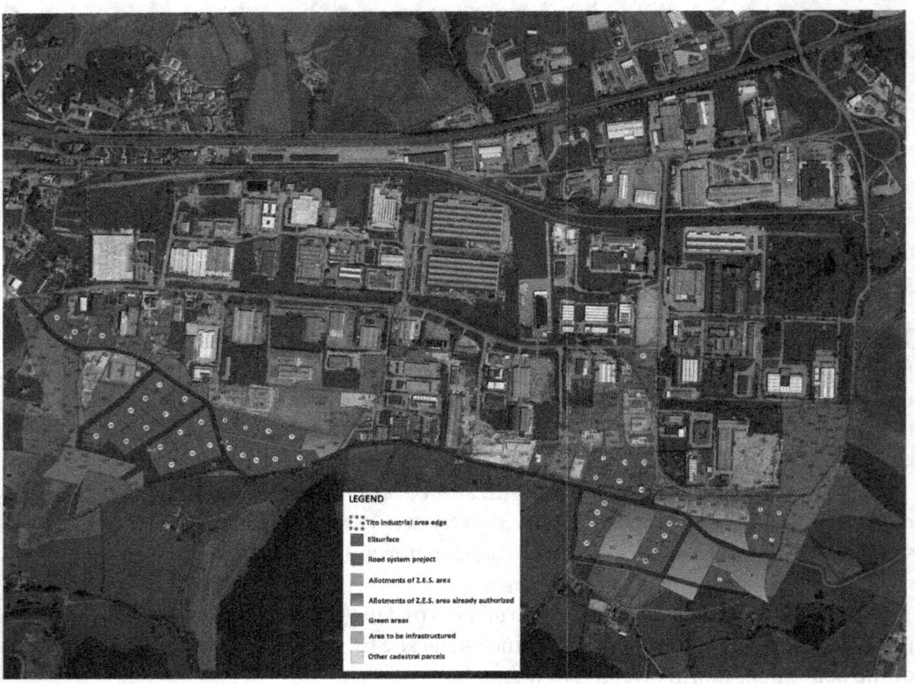

Fig. 3. Allotment of Z.E.S..area of Tito.

In the area of interest, a significant green area of 61339 square meters, already foreseen by the industrial planning instrument, has been included, providing an additional quality element.

Although the industrial area is located near Basentana Highway and the Potenza-Sicignano degli Alburni railway line to improve accessibility and encourage nationally and internationally relevant entrepreneurs to invest in the area, a helipad has also been included in the Z.E.S. area on a surface of 7000 square meters located near Cuparo farmhouse in the southernmost part of the perimeter (in brown in Fig. 3). This helipad would fill the historical accessibility gap affecting the entire area and allow for shared management among local authorities and organizations interested in its use. The organization of the road network (Fig. 4) pursues two main objectives: to facilitate access to individual lots and to enhance the connection of the industrial area with the surrounding areas. To this end, particular attention has been paid to dimensioning the road network at the individual lots to allow access to articulated vehicles. It has been designed, also, to improve the road infrastructure that connects the industrial area with the Pantano area in the Municipality of Pignola, partly located in the southern sector of the area and partly along the perimeter of the industrial area.

Fig. 4. Roadś infrastructure project of Z.E.S..area of Tito.

The extensive infrastructure investments are intended both to be a way to determine the precondition to attract new industrial operators and as a way to qualify the whole industrial site from an urban perspective. The private investments attraction represents an open program where APIBAS, institutional players, local decision-makers, and the main industrial organizations operating in Basilicata Region and at the National level must cooperate to maximize the socio-economic benefits for the whole area.

The design quality and technological features also represent a way to affirm the project's long-term sustainability from an environmental perspective [8] and a functional one.

6 Conclusions

This work concerns the latter component of the development strategy concerning the industrial settlement of Tito (PZ), which represents a primary node of the industrial infrastructure of Basilicata.

Overall, the Italian approach to developing ZESs is focused on promoting economic development and attracting foreign investment in disadvantaged areas of the country. The ZES program and other sector-specific programs offer a range of incentives and support to businesses operating within the ZESs, aiming to stimulate economic growth and create new job opportunities.

Investing in primary, efficient, and sustainable infrastructure at the ZES of Tito (PZ) service becomes a priority in this dimension of uncertainty and rapidly evolving political, economic, and social framework on a supranational scale. This project defines it on a preliminary basis since the demand for efficient and sustainable primary infrastructure, the definition of operational schemes for industrial location, and the simplification of processes that depend on a response aimed at the institutions responsible for the industrial and productive revival of the territory, become preconditions for addressing ongoing crises and directing towards development conditions defined in the ZES programming documents.

One of the main reasons that can be attributed to the causes of the proliferation of Special Economic Zones (ZESs) is the dual-level approach which, on the one hand, creates a competitive opportunity for operators due to their production location and, on the other hand, becomes a policy that deviates from the ordinary administrative/fiscal management system. This provides policymakers with an ad hoc tool to intervene in specific contexts without altering the regular regulatory framework, following a targeted action approach to address a properly documented local emergency. Policymakers resort to ZESs as investment attractors (often from foreign sources), capable of generating employment in the area and increasing exports. These benefits extend beyond the zone's boundaries, as demonstrated by specific "dynamic" effects on the surrounding regions and the local economy. Identifiable as indirect benefits, these dynamic effects emerge through interactions between the companies responsible for the ZESs and other actors in the local economy through the diffusion of skills, and they appear to have a more significant impact on medium- to long-term development in local economies compared to direct benefits [9].

A technological advantage emerges that can spill over to operators in the surrounding areas, promoting structural changes and increasing their competitiveness through a dynamic industry cluster or production district. Systemic advantages typically develop through various channels, with the most common being labor mobility between ZESs and local firms, the creation of connections with small producers in the region, the imitation of technology and management practices by local firms, and the upgrading of basic skills in the local workforce [10].

The integration of ZES firms within the local economy represents a necessary condition for such repercussions to occur [10, 11]. It is crucial to establish connections between ZES companies and those operating in the broader local context [12].

ZES firms, which in significant international experiences are typically oriented toward the global market and managed by companies outside national boundaries, have higher quality requirements in their production processes than local firms. The latter can benefit from upgrading processes and product and process innovation through partnership relationships that are established at the local level [11]. Furthermore, it is estimated that foreign firms serve as an incentive to support local production on the territory, drastically reducing the time and costs involved [13, 14].

Considering the potential benefits mentioned above, ZES policies have often sought to promote integration between foreign and local firms, aiming to generate inward connections that represent an advantage for the economic system centered around the ZES area.

The Tito Industrial Area is formally the main production area within the larger Potenza territory and therefore plays a regional role within Basilicata's industrial and artisanal system. It has an industrial tradition has accompanied the different phases of industrial settlement in Basilicata, offering an optimal location for investments in various sectors such as chemicals, metalworking, logistics, construction, and more.

Alongside the tradition of industrial settlements, there is now not only a dimension of a "production system" that measures not only the industrial presence but also a widespread system of services for the industry, but also a dimension of environmental externalities that need to be addressed, for which remediation processes are underway due to the presence of the National Interest Site (SIN).

In Tito's industrial area, complex remediation interventions are being carried out by several public bodies entitled to specific responsibilities. Through ZES investments, the industrial area becomes, as in the past, one of the main nodes of the regional industrial network, reinforcing the overall competitiveness of the whole system according to effective and sustainable growth scenarios [15, 16].

Acknowledgments. The authors are grateful to the Society of Industrial Production Areas of Basilicata (Api-Bas) and the Api-Bas technical and administrative staff for supporting the project's development.

References

1. Dvarioniene, J., Grecu, V., Lai, S., Scorza, F.: Four perspectives of applied sustainability: research implications and possible integrations. In: Gervasi, O., et al. (eds.) ICCSA 2017. LNCS, vol. 10409, pp. 554–563. Springer, Cham (2017). https://doi.org/10.1007/978-3-319-62407-5_39
2. Rodríguez-Clare, A.: Multinationals, linkages, and economic development. Am. Econ. Rev. **86**, 852–873 (1996)
3. Lauridsen, L.S.: Foreign direct investment, linkage formation and supplier development in Thailand during the 1990s: the role of state governance. Eur. J. Dev. Res. **16**, 561–586 (2004). https://doi.org/10.1080/0957881042000266624/METRICS
4. Murgante, B., Borruso, G.: Cities and smartness: a critical analysis of opportunities and risks. In: Murgante, B., et al. (eds.) ICCSA 2013. LNCS, vol. 7973, pp. 630–642. Springer, Heidelberg (2013). https://doi.org/10.1007/978-3-642-39646-5_46
5. Murgante, B., Borruso, G.: Smart cities in a smart world. In: Rassia, S.T., Pardalos, P.M. (eds.) Future City Architecture for Optimal Living. SOIA, vol. 102, pp. 13–35. Springer, Cham (2015). https://doi.org/10.1007/978-3-319-15030-7_2
6. Scorza, F., Casas, G.L., Murgante, B.: Overcoming interoperability weaknesses in e-government processes: organizing and sharing knowledge in regional development programs using ontologies. In: Lytras, M.D., Ordonez de Pablos, P., Ziderman, A., Roulstone, A., Maurer, H., Imber, J.B. (eds.) WSKS 2010. CCIS, vol. 112, pp. 243–253. Springer, Heidelberg (2010). https://doi.org/10.1007/978-3-642-16324-1_26
7. Scorza, F., Pilogallo, A., Saganeiti, L., Murgante, B.: Natura 2000 areas and sites of national interest (SNI): measuring (un)integration between naturalness preservation and environmental remediation policies. Sustain. **12**, 2928 (2020). https://doi.org/10.3390/su12072928
8. Murgante, B., Borruso, G., Lapucci, A.: Sustainable development: concepts and methods for its application in urban and environmental planning. Stud. Comput. Intell. **348**, 1–15 (2011). https://doi.org/10.1007/978-3-642-19733-8_1

9. Farole, T.: Special Economic Zones in Africa Comparing Performance and Learning from Global Experience Trade. Washington (2011)
10. Farole, T., Akinci, G.: Special Economic Zones Progress, Emerging Challenges, and Future Directions. Washington (2011)
11. Steenbergen, V., Sutton, J.: Establishing a Local Content Unit for Rwanda Policy note. (2017)
12. Amendolagine, V., Presbitero, A.F., Rabellotti, R., Sanfilippo, M.: Local sourcing in developing countries: the role of foreign direct investments and global value chains. World Dev. **113**, 73–88 (2019). https://doi.org/10.1016/J.WORLDDEV.2018.08.010
13. Javorcik, B.S.: Does foreign direct investment increase the productivity of domestic firms? in search of spillovers through backward linkages. Am. Econ. Rev. **94**, 605–627 (2004). https://doi.org/10.1257/0002828041464605
14. Javorcik, B.S., Spatareanu, M.: To share or not to share: does local participation matter for spillovers from foreign direct investment? J. Dev. Econ. **85**, 194–217 (2008)
15. Casas, G.L., Scorza, F.: Sustainable planning: a methodological toolkit. In: Gervasi, O., et al. (eds.) ICCSA 2016. LNCS, vol. 9786, pp. 627–635. Springer, Cham (2016). https://doi.org/10.1007/978-3-319-42085-1_53
16. Scorza, F., Saganeiti, L., Pilogallo, A., Murgante, B.: Ghost planning: the inefficiency of energy sector policies in a low population density region. Arch. di Stud. Urbani e Reg. 34–55 (2020). https://doi.org/10.3280/ASUR2020-127-S1003

Combining Tourism Revitalization with Environmental Regeneration Through the Restoration of Piano del Conte Lake in Lagopesole (Southern Italy)

Beniamino Murgante[1(✉)], Giuseppe Trabace[2], and Veronica Vespe[2]

[1] School of Engineering, University of Basilicata, Viale dell'Ateneo Lucano 10, 85100 Potenza, Italy
beniamino.murgante@unibas.it

[2] Studio Tecnico Giuseppe Trabace, Via San Francesco, 7, 75019 Tricarico Matera, Italy

Abstract. Lake restoration improves a degraded lake ecosystem's ecological health and water quality. It typically involves a combination of physical, chemical, and biological interventions to reduce nutrient inputs, control erosion, restore shoreline and wetland habitats, and manage invasive species. Lake restoration can be a complex process requiring careful planning, stakeholder engagement, ongoing monitoring, and adaptive management. The ultimate goal of lake restoration is to restore a healthy and resilient ecosystem that supports a diverse array of plant and animal life and recreational and cultural activities. The Piano del Conte site, a rural area in Avigliano, extends over a broad terrace at about 770 m above sea level, not far from the Lagopesole Castle. A crown of gentle hills and dense woods delimit the plain to the northeast, while to the west, it ends in a steep slope that slopes down to the Salice Valley. Lagopesole Castle is a medieval castle in the Basilicata region of southern Italy. The castle is perched on a hilltop overlooking the surrounding landscape and is surrounded by a village that has grown up around it over the centuries. Today, it is a popular tourist destination and one of the symbols of the region's cultural heritage. A regeneration program has been planned in this area based on the Piano del Conte Lake restoration and connecting this area with the castle through a bike path.

Keywords: Lake restoration · tourism revitalization · environmental regeneration

1 Introduction

Lakes are valuable resources that offer a range of benefits. They are popular sources of recreation, providing opportunities for fishing, boating, and swimming, which are popular forms of outdoor recreation. Furthermore, lakes are essential in sustaining life by providing flood protection, electricity generation, and drinking water sources. Finally, lakes are appreciated for their aesthetic beauty, providing places of solitude and relaxation.

O. Gervasi et al. (Eds.): ICCSA 2023 Workshops, LNCS 14107, pp. 575–589, 2023.
https://doi.org/10.1007/978-3-031-37114-1_40

Before human activities such as home construction, deforestation, and agriculture, the original state of a lake may not have been as pure as often assumed. According to natural geologic processes, lakes of moderate depth gradually fill and transform into wetlands over time. The degree to which a lake has transitioned along this geologic continuum, from deep to shallow, can affect its inherent water quality.

Climate, rainfall, morphology, soils, geology, and land use influence lake water quality and land use, varying across regions. To group regions with similar characteristics, ecoregions were defined based on these factors, as studied and identified by Omernik [1]. These ecoregions are based on causal and integrative factors, including land use, land surface form, potential natural vegetation, and soils. Ecoregions are based on the concept that ecosystems are spatially interconnected and that political or administrative boundaries do not necessarily define their boundaries. Ecoregions are helpful for conservation planning, biodiversity assessments, and natural resource management. They provide a framework for understanding the distribution of ecological systems across landscapes and can help guide conservation and management actions. Ecoregions are also studied in ecosystem geography, focusing on environmental systems' spatial patterns and processes and their interactions with the physical and human environments. It concerns ecosystems' distribution, structure, function, and the factors influencing their dynamics and resilience, such as climate, geology, topography, and human activities. Ecosystem geography [2] is a multidisciplinary field that draws on principles and methods from ecology, biogeography, geomorphology, hydrology, climatology, and social sciences. Its goal is to provide a spatially explicit understanding of ecosystems' functioning and support their sustainable management and conservation. To avoid the deterioration and early aging of lakes, it is essential to find an equilibrium between anthropic uses and preserving the environment [3–5].

2 Lakes Lifecycle, Restoration, and Management

The life of a lake refers to its natural lifecycle, which is influenced by various factors such as geology, climate, vegetation, and human activities. Generally, a lake is formed through natural succession, which starts with the accumulation of sediments in a depression or basin. Over time, the depression fills with water, and a new lake is born [6].

The life of a lake can be divided into several stages, including the oligotrophic stage, the mesotrophic stage, and the eutrophic stage.

During the oligotrophic stage, a lake is relatively deep, clear, and nutrient-poor, with low algae levels and aquatic plants. Depending on the lake's size and geology, this stage can last hundreds or thousands of years.

As a lake age, it gradually accumulates nutrients, such as nitrogen and phosphorus, from sources such as runoff from surrounding land or decomposing organic matter. This leads to the mesotrophic stage, in which the lake becomes shallower, with more algae and aquatic plants and abundant fish and other aquatic life.

If nutrient inputs continue to increase, the lake may enter the eutrophic stage, in which it becomes very shallow, with high levels of algae, aquatic plants, and nutrients. The water may be murky and green, and fish populations may decline due to oxygen depletion [7].

Human activities such as urbanization, agriculture, and industrialization can accelerate eutrophication and lead to premature aging and degradation of lakes. Therefore, lake management and restoration efforts often focus on reducing nutrient inputs and promoting sustainable land use practices to help preserve the life of lakes [8].

The use of a lake depends on how much people's desires align with the lake's ability to meet those desires. Limitations on desired uses of a lake, which can be prevented or rectified with appropriate management, define lake problems. This definition is crucial for creating lake management plans, as it identifies a lake problem as any restriction on desired uses by a specific group of users. To develop an effective management program, it is essential to clearly define desired uses, identify their limitations, and understand their causes. It is fundamental for preserving lake life to pursue a balance between human activities and environmental preservation [9–15].

Lake restoration, also known as lake rehabilitation, improves a degraded lake ecosystem's ecological integrity and overall health. Lake rehabilitation aims to restore the lake to a healthy, functional state that supports a diverse range of plant and animal life. This is typically achieved through a combination of techniques that address the underlying causes of degradation and improve the ecological conditions of the lake.

The specific methods used for lake rehabilitation depend on the particular needs of the lake ecosystem, which can vary widely depending on the characteristics of the lake and the surrounding watershed. However, several standard techniques are often used in lake rehabilitation efforts.

One of the primary goals of lake rehabilitation is to improve water quality [6, 16]. This can be done through various techniques, including reducing nutrient inputs, improving erosion control, and managing stormwater runoff. For example, reducing nutrient inputs may include reducing fertilizer use in the watershed, implementing best management practices on agricultural lands, or reducing wastewater discharges. Techniques to improve erosion control may consist of stabilizing shoreline areas, restoring wetlands and riparian zones, or implementing measures to reduce sedimentation.

Another critical aspect of lake rehabilitation is restoring or creating fish and wildlife habitats. This may involve adding submerged plants, creating fish spawning areas, and constructing shoreline structures to provide bird nesting areas. Techniques to improve fish and wildlife habitats may also include managing water levels and flows, controlling invasive species, and improving water quality.

Sediment removal is another technique that may be used in lake rehabilitation efforts. Sometimes, sediment buildup in a lake can significantly affect water quality and aquatic habitat. Lake rehabilitation may involve dredging or other techniques to remove sediment and restore the lake bottom to a more natural state.

Watershed management is also an essential component of lake rehabilitation. Since the health of a lake is often connected to the surrounding watershed, lake rehabilitation may involve managing land use practices and other activities in the watershed to reduce pollution and improve water quality. This may include implementing stormwater management practices, promoting sustainable agriculture practices, and reducing impervious surfaces in urban areas.

Finally, ongoing monitoring and adaptive management are essential components of lake rehabilitation efforts. Monitoring is used to assess the effectiveness of restoration efforts and make adjustments as needed. Adaptive management involves changing the rehabilitation plan based on monitoring results to ensure the rehabilitation efforts achieve the desired goals.

In summary, lake rehabilitation is a complex and multifaceted process that requires a thorough understanding of the lake ecosystem and the underlying causes of degradation. By using a combination of techniques tailored to the specific needs of the lake, it is possible to restore degraded lakes to healthy, functional ecosystems.

The terms restoration and management must be evaluated based on the expectations of the lake users and the feasible options available. Regular upkeep may be necessary to preserve water quality even after restoration efforts. The path towards sustainable progress often requires several years, involving ongoing diagnostic and feasibility analyses and successive testing and implementation of restoration procedures. In any scenario, whether improvement is likely or unlikely, a diagnostic feasibility study should be conducted to decide on one or more lake restoration and management procedures.

The present or intended utilization of the lake may not be suitable for executing specific restoration methods or may not be in line with attainable enhancements. For instance, careful consideration must be given to water supplies intended for human consumption. Using most herbicides in such supplies is prohibited, and specific restoration techniques, such as sediment removal, may necessitate costly specialized equipment to preserve the raw potable water quality.

3 Sustainable Uses of Lakes

Sustainable uses of lakes aim to balance the ecological, economic, and social benefits of the lake while protecting its natural resources and maintaining its health. Some examples of sustainable uses of lakes include:

- Recreational activities: Sustainable recreational activities such as swimming, boating, fishing, and hiking that promote appreciation of the natural environment while minimizing damage to the area.
- Ecotourism: Sustainable tourism activities that showcase the region's natural beauty and cultural heritage while supporting local businesses and communities.
- Water supply: Using the lake as a source of drinking water for local communities while protecting water quality and minimizing impacts on the lake ecosystem.
- Irrigation: Using the lake water to irrigate crops and farmland while managing water usage and preventing pollution.
- Aquaculture: Sustainable aquaculture practices that promote the conservation of fish populations and respect for the aquatic ecosystem.
- Energy production: Using the lake to generate hydroelectric power while minimizing impacts on the lake ecosystem [17, 18] and ensuring water quality.

- Scientific research: Conduct scientific research to understand better the lake's ecology, biology, hydrology, and surrounding area while supporting conservation and management efforts.

Sustainable uses of lakes require careful management to ensure that ecological, economic, and social benefits are maintained over the long term. By promoting sustainable uses of lakes, we can protect and preserve these important resources for future generations.

Some fundamental principles of sustainable lake management can be summarized in the following points:

- Comprehensive planning: Developing a comprehensive management plan that addresses the ecological, economic, and social aspects of lake management, including water quality, recreational opportunities, economic development, and cultural heritage.
- Watershed management: Managing the entire watershed that feeds into the lake, including agricultural, industrial, and urban areas, to prevent pollution and erosion.
- Water quality monitoring: Regularly monitoring the lake's water quality to detect changes in nutrient levels, pH, and temperature and implement appropriate measures to prevent or mitigate any negative impacts.
- Habitat protection: Protecting the natural habitat of the lake and surrounding area, including wetlands, shorelines, and riparian areas, to maintain biodiversity and ecological health.
- Sustainable tourism: Encouraging sustainable tourism practices that promote appreciation of the natural environment and support local businesses and communities.
- Stakeholder involvement: Engaging stakeholders, including local communities, businesses, and government agencies, in managing the lake and encouraging participation in decision-making.
- Adaptive management: Continuously evaluating the effectiveness of management strategies and adjusting them as needed to ensure the long-term sustainability of the lake.

Collaboration between various parties, including lake users, local communities, governmental organizations, and conservation groups, is necessary for the sustainable management of lakes. Lakes can be safeguarded and preserved for future generations by employing sustainable management practices.

Sustainable tourism activities for lakes aim to preserve the region's natural environment and cultural heritage while providing visitors with enjoyable and educational experiences. Several instances of environmentally friendly touristic activities for lakes include:

- Nature walks and hiking tours: Guided or self-guided tours that showcase the natural beauty of the lake and surrounding area while promoting physical activity and an appreciation for the environment.
- Wildlife watching: Opportunities to observe the diverse flora and fauna that inhabit the lake and surrounding ecosystem while encouraging visitors to respect and protect the natural environment.

- Kayaking, canoeing, and paddleboarding: These low-impact activities provide visitors with a unique perspective of the lake while minimizing disturbance to aquatic life and reducing pollution.
- Cultural tours: Tours that highlight the region's local cultural heritage and traditions while supporting local businesses and communities.
- Educational programs: Programs that provide visitors with information about the ecology, history, and management of the lake and surrounding area while promoting environmental awareness and stewardship.
- Fishing: Sustainable fishing practices that promote the conservation of fish populations and respect for the aquatic ecosystem.
- Camping and picnicking: Low-impact recreational activities that promote the enjoyment of the natural environment while minimizing damage to the area.
- Interpretive centers and museums: Educational facilities that provide visitors with information about the natural and cultural history of the region while promoting environmental awareness and conservation.

These activities can be designed to meet the needs of different types of visitors and accommodate varying physical ability levels. Promoting sustainable tourism activities makes it possible to protect lakes for future generations and produce benefits for local communities economically.

4 The Case Study

4.1 The Study Area

A lake restoration activity combined with tourism enhancement actions has been implemented in a project concerning Piano del Conte Lake close to Lagopesole castle in Avigliano municipality (Southern Italy).

The intervention area is located in the Piano del Conte locality in the municipality of Avigliano at an altitude of approximately 780 m above sea level. The fraction of Lagopesole is situated on the watershed between the Ofanto and Bradano rivers, in the municipality of Avigliano (PZ), on a hill around 829 m above sea level. Dominating the hilltop is the castle known as "Lagopesole." Frederick II built Lagopesole castle between 1242 and 1250 on a Saracen and then Norman architectural layout, as evidenced by numerous findings. The castle, constructed using ashlar stones, remains intact in its original form. It underwent restoration in the 1990s, showcasing the alterations made by Charles I of Anjou to the original Norman-Swabian design. This modification was primarily done to transform the castle into an opulent prison. Lagopesole Castle is the last castle commissioned by Frederick II and serves as a testament to his talent for selecting sites of extraordinary natural splendor. From a historical and environmental point of view, the castle represents the most visually privileged element of the surrounding landscape. Because of this, it has profoundly influenced historical, cultural, religious, and hiking tourism (Figs. 1 and 2).

The site of Piano del Conte is a rural area falling within the municipality of Avigliano and Filiano, covering a wide terrace at an elevation of about 770 a.s.l. not far from Lagopesole Castle.

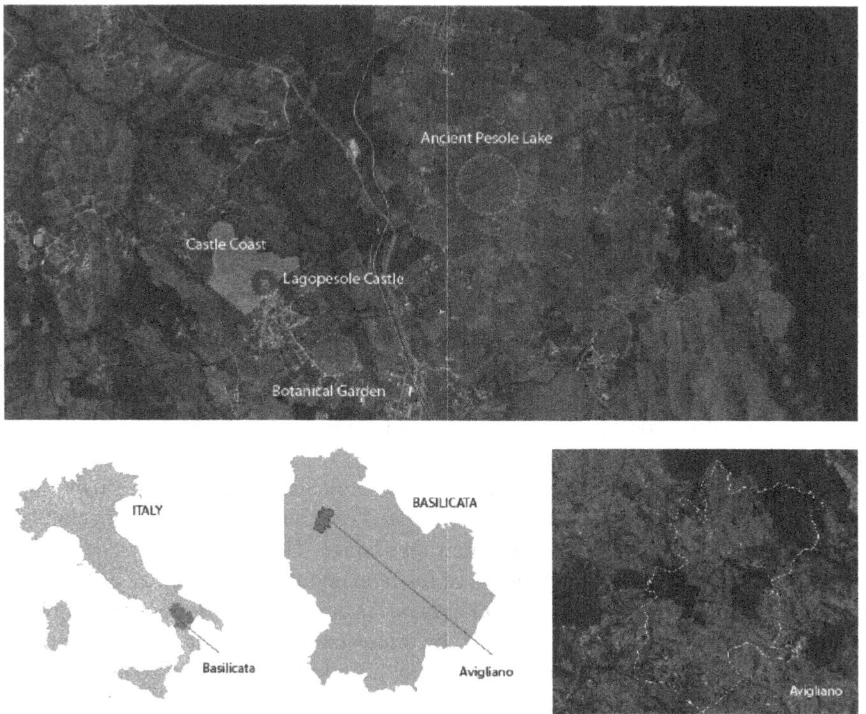

Fig. 1. Location of Lagopesole castle and Piano del Conte lake in Avigliano municipality.

Fig. 2. Piano del Conte lake in Avigliano municipality.

Piano del Conte site remains hidden from the panoramic views offered by the Potenza- Melfi highway, unlike the Lagopesole castle, located on the opposite side of the valley and clearly visible from the road axis. The site preserves the remains of the ancient "Lacus Pensilis," from which the current name of the village Lagopesole derives.

4.2 The Project

The fundamental point regarding Piano del Conte Lake recovery and environmental requalification is represented by the respect for the morphological and vegetational structure and, consequently, the restoration of the original environmental conditions.

The lake is an articulated element of environmental reconstruction in developing a methodological achievement in landscape restoration. It involves the reconstitution of a natural element that redefines the landscape and environmental framework of the Piano del Conte territory.

The first intervention to be carried out will be cleaning the lake area using appropriate means. This will be followed by cutting and removing all invasive vegetation and arranging the soil and deposits to create new lake banks. These banks have been designed based on the geological characterization of the land and the hydrological study of flood-prone areas with a return period of 1,000 years. After lake rehabilitation, the remaining portion of the municipal-owned land will be interested in regeneration interventions.

In order to make the area more accessible, a parking lot accommodating approximately 60 cars, including at least three spaces for disabled individuals, and a bicycle parking area will be created upon arrival from the provincial road.

Biking near the lake offers an exhilarating and scenic experience for outdoor enthusiasts. With the shimmering lake as a backdrop, cyclists can enjoy the fresh air and stunning views while exploring the surrounding trails and pathways. Whether it's a leisurely ride along the lakeside promenade or a more challenging off-road adventure through the nearby forests and hills, biking near the lake provides a fantastic opportunity to immerse oneself in nature and engage in a physically active and sustainable activity. Cyclists can pedal along designated bike paths, take in the beauty of the lake's shoreline, and perhaps even discover hidden gems and attractions along the way. It's a great way to combine outdoor recreation, appreciation of natural landscapes, and the joy of cycling.

The bicycle lane around the lake provides a dedicated and safe route for cyclists to enjoy the scenic beauty of the lake while engaging in their favorite activity. This designated lane, separate from vehicular traffic and pedestrian paths, allows cyclists to ride comfortably and freely, taking in the panoramic views of the water and surrounding landscapes. The bicycle lane is well-marked and designed to accommodate various skill levels, from casual riders to more experienced cyclists. The lane follows the lake's shoreline, providing continuous access to stunning vistas and recreational areas. The bicycle lane around the lake promotes a healthy and eco-friendly mode of transportation, encouraging people to cycle and enjoy the outdoors while reducing traffic congestion and carbon emissions. It also enhances safety for cyclists, separating them from motorized vehicles and providing a dedicated space for their enjoyment.

Fig. 3. Piano del Conte lake project.

The paths are divided into three types:

- Bicycle lane (orange in Fig. 3) with a width of 3.50 m and a length of approximately 2 km, made of colored permeable asphalt. It follows the catchment basin and, in some areas, deviates slightly from it to enter the sensory garden, allowing this type of user also to enjoy it.
- Main pedestrian path (red in Fig. 3) with a width of 2.50 m and a length of 2 km, which follows and defines the newly identified basin based on the conducted studies.
- A secondary pedestrian path with a width of 2.00 m connects the two aforementioned paths with various rest areas.

Within the area accessible to all users, specific areas have been identified where people can rest and take advantage of the different services and facilities. The main elements can be summarized as events, educational, playground, dog park, picnic, and outdoor fitness areas.

Events Area

This area, paved with washed stone, is equipped with steps immersed in greenery, creating a natural arena with a lake backdrop. It can host small performances, projections, outdoor parties, and exhibitions, provided they are kept within limits and compatible with the surroundings. This area also has a prefabricated wooden restroom containing facilities for men, women, and people with disabilities. A small pergola is also installed, accommodating two wooden benches, a bicycle rack, and a waste bin (Fig. 4).

Fig. 4. Events area.

Educational Area

Adjacent to the area designated for public events, a single-story building has been located for the educational area. The building is exterior wooden exterior but a reinforced concrete structure. The internal partitions have been designed to be movable, allowing the spaces to be adapted for different functions. The building also includes restrooms, with access not only from the interior but also from the exterior for general use. The café is closely connected to an external wooden pergola set amidst a grassy area. On the other side, there is a spacious interior space where tables and small gazebos will be placed to facilitate café activities. The outdoor spaces are defined by hedges that mark their boundaries. The workshops, with large windows, provide direct access to the outside, which is developed as a botanical garden consisting of twenty-two native plant species, each accompanied by informative signs placed near each plant. It represents a primary educational facility that can be modified and expanded through the activities carried out by the workshop.

Playground Area

The playground is designed for children to engage in outdoor and recreational activities. It has various play structures and amenities to promote physical activity, creativity, and social interaction.

Two equipped areas are furnished with wooden benches, waste bins, and bicycle racks. There are also two small pergolas under which two wooden benches are placed. This zone, dedicated to entertainment for young children, is slightly different from the typical playground projects, but it has been carefully crafted to integrate harmoniously with the surrounding nature.

Dog Park Area

A dog park area is a designated space specifically designed for dogs and their owners to exercise, play, and socialize in a controlled and safe environment. It offers a range of amenities and features tailored to the needs of dogs, promoting their physical and mental well-being. The dog park area aims to create a positive social experience for dogs and their owners. It allows dogs to exercise, socialize, and have fun in a controlled environment while fostering responsible pet ownership.

Picnic Area

Three pergolas with covered benches will be built in this area. Other services will be realized: a larger service box that accommodates restrooms and facilities such as a medical room, an information point, and a small bar. A prefabricated restroom block for men, women, and people with disabilities will also be included in the project. Additionally, there are other picnic benches present. An optimal design of the picnic area includes not only tables but also other essential elements. The installation of drinking fountains and the environmentally friendly choice of providing waste bins and ashtrays to combine the enjoyment of the space with full respect for the environment, avoiding the littering of bottles, packaging, and meal residues in the greenery.

Outdoor Fitness Area

The outdoor fitness area is a designated space where individuals can engage in various physical activities and exercise outdoors. It provides opportunities for people to improve their fitness, strength, and overall well-being while enjoying the natural environment. The outdoor fitness area has various fitness equipment designed for outdoor use. This includes cardio machines like ellipticals or stationary bikes, strength-training equipment such as pull-up bars, resistance stations, and balance or agility equipment. The equipment should be strategically placed to allow for proper circulation and flow of users. Fitness trails have been included in outdoor fitness areas to provide a dynamic and engaging exercise experience in natural surroundings. These trails consist of a series of fitness stations or stations that are strategically placed along a designated path or trail. Each station is equipped with exercise equipment or apparatus that targets different muscle groups and promotes various types of physical activity.

The trails cater to individuals of different fitness levels and abilities. They may offer options for beginners and advanced users, allowing individuals to progress and challenge themselves as they improve their fitness levels. Clear signage or instructions are usually provided at each station to guide users on performing the exercises correctly and safely. One of the advantages of outdoor fitness trails is the opportunity to exercise in a natural and open environment. Users can enjoy the benefits of fresh air, natural sunlight, and the beauty of the surrounding landscape while engaging in their workout routines. Its location in a beautiful area provides a refreshing and inspiring backdrop for exercise.

Sensory Garden

The project will also include a sensory garden. A sensory garden, also known as a therapeutic garden, is specifically designed to engage and stimulate the senses, providing a unique sensory experience for visitors. The garden is carefully planned and curated to incorporate various elements that appeal to the senses of sight, smell, touch, taste, and sound. Its purpose is to create a harmonious environment that promotes relaxation, healing, and well-being.

The sensory garden typically features various plants and flowers with vibrant colors, interesting textures, and captivating fragrances. These plants are selected to engage the sense of sight and smell, offering a visually appealing and aromatic experience. The garden may include visually striking elements such as colorful flower beds, blooming shrubs, and visually contrasting foliage.

The garden may incorporate different tactile elements such as soft grass, smooth stones, textured pathways, and plants with unique leaf textures to engage the sense of touch. These elements encourage visitors to interact with the garden by touching and feeling the different surfaces, fostering a sensory connection with nature.

In terms of sound, the sensory garden may include features such as wind chimes, gentle water fountains, or strategically placed plants that produce rustling sounds in the breeze. These auditory elements create a calming and soothing atmosphere, promoting relaxation and mindfulness.

Some sensory gardens also incorporate edible plants, allowing visitors to engage their sense of taste. These gardens may feature herbs, fruits, or vegetables that visitors can sample and enjoy, providing a unique sensory experience and fostering a connection to nature's bounty.

The sensory garden design considers accessibility, ensuring it is easily navigable for individuals with disabilities or mobility challenges. It may include wheelchair-accessible paths, raised beds for easy reach, and braille or tactile signs to provide information for visually impaired visitors.

Overall, a sensory garden is a carefully crafted space that offers a multi-sensory experience, promoting relaxation, stimulation, and a deeper connection with nature. It provides a therapeutic and enriching environment for individuals of all ages and abilities, allowing them to immerse themselves in the beauty and sensory delights of the natural world.

5 Conclusions

The ecological approach to the project of lake regeneration has demonstrated the significance and effectiveness of implementing sustainable practices to restore and preserve the health and functioning of the lake ecosystem. Through careful planning, scientific research, and collaborative efforts, the project has achieved its objectives and brought about positive outcomes for the lake and its surrounding environment. Incorporating ecological engineering techniques, such as establishing submerged macrophytes and creating habitat structures, has proven instrumental in enhancing the lake's environmental functions and promoting biodiversity. These measures have provided valuable habitats for various organisms, improved water clarity, and contributed to the overall health and resilience of the ecosystem.

The project has highlighted the importance of addressing key issues, such as the potential to enhance the tourism attractiveness of the area significantly.

By restoring the lake's ecological health and aesthetic appeal, these projects create a more desirable destination for tourists seeking natural beauty, recreational opportunities, and unique experiences. Clean and clear waters provide enjoyable experiences for visitors and contribute to the overall perception of the lake as a pristine and inviting environment.

Restoring diverse aquatic habitats and promoting biodiversity through ecological projects can enhance the natural and scenic values of the lake. This attracts nature enthusiasts, birdwatchers, and wildlife photographers interested in observing and interacting with the rich flora and fauna that thrive in the rehabilitated lake ecosystem.

Incorporating sustainable tourism practices and infrastructure within the lake area can further enhance its attractiveness [19, 20]. Developing well-designed biking and hiking trails, picnic areas, and viewpoint locations allows visitors to explore and appreciate the lake's surroundings while minimizing the environmental impact. Interpretive signage and educational programs can provide insights into the lake's ecological significance and foster a deeper understanding and appreciation among tourists.

Moreover, the combination of lake regeneration and tourism can have positive economic impacts on the local community [21–25]. A revitalized lake can attract more tourists, increasing visitor spending on accommodations, dining, recreational activities, and local products. This, in turn, stimulates local businesses, generates employment opportunities, and boosts the overall economy.

However, ensuring that tourism activities are managed sustainably is crucial to prevent negative impacts on the rehabilitated lake ecosystem. Implementing appropriate regulations, monitoring visitor numbers, and promoting responsible tourism practices can help maintain the lake's ecological integrity while maximizing its tourism potential.

Overall, the ecological project of lake regeneration is a successful model for promoting sustainable practices and restoring the ecological integrity of lakes. It demonstrates the effectiveness of multidisciplinary approaches, scientific research, and community engagement in achieving positive outcomes for the lake ecosystem and the surrounding communities. Continued monitoring and adaptive management will be crucial in maintaining the achieved ecological improvements and ensuring the project's long-term success.

In conclusion, lake regeneration projects have the potential to enhance tourism attractiveness by creating a healthier and more visually appealing environment, providing a range of recreational activities, and supporting local economies. By combining ecological restoration with sustainable tourism practices, lakes can become popular destinations that offer memorable experiences for visitors while preserving and showcasing their natural heritage.

Acknowledgments. The authors are grateful to Avigliano Municipality Administration and the technical staff for supporting the project's development.

References

1. Omernik, J.M.: Map supplement ecoregions of the conterminous United States. Ann. Assoc. Am. Geogr. **77**, 118–125 (1987)
2. Bailey, R.G.: Ecosystem Geography (2009). https://doi.org/10.1007/978-0-387-89516-1
3. Mitsch, W.J., Jørgensen, S.E.: Ecological Engineering and Ecosystem Restoration. Wiley (2004)
4. Pascual, U., et al.: On the value of soil biodiversity and ecosystem services. Ecosyst. Serv. **15**, 11–18 (2015). https://doi.org/10.1016/j.ecoser.2015.06.002
5. Stremke, S., van den Dobbelsteen, A.: Sustainable Energy Landscapes: Designing, Planning, and Development. Taylor & Francis (2013)
6. Scheffer, M., Hosper, S.H., Meijer, M.L., Moss, B., Jeppesen, E.: Alternative equilibria in shallow lakes. Trends Ecol. Evol. **8**, 275–279 (1993). https://doi.org/10.1016/0169-5347(93)90254-M
7. Wetzel, R.G.: Limology Lake and River Ecosystems, 3rd edn. (2001)
8. Carpenter, S.R., Caraco, N.F., Correll, D.L., Howarth, R.W., Sharpley, A.N., Smith, V.H.: Nonpoint pollution of surface waters with phosphorus and nitrogen. Ecol. Appl. **8**, 559 (1998). https://doi.org/10.2307/2641247
9. Murgante, B., Borruso, G., Lapucci, A.: Sustainable development: Concepts and methods for its application in urban and environmental planning. Stud. Comput. Intell. **348**, 1–15 (2011). https://doi.org/10.1007/978-3-642-19733-8_1
10. Beunen, R., de Vries, J.R.: The governance of Natura 2000 sites: the importance of initial choices in the organisation of planning processes. J. Environ. Plan. Manag. **54**, 1041–1059 (2011). https://doi.org/10.1080/09640568.2010.549034
11. Zoppi, C.: Integration of conservation measures concerning Natura 2000 sites into marine protected areas regulations: a study related to Sardinia. Sustainability **10**, 3460 (2018). https://doi.org/10.3390/su10103460
12. Wätzold, F., et al.: Cost-effectiveness of managing Natura 2000 sites: an exploratory study for Finland, Germany, the Netherlands and Poland. Biodivers. Conserv. **19**, 2053–2069 (2010). https://doi.org/10.1007/s10531-010-9825-x
13. Bastian, O.: The role of biodiversity in supporting ecosystem services in Natura 2000 sites. Ecol. Indic. **24**, 12–22 (2013). https://doi.org/10.1016/j.ecolind.2012.05.016
14. Lai, S., Zoppi, C.: The influence of Natura 2000 sites on land-taking processes at the regional level: an empirical analysis concerning Sardinia (Italy). Sustainability. **9**, 259 (2017). https://doi.org/10.3390/su9020259
15. Cortina, C., Boggia, A.: Development of policies for Natura 2000 sites: A multi-criteria approach to support decision makers. J. Environ. Manage. **141**, 138–145 (2014). https://doi.org/10.1016/J.JENVMAN.2014.02.039
16. Moss, B.: Ecology of Fresh Waters : Man and Medium, Past to Future. Wiley (2009)
17. Saganeiti, L., Pilogallo, A., Faruolo, G., Scorza, F., Murgante, B.: Territorial fragmentation and renewable energy source plants: which relationship? Sustain. **12**, 1828 (2020). https://doi.org/10.3390/SU12051828
18. Muzzillo, V., Pilogallo, A., Saganeiti, L., Santarsiero, V., Scorza, F., Murgante, B.: Impact of renewable energy installations on habitat quality. In: Gervasi, O., et al. (eds.) ICCSA 2020. LNCS, vol. 12253, pp. 636–644. Springer, Cham (2020). https://doi.org/10.1007/978-3-030-58814-4_50
19. Aryal, K., Ojha, B.R., Maraseni, T.: Perceived importance and economic valuation of ecosystem services in Ghodaghodi wetland of Nepal. Land Use Policy **106**, 105450 (2021). https://doi.org/10.1016/J.LANDUSEPOL.2021.105450

20. Pilogallo, A., Saganeiti, L., Scorza, F., Las Casas, G.: Tourism attractiveness: main components for a special appraisal of major destinations according with ecosystem services approach. In: Gervasi, O., et al. (eds.) ICCSA 2018. LNCS, vol. 10964, pp. 712–724. Springer, Cham (2018). https://doi.org/10.1007/978-3-319-95174-4_54
21. Scorza, F., Murgante, B., Las Casas, G., Fortino, Y., Pilogallo, A.: Investigating territorial specialization in tourism sector by ecosystem services approach. In: Stratigea, A., Kavroudakis, D. (eds.) Mediterranean Cities and Island Communities. PI, pp. 161–179. Springer, Cham (2019). https://doi.org/10.1007/978-3-319-99444-4_7
22. Chen, X., et al.: Water resources management in the urban agglomeration of the Lake Biwa region, Japan: an ecosystem services-based sustainability assessment. Sci. Total Environ. **586**, 174–187 (2017). https://doi.org/10.1016/j.scitotenv.2017.01.197
23. Scorza, F., Pilogallo, A., Las Casas, G.: Investigating tourism attractiveness in inland areas: ecosystem services, open data and smart specializations. In: Calabrò, F., Della Spina, L., Bevilacqua, C. (eds.) ISHT 2018. SIST, vol. 100, pp. 30–38. Springer, Cham (2019). https://doi.org/10.1007/978-3-319-92099-3_4
24. Sharp, H., Grundius, J., Heinonen, J.: Carbon footprint of inbound tourism to Iceland: a consumption-based life-cycle assessment including direct and indirect emissions. Sustain. **8**, 1147 (2015). https://doi.org/10.3390/su8111147
25. Eurostat: Unemployment statistics at regional level. Stat. Explain. 1–22 (2018)

A Machine Learning Method for the Analysis of Urban Italian Mobility

Gabriella Schoier(✉) and Giuseppe Borruso

DEAMS – Department of Economic, Business, Mathematic and Statistical Sciences "Bruno de Finetti", University of Trieste, Valerio, 4/1 – 34127, Trieste, Italy
{gabriella.schoier,giuseppe.borruso}@deams.units.it

Abstract. The aim of this paper is to consider a method of machine learning to analyze the problem of the sustainability of the urban transport in Italian cities. First of all we recall the definition of sustainable mobility then we present some indicators considered in our analysis.

The methodology used in this paper are decisional trees.

We both consider classification and regression trees. We have chosen two different dependent variables one for classification trees (a categorical variable: Macroregion according to NUTS 1: North West, North East, Centre, Islands and South of Italy) and one for regression trees (a quantitative variable: PM10 maximum number of days in excess of the human health protection limit foreseen for PM10). In order to test the performance of this methodology we have applied random forest.

The analysis has been performed using SAS language.

Keywords: Spatial Data Mining · Decisional Trees · Urban Mobility

1 Introduction

From the beginning of the twenty-first century, a fundamental idea has been how to extract information from big data. Big data analytics could provide opportunities to develop new knowledge to reshape our understanding of different fields and to support decision-making.

A huge amount of data i.e. big data have been collected by private and public organizations (see eg. [12, 14–16]). An example of big data collection regards urban transport. In particular, the problem of sustainability of urban transport has been recognized as a crucial economical social and political objective. To analyze the notion of urban sustainable mobility and to choose appropriate indicators it is necessary to define the notion of urban sustainable mobility and to choose appropriate indicators enabling its measurement.

The aim of this paper is to analyse urban transport mobility at province level in Italy on the base of some indicators.

The aim of this research is to understand how different variables influence urban transport mobility in the territories (provinces).

O. Gervasi et al. (Eds.): ICCSA 2023 Workshops, LNCS 14107, pp. 590–603, 2023.
https://doi.org/10.1007/978-3-031-37114-1_41

The new idea regards the application of decision trees to some indicators and random forest to test the goodness of fit.

We consider both classification and regression trees; two different dependent variables have been chosen:

- classification trees dependent variable Macroregion according to NUTS 1: North West, North East, Centre, Islands and South of Italy,
- regression trees dependent variable PM10_20 (maximum number of days in excess of the human health protection limit foreseen for PM10).

Our objective is to see how different indicators move to analyze and then monitor the sustainability of the urban transport in Italian cities in particular regarding the chosen dependent variables.

2 The Methodology: Decision Trees and Random Forest

2.1 Decision Trees

As it is well known decision trees are a part of hierarchical classification or segmentation techniques [2, 11]. These techniques have the purpose of "sorting" statistical units into the various classes of a dependent variable on the basis of the values of one or more explanatory variables.

In 1984 Breiman and others introduced an innovative segmentation technique. This technique is called Classification and RegressionTrees (CART) (see [3]). It is presented as a recursive and binary partition methodology.

The hierarchical segmentation process used in the construction of decisional trees consists in divide the statistical units in a finite number of disjoint subgroups in order to guarantee an internal homogeneity higher than that of the initial dataset and a high heterogeneity between the subgroups.

A tree has many analogies in real life, and turns out that it has influenced a wide area of machine learning, covering both classification and regression.

In decision analysis, a decision tree can be used to visually and explicitly represent decisions and decision making. As the name says, it uses a tree-like model of decisions. Though it is a commonly used tool in data mining for deriving a strategy to reach a particular goal, it is also widely used in machine learning. They are easy to interpret and make for visualizations, they make possible to reproduce work, they can handle both numerical and categorical data, they perform well on large dataset and are extremely fast.

A decision tree is a type of predictive model that has been developed independently in the statistics and artificial intelligence communities. The HPFOREST procedure creates a tree recursively. An input variable is chosen and used to create a rule to split the data into two segments. The process is then repeated in each segment, and then again in each new segment, and so on until some constraint is met. In the terminology of the tree metaphor, the segments are nodes, the original data set is the root node, and the final segments are leaves or terminal nodes. A node is an internal node if it is not a leaf. The data in a leaf determine the estimates of the value of the target variable. These estimates are subsequently applied to predict the target of a new observation assigned to the leaf.

This type of models are used for both classification and regression (see eg. [6]).

The performance of a tree can be further increased by pruning in particular by using CART (see [3]) example of indices used for pruning are Entropy and Gini for classification trees and RSS (residual sum of squares) for regression trees.

$G = 1 - \sum_j f_j^2$ Gini index

$H = - \sum_j f_j \log f_j$ Shannon index

where f_j is the relative frequency.

It involves removing the branches that make use of features having low importance. In so doing the complexity of tree is reduced and the power by reducing overfitting is increased.

The simplest method of pruning starts at leaves and removes each node with most popular class in that leaf, this change is kept if it does not deteriorate accuracy. It is also called reduced error pruning.

More sophisticated pruning methods can be used such as cost complexity pruning where a learning parameter (alpha) is used to weigh whether nodes can be removed based on the size of the sub-tree. In order to obtain the sequence of trees of decreasing dimension, one defines, for every tree $T \leq T_{max}$ a cost complexity function $R_\alpha(T)$

$$R_\alpha(T) = \widehat{R}(T) + \alpha\left|\tilde{T}\right|$$

where $\widehat{R}(T)$ estimate of rate of wrong classification,

$\left|\tilde{T}\right|$ the numbers of leaves.

2.2 Random Forest

Random forest is a high-performance method that creates a predictive model called a forest that consists of several decision trees (see [4]).

The purpose of a predictive model is to predict a target variable on the basis of independent variables/regressors.

In particular random forest trains the model using training data in which the target values are known then model is applied to observations in which the target is unknown.

If the predictions fit the new data well, the model is said to generalize well. The method has the ability to perform both classification and regression prediction. We can say that random forests are an improved extension on classification and regression trees (CART) with respect to instability and accuracy.

Random forest creates different decision trees. The differences regard the fact that the training data for a tree is a sample with replacement from the original training data and that the regressors considered for splitting a node are randomly selected from all available independent variables. Among these variables only a single one is used to form a splitting rule. The chosen variable is the one that is most associated with the target one.

Training a forest can require training hundreds of decision trees. Specifically, random forests remain relatively stable with changes in data due to the combination of many trees. Random forests are computationally simple to fit, there are no formal distributional assumptions. The Random Forest algorithm consider a forest of n trees for each tree we have to take B random sample with replacement (boostrap samples) to grow a tree then we have to select for each node indepeldently and randomly m variables from M possible variables and use them as predictors. Trees are grown until the nodes can no longer be split. These predictors are used as the "out-of-bag" (OOB) data to measure the accuracy of the model [4]. The observation is passed down these trees and it is classified in the class which obtain the majority rule, giving the OOB prediction for the observation. The error rate of all the OOB predictions is the OOB error rate of the forest.

Random forests compute the importance of variables in different ways. For classification problems the Gini criterion can be used. For a given tree, the Gini variable importance measure for a particular variable of interest is the weighted average of the decrease in the Gini impurity criteria of the splits based on this variable. This is averaged over the all the trees in the forest to get the Gini importance for the forest itself. Important variables yield high Gini variable importance measures.

Another variable importance calculation is called permutation importance. Permutation importance is based on predictive accuracy. The out-of-bag error rate is computed from both a data set obtained from permuting the values of a particular variable of interest in the "out-of-bag" OOB data and the original OOB data. The difference between these two OOB error rates gives the permutation variable importance. Important variables yield high permutation variable importance measures.

3 The Application

3.1 The Data and the Variables

The study of sustainable mobility plays an important role in the socio-economic field and it is of great importance for the politicians and the economists(see e.g. [13]).

To obtain this pourpose it is essential define the notion of sustainable mobility and to measure it. Numerous definitions of sustainable mobility are proposed, the most famous one was introduced in the Brundland report according to which: "Sustainable transport meets the mobility needs of the present without compromising the ability of future generations to meet these needs." (see [17]).

The European Conference of Ministers of Transport (see [5]) further specified the main features that a sustainable mobility system should meet, that is:

- allowing the basic access and development needs of individuals, companies and society to be met safely and in a manner consistent with human and ecosystem health, and promotes equity within and between successive generations;
- being affordable, operating fairly and efficiently, offering a choice of transport mode, and supporting a competitive economy, as well as balanced regional development;
- limiting emissions and waste within the planet's ability to absorb them, using renewable resources at or below their rates of generation, and using non-renewable resources at or below the rates of development of renewable substitutes, while minimizing the impact on the use of land and the generation of noise.

To measure the environmental sustainability of the urban mobility requires taking into account both the environmental, the economic and the social aspect [17]. Moreover, the selection process should be made explicit and should adhere, according to the COST action 356, to ten criteria: validity, reliability, sensitivity, measurability, data availability, ethical concerns, transparency, interpretability, target relevance, and actionability [11].

On the basis of these guidelines 13 indicators (reported in Table 1) have been selected and have been measured with respect to Italian provincial towns.

As regards the economic aspect three indicators have been selected: Income, Salary, Rate of Employment.

The environmental indicators chosen are six: Gasoline Fuel, Diesel Fuel, Low Emission, E-Charging Stations Density, PM_{10}, Urban Green Density.

Finally the indicators used to measure the social dimension of the Italian urban transport systems are four: Rate of Fatal Accidents, Dead Pedestrians, Vehicles Density per KM2, Population_Density.

The variables considered in this study are reported in the following Table 1 (see [7–10]).

Table 1. Indicators for Sustainable mobility of Italian cities

Name	Description
City	Province
Macroregion	Macroregion according to NUTS 1: North West, North East, Centre, Islands and South of Italy
RateFatalAccident_19	Fatality accident rate
Dead_Pedestrians_19	Pedestrians died in accidents
Population_Density_21	Popolation density
Vehicles_DensityKM2_19	Vehicle density per km^2
RateEmployment_21	Employment rate 20-64 years
Income_17	Income
Salary_20	Salary
GasolineFuel_Car_21	Petrol/gasoline vehicles %
DieselFuel_Car_21	Diesel-fuelled vehicles %
LowEmission_Car_21	Low emission vehicles %
Echarging_Stations_Density_19	Density of electric car charging columns
PM10_20	maximum number of days in excess of the human health protection limit foreseen for PM10
Urban_Green_Density_20	Urban green density

The data font is the Italian National Institute of Statistics (Istat). Some variables are not available for all the provincial towns.[1]

[1] These cities have not be considered in this analysis: Andria e Trani.

At provincial level, the most up-to-date available data refer to the year 2021 and 2019, unless the economic variables - income and salary - which refer respectively to the years 2017 and 2020, but they have been include in the analysis as they have been considered fundamental for our purpose. The criteria for the choice of each indicators inside the dimension is done as [13], i.e. the correlations within each domain, the variability indexes (i.e. coefficient of variation and the quartile difference for standardized data) and the adequacy of the indicator to the analysis to be carried out.

3.2 Classification Trees

The aim of the first part of our analysis is to consider a categorical dependent variable in order to forcast it. The dependent variable is Macroregion according to NUTS 1: North West, North East, Centre, Islands and South of Italy.

We have applied different models with and without pruning. At the end on the base of a compromise between complexity and rate of error we have chosen a classification tree with split Entropy and prune Gini index.

As we can see on the base of the model the rate of error is very low as regards the Island it is equal to zero for Centre, North West and South is less than 0.2 while for the North East is less than 0.25 see Table 2.

Table 2. Confusion matrix based on the model.

Macroregion	Centre	Islands	North East	NorthWest	South	Error rate
Centre	19	0	0	1	3	0.1739
Islands	0	13	0	0	0	0.0000
North East	1	0	17	4	0	0.2273
North West	2	0	2	21	0	0.1600
South	1	2	0	0	21	0.1250

In Fig. 1 the selected model using the Gini's index for the pruning is reported.

As one can see the number of chosen leaf according to the Gini index are 10; the value of the Gini index is 0.237.

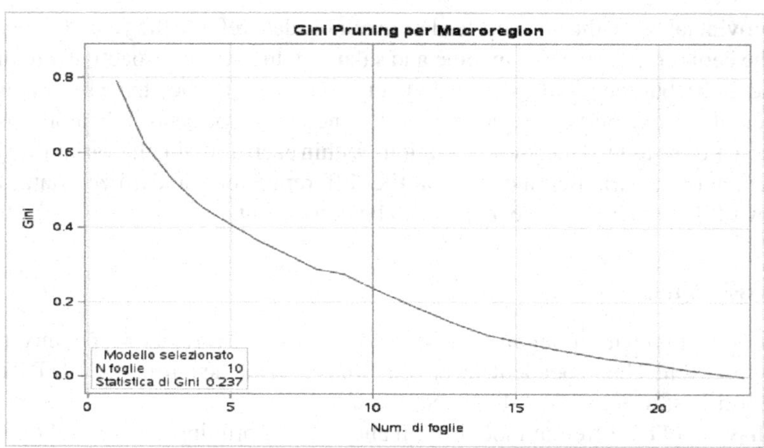

Fig. 1. The selected model using the Gini's index for pruning

The importance of the variables for the construction of the classification trees is reported in Table 3.

Table 3. Confusion matrix based on the model

Variable	Realative importance	Importance	Count
RateUnemployment_21	1.0000	4.2501	1
GasolineFuel_Car_21	0.9972	4.2381	2
Salary_20	0.7066	3.0030	2
Dead_Pedestrians_19	0.5125	2.1780	1
DieselFuel_Car_21	0.4802	2.0407	1
Vehicles_DensityKM2_19	0.4624	1.9654	1
Low_Emission_Car_21	0.2954	1.2553	1

In the Fig. 2 the obtained classification tree is produced. The leaves (terminal nodes) are: node3, node 7, node 8, node A, node B, node C while node 9 is divided in node D (terminal node) and node E which is divided in two terminal nodes: node H and node 1.

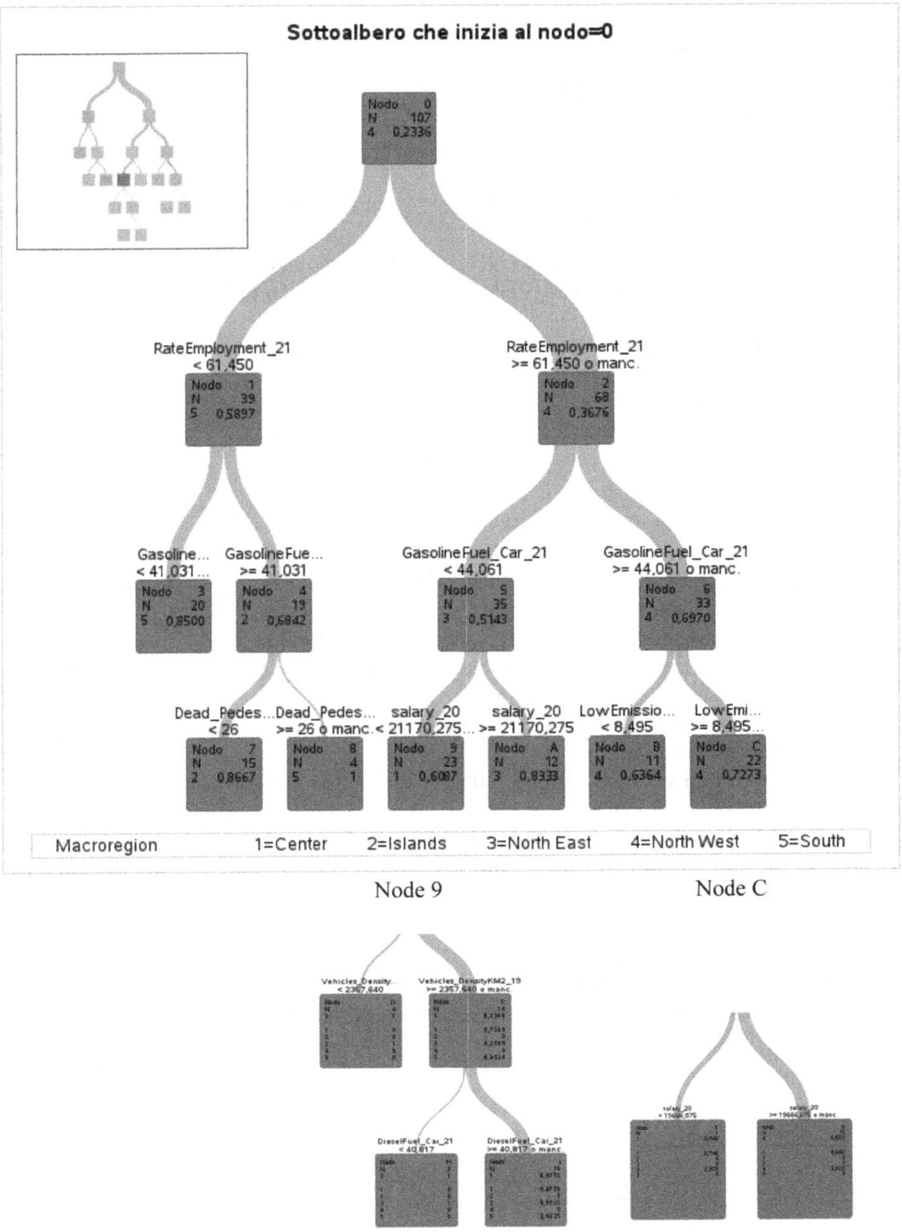

Node 9 Node C

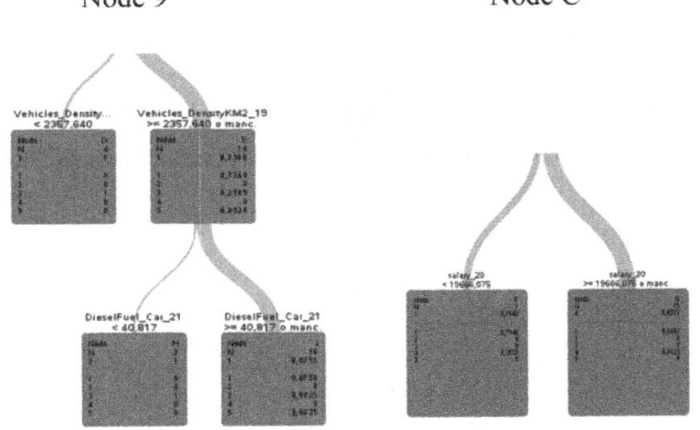

Fig. 2. Classification tree

There are 107 units in the root node (node 0).

These units are divided into 39 units with RateEmployment_21 < 61.450 (node 1) and 68 units for node 2 with RateEmployment_21 ≥ 61.450 (node 2).

Node 1 is divided in two nodes:

- node 3 (terminal node) if GasolineFuel_Car_21<41.031, twenty units assigned to class 5 (South) (prob. 0.85),
- node 4 if GasolineFuel_Car_21≥41.031, divided in two nodes:
  node 7 (terminal node) if Dead_Pedestrians_19<26 fifteen units assigned to class 2 (Islands) (prob. 0.87),
  node 8 (terminal node) if Dead_Pedestrians_19≥26 four units assigned to class 5 (South) (prob. 1).

Node 2 is divided in two nodes:

-node 5 if GasolineFuel_Car_21<44.061, divided in two nodes:
  -node 9 if Salary_20<21170,275 divided in:
   -node D (terminal node) if Vehicles_DensityKM2_19<2357,640 four units assigned to class 3 (North East) ,
  -node E if Vehicles_DensityKM2_19≥2357,640 divided in:
   -node H (terminal node) if DieselFuel_Car_21<40.817 three units assign to class 3 (North East),
   -node I (terminal node) if DieselFuel_Car_21≥40.817 sixteen units assigned to class 1 (Centre)
  -node A (terminal node) if Salary_20≥21170,275 twelve units assigned to class 3 (North East) (prob. 0.8333).
- node 6 if GasolineFuel_Car_21≥44.061, divided in two nodes:
  node B (terminal node) if Low_Emission_Car_21<8.495 eleven units assigned to class 4 (North West) (prob. 0.6364),
  node C if Low_Emission_Car_21≥8.

In order to test the classification model a random forest model has been performed. He results regarding the OOBS are reported in the next figure (Fig. 3).

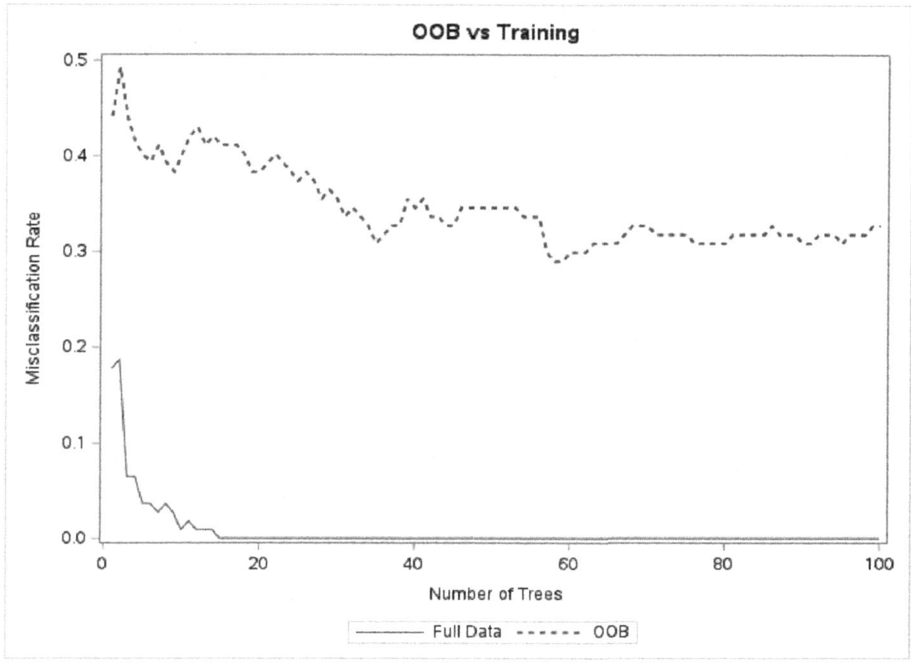

Fig. 3. OOB vs Training

3.3 Regression Trees

In order to apply regression trees we have chosen as dependent variable PM10_20 We try to predict the dependent variable on the base of the other variables that are.

We have applied different models with and without pruning. At the end on the base of a compromise between complexity and rate of error we have chosen a regresssion tree with split RSS and prune cost complexity.

We have carried out the pruning of the tree to avoid overfitting of the model on the data and to find a compromise between simplicity and discriminatory power.

As regards the pruning we have preferred cost complexity which is an algorithm based on a trade off between the complexity (size) of the tree and the error rate to prevent overfitting.

The final tree has a depth equal to 6 leaves. The ASE (Average Square Error for Regression) is given by the ratio between RSS (residual sum of squares) and the number of units of the node. In our case the ASE medium minimum is equal to 30.63 while the parameter of cost complexity is 145.4; this refers to a numbers of leaves equal to 6 (see Fig. 4).

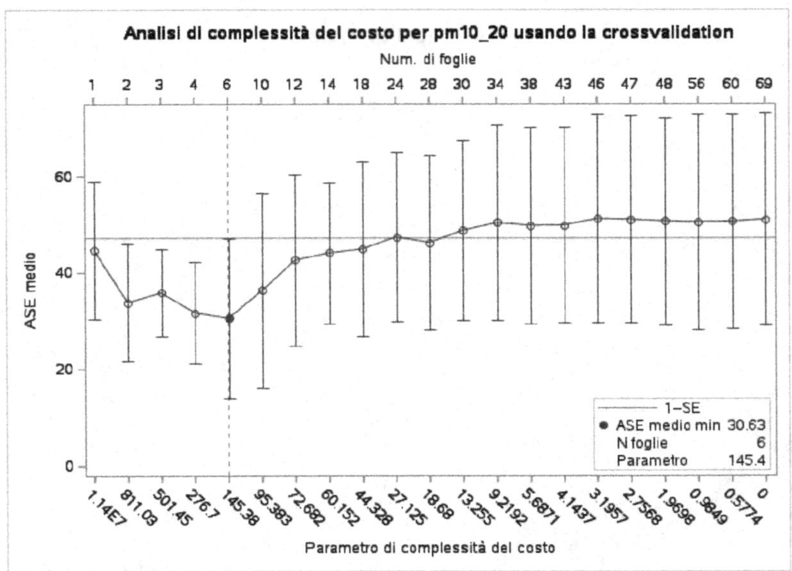

Fig. 4. The selected model using pruning costcomplexity

The final consideration regards variable importance; from Table 4 we can see which variables are the most important: Low_Emission_Car_21, Macroregion, Population_Density_21, Income_17, Dead_Pedestrians_19. The presence of the Macroregion variable shows us once again that there is actually a basic difference between the various Italian macro areas (Fig. 5).

Table 4. Variable importance.

Variable	Realative importance	Importance	Count
Low_Emission_Car_21	1.0000	36.4136	2
Macroregion	0.6583	23.9698	1
Population_Density_21	0.5745	20.9200	1
Income_17	0.3812	13.8826	1
Dead_Pedestrians_19	0.3374	12.2875	1

As regards the goodness of fit of the model with 7 leaves ASE is equal to 16.21 while the RSS is 1589.1. Using cross validation with 6 leaves ASE is 34.7613.

There are 107 provinces that have been collected. The procedure HSPLIT[2] use 98 provinces in the root node (node 0). These units are divided into 37 units with

[2] This is the procedure used by SAS language for decision trees.

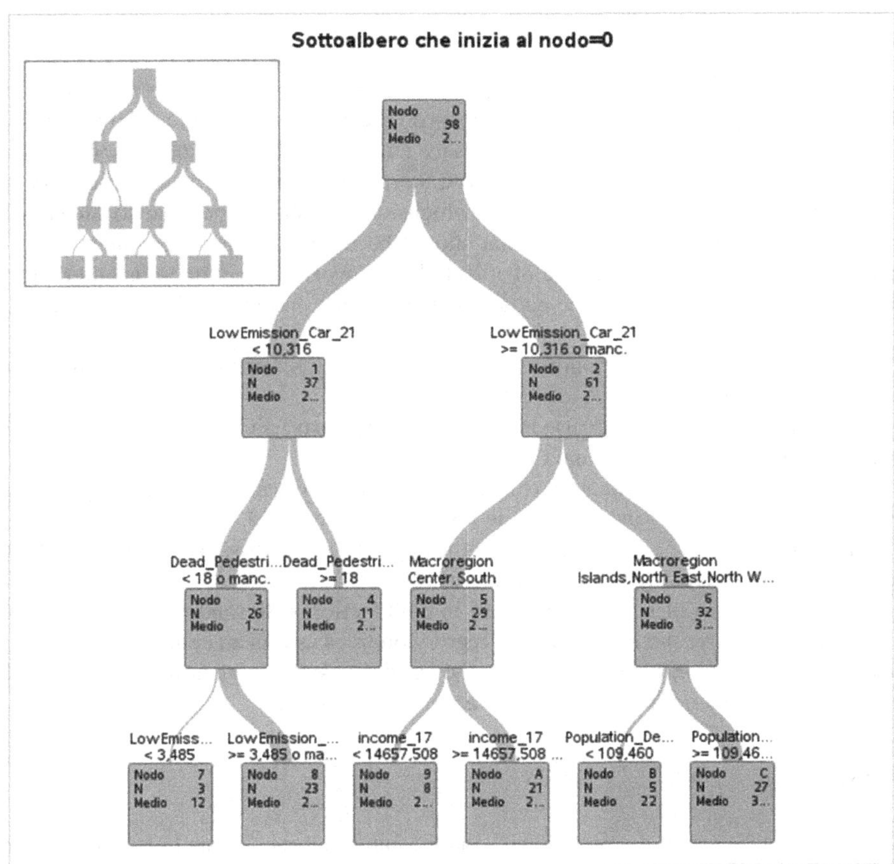

Fig. 5. Regression trees with pruning cost complexity

Low_Emission_Car_21 < 10.316 (node 1) and 61 units with Low_Emission_Car_21 $\geq$ 10.316 (node 2).

Node 1 is divided in two nodes: node 3 if Dead_Pedestrians_19 are less than 18 or there is a missing value[3] and node 4 if Dead_Pedestrians_19 $\geq$ 18. Node 4 is a terminal one while node 3 is divided by considering Low_Emission_Car_21. If Low_Emission_Car_21 < 3.485 the units are assigned to node 7 otherwise to node 8.

Node 2 is divided in node 5 if people live in Centre or South and node 6 if the live in Islands, North East, North West. Node 5 generates two leaves: node 9 if Income_17 < 14657.508 and node A if Income_17 > 14657.508. Node 6 generates two leaves: node B if Population_Density_21 < 109.60 and node C if Population_Density_21 $\geq$ 109.60.

The regression tree provides simple rules for predicting Pm10_20. This can be generalized to different data sets in fact the applications of random forest show a not elevated average squared error both in training and in OOBS.

[3] Missing values are treated using the option of HPSLIT assignmissing = similar.

4 Conclusions

In this paper we have analyzed big data, we have also illustrated processes of extraction of information from the data. In order to promote more sustainable urban transport systems it is important to be able to measure and assess the sustainability of present and future transport trends and policies. Yet, there is no general agreement both on the concept of sustainable transport and on which indexes should be used to measure it appropriately, let alone the policies that should be implemented. This comes as little surprise considering that the range of stakeholders involved are numerous and that the impacts that transport has on the economy, the society, and the environment are very complex.

Different indicators of urban transport sustainability referring to Italian provincial towns have been collected.

The statistical methodology used to analyze the Italian urban sustainability is decision trees and random forest to obtain a testing measure.

In more detail: classification trees with dependent variable Macroregion and regression trees with dependent variable PM10 have been used.

The purpose is to see if, on the basis of the previous indicators, there is the possibility of predicting the trend of variables of interest.

The applications of decision trees are in conjunction with random forest. Random forest can to improve the forecasting of regression trees as it is an elaboration of classification and regression trees that average the predictions of a large number of randomly subsampled regression trees so to obtain a more stable solution.

References

1. ANFIA (associazione nazionale filiera industria automobilistica): Cars In Use By Province And Fuel in 2021 (2021)
2. Bolasco S.: Analisi Multidimensionale dei Dati. Metodi, strategie e criteri d'interpretazione, Carrocci editore, Roma (2005)
3. Breiman, L., Friedman, J.H., Olshen, R.A., Stone, C.J.: Classsification and Regression Trees. Taylor & Francis, New York (1984)
4. Breiman, L.: Random Forest. Machine Learning, vol. 45, pp. 5–32, Kluvier Accademic Publisher, Manifactured in The Nederlands (2001)
5. ECMT: Strategy For Integrating Environment and Sustainable Development Into The Transport Policy. Adopted by the Ministers responsible for Transport and Communications at the 2340th meeting of the European Union' Council of Ministers, Luxembourg, April 4–5, 2001 (2001)
6. Gareth, J., Witten, D., Hastie, T., Tibshirani, R.: Introduzione all'apprendimento statistico. In: Salini, S., Gaito, S., Boracchi, P., Ambrogi, F., Manzi, G., Biganzoli, E. (eds) Piccin Editore (2021)
7. ISTAT(a): Nota sulle misure del Benessere Equo e Sostenibile dei territori. Anno 2021. Retrieved from October 2022 (2022) https://www.istat.it/it/files//2019/05/Nota-metodologica.pdf
8. ISTAT(b): Il BES dei territori. https://www.istat.it/en/well-being-and-sustainability/the-measurement-of-well-being/bes-at-local-level Accessed Oct 2022

9. ISTAT(c): BES-2021, Il Benessere Equo e Sostenibile in Italia. https://www.istat.it/it/files//2022/04/BES_2021.pdf. Accessed June 2022
10. Joumard, R., Gudmundsson, H.: Indicators of environmental sustainability in transport. An interdisciplinary approach to methods. INRETS, Lyon, France (2010)
11. Jan, A.K.: Data Clustering. 50 years beyond K-means. Pattern Recogn. Lett. 651–666 (2010)
12. Mayer-Schonberger, V., Cukier, K.: Big Data: A Revolution That Will Transform How We Live, Work, and Think. Mariner Books, Boston (2013)
13. Monte, A., Schoier, G.: A multivariate statistical analysis of equitable and sustainable well-being over time. Soc. Indic. Res. , 1–16 (2020). https://doi.org/10.1007/s11205-020-02392-x
14. Pubblico registro automobilistico Morti e feriti in Incidenti, Accessed 25/11/22 I.Stat
15. Schoier, G., Borruso, G.: A methodology for dealing with spatial big data. Int. J. Bus. Intell. Data Mining **12**(1), 1–13 (2017)
16. Software Testing Help: Data Mining Vs Machine Learning Vs Artificial Intelligence Vs Deep Learning (2019). http://www.intelligenzaartificiale.it/data-mining/. Accessed March 20
17. Zietsman, J., Rilett, L.R. . Sustainable transportation: Conceptualization and performance measures. (No. SWUTC/02/167403-1). Southwest University Transportation Centre, Texas Transportation Institute, College Station, Texas: Texas A & M University (2002)

Author Index

O. Gervasi et al. (Eds.): ICCSA 2023 Workshops, LNCS 14107, pp. 605–606, 2023.
https://doi.org/10.1007/978-3-031-37114-1

Printed in the United States
by Baker & Taylor Publisher Services